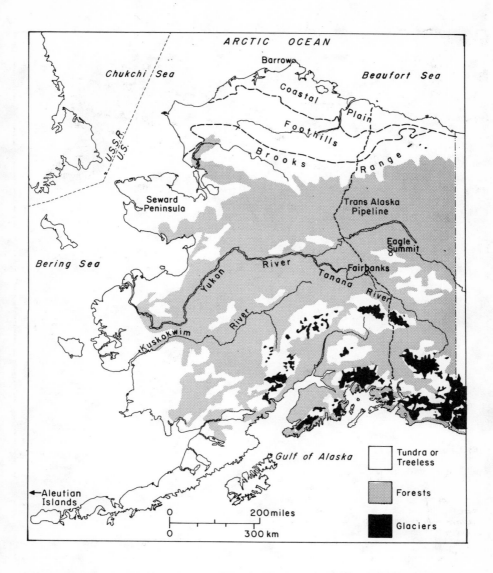

Generalized distribution of tundra, forests and glaciers in Alaska. *The physiographic provinces of the Arctic Slope are shown. (After Viereck and Little 1975.)*

AN ARCTIC ECOSYSTEM

US/IBP SYNTHESIS SERIES

This volume is a contribution to the International Biological Program. The United States' effort was sponsored by the National Academy of Sciences through the National Committee for the IBP. The lead federal agency in providing support for IBP has been the National Science Foundation.

Views expressed in this volume do not necessarily represent those of the National Academy of Sciences or of the National Science Foundation.

US/IBP SYNTHESIS SERIES ▐ 12

AN ARCTIC ECOSYSTEM
The Coastal Tundra at Barrow, Alaska

Edited by

Jerry Brown
U.S. Army Cold Regions Research and Engineering Laboratory

Philip C. Miller
San Diego State University

Larry L. Tieszen
Augustana College

Fred L. Bunnell
University of British Columbia

Dowden, Hutchinson & Ross, Inc.
Stroudsburg   Pennsylvania

Library of Congress Cataloging in Publication Data

Main entry under title:
An arctic ecosystem.
  (US/IBP synthesis series ; 12)
  Includes bibliographical references and index.
  1. Tundra ecology—Alaska—Barrow. 2. Coastal ecology—Alaska—Barrow.
3. Ecology—Arctic regions. I. Brown, Jerry. II. Miller, Philip C. III. Tieszen, Larry L.
IV. Bunnell, Fred L. V. Series: US/IBP synthesis series ; 12.
QH105.A4A77   574.5'26   79-22901
ISBN 0-87933-370-7

Distributed world-wide by Academic Press,
a subsidiary of Harcourt Brace Jovanovich,
Publishers.

FOREWORD

This book is one of a series of volumes reporting results of research by U.S. scientists participating in the International Biological Program (IBP). As one of the 58 nations taking part in the IBP during the period July 1967 to June 1974, the United States organized a number of large, multidisciplinary studies pertinent to the central IBP theme of "the biological basis of productivity and human welfare."

These multidisciplinary studies (Integrated Research Programs), directed toward an understanding of the structure and function of major ecological or human systems, have been a distinctive feature of the U.S. participation in the IBP. Many of the detailed investigations that represent individual contributions to the overall objectives of each Integrated Research Program have been published in the journal literature. The main purpose of this series of books is to accomplish a synthesis of the many contributions for each principal program and thus answer the larger questions pertinent to the structure and function of the major systems that have been studied.

Publications Committee: US/IBP
Gabriel Lasker
Robert B. Platt
Frederick E. Smith
W. Frank Blair, Chairman

PREFACE

Tundra covers about 5.5% of the land surface of the earth (Rodin et al. 1975), but justification for studying it goes far beyond its areal extent. Of the world's major ecosystems, tundra has the lowest temperatures and the shortest growing seasons. Thus we may expect to find there the limits of biological accommodation and adaptation to low temperature. Largely because of the climate, which is so inhospitable for humans and so unsuitable for traditional forms of agriculture, tundra areas have never really been developed. However, increasing demands have been placed upon tundra to provide energy, minerals, food, and recreation. Often, alternative uses of tundra resources are not compatible. There are conflicting demands for wilderness, recreation areas, development of natural resources, and retention of the traditional life-styles of the indigenous people.

The research within the U.S. Tundra Biome was developed as part of both the U.S. IBP Analysis of Ecosystems program (National Academy of Sciences 1974, Blair 1977), consisting of five Biomes (Grassland, Desert, Tundra, Western Coniferous Forest and Eastern Deciduous Forest), and the International Tundra Biome program, comprising some 14 other national study sites (Rosswall and Heal 1975, Wielgolaski 1975a, b, Bliss 1977, Heal and Perkins 1978, Sonesson 1980, Bliss et al. 1981).

It had become apparent by early 1970 that a field program centered on the coastal tundra at Barrow, Alaska, would be required to develop fully the U.S. IBP ecosystem approach. The area around Barrow had a long heritage of ecological research (Reed and Ronhovde 1971, Britton 1973, Gunn 1973), and this research contributed significantly to the planning and initiation of the U.S. Tundra Biome program (Brown et al. 1970). Because of a combination of circumstances relating to the rapidly expanding oil developments in arctic Alaska and the new wave of environmental consciousness, a modest program of basic and applied research in tundra was initiated in 1970 (Brown 1970). The following year, a full-fledged Biome program was officially recognized, with Barrow chosen for intensive ecosystem research. Prudhoe Bay, the site of major arctic oil development, became an area for comparative coastal tundra research (Brown 1975). Two alpine sites, Eagle Summit in central Alaska and Niwot Ridge in the Colorado Front Range, provided comparative data from high- and mid-latitude alpine tundras (see map inside front cover).

The 1970 field program concentrated on initiating the field design and establishing a series of field experiments and control plots. During the summers of 1971, 1972 and 1973 a vast array of field data were gathered from the Biome research area at Barrow. Summer 1974 was devoted to initial synthesis in a summer-long workshop that formed the basis of this volume, a companion aquatic volume (Hobbie 1980), and a volume on primary producers (Tieszen 1978a).

Several broad objectives guided the research design of the U.S. Tundra Biome program from its inception: 1) to develop a predictive understanding of how the tundra system operates, particularly as exemplified by the wet coastal tundra of northern Alaska; 2) to obtain the necessary data base from a variety of cold-dominated ecosystems represented in the United States so that their behavior could be modeled and simulated and the results compared with similar studies underway in other circumpolar countries; and 3) to bring basic environmental knowledge to bear on problems of degradation, maintenance, and restoration of the temperature-sensitive and cold-dominated tundra and taiga ecosystems.

The ecosystem approach and the use of ecological models were integrating and research tools of the U.S. IBP Biome studies. Miller et al. (1975) summarized the development of "box and arrow" representations of the tundra ecosystem. Modeling in the U.S. Tundra Biome program emphasized processes rather than the total ecosystem. This was done to maximize the interactions among field observation, hypothesis formulation, experimentation, and incorporation of results into working models. Such models are regarded as necessary steps leading to the eventual development of meaningful whole-ecosystem simulations.

The ecological model is a research tool, not an objective. Because of this, modeling cannot be separated from field experiments, and discussions of the two are intertwined throughout much of the volume. Bunnell (1973) emphasized the heuristic value of models that fail to predict accurately or to mimic adequately the behavior of the real world. Such failure indicates that either the model structure, certain parameter values, or the basic hypotheses are incorrect, and thus contributes directly to our understanding. Many hypotheses and model structures have been tried and modified or replaced as our understanding has developed. In this book the models that incorporate our understanding as of the mid-1970's are discussed and used to explore the behavior of organisms and processes under a variety of conditions. In some cases, the predictions of models have been subjected to testing, and results are presented. In other cases, the evaluation of model behavior remains a topic for future research.

Our intent has been to produce an integrated discussion of a tundra ecosystem rather than a collection of independent papers on its component parts. We hope that the reader will be motivated to read the book as such. Books suffer from the constraint that they are necessarily unidimensional. Although the reader may begin and end at any point, he must proceed linearly between those points. We view ecosystems as multidimensional, with complex lines of interaction and influence running throughout. In resolving this complexity into the linear structure of this volume, we have fallen back on the relatively familiar divisions of abiotic setting, primary production processes, soil and decomposition processes, and herbivory. Within each of these subdivisions, the reader will find the common theme of the limitation of rates of biological processes by low temperature and related conditions of short growing season and the presence of permafrost.

The Editors

ACKNOWLEDGMENTS

Approximately $5.5 million was expended on this program for research and logistical support. Direct financial support of the Biome-wide program was derived from three major sources: the National Science Foundation, the State of Alaska and the petroleum industry through the University of Alaska. The NSF funding was under the joint sponsorship of the U.S. Arctic Research Program (Division of Polar Programs) and the U.S. International Biological Program (Ecosystem Analysis). The Army Research Office and the Department of Energy (previously AEC and ERDA) both contributed funded projects to the Program. Industry support was provided through unrestricted grants from: Atlantic Richfield Company, Alyeska Pipeline Service Company, BP Alaska, Inc., Cities Service Company, Exxon Company, USA (Humble Oil and Refining Company), Gulf Oil Corporation, Marathon Oil Company, Mobil Oil Company, Prudhoe Bay Environmental Subcommittee of the Alaska Oil and Gas Association, Shell Oil Company, Standard Oil Company of California, Standard Oil (Indiana) Foundation, Inc., and Sun Oil Company. In addition to the directly funded support, parent institutions, almost without exception, provided their staff members with a variety of on-campus and other support, which is gratefully acknowledged on behalf of the entire program.

In a program such as this, involving hundreds of scientists and dozens of institutions and support agencies, it is difficult to present a complete list of acknowledgments. Foremost, the Office of Naval Research through its Naval Arctic Research Laboratory (NARL) at Barrow, Alaska, provided the field and laboratory support without which the U.S. Tundra Biome program would have been impossible. Two former directors of NARL, Dr. Max C. Brewer and John Schindler, deserve particular credit for facilitating the logistic support of the Tundra Biome program. Dr. Larry L. Tieszen ably served as the intensive site director at Barrow during the several summers of major activity. Alpine field support at Eagle Summit and Niwot Ridge was enhanced through the University of Alaska's Institute of Arctic Biology and the University of Colorado's Institute of Arctic and Alpine Research (INSTAAR) at its Mountain Research Station, respectively. Administratively, the Tundra Biome Center at the University of Alaska provided vital contractual and support services. Dr. George C. West, Director of the Tundra Biome Center, Dr. Keith Van Cleve, and Mr. David Witt deserve particular credit.

The Cold Regions Research and Engineering Laboratory (CRREL) of the U.S. Army Corps of Engineers provided overall management, specialized logistic and equipment support, and editorial services through an interagency agreement with NSF and in the spirit of Public Law 91-438, which authorized support of the U.S. IBP. Stephen L. Bowen, Technical Editor, and the CRREL editorial and photographic staffs were responsible for preparation of all internal Biome reports. This volume was edited and prepared through the final camera-ready copy stage by Mr. Bowen, assisted by Donna R. Murphy, Editorial Assistant, and Harold Larsen, Scientific Illustrator. Their patience, endurance and invaluable assistance over the years are sincerely acknowledged by the editors and the many Biome participants. Kathleen Salzberg, INSTAAR, provided editorial assistance on the references and prepared the subject index to this book. Sylvia Barkley verified many of the computations.

A consultant committee conducted regular reviews of the program for the NSF, and its constructive advice over the life of the program is appreciated. Members included Dr. William Mayer, Chairman, Dr. Donald Wohlschlag, Dr. Hugh Raup, Dr. William Cooper and Dr. Frederick Sparrow. In 1970 and prior to the formation of this committee, a special field review committee headed by Dr. Philip L. Johnson made recommendations for the direction of the ensuing Biome program; its foresight has been greatly appreciated. The constructive guidance of the NSF staff is also gratefully acknowledged. NSF staff members of the Ecosystem Analysis Program included, over the five-year span, Dr. Philip L. Johnson, Dr. Charles C. Cooper, Dr. John Neuhold, Dr. William Hazen, and Dr. Jerry Franklin. Dr. George Llano provided overall NSF program management on behalf of the Division of Polar Programs, and his valuable polar experience contributed significantly to the continuity of the tundra program.

This volume or its individual chapters were reviewed at several stages by the following reviewers, whose guidance and advice are greatly appreciated: Dr. Francis E. Clark, Dr. Robert S. Hoffmann, Dr. Richard T. Holmes, Dr. Albert W. Johnson, Dr. Philip L. Johnson, Dr. Robert S. Loomis, Dr. Gary A. Maykut, Dr. Samuel J. McNaughton, Dr. Atsuma Ohmura, Dr. William A. Reiners, Dr. Boyd R. Strain and Dr. Martin Witkamp.

The Biome management and the editors of this book extend a special note of appreciation to all participants in the program for their understanding and indulgence as the program evolved and during the various stages in the preparation of this volume. We especially thank those who are listed as contributors for their informal input to individual chapters. Dr. Stephen F. MacLean, Jr. provided considerable assistance in the planning and implementation of the many consumer-based projects, in organizing portions of this volume, and in numerous discussions concerning tundra structure and function.

Along with the many authors and contributors to this volume, many other investigators, undergraduates, graduate students, technicians, and support staff participated in the Tundra Biome program. Appendix 1 contains a complete list of all Biome participants and the affiliation of the principal investigators. In addition, a considerable number of international Tundra Biome members participated in various U.S. activities; these individuals are also listed in Appendix 1.

As this book goes to press, we are saddened to report that the Naval Arctic Research Laboratory has closed its doors to the support of scientific research. This results from the lack of funds to operate the Laboratory. Those of us who have literally spent hundreds of field seasons conducting field and laboratory research in the Barrow environs hope that the closure of this scientific facility on the shores of the Arctic Ocean is a temporary action and that future generations of scientists will enjoy the logistic opportunities we have been privileged to experience over the past several decades.

JERRY BROWN
Former Director, U.S. Tundra Biome
USA CRREL
Hanover, New Hampshire

CONTENTS

LIST OF AUTHORS

Vera Alexander
Institute of Marine Science, University of Alaska
Fairbanks, Alaska 99701

Sylvia A. Barkley†
Biology Department,San Diego State University
San Diego, California 92182

Roger G. Barry
Institute of Arctic and Alpine Research, University of Colorado
Boulder, Colorado 80309

Robert J. Barsdate
Institute of Marine Sciences, University of Alaska
Fairbanks, Alaska 99701

George O. Batzli
Department of Ecology, Ethology, and Evolution
University of Illinois, Urbana, Illinois 61801

Robert E. Benoit
Department of Biology, Virginia Polytechnic Institute and State
University, Blacksburg, Virginia 24061

Carl Benson
Geophysical Institute, University of Alaska
Fairbanks, Alaska 99701

W. Dwight Billings
Department of Botany, Duke University
Durham, North Carolina 27706

Jerry Brown
U.S. Army Cold Regions Research and Engineering Laboratory
Hanover, New Hampshire 03755

† Affiliation at time of participation.

Fred L. Bunnell
Faculty of Forestry, University of British Columbia
Vancouver, British Columbia, Canada V6T 1W5

F. Stuart Chapin III
Institute of Arctic Biology, University of Alaska
Fairbanks, Alaska 99701

Boyd D. Collier
Biology Department, San Diego State University
San Diego, California 92182

Patrick I. Coyne
U.S. Department of Agriculture, Southern Plains Range Research
Station, Woodward, Oklahoma 78801

S. Lawrence Dingman
Institute of Natural and Environmental Research
University of New Hampshire, Durham, New Hampshire 03824

K. R. Everett
Institute of Polar Studies, Ohio State University
Columbus, Ohio 43210

Patrick W. Flanagan
Institute of Arctic Biology, University of Alaska
Fairbanks, Alaska 99701

Philip S. Flint†
Department of Soils and Plant Nutrition, University of California
Berkeley, California 94720

Paul L. Gersper
Department of Soils and Plant Nutrition, University of California
Berkeley, California 94720

Cecil W. Goodwin
Department of Geography, Pennsylvania State University
State College, Pennsylvania 16802

Ellsworth F. LeDrew
Department of Geography, University of Waterloo
Waterloo, Ontario, Canada N2L 3G1

Martin C. Lewis
Department of Biology, York University
Downsview, Ontario, Canada M3J 1P3

Stephen F. MacLean, Jr.
Institute of Arctic Biology, University of Alaska
Fairbanks, Alaska 99701

Brent H. McCown
Department of Horticulture, University of Wisconsin
Madison, Wisconsin 53706

Orson K. Miller
Department of Biology, Virginia Polytechnic Institute and State
University, Blacksburg, Virginia 24061

Philip C. Miller
Biology Department, San Diego State University
San Diego, California 92182

David F. Murray
Institute of Arctic Biology and the Museum
University of Alaska, Fairbanks, Alaska 99701

Walter C. Oechel
Biology Department, San Diego State University
San Diego, California 92182

Frank A. Pitelka
Museum of Vertebrate Zoology, University of California
Berkeley, California 94720

Larry L. Tieszen
Department of Biology, Augustana College
Sioux Falls, South Dakota 57102

Patrick J. Webber
Institute of Arctic and Alpine Research, University of Colorado
Boulder, Colorado 80309

Gunter Weller
Geophysical Institute, University of Alaska
Fairbanks, Alaska 99701

Robert G. White
Institute of Arctic Biology, University of Alaska
Fairbanks, Alaska 99701

LIST OF CONTRIBUTORS

Rodney J. Arkley
   Department of Soils and Plant Nutrition, University of California
   Berkeley, California 94720

Mary Allessio Leck
   Department of Biology, Rider College
   Lawrenceville, New Jersey 08648

Edwin M. Banks
   Department of Ecology, Ethology and Evolution
   University of Illinois, Urbana, Illinois 61801

Dirk Barèl
   Research Institute for Nature Management
   Arheim, The Netherlands

Pille Bunnell
   Institute of Animal Resource Ecology, University of British
   Columbia, Vancouver, British Columbia, Canada V6T 1W5

Martyn Caldwell
   Department of Range Science, Utah State University
   Logan, Utah 84321

Roy E. Cameron
   Argonne National Laboratory, Environmental Statement Project
   Division, Argonne, Illinois 60439

G. Keith Douce
   Department of Entomology, University of Georgia
   Athens, Georgia 30603

Douglas A. Johnson
   U.S. Department of Agriculture, Crops Research Laboratory
   Utah State University, Logan, Utah 84322

Vera Komárková
   Institute of Arctic and Alpine Research, University of Colorado
   Boulder, Colorado 80309

Gary A. Laursen
Office of Naval Research, Arlington, Virginia 22217

Jay D. McKendrick
Agricultural Experiment Station, University of Alaska
Palmer, Alaska 99645

Herbert Melchior
Alaska Department of Fish and Game, Fairbanks, Alaska 99701

Barbara M. Murray
Institute of Arctic Biology, University of Alaska
Fairbanks, Alaska 99701

David Norton
Outer Continental Shelf Program, Geophysical Institute
University of Alaska, Fairbanks, Alaska 99701

Ronald G. Osborn†
Department of Biology, San Diego State University
San Diego, California 92182

Samuel Outcalt
Department of Geography, University of Michigan
Ann Arbor, Michigan 48104

James R. Rastorfer
Department of Biological Sciences, Chicago State University
Chicago, Illinois 60628

Emanuel D. Rudolph
Department of Botany and Institute of Polar Studies
Ohio State University, Columbus, Ohio 43210

Uriel Safriel†
Department of Zoology, Hebrew University, Jerusalem, Israel

William C. Steere
New York Botanical Garden, New York, New York 10460

Wayne Stoner†
Biology Department, San Diego State University
San Diego, California 92182

† Affiliation at time of participation.

Albert Ulrich
  Department of Soils and Plant Nutrition, University of California
  Berkeley, California 94720

Donald A. Walker
  Institute of Arctic and Alpine Research, University of Colorado
  Boulder, Colorado 80309

AN ARCTIC ECOSYSTEM

1

The Coastal Tundra at Barrow

J. Brown, K. R. Everett, P. J. Webber,
S. F. MacLean, Jr., and D. F. Murray

THE ARCTIC COASTAL PLAIN:
A GEOGRAPHIC PERSPECTIVE

The word *tundra* is broadly used to refer to the landscapes that are found above the altitudinal or latitudinal treeline. The classification of tundra has been reviewed by Barry and Ives (1974) and Murray (1978). In Alaska, lowland tundra covers large portions of the Aleutian Islands and the delta of the Yukon and Kuskokwim Rivers in the southwest, the Seward Peninsula in the west, and the Arctic Slope (see map inside front cover). Alpine tundra is found in all the mountain ranges and at elevations above about 1000 meters in upland terrain such as the Yukon–Tanana Uplands.

The Arctic Slope, that part of northern Alaska that drains to the Arctic Ocean, covers 200,000 km², an area the size of the state of Nebraska. It consists of three major physiographic provinces: the Brooks Range, the Arctic Foothills, and the Arctic Coastal Plain (Figure 1-1). These provinces differ in topography, geology, climate and history, and consequently in fauna and flora. Permafrost underlies all land surfaces at depths up to approximately 600 m.

The Brooks Range, with peaks as high as 2700 m, has cirque glaciers in its central and eastern sections. Variations in slope and topography lead to large differences in microclimate and in soil properties, and thus there are diverse habitats for plants and animals. Only the floodplains of the larger river drainages have extensive stands of a single vegetation community, usually shrub thicket. The valley bottoms contain sedge meadows and well-developed shrub tundra that is dominated by willow (*Salix lanata*, *S. pulchra*, *S. glauca* and *S. alaxensis*) and dwarf birch (*Betula exilis*). The slopes have dry meadow or heath communities dominated by *Dryas octopetala*. Above about 1800 m vascular plants are limited to protected sites, and lichen cover is discontinuous. Such areas are analogous to the polar deserts of high latitudes, and might be called alpine deserts.

1

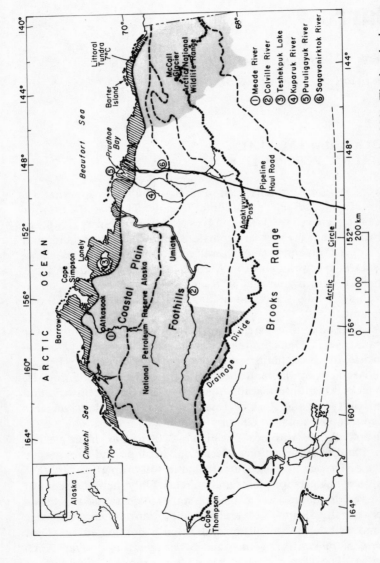

FIGURE 1-1. *Physiographic provinces of the Arctic Slope (Payne et al. 1951). The hatched area is the littoral zone which has July mean temperatures of less than 7°C (Canton 1961, Haugen and Brown 1980).*

FIGURE 1-2. *The Arctic Coastal Plain. The lakes are surrounded by marshy and polygonal terrain. The large lake (top center) is several kilometers long. (Photograph by J.J. Koranda.)*

To the north the mountains of the Brooks Range give way to the rounded summits and rolling terrain of the glaciated Foothills. Tussock tundra dominated by *Eriophorum vaginatum* with a rich assemblage of associated species, including *Salix pulchra*, *Betula exilis*, *Vaccinium vitis-idaea*, *V. uliginosum* and *Ledum decumbens*, covers vast expanses. Dry meadows and fellfields exist on the drier, exposed ridges, and sedge meadows and willow thickets in the wetter valleys and swales. The northern sections of the Foothills were not glaciated, but are similar in appearance to the tussock tundra of the glaciated southern sections.

The Coastal Plain is composed of near-shore marine, fluvial, alluvial and aeolian deposits of mid- to late-Quaternary age (Black 1964). The sediments are the products of a series of marine transgressions that encroached upon the plain. The most recent and least extensive occurred during mid-Wisconsinan time (Sellmann and Brown 1973). Large, elliptical, oriented lakes, many over 6 km long (Figure 1-2), cover up to 40% of the land surface of the northern part of the Coastal Plain. The lakes are oriented and elongated as a result of differential erosion at their north and south ends (Carson and Hussey 1962, Sellmann et al. 1975).

The relief of the Coastal Plain reflects the lakes, river terraces, ice-wedge polygons and occasional pingos. Along the 1800-km coastline relief averages 2 to 5 m, with some bluffs and cliffs exceeding 20 m. The 75-m topographic contour is taken as the boundary between the northern Foothills and the plain. Because of the very low relief and the presence of permafrost, drainage is poor and stream channels meander widely. Only one major river, the Inaru, lies completely within the plain. It flows only for a few weeks during spring melt. Other rivers that flow north through the plain originate in the foothills or mountains of the Brooks Range and generally flow throughout the summer. The largest river to traverse the Coastal Plain, the Colville River, drains 60,000 km^2 of the Foothills and western Coastal Plain (Walker 1973). It rises in the western Brooks Range and flows eastward through the Foothills, then northward across the Coastal Plain to the Beaufort Sea . The Colville intercepts drainage from the Brooks Range, and thus limits the distribution of calcareous alluvium derived from the mountains to the area south and east of the river (Figure 1-1).

The coastal climate is one of long, dry, cold winters and short, moist, cool summers (Table 1-1). At Barrow, the northernmost point in Alaska, the sun is above the horizon continuously from 10 May to 2 August, and below the horizon from 18 November to 24 January. Air temperature remains below freezing for nine months of the year and can fall below freezing during any of the three summer months. The microclimate is strongly influenced by the presence of an insulating snow cover 20 to 40 cm thick in winter, and by the underlying permafrost. A gradual warming trend begins in April and there is a definite transition toward summer conditions during May. Snowmelt, however, does not normally begin until early June. Thirty-seven percent of the annual precipitation falls as rain during the summer. The windspeed varies little during the year, averaging 5.3 m s^{-1}, with the fall months being the windiest. Fog and clouds persist through the summer; the average humidity is consistently above 80% from June through September.

Based on the 30-year normal for Barrow, the period during which daily average temperatures remain above 0 °C lasts 91 days (13 June to 12 September). By our definition the thaw season begins when there are at least three successive days with average temperatures above freezing and ends when there are at least three successive days with temperatures below freezing. This period is extremely variable and can begin as early as 1 June and end as late as the end of September. An average of 251 degree-days above 0 °C accumulates (30-year normal) and the wet tundra soils thaw to approximately 30 to 40 cm. The initiation of the plant growing season coincides with the occurrence of snow-free conditions for a particular tundra site. This date is also variable based on both season and microtopography; however, it generally follows within several days of

TABLE 1-1 *Average Air Temperature, Precipitation, Windspeed, Solar Radiation and Day Length at the Village of Barrow*

	Temp (°C)	Precip (mm)	Windspeed (m s⁻¹)	Solar radiation (MJ m⁻² day⁻¹)	Day length (hr)
Jan	− 25.9	5.8	5.0	0	0.7
Feb	− 28.1	5.1	4.9	1.6	6.8
Mar	− 26.2	4.8	5.0	7.4	11.7
Apr	− 18.3	5.3	5.2	15.5	16.7
May	− 7.2	4.3	5.2	21.9	23.1
June	0.6	8.9	5.1	23.0	24.0
July	3.7	22.4	5.2	18.5	24.0
Aug	3.1	26.4	5.5	10.8	19.0
Sept	− 0.9	14.7	5.9	5.0	13.4
Oct	− 9.3	14.0	6.0	1.7	8.6
Nov	− 18.1	7.6	5.6	0.2	2.4
Dec	− 24.6	4.8	5.0	0	0
Year	− 12.6	124.1	5.3		

Note: Radiation based on 14-year record; air temperature, precipitation and windspeed 1941–70 normal (U.S. Department of Commerce).
Source: After Bunnell et al. (1975).

the onset of positive degree-day accumulation. A portion of the microflora is active below –6 °C (Chapter 9). Thus, the period of microbial activity exceeds that of primary producers by 10 to 30 days, but rates of activity are low at such low temperatures.

The total known vascular plant flora of the Arctic Slope comprises 574 taxa. The largest number of species, 516 or 90% of the total, are found in the Foothills province (Table 1-2). Species richness is greatest in the Foothills, intermediate in the Brooks Range, and least on the Coastal Plain for each of the three major plant groups analyzed: vascular plants, mosses and hepatics. Arctic endemics, species found only north of the treeline, make up 8% of the vascular plant flora, 9% of the hepatics, and only 2% of the mosses. Data for lichens are insufficient for detailed analysis, although some recent publications are now available (Moser et al. 1979, Thomson 1979). All three plant groups show considerable floristic overlap among the provinces of the Arctic Slope and between the Arctic Slope and the region south of the latitudinal treeline. This overlap is a result of the occurrence of tundra at higher elevations south of the crest of the Brooks Range, and of some tundra species which also grow in forest habitats (Murray 1978).

The two Biome research areas on the Coastal Plain—Barrow and

TABLE 1-2 *Number of Plant and Animal Species in Different Geographic Regions of the Arctic Slope (A), Number of Species in Common Between Areas (C), and Sørenson Coefficient of Similarity* Between Areas (S)*

Plants

		Barrow	Prudhoe Bay	Coastal Plain	Foothills	Brooks Range	Total Arctic Slope	Arctic endemics	Arctic and south of treeline
Vascular plants (Hultén 1968, Murray, unpubl.)	A	124	168	308	516	330	574	45	529
	C		78	268	308				
	S		(0.53)	(0.65)	(0.73)				
	C				215				
	S				(0.67)				
Mosses (Steere 1978b)	A	177	109	245	357	347	410	9	401
	C		84	231	300				
	S		(0.59)	(0.77)	(0.85)				
	C				223				
	S				(0.75)				
Hepatics (Steere and Inoue 1978)	A	49	16	82	113	94	137	13	124
	C		11	67	80				
	S		(0.34)	(0.69)	(0.77)				
	C				58				
	S				(0.66)				

Animals

Taxon (References)	A	C	S	C	S			
Birds (Kessel and Cade 1958, Pitelka 1974, Norton et al. 1975, Bergman et al. 1977)	28, 39; 45, 45, 50	28; 24	(0.77); (0.53)	36, 19	(0.76), (0.40)	76	35	41
Mammals (Bee and Hall 1956)	10, 14; 16, 19, 22	10; 15	(0.83); (0.86)	18, 14	(0.88), (0.74)	24	5	19
Acari (MacLean et al., unpubl.)	80, 86, 86	56	(0.68)	58, 53	(0.67), (0.64)	127	Unknown	93+
Collembola (Fjellberg, unpubl.)	80, 79, 62	52	(0.65)	51, 43	(0.72), (0.61)	115	6+	76+
Homoptera (MacLean and Hodkinson 1980; MacLean, unpubl.)	1; 7, 26, 12	7	(0.42)	10, 5	(0.53), (0.53)	28	Unknown	17

*Sørenson Coefficient of Similarity is $QS = 2j/a + b$, where a is number of species in first sample, b is number of species in second sample, and j is number of species shared by the two samples (Sørenson 1948).

Prudhoe Bay—have only a limited subset of its total flora. This is a reflection of the particularly severe summer climatic conditions that exist near the coast, but moderate inland across the plain to the south. This zone of littoral tundra (Figure 1-1) is characterized by low species diversity, dominance of grasses and sedges (Cantlon 1961), rarity of tussock tundra, and the absence of erect shrubs. The limit of littoral tundra follows roughly the 7 °C July mean temperature isotherm.

The floras of the coastal tundras at Barrow and at Prudhoe Bay are strikingly dissimilar, with Sørenson Coefficients of Similarity (Sørenson 1948) that are much lower than those describing the comparisons between provinces (Table 1-2). The Barrow peninsula is dominated by wet, acid soils. The Prudhoe Bay region, in contrast, is influenced by two large rivers, the Sagavanirktok and Kuparuk, that originate in the mountains and contribute carbonates to the soils. However, even in this region, acid soils occur beyond the influence of the rivers.

Differences in parent materials and topography have a marked effect on the vegetation of the two regions. The lichen genera *Cladina* and *Cladonia*, which are associated with acid soils, are represented by 19 taxa in the Barrow region, but only 4 at Prudhoe Bay. The species *Collema tunaeforme*, *Evernia perfragilis* and *Fulgensia bracteata*, which are characteristic of calcareous substrates, are present at Prudhoe Bay but not at Barrow. The absence of sphagnum mosses and the scarcity of polytricaceous mosses around Prudhoe Bay are examples of probable pH control of distribution in the bryoflora (Steere 1978a). The effect of pH on vascular plants is noticeable in the distribution of *Carex* species; the calciphiles *C. atrofusca*, *C. membranacea* and *C. misandra* are common in the vicinity of Prudhoe Bay but are absent from the Barrow area (Murray 1978, Walker and Webber 1979). A rich arctic-alpine floristic element is found on the numerous exposed and well-drained habitats that form on the coarse-textured soils of river banks, gravel bars, dunes and pingos close to Prudhoe Bay. The vegetation in this area shows a greater affinity with that of more southerly tundra than does the vegetation of the Barrow peninsula.

The terrestrial vertebrate fauna of northern Alaska is composed entirely of homeothermic birds and mammals and lacks the heterothermic reptiles and amphibians which extend well into the Asian Arctic. Pitelka (1974) listed 189 species of birds for the Arctic Slope, 76 of which are considered to be regular breeders (Table 1-2). Because of the mobility of birds, there are many records of accidental or casual visitors to the Arctic Slope. The number of species is very similar in the three physiographic provinces: 45 species are found in both the Coastal Plain and Foothills, and 50 in the Brooks Range. However, the composition of the bird fauna changes considerably from the coast to the mountains. Thirty species of waterfowl and shorebirds and three species of passerine birds occur on the Coastal Plain, while in the Brooks Range passerines account for 21 species and waterfowl and shorebirds for 18 species (Kessel and Cade 1958, Pitelka 1974). Only 13 bird species breed regularly in all three provinces. Thirty-five species, or 46% of the regular breeders, are limited in their breeding distribution to the Arctic Slope. Thus the avifauna exhibits a much higher level of endemism than does any other animal or plant group. The breeding bird faunas of the Barrow and Prudhoe Bay regions are more similar than their floras.

The Arctic Slope is well known for its wildlife resources, which include dall sheep (*Ovis d. dalli*), wolves (*Canis lupus*), grizzly and polar bears (*Ursus arctos* and *U. maritimus*), wolverines (*Gulo gulo*), moose (*Alces alces*) and caribou (*Rangifer tarandus*), as well as golden eagles (*Aquila chrysaetas*) and peregrine falcons (*Falco peregrinus*). Musk oxen (*Ovibos moschatus*) were a part of the fauna until the mid- to late 1800s, when they were eliminated by man. They have been successfully reintroduced to the Arctic Slope in the Arctic National Wildlife Range and near Cape Thompson (Figure 1-1), and can once again be considered resident mammals of the Coastal Plain and Foothills. Bands of caribou from two major herds roam the Arctic Slope, and have always been important in the economy of the Eskimo.

The terrestrial mammal fauna of the Arctic Slope is limited to about 24 species. The number of species present increases from the Coastal Plain to the Brooks Range. All of the species of the Coastal Plain except polar bears live in the Foothills as well, and all but polar bears and musk oxen live in the mountains of the Brooks Range. Faunal overlap between provinces is very high, as is overlap between the fauna of the Arctic Slope and more southerly locations. Only 5 of the 24 terrestrial mammals are endemic to arctic tundra.

Microtine rodents are a substantial part of the mammal fauna. Whereas in the Canadian Arctic Archipelago only the collared lemming (*Dicrostonyx groenlandicus*) is found, on the Coastal Plain at Barrow there are two species, the collared and the brown lemmings (*Lemmus sibericus, = trimucronatus*). At Prudhoe Bay, and inland from the coast, these two species occur together with the tundra vole (*Microtus oeconomus*). And these microtines are joined by the red-backed mouse (*Clethrionomys rutilus*) in the foothill tundra and by the singing vole (*Microtus miurus*) in rocky habitats of the southern Foothills and the Brooks Range.

The adjacent Arctic Ocean is rich in marine mammals such as ringed and bearded seals (*Phoca hispida* and *Erignathus barbatus*), walrus (*Odobenus rosmarus*), and bowhead and beluga whales (*Balaena mysticetus* and *Delphinapterus leucas*). The marine mammals, probably more than any other resource, were responsible for the development of the rich culture of the people living along the arctic coast of Alaska.

The invertebrate fauna of the Arctic Slope is poorly known. However, the recently built road from interior Alaska to the Prudhoe Bay oilfield has provided access to collecting sites along a latitudinal transect, allowing study of the distribution of invertebrates. Soil mites (Acari) and springtails (Collembola) are among the most diverse of the invertebrates; 127 mite species and 115 Collembola species were recorded along the transect (Table 1-2). Since these data come from a limited number of samples, they do not represent the total fauna of the Arctic Slope. The number of species recorded from the three physiographic provinces is similar. The most Collembola species are found in the Foothills and Coastal Plain, while the Acari are most diverse in the Brooks Range and the Foothills. Overlap between provinces is high. Recently, MacLean et al. (1978) showed that the mite and Collembola species from a coastal tundra site in northern Chukotka, in northeast Asia, overlapped considerably with the fauna of the Arctic Slope. Fifty-nine of ninety mite species and 50 of 79 Collembola species found in the Chukotkan tundra have also been found in Alaska.

In contrast to the distribution of soil microarthropods, many other invertebrate groups increase in number of species from the Coastal Plain to the Brooks Range. For example, at Barrow there are only small numbers of a few species of herbivorous insects, including only a single species of the plant-sucking Homoptera, which is an important group worldwide. However, the number of species of herbivorous insects increases almost four-fold from the Coastal Plain to the Foothills along the road transect, then declines markedly from the Foothills to the Brooks Range. The distribution parallels that of the vascular plants on which the insects feed. However, the distribution of host plants is clearly only one factor in herbivore distribution, since these plant species are commonly found farther north than their characteristic herbivores.

BARROW RESEARCH AREA

Location

The Barrow peninsula is situated at the northern extremity of the Coastal Plain (71°18 'N, 156°40 'W). It is a triangular-shaped land mass bounded by the Chukchi Sea on the west and the Beaufort Sea and Elson Lagoon on the east (Figure 1-3). The earliest known site of human habitation, Birnirk, was submerged by an encroaching sea some 1200 to 1500 years ago (Ford 1959). The present village of Barrow (population 2700) is the largest Eskimo settlement in the State of Alaska.

Since 1920 the National Weather Service has operated a first-order weather station at Barrow. About 6 km north of the village there are

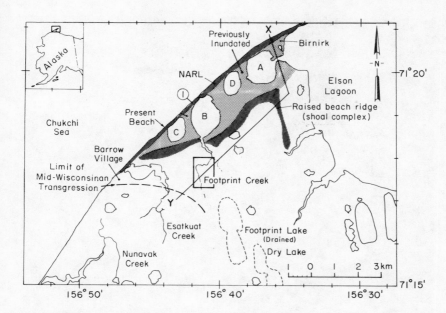

FIGURE 1-3. *Physiographic and historical features of the Barrow penin-sula. A) North Salt Lagoon, B) Middle Salt Lagoon, C) South Salt Lagoon, D) Imikpuk Lake, 1) Drainage channel for Middle Salt Lagoon. The shaded area around the lagoons and Imikpuk Lake is now tundra, but was previously a large embayment. The box outlines the Biome area shown in Figures 1-7, 1-11 and 1-12. Point Barrow is 5.8 km northeast of Birnirk. X-Y indicates the approximate location of the cross section shown in Figure 1-6.*

several government-operated facilities, including the Naval Arctic Re-search Laboratory (NARL), which has supported research on tundra ecology since 1947 (Reed and Ronhovde 1971, Britton 1973, Gunn 1973). In the 1940s and early 1950s Barrow was the main supply base for the ex-ploration of Naval Petroleum Reserve No. 4, redesignated National Pe-troleum Reserve, Alaska, in 1976. It also was a supply station during the construction of distant early warning sites (the DEW line) in the 1950s.

The coastal tundra at Barrow has low relief and is dominated by a pattern of ice-wedge polygons, shallow oriented lakes, drained lake basins and small ponds. Elevations range from sea level to 5 m along the northern shores of Elson Lagoon and rise to greater than 10 m south-westward across the peninsula. North of 71°15 ', approximately 65% of the surface is covered by polygonal ground (Sellmann et al. 1972), and half of this consists of high-centered or low, flat-centered polygons. The

FIGURE 1-4. *Aerial view looking north across the U.S. Tundra Biome research area. The ice-covered Arctic Ocean is in the background. The Naval Arctic Research Laboratory camp complex is in the upper right corner. The ice-covered water body is Middle Salt Lagoon. Polygonal terrain is visible in the foreground. (CRREL photograph.)*

remainder of the landscape contains recently drained lake basins, gently sloping terrain and lakes.

In 1970 an area 3 km from the sea near NARL was selected for the main U.S. International Biological Program Tundra Biome research effort (Figure 1-4). The area contains a sequence of drained lake surfaces (Figure 1-5). A small entrenched stream, Footprint Creek, flows across the northern portion and its marshy feeders, together with polygon troughs, drain the western and southern portion. The drainage area north of the creek consists of gentle, hummocky slopes and high-centered polygons with deepened troughs along with non-patterned meadows and mixed high- and low-centered polygons.

Three primary terrestrial sites and one aquatic site were established (Figure 1-5):

Site 1, immediately north of Footprint Creek, was used for a series of experimental simulations of human-induced impacts: heated soils, oil spills, physical disruption and greenhouse effects.

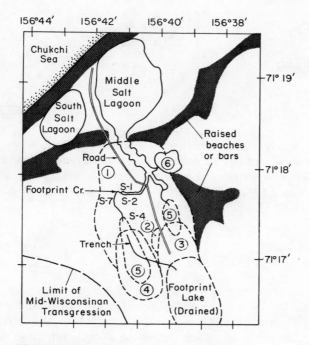

FIGURE 1-5. *U.S. Tundra Biome intensive research area (S-1, S-2, S-4, S-7) and associated landscape features. 1) oldest basin, 2-5) intermediate aged basins, 6) youngest basin. Footprint Lake was drained in 1950 through a bulldozed trench.*

Site 2, immediately south of Footprint Creek, was chosen for its relatively uniform wet meadow. Control plots and experiments to simulate natural perturbations, including changes in grazing and nutrient regime, were established.

Site 4, south of site 2, was selected for its microtopographic diversity and included a number of plots that contained representative polygonal terrain.

These three sites constitute the "Biome research area" referred to in this book.

Site 7, west of Footprint Creek, contained well-developed, low-centered polygons filled with water that were used for aquatic studies (Hobbie 1980).

Locations of plots and sample areas within these and related sites are shown on the map in Appendix 2.

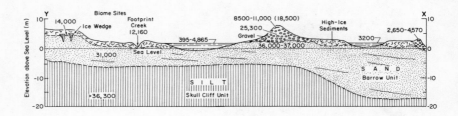

FIGURE 1-6. *Idealized geologic cross section across the Barrow penin-sula showing location and age of radiocarbon-dated organic materials (see Figure 1-3 for the approximate location of the section). The radio-carbon dates in years BP are from Brown (1965) except 18,500 from Everett (unpubl.) and 12,160 from Lewellen (1972).*

Geologic History

The general course of events over the past 25,000 years has been re-constructed on the basis of local and regional stratigraphic and geo-morphic data and correlations (Lewellen 1972, Sellmann and Brown 1973). Figure 1-6, an idealized section across the Barrow peninsula that incorporates radiocarbon dates and stratigraphic information, illustrates the major geologic units and surface features. The materials shown in the upper part of the cross section were deposited or reworked by an inva-sion of the sea that extended inland to about the current 8-m elevation. This elevation is not precise, since the surface relief changed as the sedi-ment refroze, producing an increase in volume due to the formation of ground ice. During this transgression, which occurred approximately 25,000 to 35,000 years ago (mid-Wisconsinan time), the surface of the ex-isting permafrost would have been lowered, but permafrost probably did not disappear entirely. Subsea permafrost is currently found to depths of over 100 m offshore from the present coastline (Lachenbruch and Mar-shall 1977, Lewellen 1977).

With the retreat of the sea, a gravelly beach ridge–shoal complex built up north and east of the Biome research area. This ridge complex currently reaches elevations of 6 to 8 m. North of the ridge, but landward of the present-day active beach, an embayment formed which persists in fragmented form as the lakes and sloughs from Elson Lagoon to Barrow Village. Until 1945 these lakes and sloughs were connected during peri-ods of high water at approximately the 2.5-m elevation. At that time, Middle Salt Lagoon was artificially drained to prevent flooding around NARL and the level of the slough was decreased to nearly sea level (Fig-ure 1-3).

As the area occupied by the Biome research sites was exposed by a late glacial regression of the sea, geomorphic processes related to extreme cold climate again developed. The sediments that had thawed beneath the shallow waters of the sea refroze to form a thick and continuous permafrost section. Presumably, ice wedge formation was active under the arctic climate that existed at that time, and has continued to the present. Evidence from pollen recovered from a buried ice wedge and radiocarbon dating of organic matter immediately west of the Biome research area indicates that by at least 14,000 BP a tundra as cold as at present, but somewhat drier, existed (Colinvaux 1964, Brown 1965). Fecal pellets of microtine rodents recovered in the same ice wedge sample indicate the presence of these small mammals at that time. Since ice wedges were actively growing 14,000 years ago, it is reasonable to assume that the thaw lake cycle (Britton 1957) as we know it today was also an active geomorphic process then. The detailed historical reconstruction of the Biome research area that follows is based upon this assumption.

In the Footprint Creek drainage a lacustrine peat immediately overlying the marine sediment at 2.2 m elevation has been radiocarbon dated at 12,160 ±200 years (Figure 1-6). This date provides a maximum age for the thaw lake. And since this peat directly overlies marine sediment, it probably also dates one of the earliest thaw lakes in the area. Aerial photographic interpretation suggests that the entire area was originally covered by one large lake (Figure 1-5). The shoreline of this lake abuts the surrounding uplands at an elevation of 5.5 m on both the east and west sides. The topographic high point on the west is known to contain large quantities of segregated ice and ice wedges (Brown 1965) and is probably a remnant of the primary land surface. The net effect of this early lake was to thaw the ice-rich permafrost to a depth of 3 m and rework materials of the type still found to the west. In the process most of the sea salts were removed from the sediments that form the parent material of the present soils.

The initial lake probably drained as headward erosion of the Middle Salt Lagoon slough cut through a shallow pass in the elevated beach ridge–shoal complex. With this draining or lowering of the lake level, the newly exposed lake sediments refroze, tundra vegetation developed, and a new cycle of ice wedge formation began.

In time, smaller lakes developed in this large lake basin. Each lake drained as headward erosion of the small tundra-covered stream channels intercepted the borders of the lake basins. The youngest and smallest lake apparently formed the basin within which the ponds studied in the Biome aquatic program are situated (site 7; Hobbie 1980). The present-day polygonal ground is not only the product of current ice wedge formation, but probably represents previous cycles of ice wedge growth, both on land and under shallow lakes or ponds. The Biome research area is slightly higher than the pond-covered areas to the east and west, suggesting that it is older. It is unlikely that more than one major lake has occupied the area of the terrestrial research sites, but the adjacent aquatic research site has gone through at least three lake cycles.

The activities of man have led to significant changes in the Biome research area since the mid-1940s. The tracks of off-road vehicles have produced thermal disturbance and subsequent formation of small ponds at ice wedge intersections, shifts in vegetation composition and, in some cases, severe erosion. More dramatic is the alteration in drainage caused by the lowering of Middle Salt Lagoon to sea level and the complete draining of Footprint and Dry Lakes in 1950. These actions created a new erosional base level in the basin (Figure 1-5). Prior to this lowering, the water level in Middle Salt Lagoon stood at approximately 2.5 m elevation. Since then there has been massive and rapid headward erosion as Footprint Creek readjusts to the new base level conditions (Lewellen 1972). After the water level was lowered, the floor of the previously flooded valley was exposed and Footprint Creek entrenched further to form the present marginal terrace. The gravel road on the east side of the Biome research area has caused some ponding and melting of ice wedges.

TERRAIN SUBDIVISIONS AND FORMATION

Although tundra might appear to be a featureless plain, it actually possesses a considerable variety of landforms, both on meso- and microscales, and is an extremely dynamic landscape (Britton 1957). The Biome research area and areas immediately adjacent to it consist of several major terrain units, each composed of characteristic landforms and associated microtopographic units (Figure 1-7). Adjacent to Footprint Creek are alluvial terraces, floodplains, and steep- and gently sloping stream banks. Immediately to the south are the weakly developed polygons that compose much of site 2 (Figure 1-4). Site 4, farther to the south, consists of a highly polygonized landscape containing both high-centered and well-developed low-centered polygons (Figure 1-8).

Polygons give rise to several microtopographic units—rims of low-centered polygons, tops of high-centered polygons, basins (centers) of low-centered polygons, and polygon troughs—and to a diverse range of soil types, vegetation, and habitats. These recur over short distances, commonly on the order of several meters (see Figures 1-8 and 1-9). Since the troughs are interconnected they serve as pathways for the movement of water, nutrients and plant litter, especially during snowmelt. In winter they are extensively used by lemmings under the deeper snow and low density depth hoar (Chapter 2). The basins of low-centered polygons are relatively poorly drained and many are areas of continuing organic

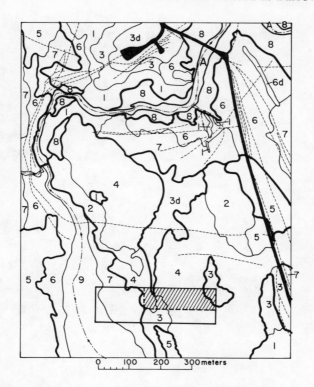

FIGURE 1-7. *Landscape map of the Tundra Biome research area. The area mapped is the same as that in Figures 1-11 and 1-12. The black areas are gravel roads and pads. The dashed lines indicate off-road vehicle trails present in 1971. Heavy solid lines outline the major soil complexes, associations, and units (Figure 1-11). The rectangle is commonly referred to as site 4. Details of the hatched rectangle are shown in Figure 1-8.*

1) High-centered polygons, relief ≥1 m.
2) Mixed high-centered and low-centered polygons, relief ≤0.5 m, frost boils common.
3) High-centered polygons, broad trough, relief <0.5 m.
4) Low-centered polygons, relief ≤0.5 m.
5) Large, low-centered polygons, many orthogonal, relief ≤0.5 m.

6) Large, high-centered polygons, narrow troughs, relief 0.1 to 0.5 m.
7) Polygonal pattern, relief <0.1 m.
8) Sloping areas (2 to 6%) marginal to streams, frost boils and discontinuous polygonal cracks.
9) Vegetation-covered waterway, discontinuous polygonal cracks.
A) Alluvium.
d) Disturbed area.

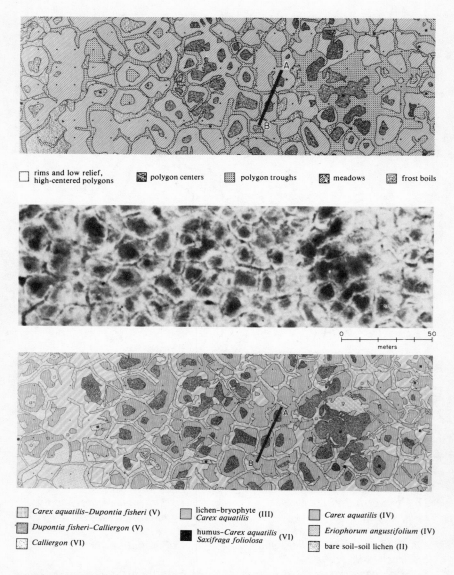

rims and low relief, high-centered polygons   polygon centers   polygon troughs   meadows   frost boils

0   meters   50

Carex aquatilis–Dupontia fisheri (V)   lichen–bryophyte *Carex aquatilis* (III)   *Carex aquatilis* (IV)

Dupontia fisheri–Calliergon (V)   humus–*Carex aquatilis Saxifraga foliolosa* (VI)   *Eriophorum angustifolium* (IV)

Calliergon (VI)   bare soil–soil lichen (II)

FIGURE 1-8. *Vertical photograph (center), soils (top), and vegetation (bottom) of a portion of the site 4 grid. (After Walker 1977).* The complexity of the microtopography decreases from right to left. Mixed high- and low-centered polygons are on the extreme right. The center portion is mostly well-developed low-centered polygons. The dark colored centers may contain standing water following snowmelt and during wet summers. The rims of polygons are outlined in lighter tones. Troughs are linear elements, dark where they are very moist or contain standing water. The left third consists of polygons with little or no microrelief contrast. See Figures 1-7, 1-11, and 1-12 for the relationship of the grid location to the terrain, soils, and vegetation of the entire research area. See Figure 1-9 for features on transect A–B.

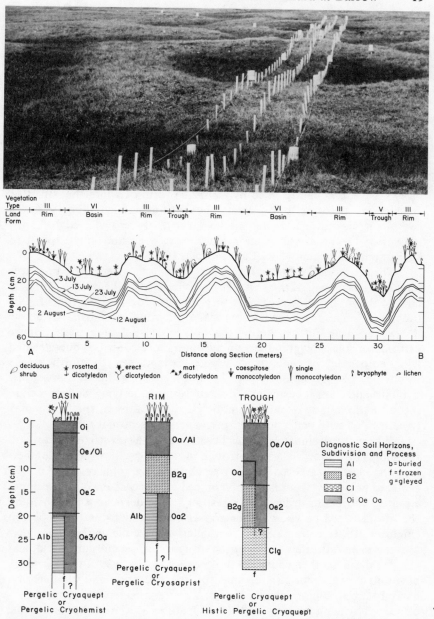

FIGURE 1-9. *Ground oblique photograph of a low-centered polygon, its microtopographic profile and thaw depths, and idealized soil profiles for each microtopographic unit (basin, rim, and trough). The profile and thaw depths are lines established by the wooden stakes shown in the photograph. Progression of depth of soil thaw is for summer 1973.*

accumulation. The rims of low-centered polygons, the tops of high-centered polygons, and particularly the outer edges of both are more exposed to summer and winter microclimatic extremes. Since polygonal terrain forms the basis for much of the biological and pedological variation found in wet coastal tundra, a brief review of its development follows.

Shallow, narrow troughs averaging 0.5 m deep by 1 to 2 m wide and underlain by ice wedges form the outlines of polygons having diameters that range from a few meters to more than 30 m (average 12 m). Ice wedges develop as a result of cracking of the ground due to contraction during periods of intense and rapid winter cooling. The narrow thermal cracks are subsequently filled by ice in the form of winter hoarfrost or from spring meltwater that freezes. The cracking and ice filling, repeated over many centuries, results in the growth of vertical wedge-shaped masses of ice which penetrate many meters deep and may expand to several tens of meters wide (Lachenbruch 1962).

The increase in volume caused by the expanding ice wedges produces buckling or heaving of the surfaces on either side of the wedges and parallel to them. The ridges or rims so produced, together with melting of the tops of the wedges, cause depressions or troughs immediately above the wedges that further define the polygonal surface pattern (Figure 1-10). As a rule, polygonal terrain becomes more deformed and elevated with the passage of time, as ice wedges expand laterally and polygons subdivide, i.e. secondary ice wedge cracks form within the polygons. Troughs and central basins may deepen as the underlying wedges melt in response to climatic or microclimatic changes. Many of the basins may remain filled with water to form permanent or seasonal ponds.

Where the drainage level has been lowered, as on stream banks and the shores of drained lakes, the trough produced by thawing of ice, thermokarst, and thermal erosion may result in topographic reversal of low-centered polygons. That is, a polygon center that was once low becomes elevated and better-drained with respect to the deepening troughs, and the low-centered polygon is thus converted to a high-centered polygon (Figure 1-10). In extreme cases, particularly where the underlying mineral soil is sandy, the depression of the troughs may be more than 1 m, and the raised centers then consist of dry, peaty soil. Because of their elevated position, the raised areas are vulnerable to desiccation and wind erosion as well as to slumping into the troughs. These processes appear to be accentuated by lemmings, which find the features ideal nest sites and riddle them with burrows, causing further desiccation and oxidation of the peat. In situations where organic materials are removed altogether, the depth of summer thaw increases and frost heaving may convert the surface to small, bare frost scars or boils, or into hummocks.

The sequence of events just described produces the contrasting types

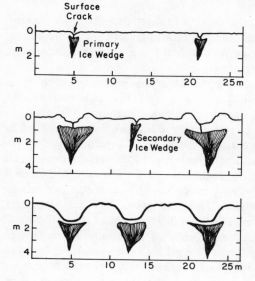

FIGURE 1-10. *Idealized evolution of polygonal ground from initial stage (top) to low-centered polygon (middle) and finally high-centered polygon (bottom). (Modified from Drew and Tedrow 1962 and French 1976.)*

of polygon systems seen on the Biome research area: the large, low-centered, rectangular type (orthogonal) polygons, many of whose centers are permanently water-filled, and the smaller and presumably older nonorthogonal type that shows a gradation of forms, including those with highly elevated centers or tops, broad, flat centers, and low-centered basins (Outcalt 1974). The more complex nonorthogonal polygons cover over 75% of the Biome research area.

The microrelief pattern superimposed on the regional topographic and moisture gradients within the Biome research area creates diverse edaphic and biotic conditions which are further illustrated in the following sections.

SOILS: DESCRIPTION AND DISTRIBUTION

Despite the widespread development of polygonal ground most of the soils in the Biome research area have formed on flat to very gently sloping topography under cold, moist conditions that favor the accumulation of organic matter. A high proportion of the soils have a tripartite morphology: a histic or organic-rich surface horizon; a horizon of silty clay to silt loam textured mineral material, commonly gleyed and with variable amounts of included or enmixed organic materials; and an underlying perennially frozen organic-rich horizon that is commonly coextensive with the horizon above. The sequence of horizons has been interpreted as reflecting the burial of organic materials by lacustrine sediments as a result of the thaw lake cycle or in some cases by frost heaving (Tedrow 1977). The surface horizon and mottling within the mineral horizons are the product of the current soil-forming processes of organic matter accumulation and gleization.

Two soil orders are represented within the Biome research area: Inceptisols, mineral soils with poorly differentiated horizons, and Histosols, soils composed primarily of organic materials (Soil Survey Staff 1975). Because of the high moisture, the Inceptisols are classified as aquepts. Histosols are differentiated taxonomically into suborders reflecting the state of decomposition of their organic materials. Because all the soils have a cold temperature regime the prefix *Cry* is added to each subgroup name. The term *Pergelic* preceding the subgroup name indicates the presence of permafrost. The term *Histic* indicates the peaty character of the surface 25 cm. The areal distribution of the soils or soil combinations is related to landscape units of the Biome research area (Figure 1-11). Weakly leached soils (Pergelic Cryochrepts), represented by the Arctic Brown Soil (Tedrow and Cantlon 1958), are present only on coarser-textured deposits on primary land surfaces such as beach ridges (Figure 1-3) and are not represented within the Biome research area.

The soils, much like the vegetation, are arranged along a topographic gradient ranging from the relatively freely drained and weakly leached Pergelic Cryochrepts (Arctic Brown Soils) to soils developed under conditions of extreme wetness, such as some Pergelic and Histic Pergelic Cryaquepts (Half Bog Soils). Intermediate and somewhat better-drained elements of the topographic–moisture gradient also have Histic Pergelic Cryaquepts and Pergelic Cryaquepts (Meadow Tundra Soils) developed in association with weakly expressed low-centered polygons and low relief high-centered polygons.

Where the low-centered polygonal pattern is strongly developed, an association of soils occurs that is closely related to the elements of that pattern (Figure 1-9). Within the depressed polygon centers (basins), moderately decomposed organic materials constitute Pergelic Cryohemists (organic soils with more than 40 cm of organic materials—Histosols). On the rims of low-centered polygons the soils may be Pergelic Cryosaprists made up of highly decomposed organic materials, extensions of the basin Cryohemists, elevated and oxidized as the polygon rim expanded in response to ice wedge growth, or Pergelic Cryaquepts, little differentiated, mottled mineral soil with widely ranging amounts of organic materials. The latter are more common toward the troughs and show the effects of ice wedge expansion by the disruption of their horizons and enmixing of mineral and organic materials.

Within the polygon troughs the soils may be Pergelic Cryaquepts, composed of coarse, fibrous organic material overlying gray or mottled materials. Where the fibrous organic material reaches a thickness of 25

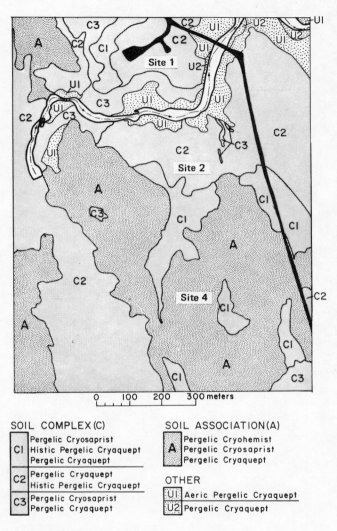

SOIL COMPLEX (C)

C1	Pergelic Cryosaprist Histic Pergelic Cryaquept Pergelic Cryaquept
C2	Pergelic Cryaquept Histic Pergelic Cryaquept
C3	Pergelic Cryosaprist Pergelic Cryaquept

SOIL ASSOCIATION (A)

A	Pergelic Cryohemist Pergelic Cryosaprist Pergelic Cryaquept

OTHER

U1	Aeric Pergelic Cryaquept
U2	Pergelic Cryaquept

FIGURE 1-11. *Generalized soils map of the Biome research area. Soil complexes (C) include two or more soils with no consistent spatial relationship. Soil associations (A) consist of two or more soils (three at Barrow) in a predictable spatial arrangement, e.g. associated with polygon rims, centers and troughs. In other areas (U) a single soil dominates. Details of the soils for site 4 are shown in Figures 1-8 and 1-9.*

TABLE 1-3 *Characteristics of the Principal Soils of the Biome Research Sites 1, 2 and 4*

| Soil taxon | Most commonly associated landform element and soil combination | Most commonly associated vegetation type(s) | Snow depth range, June 73 (cm) | Thaw depth 3-16 Aug 1970-73 (cm) | Summer avg temp, 7.5 cm (°C) | Surface organic horizon thickness (cm) | Surface organic C content (%) | Soil properties (0-10 cm) | | | | CEC based on sum of bases (meq 100 g⁻¹) |
								Moisture, 1972 (% dry wt)	Bulk density (g cm⁻³)	Sand:silt ratio	Reaction (H₂O paste)	
Pergelic Cryaquept	Frost boil (A)[1]	II[2]	ND[5]	40-60	ND	0.0-0.5	≤22	ND	ND	ND	ND	57
	Wet meadow (C2)	V, VI, VII	27-35	27-30	6.3	11-12	37-45	428	0.18	0.05-0.24	5.4	34
Histic Pergelic Cryaquept	Polygon rims–dry meadow (A, C1)	III	15-18	24-35	7.3	5-25	7-31	61	0.64	0.12-11.2	5.8	66
	Polygon troughs (A, C2)	IV, V	33-43	29-36	8.0	10-28	10-43	140	0.50	0.22-0.54	5.4	44
Pergelic Cryohemist	Moist meadow (C2)	IV	16-26	30-33	6.8	5-8	21-24	151	0.43	0.12-0.40	5.5	61
	Polygon centers (A)	III, IV, VI	45-46	29-37	7.7	8-45+	40-48	263	0.26	0.17-0.35	5.1	58
Pergelic Cryosaprist	High-centered poly-gons (C3)	I	0	36	ND	30+	29	77	0.33	0.37	4.9	50
	Aeric Pergelic Cryaquept (U1-U2)	II	2-6	40-49[3]	6.8	0.5-3	5-10	49	0.92[4]	0.18-1.87	ND	ND

1—Refer to Figure 1-11.
2—Refer to Table 1-4 and Figure 1-12.
3—Sandy alluvial soil, not included, may thaw to 90 cm.
4—Data 0-5 cm (probably somewhat lower values than 0-10 cm depth).
5—Not determined.

cm, the soils are considered Histic Pergelic Cryaquepts. Rarely is the organic material of sufficient thickness that Pergelic Cryohemists or the very fibrous Cryofibrists can be recognized. This association of soils repeats from polygon to polygon.

On the centers of prominent high-centered polygons Pergelic Cryosaprists are found. They are the products of oxidation of Pergelic Cryohemists of the former polygon basin. Lighter-colored Aeric Pergelic Cryaquepts are found on the coarser-textured and better-drained mineral soil slopes marginal to Footprint Creek.

The maximum thaw depths encountered across the entire Biome research area ranged between 24 and 60 cm (Table 1-3). Thaw variation as a function of microrelief showed less deviation from the mean early in the season than later in the summer, when site characteristics had had time to exert their full influence. However, thaw differences between rims of low-centered polygons and centers of high-centered polygons decrease during the season as the tundra surface becomes generally drier. Measurements of mean mid-August thaw depth from 1970 to 1974 in 10 control plots on the *Carex–Oncophorus* meadow (site 2) showed only a 2-cm difference between years (25.2, 26.9, 26.7, 24.7 and 24.7 cm). The small difference in mean depth between summers with quite different meteorological conditions indicates that the soil that remains near saturation is subject to a relatively small mean fluctuation in thaw. However, for a more diverse terrain some 4 km to the northeast, Brown (1969) measured average thaw between 33 and 43 cm over the period 1962 to 1966.

VEGETATION

Sedge meadows cover about three-quarters of the Biome research area (Webber 1978) (Table 1-4, Figure 1-12). The meadows are dominated by a single species, *Carex aquatilis*, and commonly have only a few secondary species, such as *Eriophorum angustifolium, E. scheuchzeri* and *Dupontia fisheri*. They also have a large moss component consisting of species of *Calliergon* and *Drepanocladus*. Lichens are a minor component of these meadows (Murray 1978). Complete species nomenclature for the Biome research area is given in Murray and Murray (1978).

The most striking feature of the vegetation is that it changes character every few meters in response to change of microtopography and drainage (Figure 1-8). The vegetation changes are best indicated by variations in the subordinate species, especially the mosses and grasses. Thus the ubiquitous *Carex aquatilis* dominates the meadow vegetation types which occur along a moisture gradient from dry to wet.

Eight major vegetation types were recognized and mapped (Figure

TABLE 1-4 *The Eight Vegetation Types of the Biome Research Area*

Vegetation type	Dominant species*	Characteristic microtopographic units	Area (%)
Luzula heath (I)	*Luzula confusa, Potentilla hyparctica, Alectoria nigricans, Pogonatum alpinum, Psilopilum cavifolium*	Tops of high-centered polygons	3
Salix heath (II)	*Salix rotundifolia, Arctagrostis latifolia, Saxifraga nelsoniana, Sphaerophorus globosus, Brachythecium salebrosum*	Rims of low-centered polygons and creek banks	7
Carex–Poa meadow (III)	*Carex aquatilis, Poa arctica, Luzula arctica, Cetraria richardsonii, Pogonatum alpinum*	Rims of low-centered polygons and dry, relatively undeveloped polygonized sites	41
Carex–Oncophorus meadow (IV)	*Carex aquatilis, Oncophorus wahlenbergii, Dupontia fisheri, Peltigera aphthosa, Aulacomnium turgidum*	Moist, flat sites and drained polygon troughs	21
Dupontia meadow (V)	*Dupontia fisheri, Eriophorum angustifolium, Cerastium jenisejense, Peltigera canina, Campylium stellatum*	Wet, flat sites and polygon troughs	7
Carex–Eriophorum meadow (VI)	*Carex aquatilis, Eriophorum russeolum, Saxifraga foliolosa, Calliergon sarmentosum, Drepanocladus brevifolius*	Basins of low-centered polygons and pond margins	15
Arctophila pond margin (VII)	*Arctophila fulva, Ranunculus pallasii, Ranunculus gmelinii, Eriophorum russeolum, Calliergon giganteum*	Pond and stream margins	2
Cochlearia meadow (VIII)	*Cochlearia officinalis, Phippsia algida, Ranunculus pygmaeus, Stellaria humifusa, Saxifraga rivularis*	Snowbeds, creek banks and creek sides	4

*Species are listed in order of amount of cover.

26

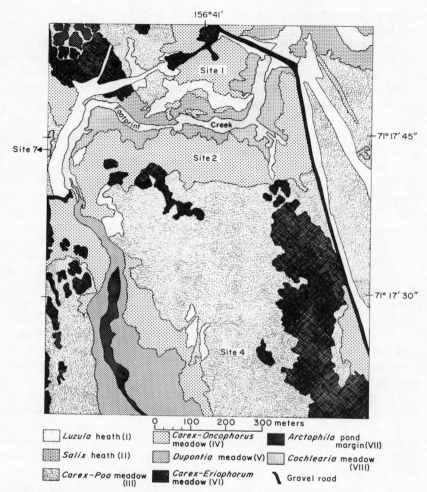

FIGURE 1-12. *Vegetation map of the Biome research sites. The types have been coded according to their most abundant vegetation. The details of the vegetation for site 4 are shown in Figure 1-8. (After Webber 1978.)*

1-12) and an estimate of the area occupied by each type was computed (Table 1-4; Webber 1978). *Luzula* heath (Type I), which occupies only 3% of the Biome research area, is characteristic of high-centered polygons and some raised beaches. The low density of species and individuals within the *Luzula* heath is due to dryness, elevation above the water table, thin snow cover, and exposure to winds. The characteristic growth-forms present are caespitose graminoids and lichens. Characteristic species include *Luzula confusa, Potentilla hyparctica, Alectoria nigricans* and *Pogonatum alpinum*.

Salix heath (Type II) is characteristic of the sloping creek banks and the centers of some low-centered polygons which drain readily. It occupies 7% of the research area. *Salix rotundifolia*, a prostrate deciduous shrub, *Arctagrostis latifolia* and *Saxifraga nelsoniana* characterize this type. The *Salix* heath has the highest number of forbs (22) and the highest overall number of species (70) of any of the vegetation types. The sandy soil associated with *Salix* heath is usually well drained and has the greatest seasonal depth of thaw.

Carex–Poa meadow (Type III) is the most extensive vegetation type, covering 41% of the research area. Bryophytes, primarily mosses, and lichens cover relatively larger areas than do the graminoids. The mosses *Pogonatum alpinum* and *Dicranum elongatum* and the lichens *Cetraria richardsonii* and *Dactylina arctica* are characteristic species. The *Carex–Oncophorus* meadow, *Dupontia* meadow, and *Carex–Eriophorum* meadow all have the same superficial meadow physiognomy. The *Carex–Poa* meadow is separated from the other meadow vegetation types by the abundance of *Poa arctica*, which is prominent when in flower, and by the presence of a high lichen diversity. *Carex–Poa* meadow is best developed in the drier parts of the polygonized sedge meadow complex where large, flat, and sometimes slightly raised low-centered polygons with barely discernible troughs occur. The *Carex–Poa* meadow is also common on hummocky rims of low-centered polygons in wetter areas and in areas with pronounced polygon development.

Carex–Oncophorus meadow (Type IV), the second most extensive vegetation type, occupying 21% of the map area, develops on moister sites than the *Carex–Poa* meadow.It occurs on flat polygon centers and in drained, shallow polygon troughs. It is distinguished from *Carex–Poa* meadow on the basis of reduced lichen cover and the presence of mosses such as *Calliergon sarmentosum, Oncophorus wahlenbergii*, and *Aulacomnium turgidum*, and of *Dupontia fisheri* and *Peltigera aphthosa*. The *Carex–Oncophorus* meadow has the greatest number of graminoid species and was the vegetation type most intensively studied during the Tundra Biome program.

Dupontia meadow (Type V) occupies 7% of the mapped area. It is characteristic of flat, slowly draining sites and wet polygon troughs. *Eriophorum russeolum* is also common in this type, but the low cover of *Carex* and the greater abundance of *Dupontia* and *Eriophorum angustifolium* distinguish it from the other meadow types. Woody dicotyledons are essentially absent but several forbs occur. *Cerastium jenisejense, Stellaria edwardsii* and *S. laeta* may form distinctive mats, and *Saxifraga cernua* is a common erect forb.

The vegetation that composes the *Carex–Eriophorum* meadow

(Type VI) is variable. This type includes the sparse vegetation of the basins of low-centered polygons as well as the more abundant vegetation of some pond margins. It has no woody species, and only a few lichens. *Saxifraga foliolosa* is characteristic of the basins and *Calliergon sarmentosum* is characteristic of the pond margins. *Drepanocladus brevifolius* is common throughout this type. Low species diversity, thick organic mat, and highly organic soils distinguish Type VI from the other meadow types. Spring snow cover on this type is moderately deep and late to recede.

The vegetation type termed *Arctophila* pond margin (Type VII) is also found in slow-flowing streams and is the most distinct of the principal types, although it occupies only 2% of the area. Woody plants and lichens are totally absent. Single-shooted graminoids, erect forbs and bryophytes all contribute to this vegetation type, although the emergent grass *Arctophila fulva* is characteristic. *Ranunculus pallasii* and *Caltha palustris* are occasionally present. The pleurocarpous mosses *Calliergon giganteum* and *Drepanocladus brevifolius* are the principal bryophytes. Late in the growing season the substrate of *Arctophila* pond margin may occasionally become anaerobic and have a characteristic odor of hydrogen sulfide.

The *Cochlearia* meadow (Type VIII) is a rudimentary community that develops on recent alluvium in the creek bed that crosses the Biome research area, where snow commonly accumulates and remains late in the growing season. The sandy, moist alluvial soil of the *Cochlearia* meadow thaws deeply and the active layer may exceed 1 m in late summer. This vegetation type is floristically rich, but extremely variable. *Cochlearia officinalis*, *Phippsia algida* and *Stellaria humifusa* are the principal species present.

The variations in vegetation and soil across microtopographic features are a dominant aspect of the coastal tundra at Barrow. Many of the following chapters deal with the structure and function of tundra organisms across these unique landscape units.

2

Climate, Snow Cover, Microclimate, and Hydrology

S. L. Dingman, R. G. Barry, G. Weller,
C. Benson, E. F. LeDrew, and C. W. Goodwin

INTRODUCTION

The environmental conditions within a few meters above or below the ground surface constitute the microclimate of a region, and it is to these conditions that most terrestrial organisms must adapt. The microclimate is characterized by the radiation, temperature, and moisture regimes of the near-surface atmospheric and soil layers. These regimes are determined largely by the regional climate, as modified by local topography and by the vegetation cover.

Quantitatively, the microclimate is described by the energy and water balances at the surface. These balances are complexly related. The net radiation input to the land surface provides the energy that is utilized in surface physical and biological processes. The energy balance expresses how this energy is partitioned, and the water balance is determined by the energy balance. At the same time, the water balance influences the magnitude of the energy balance components through latent heat exchanges and through the effects of snow on surface conditions.

For comparison, descriptions of radiation, energy and water balances at other arctic sites can be found in Ohmura (1972), Weller and Holmgren (1974a and b), Woo (1976), Ohmura and Muller (1976), Stewart and Rouse (1976), Courtin and Labine (1977), Rydén (1977), and LeDrew and Weller (1978). Dingman (1973) published an annotated bibliography covering much of the pre-1972 literature on the water balance in arctic and subarctic regions.

CLIMATE

Climatic Setting

Traditionally, areas where the average temperature of the warmest month is below 10 °C have been identified as having a tundra climate

(Köppen 1936). More recently, temperature data were used to identify air masses, and Bryson (1966) showed that arctic tundra areas in North America have at least a 50% frequency of arctic air in July. The median location of the Arctic Front in July corresponds approximately with the northern limit of boreal forest (see map inside front cover), although in eastern North America the definition of the frontal zone and its relationship with vegetation boundaries is less certain (Barry 1967). The exact causal relationship between this frontal position and the biota remains uncertain, but the lack of trees in the arctic tundra must be attributable in part to the poleward decline of available surface energy. Annual net radiation at the treeline is about 670 MJ m^{-2} in Alaska and 750 MJ m^{-2} in central Canada, and decreases to 400 to 600 MJ m^{-2} over the tundra (Hare and Ritchie 1972).

The general weather conditions in northern Alaska are a result of the patterns of atmospheric circulation. The mean sea level pressure map shows that in winter Alaska is influenced by easterly arctic airstreams associated with a deep low over the Aleutians and a ridge of high pressure from the Mackenzie Valley across the Arctic Ocean towards eastern Siberia. A ten-year analysis of daily weather maps by Putnins (1966) illustrates the winter maximum of anticyclonic patterns with high pressure cells predominantly to the north and east of Alaska.

Winter conditions at Barrow are similar to those over most of the Arctic Slope, but during summer its coastal location gives it a modified arctic tundra climate (Watson 1959, Searby and Hunter 1971). The temperature regime north of the Brooks Range is continental, with an annual range of 32 °C for monthly mean temperatures (Table 2-1). Extreme maxima and minima have ranged between 26 °C and −49 °C at Barrow, and between 39 °C and −61 °C (unofficial reading) at Umiat in the central Colville River Valley (Conover 1960). Mean daily temperatures are below −20 °C at Barrow from December through March. February is the coldest month, with 90% of hourly temperatures below −18 °C (Rayner 1960a, b). The severe temperatures are accompanied by moderate wind speeds, averaging 5 m s^{-1}, which often cause blowing snow. In contrast to inland localities, the wind is seldom calm at Barrow; speeds above 12 m s^{-1} are also infrequent (Figure 2-1). Winds along the arctic coast are easterly except in the vicinity of Barter Island, where the regional topography frequently causes strong westerly winds in winter (Schwerdtfeger 1975).

The winter temperature regime is closely related to the presence of a surface temperature inversion which has an average intensity of about 12 °C over a vertical distance of 750 m (Bilello 1966). A ground-based inversion is present on 62% of winter days, and for half of these days the inversion layer is more than 1000 m thick (Holzworth 1974). The resulting stability of the lower troposphere implies that day-to-day temperature changes are largely determined by changes in cloud cover and the

TABLE 2-1 *Monthly and Annual Values of Temperature and Precipitation for Alaskan Arctic Coastal Stations Within the Period of Biome Investigations*

Year	J	F	M	A	M	J	J	A	S	O	N	D	Annual
Temperature (°C)													
Barrow													
1970	-24.7	-27.2	-28.0	-19.4	-7.2	3.2	0.5	1.7	-3.5	-17.5	-20.1	-23.4	-13.8
1971	-28.6	-32.3	-27.9	-20.3	-8.1	4.7	1.7	0.8	-0.2	-9.9	-18.1	-24.1	-13.5
1972	-26.8	-28.4	-28.7	-20.2	-7.7	6.1	0.3	4.8	-0.4	-6.1	-17.0	-19.4	-11.9
1973	-25.3	-25.1	-29.3	-19.3	-7.2	4.3	0.7	4.3	1.1	-7.0	-13.4	-20.8	-11.4
1941-70	-25.9	-28.1	-26.2	-18.3	-7.2	3.7	0.6	3.1	-0.9	-9.3	-18.1	-24.6	-12.6
Barter Island													
NWS normal	-26.2	-28.4	-25.9	-17.7	-6.1	4.4	1.2	3.8	-0.2	-8.7	-17.7	-24.7	-12.2
Prudhoe Bay													
1970	-27.6	-28.9	-29.2	-18.6	-7.2	2.1	5.4	4.8	-2.5	-17.2	-19.5	-27.6	-13.9
1971	-32.9	-37.1	-29.7	-21.7	-6.8	4.1	7.2	2.7	-0.5	-13.6	-20.7	-28.4	-14.8
1972	-29.4	-32.4	-31.5	-21.5	-7.3	2.2	6.3	5.7	-1.8	-8.6	-18.4	-22.7	-13.3
1973	-26.9	-28.7	-33.7	-19.1	-5.4	2.2	6.8	6.4	1.7	-10.4	-17.4	-22.6	-12.3
Average	-29.2	-31.8	-31.0	-20.2	-6.7	2.6	6.4	4.9	-0.8	-12.5	-19.0	-25.3	-13.6
Precipitation (mm)													
Barrow													
1970	1.8	2.3	1.5	3.8	2.3	0.5	3.8	8.9	3.6	4.1	11.9	2.3	46.7
1971	4.6	3.3	4.1	0.5	6.4	3.1	24.9	8.9	4.3	9.1	4.3	4.6	78.0
1972	1.3	4.8	T	0.3	1.5	1.3	2.8	28.5	33.8	33.6	10.9	4.3	125.0
1973	1.8	4.1	1.0	13.2	4.8	19.8	26.9	55.9	29.0	14.2	9.1	2.3	182.1
1941-70	5.8	5.1	4.8	5.3	4.3	8.9	22.4	26.4	14.7	14.0	7.6	4.8	124.1
Adjusted*	9.3	8.2	7.7	8.5	6.9	9.8	24.6	29.0	23.5	22.4	12.2	7.7	169.8
Barter Island													
NWS normal	13.9	8.4	6.6	5.8	7.9	13.5	28.5	32.5	22.6	20.6	11.4	7.4	179.0
Adjusted*	22.2	13.4	10.6	9.3	12.6	14.8	29.6	35.8	36.2	33.0	18.2	11.8	247.5

*Basis for adjustment is discussed in text.
Source: Barrow and Barter Island—U.S. Department of Commerce; Prudhoe Bay—Brown et al. (1975).

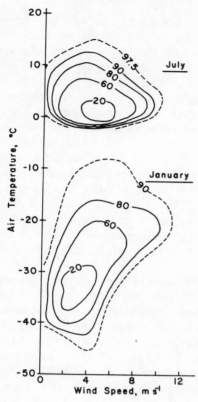

FIGURE 2-1. *Cumulative frequencies of hourly air temperatures and wind speeds at the village of Barrow, 1945–54. The frequencies are expressed as the cumulative percentage frequencies of the total distribution. (After Rayner 1960a, b.)*

effect of clouds on infrared radiation, rather than by changes of air mass. Deep Pacific cyclones affect southern Alaska and the Bering Sea but seldom penetrate to the Arctic Slope. When they do, the frontal systems tend to move above the 1000- to 1500-m-deep inversion layer and may not affect the weather at the surface.

The persistence of anticyclonic conditions during late winter leads to clear skies and the receipt of a high percentage of the possible solar radiation. The mid- to late winter period has an average of 10 or more days per month with clear skies, associated with the 45 to 50% frequency of anticyclonic patterns.

Temperatures begin to rise in late winter but lag 4 to 6 weeks behind the increase in solar radiation. The mean daily temperature is above freezing from June through August, but fails to reach 5°C even in July as a result of coastal cloudiness and the effect of the Arctic Ocean. The Arctic Ocean maintains a cover of close pack ice in summer except for open water areas which extend some 30 to 100 km from the coast by August or September. Even in August the open water is only about 3°C (Searby and

Hunter 1971). This cold surface cools the lowest layers of the atmosphere, thus providing a source of cool air and sea breeze conditions (Moritz 1977, Walsh 1977). Forty-three percent of hourly temperatures in July are at or below 0 °C (Rayner 1960a, b), and on the average there are only 91 days with a mean daily temperature above 0 °C each year.

Cloudiness increases during May and June as moisture becomes available from open areas in the sea ice. Fog formed over the Arctic Ocean drifts inland, often as low stratus that forms following warming of the surface air. Convective activity further modifies the cloud type to stratocumulus. At the coast, heavy fog occurs on about one day in three from June through August. In May and June this fog and cloud cover reduce the proportion of possible solar radiation actually received at the surface and depress temperatures near the coast. Simulations by Lord et al. (1972) show the importance of such cloud cover in suppressing the diurnal range of temperature at the surface. However, until snowmelt the effect of cloud cover is in part offset by the multiple reflections between the snow surface and the clouds.

During the summer temperatures increase from the coast inland. The mean daily temperature in July at Umiat for the years 1947-53 was 12 °C. This inland warmth was demonstrated in July 1966 when the air temperature at the coast averaged 10.6 °C when winds were southerly and 2.7 °C when winds were off the ocean (Weaver 1970, Barry et al. 1976, Myers and Pitelka 1979). According to Brown et al. (1975) the mean temperature gradient inland from the arctic coast is 6 °C per 100 km, although they suggest that much of this warming occurs close to the coast where the gradient may be two to three times greater (Walsh 1977). The tundra at Barrow is typical of the very cool, moist zone in the immediate vicinity of the coast. In the Prudhoe Bay region, the area south of the bay is transitional to the warmer inland zone which extends into the Foothills, but still is significantly cooler than locations 20 km or more inland (Walker and Webber 1979). Average thawing indices, the sum of the positive differences between daily mean temperature and 0 °C, for 1970-73 are 304 at Barrow but 477 at Prudhoe Bay (Brown et al. 1975).

From July through September the strong temperature gradient from the snow-free land to the cold, largely ice-covered Arctic Ocean sets up a horizontal density gradient that is referred to as the Arctic Front. An average of four weak lows per month travel eastward along this frontal zone from the Siberian arctic coast. About 35% of the annual precipitation falls, mainly as rain, during these three months in association with these systems (Table 2-1). The Arctic Front is generally at a height of 300 to 700 m over the coast, and reaches the ground about halfway between the coast and the Foothills (Conover 1960). When the front moves inland, the shallow layer of arctic air that covers the whole Arctic Slope produces cold, foggy weather. This air tends to advance up the river valleys so that hilltops a few hundred meters in elevation may be warmer than the valleys below. Less frequently, the front retreats poleward and thus allows the entire area to be warmed by land winds. An analysis of the Arctic Front by Streten (1974), using very high resolution radiometer (VHRR) imagery from the NOAA-2 satellite, showed considerable variability in cloudiness associated with the frontal zone. It also confirmed the front's northward advance from early to midsummer, as determined by Barry (1967), and its southward retreat by August. By October, the circulation regime has reverted back to its winter mode as the arctic inversion redevelops over the snow-covered land.

Annual precipitation on the Arctic Slope is light, although data are inadequate to describe regional trends in any detail. Clebsch and Shanks (1968) found that amounts in July and August 1956 were 50% greater at stations located 2, 15 and 55 km inland than at the first-order weather station at Barrow. Theoretically, easterly airflow along the arctic coast should tend to produce divergence and suppression of precipitation over the coastal strip (Bryson and Kuhn 1961), although this effect is less in higher latitudes than in low latitudes. At the present time, data on surface and upper winds and on precipitation amounts are inadequate to test this hypothesis. Total precipitation is undoubtedly higher to the south and in the Brooks Range, with an estimated 500 mm falling on the upper McCall Glacier at 2275 m (Wendler et al. 1974). Kilday (1974) indicated that annual totals exceed 500 mm over most of the Brooks Range and are 1000 mm in the wettest eastern section. In the coastal tundra at Barrow, rainfall intensity is low, with frequent drizzle and light snow falling during May and June from the coastal stratus clouds. Freezing rain also occurs during this season as well as during the autumn transition. The maximum 6-hour total rainfall recorded is 15 mm (Miller 1963); a 24-hour snowfall of 38 cm has been recorded in October.

Interannual Variability and the
Representativeness of the Biome Years

The interannual variability, expressed by the standard deviation of mean monthly temperature, is approximately 3 °C during the winter months, October through February, but declines to just over 1 °C in July and August. The winter variability is associated with shifts in the Arctic Frontal zone. The extreme variations from the 1924-73 mean occurred in January 1930, with a deviation of +11.4 °C, and January 1925, with a deviation of -8.1 °C. During the summer months there is less departure from the long-term average; the extremes are +4.9 °C in August 1954 and -3.6 °C in August 1956.

Another approach to calculating interannual variability using cumu-

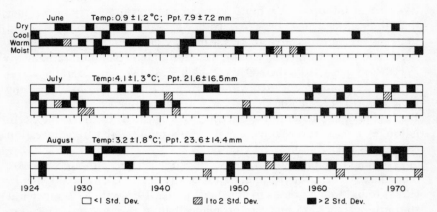

FIGURE 2-2. *Summary of deviations of temperature and precipitation from monthly means (1924–73) during summer months for the village of Barrow.*

lative thawing degree-days has been taken by Myers and Pitelka (1979). They demonstrated that 7 of the 26 years from 1950 to 1975 deviated more than 100 cumulative degrees Celsius from the average daily mean temperature. Early spring and late July and August are shown to vary more from year to year than June and early July. The high variability in August is related to the strong contrasts between temperatures associated with winds blowing over the Beaufort and Chukchi Seas or over land. Hence, climatic conditions near the coast are closely determined by atmosphere–ocean–ice interactions (Barry et al. 1976). The precipitation data, which are subject to measurement problems, have much greater interannual variability.

The long-term patterns of some individual months indicate that the mean departure for December 1932-41 was +2.0°C, whereas that for December 1953-61 was -2.2°C; this difference is significant at the 2% level by Student's *t*. For June, the period 1925-32 had a departure of +1.3°C; this difference is significant at the 5% level. There are no comparable shifts for July or August, although July 1959-70 averaged 0.8°C below, and August 1959-71 0.9°C below, the respective 1924-73 mean values. When running-mean techniques are used on individual summer months at 5-year intervals, there are suggestions that the mid-1950s and the late 1960s were cooler than the long-term means. Rogers (1978), using a linear regression of thaw season degree-days against time, found a summer cooling trend over the 56-year period of air temperature records at Barrow. In terms of the departure of total precipitation from the 1924-73 monthly averages, there was a tendency for more dry months in summer between 1964 and 1972, whereas the 1950s were generally wetter

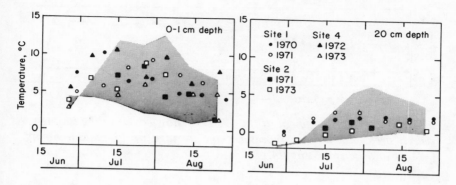

FIGURE 2-3. *Ten-day mean soil temperatures at the Biome research area as measured during 1970–73 and simulated for the extreme years during 1960–73. The shaded area represents the range of the simulated soil temperatures for the warmest year, 1968, and the coldest year, 1969.*

than average (Figure 2-2).

A major question in any short-term observational program is how representative the data are with respect to long-term conditions and trends. During the 4 years of Biome measurements the positive departures of temperature from the long-term summer observations were especially pronounced during 1972: +2.4°C in July and +1.7°C in August (Figure 2-2, Table 2-1). Precipitation also varied from the long-term averages during the research period: July was much drier than average in 1970 and 1972, and slightly wetter than average in 1971 and 1973.

In order to compare the representativeness of soil temperatures during the Biome years with those in the previous decade when temperatures were not measured, a surface equilibrium temperature model was used to simulate soil temperature and thaw for the period 1960–73. The model, a modification of one developed by Outcalt et al. (1975) to simulate annual snow and soil thermal regimes, predicted daily soil temperatures on a 5-cm grid for the 14-year period. The actual data obtained for the Biome years are within the predicted extremes of simulated soil temperatures (Figure 2-3). Therefore it is reasonable to assume that soil temperatures observed during the 1970-73 Biome period are within the range of variation normally encountered on the tundra at Barrow.

SNOW COVER

Most plants and animals are small enough to live within the protective blanket of snow, and larger predators and herbivores depend,

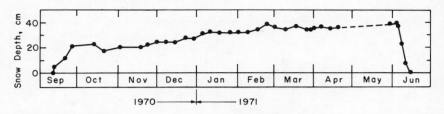

FIGURE 2-4. *Development of the 1970–71 snow cover on the Biome research area. Each point represents the average of 15 measurements. (Weller and Benson, unpubl.)*

directly or indirectly, on food-chain members harbored within the snow cover. Thus a knowledge of snow distribution and structure is an essential part of the understanding of tundra ecology (Pruitt 1960, Formozov 1961). The most detailed work on the nature of the snowpack on the Alaskan Arctic Slope is reported in Benson (1969) and Benson et al. (1975).

The major surface processes during the winter are the accumulation of snow, its redistribution by wind, and the transfer of mass and energy within the snowpack. Over most of the tundra at Barrow, the snow builds to a thickness of about 20 cm within 10 to 20 days after freeze-up, following which it continues to increase very slowly in thickness (Figure 2-4). The initial snow cover markedly reduces surface roughness and permits more effective snow drifting. Snow is deposited in drift traps and, as the winter progresses, the surface relief becomes more and more subdued.

With the establishment of the snow cover and the virtual disappearance of solar energy input at the surface the net radiation becomes negative. The radiational cooling at the surface sets up fairly steep temperature inversions above the ground, so that both atmosphere and ground supply heat to the surface, one by eddy diffusion, the other by conduction. These conditions induce a flow of heat and moisture from the soil surface upward through the snowpack, driven in part by wind and barometric fluctuations (Benson 1969). There is a consequent general drying of the upper soil layers and formation of depth hoar in the snowpack. This results in a net gain of moisture in the snow because of the upward transport of water. Some condensation at the snow surface also adds to the mass of the snow (Weller and Holmgren 1974a).

Although fresh snow continues to accumulate throughout the winter, the steady winds constantly reshape the pattern of the snow cover. Across the smoothed surface, barchan-type dunes form and move during storm periods. During less windy periods, these dunes stabilize and become drift traps for future storms. Exceptionally high winds may

TABLE 2-2   *Types of Snow Found on the*
Windblown Arctic Coastal Plain

Snow type	Range of grain size (mm)	Range of density (g cm⁻³)*
Fresh new snow, variable crystal forms	0.5 to 1.0 sometimes <0.5	0.15 to 0.20
Hard, fine-grained wind slab	0.5 to 1.0	0.35 to 0.45
Medium-grained snow	1 to 2	0.23 to 0.35
Depth hoar: soft, coarse, loosely bonded crystals	5 to 10	0.20 to 0.30

*The density ranges are approximate, but they indicate the differences one may expect between the various layers.

remove or reshape the old dunes and even reexpose some of the vegetation. The interaction of wind effects and transfer processes within the snowpack produces four snow types (Table 2-2) and four typical snow structures:

1. A hard, fine-grained, high density, windpacked layer overlying a soft, coarse-grained, low density layer. The upper layer is frequently a wind slab; the lower is almost entirely depth hoar. This two-layer structure is the most common, being present over about 80% of the open tundra.
2. The hard wind slab layer alone, found over about 15% of the open tundra.
3. The soft depth hoar alone, covering about 5% of the open tundra.
4. A complex, deep snowpack, largely wind slab and medium-grained snow, in natural drift traps such as creek bottoms.

The development of the two-layer structural type as seen in Figure 2-5 is a direct consequence of the depositional history of the snow. The rapidly deposited snow layers of September contain few significant wind slabs and are the primary units in which depth hoar develops. As the season progresses, the wind causes very hard snow layers to form as small increments of new snow are added. Admixtures of silt or fine sand from exposed roads or dunes, or of particles of vegetation, strengthen wind slabs.

The continual heat flux from the soil below the snow keeps the soil/snow interface temperature above that of the upper snow surface. This

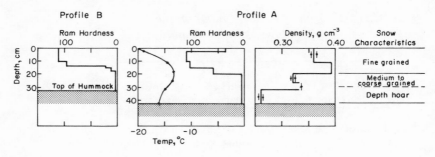

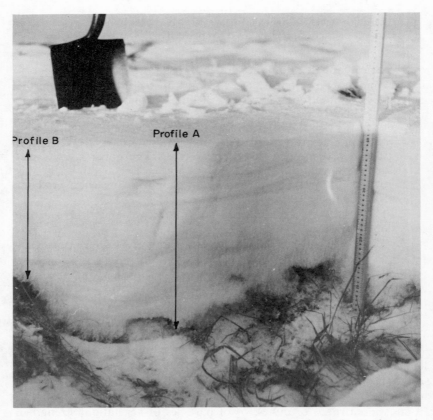

FIGURE 2-5. *Profile of the snow cover showing depth hoar above the vegetation and ice layers, and plots of physical properties. ("Ram hardness" is a measure of the snow's resistance to the penetration of a cone under an impact of known energy.) (After Benson 1969.)*

temperature gradient is accompanied by a vapor pressure gradient, which results in upward transfer of water vapor accompanied by recrystallization of the lower part of the snowpack into depth-hoar crystals. Most of the mass removed from the lower part of the snow cover is redeposited in the colder upper part, where it aids in the development of wind slabs. The rate of mass transfer within snow in interior Alaska, where stronger temperature gradients persist in the snow, has been calculated by Trabant and Benson (1972) and is on the order of 0.02 to 0.03 g cm^{-2} day^{-1}.

The depth hoar layer is so fragile that it often disintegrates with the slightest disturbance, causing the collapsed snow or snowquakes commonly observed when one walks in an undisturbed area. These snowquakes are first observed in November and then with increasing frequency until April, and are generally restricted to a few thousand square meters in area because of the support afforded by hummocky microrelief.

The second structural type, a hard layer of snow without underlying depth hoar, develops after wind erosion entirely removes the snow cover from a small area. Subsequently, a new wind slab forms almost directly on the surface. This process has been observed during a single storm, i.e. as the winds shift slightly in direction, an area may change from an erosional regimen to one of deposition. Rarely does an area remain denuded of snow for long.

The third structural type is rare and occurs only when wind erosion removes the wind slab layers, leaving the depth hoar. The structure may be somewhat stabilized by a thin wind crust, which is usually removed or covered by the next wind event.

Almost any irregularity on the surface serves as a drift trap, at least under some wind conditions. The snow depth is generally related to the height of the vegetation. Snow is also caught in the low areas between polygons, which generally become filled by mid-October. Along the coast drifts often exceed 4 m in depth. However, the most extensive drifts accumulate in stream channels incised a meter or more below the tundra surface. For example, on the Meade River at Atkasook drifts are often several kilometers long, up to 20 m wide, and 10 m deep.

The large drifts that form on the banks of rivers and lakes are separated into two groups, one formed by storm winds from the west which bring most of the new snow and the other by the prevailing northeasterly winds. The general shapes of the drifts are reproduced each year. The sizes and shapes of the prevailing-wind drifts are virtually independent of the amount of snowfall. However, the sizes of storm-wind drifts vary significantly with the amount of snowfall. As an example of this process cross sections of drifts on the banks of the Meade River were measured between 1962 and 1973 (Figure 2-6). Drifts caused by storm winds were at

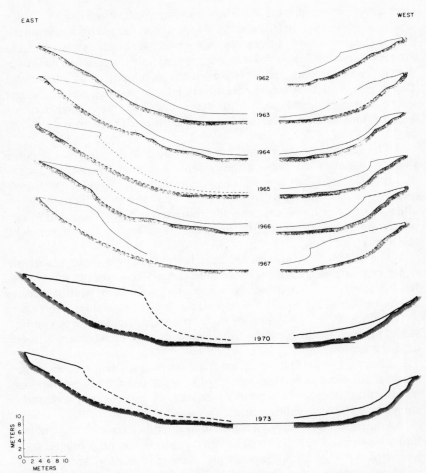

FIGURE 2-6. *Profiles of snowdrifts on the banks of the Meade River at Atkasook (70°29'N, 157°24'W) as seen from the north. The drifts on the west side are formed by storm winds from the west and vary in size with the amount of snowfall. The drifts on the east side are formed by prevailing winds from the east and are virtually independent of the amount of snowfall. (After Benson 1969.)*

a minimum in 1964 and a maximum in 1967, while prevailing wind drifts were nearly constant in size (Benson 1969).

By early December and until the following spring melt, diurnal changes in air temperature do not appreciably influence the soil thermal regime. The insulating effect of the winter snow causes the amplitude of daily temperature fluctuations to decrease with depth and results in

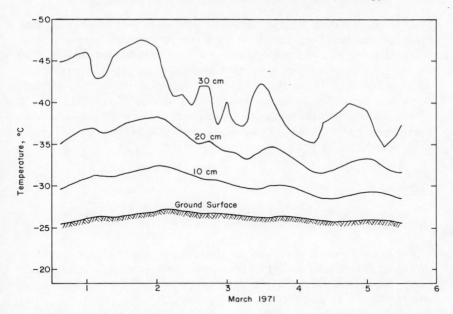

FIGURE 2-7. *Temperatures in the snow during 1-6 March, the coldest period in 1971. The numbers on the graphs give the distance above the ground surface at which snow temperatures were measured.*

warmer conditions at the snow/ground interface (Figure 2-7). Although the temperature at the air/snow interface during the 6 days shown in Figure 2-7 ranged between –47°C and –35°C, the temperature at the snow/soil interface stayed within a degree or two of –26°C. The snow temperature phase lag and amplitude attenuation indicate that the effective thermal diffusivity of the snow is larger by a factor of 3 to 4 than that of the organic materials just below the snow/soil interface. Thus, the rather stable and relatively warm thermal environment at the snow/ soil interface is produced by the mass of snow overlying the interface and not by the thermal properties of the snow cover per se. Increasing depths of snow favor a more moderate snow/soil interface environment, with reduced temperature extremes and a higher mean temperature.

The typical two-layer snow structure is the most favorable environment for small mammals like lemmings. The loose depth-hoar layer gives little resistance to burrowing, and the hard wind slab provides protection from wind and from predators. At a snow fence site (Slaughter et al. 1975, Outcalt et al. 1975), where the maximum snow depth was increased to nearly 2 m by drifting, there was evidence of much more intense lemming activity and nesting than on the surrounding tundra, where the natural snow depth was less than 0.5 m. Other mobile organisms also seek out natural deep snow areas to take advantage of the more moderate interface climate. Deep-drifted snow in narrow gullies, between high-centered polygons, and near ponds is a favorable winter habitat. The other two structural types, hard snow and soft snow alone, are relatively unfavorable sites. When the wind slab is very near the surface it effectively cuts off the area; no burrowing was found in hard wind slabs. If only a depth hoar layer remains after removal of the wind slab, low temperatures occur at the soil/snow interface because of the high air permeability of the depth hoar.

MICROCLIMATE

Definition of Microclimate Seasons

A characteristic succession of physical processes is observed each year on the tundra: establishment of the winter regime through large radiant energy losses, modification of the snowpack just prior to melting, generally rapid melting and consequent large runoff, high evaporation from the water-covered tundra after snowmelt, and the relatively dry summer regime followed by freeze-up. This progression is accompanied by a characteristic pattern in the relative magnitudes of the components of the radiation, energy, and water balances that provides a convenient basis for identifying six seasons: winter, pre-melt, melt, post-melt, summer, and freeze-up (Weller and Holmgren 1974a). Although the starting dates and durations of these seasons vary from year to year, it is possible to specify typical values (Figure 2-8).

Earlier studies at Barrow have suggested somewhat different bases for dividing the year into seasons: Kelley and Weaver (1969) defined six seasons based on soil–temperature regime, and Maykut and Church (1973) described four seasons based on variations of surface albedo.

Figure 2-8 shows the magnitudes and signs of the energy-balance components typical of each season. The radiation balance is negative during the winter, and positive during the rest of the year. The hydrologic regime is dominated by increasing storage during the freeze-up, winter and pre-melt seasons, by runoff during the melt season, and by evapotranspiration during the post-melt and summer seasons.

Radiation Balance

The radiation balance describes the partitioning of radiant energy into incoming and absorbed solar radiation, longwave incoming radiation, and longwave outgoing radiation at the earth's surface as follows:

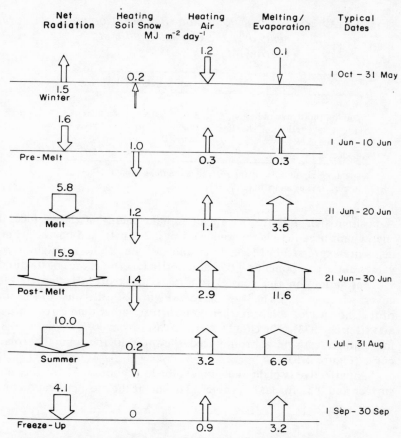

FIGURE 2-8. *Heat balances of the coastal tundra at Barrow for six different seasons. The width and direction of the arrows indicate magnitude and direction of energy flux. The numbers at the base of each arrow give typical rates in MJ m⁻² day⁻¹ (1 J = 0.239 cal). Evaporation rates are for open water. (After Weller and Holmgren 1974a.)*

$$R_n = Q(1 - \alpha) + (\theta\!\downarrow - \theta\!\uparrow)$$

where R_n = net radiation (shortwave plus longwave)
Q = incoming shortwave radiation or insolation (0.3 to 3 μm wavelength)
α = surface reflectivity (albedo)
$\theta\!\uparrow$ = longwave outgoing radiation (2 to 100 μm wavelength)
$\theta\!\downarrow$ = longwave incoming radiation (2 to 100 μm wavelength).

TABLE 2-3 *Annual Radiation Balance Compo-*
nents over the Coastal Tundra at
Barrow (MJ m^{-2} yr^{-1})

Component	Land	Lakes	Average*
Incoming shortwave radiation, Q	3200	3200	3200
Net longwave radiation, $\theta\!\downarrow - \theta\!\uparrow$	−1000	−1010	−1005
Net radiation, R_n	450	540	500
Albedo, α	0.55	0.52	0.53

*Assuming about 50% of the surface is land and 50% is lakes.
Source: Maykut and Church (1973).

A positive sign indicates a gain of radiant energy at the surface. The energy unit used here is the joule (1 J = 0.239 cal), and balance components are expressed in MJ m^{-2} per unit of time. Table 2-3 gives average values of the components of the radiation balance over the coastal tundra.

Insolation on the coastal tundra is markedly affected by cloud cover, which averages 68% at Barrow (Figure 2-9). Because of this, most of the shortwave radiation received is diffuse rather than direct (Maykut and Church 1973). The cloud cover increases from 40% in winter to 85% in summer, causing a pronounced skewness in the annual insolation curve (Figure 2-10).

An effective (weighted average) albedo is about 0.55 for the tundra surface and 0.52 for lakes (Table 2-3). One of the most critical factors in

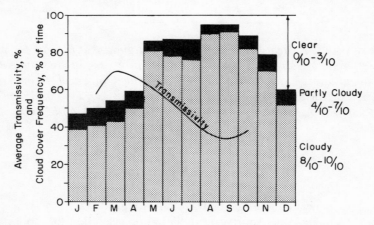

FIGURE 2-9. *Cloud cover conditions (bars) and transmissivity for coastal tundra. Transmissivity from Maykut and Church (1973), cloud cover from University of Alaska (1975).*

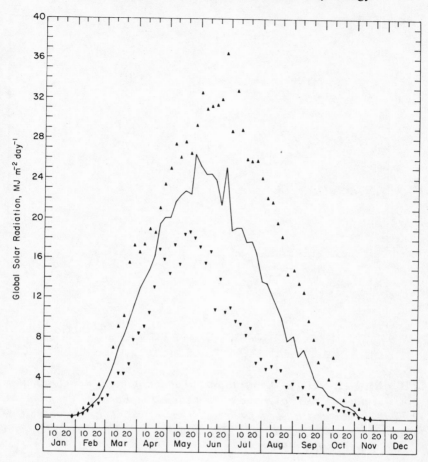

FIGURE 2-10. *Mean (—), maximum (▲) and minimum (▼) incoming shortwave solar radiation for five-day intervals over the coastal tundra at Barrow. The data are based on 1962 and 1964-66 from Kelley et al. (1964), Lieske and Stroschein (1968), Weaver (1969, 1970), Maykut and Church (1973), and LeDrew and Weller (1978).*

determining the surface climate is the large annual variation in albedo that coincides with the establishment and decay of the annual snow cover. Winter albedo values are 80% to 90%, depending on variations in the character of the snow surface caused by fresh snowfalls and wind-packing. Albedo decreases in early June as a result of the progressively thinning snowpack and the appearance of bare patches (Weller and Holmgren 1974a), and drops to approximately 15% within a week or so

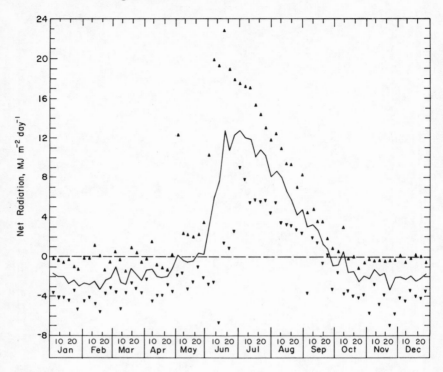

FIGURE 2-11. *Mean (—), maximum (▲) and minimum (▼) net radiation for five-day intervals over the coastal tundra at Barrow. The data are based on 1962 and 1964-66 from Kelley et al. (1964), Lieske and Stroschein (1968), Weaver (1969, 1970), Maykut and Church (1973), and LeDrew and Weller (1978).*

as the snow melts from the land surface. Over lakes the ice cover extends this transition to two or three weeks. During the snow-free period, the average albedo generally varies between 10 and 20%, with large spatial variations. During freeze-up, the albedo fluctuates between 18% and 60% as snow falls and melts; the permanent snow cover forms by early October.

Maykut and Church (1973) found that incoming longwave radiation for three years averaged 7440 MJ m^{-2} yr^{-1}, which is more than twice the annual receipt of incoming shortwave solar radiation (Table 2-3). The longwave input exceeds the shortwave in every month except April and May (Lieske and Stroschein 1968). The longwave radiation balance is at a minimum during the coldest part of the year when cloud cover is at a minimum (February and March), and maximum values are reached during the summer months when cloud cover increases and cloud temperatures are highest.

The net longwave flux is negative for each of the seasons and for the year (Table 2-3). Positive net incoming longwave flux occurs only occasionally when warm stratus clouds are advected over a cooler tundra surface. The loss of longwave radiation from lakes is less than that from the tundra during June, because of residual ice and the lower temperatures of the lakes. However, the reverse is true from July to October as a result of higher temperatures due to the greater absorption of insolation.

Between October and April the radiation balance is dominated by the negative net longwave radiation; near the end of May the balance becomes positive (Figure 2-11). After snowmelt, when albedo has decreased dramatically, the net shortwave gain exceeds the net longwave loss by a factor of four (Maykut and Church 1973). Maximum average net energy receipt of about 12 MJ m^{-2} day^{-1} occurs during the period 15-19 June. After mid-August, the absorbed radiation gradually decreases with decreasing day length and solar altitude, becoming negative again in late September–early October.

Energy Balance

The partitioning of the net radiation at the surface is described by the energy-balance equation:

$$R_n + H + L + G = 0$$

where R_n = net radiation
H = net exchange of heat with atmosphere by conduction/convection (sensible heat flux)
L = net exchange of latent heat with atmosphere (vaporization and latent heat used in melting)
G = net exchange of heat with snowpack and/or soil.

Estimates of average energy-balance components for the coastal tundra at Barrow were developed from several sources, and are summarized in Table 2-4. Differences in the various values probably reflect real differences in the energy balance between 1957-58, 1962-66 and 1971-72, but also include variations due to different measuring techniques as well as procedures for the calculations.

The energy used in melting snow is about 35 MJ m^{-2} yr^{-1}, assuming that a snow water equivalent of 106 mm (see below) is melted annually. It is generally assumed that there is no net heating or cooling of the ground, so the average annual value of G represents energy used in warming the snowpack. This assumption is consistent with the findings of Kelley and Weaver (1969) at Barrow; however, Lachenbruch and Marshall (1969)

TABLE 2-4 Comparison of Monthly, Seasonal and Annual Values ($MJ\ m^{-2}\ day^{-1}$) of the Energy Balance Components for the Coastal Tundra at Barrow

Month	Season according to energy balance	Net radiation R_n — Maykut & Church 1962-66	Net radiation R_n — Mather & Thornthwaite 1957-58	Net radiation R_n — Weller & Holmgren 1971-72	Convective heat H — Mather & Thornthwaite 1957-58	Convective heat H — Weller & Holmgren 1971-72	Latent heat L — Mather & Thornthwaite 1957-58	Latent heat L — Weller & Holmgren 1971-72	Subsurface heat G — Mather & Thornthwaite 1957-58	Subsurface heat G — Weller & Holmgren 1971-72
Sept	Freeze-up	2.1	1.6		-1.1		-0.7*	-3.2	0.2	0
Oct		-1.4	-0.8		0.2		-0.2		0.8	
Nov		-2.1	-2.8		1.8*		0		1.0	
Dec		-2.2	-2.6		1.6*		0		1.0	
Jan	Winter	-2.0	-1.2		0.6*		0		0.9*	
Feb		-2.2	-3.0		2.7*		0		0.3	
Mar		-2.1	-1.2		1.0*		0		0.2	
Apr		-1.8	-1.7		1.7*		0		0	
May		-0.5	2.7		-1.4		-1.0*		-0.3	
(Winter mean, brace)		-1.8	-1.3	-1.5	1.0	1.2	-0.1	0.1	0.5	0.2
1-10 June	Pre-melt	9.1	12.1	1.6		-0.3				
11-20 June	Melt			5.8 (7.8)	-3.6	-1.1 (-1.4)	-6.0	-0.3 / -3.5 (-5.1)	-2.5	-1.0 (-1.2)
21-30 June	Post-melt			15.9		-2.9		-11.6		-1.4
July	Summer	11.0	12.0	10.0	-6.2		-4.9*		-0.9	
Aug		6.6	6.6		-3.7		-2.2*		-0.7	
(Summer mean, brace)		8.8	9.3		-5.0	-3.2	-3.6	-6.6	-0.8	-0.2
Annual	($MJ\ m^{-2}\ day^{-1}$)	1.2	1.8	1.6	-0.5	0.1	-1.3	-1.7	0	0
mean	($MJ\ m^{-2}\ yr^{-1}$)	440	660	580	-200	30	-470	-620	0	0

*Estimated.

Note: A negative sign indicates an energy flux away from the surface, a positive sign an energy flux towards the surface.

Source: Mather and Thornthwaite (1958), Maykut and Church (1973), and Weller and Holmgren (1974a).

showed that average ground temperature has increased 4 °C since 1850, so the assumption is not strictly true over several decades. The energy required to warm the snowpack from its typical winter temperature of −30 °C to the melting point is about 7 MJ m^{-2}.

The net radiation value of 440 MJ m^{-2} yr^{-1} measured by Maykut and Church (1973) is probably the most reliable mean value, since it represents measurements over five years. However, it should be noted that the data of Weller and Holmgren (1974a) indicate a radiation balance of about 580 MJ m^{-2} yr^{-1} and Mather and Thornthwaite's (1958) values are even higher. Most of the radiant energy available at the surface is transferred to the atmosphere by conduction and convection (H). During winter, this exchange is positive, i.e. the air is warmer than the snow surface and the snow is warmed. Convective exchange becomes negative as the snowpack ripens in late May and early June, with the rate of energy loss increasing to a peak during the summer and declining again during freeze-up.

During the winter, there is a minor net gain of latent-heat energy due to condensation, and some sublimation occurs prior to and during snow-melt. Open-water evaporation rates are estimated to be about ten times larger than transpiration rates, and the rate of evapotranspiration typically peaks in late June when the tundra is still water-saturated and available radiant energy is at its peak.

There is a net flow of energy from the ground to the snowpack (G) during the winter, when snow and soil temperatures are higher than surface temperatures. As the net radiation increases and surface temperatures rise in May, this flow reverses, and most of the available energy is used to warm the snow and soil. After melt, downward heat flow continues as the active layer thaws and warms. Typically over 90% of the thaw occurs by mid-July (Kelley and Weaver 1969). The energy used to warm and thaw the soil in spring must, on the average, be balanced by an upward movement of latent and sensible heat during freeze-up in September.

HYDROLOGY

Water Balance

The water-balance equation at the surface for a specified period of time is expressed as:

$$P = E + R + I + \Delta S$$

where P = precipitation

E = net evapotranspiration
R = runoff
I = net infiltration
ΔS = change in surface storage of water in the area considered.

As with the energy balance, it is assumed that surface storage is neither increasing nor decreasing, so that the average annual value of ΔS is zero. In addition all the water that infiltrates eventually ends up as runoff or evapotranspiration, so that $I = 0$ for long-term average conditions. Precipitation and runoff are estimated using standard techniques. For average annual data, evapotranspiration is then found by subtraction. For shorter periods, information on evapotranspiration is based on measurements of evaporation from pans or small ponds, on the energy calculated to be available for evaporation via the energy balance equation, or in a few cases on observations of soil moisture (which may also be used to estimate I). Data on short-term changes in storage are in some cases available in the form of records of the changes in elevation of tundra ponds (Hobbie 1980).

The average annual precipitation recorded (1941-70) at the Barrow National Weather Service Station is 124.1 mm (Table 2-1), but it is known that this recorded amount is less than the true amount. Comparisons of the water equivalent of the tundra snowpack (Black 1954, Benson 1969) show that actual snowfall exceeds the amounts recorded at the Barrow gage because of the effects of wind on the gage catches. A summary of data for six winters (Table 2-5) suggests that, on the average, the true value is 1.6 times the recorded value. Although data have indicated that summer precipitation measurements do not need to be adjusted for wind effect on gage catch, Brown et al. (1968) found that a correction should be made for the effects of traces. Traces, recorded when precipitation is less than 0.13 mm in a measurement period, have been summed as zero values (Table 2-1). Brown et al. (1968) found that the measured summer precipitation should be multiplied by 1.1 to give the actual value.

Thus, the average annual precipitation value of 170 mm is estimated by multiplying the National Weather Service data by 1.1 for the months June through August and by 1.6 for the other nine months, when precipitation is assumed to be in the form of snow (Table 2-1). The estimate of total precipitation is consistent with most detailed studies of the region's precipitation and water balance, including those of Black (1954), Mather and Thornthwaite (1958) and Brown et al. (1968). Corrected values (Table 2-1) show a precipitation maximum in August and a secondary maximum in January. On the average, about 63% (106 mm) of the annual precipitation falls as snow (September through May) and 37% (64 mm) as rain (June through August) at Barrow. At Barter Island, an average of 68% (167 mm) falls as snow and 32% (80 mm) falls as rain. The

TABLE 2-5 *Water Equivalent of Snow on the Nearby Coastal Tundra Compared with Precipitation Records at the National Weather Service Station, Barrow, Alaska*

| | Measurements on tundra | | | NWS gage |
Year	Avg depth (mm)	Avg density (g cm^{-3})	Avg water equivalent (mm)	1 Sept–31 May water equivalent (mm)
1962–63	350	0.42	144 ± 17	141
1969–70	170	0.36	61 ± 7	32
1970–71	350	0.36	126 ± 14	41
1971–72	300	0.36	108 ± 12	30
1972–73	330	0.36	119 ± 13	110
1973–74	340	0.36	122 ± 14	68
Average*			113 ± 28	70 ± 42

* ± standard deviation.

correction factor of 1.6 is a minimum value for Barrow and the remainder of the Coastal Plain since it is based on the amount of snow remaining on the open tundra after some has blown away and concentrated in drifts. Recent experience with Wyoming snow shields indicates that the correction factor may be about 3 rather than our conservative estimate of 1.6.

Significant unfrozen zones underlie the Colville River and other large rivers (Williams 1970), and these may be conduits for substantial runoff that originates in the Brooks Range and the northern Foothills. However, because most of the Coastal Plain is underlain by permafrost that extends from a depth of about 0.5 m to depths of several hundred meters, it can be assumed that all runoff from the tundra occurs via surface streams. Thus, runoff may be estimated from the discharge records of streams whose drainages are confined to the Coastal Plain. Such data are limited, as regular U.S. Geological Survey stream gaging programs began in the area only in 1970. Data collected for entire water years (October to September) and adjusted for year-to-year precipitation variations indicate that average annual runoff from the Coastal Plain is about 110 mm. Because of measurement difficulties, discharge data are subject to uncertainties of 15 to 25%.

In May, much of the evaporative heat loss is due to sublimation from the snow. During the post-melt season, the greatest proportion of total evapotranspiration is evaporation from open water, while transpiration increases in importance in July and August. Subtracting

TABLE 2-6 *Summary of Streamflow Data and Time Concentration of Runoff for Streams Draining the Coastal Plain*

Stream	Drainage area (km²)	Water year	Annual runoff (mm)	Precipitation (% of normal)*	Monthly runoff Percent mean annual runoff occurring in				Duration of concentrated runoff period (days)†	Maximum daily runoff (% of annual)
					June	July	Aug	Sept		
Nunavak Creek, Barrow	7.23	1972–73	166	167	66.7	17.6	13.2	2.4	13	9
		1973–74	150	75	80.0	18.0	1.9	1.0	6	14
		1974–75	70	99	80.5	17.8	1.7	0	5	10
		1975–76	65	48	81.7	15.9	1.6	0.8	9	8
Esatkuat Creek, Barrow	3.66	1972–73	200	167	61.0	3.0	23.0	14.0	8	9
Esatkuat Lagoon, Barrow	9.12	1972–73	154	167	81.0	1.0	18.0	0	5	16
Putuligayuk River, Prudhoe Bay	456	1970–71	76	63(96)	97.7	1.6	0.4	0.3	3	31
		1971–72	93	74(80)	83.6	5.2	3.4	7.7	3	23
		1972–73	71	167(66)	91.0	2.6	3.2	3.1	3	30
		1973–74	53	75(46)	93.7	5.4	0.4	0.3	5	20
		1974–75	66	(36)	91.9	6.2	0.6	1.3	5	13
		1975–76	112	(65)	89.7	9.5	0.4	0.3	5	13

*Expressed as percentage of the measured 1941–70 average at the Barrow National Weather Service Station (124.2 mm). Numbers in parentheses are percentage of the 1949–73 average at the Barter Island National Weather Service Station (179.3 mm).

†The length of the period (consecutive days) during which half the annual runoff occurred.

Source: Streamflow data from U.S. Geological Survey (1971–1976).

estimated average runoff (110 mm) from estimated average precipitation (170 mm) gives a value of 60 mm yr^{-1} for average annual evapotranspiration. However, this estimate absorbs the inaccuracies of the other two measurements and therefore has wide confidence intervals. In fact, other data suggest that the actual value of evapotranspiration is substantially higher. Annual Class-A pan evaporation in the Barrow area is about 160 mm (Brown et al. 1968); reducing this by a standard pan coefficient (0.6 to 0.7) gives a range of 96 to 112 mm yr^{-1} for evaporation from a well-watered surface. The energy balance data of Weller and Holmgren (1974a) indicate evaporation rates of 4.8 mm day^{-1} for the post-melt period and 2.7 mm day^{-1} during the summer season; if these rates are considered average, an annual total of 210 mm is calculated. Stewart and Rouse (1976) found that daily evapotranspiration from both wet and dry tundra surfaces can be well estimated from net radiation and air temperature. Application of their method using typical values for Barrow suggests an annual total of about 140 mm.

Interestingly, Stewart and Rouse (1976) found that evaporation from a relatively dry tundra surface averaged 80% of that from the wet surface (standing water) under the same temperature and radiation conditions. This is apparently due to the fact that, as noted in Chapter 3, only 14 to 20% of the evapotranspiration from the land is due to transpiration from vascular plants. The remainder is evapotranspiration from mosses, which are often wetted by fog and dew and have low resistance to water loss.

These considerations therefore indicate that either the estimate of regional average precipitation is too low, or the estimate of runoff is too high, or both. It is likely that failure to account for occult precipitation (fog, dew) is a significant source of error. In any case, it is important to realize that substantial uncertainties remain in our understanding of arctic water balances, even in regions of relatively intensive study.

Runoff is concentrated into a short period of time (Table 2-6). Although the data are limited, there is a definite suggestion that runoff is more time-concentrated in larger drainage basins. This is the opposite of what would normally be expected, and may be due to the formation and breakage of ice jams on the large streams.

Actual data on infiltration are very limited, but it is possible to infer the general nature of the intra-annual variation. In winter, an upward moisture gradient is established, so that there is exfiltration in the form of vapor for much of the year. During and immediately after melt, water infiltrates in liquid form, to the extent that soil moisture capacity is virtually reached. Through the summer, most of the water falling as precipitation infiltrates, and most of this is subsequently evaporated and transpired.

Surface storage increases through the winter as snow accumulates and water vapor transported upward from the soil condenses in the snowpack. Most of the snow is depleted within the few days of the melt period, but part of the snow is converted to liquid water storage in puddles, ponds and lakes. This storage, in turn, is gradually reduced by evaporation through the summer. Persistent snowdrifts in stream valleys may contribute small amounts of stream flow well after the general melt is completed.

Thermal and Hydrologic Processes During Snowmelt

As the radiation balance becomes positive around 1 June, the snowpack warms or ripens and the underlying soil begins to warm. Incoming shortwave solar radiation reaches its maximum values in May, as atmospheric transmissivity is high. However, albedo still exceeds 80%, so that most of this radiation is reflected. About 60% of the available radiant energy is used to warm the snowpack and soil (Figure 2-8). Snowmelt begins at the surface when air temperatures rise above 0 °C. Heat is transferred downward in the snow by conduction and as sensible and latent heat associated with liquid water movement. It appears that the latter process is responsible for much of the warming of the snowpack, and also contributes to warming of the soil. The percolating meltwater refreezes in the colder snow, liberating latent heat and forming a complex network of ice glands, lenses and layers. Benson et al. (1975) calculated that about 1.9 MJ m^{-2} of heat is transported downward for each 1 cm of ice thickness formed. With the estimated cold content at this time of 2.3 MJ m^{-2}, the formation of ice layers totaling a little over 1 cm thick would suffice to warm the snow to 0 °C. Weller et al. (1972) described the 1971 melt in the coastal tundra at Barrow, and reported that melting converted an 8 °C temperature gradient across the snowpack to near isothermal conditions within 2 to 3 days. The soil temperature also rose steeply during this period.

Initially, the ice layers tend to form at the top of the depth hoar layer, but as the pre-melt season progresses they are found at the base of the snowpack (Benson et al. 1975). The two-layer structure thus breaks down and the density of the pack becomes vertically uniform. Typically, the density of ripe snow is between 0.4 and 0.5 g cm^{-3}. The disappearance of the depth hoar layer and the flooding of low areas as melt progresses are major environmental changes for lemmings. They are forced out of the protective snow cover and become subject to environmental extremes and avian predation, with consequent high mortality (Bunnell et al. 1975).

The changes in water content and density of the snowpack during the pre-melt season cause the albedo to decrease from its winter value of about 85% to about 75% just before the melt season begins (Maykut and Church 1973).

Virtually every aspect of the surface environment changes dramatically during the brief melt season. These changes are rapid because of the relatively high insolation rates during the long days and the operation of positive feedback loops affecting the radiation and energy balances. The energy available at the surface increases by a factor of 3.6, and about 60% of this is used in melting (Figure 2-8).

Once the snowpack is isothermal at 0 °C, the further addition of energy produces meltwater that does not refreeze. Initially, this water fills voids in the snowpack and reduces the albedo, typically to values near 50%. Reduction in the albedo increases the absorption of solar radiation, which increases the melt rate.

Snowpacks can hold about 5% of their water equivalent as liquid water (Anderson and Crawford 1964). For the coastal tundra this would amount to about 5 mm of water, which can be produced in a period of a few hours at the rates at which radiant energy enters the snowpack during melt. Once this capacity is filled, the snowpack is ripe and further melt produces runoff at the snow/ground interface or over ice lenses and layers. As meltwater accumulates in low-lying areas and produces slush, the albedo is further reduced and the melting accelerated.

Snow-free patches generally appear within a day or so of the onset of melting and initiate the operation of another positive feedback loop. The albedo of the exposed areas is 10 to 15%, so they absorb four to five times as much radiant energy as the snow-covered ground. This additional energy produces local heating of the air and local advection of heat to the surrounding snow, which further accelerates melting (Weller et al. 1972, Weller and Holmgren 1974a).

The upper layer of the soil generally begins to thaw a few days before snowmelt is complete. This layer typically has been desiccated by loss of water to the snowpack during the winter, so that some infiltration of snowmelt water occurs. Data of Guymon (1976) indicated that this infiltration was most significant in poorly drained areas. However, most of the snowmelt water runs off to streams and lakes after ponds and polygon troughs are filled.

A large fraction of the total annual runoff occurs within a few days (Table 2-6). The spring runoff sequence on the Coastal Plain has been described by Johnson and Kistner (1967), Lewellen (1972), Holmgren et al. (1975) and Hobbie (1980), and for the through-flowing Colville River by Arnborg et al. (1966). In stream channels, the first flow is over ice that is frozen fast to the bottom. The sediment load of this initial runoff is very low. But as the flow increases toward its peak, the channel ice is eroded and melts free from the bottom, generally dislodging large amounts of sediment. In the larger rivers, ice jams frequently occur, damming flow until sufficient head builds up to dislodge them and cause sudden catastrophic flooding downstream. There is considerable bank erosion at such times, due to the thermal/mechanical action of the water and the mechanical action of the ice masses.

Loss of the winter snow cover proceeds from the Brooks Range northward across the Foothills and Coastal Plain. As indicated on the satellite view of the eastern portion of the Arctic Slope (Figure 2-12), the major valleys of the Brooks Range are seen to be more or less snow-free. But close inspection reveals that many of the gullies on the mountain-sides are filled with snowdrifts that extend to the valley bottoms. In the Foothills the ridges melt out first, leaving snow in the gullies. Meltwater collects in the larger valleys, reducing albedos and accelerating melting there. Thus the major rivers have developed, or are in the process of developing, continuous open-water streams and generally appear as dark bands, probably because of flooded areas and because melting is further advanced. Many lakes appear darker than their surroundings, also because of standing water on the ice. The larger rivers flood their deltas and the sea ice, forming large overflow plumes.

Attempts have been made to model the snowmelt runoff process on the Coastal Plain for watersheds ranging in size from 3.8 km² to 13,890 km² (Carlson et al. 1974, Dingman, unpubl.). The models used have consisted of a snowmelt generator driven by climatic input and a simple storage model to transform snowmelt input to streamflow output. The basic form of the storage model is:

$$q_t = K(S_t - S_0)^n$$

where q_t = runoff during period t
K and n = storage parameters
S_t = snowmelt during period t
S_0 = the amount of melt that is absorbed into "dead" storage (filling lakes, ponds, troughs and soil pores).

Using a simple snowmelt model, Dingman (unpubl.) accounted for melt due to absorption of shortwave radiation only. Hourly melt was routed through the storage model to simulate measured runoff in Esatkuat Creek near Barrow (drainage area = 3.8 km²). The parameters K and n were estimated from examination of the measured runoff hydrograph for the area. The value of n was taken as unity, so the storage model was effectively a linear reservoir. When modification was made to account for the irregular distribution of snow depths over the watershed, the model appeared to be quite successful (Figure 2-13).

Carlson et al. (1974) simulated snowmelt from three large Arctic Slope rivers—the Putuligayuk (456 km²), the Kuparuk (9210 km²), and

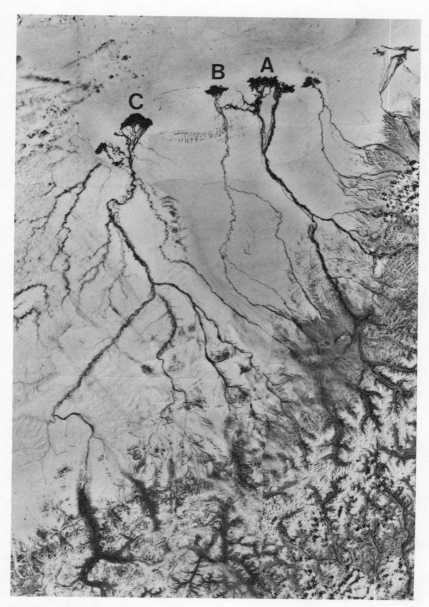

FIGURE 2-12. *Landsat satellite mosaic of a portion of the Arctic Slope for the period 27 May to 6 June 1973. Note melting in the river valleys and the meltwater plumes of the Sagavanirktok (A), Kuparuk (B) and Colville (C) Rivers. Early snowmelt induced by the Prudhoe Bay road network can be seen between the Sagavanirktok and Kuparuk Rivers.*

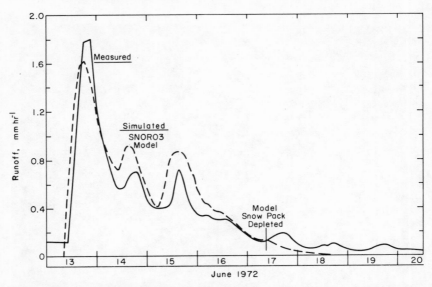

FIGURE 2-13. *Simulated and measured snow runoff in Esatkuat Creek near the village of Barrow, 13-20 June 1972. (Dingman, unpubl.)*

TABLE 2-7 *Values of Model Parameters for Four Arctic Coastal Plain Watersheds*

	Area (km²)	Year	K (hr⁻¹)	L (days)
Esatkuat Creek	3.8	1972	0.088	0
Putuligayuk River	456	1970	0.014	3
		1971	0.014	4
Kuparuk River	9,210	1970	0.012	2
		1971	0.008	2
Sagavanirktok River	13,980	1971	0.008	8

the Sagavanirktok (13,890 km²). Their snowmelt model included energy exchanges due to solar radiation, convection, longwave radiation and other modes. The calculated melt was routed through a linear storage reservoir ($n = 1$), and then delayed for a specified lag period. Values of the parameter K and the lag period L (Table 2-7) were determined by an optimization procedure to reproduce the runoff measured at the gaging station. The values of K decrease with watershed size, and the values of L

tend to increase, as would be expected.

Based on energy considerations, Weller and Holmgren (1974a) concluded that evaporation accounted for only 2% of the total ablation when the snow cover was still complete, but up to 13% when bare patches appeared. They noted also that condensation on the snow surface was likely when air temperature rose above 0°C. Johnson and Kistner's (1967) measured pan evaporation rates of up to 0.47 mm hr^{-1} at midday during snowmelt near Meade River indicate that open-water evaporation begins to become important at this time.

Post-melt, Summer Hydrology, and Related Processes

Immediately following snowmelt, the coastal tundra is largely covered with water. However, snowdrifts remain in river channels and most lakes are still ice-covered. The albedo of the surface is 10-15%, causing the net radiation to jump almost an order of magnitude from its pre-melt value, and all energy-balance components are at or near their maxima (Figure 2-8). Over the ice-covered lakes the dramatic reduction of albedo extends over a period of two to three weeks. Once the ice cover disappears, the lakes have a somewhat lower albedo than the land surface and absorb more solar radiation.

During the post-melt season, over 70% of the available energy is utilized in evaporating the extensive surface water. Water balance considerations and data on evapotranspiration during the summer season (see below) suggest that an average of 10 mm ($\cong$ 1 mm day^{-1}) evaporates during this 10-day period. This value is consistent with the average pan evaporation rates of 2.77 mm day^{-1} and 1.72 mm day^{-1} measured by Miller et al. (1980) in late June of 1972 and 1973, respectively, if a pan coefficient is applied and if less than 100% of the surface is considered to be evaporating. Weller and Holmgren (1974a) estimated considerably higher rates, 4.2 to 4.6 mm day^{-1}, on the basis of energy considerations alone.

Warming of the soil begins during the pre-melt period, but there is no significant thawing until the post-melt season. Thaw is very rapid initially, and can be expressed by an equation of the type applied to a relatively dry upland soil by Kelley and Weaver (1969):

$$Z = L[1 - \exp(-at)]$$

where Z = depth of thaw (cm)
   t = time in days
   a = empirical constant (1970 value = 0.067 day^{-1}; 1971 value = 0.047 day^{-1}; 1972 value = 0.082 day^{-1})

L = empirical constant = maximum thaw depth (35 cm in 1970; 37.5 cm in 1971; 63.3 cm in 1972).

Note that there is considerable year-to-year variation in the thaw progression; this variation can be correlated with cumulative net radiation during the early summer. There is also marked spatial variation in thaw progression due to soil type.

As the summer season begins in late June or early July, net radiation decreases. This is due to the passing of the summer solstice, an increase in cloudiness (Figure 2-9), and an increase of the albedo of the tundra to an average of about 19% as the surface dries. Evaporation still consumes the largest portion of the available energy, but convective heat loss increases in importance (Figure 2-8). Diurnal variations in soil temperature are greatest during this period as a result of strong diurnal changes in radiation under snow-free conditions (Kelley and Weaver 1969).

Summer soil temperatures vary across microtopographic positions and during the summer these differences reflect variations in albedo, microclimate and soil properties, particularly those related to moisture content. Elevated rims of low-centered polygons are sometimes cooler due to wind, while troughs and basins are warmer. However, at other times, increased evaporation and transpiration from the more vegetated and/or wetter troughs may result in lower temperatures there (Figure 2-14). Maximum differences occur under clear sky conditions during early afternoon with 8°C differences observed at the 1-cm depth between cooler rims and warmer basins and troughs of low-centered polygons (Goodwin 1976). Nighttime difference decreases 2 to 3°C. Although diurnal and seasonal soil temperatures follow closely changes in air temperature, other climatic factors such as cloud cover modify the magnitude of the difference between them. For example, soil temperatures at 1 cm depth for rims, troughs and basins at site 4 averaged 8.7°C in July 1972 and 5.6°C in July 1973. Average monthly air temperatures for July 1972 were only 1.8°C higher than 1973 (Table 2-1). Increased radiational warming accounted for most of the increased soil temperature.

Evapotranspiration rates decrease from the post-melt season because of the decrease in water on the surface and the decrease in available energy (Weller and Holmgren 1974a). Studies have consistently shown a near balance of precipitation with evapotranspiration during the summer (Mather and Thornthwaite 1958, Brown et al. 1968, Guymon 1976). About 80% of the annual evapotranspiration occurs during the 1 July–31 August season. Comparisons of total evapotranspiration and pan evaporation indicate that water losses from moist vegetated surfaces are approximately the same as those from open water. Koranda et al. (1978) measured overall loss rates from soil as 4.6 to 5.6 mm day^{-1}, compared with open-pan evaporation of 3 mm day^{-1}. Based on Miller et al. (1976)

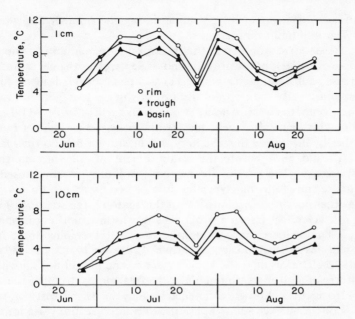

FIGURE 2-14. *Seasonal course (5-day means) of 1972 summer soil temperature on the trough, rim and basin of a low-centered polygon at 1 cm and 10 cm depth. (After Bunnell et al. 1975.)*

a calculated evaporation rate for a standard day (12 July 1973) was 2.3 mm, while average pan evaporation rate was 2.3 mm day⁻¹ for 10 to 16 July. In all cases, transpiration made up only a small fraction (7% to 15%) of total water loss. These observations are consistent with those of Rouse et al. (1977) who found evapotranspiration from a shallow tundra lake and a wet sedge tundra essentially identical.

Soil temperature–moisture studies (Guymon 1976) showed negligible vertical water movement in the mineral soil during the summer. This suggests that virtually all rain falling on the dry tundra infiltrates only into the surface organic layer and is subsequently evaporated and transpired. Runoff originates from rain falling directly on ponds and streams and on adjacent low areas where the water table is at or near the surface.

The runoff data of Brown et al. (1968) show zero flow during extended periods of no rainfall, indicating that the thawing active layer is not a source of stream flow. Similarly, records of pond levels (Brown et al. 1968, Hobbie 1980), pond chemistry (Brown et al. 1968), and lake levels (Kane and Carlson 1973) indicate that in the absence of inlet and outlet streams, changes in their volume during the summer are caused solely by rainfall and evaporation.

The freeze-up season marks the transition from summer to winter. By the time of freeze-up, towards the end of September, the net radiation has decreased substantially (Figure 2-11) as a result of much lower solar elevation and greatly reduced duration of daylight—13.5 hours in mid-September compared with 24 hours two months earlier (Table 1-1). Light snowfalls, which generally melt, may temporarily reduce the net radiation further by increasing the albedo of the tundra; the albedo fluctuates between 18 and 60% before the establishment of the "permanent" winter snowpack. The bulk of the available radiation energy is used in melting these snowfalls, but typically little or no runoff results.

The other major physical process of this season is the freezing of the thawed soil layer. As freezing progresses downward, and occasionally upward, a steadily increasing slab or sandwich of soil remains isothermal as the latent heat of fusion is being extracted (Brewer 1958, Nakano and Brown 1972). The result is the *zero curtain* or the period during which temperatures at a given depth remain at the freezing point. Once the soil is totally frozen the cold wave can penetrate into the permafrost. Diurnal variations of the surface soil temperature decrease because variations in air temperature and insolation are smaller and snow depth is increasing.

SUMMARY

Data collected prior to and during the Tundra Biome program provide a reasonably complete and consistent picture of the climate, microclimate and hydrology of the coastal tundra of northern Alaska. The average net radiation at the surface is between 420 and 450 MJ m^{-2} yr^{-1}. Of this, 55% is sensible heat transferred to the air, 36% is used in evapotranspiration, 7% is used to melt snow, and 2% is sensible heat transferred downward to snow and soil.

Two-thirds of the year is characterized by a negative net radiation balance, very low surface temperatures, and a gradually increasing snowpack subject to substantial drifting. The snow reduces extremes of temperature and wind at the ground surface, providing a more moderate microclimate for surface- and near-surface-dwelling organisms.

When the net radiation balance becomes positive in late May, the snowpack, upper soil, and air temperatures approach the freezing point. Surface melting of the snow redistributes water and heat downward, causing the first in a series of rapid changes in the immediate surface environment. Profound changes occur over the few days when the snowpack melts and the upper layers of the soil thaw. During this time there is a rapid increase in net radiation, which is accelerated by decreasing snowpack albedo and then by the absorption of heat by the exposed ground surface. In a few days, the snowpack has disappeared except for larger drifts. Most of the meltwater runs off, and streams are in flood condition as 50% or more of the annual flow volume is discharged in a few days. The ground is covered with extensive areas of shallow surface water. Net radiation is at a maximum during this post-melt period, and most of the energy is used in evaporation.

The short summer season is subject to relatively small interannual variability in temperature but large variability in precipitation. About two-thirds of the net radiation is used in evapotranspiration, and the rest in heating the air. The depth of thaw in the soil approaches its maximum near the beginning of August. There is a near balance between precipitation and evapotranspiration, but significant runoff may occur in wetter years. Only about 10% of the evapotranspiration is transpiration. The remainder is evaporation from soil and interception from plant surfaces. Significant evaporation takes place from lakes and ponds, as well.

Net radiation is still positive but small in September. Air temperatures drop consistently below 0°C and the soil begins to freeze from below and above. Precipitation is largely in the form of snow, but intermittent melting often occurs. By the end of September, the net radiation becomes negative, the soil active layer may be completely frozen, and the permanent snowpack is becoming established.

3

Biophysical Processes and Primary Production

P. C. Miller, P. J. Webber,
W. C. Oechel, and L. L. Tieszen

INTRODUCTION

During most of the year the arctic tundra is covered with snow, and the exchange of heat at the earth's surface through radiation, convection and evaporation involves only physical components of the environment. However, during the short snow-free period the vegetation becomes a significant exchange surface. The vegetation influences the partitioning of incoming energy into evaporation, convection and soil heat conduction. The vegetation also accumulates the biomass on which the plants themselves and the other ecosystem components depend for energy. This chapter discusses the rates of primary production, the standing crop, and the partitioning of incoming energy by the vegetation. The interactions between diverse environmental factors and specific canopy and plant properties affecting plant temperatures are integrated in the energy budget equation (Gates 1962, 1965, Parkhurst and Loucks 1972, and others):

$$Q_a + \theta_a = \theta + G + H + LE + M$$

where Q_a = incoming shortwave radiation absorbed by the plant
θ_a = longwave radiation absorbed by the plant
θ = longwave radiation emitted by the plant
G = net heat flux into the soil or moss layer
H = heat exchanged by convection
LE = evaporative loss of energy by transpiration from vascular plants or the evaporative loss of energy from moss surfaces
M = metabolic term to account for energy used in photosynthesis or produced in respiration.

The energy exchange processes are significant in determining the rates of primary production, the temperatures of the plants and soil, and the rates of water loss from vascular plants and mosses. The metabolic term is small relative to the total energy exchanged by physical processes, but is important in maintaining all biological processes. The effect of the energy exchange processes is mainly through absorbed solar energy for photosynthesis and through influences on plant temperatures. Temperatures at the Biome research area, even during the growing season, are almost always below the optimum for physiological processes in most plants. Therefore, physiological adaptation of plants to low temperatures, and morphological adaptation that increases plant temperature, should be more evident in the vegetation of the coastal tundra at Barrow than in temperate regions.

PRIMARY PRODUCTION IN THE BARROW WET MEADOW TUNDRA

Standing Crop and Primary Productivity

Primary productivity in the tundra at Barrow has been estimated by the harvest method for the aboveground vascular vegetation (Webber 1978), by cuvette measurements for vascular plants (Tieszen 1975, 1978b) and mosses (Oechel and Sveinbjörnsson 1978), by photosynthesis models for vascular plants (Miller et al. 1976) and mosses (Miller et al. 1978a), and by the aerodynamic method for the total ecosystem (Coyne and Kelley 1975). Based on these different measurements, gross above- and belowground primary production for the Biome research area in 1972, a year of nearly normal temperature and precipitation, was 465 gdw m^{-2}, including 358 gdw m^{-2} for vascular plants, 106 gdw m^{-2} for mosses, and about 1 gdw m^{-2} for lichens.

Net primary productivity, which is gross productivity minus the estimated respiratory costs for plant maintenance and growth, was about 230 gdw m^{-2} yr^{-1}, including 162 gdw m^{-2} yr^{-1} for vascular plants, 66 gdw m^{-2} yr^{-1} for mosses, and less than 1 gdw m^{-2} yr^{-1} for lichens. For these calculations growth respiration was calculated as 0.3 of the new biomass for both vascular plants and mosses. Maintenance respiration was calculated as 0.0054 gdw gdw^{-1} day^{-1} for 35 days for aboveground vascular material, 0.0027 gdw gdw^{-1} day^{-1} for 60 days for belowground vascular material, and 0.003 gdw gdw^{-1} day^{-1} for 60 days for mosses. The daily maintenance cost was calculated using protein percentages of 9, 4.5 and 4.8 for above- and belowground vascular and moss material respectively (Penning de Vries 1974, Chapter 5). The overall value is composed of the separate productivities of different plant growth forms in eight vegetation

TABLE 3-1 Net Productivity and Respiration Rate (gdw m⁻² yr⁻¹) of Different Plant Growth Forms for Eight Vegetation Types Recognized for the Coastal Tundra at Barrow

				Vegetation type					
	Luzula heath I	Salix heath II	Carex–Poa meadow III	Carex–Oncophorus meadow IV	Dupontia meadow V	Carex–Eriophorum meadow VI	Arctophila pond margin VII	Cochlearia meadow VIII	Average for the coastal tundra at Barrow
No. of stands per type	1	5	11	6	6	8	2	4	
Net productivity									
Aboveground vascular plants									
Graminoids	9	4	28	41	48	42	76	33	33
Forbs	4	5	1	3	3	2	39	14	3
Woody dicotyledons	5	16	10	1	1	0	0	0	6
Total	18	25	39	45	52	44	115	47	42
Total belowground vascular plants	57	47	114	142	217	132	103	51	120
Cryptogams									
Bryophytes	9	4	137	22*	11	21	10	11	66
Lichens	1	3	4	†	0	0	1	1	2
Total (est.)*	10	7	141	22	11	21	11	12	68
Total primary production (est.)*	85	79	294	209	280	197	228	110	230
Maintenance respiration									
Aboveground vascular plants	4	8	12	9	9	7	22	9	10
Belowground vascular plants	93	76	130	161	211	171	84	25	138
Mosses	3	1	44	7	3	7	3	4	21
Growth respiration									
Aboveground vascular plants	5	8	12	14	15	13	35	14	13
Belowground vascular plants	17	14	34	43	65	40	31	15	36
Mosses	3	1	41	7	3	6	3	3	20
Gross productivity									
Aboveground vascular plants	27	41	63	68	76	64	172	70	65
Belowground vascular plants	167	137	278	346	493	343	218	91	294
Total vascular plants	194	178	341	414	569	407	390	161	359
Mosses	15	7	222	36	17	34	16	18	106
Total	209	185	563	450	586	441	406	179	465

*Estimates are based on harvests at the period of peak aboveground vascular biomass and seasonal CO₂ gas exchange estimates in 1972. Values are means from the stands in each vegetation type.

† indicates less than 0.5 g.

Source: Webber (1978), Rastorfer (1978), Oechel and Sveinbjörnsson (1978) and Williams et al. (1978).

types recognized at Barrow, weighted by the surface area of each type (Table 3-1).

Net aboveground primary production of vascular plants at Barrow in 1972, estimated by the harvest method and averaged according to the relative surface area of the different vegetation types, was 42 gdw m^{-2} (Webber 1978, Table 3-1). Aboveground production of vascular plants ranged between 18 gdw m^{-2} for *Luzula* heath and 115 gdw m^{-2} for *Arctophila* pond margins. Eighty-four percent of the area had aboveground vascular plant production of 39 to 51 gdw m^{-2}. Although the average productivity within a tundra region is frequently near the low end of the range of productivities of the vegetation types in that region (Beschel 1970, Webber 1971), the average in the coastal tundra at Barrow is near the middle of the range for the vegetation types near Barrow because this area is dominated by reasonably productive vegetation types. The least productive vegetation type, the *Luzula* heath, occupies 3% of the entire area.

Aboveground vascular plant productivity increased along a moisture gradient from the tops of high-centered polygons to pond and stream margins. The wetter areas have reduced soils and moderately high phosphate levels and are dominated by graminoids. The productivity of forbs was highest in dry areas with moderate levels of phosphate and more oxidized soils, but productivity rarely exceeded 6 gdw m^{-2} yr^{-1}. The productivity of woody dicotyledons was also highest in dry oxidized areas with moderate levels of phosphate, and was about 20 gdw m^{-2} yr^{-1}. Bryophyte productivity, calculated as 56% of the green biomass or about 66 gdw m^{-2} yr^{-1} (Oechel and Sveinbjörnsson 1978), differed widely in the different vegetation types, with the highest rates in the mesic meadow where many acrocarpous mosses such as *Dicranum elongatum* and *Pogonatum alpinum* are abundant. The principal factor controlling the distribution of bryophytes appears to be slight differences in microrelief, moderated by the vascular plant canopy, which influence the moss and soil moisture regimes (Webber 1978, Oechel and Sveinbjörnsson 1978, Stoner et al. 1978b).

Belowground productivity estimated from the belowground biomass (Webber 1978, Table 3-2) and from longevities of belowground plant parts (Shaver and Billings 1975, Billings et al. 1978, Chapter 5) was 120 gdw m^{-2} yr^{-1}. The belowground productivities ranged between 47 and 217 gdw m^{-2} yr^{-1} from the *Luzula* and *Salix* heaths to the *Dupontia* meadow. The ratio of above- to belowground productivities varied from about 1:1 to 1:4 and averaged 1:2.9. Dennis (1977), using a regression approach, estimated that belowground productivity was 143 gdw m^{-2} yr^{-1} in 1971.

Total standing crop of live and intact dead plant material was 5292 gdw m^{-2}, weighted by the relative area of the different vegetation types (Table 3-2). The standing crop was dominated by graminoids, bryophytes

TABLE 3-2 Above- and Belowground Standing Crops (gdw m⁻²) for Eight Vegetation Types Recognized for the Coastal Tundra at Barrow

| | Vegetation type | | | | | | | | |
	Luzula heath I	Salix heath II	Carex–Poa meadow III	Carex–Oncophorus meadow IV	Dupontia meadow V	Carex–Eriophorum meadow VI	Arctophila pond margin VII	Cochlearia meadow VIII	Average for the coastal tundra at Barrow
No. of stands per type	1	5	11	6	6	8	2	4	
Percentage of surface area	3.0	7.2	41.0	20.9	6.9	14.6	2.3	4.1	100
Aboveground biomass									
Graminoids	9	4	31	41	49	43	79	33	35
Forbs	5	5	1	3	3	2	40	15	4
Woody dicotyledons	5	31	31	3	1	0	0	0	16
Total vascular plants	18	40	63	47	53	45	119	48	55
Bryophytes	16	8	244	40	19	37	18	20	117
Lichens	15	37	55	5	11	0	0	14	28
Total non-vascular plants	31	45	299	45	30	37	18	34	145
Total aboveground	50	85	362	92	83	82	137	82	200
Belowground biomass									
Stem bases	113	0	64	260	77	111	2	3	106
Live rhizomes	59	108	110	91	220	77	43	44	103
Live roots	399	363	626	645	1008	866	466	106	641
Total belowground	571	471	800	996	1305	1054	511	153	849
Total biomass	621	556	1162	1088	1388	1136	648	235	1050
Above:Belowground vascular biomass ratio	1:30	1:12	1:13	1:21	1:14	1:24	1:4	1:3	
Aboveground:root biomass ratio	1:20	1:9	1:10	1:14	1:19	1:19	1:4	1:2	
Aboveground dead vascular									
Standing dead	57	33	31	36	51	43	36	32	36
Litter and prostrate dead	41	127	121	67	75	47	64	85	91
Belowground intact dead	2805	1400	6367	3370	2106	2951	1228	291	4116
Total	3524	2116	7681	4561	3620	4177	1976	643	5293

Note: Standing crops were harvested at the period of maximum aboveground biomass in 1972. Values are the means of the stands within each vegetation type. Belowground biomass is based on three stands per type when possible.
Source: Webber (1978).

and dead material. At peak season the average dry weight of above-ground plant material was: graminoid biomass 35 gdw m^{-2}, forb biomass 4 g m^{-2}, woody dicotyledon biomass 16 g m^{-2}, bryophyte biomass 117 g m^{-2}, lichen biomass 28 g m^{-2}, vascular standing dead 36 g m^{-2}, vascular litter and prostrate dead 91 g m^{-2}, and belowground intact dead 4116 g m^{-2}. The aboveground vascular standing crop averaged 54 gdw m^{-2}, and ranged between 19 and 119 gdw m^{-2}, depending on the vegetation type.

Primary productivity in the *Carex–Oncophorus* meadow vegetation type (Biome research site 2) was estimated from cuvette photosynthesis measurements on vascular plants and mosses, by canopy photosynthesis models for vascular plants and mosses, and by the aerodynamic method. In this vegetation type, gross primary productivity, estimated by the harvest method and by respiration costs, was 450 gdw m^{-2} yr^{-1}, including 414 gdw m^{-2} yr^{-1} for vascular plants and 36 gdw m^{-2} yr^{-1} for mosses. Net primary productivity was 209 gdw m^{-2} yr^{-1}, including 187 gdw m^{-2} yr^{-1} for vascular plants and 22 gdw m^{-2} yr^{-1} for mosses. The respiratory cost for growth of above- and belowground tissues was 57 gdw m^{-2} yr^{-1}, and the respiratory cost for maintaining these tissues was 170 gdw m^{-2} yr^{-1}. The growth and maintenance costs for mosses were 6.6 gdw m^{-2} yr^{-1} and 7.2 gdw m^{-2} yr^{-1}, respectively.

The gross primary productivity for vascular plants of 414 gdw m^{-2} yr^{-1} was equivalent to a carbon dioxide uptake of 609 g CO_2 m^{-2} yr^{-1}. The conversion was made using glucose as a base to be consistent with the calculation of growth respiration (Penning de Vries 1974). Based on his cuvette measurements, Tieszen (1975) estimated carbon dioxide uptake at 602 g CO_2 m^{-2} yr^{-1}. Using the canopy photosynthesis model Miller et al. (1976) estimated 610 g CO_2 m^{-2} yr^{-1}. The simulated gross primary productivity for mosses was equivalent to a carbon dioxide uptake of 53 g CO_2 m^{-2} yr^{-1} (Miller et al. 1978a), which is only slightly lower than the cuvette measurement of Oechel and Sveinbjörnsson (1978) of 57 g CO_2 m^{-2} yr^{-1}. The gross primary productivity for the community of vascular plants and mosses was 667 g CO_2 m^{-2} yr^{-1}, which was similar to the estimate by the aerodynamic method (Coyne and Kelley 1975) of 632 g CO_2 m^{-2} yr^{-1}. The general agreement of these estimates for Biome research site 2 gives support to the calculations for the other vegetation types and for the coastal tundra at Barrow as a whole.

Seasonal Progression of Primary Productivity

The seasonal progression of primary productivity was estimated in the *Carex–Oncophorus* meadow (site 2) by periodic harvests of aboveground material, periodic photosynthesis measurements in cuvettes, simulations based on photosynthesis, light and temperature relations, and the aerodynamic method (Dennis 1968, Tieszen 1972a, b, 1975, 1978b, Coyne and Kelley 1975, Miller et al. 1976, Dennis et al. 1978, Oechel and Sveinbjörnsson 1978).

Estimates of carbon dioxide incorporation with the cuvette and the simulation model showed a constant increase in carbon dioxide uptake from the beginning of the season to mid-July (Figure 3-1). The aboveground harvests for the first 30 days of the season showed a constant rate of carbon incorporation that was approximately equal to the initial rates estimated by the cuvette and by the model (Figure 3-1). During the remainder of the season the rate of carbon dioxide uptake by vascular plant tops declined. The comparison indicated that during the first 30 days, when net photosynthesis by the canopy was increasing, the rate of photosynthate allocation to aboveground biomass productivity was constant and the allocation to belowground parts was increasing. In spite of this allocation to belowground parts, the weight of the belowground parts decreased because of respiratory costs associated with maintenance (Chapter 5). During the second half of the season, when green tissues were gradually senescing, both net photosynthesis by the canopy and aboveground production rates were decreasing at about equal rates, and allocation to belowground parts continued. During this period belowground weights were increasing (Chapter 5). Net photosynthesis in the latter part of the season remained greater than the rate required to maintain aboveground biomass at peak season levels. The reduction in aboveground biomass must have been triggered by intrinsic controls. By 4 August, the standing crop of live aboveground biomass had begun to decline from the peak season level. Aboveground production was becoming negative, indicating mobilization of aboveground organic and/or inorganic nutrients and translocation of these nutrients to belowground parts. Mosses show a more or less constant rate of seasonal CO_2 incorporation (Oechel and Sveinbjörnsson 1978). High early season carbon uptake makes mosses active at a time when vascular plants are not highly productive (Figure 3-1, Miller et al. 1978a).

The seasonal course of atmospheric carbon dioxide flux, estimated by the aerodynamic method, showed a fairly constant rate of carbon dioxide removal from the atmosphere during the first 20 days of the season, indicating that most of the carbon dioxide incorporated in net photosynthesis was counterbalanced by plant root and soil respiration. From about 10 July to 25 July, atmospheric carbon dioxide flux increased, suggesting that respiratory sources of carbon dioxide were insufficient to maintain the observed increase in net photosynthesis. During August, when net photosynthesis declined, ecosystem respiration sources gradually assumed greater importance and carbon dioxide flux from the atmosphere declined.

Net photosynthesis, and consequently primary production, was lim-

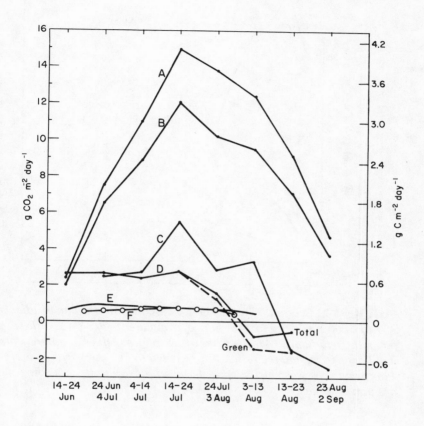

FIGURE 3-1. *Seasonal course of carbon incorporation in the moist meadow tundra estimated by independent approaches during 1971 or 1973. A—vascular plant carbon incorporation estimated by a canopy simulation model (Miller et al. 1976). B—vascular plant carbon incorporation estimated from cuvette measurement of photosynthesis, corrected for shading (Tieszen 1975). C—community net carbon incorporation estimated by the aerodynamic method (Coyne and Kelley 1975). D—vascular plant carbon incorporation estimated from periodic harvests (Tieszen 1975). E—moss carbon incorporation estimated from simulation model for 1973 (Miller et al. 1978a). F—green moss carbon incorporation estimated from cuvette measurements of photosynthesis for 1973 season. (After Oechel and Sveinbjörnsson 1978.)*

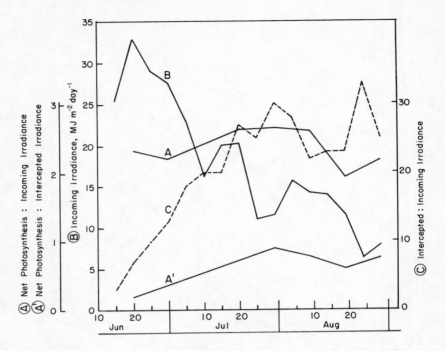

FIGURE 3-2. *Seasonal courses in 1971 of incoming solar irradiance, 300 to 3000 nm (B) and the ratio of simulated net photosynthesis to incoming irradiance (A), the ratio of net photosynthesis to intercepted irradiance (A'), and the ratio of intercepted to incoming irradiance (C). Photosynthesis was calculated in terms of energy units, and the ratios are dimensionless.*

ited strongly by the availability of photosynthetic tissue and interception and absorption of solar radiation throughout most of the season (Figure 3-2). Carboxylation data (Chapter 4) suggested a maximum photosynthetic capability around mid-July, which, combined with a maximum live foliage area index around the first day of August, should have given peak community photosynthesis around or preceding the first day of August. This trend was predicted by the simulations.

VERTICAL DISTRIBUTION OF BIOMASS AND CANOPY STRUCTURE

The canopy structure affects the microclimate and soil temperature by intercepting and emitting radiation and decreasing the vertical transport of heat and water vapor. Soil surface temperatures affect the air temperatures immediately above the surface and the deeper soil temperatures. Thus there is an interacting system comprising 1) the vertical profiles of leaf area index, leaf inclination, leaf width, leaf absorptance, leaf conductance to water loss, and stem area index; 2) the absorptance of the soil and the properties of the soil affecting heat conduction; 3) the profiles of the processes of energy exchange; and 4) the profiles of plant temperature.

During the course of the growing season, the foliage area index of the canopy of the *Carex–Oncophorus* meadow develops from zero at the beginning to between 0.8 and 1.2 by the last half of July (Caldwell et al. 1974). (The foliage area index was calculated as the total of the leaf and stem area indices, m² plant surface per m² ground, one side of the leaf considered.) In years without intensive lemming grazing the standing dead material with a foliage area index of 0.3 to 0.5 was present throughout the season but was most conspicuous early in the season. Litter with an area index of 0.3 to 0.5 was concentrated within 2 cm above the moss surface. Standing dead material and litter included dead material in various stages of decay from several previous years. From mid-July to the end of the growing season leaf material produced in the current year senesced and was added to the crop of standing material. New leaves grow from the stem base, located in the moss layer, and must grow through the shade cast by the dead material. From above, the appearance and albedo of the canopy were dominated by the light brown dead material until early June when the darker green live material began to predominate in the upper levels. However, the conversion from light to dark color was not complete because the current year's growth senesces and turns light brown before the new leaves dominate the canopy.

The graminoids (*Dupontia fisheri*, *Carex aquatilis* and *Eriophorum angustifolium*) developed the highest foliage area index, about 0.2–0.4 (Figure 3-3). However, foliage area indices and mean inclinations vary systematically across microtopographic units and were highest near the wet end of the gradient (Caldwell et al. 1974, Dennis et al. 1978). In standing water, foliage area indices of pure stands of *Dupontia* and *Arctophila fulva* were as high as 5.2 and 8.5, respectively. At the other extreme, the centers of low-centered polygons, occupied predominantly by *Carex*, had foliage area indices of 0.1 to 0.2. The seasonal progression of aboveground biomass increased with the foliage area and was 80 to 100 g m⁻² by late July in the moist meadow studied.

The foliage areas were not uniformly distributed vertically in the canopy. Foliage was concentrated in the lowest 5 cm of the canopy (Figure 3-4) and in late July was stratified by species and growth form, with the grasses and sedges growing above the dicotyledonous plants. Most of the leaves and stems were steeply inclined, with angles 60° to 90° from

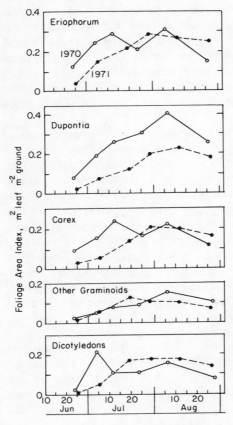

FIGURE 3-3. *Seasonal progression of the development of the foliage area index of leaves plus stems of* Eriophorum angustifolium, Dupontia fisheri, Carex aquatilis, *other graminoids, and all dicotyledonous plants in 1970 and 1971.*

the horizontal (Figure 3-5). *Carex* was the most steeply inclined, with most leaves inclined 80° to 90° from the horizontal, followed by *Dupontia* with inclinations between 50° and 90°, and *Eriophorum* with foliage distributed almost equally through all leaf inclinations. The dicotyledons and understory plants, for example, *Salix pulchra* and *Petasites frigidus*, usually have more horizontally inclined leaves. By late July the canopy of the grasses and sedges was made up of the leaves and stems of the individual tillers, each with four to six new leaves and the dead leaves of past years. The density of individual tillers was 2600 to 4800 m^{-2} (Dennis et al. 1978).

Belowground live biomass was 5 to 10 times that above ground and was concentrated near the soil surface. Over 50% was in the upper 5 cm of soil and over 80% in the upper 10 cm (Dennis 1977, Dennis et al. 1978) (Figure 3-6). In the upper 5 cm, stem bases made up 8 to 22% and rhizomes 9 to 25% of the belowground biomass. The remaining biomass

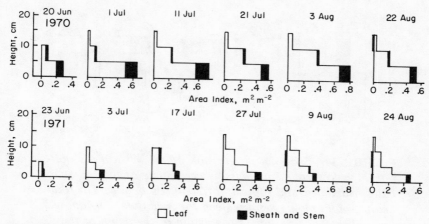

FIGURE 3-4. *Seasonal progression of leaf area index, sheath and stem area index, and inflorescence area index during 1970 and 1971. Inflorescence area index is shown by the shaded area to the left of the vertical axis.*

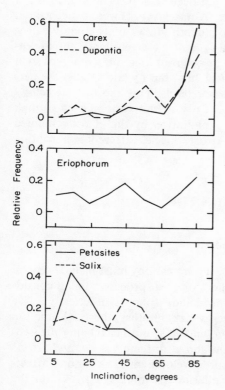

FIGURE 3-5. *Relative frequency of leaf inclinations (degrees from the horizontal) for five common species in wet meadow tundra:* Dupontia fisheri, Eriophorum angustifolium, Carex aquatilis, Petasites frigidus *and* Salix pulchra.

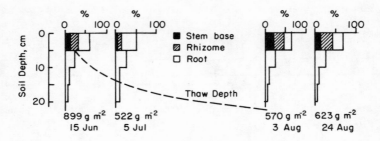

FIGURE 3-6. *Seasonal progression of the vertical distribution of belowground biomass as percentage of total in stem bases, rhizomes, and roots at different soil depths. The total belowground biomasses are given for each date. The dashed line indicates the seasonal progression of the depth of thaw. (After Dennis 1977, Dennis et al. 1978.)*

was composed of roots. Between 5 and 10 cm most of the biomass consisted of roots, since stem bases did not occur below 5 cm and rhizomes made up less than 1% of the biomass. Although roots were concentrated in the upper 10 cm, they occurred to a depth of 25 cm. The relative proportion of the different belowground parts at a given depth varied seasonally. The percentage of the total belowground biomass that was stem bases and rhizomes was lowest in early July, but by late August the percentage had increased to the early season levels. Thus most of the belowground biomass was in thawed soil early in the season, even though the total soil volume available for exploitation by the plants remained constrained by the underlying permafrost. Species differences in rooting patterns are discussed in Chapter 5.

INFLUENCE OF THE CANOPY ON THE PHYSICAL ENVIRONMENT

Interception and Absorption of Radiation

A discussion of radiation in the tundra canopy must include several wavelength bands, depending on the biological processes being considered. Radiation in the 300- to 700-nm band, "photosynthetically active radiation" or PAR, provides energy for photosynthesis. Radiation between 300 and 3000 nm (insolation) and 9000 and 11,000 nm (infrared) provides energy that warms the plant above air temperature, and affects the rates of metabolism, growth, and development. The canopy affects the spectral composition of the radiation (Lemon 1963). Within the canopy solar irradiance decreases because of interception and absorption by the leaves, stems and dead material, while infrared irradiance commonly increases because the leaves usually radiate more than the sky does. Most of the photosynthetically active radiation is absorbed and not reflected or transmitted (Stoner et al. 1978a). Thus, from the point of view of the irradiance absorbed for photosynthesis, only the solar irradiance penetrating to a leaf without interception is considered. But from the point of view of the total energy exchanged by a leaf and an analysis of leaf temperature, the reflected solar and infrared radiation must be included.

Simulation models for irradiance in vegetation canopies have been developed for lower latitudes for vegetation with well developed, homogeneous canopies (deWit 1965, Anderson 1966, Duncan et al. 1967) and have been applied to the tundra (Miller et al. 1976, Ng and Miller 1977, Stoner et al. 1978c, Tieszen 1978c). Stoner et al. (1978a) showed that the simulation model used previously (Miller et al. 1976, Ng and Miller 1977) predicted the vertical distribution of photosynthetically active radiation well in northern latitudes, so that the basic equations appear valid. For canopy energy exchange, incoming shortwave radiation was divided into downward streams of direct beam and diffuse, and an upward stream of reflected radiation. Infrared radiation was divided into downward and upward streams. Canopy properties affecting the interception and penetration of solar radiation in the canopy included the inclination of the leaves from the horizontal, the distribution of leaf and stem area, and the reflectivities of leaves, stems and dead material. In addition the altitude of the irradiating source affected the interception and penetration of radiation.

The simulation models were used to estimate the partitioning of solar and infrared radiation in the canopy. Of the incoming direct solar beam, about 86% was intercepted in the canopy; the rest passed through to the soil or moss surface (Figure 3-7). The canopy appeared more transparent to diffuse solar radiation because of the scattering and downward reflection of direct beam radiation. The diffuse radiation reaching the soil–moss surface was 36% of the incident diffuse above the canopy because of the additional loss to scattering. About 18% of the incoming solar was reflected back, most of the reflected amount coming from the canopy rather than the soil–moss surface. Some absorbed solar radiation was emitted as infrared. Infrared radiation was lost from the canopy both upwards and downwards. However, the canopy received more infrared from the soil–moss surface than it lost to the sky. The net radiation in the canopy was about twice that of the soil–moss surface.

Of the net radiation absorbed by the canopy, 80 to 90% was lost by convection and 10 to 20% was lost by evaporation. Bowen ratios—convectional heat loss divided by evaporative heat loss —for the canopy were 4 to 9. Transpiration was low because of the nearly saturated air

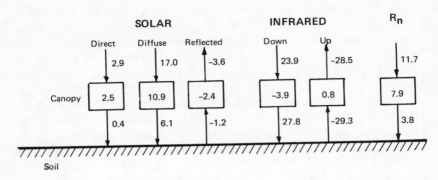

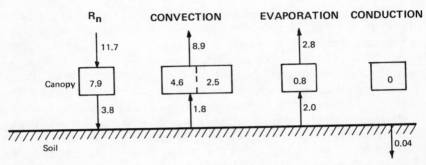

FIGURE 3-7. *Partitioning of incoming solar and infrared irradiance (MJ m⁻² day⁻¹) by the canopy and soil in the meadow vegetation type. Convectional loss is divided into that lost from standing dead material (4.6 MJ m⁻² day⁻¹) and that lost from green leaves (2.5 MJ m⁻² day⁻¹). (After Stoner et al. 1978b.)*

with relative humidities of 90 to 100% within the canopy. The high relative humidity was caused by the high rates of evaporation from the moss, and by the convectional loss of radiation that was intercepted by standing dead material. At the moss surface 30 to 50% of the absorbed radiation was lost by convection and 50 to 70% by evaporation. Conduction accounted for less than 1% of the incoming solar radiation. Of the total water lost by evapotranspiration from the wet meadow 14 to 20% was lost by transpiration from the vascular plants. The remainder was lost by evapotranspiration from the moss understory (Miller et al. 1976, Ng and Miller 1977, Stoner et al. 1978b). This partitioning of water loss was confirmed in field studies with tritiated water (Koranda et al. 1978).

During the growing season the fraction of incoming radiation intercepted by the *Carex-Oncophorus* meadow canopy increased as the foliage area index increased, while the intercepted radiation per unit of foli-

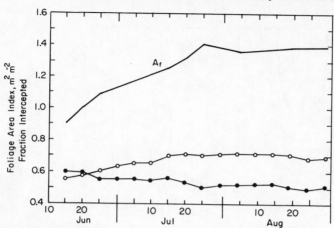

FIGURE 3-8. *Seasonal progression of total foliage area index (live plus dead, A_f) and the fraction of incoming beam irradiance intercepted by the canopy (○) and by a unit foliage area (●).*

age area decreased because of increased self-shading (Figure 3-8). On 21 June, when solar irradiance was potentially the greatest, the fraction of incoming radiation intercepted by live leaves in the *Carex–Oncophorus* meadow was almost zero because of the small foliage area index, but the irradiance per unit foliage area was large. The irradiance per unit foliage area decreased dramatically during the season when the standing dead material was absent, but less dramatically when a constant standing crop

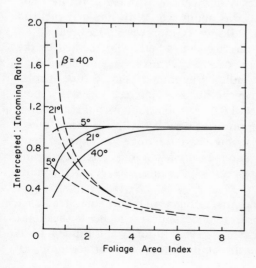

FIGURE 3-9. *Ratio of intercepted to incoming beam irradiance per unit ground surface (—) and per unit of foliage surface (- -) at three solar altitudes (β) with different foliage area indices.*

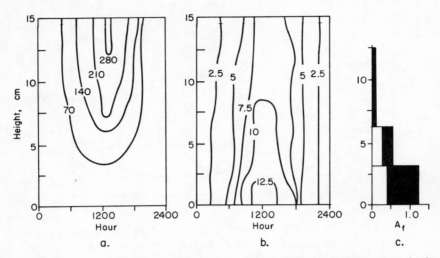

FIGURE 3-10. *a) Isopleths of solar irradiance (300 to 3000 nm) absorbed by leaves (J m^{-2} s^{-1}) at different heights in the canopy through the day on about 15 July 1971. b) Isopleths of leaf temperatures through the day for 15 July. c) Vertical profiles of live (■) and dead (□) foliage area indices (A$_f$).*

of dead material was present. Interception by evergreen shrubs was more constant through the growing season than was interception by grasses and sedges because shrub leaf and stem areas were more constant. Thus photosynthesis was possible earlier in the season in evergreen shrubs. On 21 June, the interception efficiency of a canopy with leaves inclined 65° and a foliage area index of 1.0 was about 0.6. With similarly inclined leaves and foliage area index of 2.0, interception was about 0.96.

The fraction of incoming direct beam radiation intercepted by the canopy increased as solar altitude decreased; thus interception was high with relatively low foliage area indices (Figure 3-9). On 21 June at solar midnight with the sun 5° above the horizon, interception was almost complete with foliage area index of 0.5. At solar noon with the sun about 40° above the horizon, interception was only 0.3 with the same foliage area index. At this time complete interception required a foliage area index of about 4.0. The *Dupontia* and *Arctophila* stands, after developing foliage area indices of 5 and 8 respectively, should intercept all incoming solar radiation.

Leaf absorptances were lower in regions with higher solar irradiance than in regions with lower solar irradiance, and were higher in the alpine than in the Arctic (Billings and Morris 1951, Mooney and Billings 1961, Mooney and Johnson 1965). In the simulation models for vegetation of

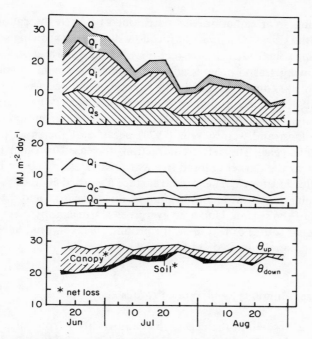

FIGURE 3-11. *Seasonal progression of incoming solar irradiance (Q), quantity reflected up from the canopy (Q_r), quantity intercepted by the canopy (Q_i), quantity absorbed by the soil (Q_s), quantity absorbed by the canopy (Q_c), and quantity absorbed by the photosynthetic tissue (Q_a) and of downward and upward infrared irradiance (θ). The net infrared loss is partitioned by source.*

the coastal tundra at Barrow (Miller and Tieszen 1972, Miller et al. 1976, Ng and Miller 1977), absorptances of 0.5 for live leaves and stems and 0.4 for dead leaves were used. Chlorophyll concentrations in the vegetation at Barrow were similar to those of temperate plants (Tieszen 1972b).

Absorbed solar radiation per unit leaf area was highest at the top of the canopy throughout the day and through the growing season (Figure 3-10). However, even at the top of the canopy absorbed irradiances were near or below light saturation for photosynthesis, indicating that photosynthesis was usually light-limited (Chapter 4). One might anticipate greater leaf areas at canopy levels where photosynthesis was greater. But most of the live leaf area was concentrated at the bottom of the canopy and most of the solar radiation on a ground area basis was absorbed near the ground surface.

The incoming solar radiation was partitioned between the canopy and the soil for the *Carex–Oncophorus* meadow during the growing season. The incoming solar radiation was relatively high in June and became lower as the growing season progressed. The fraction of incoming solar radiation (300 to 3000 nm) absorbed in the canopy varied because of the different live and dead leaf area indices, but increased through the season as the live leaf area increased (Figure 3-11). The lowest interception occurred in the coldest and wettest year (1973) because of the small leaf area index in that year. The reflected fraction decreased through the growing seasons as the darker colored live leaf area extended above the lighter colored dead leaf area. The ground surface absorbed 50 to 60% of the incoming solar radiation at the beginning of the season and 40 to 50% by the end of the season. Under an evergreen shrub canopy, with its more even seasonal course of leaf area, the ground surface would have a more uniform seasonal course of radiation absorption.

Air Temperature, Humidity, and Wind Profiles

Air temperatures within the vegetation canopy differ from air temperatures above it because of the heat exchanged between the air, soil surface, leaves and stems. The vertical profile of air temperatures through the canopy depends upon the absorption of radiation vertically through the canopy, which depends on the solar altitude and the profiles of leaf and stem area. With low solar altitudes, when the solar radiation is intercepted mostly near the top of the canopy, the air is warmest at the top of the canopy. With high solar altitudes, solar radiation penetrates to the ground surface and the air near the ground surface is warmed more than the air higher in the canopy. These patterns are consistent with measurements of Weller and Holmgren (1974a) at Barrow and Larcher et al. (1973) in the Austrian alpine tundra. Because net radiation is positive through the 24-hour arctic summer day, surface temperatures and air temperatures near the ground are usually higher than air temperatures above the canopy or near the top of the canopy, in contrast to the diurnal patterns of air temperatures in lower latitudes. The difference between surface and above-canopy air temperatures can be up to 20 °C in the *Carex–Oncophorus* meadow and up to 30 °C on drier beach ridges (Kelley and Weaver, unpubl.).

Similarly, air humidities within the canopy differ from those above it. Evaporation from the ground surface increases the humidity near the ground surface and transpiration from leaves increases the humidity of the air within the canopy. The exact profile has not been measured because such measurements involve difficult logistic problems in the low canopy of the coastal tundra vegetation. The humidity difference should be close to the difference between the saturation vapor density at the temperature of the ground surface and the humidity of the air.

Heat and humidity of the canopy air are exchanged vertically by processes of turbulent transfer, which are related to wind and to foliage area in a complex manner (Monteith 1974). The *Carex-Oncophorus* meadow canopy, with its small leaf area at the top and larger leaf area at the bottom, has a rapid exchange of air near the top of the canopy and slower exchanges near the ground. Weller and Holmgren (1974a) measured wind profiles through the canopy with a hot wire anemometer. Foliage area indices were not measured at the same time, but assuming that the foliage area index was between 1 and 2, and that wind decreases exponentially with the foliage area index, an extinction coefficient for wind of 1 to 1.5 (foliage area index)$^{-1}$ is appropriate. Wind has been shown to affect stomatal opening, photosynthesis, and transpiration (Caldwell 1970a,b, Grace and Thompson 1973), and has been implicated in reducing growth by lowering plant temperatures (Warren Wilson 1966a).

Effect of Plant Properties and Environmental Factors on Leaf Temperatures

The influence of plant form on plant temperature was suggested previously. Krogg (1955) found that willow catkins with transparent hairs reflected solar radiation to the inner surface while trapping the infrared radiation. The inner surface was dark, increasing the absorption of solar radiation. As a result, catkin temperatures were several degrees above ambient temperatures. Hocking and Sharplin (1965) noted that flower shapes are sometimes parabolic, focusing the sun's rays into the center of the flower. The warmer center may then attract pollinators or speed development of reproductive parts. The influence of plant properties on plant temperature can be simulated by defining the environmental variables and solving the energy budget equation for plant temperature. Such simulations indicated that leaf temperatures may increase 0.07 °C per percent change in leaf absorption, 0.2 °C per mm change in leaf width, and 2 to 3 °C per s cm^{-1} change in leaf resistance at low leaf resistances (Figure 3-12). Leaf temperatures can be expected to rise with decreased wind speed at low wind speeds, but be relatively unaffected by changes in air humidity.

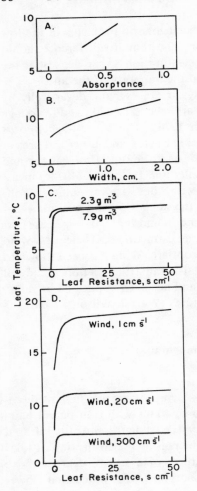

FIGURE 3-12. *Effect on simulated leaf temperatures on about 10 July (5-day mean) at solar noon of changes in A) leaf absorptance, B) leaf width, C) leaf resistance to water loss at two ambient vapor densities, and D) leaf resistance to water loss at three wind speeds. The standard environmental conditions used were: total solar irradiance 560 J m⁻² s⁻¹, infrared radiation from the sky 280 J m⁻² s⁻¹, air temperature 6.0°C, wind speed 1.0 m s⁻¹ and vapor density of the air 7.9 g m⁻³.*

Influence of the Canopy on the Soil Thermal Regime

The moss or soil surface temperature is the interface between the aerial and soil thermal regimes. In natural and modified vegetation canopies, thaw depth was shallower with higher foliage areas (Brown et al. 1969, Linell 1973, Ng and Miller 1977). In field experiments (Ng and Miller 1977), thaw depth on 1 August decreased 3 cm with an increase in foliage area index of 1.0 on the control plots. These shallower thaw depths reduce the available minerals and water for the plants, and lower temperatures of the roots.

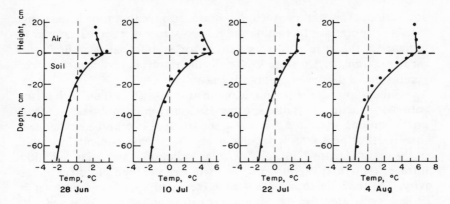

FIGURE 3-13. *Profiles of air and soil temperature at different times of the year in the moist meadow canopy. Points show measured values of daily mean temperature. Curves give results of simulations. (After Miller et al. 1976, Ng and Miller 1977.)*

Ng and Miller (1975, 1977) presented a model of canopy processes, ground surface heat exchange, and soil heat conduction based on microclimate and foliage area profiles measured in 1973. The model predicted the seasonal course of soil temperature well, except during a period of snow (Figure 3-13). The simulation indicated that in the *Carex–Oncophorus* meadow, evaporation from the wet moss–soil surface can account for over 80% of the latent energy lost with low and ambient foliage area indices (0.5 and 1.9), but that evaporation can decrease to 40 to 75% of the energy lost with a foliage area index of 4.6. The amount of the decrease depended on the extinction coefficient for turbulent transfer; the coefficients used, 1.0 and 0.5 respectively, were within the range of measured values. With a dry ground surface and foliage area indices of 0.5 and 1.9, convection accounted for over 90% of the energy lost from the ground, but at the high foliage area index convectional loss was 77 to 84%, depending on the turbulent exchange extinction coefficient (1.0 and 0.5, respectively). Under normal or wet conditions with a turbulent exchange extinction coefficient of 0.5, convection added energy to the surface with all foliage area indices. But using an extinction coefficient of 1.0, convection added energy only with the low and ambient foliage area indices. Using the extinction coefficient of 0.5, both the energy conducted into the ground and the depth of thaw decreased with the higher foliage area index. However, the converse occurred with an extinction coefficient of 1.0. These results have the common basis that decreasing the extinction coefficient for turbulent transfer increases the turbulent transfer at the soil surface and increases heat loss due to evaporation and convection. However, convection is more sensitive to turbulent exchange than is evaporation. Increasing the foliage area index decreases solar irradiance at the surface, increases the absorbed infrared, and diminishes turbulent transfer. Decreased soil moisture results in higher surface temperatures and decreases evaporative heat losses.

Simulations of the seasonal course of the depth of thaw with different environmental conditions, using 1973 environmental data as standard conditions, indicated decreasing sensitivity, i.e. centimeter change in thaw depth at peak season per unit change in the environmental variable, in the order (Figure 3-14): diffuse solar radiation, total solar radiation, infrared radiation, vapor density, air temperature, and turbulent diffusivity. The thaw depth at peak season increased with increased solar irradiance, infrared irradiance, and air temperature, but decreased with turbulent exchange and air humidity. The seasonal course of thaw depth with different values for ecosystem properties indicated that the thaw depth was most sensitive to changes in thermal conductivity of the organic layer, air resistance near the ground, thickness of the organic layer, and leaf inclination, and was least sensitive to the reflectance of the surface under the vascular canopy. Expressed in terms of the expected accuracy of the instruments used to measure the variables, the sensitivities were in the order (most sensitive to least sensitive): thermal conductance of the organic layer, thickness of the organic layer, vapor density, diffuse solar radiation, total solar radiation, infrared radiation, leaf inclination, air temperature, ground air resistance, turbulent diffusivity, leaf area index, and ground surface reflectance. Changing the vertical distribution of the foliage area index had little effect on the air temperature and humidity profiles.

The general trends in sensitivity were the same in another set of simulations involving a plot from which the canopy was removed. The depth of thaw was more sensitive in the clipped plot than in the control plot to solar radiation, ground surface reflectance, boundary layer resistance at the ground surface, and the thickness of the organic layer. Thaw was less affected by infrared radiation in the clipped plot than in the control and showed about the same sensitivity in the two plots with regard to air temperature and thermal conductivity. These changes in sensitivity relate to the attenuation of solar radiation and turbulent transfer by the canopy. The thaw development under horizontal leaves, as contrasted with more vertical leaves, decreased because of the decreased penetration of solar radiation with horizontal leaves. The thaw deepens with increasing boundary layer resistance or vapor density because both suppress evaporation, and increase surface temperature and conduction.

The simulations indicate that as the vascular canopy develops, and standing dead or live and dead moss material accumulates, the depth of thaw decreases and the potential volume that can be exploited by the

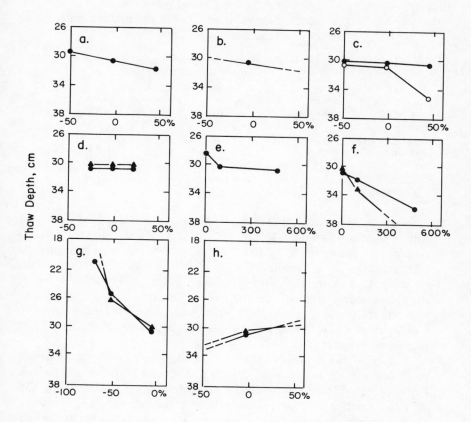

FIGURE 3-14. *Simulated sensitivities of the depth of thaw on 8 August to changes in various canopy parameters. The parameters were changed from the standard case values by the percentage indicated on the abscissa, except for the boundary layer resistances of the soil surface and the resistance of the soil to evaporation. The canopy parameters are a) leaf inclination, b) foliage area index, c) extinction coefficient for turbulent exchange, d) soil surface reflectance, e) relative humidity of the effective evaporating surface of the soil, f) boundary layer resistances of the soil surface, g) conductivity of the organic layer, and h) depth of the organic layer. In (c) the sensitivity of the thaw depth to the extinction coefficient for turbulent exchange was calculated with midseason foliage area indices of 1.56 (○) and 4.68 (●). Otherwise, where two lines are given, ▲ indicates sensitivities run with the foliage area index of a canopy from which the foliage was removed. Dashed lines indicate end points off scale. (After Ng and Miller 1977.)*

TABLE 3-3   *The Effect of a ± 20% Change of Initial Conditions after 100 Simulated Years, Expressed as Percentage Change from the Standard Case*

Variable changed initially	Effect on variable after 100 years (%)				
	Organic mat thickness	Thaw depth	Annual phosphorus release	Live aboveground standing crop	Foliage index
Organic mat thickness	± 16	± 3	+ 2 to –4	± 5	+ 4 to –7
Thaw depth	± 6	± 17	± 17	± 28	± 26
Live aboveground standing crop	0	0	0	0	0

Source: Miller (1978).

roots of plants for water and minerals decreases. The depth of thaw on 1 August decreased about 1.3 cm per unit increase in foliage area index in simulations, compared to 1.5 to 0.1 cm per unit foliage area index in field measurements. It is possible that without a periodic removal of the standing dead material by lemmings the vegetation composition would shift to shallow-rooted species such as mosses, lichens and *Dupontia* or to evergreen forms requiring less nutrients. Decreased thaw depth and increased moss has occurred in long-standing exclosures in the vicinity of the Biome research area.

Some of the interactions between foliage area index, thaw depth, phosphorus availability, plant growth and accumulation of soil organic matter were explored in a simplified ecosystem model (Miller 1978). Coefficients relating the annual change in each compartment to the state of the system were estimated from the understanding at the time of the processes involved. The initial values for the organic mat thickness and thaw depth influenced several variables after 100 simulated years, but changes in initial values for standing dead and live vegetation had little effect (Table 3-3). The simulations support the notion that subtle changes in the tundra may persist for many years, although in its grosser features the system appears unchanged. Parameters defining phosphorus cycling were critical in influencing the system. Changing the initial amounts of standing dead and live plant biomass by ± 20% had no effect but changing the initial thickness of the organic mat by ± 20% caused long-lasting changes in several variables. Changing the initial thaw depth by ± 20% changed the peak season thaw depth, phosphorus release, standing crop, foliage area index, and organic mat thickness. The state of the system after 100 years was influenced by changing parameters defining transfers, especially those affecting phosphorus release. Periodic clipping of aboveground standing crop by lemmings stabilized the system, although varying the period between clippings from 3 to 5 years had little effect.

CONTROL OF EVAPOTRANSPIRATION BY PLANTS AND PLANT–WATER RELATIONS

The control of water loss by the plants affects both surface energy exchange processes and plant physiological processes. The maintenance of turgor is essential for photosynthesis, respirative growth, and development (Hsaio 1973). Various aspects of the plant water relations are affected at temperatures well above those typical at the Barrow research sites, including water absorption (Kuiper 1964), plant growth and osmotic potential of the leaves (Kleinendorst and Brouwer 1970) because of decreased root permeability. The relative water content and growth of alpine and subalpine species were reduced by soil cooling, although net photosynthesis and transpiration were unaffected (Anderson and McNaughton 1973). Stomatal opening in temperate plants was inhibited at leaf temperatures lower than 10 °C (Kuiper, cited by Ketellapper 1963, Courtin and Mayo 1975).

The flow of water was viewed in a simple model of the soil–plant–atmosphere continuum (Stoner and Miller 1975, Ehleringer and Miller 1975, Miller et al. 1976). Water flows through the roots and stems to the leaves because of a difference in the water potentials of the soil and leaves, and is lost to the air because of a difference in the vapor densities of the leaves and air. The flow of water through the plant is restricted by the resistance of the root–soil system to water uptake and the resistances of the leaves and leaf air boundary layer to water vapor diffusion. Mosses were viewed similarly except that water uptake is mainly on the surface of the moss, liquid water is absorbed through the surface, and water loss from the tissue is suppressed when a surface film of water is present (Miller et al. 1978a, Stoner et al. 1978b).

Water Relations of Vascular Plants

The partitioning of absorbed energy into convection and evaporation is controlled by stomatal closure, which occurs to prevent low water contents and detrimental water potentials, either of which may be harmful (Jarvis and Jarvis 1963). Leaf resistances increased abruptly with relative water contents below about 91% in *Arctophila*, 80 to 89% in *Dupontia*, *Potentilla hyparctica* and *Salix pulchra*, and 72% in *Eriophorum angustifolium* (Figure 3-15) (Stoner and Miller 1975). Species in other regions are similar, i.e. between 80 and 89% for *Caltha leptosepala* and *Bistorta bistortoides* (Ehleringer and Miller 1975), 85 and 90% for alpine plants (Anderson and McNaughton 1973), and 90% for *Populus tremula*

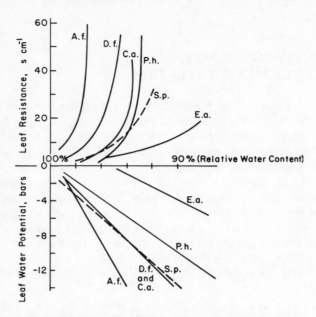

FIGURE 3-15. *The relationships between relative water content and leaf resistance and between relative water content and leaf water potential for* Arctophila fulva *(A.f.),* Dupontia fisheri *(D.f.),* Carex aquatilis *(C.a.),* Eriophorum angustifolium *(E.a.),* Potentilla hyparctica *(P.h.), and* Salix pulchra *(S.p.). (After Miller et al. 1978b.)*

and *Betula verrucosa* (Jarvis and Jarvis 1963). The similarity of these levels in different environments and species indicates that most vascular plants maintain leaf water contents of more than 80 to 90% of their turgid water content. The relation between water potential and water content of the leaves also differed among the species in the *Carex-Oncophorus* meadow (Stoner and Miller 1975). *Arctophila* showed the highest rate of change of leaf water potential with a change in relative water content (Figure 3-15). *Eriophorum* had the lowest.

Leaf water potentials of grasses, sedges and soft-leaved forbs were near 0 bars with low transpiration rates during the night, even though the sun is above the horizon 24 hours a day. These leaf water potentials were higher than those of well-watered fell-field plants maintained in saturated air in the laboratory, including *Dryas integrifolia* (–10 to –15 bars), *Saxifraga oppositifolia* (–10 bars), and *Dryas octopetala* (–13 bars) (Courtin and Mayo 1975). Soil water potentials within the root zone were always greater than –0.5 bar. During the relatively warm, dry summer of

1972, midday water potentials reached -28 bars in *Dupontia*, -25 in *Carex*, and -13 in *Poa arctica*. But in the relatively wet, cold summer of 1973, water potentials were above -15 bars (Stoner and Miller 1975). In other studies water potentials of soft-leaved forbs were similar, above -10 bars in *Thlaspi alpestre* (Rochow 1967) and above -11 bars in *Caltha leptosepala* (Kuramoto and Bliss 1970), but those of evergreen dwarf shrubs and trees were lower, -35 bars in *D. integrifolia* (Courtin and Mayo 1975), -60 bars in *D. integrifolia*, -54 in *Picea englemanii*, -35 to -54 in *S. oppositifolia*, -62 in spruce, and -54 in *Diapensia lapponica* (Courtin 1968).

Leaf resistances of arctic and alpine plants were also similar to those of temperate zone plants (Miller et al. 1978b). Minimum leaf resistances in the coastal tundra at Barrow were 1 to 3 s cm^{-1}. Cuticular resistances were 12 to 39 s cm^{-1}. Leaf resistances decreased as temperatures rose to 15 °C. The light response curve for stomatal opening indicates that minimum leaf resistances of 1 to 2 s cm^{-1} were approached at 140 J m^{-2} s^{-1} (400 to 700 nm) in plants grown at 5 °C in the laboratory (Figure 4-4). In the field open stomata occurred at 70 J m^{-2} s^{-1} (400 to 700 nm). Ehleringer and Miller (1975) reported minimum leaf resistances at 140 to 210 J m^{-2} s^{-1} solar irradiance (300 to 3000 nm) in the alpine tundra on Niwot Ridge for *Caltha leptosepala* and *Bistorta bistortoides*. Courtin and Mayo (1975) reported high minimum resistances for *Dryas integrifolia*. With reasonable conversions between incoming shortwave and photosynthetically active radiation, it can be demonstrated that tundra plants at Barrow open stomates at lower light intensities than do alpine plants.

The root–soil resistance to water uptake of an entire plant included the root's permeability to water uptake, and the total root mass. Root resistances measured in situ were 0.6 to 1.7×10^6 bar s cm^{-1}. Root resistances decreased in the order *Dupontia, Carex* and *Eriophorum*, which had rooting depths of 15, 20 and 25 cm, respectively. Field measurements on coastal tundra species and laboratory measurements on alpine species indicated that root resistances were independent of root temperatures but related to transpiration rates (Stoner and Miller 1975, Caldwell et al. 1978). *Typha latifolia*, from high elevations, showed no change in relative water content with changes in root temperature between 20° and 30 °C, while plants from low elevations showed decreases (McNaughton et al. 1974). Taken as a whole, these data support the idea that species from colder climates have lower root resistances at low temperature.

Water Relations of Mosses

Water relations of mosses differ from those of vascular plants, partly because mosses show little control over tissue moisture status. Mosses lack roots and, except for genera such as *Polytrichum* and *Pogonatum*, most mosses lack the functional equivalent. The moisture supply in the soil is largely unavailable, and moss tissue water contents can vary widely. The movement of liquid water occurs primarily as a result of capillarity on the outside of the plant (Bowen 1931, 1933, Magdefrau 1937, Anderson and Bourdeau 1955), and is probably limited to within 1 to 2 cm above the water surface (Anderson and Bourdeau 1955). Water absorption from the capillary stream can take place at the leaf bases, leaf traces, and especially at the thin-walled cells at the plant tip (Bowen 1933). Rapid absorption is aided by the lack of cuticle in most species (Vaizey 1887, Czapek 1899, Kressin 1935, Patterson 1943), a feature which also facilitates desiccation. Water vapor is absorbed less than liquid water. In a saturated atmosphere mosses generally only reach water contents (g water gdw⁻¹) of 30 to 60%. At 95% relative humidity, water contents of 50% were reported (Patterson 1943), whereas the water content of mosses placed in liquid water for a few minutes may be 300 to 700% (Muller 1909). Anderson and Bourdeau (1955) found that both *Atrichum* and *Polytrichum* failed to become turgid in relative humidities of up to 100% and that turgid mosses wilted at 95% relative humidity. However, the mosses became turgid minutes after liquid water was added. It appears, therefore, that mosses less than 1 to 2 cm high may acquire water through capillary movement from the soil surface or through the addition of liquid water in the form of rain, dew or fog. Taller mosses must rely almost solely on aerial transport of liquid water in the form of rain, dew or fog for active growth and photosynthesis. Possible exceptions are the Polytrichaceous species which, especially at relatively high humidities, may maintain turgidity through the transport of water from the underlying organic or soil layer, within and along the stem. In the tundra at Barrow, moss shoots were usually less than 2 cm in height above the soil surface. The frequent saturation of the soils and the high incidence of rain, fog and dew suggested that both capillary movement of water from the soil surface and the application of liquid water directly to the moss surface were important in supplying moisture to the moss.

Transpiration rates in mosses are potentially much higher than in vascular plants because of low resistance to water loss. *Calliergon sarmentosum* is a mesic to hydric species and showed little resistance to desiccation. *Pogonatum alpinum* occurred in xeric to mesic locations and showed numerous xerophytic adaptations, including a well-developed cuticle, the ability to roll the tissue margins over the photosynthetic lamellae during desiccation, and the ability to fold the leaf tissue against the stem. Oechel and Sveinbjörnsson (1978) showed that with water contents of 400%, a temperature of 24 °C, relative humidity of 20%, and wind speed of 1.7 m s⁻¹, *Calliergon* lost 0.23 g H₂O gdw⁻¹ min⁻¹ and *Pogonatum* only lost 0.03 g H₂O gdw⁻¹ min⁻¹. Both air resistances and tissue resistances of the moss canopy were low when expressed on an areal basis. Air resistances were similar for *C. sarmentosum* and *Dicranum elongatum* and ranged from 0.9 to 1.0 s cm^{-1} respectively at a wind speed of 4.5 m s^{-1}. *P. alpinum* had an air resistance of only 0.3 s cm^{-1} at 4.5 m s^{-1}, presumably as a result of the very rough canopy (Alpert and Oechel, unpubl.).

All moss species showed little tissue resistance to water loss (less than 0.5 s cm^{-1}) at the field water contents commonly observed (Figures 3-16 and 3-17). As tissue desiccated *C. sarmentosum* increased resistance to water loss only slightly. At the moisture compensation point for photosynthesis (75% w.c.), *C. sarmentosum* showed a leaf resistance of only 0.84 s cm^{-1}. *P. alpinum*, on the other hand, had a higher resistance of greater than 3.0 s cm^{-1} at its moisture compensation point for photosynthesis (60% w.c.). At a water content of 200%, the resistance in *Pogonatum* was the lowest of all species, 0.3 s cm^{-1}. However, resistance increased to 3.2 s cm^{-1} at 75% water content. The low resistance at high water contents of *Pogonatum alpinum* may partially be the result of the photosynthetic lamellae present on the leaf surface. As desiccation proceeds, the rolling of the tissue margins over the photosynthetic lamellae and the appression of the leaf tissue against the stem increased the leaf resistance. The more responsive nature of resistance to drought in *Pogonatum* and *Polytrichum* species is presumably an important adaptation to the more xeric sites where they often occur.

The colony growth form has been found to increase the rate of water uptake over that achieved by individual shoots. *Pogonatum* represents the less dense turf growth form, and water uptake rates were dictated primarily by the response of single shoots. *Calliergon*, on the other hand, develops a carpet growth form with high shoot density. In *Calliergon sarmentosum* water is held on the tissue surface and the colony form is much more important in controlling water uptake and loss than in *Pogonatum* (Gimingham and Smith 1971). However, it appears that appreciable water can be taken up via the tissue bases on both species. These rates of water uptake vary considerably. *Pogonatum*, for example, had a low rate of uptake, as shown by the length of time required to recover 50% of the total water content (WC$_{50}$). The rate of water uptake from air-dried status to WC$_{50}$ was 0.24 g H$_2$O gdw^{-1} min^{-1} when the bases were immersed in water to a depth of 2 mm and 0.01 g H$_2$O gdw^{-1} min^{-1} when the apexes were immersed to 2 mm. Carpets of *Calliergon* took up water much more rapidly and to a larger extent. Water was taken up via the apexes at a rate of 4.05 g H$_2$O gdw^{-1} min^{-1} and WC$_{50}$ was reached in 1.2 minutes. Water uptake via the bases was faster at a rate of 12.9 g H$_2$O gdw^{-1} min^{-1} with WC$_{50}$ achieved in only 0.3 minute (calculated from Gimingham and Smith 1971). The rates of water uptake for these two moss species approximate the range of extremes found at Barrow.

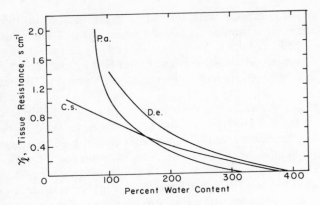

FIGURE 3-16. *The relationship between water content and leaf resistances in three moss species:* Pogonatum alpinum *(P.a.) from Eagle Creek, Alaska (Alpert and Oechel, unpubl.);* Dicranum elongatum *(D.e.) from Barrow; and* Calliergon sarmentosum *(C.s.) from Barrow. (After Oechel and Sveinbjörnsson 1978.)*

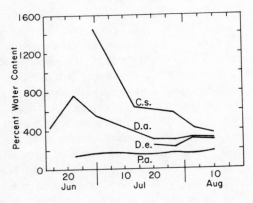

FIGURE 3-17. *The seasonal course of the tissue water contents in four moss species:* Calliergon sarmentosum *(C.s.),* Dicranum elongatum *(D.e.),* Dicranum angustum *(D.a.), and* Pogonatum alpinum *(P.a.). (After Oechel and Sveinbjörnsson 1978.)*

The low irradiance, low temperature, and low evapotranspiration helped maintain the turgidity of moss tissue. *Pogonatum* had favorable moisture levels throughout some summers, 150% to 200% water content, which were sufficient to maintain photosynthesis at near optimal levels (Oechel and Collins 1976, Sveinbjörnsson 1979). *Calliergon* occurred primarily in troughs and wet meadow areas and was often submerged or inundated with water early in the year, resulting in water contents greater than 1400%. As the season progressed, water levels dropped and water contents declined to 400% (Figure 3-17). Even at this level, photosynthesis was at near-maximum rates.

Locally, however, tissue moisture relations affected species distribution and survival. The moisture regimes of rims of low-centered polygons appeared to restrict the growth of *Calliergon* in those areas, and the wet nature of many *Calliergon* habitats would depress photosynthesis in *Pogonatum* if it occurred there (Oechel and Collins 1976).

Local populations of all species, and especially of *Calliergon*, became desiccated at various times during the summer. Populations on sides and tops of high-centered polygons drained free of water early in the summer and became desiccated. Individuals growing on the sides of polygon troughs that were water-filled early in the season were especially prone to desiccation. Also, periods of drought had a major influence on bryophyte growth and survival. An exceptionally warm, dry period of several weeks in 1972 resulted in the death of numerous individuals of *Pogonatum* and *Calliergon*. Damage was delayed and less extensive in *Pogonatum* than in *Calliergon*. At the end of the drought period, large areas of *Calliergon* mats recovered by initiating new shoots from existing material (Oechel and Collins 1976). Because of water uptake through the deep stems of *Pogonatum*, this species can maintain turgidity in the absence of standing water or precipitation for much longer periods than the other species examined (Oechel, unpubl.).

SIMULATION OF PLANT–WATER RELATIONS

The dynamics of vascular plant–water relations were simulated for the June–August period in 1970-73 (Stoner and Miller 1975). Simulations for 1973, which was cold and wet relative to the long-term average, indicated that leaf resistances of *Arctophila* and *Potentilla* decreased in the early morning, then increased in midmorning to a plateau which continued through the day. *Dupontia* resistances increased to a maximum at midday and decreased in the afternoon. *Salix* and *Eriophorum* showed slight increases in leaf resistance at midday, while *Carex* leaf resistances were low throughout the day. The increase in leaf resistances in the middle of the day reflected the sensitivities of leaf resistance and leaf water

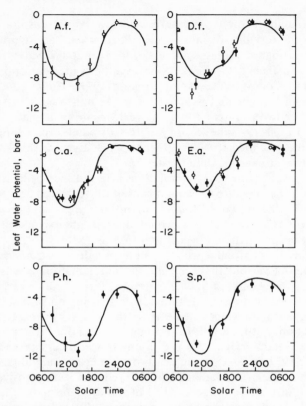

FIGURE 3-18. *Diurnal courses of leaf water potential for 29–30 July 1973 for* Arctophila fulva *(A.f.)*, Dupontia fisheri *(D.f.)*, Carex aquatilis *C.a.)*, Eriophorum angustifolium *(E.a.)*, Potentilla hyparctica *(P.h.) and* Salix pulchra *S.p.). Measured (○ = individuals in troughs, ● = individuals on polygon tops) and simulated (—) values are given. Vertical lines are the 95% confidence intervals. (After Stoner and Miller 1975.)*

potential to leaf water content. The simulated courses of leaf water potential generally followed the observed courses (Figure 3-18). Simulations for 1972, which was relatively warm and dry, indicated stomatal closure occasionally in *Carex* and frequently in *Dupontia* (Figure 3-19). Complete stomatal closure occurred in *Dupontia* for short periods. In 1973, *Dupontia* usually was partially stressed; *Carex, Eriophorum* and *Salix* had little or no stress while *Arctophila* and *Potentilla* showed complete stomatal closure.

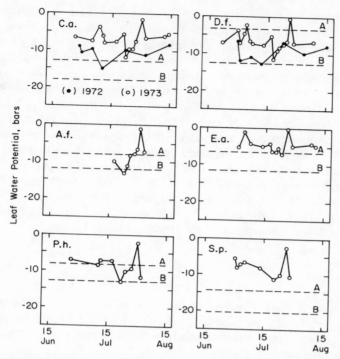

FIGURE 3-19. *Seasonal courses of midday leaf water potentials for* Carex aquatilis *(C.a.),* Dupontia fisheri *(D.f.),* Arctophila fulva *(A.f.),* Eriophorum angustifolium *(E.a.),* Potentilla hyparctica *(P.h.) and* Salix pulchra *(S.p.) in 1972 and 1973. Water potentials at which leaf resistances are three times the minimum (A) and infinite (B) are given. (After Stoner and Miller 1975.)*

Measurements of photosynthesis in the field (Tieszen 1975, 1978b) indicated a midday depression in carbon dioxide uptake, which was related to a slight stomatal closure (Tieszen 1978b). Thus water stress may limit vascular plant production at Barrow by increasing stomatal resistance and decreasing photosynthesis. The role of water in limiting production via its effect on growth has not been studied. The species, in decreasing order of their sensitivity to water stress, were *Arctophila, Dupontia, Carex, Salix, Potentilla* and *Eriophorum*.

The water relations of the mosses *Dicranum* and *Calliergon* were simulated in the open or under a vascular plant canopy along a substrate moisture gradient (Stoner et al. 1978b). The canopy tended to increase available water by reducing the vapor density gradient between the mosses and the air but also tended to decrease the available water by intercepting 30% of the summer precipitation. The significance of the counteracting tendencies varied with the substrate water potential. Both *Calliergon* and *Dicranum* showed similar seasonal courses of water content with and without the canopy and with different substrate water potentials. With substrate water potentials of –1 bar both species had a higher water content under the canopy than in full sun. The effect of the canopy on plant water potential was much reduced at a substrate water potential of –5 bars. During the late-summer dry period interception of precipitation reduced the water reaching the surface, and moss in the full sun had higher water contents than did moss under the canopy. The water contents of *Dicranum* had the same pattern as *Calliergon*, although the effect of the canopy in reducing evaporation was less because of the higher resistances of *Dicranum* to water loss.

SUMMARY

In summary, in 1972, a year of near normal temperatures and precipitation, calculated gross primary production above and below ground, averaged for the whole Barrow region, was about 465 gdw m^{-2}, including 358 gdw m^{-2} for vascular plants, 106 gdw m^{-2} for mosses, and 1 gdw m^{-2} for lichens. Net primary production was about 230 gdw m^{-2}, including 162 gdw m^{-2} for vascular plants, 66 gdw m^{-2} for mosses and less than 1 gdw m^{-2} for lichens. The average net primary production above ground was 108 gdw m^{-2}. Belowground production was about 120 gdw m^{-2}.

In the *Carex–Oncophorus* meadow vegetation type, in which most research was concentrated, gross primary productivity was 450 gdw m^{-2} yr^{-1}, including 414 gdw m^{-2} yr^{-1} for vascular plants and 36 gdw m^{-2} yr^{-1} for mosses. Net primary productivity was 209 gdw m^{-2} yr^{-1}, including 187 gdw m^{-2} yr^{-1} for vascular plants and 22 gdw m^{-2} yr^{-1} for mosses. The respiratory cost for maintaining the above- and belowground vascular biomass was 170 gdw m^{-2} yr^{-1} and the respiratory cost for growing new biomass was 57 gdw m^{-2} yr^{-1}. For mosses the maintenance and growth costs were each 7 gdw m^{-2} yr^{-1}. The gross primary productivity of vascular plants was equivalent to a carbon dioxide incorporation of 609 g CO_2 m^{-2} yr^{-1}.

The plant canopy of the *Carex–Oncophorus* meadow interacts with various biophysical factors to affect production and water loss. Several features of the *Carex–Oncophorus* meadow canopy structure act to increase plant temperatures, which are usually below optimum for physiological processes in these tundra species. The steeply inclined leaves of the grasses and sedges and the accumulated standing dead material increase the interception of radiation in the canopy, and by convecting this energy warm the canopy air. The increased leaf temperatures increase transpiration, photosynthesis, biosynthesis and leaf expansion. Even in these wet soils, the species show water stress, indicated by high leaf resistances, and patterns of distribution related to soil water. Increased interception in the canopy causes decreased absorbed energy at the moss and ground surface, producing lower moss temperatures, lower soil temperatures and shallower thaw depth. The latter two effects should reduce growth at the stem base, growth of roots, and the amount of nutrients made available by decomposition. Reduced nutrient uptake and reduced activity at the stem base should reduce leaf growth. This sequence of events should have a stabilizing influence on foliage area index. The low foliage area early in the growing season in the *Carex–Oncophorus* meadow, relative to an evergreen shrub canopy with the same foliage area at peak season, should increase soil thaw and nutrient availability and partially compensate for the increased energy required to thaw waterlogged soils.

4

Photosynthesis

L. L. Tieszen, P. C. Miller, and W. C. Oechel

INTRODUCTION

The interception of solar radiation and the conversion of that energy by photosynthesis into stable organic forms is essential for the maintenance and growth of plants as well as for their vegetative or sexual reproduction. Accumulating information on photosynthesis of tundra plants suggests that this process is highly adapted to the extreme conditions of the tundra. This chapter describes photosynthesis in the coastal tundra at Barrow and the sensitivity of carbon dioxide assimilation to abiotic and biotic factors. Response patterns and internal and external controls over photosynthesis in vascular plants and mosses are described in an attempt to quantify those factors that govern rates of carbon dioxide uptake. The objectives of Chapter 4 are to understand the controls over photosynthesis, analyze the sensitivity of the system, and estimate community productivity as reviewed in Chapter 3.

Photosynthesis is a photochemical, diffusion, and enzymatic process with a rate controlled by intrinsic and extrinsic factors. The process is basically similar in all vascular plants and mosses, although variations in component dark reactions have evolved and are most notable in the distinctions between C_3 and C_4 plants (Hatch et al. 1971). Tundra vegetation consists mainly of C_3 plants (Tieszen and Sigurdson 1973), and no significant differences would be expected in the basic mechanisms between C_3 plants in the Arctic and C_3 plants in more temperate climates. However, component reactions, e.g. at the enzyme level, have probably evolved and could be manifest as quantitatively different response patterns.

The amount of carbon dioxide assimilated is a function of the maximum capacity (rate) for carbon dioxide uptake, which may be related to intrinsic factors such as component enzyme levels (Treharne 1972), the concentrations of ribulose-1,5-diphosphate, nutrient status, innate leaf growth, or development patterns. The extent to which this maximum capacity is realized is a function of the microenvironment within the canopy (see Chapter 3.). At the cell and leaf level, responses to light, temperature and water are most crucial in determining the rate of photosynthesis. Nutrients can limit leaf carbon dioxide uptake at the cell level by affecting the internal capacity and at the plant and canopy level by affecting the allocation for the production of more photosynthetic tissues. Similarly, grazing will alter this pattern directly by removing established tissues at various developmental stages. Most of these interactions are discussed in this chapter and have been incorporated into a canopy photosynthesis model (Miller et al. 1976).

INTRINSIC FACTORS AFFECTING CARBON DIOXIDE EXCHANGE

Maximum Rates and Growth Forms

The maximum photosynthetic rates for expanded blades range between 7 and 31 mg CO_2 dm^{-2} hr^{-1} (Table 4-1) or nearly as widely as those of vascular plants in other Biomes (Tieszen and Wieland 1975). Within the tundra, however, similar species, e.g. *Carex* spp. at Barrow and Devon Island, Canada (Mayo et al. 1977), show very comparable rates. Furthermore, photosynthetic rates show a distinct relationship to growth forms. The rates are highest in graminoid types and forbs ($\sim$30 mg CO_2 dm^{-2} hr^{-1}), slightly lower in some of the deciduous dwarf shrubs ($\sim$20 mg CO_2 dm^{-2} hr^{-1}), except for *Salix* species which tend to be higher, and still lower among the evergreen dwarf shrubs (7 mg CO_2 dm^{-2} hr^{-1}) such as *Cassiope tetragona, Ledum decumbens,* and *Vaccinium vitis-idaea* (Johnson and Tieszen 1976). Photosynthesis rates in vascular plants are equivalent to rates of similar growth forms in more temperate zones (Table 4-2), suggesting that these species are adapted genetically or physiologically to the low ambient temperatures. As expected, photosynthetic rates are much lower in mosses than in vascular plants (Table 4-2), ranging between 1.0 and 4.4 mg CO_2 gdw^{-1} hr^{-1} (Oechel 1976, Oechel and Collins 1976, Oechel and Sveinbjörnsson 1978). Although the rates of different moss species vary widely, they are similar to those of temperate,

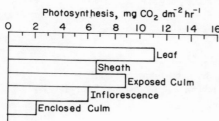

FIGURE 4-1. *Photosynthetic rates of various plant parts of* Dupontia fisheri *near mid-season. The rates were determined with the* ^{14}C *system. N = 8. (After Tieszen and Johnson 1975.)*

TABLE 4-1 *Maximum Photosynthetic Rates of Field-grown Tundra Plants at the Tundra Biome Research Area under Ambient Light and Temperature Regimes*

Species	Leaf area basis ($mg\ CO_2\ dm^{-2}\ hr^{-1}$)	Dry weight basis ($mg\ CO_2\ gdw^{-1}\ hr^{-1}$)
Barrow		
Graminoids[1]		
Alopecurus alpinus	16	35
Arctagrostis latifolia	14.7	37
Arctophila fulva	19.6	34
Calamagrostis holmii	12.6	33
Carex aquatilis	18.5	24
Dupontia fisheri	17.1	25
Eriophorum angustifolium	20.9	
Elymus arenarius	30.8	33
Hierochloe alpina	7	12
Poa arctica	11.5	14
Poa malacantha	10.1	
Forbs[1]		
Petasites frigidus	13.4	17
Ranunculus nivalis	18	21
Deciduous dwarf shrubs[1]		
Salix pulchra	28	
Mosses[2]		
Pogonatum alpinum		4.4
Calliergon sarmentosum		2.7
Polytrichum commune		2.9
Dicranum angustum		1.0
Dicranum elongatum		1.3
Niwot Ridge		
Graminoid[3]		
Deschampsia caespitosa	21.3	
Forbs[3]		
Geum rossii	26.7	
Kobresia myosuroides	21.3	

[1]Tieszen (1973, 1975, unpubl.) and Tieszen and Johnson (1975.
[2]Oechel (1976), Oechel and Collins (1976), and Oechel and Sveinbjörnsson (1978).
[3]Johnson and Caldwell (1974).

TABLE 4-2 *Maximum Photosynthetic Rates of the Major Plant Growth Forms Among all Biomes*

Species	Leaf area basis (mg CO_2 dm^{-2} hr^{-1})	Dry weight basis (mg CO_2 gdw^{-1} hr^{-1})
Herbaceous plants		
Cultivated with C_3 pathway[1]	20–35	30–60
Herbs from sunny habitats[1]	15–60	30–90
Herbs from shaded habitats[1]	4–16	20
Tundra graminoids[2]	7–31	18
Tundra forbs[2]	13–18	15
C_4 plants[1]	30–70	40–120
Succulents[1]	4–12	8
Submerged macrophytes[1]	4–6	
Woody plants		
Deciduous broad-leaved trees[1]		
Sun leaves	10–25	15–30
Shade leaves	6–15	
Tundra deciduous dwarf shrubs, average[2]	13	15
Tundra evergreen dwarf shrubs, average[2]	7	5
Evergreen broad-leaved trees[1]		
Sun leaves	10–16	6–10
Shade leaves	3–8	
Semi-arid sclerophyllous shrubs[1]	4–12	4–6
Evergreen conifers[1]	4–12	3–15
Mosses		
Tundra mosses[3,4]		0.1–4.4
Temperate mosses[4]		1.1–3.5
Temperate epiphytic mosses[4]		0.6–1.5
Lichens[4]		0.3–3.9

[1]Šesták et al. (1971).
[2]Tieszen et al. (1981).
[3]Kallio and Heinonen (1973), Oechel (1976), Oechel and Collins (1976), Oechel and Sveinbjörnsson (1978).
[4]Kallio and Kärenlampi (1975).

subarctic and antarctic mosses (Stålfelt 1937, Hosokawa et al. 1964, Rastorfer 1972, Kallio and Kärenlampi 1975).

The proportion of shrubs decreases and that of graminoids increases with increasing latitude in tundras. This may reflect the higher ratio of potentially productive to supporting tissue (e.g. stems) in the graminoid growth form. In *Dupontia* the leaf is obviously the most important photosynthetic component; however, other components (Figure 4-1) are photosynthetically active and contribute to the total amount of carbon dioxide incorporated. Mosses and lichens represent an extreme development of this trend since nearly all tissues are photosynthetic. Thus at high latitudes plants are selected which either have little nonphotosynthetic tissue or are highly opportunistic in their CO_2 uptake.

Enzyme Levels and Component Resistances

The maximum rates of carbon dioxide uptake among all vascular species are highly correlated with specific leaf density or thickness ($r = +0.83$) and with carboxylation activity ($r = +0.76$, $N = 54$) (Tieszen 1973). Chabot et al. (1972) noted an acclimation response of *Oxyria digyna* that resulted in higher carboxylation levels at low temperatures, and Treharne (1972) suggested a causal relationship between carboxylation activity and photosynthesis. Their data suggest that the range in carbon dioxide uptake potential is determined by differences in carboxylation activity. Further support is provided by data from the Biome research area, which showed high correlations between photosynthesis near light saturation and carboxylation activity among all leaves throughout the season (*Dupontia*, $r = +0.74$, $p > 0.97$; *Carex*, $r = +0.81$, $p > 0.99$; *Eriophorum*, $r = +0.75$, $p > 0.99$). Therefore, species differences and seasonal patterns are directly related to carboxylation activity. Since ribulose-1,5-diphosphate carboxylase is a substantial portion of total cell protein (Huffaker and Peterson 1974), this enzyme also accounts for the major changes of nitrogen content through the season.

The high correlation of maximum photosynthesis with carboxylation activity further suggests that differences in photosynthetic rates are related more to differences in some component of the mesophyll resistance than to leaf resistance. In the field, minimum leaf resistances for *Dupontia* are generally less than 2 to 3 s cm^{-1}, whereas minimum mesophyll resistances are rarely below 7 s cm^{-1} and are often well above 12 s cm^{-1}. Similar values for *Carex, Eriophorum angustifolium, Salix pulchra* and *Petasites frigidus* support this contention. This trend is even more pronounced in mosses, where leaf resistances are generally less than 1 s cm^{-1} but mesophyll resistances are large (Oechel and Sveinbjörnsson 1978).

Growth Rate and Developmental Stage

Photosynthetic competence is a function of leaf development, increasing as the leaf elongates or expands until a mature stage is attained. The leaf usually remains at full competence until senescence occurs and carbon dioxide uptake ability decreases as proteins and other materials are hydrolyzed and mobilized. Obviously, the dynamics of leaf photosynthesis will vary with plant growth forms as patterns of leaf development and retention vary. In *Dupontia* exsertion is followed by an elongation period of 20 to 22 days, followed by a shorter period of 8 to 10 days during which the growth rate is near zero. At the end of this period, the leaf initiates senescence and in about 25 to 30 days it is dead. Thus, in comparison with other growth forms where the mature phase may last more than one growing season, *Dupontia* has a short period of maximal photosynthesis (Johnson and Tieszen 1976). *Carex* and *Eriophorum angustifolium* have somewhat longer mature periods than *Dupontia*, while moss tissue may remain photosynthetically active for at least 3 years (Collins and Oechel 1974).

Photosynthetic activity of vascular plants does not occur beneath the winter snow even though substantial carboxylation activity is present (Tieszen 1974). Thus photosynthesis begins concurrently with growth, which is initiated within one day of snowmelt. This has now been confirmed in the Arctic not only for graminoids but also for *Dryas* (Mayo et al. 1977), which remains inactive until snowmelt. This is not unexpected since the plant temperatures beneath late-winter snow may approximate the permafrost temperature, thereby presenting a distinct contrast with conditions that may occur in mid-latitude alpine areas. As meltwater percolates through the snowpack, however, temperatures abruptly approach 0 °C (Tieszen 1974).

Following snowmelt, leaf expansion and growth of *Dupontia* occur rapidly and are accompanied by the development of photosynthetic competence. The first leaf elongates and exserts some chlorophyllous tissue produced the previous season. This tissue never becomes very active although it does make a positive contribution to the carbon balance. By about 19 June, however, the second and third leaves have elongated and they are soon active (see Chapter 5). Although the sequential pattern of photosynthesis is somewhat obscured by the short growing season, successive leaves become more active as the season progresses. This general ontogenetic leaf pattern is similar to that of other graminoids, and results in a sequence of developing photosynthetic competence as leaves elongate or enlarge, a period of maximal photosynthetic competence associated with maturation, and a subsequent decline in photosynthetic competence as senescence develops (Johnson and Caldwell 1974, Johnson and Tieszen 1976, Tieszen 1978b).

In a short growing season a sequential leaf pattern seems costly since it requires a large investment in synthetic and growth processes (see Chapter 5). Although it does replace leaves at successively higher positions in the canopy in more favorable radiant flux (but less favorable thermal) environments, this pattern must have other selective value, e.g. as a mechanism for withstanding acute or chronic grazing pressures.

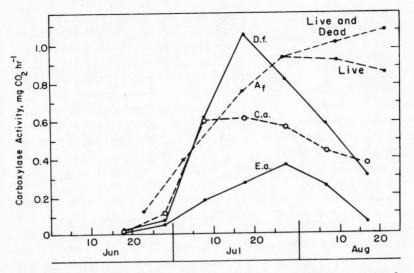

FIGURE 4-2. *Seasonal progression of the carboxylation activity for entire tillers (summation of leaf activity times leaf area) in 1971 of: Dupontia fisheri (D.f.), Carex aquatilis (C.a), Eriophorum angusti-folium (E.a.), and the total foliage area index (A_f) of the community. The foliage area indices of the species are given in Figure 3-3. Absolute rates not directly comparable among species. (After Tieszen 1978b.)*

On both a daily and seasonal basis, leaf photosynthetic rates are highly correlated with carboxylation activity (Tieszen 1978b). The integration of carboxylase activity among all leaves suggests that on a tiller basis the greatest potential for photosynthesis occurs well before the time of maximum standing crop or leaf area index (Figure 4-2). Although the greatest conversion efficiency on a green leaf area basis should occur on 20 July, the increased canopy or tiller density later in the season results in a greater efficiency on a land basis. Mosses begin each season with a high proportion of chlorophyllous tissue which may equal 50% of the maximum for the season. This tissue is photosynthetically competent under the snow, with potential in situ photosynthesis rates of about 25% of the normal seasonal maximum (Tieszen 1974, Oechel and Sveinbjörnsson 1978). In contrast to vascular plants, the photosynthetic moss tissue does not decrease in activity during the growing season (Oechel 1976), but net photosynthesis is reduced as the tissue ages. Early in the season photosynthesis is carried out by tissue from the previous 1 or 2 years. This pattern permits early season photosynthesis but at rates for 2- and 1-year-old tissue of only 40% to 75% of new tissue, respectively (Collins and

Oechel 1974). As the season progresses, new tissue is produced with high photosynthetic capacities. The moss growth pattern has the potential for significant late season photosynthesis since no end-of-season senescence is observed. However, mortality of older age classes is high, and the amount of older tissue decreases markedly at ages greater than 1 year (Collins and Oechel 1974).

Nutrients

Nutrients can limit photosynthesis at the leaf and plant level if the allocation for photosynthetic structures exceeds the support capabilities of available nutrients. Under field conditions *Dupontia* appears to control allocation to produce a complement of photosynthetic structures operating at near optimal capacities. The main response to chronic and intense fertilization (Schultz 1964) was an increase in productivity due to the stimulation of greater plant density (Dennis et al. 1978) and a two times greater leaf area index. Although fertilizer stimulated a slight increase in leaf width in *Dupontia*, there was no significant difference in carboxylation activity and presumably no difference in leaf photosynthesis. The short-term responses at site 2 were similar (Dennis et al. 1978) and resulted in statistically significant, but small, increases in plant phosphorus and potassium, but not nitrogen (Chapin et al. 1975).

In an attempt to document the spatial variability of photosynthesis and to determine the extent to which large changes in production were associated with changes in photosynthetic rates, a study was made along a productivity and growth form gradient (Tieszen, unpubl.). Although aboveground production ranged from 21 g m^{-2} in the basins of low-centered polygons to 215 g m^{-2} in a disturbed vehicle track, there were no significant ($p = 0.95$) correlations among photosynthesis and soil or leaf potassium, nitrogen and phosphorus (Tieszen 1978b) (Table 4-3). This

TABLE 4-3 *Range of Nutrient Concentrations in Leaves (%) in which Photosynthesis was Independent of Leaf Nutrient Concentration (P = 0.95)*

	Dupontia fisheri	*Carex aquatilis*	*Eriophorum angustifolium*
Nitrogen	1.83–3.28	2.74–3.28	1.50–3.21
Phosphorus	0.07–0.24	0.07–0.40	0.15–0.31
Potassium	0.64–1.59	0.55–1.55	0.45–1.14

independence of photosynthesis and potassium, nitrogen and phosphorus over a large range of field concentrations provides strong evidence for precise control of allocation in response to available nutrients. Plants of the coastal tundra at Barrow do not appear to produce additional leaf area unless they can operate at near maximal capacity. Thus, under field conditions, plants seem to avoid nutrient limitations of photosynthesis by limiting the amount of photosynthetic tissue within the support capabilities of the available nutrients (see also Chapter 5). Ulrich and Gersper (1978), however, show that these plants are always on the borderline of being nutrient-limited; and the addition of phosphorus and nitrogen clearly stimulates production (Chapin et al. 1975, Dennis et al. 1978).

EXTRINSIC FACTORS AND THE RATE OF PHOTOSYNTHESIS

Light

Arctic tundras have often been described as light-limited ecological systems. Daily totals of irradiance can be high at Barrow, but instantaneous irradiances are generally low because of the low sun angle and frequent cloudiness. Light response curves for vascular plant species are

TABLE 4-4 *Irradiance (300 to 3000 nm) Required for Photosynthesis to Equal Respiration as Determined from Field Measurements at Temperatures near 0°C*

Species	Irradiance $(J\ m^{-2}\ s^{-1})$
Vascular plants	
Dupontia fisheri	16.7 ± 2.1
Carex aquatilis	9.1 ± 0.7
Eriophorum angustifolium	9.1 ± 0.7
Salix pulchra	14.0 ± 2.1
Vascular plant mean	12.6 ± 3.5
Mosses	
Pogonatum alpinum	9.1 ± 2.1
Calliergon sarmentosum	10.5 ± 3.5
Dicranum angustum	5.6 ± 2.8
Dicranum elongatum	10.5 ± 4.2
Polytrichum commune	11.2 ± 1.4
Moss mean	9.1 ± 2.1

similar (Tieszen 1973) and tend to approach saturation at 280 to 350 J m^{-2} s^{-1} (400 to 700 nm). These saturation requirements are sufficiently high that leaves are rarely light-saturated in situ, which suggests that the entire canopy might be responsive to increased irradiance.

Individual leaves of tundra plants require very low light for carbon dioxide compensation, 5.6 to 7 J m^{-2} s^{-1} (400 to 700 nm) (Tieszen 1973, Mayo et al. 1977). Under field conditions, whole shoots possessed similarly low compensation requirements (Table 4-4), especially at low temperatures. Although the respiratory capacities of these tundra plants are high, the combination of efficient photosynthesis and low daily temperatures often resulted in the maintenance of a positive carbon budget for 24 hours (Tieszen 1975). The close coupling of the daily course of carbon dioxide uptake to irradiance implies a direct dependence even during midday hours. This is further documented by the significant positive regression between daily carbon dioxide uptake and daily irradiance which is discussed later.

This light dependence may be mainly a vascular plant phenomenon

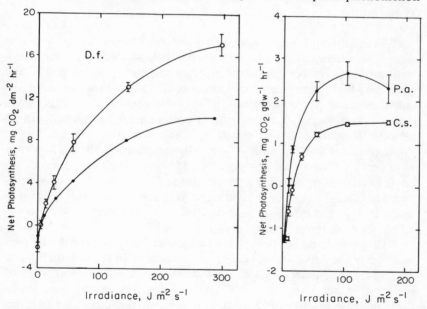

FIGURE 4-3. *The response of photosynthesis to irradiance (400-700 nm) in* Dupontia fisheri *(D.f.),* Pogonatum alpinum *(P.a.), and* Calliergon sarmentosum *(C.s.). The curves for* D. fisheri *are from the field (○) and from plants grown in the laboratory at 5°C (●). The curves for the mosses are from field-collected samples measured in the laboratory. Note the different vertical scales. Standard errors are shown by the vertical bars. (After Tieszen 1974, 1975, Oechel and Collins 1976.)*

since arctic mosses tend to reach light saturation at lower radiant fluxes than vascular plants—98 J m^{-2} s^{-1} (400 to 700 nm) (Figure 4-3). Mosses are generally light-saturated for most of the midday periods. The tendency for light intensities above saturation to reduce the rate of photosynthesis in *Pogonatum alpinum* may be a result of photo-inhibition or photo-oxidation of the photosynthetic apparatus (Oechel and Collins 1976). This pattern is in contrast to graminoids, which increase photosynthesis to radiation levels approaching full sunlight, and represents a major response difference between *Pogonatum alpinum*, especially populations from low light environments, and the graminoids. The different light saturation requirements result in different daily responses between mosses and vascular plants. During the season, mosses show only a slight daily dependence of photosynthesis on total daily irradiance (Oechel and Sveinbjörnsson 1978), in marked contrast to vascular plants (Tieszen 1975).

Temperature

An effective photosynthetic system at low ambient temperatures is essential for maintaining a positive carbon balance. Although mean ambient air temperatures during the growing season are less than 4 °C and graminoid leaf temperatures are closely coupled to air temperatures, detailed studies at Barrow (Tieszen 1973, 1978b) and in other areas (Mayo et al. 1977) have shown a temperature optimum for leaf photosynthesis between 10 and 15 °C and significant carbon dioxide uptake at 0 °C. Photosynthesis in *Dupontia* is generally active until the leaf freezes, which may not occur until –4 to –7 °C. However, the destruction of enlarging cells was observed at a temperature of –4 °C, which usually represents the lower limit of photosynthesis. Very low temperatures are infrequent in July and do not appear to affect carbon dioxide uptake as significantly as other growth processes.

The underlying physiological and biochemical bases for the temperature response curve are not clear. All resistances in the graminoids, including leaf resistance, remained low down to 5 °C (Figure 4-4). Leaf resistance did not increase at 0 °C. At higher temperatures there was a slight increase in leaf resistance but the mesophyll components of resistance became significantly more important, indicating an internal diffusion or carboxylation limitation to photosynthesis. A substantial increase in light respiration may account for the net photosynthesis decrease at temperatures greater than 15 °C.

Mosses also have relatively high photosynthetic rates at low temperatures (Figure 4-5). Temperature responses are similar to those observed in vascular plants with temperature optima between 10 and 19 °C (Oechel

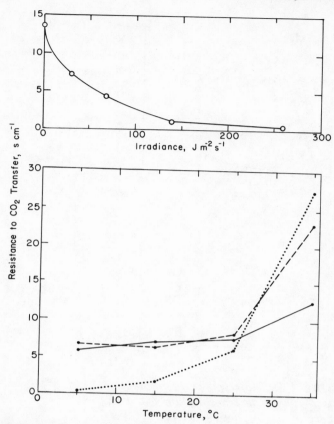

FIGURE 4-4. *Relationships of the resistance to CO_2 transfer to irradiance and temperature. The resistances include leaf (stomatal and cuticular) (—), cell wall (---) and carboxylation (. . .). The plants were grown in growth chambers at 5°C. (Tieszen, unpubl.)*

1976, Oechel and Collins 1976). Rates are only slightly decreased at 5°C. *Pogonatum* photosynthesizes at 55% of the maximum rate at 0°C. The high rates of photosynthesis at low temperatures are of obvious adaptive significance, since tissue temperatures frequently drop to between 5 and 0°C during the growing season. Continuous sunlight results in positive net photosynthesis during these periods.

Temperature optima from 10 to 19°C seem high; however, during periods of high irradiance, moss tissue temperatures exceed air temperature. In 1973, midday tissue temperatures were above 5°C 87% of the time and above 10° 44% of the time. In 1972, which was warmer and

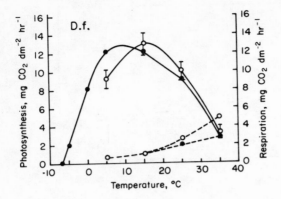

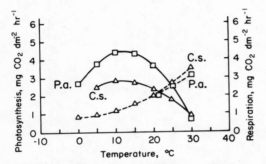

FIGURE 4-5. *The response of photosynthesis (—) and dark respiration (- - -) to temperature in* Dupontia fisheri *(D.f.),* Pogonatum alpinum *(P.a) and* Calliergon sarmentosum. *(C.s.). The curves for* D. fisheri *are from the field (○) and laboratory (●). The curves for* P. alpinum *and* C. sarmentosum *are for field-grown samples measured in a field laboratory. (After Tieszen 1973; unpubl.; Oechel and Collins 1976.)*

drier, temperatures were above 10 °C at midday 73% of the time and reached as high as 30 to 35 °C. However, in 1974 tissue temperatures above 20 °C were seldom measured (Oechel 1976, Oechel and Collins 1976). The broad temperature responses of arctic bryophytes make them well adapted to the wide range of tissue temperatures encountered in the Arctic. However, at least in the case of *Dicranum*, simulation modeling indicates that the relatively high values for temperature optima for photosynthesis result in a seasonal depression of photosynthesis of about 25% (Oechel et al. 1975).

Photosynthesis in vascular and nonvascular plants appears well adapted to the low temperatures, although the mechanism for this is not known. Low temperatures, therefore, must exert relatively greater effects on growth and developmental processes, possibly including respiration. At low temperatures all processes function in an integrated manner, suggesting a general adaptation to low temperatures rather than specific changes at the enzyme level.

Water

The water relations of the wet meadow are particularly conducive to bryophyte growth. Low temperatures, low radiation, and precipitation greater than evapotranspiration maintain hydrated tissues, resulting in high photosynthetic rates and avoiding tissue damage due to desiccation. The photosynthetic responses of mosses to water content reflect the water relations of the microtopographic units (Figure 4-6). *Pogonatum alpinum*, which occurs in drier areas and is a more drought-resistant species than *Calliergon sarmentosum*, reached photosynthetic compensation at 60% water content, and optimal rates were observed at 200% to 350% water content. *Calliergon*, which occurs in wetter areas including polygon troughs and the wet meadows, appears to require higher moisture contents to reach compensation (about 75% w.c.) and maximum photosynthesis (about 400 to 500% w.c.) than does *Pogonatum*. Both species generally remain hydrated, allowing photosynthesis to proceed to near maximal rates. Polygon troughs that have drained free of standing water

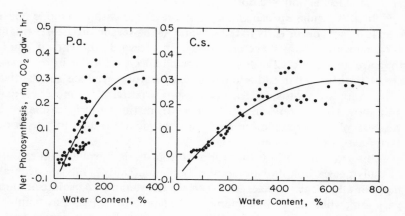

FIGURE 4-6. *Response of photosynthesis to water content (percentage of dry weight) in* Pogonatum alpinum *(P.a.) and* Calliergon sarmentosum *(C.s.). (After Oechel and Collins 1976.)*

and occasional summers with warm, dry periods (e.g. 1972) can result in the desiccation of mosses. However, these conditions are relatively uncommon. As indicated in the previous chapter, the vascular plants maintain low leaf resistances and generally high water potentials. Although occasional midday stomatal closure is seen, water is generally not limiting to carbon dioxide uptake in these *Carex–Oncophorus* meadow forms.

Diurnal and Seasonal Patterns of Carbon Dioxide Exchange

The daily and seasonal trends of photosynthesis integrate the response patterns of the plant to environmental variables with the plant's seasonal ontogenetic pattern. The early season pattern is characterized by positive rates of photosynthesis throughout the day in both vascular plants and mosses. (Oechel and Collins 1973, Tieszen 1975, Oechel and Sveinbjörnsson 1978). However, at the time of snowmelt the foliage area index is near zero for vascular plants. Immediately after snowmelt vascular tissues develop photosynthetic competency, elongate, and begin to produce an intercepting canopy (Tieszen 1975, Dennis et al. 1978, Tieszen 1978b). Mosses, on the other hand, have tissues that may overwinter 1 or 2 times (Collins and Oechel 1974) and can continue photosynthesizing as soon as they become snow-free, although at reduced rates. The relatively large moss biomass at the beginning of the season can result in high rates at a time when the vascular canopy is just developing (Miller et al. 1976, Oechel and Sveinbjörnsson 1978).

In all vascular species the highest values for carbon dioxide uptake on a leaf basis occur early in the season. As the season progresses (Figure 4-7), maximum values become lower, and towards the end of August they are near 5 mg CO_2 dm^{-2} hr^{-1} for all species. Earlier in the season periods with similar radiation and temperature produce substantially higher rates of photosynthesis. The response patterns for mosses (Figure 4-8) show some interesting differences from the patterns displayed by vascular plants, including more negative "night" values and depressed early-season rates in some species.

Integrating hourly values for a 24-hour period provides an estimate of daily net carbon dioxide uptake by plants. Daily totals are generally high for all vascular species, even early in the summer. Absolute amounts vary somewhat, depending upon specific light and temperature combinations, and are greatest on days of high solar irradiance. Carbon dioxide incorporation correlates more highly with daily totals of radiation than with temperature. Photosynthetic efficiencies for the entire season are about 1% for the graminoids and 1.7% for *Salix* (Table 4-5). An extrap-

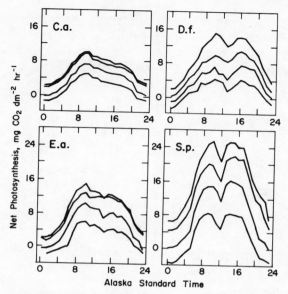

FIGURE 4-7. *Seasonal progression of the daily course of net photosynthesis in 1972. The upper curve represents the period 25 June to 4 July and lower curves are at successive 10-day intervals predicted by regression equations for* Dupontia fisheri *(D.f.),* C. aquatilis *(C.a.),* E. angustifolium *(E.a.) and* S. pulchra *(S.p.). (After Tieszen 1975.)*

TABLE 4-5 *Mean Daily Totals of Net CO_2 Uptake by Leaves (in mg CO_2 dm^{-2} day^{-1}) by Important Vascular Species Through Summer 1972 (from regression estimates of Tieszen 1975) and Efficiencies of Conversion (in parentheses, in percent)*

Period	Dupontia fisheri	Carex aquatilis	Eriophorum angustifolium	Salix pulchra
25 June–4 July	235 (0.94)	149 (0.90)	215 (0.86)	401 (1.60)
5 July–14 July	190 (1.09)	142 (0.81)	186 (1.07)	361 (2.07)
15 July–24 July	163 (0.90)	149 (0.83)	196 (1.10)	318 (1.78)
25 July–3 Aug	105 (1.03)	116 (1.14)	143 (1.41)	234 (2.31)
4 Aug–13 Aug	113 (0.85)	89 (0.67)	125 (0.94)	204 (1.53)
14 Aug–23 Aug	80 (0.74)	73 (0.68)	103 (0.95)	146 (1.34)
24 Aug–3 Sept	41 (0.64)	43 (0.69)	62 (0.96)	72 (1.11)

Efficiency is the ratio of the energy fixed per unit leaf area to the intercepted irradiance per unit leaf area.

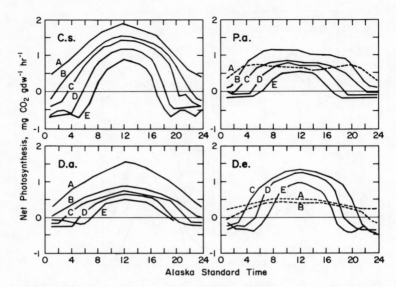

FIGURE 4-8. *Diurnal patterns of CO₂ flux for alternate 10-day periods through the 1973 growing season simulated for* Pogonatum alpinum *(P.a.),* Calliergon sarmentosum *(C.s.),* Dicranum elongatum *(D.e.), and* Dicranum angustum *(D.a.). The environmental input was the 10-day average for the hour simulated. Periods began on 24 June (A), 14 July (B), 3 Aug (C), 23 Aug (D), and 12 Sept (E). (After Miller et al. 1978a.)*

olation of the linear equation relating daily totals of carbon dioxide uptake to radiation suggests that for the three graminoids slightly less than 4.2 MJ m⁻² day⁻¹ is required to compensate for daily aboveground respiratory carbon dioxide losses. The value is somewhat greater than the compensation points actually measured during night runs, and may suggest a higher respiration rate during daytime than at night.

Late in the season the combination of shorter photoperiods, reduced irradiances, a developing senescence, and self shading results in a decrease in the daily incorporation of carbon dioxide. Thus, by 25 August, daily photosynthetic totals for some graminoids are well below 50 mg CO₂ dm⁻² day⁻¹.

A multiple linear regression analysis (Tieszen 1975) suggests that in all species there is a highly significant change in photosynthesis which is independent of the seasonal changes in radiation for the entire plant, which could be caused by an increase in the proportion of supporting or other non-chlorophyllous tissues, developing senescence, or other phenomena. The overall seasonal trend of photosynthesis is one of decreasing diurnal amplitude and of decreasing photosynthetic input. However, photosynthetic efficiency computed on a land area basis remains high and attains its maximum between the middle of July and the first week in August, which agrees with tiller carboxylation data (Figures 4-2 and 5-16). Maximum efficiencies are above 1% for the graminoids and attain 2.3% for *Salix pulchra*.

Early in the season, while light intensity is high and often above saturation, mosses under simulated canopies show rates of carbon dioxide incorporation similar to those of mosses growing in open areas. During this period, protection from photoinhibition and higher rates at midday under reduced sunlight offset the effects of reduced levels of carbon dioxide incorporation during the evening. However, as the light intensity decreases, especially during the period around solar midnight, and as dark respiration increases, relative rates of carbon dioxide incorporation by mosses under the canopy decrease. When midday radiation values are high, advantage is conferred through shading, but if midday radiation values are below saturation, there is a lowering of photosynthetic rates at midday in response to shading. During evening hours photosynthesis is also lowered by shading, often below the compensation point, and the period of dark respiration is increased as a result.

The mosses differ from vascular plants in their levels of energy capture. The mosses are much lower in overall efficiencies than are vascular plants, except under periods of low radiation when the percentage of energy capture increases. They also differ from vascular plants in that mosses show no decreasing efficiencies at the end of the season resulting from senescence. Moss photosynthesis shows less seasonal variation than does vascular plant photosynthesis, but both have equally marked diurnal changes. Light intensity as well as water status are important controlling factors in moss photosynthesis.

Other Factors

Other factors could potentially influence photosynthesis and alter the daily and seasonal courses just described. Plant pathogens, for example, commonly inhibit photosynthesis by damaging chloroplasts and/or by destroying proteins. Pathogens are not obvious on plant species of the tundra at Barrow. One of the most striking impressions given by the vegetation is the absence of leaf lesions. Root nematodes are present and fungi become active after the leaf senesces, but neither of these relationships affects photosynthesis directly. Grazing may also influence the photosynthetic response patterns, but mainly by altering the relative number of young, mature and senescent leaves. These phenomena and the role of acclimation are discussed in the following sections.

SIMULATION ANALYSIS OF PHOTOSYNTHESIS
AND VASCULAR CANOPY INTERACTIONS

Models

Vascular Plant

Previous discussions of photosynthesis have considered the physiological responses of single leaves, tillers or moss mats to independent biotic and abiotic factors. In plant communities these factors do not operate independently. They result from complex feedbacks involving regional climate, canopy structure, and the process of carbon dioxide uptake. In an attempt to quantify these relationships and to determine their relative and absolute importance, they have been incorporated into an interactive model called Stand-Photosynthesis which is basically an outgrowth of models discussed earlier (Miller and Tieszen 1972, Miller et al. 1976, Stoner et al. 1978b).

The stand photosynthesis model is based on the fluxes of carbon dioxide, water, and heat for a single leaf located in the canopy in profiles of direct and diffuse solar and infrared radiation, wind, air temperature, and vapor density. The canopy consists of horizontal strata of live and dead leaves, stems, and reproductive structures. The vegetative canopy produces profiles of solar and infrared radiation, by intercepting, absorbing, and emitting radiation, which are calculated for each stratum. Similarly, the canopy effects on wind, air temperature, and humidity are

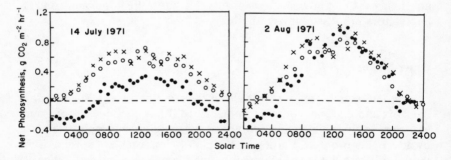

FIGURE 4-9. *Comparison of net CO_2 exchange from field cuvette (○), simulation (×), and aerodynamic estimates (●). The aerodynamic data represent flux from the atmosphere only. The cuvette measurements and simulations are for vascular plants. Cuvette data from Tieszen (1975), aerodynamic data from Coyne and Kelley (1975), simulations from Miller et al. (1976).*

calculated as described previously. The energy budget is solved for each stratum, and the partitioning of energy exchange by convection and transpiration is determined for stems and leaves. Transpiration is the resultant relative saturation deficit which affects leaf water potential and thereby leaf resistance and the carbon dioxide diffusion pathway. Photosynthesis on a leaf area basis is calculated for sunlit and shaded leaves and stems in each stratum. In this model the internal resistances depend on solar radiation and temperature.

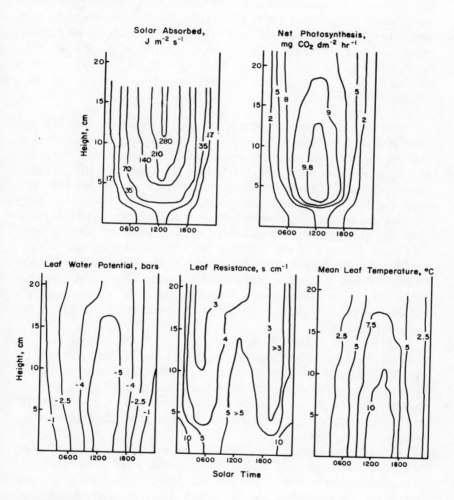

FIGURE 4-10. *Isopleths showing the simulated daily course of various plant responses to environmental conditions through the canopy for a 5-day period beginning 15 July 1971. (After Miller et al. 1976.)*

The output for the canopy model was validated with production data (Miller and Tieszen 1972) and more recently with photosynthesis data from both field cuvette experiments and an assessment of community carbon dioxide exchange (Miller et al. 1976). Daily courses were generally similar (Figure 4-9) as were the estimates of seasonal incorporation. Production data were simulated for various periods throughout a growing season and, in some cases, for a variety of seasons. Sensitivity analyses of several environmental parameters were made with a standard day (Figure 4-10) that represents the mean input data for the 5-day period beginning 15 July 1971. The standard day represents midseason conditions in 1971; mean temperatures and solar radiation used in the model are near the means for the four years of the field program.

Moss

The moss simulation model is similar in concept to the vascular plant model (see Miller et al. 1978b). Photosynthesis and transpiration follow from the solution of the energy budget equation, with the inclusion of appropriate physiological relations. The input climatic data consist of solar and infrared irradiance, air temperature, air humidity and wind speed. The vascular canopy is composed of leaves, stems and standing dead material of different species, each defined by inclination and by vertical profiles of area per unit area of ground. Solar and infrared radiation from the sun and sky are intercepted by the canopy and produce profiles of direct, diffuse reflected solar, and reflected infrared radiation within the canopy. The air temperature and humidity above the canopy at the moss surface interact with the canopy structure, wind profile, and radiation profiles to produce profiles of air temperature, humidity and leaf temperature.

At the moss surface the receipt of net radiation is balanced by heat exchanges due to convection, evaporation and conduction. The convectional heat exchange occurs by turbulent exchange of air from the surface across a surface boundary layer and across a bulk canopy air layer to a reference height in the canopy. Surface evaporation is related to the turbulent exchange of water vapor across the surface boundary layer and bulk canopy air layer.

Moss photosynthesis is related to solar irradiance, tissue temperature and water status. Solar and infrared irradiance, air temperature, humidity, and wind velocity affect the plant water status through their effect on leaf temperature and transpiration. The plant water status influences the rates of transpiration and photosynthesis through their common resistance to water and carbon dioxide diffusion. Water, in the form of precipitation and dew, that is not intercepted by the vascular canopy is added to the moss surface water film. Water flows between the green moss surface and the non-green moss and peat layers below. Surface water can be evaporated directly or absorbed into the moss tissue, to be lost by transpiration later.

The seasonal progression of microclimate and production was simulated using a standard set of climatic conditions and deviations from the standard. The standard input climate is based on climatic and microclimatic data collected at the Biome research area during summer of 1973. Climate data were adjusted using long-term records to produce two other sets of conditions which were each 3 standard deviations above or below the standard temperature conditions. The two contrived climates are hereafter referred to as hot and cold. The microclimatic data from 1973 have been used in other studies (Ng and Miller 1975, Stoner and Miller 1975, Miller et al. 1976, Ng and Miller 1977, Stoner et al. 1978b) and were used here as the standard case to aid in interpreting the results.

Simulation Results

Temperature Relationships

Analyses suggest that the vascular plant photosynthetic system has adapted to function at near maximal capacities under existing temperatures of the coastal tundra at Barrow while maintaining a leaf temperature optimum above mean ambient temperatures (Figure 4-11). Large amounts of leaf area occur in positions of the canopy where temperatures are ameliorated at times of the day when irradiances are high enough for carbon dioxide uptake to respond to temperature. Furthermore, since within-season temperature changes are small, the results suggested that seasonal acclimation responses, i.e. compensatory shifts in the response curve, are not necessary to maintain high daily photosynthesis rates. Strong acclimation responses have not been seen in the Barrow tundra plants (Oechel and Sveinbjörnsson 1978, Tieszen 1978b).

As the temperature optimum for photosynthesis increases, the stratum which supports the highest photosynthetic rates on a leaf area basis shifts to lower levels in the canopy (Figure 4-12). However, the total daily photosynthesis rate of each stratum remains similar, because strata with high irradiance and potentially high photosynthetic rates have less leaf area than do strata at the base of the canopy. The model simulations suggest that dwarf shrubs and cushion plants should be characterized by higher optimum temperatures for photosynthesis than the graminoids, which are more closely coupled to ambient air temperatures.

In part, plants are capable of effective photosynthesis because the response curves are broad enough that with an optimum of 15 °C rates

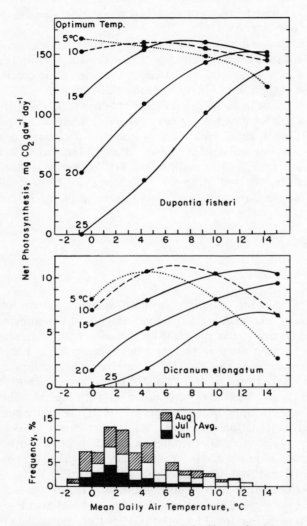

FIGURE 4-11. *The simulated effect of various temperature optima for photosynthesis on daily net photosynthesis of* Dupontia fisheri *and* Dicranum elongatum *at varying mean daily air temperatures. Also presented is the frequency of days with the indicated mean temperatures during 15–30 June, July and August, 1970–73. (After Oechel et al. 1975 and Miller et al. 1976.)*

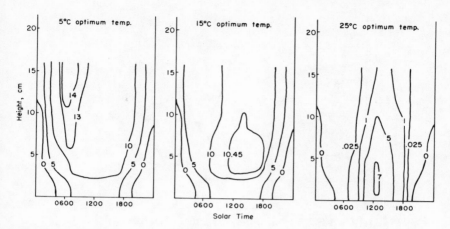

FIGURE 4-12. *Isopleths of simulated net photosynthesis (mg CO_2 dm^{-2} hr^{-1}) through the day at different levels in the canopy, using the stand photosynthesis model with different temperature optima. (After Miller et al. 1976.)*

are still positive at 0 °C. The significance of the breadth and shape of the response curve is illustrated by simulations in which the curve was enhanced or depressed at 0°C. When the response at low temperatures was increased so rates at 0 °C were increased 100%, the daily increase was only 7%. When the rates were decreased by 50% at 0 °C, daily photosynthesis was reduced only 3%. If, however, the curve was depressed so carbon dioxide uptake at 0 °C was zero, daily uptake was reduced 27%. Thus a photosynthetic capability at 0 °C is very important, and it appears that the *Dupontia* response curve is well-adapted to prevailing temperatures.

Carbon dioxide uptake is much more temperature-sensitive in mosses than in graminoids. In simulations where the temperature optimum for photosynthesis is varied and the shape of the response surface held constant, a temperature optimum of 5 °C yields the highest uptake rates for the most frequently observed temperatures 1–3 °C (Figure 4-10). Uptake is suppressed only slightly at a temperature optimum of 10 °C under these conditions. However, temperature optima of 15 °C and higher result in large depressions in carbon uptake at ambient temperatures below 10 °C. The high temperature optima typical of the mosses result in significant losses of carbon. For example, the observed temperature optima of 11 to 19 °C in *Dicranum* result in a seasonal carbon uptake 25% lower than that possible with lower optimum temperatures (Figure 4-13) (Oechel et al. 1975). Other moss species at the Biome research area show similar patterns (Oechel 1976, Oechel and Sveinbjörnsson 1978). The temperature optimum in *Dicranum elongatum* does not acclimate season-

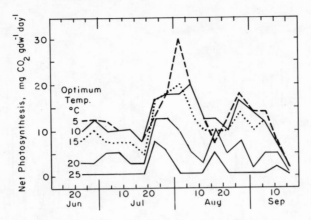

FIGURE 4-13. *The simulated effect of different temperature optima on the seasonal course of net photosynthesis in* Dicranum elongatum. *The environmental input data are from 1973. (After Oechel et al. 1975.)*

ally in a manner that would maximize carbon uptake, despite the fact that the low temperature optima necessary to maximize carbon uptake in *Dicranum* have been observed in *Dicranum fuscescens* in the Subarctic (Hicklenton and Oechel 1976). The controls on low temperature acclimation are not understood. The carbon uptake benefits of such acclimation or genetic adaptation are known, but the costs are not.

Because of the temperature sensitivity in mosses, they should be affected more by climatic temperature changes than are the vascular plants. Compared to the standard climate, photosynthesis in the simulated cold climate described above decreased from 22% in *Dicranum* to 72% in *Calliergon*. Under the hot climate photosynthesis increased slightly in *Dicranum*, relative to the standard year. Photosynthesis decreased in *Calliergon*, because of water stress induced by the higher temperatures. Although mosses are more temperature-limited than are vascular plants, increased temperatures may reduce the success of certain species of moss by creating an unfavorable moisture balance (Stoner et al. 1978b).

Maximum Rates and Competency

Simulations show that *Dupontia* is very sensitive to the light-saturated rate of photosynthesis (Figure 4-14). Doubling the rate of light-saturated photosynthesis results in a 58% increase in daily uptake of carbon, whereas a reduction of the saturated rate to 25% results in a reduc-

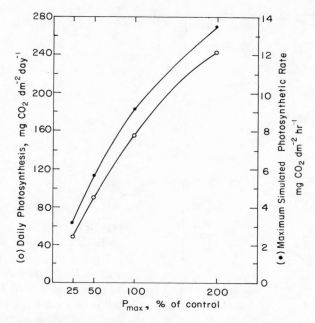

FIGURE 4-14. *Simulations of the effect of the light-saturated rate of photosynthesis (P$_{max}$) on daily photosynthesis and maximum simulated rates using conditions for the standard day.*

tion to 32% of the control rate. As was indicated earlier, one of the compensatory adjustments of these vascular plants is the maintenance of photosynthetic rates comparable to temperate region plants. The model assumes maximum competency in all photosynthetic leaves, an assumption which leads to at least a slight overestimate of uptake. The justification for this assumption was that developing leaves with incomplete competency are located near the base of the canopy where irradiance is reduced; the error resulting from light-saturated responses is therefore minimized.

Irradiance

The sensitivity of daily photosynthesis to daily irradiance (Figure 4-15) illustrates that the mean daily photosynthetic rate approaches saturation near 25 MJ m^{-2} day^{-1}. *Dupontia*, therefore, approaches maximum daily photosynthesis rates at the upper range of daily intensities received. For major portions of the season the leaves are light-limited and would

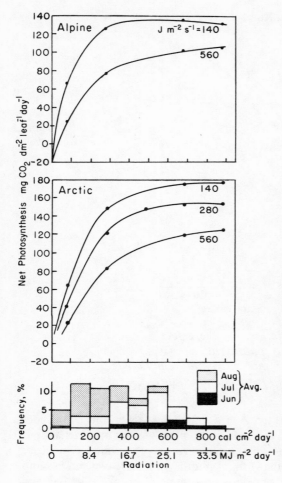

FIGURE 4-15. *The simulated response of daily total net photosynthesis to daily irradiance and saturation irradiance (indicated below curve). Also indicated is the frequency of daily irradiances for 15-30 June, July and August 1970-73. (Other input = standard day.) Simulations of the effects of varying requirements for saturation are also shown. (After Miller et al. 1976.)*

remain so even if they saturated at 140 J m^{-2} s^{-1}. In the alpine similar response curves and equivalent daily total irradiance result in less carbon dioxide uptake because at solar noon, when the irradiances are substantially greater, plants become saturated, and water stress often develops.

Vapor Density, Soil Water Potential, and Root Resistance

Cuvette data and the simulations indicate that water stress develops to a sufficient extent to cause some stomatal closure and therefore occasional reductions in the photosynthesis of vascular plants. However, the field data and vascular plant simulations suggest that such water stress occurs infrequently and only when leaf temperatures and/or irradiances are significantly higher than the mean. *Dupontia* may have allocated sufficient resources to root absorptive tissue to meet the demands of the evaporative leaf surfaces.

The water vapor density gradient is one of the factors determining the rate of water loss. The gradient is normally small because the air is nearly saturated and the leaves are close to air temperature. Simulations, in which air water vapor density was varied from –40% to +30% of ambient, indicate a slight sensitivity of –9% to +9% change in photosynthesis to changes in the water vapor density gradient. This effect was related to lower leaf water potentials and higher leaf resistances as the water vapor density gradient increased. Transpiration losses also increased as the gradient increased, to the maximum simulated, resulting in an increase in water loss of 42% in the upper part of the canopy, 26% in the center, and 21% at the bottom. The greater increase at the top of the canopy was because the gradient of water vapor density from the air to the leaf became more important than the higher leaf temperatures at the bottom of the canopy.

The slight increase in leaf resistance and the associated slight decrease in photosynthesis when transpiration changes are large suggests that root resistance in *Dupontia* is small relative to the water requirements. Increasing root resistance by 50% results in less than a 6% reduction in daily photosynthesis. The reduction is caused by a midday decrease of –2.6 to –3.8 bars in leaf water potential at the top of the canopy and a decrease of –3.7 to –4.9 bars at the canopy bottom. However, leaf water potentials increase to standard day values near solar midnight as the plant regains its water deficit. These simulations strongly suggest that *Dupontia* is sensitive to periods of high water demand but that it can normally supply the amount of water required to keep stomates open. Although this is in agreement with data for *Carex* from both Barrow and Devon Island, it contrasts sharply with *Dryas* (Mayo et al. 1977), which shows decreased rates of uptake, associated with low water potentials, at high temperatures.

Calliergon is more sensitive to a decrease in soil moisture levels than are the other moss species analyzed. For *Dicranum elongatum*, *Dicranum angustum* and *Pogonatum alpinum*, simulations indicate a 25% decrease in photosynthesis associated with a 10-bar decrease in soil water potential (from 0 to –10 bars). Under the same conditions, *Calliergon* undergoes an 80% decrease in photosynthesis. *Calliergon* appears to be much more dependent than the other species on a liquid water film and on standing water to maintain a beneficial moisture status (Figure 4-16).

Calliergon takes up water poorly from depth and displays low resistances to water loss when compared to the other species. In the *Dicranum*

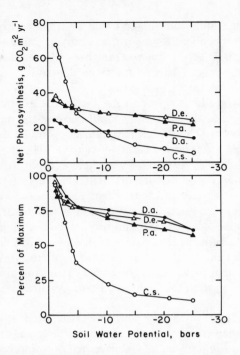

FIGURE 4-16. *Simulated annual net photosynthesis at different soil water potentials expressed in absolute terms and as a percentage of maximum for four arctic moss species:* Pogonatum alpinum *(P.a)*, Calliergon sarmentosum *(C.s.)*, Dicranum elongatum *(D.e.)*, *and* Dicranum angustum *(D.a.). (After Miller et al. 1978a.)*

species examined, the mat growth form plays an important role in water retention by increasing the apparent air resistance to water loss and in aiding water uptake by maintaining a nearly saturated environment at the base of the photosynthetically active zone. In *Pogonatum*, xeromorphic adaptations of tissues that are deeply rooted in the substrate and are efficient in translocating moisture are important in maintaining advantageous moisture balances under xeric conditions (Miller et al. 1978a).

Calliergon's susceptibility to xeric conditions is shown by the effect of a hot season. At soil water potentials of –5 bars and less, *Calliergon* shows net carbon dioxide loss in the hot climate. By comparison, *Dicranum* and two vascular plant species show little suppression by photosyn-

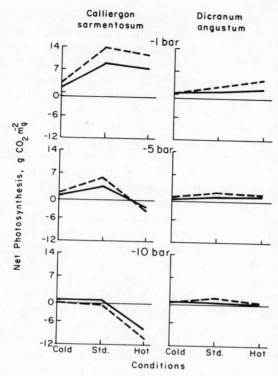

FIGURE 4-17. *Annual net photosynthesis for* Calliergon sarmentosum *and* Dicranum angustum *at different substrate water potentials for three simulated seasons and conditions ("cold," standard, "hot") for moss in full sun (—) and under the canopy (--). (After Stoner et al. 1978b.)*

thesis in the hot climate as compared with the standard climate (Figure 4-17).

Canopy Architecture Effects

Previous simulations and field data have shown the importance of physiological parameters and the dependence of photosynthesis on certain environmental variables. Since these variables are influenced by structural features of the plants as well as by physical features of the canopy, their potential influence on photosynthesis needs to be understood.

The graminoid leaf, especially in the single-shooted growth form, is closely coupled to air temperature. The temperature correspondence is mainly a result of the low boundary layer resistances associated with narrow leaves and the generally turbulent wind conditions of the Biome research area. As leaf width increases, leaf temperatures should increase and more closely approach the temperature optimum for photosynthesis. However, at the same time, the water vapor density gradient between the air and the leaf, and the transpiration rate, increase, resulting in a potentially large water deficit and in a decrease in leaf water potential. Altering leaf width from 4 to 15 mm under standard conditions has no effect on carbon dioxide uptake. The radiation load is low; therefore the leaf temperature remains close to the air temperature.

The rate of photosynthesis for any given leaf will also vary as a function of its position in the canopy, since irradiance and leaf temperatures are markedly influenced by the canopy. Leaves at the top of the canopy protrude above the standing dead material and are occasionally light-saturated although they are usually at low temperatures. The trends are reversed for the leaves positioned at the bottom of the canopy. Because of the effect of canopy density on thermal and radiance properties, the foliage area index will determine the range of photosynthesis rates by all leaves. Increasing live foliage area will reduce available light, since the absorptivity of visible wavelengths by live leaves is high. Mean photosynthetic rates should decrease, although stand photosynthesis should increase up to a maximal foliage area index. Beyond this point self-shading should result in a decrease in carbon dioxide uptake. Mean leaf photosynthetic rates decrease as the live foliage area index exceeds 0.74 (Figure 4-18). With a live foliage index of 1.0, a common upper value, mean leaf rates are decreased to 14% of the open canopy, a decrease which results principally from the absorption of radiation by the live leaves, resulting in high light extinction in the canopy. Thus, with a foliage area index of 1.0 or higher, relatively few leaves in the 10 to 15 cm stratum are saturated and then for only 1 hour around solar noon. Although mean photosynthetic rates on a foliage area basis continue to decrease, community uptake increases up to a foliage area index of from 3 to 6. With a foliage area index of 6 as much as 34 g CO_2 m^{-2} day^{-1} is assimilated. In terms of carbon dioxide exchange, a foliage area index as high as 8, which has been measured (Dennis et al. 1978), can be supported by the graminoid vegetation. With such a high foliage area index the lower leaves are in a negative carbon balance. Canopy architecture becomes increasingly important in affecting photosynthesis at high foliage areas. In the standard canopy with a dead area index of 1.24, photosynthesis increases at all times of the day as leaf inclination increases.

One of the characteristic features of graminoid canopies, especially in the absence of lemmings, is the accumulation of standing dead mate-

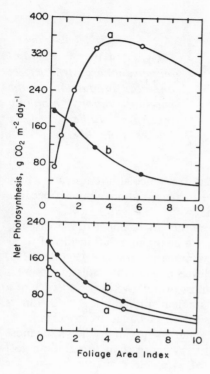

FIGURE 4-18. *A simulation illustrating the effect of increasing live (upper graph) and dead (lower graph) foliage area index on photosynthetic rates per unit ground area (a) and per unit leaf area (b). Other input is for the standard day. In the upper graph, ground area rates are the sum of all vascular plants. In the lower graph ground rates are for* Dupontia *only with a foliage area index of 0.125 in the presence of a total live foliage area index = 0.744 plus a dead foliage area index given. (After Miller et al. 1976.)*

rial (Tieszen 1972b). As an intercepting and emitting component in the canopy, the effect of the accumulation of standing dead material on photosynthesis and soil thaw could be quite significant. But because of the decreased absorptivity of the dead material its effects on photosynthesis are less than that of live material (Figure 4-18). In the simulations a dead foliage area index of 5.0, 2 to 3 times that usually measured in the field, results in a 64% reduction of photosynthesis. Accumulation of dead material has a depressing effect on photosynthesis, which is minimized as long as winter snows and some decomposition reposition this potentially intercepting material at the bottom of the canopy. At the bottom of the canopy, however, the effects of dead material will be greater in *Dupontia* than most other species, since *Dupontia* has more leaf area near the base of the canopy.

Canopy relationships also have profound effects on mosses. A vascular plant canopy under moist conditions reduces the carbon dioxide uptake by mosses from the levels simulated in the open. The canopy reduces radiation and temperature at the moss surface, which would tend to decrease photosynthesis, especially during periods of low radiation. The canopy also reduces turbulence and results in a lowered vapor density gradient between the moss and the air. Therefore the reduction in car-

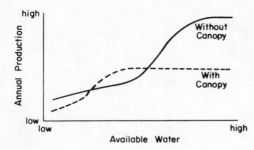

FIGURE 4-19. *A diagrammatic summary of the effect on moss production of the vascular canopy along a moisture gradient. (After Stoner et al. 1978b.)*

bon dioxide uptake due to the lowered irradiance and temperature may be more than compensated for by the increased photosynthesis because of the improved tissue moisture status.

The result of an interplay between the environment in the vascular canopy and the moss–water relation is a changing relationship of moss production and canopy cover along a moisture gradient (Figure 4-19). The simulations indicate that at high levels of available moisture, there is no water limitation, and mosses are most productive in the absence of a vascular plant canopy under full ambient radiation. Production is limited by light, and plant resistances to gas exchange are important. At moderate moisture availability, a vascular plant canopy increases moss production by decreasing evaporation by more than the amount lost through interception. At low levels of available moisture, mosses are most productive in the absence of a canopy. In this situation, a canopy intercepts much of the precipitation available and mosses are seldom hydrated. Under these conditions, brief periods of light precipitation are not effective in penetrating the canopy to hydrate the moss tissue (Stoner et al. 1978b). These results should be viewed as speculative because of uncertainties in the interception model and in the water uptake relationships in mosses. The water relationships of mosses are poorly understood compared with the level of understanding of moss photosynthesis.

Grazing

Grazing is an important biotic interaction that affects the photosynthetic rates and patterns described above. In the absence of a peak in the lemming population, the grazing pattern in the coastal tundra at Barrow results in the removal of some vegetation, usually as tiller units or shoots, near the moss surface. Thus, photosynthetic tissues at various stages of photosynthetic competency are removed and consequently seasonal production is reduced. Heavy grazing, especially in late winter or early spring, removes the canopy, including standing dead and live material. Thus, the microenvironment surrounding the photosynthetic leaves

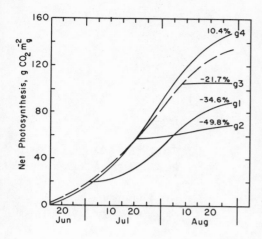

FIGURE 4-20. *Simulated responses of a* Dupontia fisheri *tiller to grazing. Leaf photosynthetic rates were estimated for 1971 environmental data and 1972 leaf growth data. Grazing was simulated by the complete removal of photosynthetic tissue. The numbers represent the percent change in seasonal CO_2 uptake resulting from four grazing events.*

is altered dramatically. Leaves near the moss surface are exposed to more intense radiation and have lower temperatures, since convectional losses are greater (Figure 4-20).

Early season grazing by lemmings has little effect on photosynthesis in *Dupontia* because photosynthetically competent tissues are not available to be harvested and because mean photosynthetic rates of new tissues increase in a more open canopy. Midseason grazing, however, is very detrimental to seasonal carbon dioxide uptake. In plants grazed in midseason, carbon dioxide uptake was 42% less than in ungrazed plants. This results mainly because photosynthesis is limited by the available leaf area, and grazing at midseason removes photosynthetic tissue at a time when its contribution is greatest. In addition to the major effect on ecosystem carbon balance, grazing reduces storage reserves (Tieszen and Archer 1979), which will affect plant performance for one or more growing seasons. We have not assessed the occasional severe grazing pressure which can result in rhizome and stem base destruction. This may have dramatic effects on population structure.

Seasonal Course of Carbon Dioxide Uptake

Primary production varies both spatially and from season to season. Since the rate of net photosynthesis is not strongly depressed because of the low temperatures, other factors must account for major portions of the variation. The primary factors limiting primary production or canopy development appear to be: 1) the length of the growing season (see Figures 3-1, 3-2), which is dictated by the duration of snow cover and related to topography and seasonal radiation patterns, and 2) the alloca-

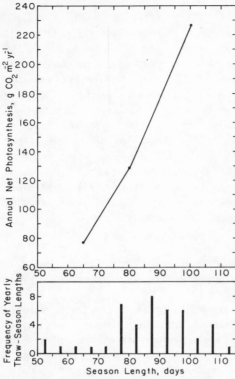

FIGURE 4-21. *The simulated effect of season length on annual net photosynthesis for* Dupontia fisheri *in the canopy of the* Carex–Oncophorus *meadow. The frequencies of yearly thaw season lengths of periods with above 0°C mean daily temperatures for the years 1922 to 1973 are given also. Other input is for the standard season. (After Miller et al. 1976.)*

tion of carbohydrates for leaf production which, in the coastal tundra at Barrow, is controlled to a large extent by the availability of soil nutrients, principally nitrogen and phosphorus. The spatial pattern of aboveground primary production reflects these topographic and nutrient relationships; and the magnitude of production depends upon climatic factors. Simulating the seasonal courses of carbon dioxide uptake for *Dupontia fisheri* can be used to assess the response of the graminoids to some of these variables.

Season length was simulated by initiating the season earlier or later than the 15 June date used for 1971. Environmental factors and rate of canopy development were assumed to be the same as in the 1971 simulation. Under these conditions, there is a marked effect of season length on total carbon uptake (Figure 4-21), primarily because plants can more fully utilize the high levels of radiant energy at the time of the solstice. During the simulated long season, *Dupontia* attained a foliage area index of 0.22 on 4 August, nearly 30% greater than the standard season. Conversely the foliage area was reduced by 30% during the short season. Unfortunately, long-term field observations covering this range of season lengths are not available for comparison with productivity estimates. Production and carbon dioxide uptake are increased in the short season if the canopy delays senescence and continues to develop until a standard canopy is attained. The simulations and an analysis of the seasonal course of CO_2 uptake (Figures 3-1, 3-2) suggest that production is very sensitive to the rate of allocation to leaves. We have estimated (Tieszen 1978b) that a 25% increase in leaf production results in a 45% increase in CO_2 uptake. Thus, it appear that both the date of initiation and the pattern of canopy development are among the most important factors controlling CO_2 uptake and primary production.

Variations in the amount of radiant energy received during a season of constant length affect seasonal uptake and production. An increase in incoming solar radiation equivalent to one standard deviation results in a 13% increase in uptake.

The overall sensitivity of the carbon dioxide uptake system to temperature variations is much less significant. Decreasing temperatures by one standard deviation results in a mean temperature of $+3.0\,°C$, or $2.3\,°C$ lower than the long-term mean, but reduces carbon dioxide uptake by only 1.4%. Early in the season, low temperatures inhibit carbon dioxide uptake on a leaf basis. However, the small foliage area at this time makes its effect on the total season budget nearly negligible. Increasing temperatures by one standard deviation increases carbon dioxide uptake by only 0.4% (Tieszen 1978b).

In order to determine the effect of several factors interacting simultaneously, two seasons were simulated, one warmer and brighter than the mean and one colder and with less irradiance than the mean. The warmer season with higher irradiance resulted in an 11% increase in carbon dioxide uptake whereas the colder season with less irradiance reduced carbon dioxide uptake by 17%. If these patterns are associated with changes in rates of allocation, the effect is great. When the warmer, brighter season was combined with a 20% increase in live foliage area index, net photosynthesis increased 53%. When the colder, darker season was combined with a similar decrease in the foliage area, net photosynthesis decreased by 41%. The carbon dioxide uptake system, however, appears relatively insensitive to temperature, is quite dependent on radiant energy, and is very dependent on allocation to photosynthetic tissue. The sensitivity of allocation to various environmental factors must now be understood because photosynthesis, per se, functions quite well at the prevailing ambient temperatures.

SUMMARY

The photosynthetic rates of plants of the coastal tundra at Barrow show consistent patterns among growth forms that are comparable to similar plant types in more temperate zones. Maximal rates of carbon dioxide uptake are greatest in leaves of short duration, for example grasses and forbs, and are lowest in the evergreen dwarf shrubs, mosses and lichens. The dominant graminoids attain rates around 17 to 21 mg CO_2 dm^{-2} hr^{-1} and the mosses 1 to 5 mg CO_2 gdw^{-1} hr^{-1}.

Leaves rapidly develop photosynthetic competency following snow-melt, and maximal rates are highly correlated with carboxylation activity. The continuous irradiance and a relatively open canopy result in high daily rates of carbon dioxide uptake. Net rates for whole plants are highest in early July, 200 to 400 mg CO_2 dm^{-2} hr^{-1}, and decrease progressively until early September as senescence progresses, self-shading increases, and the irradiance decreases following the summer solstice. Efficiencies of energy conversion are above 1% for the graminoids and are as high as 2.3% for *Salix pulchra*. The net seasonal incorporation is 602 g m^{-2}, a field value corroborated by the aerodynamic assessment of carbon dioxide exchange and the simulation model. Approximately two-thirds of the seasonal incorporation occurs after the canopy has developed and has replenished belowground reserves.

Plants are well adapted to prevailing tundra environments. The vascular plants and mosses have similar, low light compensation requirements (5.6 to 15.8 J m^{-2} s^{-1}, 400 to 700 nm), but differ with respect to light saturation. Grasses saturate around 279 J m^{-2} s^{-1} and mosses saturate around 98 J m^{-2} s^{-1}. On a daily basis vascular leaves are rarely light-saturated, but mosses may be inhibited by high irradiances, especially in open canopies.

Temperature optima for leaf carbon dioxide uptake are commonly around 15 °C or well above mean ambient temperatures. The high uptake efficiencies on a daily and seasonal basis suggest that this optimum allows plants to function effectively under climatic conditions of the coastal tundra at Barrow. Simulations confirm that a temperature optimum of 15 °C allows vascular plants to take up carbon dioxide efficiently across the range of temperatures experienced. This occurs in part because the leaf area is concentrated at the base of the canopy where leaf temperatures are higher and because the leaves often function on the light-dependent portion of the light response curve. Seasonal temperature acclimation is not apparent. Mosses, however, show a greater sensitivity to temperature changes and a greater vulnerability to water loss. Thus, they show more frequent water stress than the vascular plants, which are rarely water-stressed even though leaf resistances are low. This results from a low evaporative demand and a high soil water potential.

Annual carbon dioxide uptake and net primary production are mainly limited by the availability of photosynthetic leaf area. In a typical season, photosynthesis on a land area basis is strongly limited because the canopy is not well developed until late July when solar irradiance is already decreasing. Season length, or more precisely, the date of snowmelt, is an important factor dictating the extent of canopy development and therefore the uptake of carbon dioxide.

Spatially, the uptake of carbon dioxide is under a similar control. The productivities of the vegetation types are largely a function of the plant densities or foliage area indices, which are determined by the moisture and nutrient (mainly phosphorus) gradients. Wetter and more fertile areas are more productive because the plants composing the vegetation types in these areas allocate more carbon for photosynthetic tissues. The photosynthetic rates on a leaf basis of a given growth form remain comparable across a wide range of microtopographic units.

5

Control of Tundra Plant Allocation Patterns and Growth

F. S. Chapin III, L. L. Tieszen, M. C. Lewis,
P. C. Miller, and B. H. McCown

INTRODUCTION

There is no significant difference in photosynthetic potential among populations in the three major graminoid species in the coastal tundra at Barrow (Chapter 4), and all populations receive the same low solar irradiance. Nevertheless, there is as much as a ten-fold difference in standing crop among these same populations. Clearly, growth and primary production are limited by more than plant photosynthetic potential or energy available for photosynthesis. This chapter seeks to explain how tundra plants control allocation patterns and growth to successfully exploit the cold-dominated, nutrient-limited environment of Barrow.

Carbon and minerals may be allocated to: 1) leaf and stem growth, which exerts a direct positive feedback on canopy photosynthesis by augmenting the quantity of photosynthetic tissues; 2) root production, which increases the capacity of the plant to absorb water and nutrients; 3) rhizome production, which leads to vegetative reproduction and additional photosynthetic tissue and provides for carbon and nutrient storage; and 4) inflorescences, which can lead to the dispersal and establishment of genetically distinct individuals. The balance and timing of these alternative allocation pathways determine the pattern of plant growth and reproduction and the relative supply of carbon, water and nutrients that the plant acquires. We place special emphasis on *Dupontia fisheri*, which typifies the non-caespitose or single graminoid growth habit that constitutes the major part of the coastal tundra vegetation at Barrow (Chapter 3, Tieszen 1972b).

140

GROWTH PATTERNS OF TUNDRA GRAMINOIDS

Growth Form of *Dupontia fisheri*

Dupontia, like most grasses, consists of a prostrate, subterranean branched stem (rhizome), aerial shoots, and roots produced from below-ground nodes (Figure 5-1). Each new tiller is initiated from an axillary bud of a leafing node. As the bud develops and the rhizome elongates below ground, the tiller is termed a "V0," a tiller containing only rhizome phytomers. At Barrow a V0 tiller seldom reaches the stage of leaf exsertion in its first season of growth, whereas mid-latitude grasses generally exsert leaves in the same season that rhizome growth begins (e.g. Koller and Kigel 1972). During the second growing season, when the shoot appears above ground, the tiller is designated "V1," a tiller in its first season of shoot production. The tiller then produces three or four new leaves each year. Tillers in their second, third and fourth years of growth above ground are designated "V2," "V3," and "V4," respectively.

A second V0 and sometimes a third or fourth may be produced by any tiller in its first year of leaf production. These subsequently produced tillers are designated as "primes" (for example V0 ', V1 ') to indicate their age class and relationship to other members of that class. Sub-

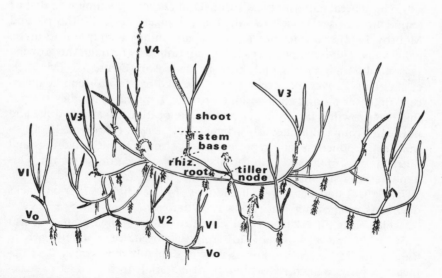

FIGURE 5-1. *Typical tiller system of* Dupontia fisheri *showing age classes of component tillers. The letter V with associated number indicates the age class of the tiller (see text). (From Allessio and Tieszen 1975a.)*

sequent development of "primes" may be slower, and they may take one year longer to complete their life cycles. Production of prime tillers is the means by which a tiller system branches, although prime tillers often do not produce daughter tillers and become "dead ends" or side branches of the main rhizome axis (Figure 5-1).

After production of approximately 18 nodes, the apical meristem typically differentiates into an inflorescence. The last four nodes and the inflorescence normally develop in the third (V3) or fourth (V4) season of aboveground growth, although induction and initiation occur at the end of the preceding season (Mattheis et al. 1976). The last growing unit develops into the flag leaf and the elongated lower internode of the culm. After flowering, the shoot dies. The tiller rhizome and roots continue to live for several years and may occasionally produce V0 tillers (Allessio and Tieszen 1975a, Shaver and Billings 1975).

The tiller system comprises all the vegetative offshoots of the original seedling or tiller, and in the tundra at Barrow consists of more than 20 to 30 tillers. Living tillers are often interconnected by dead rhizomes.

Seasonal Growth Patterns

Shoot Growth

The general pattern of leaf turnover in *Dupontia* is similar to that of temperate grasses (Evans et al. 1964, Langer 1966, Milthorpe and Moorby 1974) and does not represent any unique adaptation to arctic conditions. *Dupontia* produces leaves continuously through the growing season, although more rapidly early in the season (Figure 5-2) (Mattheis et al. 1976). Leaves that are not fully exserted by season's end lie quiescent until spring and then resume growth. Laboratory studies suggest that leaf growth is largely supported by reallocation of carbohydrate and nutrients from simultaneously senescing old leaves (McCown 1978), so that leaf production may represent a large sink for carbohydrates and nutrients only in the spring of the first year of aboveground growth. This hypothesis is supported by ^{14}C labeling studies (Allessio and Tieszen 1975a, 1978) and computer simulations (Miller et al. 1978c) but lacks documentation of nutrient reallocation patterns.

Flowering tillers differ from vegetative tillers in their pattern of leaf turnover in that all leaves of flowering tillers senesce relatively early in the season. The accelerated senescence presumably represents a developmentally programmed redistribution of materials to reproductive structures, as in temperate graminoids (Williams 1955). Thus the pattern of shoot growth of *Dupontia* may maximize reutilization of nutrients from senescing leaves.

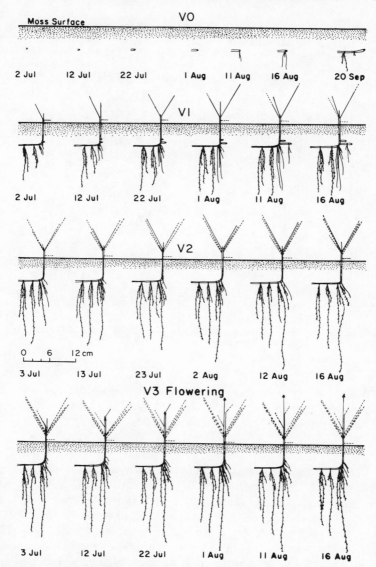

FIGURE 5-2. *Seasonal growth patterns of* Dupontia *tillers of different age classes. Leaves are represented by lines inclined at 62°, the mean leaf inclination for* Dupontia; *the solid portion of the line represents green leaf length and the dashed portion represents senesced length. The most recently exserted leaf is inclined 90° until fully exserted. The inflorescence is represented with an arrow. [Drawn from data collected for shoots (Mattheis et al. 1976), roots (Allessio and Tieszen 1975a, Shaver and Billings 1975), and V0 tillers (Lawrence et al. 1978) in 1973.]*

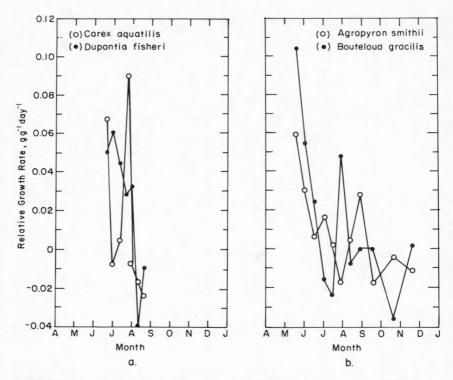

FIGURE 5-3. *Mean relative growth rates of graminoids observed in situ in a) tundra (calculated from Tieszen 1972b), and b) temperate grassland at Cottonwood, S.D. (Lewis et al. 1971).*

The most striking feature of plant growth at Barrow is the high production rate at low temperatures. Graminoids in the Biome research area have relative production rates (g g^{-1} day^{-1}) comparable to those of some dominant grasses of a mid-latitude grassland, in spite of a 15 to 20°C difference in average air temperature during the growing season (Figure 5-3). The principal difference in their patterns of production is not the rate of growth but the short period during which growth occurs in the tundra. The capability of tundra plants to grow effectively at low temperature is further seen in controlled environment experiments where graminoids from Barrow exhibit maximum rates of leaf initiation, elongation, and hence growth at 15°C (Tieszen, unpubl.). This is comparable to the optimum temperature for growth of some alpine grasses (Scott 1970), but some 10 to 15° cooler than the optimum growth temperature of temperate zone grasses (e.g. Evans et al. 1964, Warren Wilson 1966a). However, the 15°C temperature optimum for growth of tundra graminoids is 5 to 10°C higher than average summer shoot temperature in the field. Transplant studies show that Barrow graminoids and other arctic species do grow faster in warmer climates (Warren Wilson 1966a, Chapin and Chapin, pers. comm.) than in their natural environment, indicating that arctic plant growth is limited in part by temperature despite adaptations that permit rapid growth at low temperature.

The similarity of relative production rates between tundra and mid-latitude grasses in the field suggests that the metabolic cost associated with this production (i.e. growth respiration) may also be similar, assuming comparable production efficiencies. This hypothesis is supported by laboratory studies showing that arctic plants have a higher respiratory rate than mid-latitude plants when measured at some standard temperature, but that the respiration rates of various populations at their respective habitat and growth temperatures may be comparable (Mooney and Billings 1961, Billings et al. 1971). High rates of mitochondrial oxidation are the cause of high respiration rates measured in intact plants (Klikoff 1966). Because respiration is temperature-dependent, a high respiratory capacity would be required for arctic plants to maintain their observed growth rates at low ambient temperature. The high respiratory capacity of arctic plants is determined both genetically and environmentally, although genetic factors appear more important than acclimation in explaining this temperature compensation (Klikoff 1966, Billings et al. 1971).

Many authors (e.g. Bliss 1962a, Billings and Mooney 1968) have commented upon rapid spring shoot growth of tundra species. However, Warren Wilson (1966a) found lower growth rates in the high Arctic than in England. Further critical studies of relative growth rates of arctic plants are needed.

Rhizome Growth

Simulations suggest that the rapid early-season leaf growth of *Dupontia* is correlated with a corresponding decrease in the biomass of the rhizome and to a lesser degree of the stem base (Figure 5-4). This has been corroborated in measurements of temperate and upland tundra sedges (Bernard 1974, Chapin et al. 1980). Later in the season there is substantial allocation of biomass to belowground organs and probably a retrieval of materials from senescing leaves to the rhizome and sheath/stem base in preparation for the following season. This agrees with conclusions of the carbon dioxide budgets (Chapter 12) and ^{14}C and ^{32}P autoradiography (Allessio and Tieszen 1975a, Chapin and Bloom 1976). The main growth phase of new V0 tillers is from mid-July onward in contrast to the mid-June onset of leaf production. The delay of below-

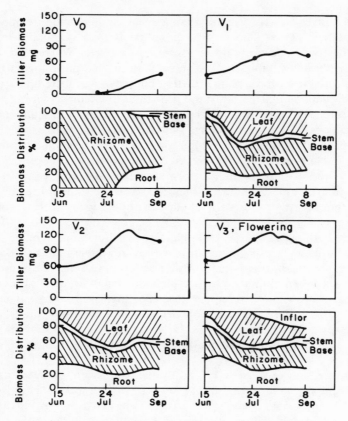

FIGURE 5-4. *Simulated seasonal biomass pattern of different plant parts of* Dupontia fisheri *tillers of different ages. (After Stoner et al. 1978d, Lewis, unpubl.)*

ground growth behind aboveground growth is common to temperate and other arctic graminoids and presumably is a consequence of programmed reallocation of resources from one plant part to another (Evans et al. 1964, Auclair et al. 1976, Callaghan 1976, Chapin et al. 1980). The soil reaches maximum temperature later in the season than does air, and this may have further selected for asynchrony of above- and belowground growth. Simulations suggest that rhizome weight in flowering tillers continues to decline through the entire season, coincidental with the growth of the culm and inflorescence. Although the overall seasonality of rhizome growth is probably genetically programmed, the absolute growth rate is subject to environmental modification. In contrast to the temperate graminoids investigated, *Dupontia* is capable of active rhizome growth at soil temperatures at least as low as 4 °C (McCown 1978).

Root Growth

Primary root primordia begin accumulating new photosynthate in the spring while the soil is still frozen (Dadykin 1954, Allessio and Tieszen 1975a, 1978), but growth and elongation do not begin until after soil thaw. In *Dupontia* elongation of primary roots is complete by late July, whereas other major graminoids of the tundra continue primary root elongation throughout the growing season (Shaver and Billings 1975). *Dupontia* initiates two to four roots per rhizome node. Autoradiography shows that these roots remain functional throughout the life of the tiller, frequently remaining alive even after the shoot dies (Allessio and Tieszen 1975a). A few shorter, slender roots are initiated in later seasons from the nodes of older leafing phytomers and elongate upward between the dead sheaths; they may be important in retrieving leached nutrients from stem flow. Primary roots of *Dupontia* do not elongate after their first season (Shaver and Billings 1975). Toward the end of the first season lateral roots are initiated with a larger surface-to-volume ratio (Shaver and Billings 1975). As with primary roots, these roots actively accumulate new ^{14}C photosynthate much earlier in the season than they commence visible elongation (Allessio and Tieszen 1975a).

Root biomass in the tundra at Barrow shows more variation both among and within microtopographic units than between sample dates. Therefore the seasonality of root production is difficult to determine by the harvest method (Dennis and Johnson 1970, Dennis 1977, Dennis et al. 1978). ^{14}C translocation studies (Allessio and Tieszen 1975a) and direct observations of root elongation (Shaver and Billings 1975) suggest that much of the root production for the wet meadow tundra occurs in July and August, after the early flush of leaf production. It appears that early in the season new photosynthate is allocated primarily to new shoot growth, and that the root growth that does occur at this time proceeds largely at the expense of rhizome carbohydrate reserves acquired in previous seasons. In the community as a whole, approximately 25% of the root biomass (i.e. 100 g m^{-2}) may turn over each year (Shaver and Billings 1975). This percentage is considerably lower than that found in many temperate ecosystems such as the eastern deciduous forest (Harris et al. 1977), but is approximately the same as that reported for grassland communities (Dahlman and Kucera 1965). The seasonality of root loss through senescence is not known, but loss is assumed to occur largely during winter. Because of the large ratio of belowground to aboveground biomass, roots and rhizomes constitute a major carbon and nutrient input to the saprovore food chain and are probably a relatively more important carbon–nutrient source than in temperate ecosystems (Chapter 12).

Roots of tundra plants, of necessity, grow at temperatures below 5 °C and can resume active elongation even after being temporarily frozen (Billings et al. 1977). Graminoids at Barrow have lower optimum temperatures for root initiation, elongation, and hence production than do comparable temperate species, when grown in the growth chamber (Chapin 1974a). In part due to low temperature sensitivity of root growth, root production in the field is not correlated with root temperature but appears to be controlled largely by photoperiod (Shaver and Billings 1977). For example, elongation of primary roots in *Dupontia* occurs during the first half of the growing season when root temperatures are lowest. Secondary root production predominates in August (Shaver and Billings 1975, 1977). In *Eriophorum angustifolium* most of the root tips are close to the retreating permafrost table, so the zone of most rapid elongation occurs in the coldest soil.

The primary roots of all graminoids at Barrow have large diameters and contain aerenchyma. These roots transport sufficient oxygen to produce an aerobic rhizosphere (Barsdate and Prentki, unpubl.) in a soil that is frequently oxygen-deficient. Because tundra plants are effective in transporting oxygen to roots, it is unlikely that metabolism of primary roots is ever limited by an inadequate oxygen supply. The root diameter probably results from a balance between selection for large diameter for adequate oxygen transport and selection for large surface-to-volume ratio for effective nutrient absorption (Chapin 1978). Both *Dupontia* and *Carex* produce secondary roots with small diameter, which are found primarily in the surface aerobic soil horizons and are important in nutrient absorption because of their large surface-to-volume ratio. These thin roots probably meet most of their oxygen requirement with soil oxygen rather than by diffusion through the primary roots. The small diameter rooting strategy allows continued exploitation of the surface soil horizon with a minimal carbon investment (Chapin 1978).

Graminoids at Barrow produce very few root hairs in the field, as is typical of aquatic and emergent plants (Sculthorpe 1967). Root hairs presumably require an external oxygen supply for proliferation and maintenance and for this reason are of minimal importance in Barrow tundra.

ALLOCATION OF CARBON COMPOUNDS

Seasonal Patterns

Growth and production depend in part upon availability of photosynthate in the form of total nonstructural carbohydrate (TNC), a pool that includes sugars and storage polymers. The TNC concentrations in leaves, stem bases and rhizomes of *Dupontia* are quite high, ranging

TABLE 5-1 *Biomass and Carbohydrate Composition of V2 tillers of* Dupontia fisheri

Plant part	Biomass (mg part⁻¹)	TNC (% dw)	TNC (mg part⁻¹)	Lipid (% dw)	Lipid (mg part⁻¹)	Other†† (mg part⁻¹)
		19–30 June				
Blade	5*	26*	1.3	16	0.8	2.9
Stem base	9*	24*	2.2	6	0.5	6.3
Rhizome	33*	36	11.9	6	2.0	19.1
Root	40†	8‡	3.2	10	4.0	32.8
Total (mg)	87		18.6		7.3	61.1
% of total plant pool			21.4		8.4	70.2
		1–15 Aug				
Blade	35*	20	7.0	7	2.5	25.5
Stem base	10*	44*	4.4	4	0.4	5.2
Rhizome	20*	40*	8.0	5	1.0	11.0
Root	40†	2‡	0.8	4	1.6	37.6
Total (mg)	105		20.2		5.5	79.3
% of total plant pool			19.2		5.2	75.5
		23 Aug–20 Sept				
Blade	5**	19*	1.0	5	0.3	3.7
Stem base	20*	40*	8.0	6	1.2	10.8
Rhizome	33*	42*	13.9	5	1.7	17.4
Root	40†	5‡	2.0	6	2.4	35.6
Total (mg)	98		24.9		5.6	67.5
% of total plant pool			25.4		5.7	68.9

* Lewis and Tieszen (unpubl.).

†Estimated as 30 to 40% of total biomass at peak season (from McCown 1978); seasonal changes assumed negligible with senescence equal to production.

‡ McCown (1978).

** Estimated as equal to early season.

†† By subtraction.

between 20 and 40% of the total dry weight (Shaver and Billings 1976, McCown 1978, McKendrick et al. 1978) (Table 5-1, Figure 5-5). High TNC levels are typical of arctic and alpine species (Russell 1940, Mooney and Billings 1960, Warren Wilson 1966a, Fonda and Bliss 1966, but see Payton and Brasch 1978). This raises the question of whether tundra plants have a carbon/energy surplus or whether there is strong selection to maintain high TNC levels in spite of high growth demands for TNC. Russell (1940), Warren Wilson (1966a) and Haag (1974) concluded that low temperature somehow prevented carbohydrate use in growth and respiration, resulting in large sugar accumulations. We suggest that inadequate nutrient supply is a major factor limiting use of carbohydrates in growth. Although there is considerable interhabitat variation in production along a gradient of nutrient availability at the Biome research

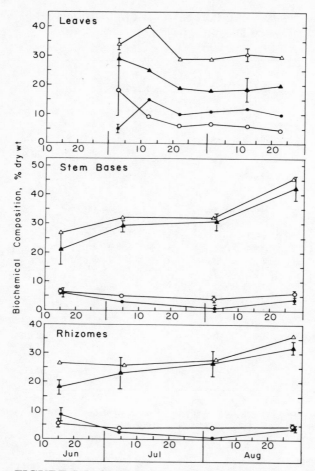

FIGURE 5-5. *Seasonal changes in concentrations of total nonstructural carbohydrates (△), polysaccharides (▲), lipids (○) and sugars (●) in leaves of* Dupontia fisheri *and in stem bases and rhizomes of composite samples of all moist meadow graminoids. Vertical bars indicate standard error. (After McCown 1978.)*

area (Tieszen, unpubl.), populations show markedly similar TNC concentrations (Table 5-2). Total nonstructural carbohydrate concentration tends to be higher in habitats with low tissue phosphorus and low production. These observations suggest that *Dupontia's* growth is limited more strongly by nutrients than by carbohydrate availability. Computer

TABLE 5-2   *Variability of Chemical Composition, Production, and Photosynthetic Potential in Leaves and Rhizomes of* Dupontia fisheri *Along a Moisture–Nutrient Gradient*

	Coefficient of variation (%)	
	Leaves	Rhizomes
Concentration		
Nitrogen	19.2	42.5
Phosphorus	37.0	64.9
Potassium	33.5	46.3
Calcium	33.1	51.0
Total nonstructural carbohydrate	16.4	3.6
Total community production	62.0	—
Photosynthetic potential	17.0	—

Source: Calculated from Tieszen (unpubl.).

simulations suggest a similar conclusion, i.e. that an increased photosynthetic rate, and hence increased TNC availability, would increase production at Barrow but that this TNC limitation of growth is less marked than is limitation by nutrients (Miller et al. 1976, 1979). It appears that although arctic tundra plants grow in a low radiation environment, carbohydrate availability does not unduly limit growth.

In mature shoots of *Dupontia* storage polysaccharides constitute the bulk of the TNC pool (Figure 5-5) (McCown 1978), in contrast to the predominance of sugars observed in other arctic and alpine species (Mooney and Billings 1960, Fonda and Bliss 1966, Warren Wilson 1966a). These reserves may be important for periods of intensive grazing. Although soluble carbohydrates are generally less than 15% of dry weight in Barrow graminoids, these levels are nonetheless high in comparison with temperate plants, and may contribute to the frost tolerance (Weiser 1970) that allows arctic plants to survive subzero temperatures at any time during the active growing season (Sørenson 1941). In *Dupontia* the rhizome is the largest compartment for TNC storage. From 40 to 65% of the total TNC is located in the rhizome throughout the year (Table 5-1). Fructosans rather than starch are the main storage polysaccharide in arctic (McCown 1978) and cool temperate (White 1973) grasses.

Tissue age strongly influences both the types and amount of carbohydrate present. In new roots and in the rhizomes and stem bases of young tillers, monosaccharides are the predominant carbohydrate, reaching concentrations as high as 40% dry weight (Shaver and Billings

1976). In these tissues carbohydrates play an active metabolic role, providing the energy necessary for rapid growth in a short growing season and protecting important tissues from freezing. It is mainly in the mature tillers that carbohydrate storage as polysaccharide becomes important. Hence, high TNC levels in plants at Barrow may reflect quite different processes, depending upon tissue age (Shaver and Billings 1976).

There is a gradual accumulation of carbohydrate reserves in rhizomes and shoots as the growing season progresses (Figure 5-5). Overwintering green leaf sections enclosed within the sheath bases may be important reservoirs for respiratory energy and precursor molecules utilized during the rapid production of photosynthetic tissue in spring (McCown 1978) and are an important energy source for grazers during the winter and spring months. In early spring sugar levels are high, presumably the result of hydrolysis of the polysaccharides built up the previous autumn (Shaver and Billings 1976, McCown 1978). After the period of rapid leaf production in June, sugar levels drop and do not rise again until autumn. The seasonal pattern of lipids is unclear. In 1970 early season levels of leaf lipids were unusually high (17%), but rapidly dropped to a constant level of 6% (McCown 1978). In other years lipid levels remained low throughout the growing season (Figure 5-5). High lipid levels in early spring could reflect energy storage (Bliss 1962b, Hadley and Bliss 1964) or could reflect small cell size and the abundant membrane lipid associated with meristematic tissue and high metabolic activity (Kedrowski and Chapin 1978). Early season lipids appear to have a lower melting point than those observed later and hence would function effectively in membranes at lower temperatures (McCown 1978).

The TNC concentration of *Dupontia* exhibits greater seasonal stability than that of temperate plants (McKendrick et al. 1975, McCown 1978), a feature of arctic plants also noted by Warren Wilson (1966a). The seasonal constancy of TNC pool size reflects a seasonal stability of allocation patterns as demonstrated by ^{14}C translocation studies in *Dupontia*. From snowmelt until time of maximum aboveground biomass (which was the duration of the study) new photosynthate is largely retained in the shoot where it is synthesized, presumably to support the continuing production of new leaves through the season (Figure 5-6) (Allessio and Tieszen 1975b). Except in V1 tillers, which are in their first year of aboveground growth and which produce the majority of new roots and rhizomes, there is relatively little translocation of photosynthate to belowground structures during this first half of the season. Moreover, production of new leaves by a tiller is largely self-supported and is relatively independent of carbohydrate reserves stored below ground. Even reproductive tillers are largely self-sufficient and do not withdraw large quantities of photosynthate from their own or neighboring rhizomes (Allessio and Tieszen 1975a). These observations indicate a

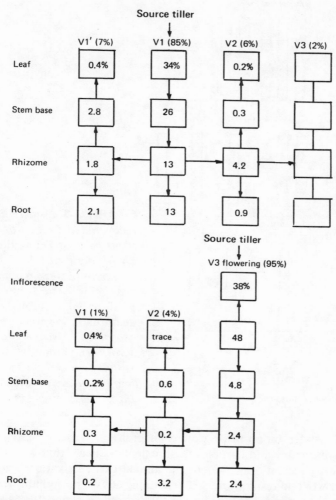

FIGURE 5-6. *Distribution of* ^{14}C *in tillers and plant parts of a* Dupontia fisheri *tiller system after the source tiller (V1 or V3 flowering) was labeled. (After Allessio and Tieszen 1975a.)*

substantial degree of tiller independence and suggest that the large belowground carbohydrate reserves may serve primarily to support late-season root growth and maintenance and as a reserve for rapid leaf growth in the event of grazing rather than to support the normal course of leaf growth as had been previously assumed (Mooney and Billings 1960, Fonda and Bliss 1966). However, leaf growth in the spring may be

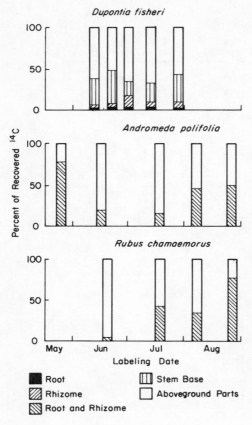

FIGURE 5-7. *Distribution of recovered* ^{14}C *in different plant parts of* Dupontia fisheri *in mesic meadow tundra at Barrow (Allessio and Tieszen 1975a) and* Andromeda polifolia *and* Rubus chamaemorus *in an arctic mire at Stordalen, Sweden (Johansson 1974).* Dupontia *was harvested two days after labeling; the others were harvested three weeks after labeling.*

highly dependent upon belowground mineral reserves.

Gas exchange and harvest measurements indicate that over the entire growing season only 34% of the annual carbon fixation is used in shoot growth and respiration. The remaining 66% is presumably translocated below ground, perhaps late in the season, to support growth and maintenance of roots and rhizomes. A downward translocation of this magnitude would be necessary to provide the energy source for the substantial root and rhizome respiration measured by Peterson and Billings (1975).

The retention of radiocarbon in shoots of labeled tillers and the seasonal stability of the allocation pattern in *Dupontia* differ strikingly from the allocation patterns of other growth forms (Figure 5-7) (Johansson 1974). In *Andromeda polifolia*, an evergreen shrub growing in Swedish tundra, 75% of the fixed carbon was translocated below ground early in the season. As leaf growth began, a larger proportion of the ^{14}C was retained in the shoot. Finally, at the end of the season, fixed carbon

was allocated above and below ground in approximately equal proportions (Figure 5-7). *Rubus chamaemorus* from Sweden had an allocation
pattern consistent with its deciduous habitat. During the leaf production
phase, virtually all the assimilated carbon was retained in the shoot, as in
the actively growing *Dupontia* shoot. As the season progressed, an increasing proportion of the photosynthate was translocated below ground
(Figure 5-7). Clearly, the allocation patterns of these three species are
closely tied to their growth forms, phenological calendars, and locations
of storage.

Environmental Influence upon Allocation Pattern

Environmental factors affect allocation pattern as well as the total
quantity of production . High root-to-shoot ratios of plants observed in
the field at the Biome research area (Dennis and Johnson 1970, Chapin
1974a, Dennis 1977, Dennis et al. 1978, Webber 1978) may indicate
greater environmental limitation upon shoot than root growth (Dennis
and Johnson 1970) or more likely reflects a genetically and environmentally controlled allocation of biomass to nutrient absorptive tissue
(Chapin 1974a), as observed in laboratory studies (Brouwer 1965, Davidson 1969). Low root temperature may indirectly result in a high root-to-
shoot ratio by decreasing rates of nutrient uptake, thus lowering the nutrient status of the plant, i.e. low root temperature and low nutrient
status may influence allocation through similar mechanisms (Patterson
et al. 1972, McCown 1975). Laboratory studies indicate that the increase
in root-to-shoot ratio resulting from an impoverished nutrient status
serves to increase nutrient supply and decrease nutrient demand, thus
compensating for the nutrient deficiency (e.g. Leonard 1962, Brouwer
1965). Direct field evidence for this comes from long-term fertilization
studies at Barrow, where after 10 years of fertilization, the root-to-shoot
ratio was reduced from 7:1 to 3:1 (Dennis 1977). McCown (1978) observed that the root-to-shoot ratio of *Dupontia* was less affected by root
temperature than was that of the temperate grass *Poa pratensis*. A
relatively inflexible root-to-shoot ratio is typical of slowly growing
species (Grime 1977).

When growth is strongly nutrient-limited, nonstructural carbohydrates accumulate to high levels (Leonard 1962) as observed in *Dupontia*
at the Biome research area (Shaver and Billings 1976, McCown 1978).
TNC levels are reduced, and shoot growth is enhanced by fertilization, a
further indication of the importance of nutrients in limiting production
in the tundra (McKendrick et al. 1978).

The number of daughter tillers (V0's) initiated is positively correlated

TABLE 5-3 *Correlation of Production Parameters with Nutrient Composition of the Plant Part in Tillers Sampled along a Moisture–Nutrient Gradient*

	Production parameter		
	No. leaves tiller^{-1}	Leaf length	No. V0 (mature tiller)$^{-1}$
Carex aquatilis			
Nitrogen	−0.21	−0.29	—
Phosphorus	0.49	0.52	—
Dupontia fisheri			
Nitrogen	0.10	−0.51	0.80*
Phosphorus	−0.12	0.37	−0.69†
Eriophorum angustifolium			
Nitrogen	0.47	−0.06	—
Phosphorus	0.45	0.59	—

Note: Numbers are correlation coefficients.
*Significant at the 0.05 level of probability.
†Significant at the 0.01 level of probability.
Source: Calculated from Tieszen (unpubl.).

with nitrogen concentration and negatively correlated with phosphorus concentration (Table 5-3), whereas leaf length shows the reverse correlation. No clear trend is evident with leaf number. This suggests that the intercalary and rhizome meristems respond quite differently and perhaps are limited by different nutrient balances. Apparently, leaf intercalary meristems are stimulated by favorable phosphorus status and/or a low nitrogen-to-phosphorus ratio. A high phosphorus content might be anticipated in meristematic cells because of the high requirement for membrane phospholipid and phosphorylated sugars. The high leaf meristematic activity under such nutritional circumstances would lead to strong apical dominance and could partially explain the concomitant low rates of rhizome growth and vegetative reproduction.

Translocation is inhibited by low temperature only temporarily, even in temperate plants (Swanson and Geiger 1967). Temperature does influence the rate of active loading and unloading of phloem cells, an effect that is indistinguishable from the temperature effect upon source and sink strength (Crafts and Crisp 1971). In contrast to temperate plants, *Dupontia* is capable of translocating ^{14}C to root and rhizome primordia frozen in soil (Allessio and Tieszen 1975a), as discussed above. Similarly, low temperature inhibits translocation of sugars from leaves in C_4 grasses growing at their upper elevational limit but not in alpine gram-

TABLE 5-4 *Plant Responses in Warm (1972) and Cold (1973) Growing Seasons*

| | Temperature (°C) | | | Biomass[4] (g m⁻²) | Net annual photosynthesis[5] (g CO_2 m⁻² yr⁻¹) | Phosphorus in *Dupontia* leaves[6] | | Phosphorus uptake[7] [μmoles hr⁻¹ (g fresh wt root)⁻¹] |
	Air[1]	Canopy[2]	Soil[3]			(% dry wt)	(mg tiller⁻¹)	
1972	5.1	8.1	5.0	125 ± 19	620	0.163 ± 0.017	0.105	0.041
1973	4.0	5.5	3.1	93 ± 13	450	0.526 ± 0.068	0.105	0.039
Difference	1.1	2.6	1.9	32	170	0.363	0.0	0.002
% difference	−22	−32	−38	−25	−27	+223	0	−5

[1] U.S. Department of Commerce, Barrow.
[2] Miller and Stoner (unpubl.), Miller et al. (1976).
[3] 5-cm depth (MacLean 1975a).
[4] Average of 16 sites along a nutrient gradient (Tieszen, unpubl.).
[5] Miller et al. (1976).
[6] Average of 10 sites along a moisture–nutrient gradient (Tieszen, unpubl.).
[7] Uptake calculated for *Dupontia fisheri* in a solution of 1.0 μM inorganic phosphate (Chapin and Bloom 1976).

inoids in Wyoming (Wallace and Harrison 1978). Thus, it appears that the effects of low temperature upon allocation in tundra plants are involved more with growth processes than with inhibition of carbohydrate and nutrient transport. Data in support of this hypothesis are largely inferential, and direct experimental evidence is needed.

Roots are more strongly buffered against temperature variation from one growing season to another than is the plant canopy, and shoot growth increases more rapidly with increasing temperature than does nutrient uptake. For these two reasons, in a warm growing season production is greater and the demand for nutrients outstrips the slightly enhanced supply. The situation is aggravated by the asynchrony of shoot production and nutrient uptake, the bulk of the nutrient uptake occurring after shoot production is largely complete (Chapin and Bloom 1976). The asynchrony is demonstrated by a comparison of the 1972 and 1973 growing seasons (Table 5-4) and suggests the following hypotheses:

1. In tundra communities, warm years will result in greater nutrient deficiency than will cold years. Nutrient deficiency will be particularly severe with respect to phosphorus because phosphorus absorption is more strongly affected by temperature than is absorption of other nutrients (Nielsen and Humphries 1966). The effect upon nutrient content of yearly temperature differences will be particularly pronounced in tundra underlain by permafrost, where the temperature gradient is most pronounced from the canopy to the bottom of the rooting zone.

2. Changes as slight as 1 °C in air temperature above the plant canopy are sufficient to profoundly alter the nutritional status of plants. Data from the Biome research area indicate the sensitivity of allocation pattern to small changes in environmental parameters. Similar conclusions were independently reached by Wielgolaski et al. (1975) in studies of the Norwegian alpine.

In summary, studies of carbohydrate allocation suggest that plants of the coastal tundra at Barrow have compensated for the effects of low temperature by allocating a large proportion of their biomass to nutrient-absorptive and belowground storage tissues. The high TNC levels suggest that growth of ungrazed tundra plants is not unduly carbohydrate-limited.

CARBON COST OF PLANT GROWTH

Concepts

The carbon fixed through photosynthesis can be converted to new biomass, but there are certain energy costs of producing and maintaining an increment of biomass that must be considered in order to understand patterns of carbohydrate allocation. The rate of change in live biomass of a plant compartment is the balance between the rates of photosynthesis, respiration, and death and the net translocation flux to that compartment. Growth also involves the accumulation and incorporation of nutrients. The rate of change in nutrient content of a plant compartment is the balance among the rate of uptake from soil, the net translocation flux, and losses from the living system due to leaching, exudation, grazing and death. There is inadequate information currently available to allow growth to be analyzed in terms of nutrient costs.

Respiration provides energy for a number of distinct metabolic processes and can be separated into at least three components: maintenance respiration, growth respiration and translocation respiration. Maintenance respiration provides the energy required to sustain the existing live biomass at its present level of metabolic activity. Maintenance respiration includes the energy requirement of basic metabolic processes and the replacement or turnover of structural and functional substances, particularly of proteins, and is assumed to be proportional to protein content and turnover (Penning de Vries 1975). The proportionality constants of maintenance respiration have been calculated (Miller 1979) for various plant parts according to the relationship derived for crop plants (McCree 1974, Penning de Vries 1975) and corrected for values measured in plants from the Biome research area (Chapin et al. 1975, Billings et al. 1978). The relatively high protein content of graminoids in the tundra at Barrow (Chapin et al. 1975) suggests a high maintenance respiration and is in agreement with the high shoot respiration rates measured (Tieszen 1975). Leaves have a higher proportionality constant of maintenance respiration (0.012) than do roots or rhizomes (0.006) because of higher protein content, which is consistent with the higher respiration rate measured in leaves than in roots.

Growth respiration provides the energy required to synthesize various components of new tissues from glucose (Penning de Vries 1972b; Table 5-5). Although plants contain a variety of sugars that function as metabolic intermediates, these will be viewed as glucose equivalents for the sake of simplicity. The investment in new tissue is equal to the quantity of glucose equivalents contained in the added biomass plus that glucose respired in the synthetic process, the growth respiration (Figure 5-8). The total growth respiration for production of new biomass is calculated from the increase in biomass and a constant c that apportions the cost of synthesis among the biochemical constituents of the new tissue (Table 5-5):

$$c = 1.15(\% \text{ lignin}) + 0.17(\% \text{ cellulose}) + 2.03(\% \text{ lipids}) +$$

$$+ 0.59(\% \text{ protein}) + 0.17(\% \text{ polysaccharide}) + 0.09(\% \text{ sucrose}).$$

TABLE 5-5 *Costs of Synthesis and Breakdown, and Biochemical Composition, of Different Plant Parts of* Dupontia fisheri

Biochemical constituent	Investment in synthesis* (g glucose g⁻¹ product)	Maximum glucose regained during senescence* (% of original)	Minimum loss in senesced tissue† (% of original)	Biochemical composition** (% of nonmineral dry wt)		
				Leaf	Rhizome	Root
Sucrose	1.09	98	2	13	3	2
Storage polysaccharide	1.17	95	5	7	37	0
Protein	1.59	56	44	18	7	6
Lipid	3.03	46	54	7	5	4
Cellulose	1.17	0	100	51	42	80
Lignin	2.15	0	100	5	6	8
Total cost (g glucose) of synthesizing 1 g of tissue:				1.28	1.30	1.30
Maximum glucose potentially regained during senescence†:				0.40	0.55	0.11

*Based on Penning de Vries (1972b, 1974) and Penning de Vries et al. (1974).

†Assumes no leaching and total breakdown of all compounds except cellulose and lignin.

**Sucrose (McCown 1978); polysaccharides (TNC-sugars) (McCown 1978); protein estimated from nitrogen (Chapin et al. 1975); lignin (Penning de Vries 1972b, White et al. 1975); cellulose estimated as remainder.

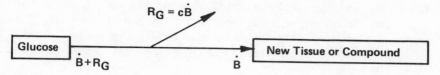

FIGURE 5-8. *Processes of growth and growth respiration. When new tissue is created, glucose is metabolized, some glucose appearing in the form of the new biochemical compounds (Ḃ), and some being lost (R_G) as it supplies energy for the synthesis of these compounds. For example, to produce 1 g of lignin (Ḃ), 2.15 g of glucose is used (Ḃ + R_G) and R_G involves 1.15 g of glucose. Other compounds use varying amounts of glucose per gram, as listed in Table 5-5. R_G is calculated for each compound by subtracting the gram of product from the total gram of glucose used. The total R_G for creating new tissue is found by summing the R_G's for synthesizing each compound, weighting each by the percentage composition.*

Tundra graminoids have a relatively low lignin content and a relatively high polysaccharide and sugar content and hence may be able to produce more biomass per unit carbon fixed than can temperate counterparts. More complete data on chemical composition of tundra graminoids are needed to verify this hypothesis.

Translocation is a vital process requiring energy, particularly for the loading and unloading of phloem elements, and energy cost is proportional to the translocation rate; available estimates (Penning de Vries et al. 1974) suggest a value of 0.05 for the proportionality constant. Because both loading and unloading costs are involved, 1 g of glucose will be required to translocate 10 g from source to sink. Because of the high belowground-to-aboveground biomass ratio of tundra graminoids, more of the maintenance and growth respiration occurs in nonphotosynthetic tissues than would be the case in their temperate counterparts. Hence, translocation respiration may be relatively more important in tundra than in temperate graminoids.

The carbon cost involved in growth is partially regained during senescence when some of the biomass components are broken down and retranslocated to storage areas to support future growth. Remobilization is not complete, and different classes of compounds are remobilized to different extents (Table 5-5).

Sucrose and the various storage polysaccharides require a minimal energy investment for synthesis and subsequent breakdown. In contrast, lipid requires a major energy investment, half of which is lost during reconversion to glucose. Although complete conversion of lipid to glucose is unlikely in any system, it is clear that lipid is a costly compound to synthesize and would be utilized as an energy source primarily where space or weight is limited, as in a seed. Plants growing in permafrost soils have larger amounts of membrane lipid but smaller amounts of storage lipids than do plants in warm soil (Kedrowski and Chapin 1978). The high lipid content reported for arctic and alpine plants (Bliss 1962b) is probably associated with membrane lipid for metabolism or for anti-herbivore defense, such as resins, and not with an energy storage function, as previously assumed.

Lignin and cellulose, two important structural compounds, also differ strikingly in their carbon cost of synthesis. Neither is significantly broken down for retranslocation during senescence. Lignin should be an important component of a tissue only where strong support is essential or where selection has led to strategies to discourage herbivory. Neither selective force appears to have led to a high lignin content in tundra graminoids.

The implications of biosynthetic cost for successful adaptation to the tundra environment are discussed in Chapter 6.

It is of interest, especially when considering the relatively anaerobic soil conditions of the coastal tundra, that biosynthetic processes under anaerobic conditions are 18-fold less efficient because of the incomplete oxidations that can be performed. In addition, toxic end products must be excreted, requiring additional energy expenditures. Although the native graminoids appear to have efficient oxygen transport systems and thus circumvent such problems, introduced plants and some dicotyledons may be severely stressed by the saturated soils and anaerobic conditions characteristic of many arctic soils.

Biomass Flux Analyses for *Dupontia*

A detailed picture of the fluxes involved in growth and allocation of carbohydrates and nutrients through the season can be built from simulations of the seasonal courses of dry matter accumulation, percentage composition, and metabolic cost estimates in *Dupontia* (Figure 5-9). Estimates of photosynthesis and respiration derived from the flux analysis can be compared with direct measurements of net photosynthesis and respiration. Analyses of this type are essential to a thorough understanding of the way the plant uses available resources to grow and produce offspring in a particular environment. Biomass changes provide an indication of biosynthetic activity but the costs of biosynthesis, translocation, uptake, and maintenance must be known to truly understand the allocation pattern and overall physiological balance. The following description is based upon simulations of translocation, respiration and growth.

In a newly initiated tiller (V0), simulated rates of translocation and growth generally increase steadily through the season until about 20 August. Subsequently, the rate of growth falls as maintenance respiration

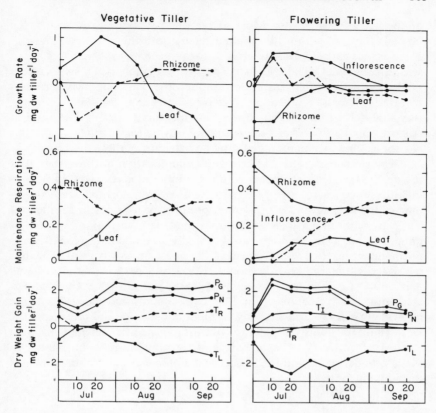

FIGURE 5-9. *Simulated seasonal changes in rates of growth and maintenance respiration, and in dry weight gain by gross (P_G) and net (P_N) photosynthesis, and translocation to rhizomes (T_R), leaves (T_L) and inflorescences (T_I) for vegetative (V2) and flowering tillers of* Dupontia *during 1973. (Calculated from Lawrence et al. 1978.)*

increases in parallel with biomass. The translocation rate represents a net import from other members of the system, because there are no leaves and hence no photosynthesis in a V0.

Simulations suggest that the rhizome of a vegetative tiller (Figure 5-9) has a significantly negative growth rate, i.e. decreases in weight, through July and recovers through August and early in September. The simulated seasonal course of growth in blade tissue is negatively correlated with growth of the belowground organs, changing from positive values early in the season to negative ones in late August. Calculations predict accurately the observed seasonal changes in biomass. The simulated seasonal changes in maintenance respiration reflect changes in size of the live compartments. Most of the photosynthate produced in the blade is retained within this compartment. Both the stem base and rhizome export carbohydrate in early July but become net importers as the season progresses. The calculated rate of net photosynthesis increases gradually through the season even though the blade biomass decreases from early August onward. Net photosynthesis rates calculated from the flux analyses are consistently lower than measured rates until the end of August but then persist at unexpectedly elevated levels until freeze-up. No convincing explanation can now be offered for these discrepancies.

The simulated patterns of growth and allocation in flowering tillers (Figure 5-9) contrast strikingly with those in vegetative tillers. In flowering tillers the growth rate of the rhizome is strongly negative at the beginning of the season, and the rhizome continues to lose weight throughout the season, although it never assumes the role of a major exporter of photosynthate. The stem base grows rapidly and blades develop their exporting capacity early in the season. The phase of positive leaf growth is truncated compared with vegetative tillers and never attains the same maximum rate. The second, smaller peak in leaf growth may be associated with the production of the flag leaf. The inflorescence exhibits the highest growth rate, particularly through midseason, and represents the largest sink for photosynthate. In contrast to vegetative tillers, there is no late-season recovery of stem base and rhizome because the photosynthetic rate decreases and inflorescence maintenance respiration increases throughout the season.

Implications of Biomass Flux Analysis

Simulations suggest that although the rhizome rapidly decreases in weight early in the season, there is relatively little upward translocation of reserves at this time. Maintenance respiration accounts for the major change in rhizome weight. In general, these simulations suggest that the rapid early-season development of leaves is self-sustaining and that remobilization of reserve carbohydrates is of minor importance. This conclusion is supported by evidence from radiocarbon and carbohydrate analyses and contrasts strongly with earlier conclusions concerning arctic and alpine forbs. Russell (1940), Mooney and Billings (1960) and Fonda and Bliss (1966) concluded on the basis of correlations between growth and changes in carbohydrate levels that rhizome reserves were utilized to support rapid spring shoot growth. Further research is necessary to determine whether the difference in conclusions results from differences in methods and interpretation or from differences between graminoid and forb growth patterns and phenology.

Simulations, seasonal measurements of TNC, and autoradiography all suggest that the large pools of nonstructural carbohydrate contained in belowground structures of *Dupontia* are not redistributed to any great extent through the growing season and mainly provide substrate for maintenance respiration and, except in the reproductive tillers, are replenished during August and September in readiness for metabolism the following season. Simulations support ^{14}C translocation studies (Allessio and Tieszen 1975b) showing that inflorescence development is self-sustaining and not dependent on reserve utilization, even though the rhizome rapidly loses weight early in the season. Later development of the inflorescence may well depend on photosynthesis produced by its own chlorophyllous tissue.

NUTRIENT ABSORPTION

Seasonal Patterns

The high levels and relatively stable pool size of nonstructural carbohydrate strongly suggest that nutrient availability, absorption rates and/or translocation rates are among the important factors limiting plant growth at Barrow. The nitrogen and phosphorus status of the soils is quite low (Chapter 7). More than 99% of the nitrogen and phosphorus present in the rooting zone is organically bound and available to plants only after being released by decomposition, a process that occurs slowly at low temperatures and low oxygen levels. Nitrogen is frequently cited as a key limiting nutrient at the Biome research area and in other tundra systems (Russell et al. 1940, Warren Wilson 1957, Bliss 1966, McKendrick et al. 1978). Exchangeable ammonium, the principal ionic form of nitrogen, remains seasonally constant in the rooting zone but increases through the growing season in lower soil horizons (Flint and Gersper 1974), suggesting that nutrient absorption by plants has a significant impact upon soil nutrient dynamics. In contrast to nitrogen, available soil phosphorus and potassium decrease in concentration through the growing season (Barèl and Barsdate 1978), suggesting that phosphorus and potassium will be absorbed by plants earlier in the season than will nitrogen.

An important asynchrony is apparent in environmental favorability for aboveground and belowground plant processes. Light and air temperature regimes are most favorable for photosynthesis immediately following snowmelt, whereas soil temperatures and thaw depth increase until late July or early August. Seasonal changes in depth of thaw, soil temperature, and the quantity and activity of root biomass influence the seasonal pattern of nutrient absorption. However, simulations suggest that these parameters are less important than seasonal changes in soluble

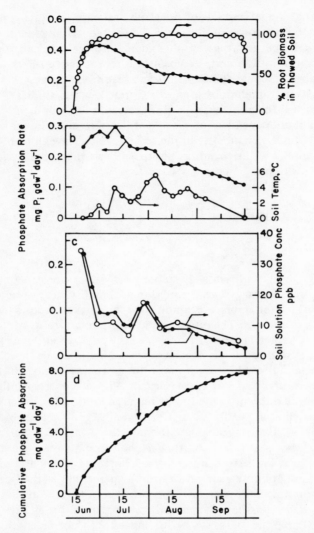

FIGURE 5-10. *Predicted rate of phosphate absorption per gram of* Dupontia fisheri *root during the 1973 growing season. a) Measured phosphate absorption capacity of roots corrected for percentage of root biomass present in thawed soil (calculated from Dennis 1977). b) Absorption rate in* a *corrected for soil temperature (MacLean 1973). c) Absorption rate in* b *corrected for soil solution phosphate concentration (Barèl and Barsdate 1978). d) Predicted cumulative phosphate absorption per gram of root during the growing season. Vertical arrow indicates date when net downward translocation of phosphorus from shoots to belowground storage organs begins. (After Chapin and Bloom 1976.)*

soil phosphorus in determining the seasonal pattern of phosphorus uptake (Chapin and Bloom 1976). The seasonal pattern of phosphorus release from decomposers is probably the single most important factor governing phosphorus availability and therefore phosphate uptake by vascular plants (Chapin et al. 1978). Absorption of phosphate continues actively until late September when the soil begins freezing from the surface downward (Figure 5-10). More than 40% of the total phosphorus absorbed by a given root biomass is acquired after 25 July, the date when shoots begin a net downward translocation of phosphorus for belowground winter storage. Clearly, aboveground phenological patterns are an inaccurate gauge for determining periods of plant activity. Because total root biomass increases through the growing season, end-of-season nutrient absorption is probably even more important than the above discussion would indicate.

Physiological Basis

Tundra graminoids differ from their temperate counterparts in having higher phosphate absorption rates under standard measurement conditions (Figure 5-11). Furthermore, tundra plants maintain substantial rates of phosphate absorption at temperatures that would inhibit active uptake by most temperate plants (Sutton 1969, Chapin 1974a, Carey and Berry 1978). For example, *Dupontia* grown in the field still maintains 35% of its 20 °C phosphate absorption rate at 1 °C (Chapin and Bloom 1976), which suggests that tundra plants actively absorb phosphate from cold soils and do not depend upon daily or seasonal warming of the soil to fulfill their phosphate requirements. Phosphate absorption by tundra plants is relatively insensitive to temperature changes and has an optimum temperature of at least 40 °C. It would appear that the phosphate absorption process in graminoids has adapted to low temperature by a decrease in temperature sensitivity below optimum temperature, by an increased affinity of roots for phosphate at low temperatures (Chapin 1977), and by an increase in uptake rate at all temperatures, but not by any change in temperature optimum. Similar conclusions were reached for the photosynthetic process (Chapter 4). The ability to acclimate in compensation for temperature changes is not well developed in plants at Barrow, as might be anticipated in a thermally stable environment such as the tundra soil (Chapin 1974b). The overall effects of temperature upon rate of phosphate absorption by *Dupontia* are such that the rate at the bottom of the soil profile (0.2 °C) is approximately 75% of the rate at the top of the profile (5.0 °C) (calculated from Chapin and Bloom 1976).

A plant's capacity to absorb nutrients depends upon its nutrient status and allocation pattern. Plants with low concentration of an essen-

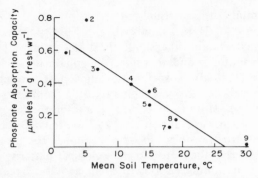

FIGURE 5-11. *Phosphate absorption capacity (*V_{max}*) of roots grown and measured at 5 °C in relation to the July mean soil temperatures of the site. 1)* Eriophorum angustifolium, *Barrow, Alaska; 2)* Dupontia fisheri, *Barrow, Alaska; 3)* Carex aquatilis, *Barrow, Alaska; 4)* Eriophorum scheuchzeri, *Fairbanks, Alaska; 5)* Scirpus microcarpus, *Los Gatos, California; 6)* Eleocharis palustris, *Fairbanks, Alaska; 7)* Carex aquatilis, *Circle Hot Springs, Alaska; 8)* Eleocharis palustris, *Corvallis, Oregon; 9)* Scirpus olneyi, *Thousand Palms, California. (After Chapin 1974b.)*

tial nutrient develop a high capacity to absorb that nutrient (Hoagland and Broyer 1936, Cole et al. 1963). For example, individuals of *Carex* with a high phosphate status had lower capacities for phosphate absorption (Chapin and Bloom 1976).

Soil oxygen, which appears to be a major determinant of plant distribution at Barrow, has a direct impact upon absorption of both essential and toxic nutrients. Graminoids have well-developed aerenchyma that transports sufficient oxygen to the rooting zone to create an aerobic zone around each root (Barsdate and Prentki, unpubl.). Many dicotyledons lack aerenchyma and are excluded from the wetter habitats. The oxygen in the aerobic soil zone around a root decreases the solubility of toxic heavy materials. In spite of this relatively aerobic rhizosphere, graminoids absorb sufficient iron and manganese to reach levels that would approach toxicity in crop plants (Ulrich and Gersper 1978). Nothing is known about the influence of these minerals on tundra plant growth.

The uniform distribution of nutrient absorptive capacity along

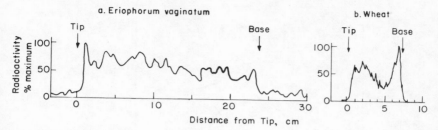

FIGURE 5-12. *Distribution of phosphate uptake rate along roots of* Eriophorum vaginatum *(Chapin 1974a) and wheat (Bowen and Rovira 1967).*

graminoid roots (Chapin 1974a) reflects the lack of a well-defined root hair zone (Chapin 1978), a consequence of the anaerobic soil conditions. The maintenance of absorptive capacity along the entire length of *Eriophorum vaginatum* roots is a striking difference from temperate grasses (Figure 5-12) and may be selected for by the moist soil environment, where suberization to prevent water loss and consequent loss of absorption capability is disadvantageous.

NUTRIENT ALLOCATION

Seasonal Patterns

Since nutrients are among the prime factors affecting carbohydrate allocation, it is important to know how nutrients are allocated within the plant and the factors that control this allocation. Graminoids at Barrow begin the growing season with a small amount of overwintering green material. Translocation of nutrients to these shoots presumably begins at or before snowmelt, coincident with the initial carbohydrate translocation to shoots. Early in the season the nitrogen and phosphorus concentrations of aboveground tissues are quite high (Figure 5-13) and the nitrogen-to-phosphorus ratio is relatively low. This suggests that a large proportion of the tissue is actively growing and metabolizing and hence has a high phosphorus requirement for membrane phospholipid and phosphorylated intermediates. As leaves approach maturity, they develop more structural material, as indicated by the seasonal increase in percentage calcium (Chapin et al. 1975). The increase in structural material causes percent nitrogen to decline (Figure 5-13a), though the total aboveground standing crops of nitrogen and phosphorus are increasing (Figure 5-13b). Phosphorus follows the same pattern as nitrogen. The net transfer of nitrogen and phosphorus to shoots continues until 25 July, ten

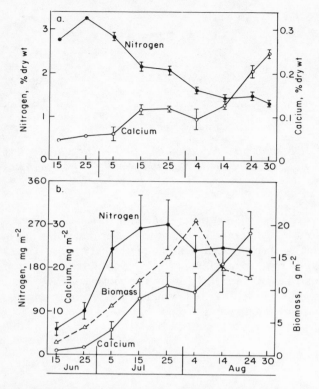

FIGURE 5-13. *Seasonal course of (a) percentage nitrogen and calcium and (b) standing crop of nitrogen, calcium, and biomass in* Dupontia *sampled from moist meadow tundra. (After Chapin et al. 1975, Chapin 1978.)*

days before the maximum standing crop of biomass is achieved. The most rapid transfer of nitrogen to the shoots occurs during the first three weeks of the growing season (Figure 5-13), at which time the activity of old roots would be minimized by poor aeration and low temperatures. It is probable that most of the early-season aboveground nitrogen and phosphorus comes from stored reserves rather than from current-season absorption by roots as demonstrated for upland tundra (Chapin et al. 1980). The bulk of all plant nutrients are located below ground (Table 12-3), such that seasonal changes in aboveground standing crop involve at most 20% of the total plant nutrient content.

Precipitation and dew drip continually leach nutrients (particularly potassium) from shoots at a rate that depends upon local weather conditions and the solubility of the different elements. Nitrogen and phos-

TABLE 5-6 *Estimated Nutrient and Standing Crop Removed from Shoots by Retranslocation Below Ground*

	Percentage of maximum standing crop removed				
	Biomass*	Nitrogen	Phosphorus	Potassium	Calcium
Carex aquatilis	43	21	44	25	0
Dupontia fisheri	38	53	55	64	0
Eriophorum angustifolium	34	43	61	48	0
Graminoid	35	48	45	42	0
Dicotyledon	33	65	78	76	0
Community average	34	40	49	44	0

Note: Assumes that all nutrient disappearance from time of maximum standing stock of nutrients until 24 August results from retranslocation.
*Calculated from Tieszen (1972b).
Source: Chapin et al. (1975).

phorus are probably leached slowly (Tukey 1970, Morton 1977) so that the decrease in aboveground concentration of nitrogen and phosphorus after 25 July must be due primarily to downward translocation.

Because of downward translocation, shoots begin acting as a nutrient source rather than a nutrient sink even before peak standing crop is achieved (Figure 5-13). Graminoids retranslocate more than 40% of their maximum aboveground standing crop of nutrients below ground before the end of August (Table 5-6), a quantity comparable to that observed in other communities (Goodman and Perkins 1959, Morton 1977, Chapin et al. 1980). Autoradiography indicates that phosphorus, which is absorbed in late season (September), is stored in the rhizome/stem base rather than being translocated to other plant parts (Chapin and Bloom 1976). Clearly, nutrient storage plays an essential role in the strategy of tundra graminoids.

Effect on Shoot Growth and Photosynthesis

The pronounced increase in aboveground plant production when nutrients are added to the tundra system indicates that growth is strongly limited by nutrients under natural conditions (Russell et al. 1940, Schultz 1964, Bliss 1966, Haag 1974, Chapin et al. 1975). Nitrogen and phosphorus have been specifically identified by field fertilization studies as two of the most important limiting nutrients in the tundra at Barrow (McKendrick et al. 1978). Yet the precise nature of the effect of these two nutrients upon production remains unclear. Phosphorus and nitrogen concentrations in young leaves of *Dupontia* collected in the field were

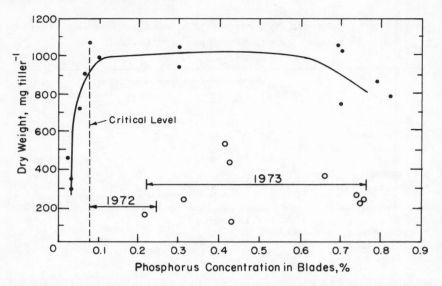

FIGURE 5-14. *Tiller weight of aboveground material of* Dupontia fisheri *in relation to the phosphorus concentration of the leaf blades (after Ulrich and Gersper 1978) and the range of concentration measured in the field in 1972 and 1973 (Chapin et al. 1975, Tieszen, unpubl. data). In the laboratory, experimental plants (●) were grown in solution culture with different phosphorus concentrations and the total leaf phosphate was estimated from measurements of acid-soluble phosphate. Field measurements of biomass and nutrient concentration (○) were made in the moisture–nutrient gradient.*

always higher than the critical level necessary for maximum growth in the laboratory (Figure 5-14). Moreover, weights of field plants were consistently below those of laboratory plants when either nitrogen or phosphorus was tested in the laboratory as the only factor limiting growth (Ulrich and Gersper 1978). Laboratory studies on plant critical levels suggest two hypotheses: 1) nitrogen and phosphorus never act as the sole limiting factor in the field but are both among a complex of limiting factors, and 2) tundra graminoids never produce nutrient-deficient tissues, but rather limit growth rate. Graminoids at Barrow produce new tissue only if an adequate quantity of nitrogen and phosphorus is available for maximal development and presumably for optimal function. Environmental factors such as nutrients restrict growth rather than compromise the effectiveness of new tissues that are produced. Agricultural crops and species from fertile habitats differ substantially in this regard, responding to nutrient stress with deficiency symptoms and reduced respiration and photosynthesis (Chapin 1980a).

In spite of a 15-fold variation in soil solution phosphate concentration and a 6-fold variation in leaf phosphorus between microtopographic units, leaf phosphorus concentration shows no correlation with photosynthetic rate (Chapter 4), suggesting that the photosynthetic apparatus of a graminoid is relatively insensitive to changes in phosphate concentration. In contrast, shoot production is positively correlated with 1) availability of soil phosphorus, 2) capacity of the plant to absorb available phosphorus (Chapin 1978), and consequently 3) concentration of phosphorus in leaves (Table 5-3). The correlations suggest an intimate association between the phosphorus nutrition of the plant and growth under natural conditions in the field. However, the nature of the relationship between phosphorus nutrition and growth requires further study.

The maximum nitrogen and phosphorus contents of graminoids at Barrow are as high as or higher than those of native temperate zone graminoids (Chapin et al. 1975). This might be anticipated because of a low percentage of structural material. Nitrogen requirements may be high in tundra plants because of high enzyme complements, as discussed previously. A high phosphorus complement may result from 1) a high incidence of polyploidy (Johnson and Packer 1965) and consequently high DNA content, and 2) high concentrations of membrane phospholipid to support metabolism and convey cold tolerance (de la Roche et al. 1972, Thomson and Zalik 1973, Kedrowski and Chapin 1978). *Dupontia* probably has a higher proportion of its phosphorus tied up in structural material, DNA and phospholipid than do temperate plants (Figure 5-15). The total phosphorus complement of leaves varies considerably through the season and between habitats of different phosphorus status. Plants with low phosphorus content may have as much as 85% of their phosphorus complement structurally bound and have essentially the same phosphorus composition as standing dead material (Figure 5-15).

Along a nutrient gradient nitrogen concentration of mature leaves is not correlated with photosynthetic potential. The percentage change in carboxylation activity from early season to mid-season and then from mid-season to end-of-season is greater than the corresponding change in nitrogen content, indicating that early and late in the season a higher proportion of shoot nitrogen is bound as structural protein and as nonphotosynthetic enzymes than at mid-season (Figure 5-16). This may partially explain the low photosynthetic rates early in the growing season (Chapter 4). The parallel decrease in carboxylation activity and total nitrogen content in the latter half of the growing season suggests that ribulose diphosphate carboxylase is broken down more rapidly than it is synthesized after mid- to late July and that the nitrogenous breakdown products are translocated out of the shoot at this time. The decrease in total carboxylation activity and shoot nitrogen after mid- to late July indicates a strong selection for early senescence and downward translocation of

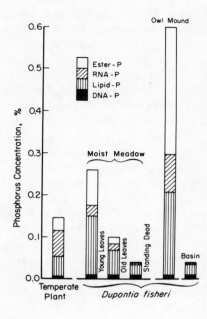

FIGURE 5-15. *Estimated compart-mentalization of phosphorus into various classes of compounds in shoots of a temperate plant (Bieleski 1973) and* Dupontia fisheri *from three microsites. Ester-P includes inorganic-P and was determined by a weak acid extraction (Ulrich and Gersper 1978). Lipid was measured (McCown 1978) and assumed to contain the same proportion of phospholipid as cold-acclimated winter wheat seedlings (de la Roche et al. 1972). Phosphorus in DNA is assumed to be constant in* Dupontia *and 40% greater than that observed in temperate grasses (Bieleski 1973). The phosphate contained in RNA was determined by subtraction.*

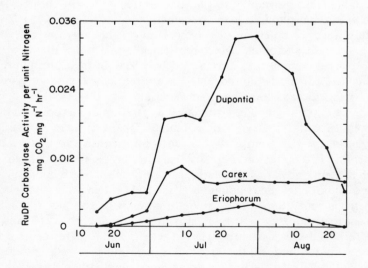

FIGURE 5-16. *Seasonal course of ribulose diphosphate carboxylase activity per unit nitrogen in leaves of* Dupontia fisheri, Carex aquatilis *and* Eriophorum angustifolium. *(Calculated from Tieszen 1975, Chapin et al. 1975.)*

nitrogen, despite the importance of length of photosynthetic season in limiting total·carbon gain (Chapter 4, Miller et al. 1976). At Barrow, the probability of a killing frost increases after early August and may select for downward nutrient translocation at this time to minimize the probability of large nutrient losses. Moreover, root and rhizome growth is quite active in late July, and the belowground demand for nitrogen may be met in part by nitrogen translocated from leaves (Chapin et al. 1980).

REPRODUCTIVE ALLOCATION AND POPULATION STRUCTURE

Tiller Interaction

Growth and allocation patterns have been discussed in terms of a single tiller unit. However, the tiller system is the genetic unit in *Dupontia*, and it responds to selection and interacts to maximize short-term carbon and nutrient gain and long-term reproductive success for the entire tiller system.

^{14}C and ^{32}P translocation studies (Allessio and Tieszen 1975b, Chapin and Bloom 1976) indicate that although mature tillers act largely as independent physiological units, there is still considerable translocation from old V2 and V3 tillers to young V0 and V1 tillers that have little or no photosynthetic tissue. Experiments in which individual tillers are severed from the tiller system corroborate these conclusions (Mattheis et al. 1976). Only tillers in their first season of leaf production were highly dependent upon other members of the tiller system for normal seasonal growth. Mature tillers initiated and supported more daughter tillers when their reserves were not tapped by the tiller system (Mattheis et al. 1976). Tiller interdependence may be particularly important during regrowth following grazing. Similar intertiller relationships have been observed in temperate grasses (Evans et al. 1964, Marshall and Sagar 1968).

Neighboring tillers compete for available resources. Nutrients are probably more critical than carbohydrates in governing dry weight increases of tillers. Even young tillers have high available carbohydrate concentrations. The number and the length of new V0 rhizomes are strongly correlated with rhizome nutrient concentration (Table 5-3). Clearly, the nutritional status of the plant governs the balance between growth of an individual shoot and vegetative propagation and hence has profound effects upon population structure.

Population Dynamics

New shoot production and the interaction between members of a single tiller system are important primarily because of implications for population structure. Each tiller may draw upon the resources of older tillers to colonize, grow and reproduce, particularly during its first two years, thus minimizing carbon costs of growth and respiration and the risks of mortality during the early stages of growth. Unlike *Carex bigelowii* (Callaghan 1976) *Dupontia* tillers show minimal mortality until after flowering occurs in V3 or V4 tillers. Consequently, V0, V1, V2 and V3 tillers have similar frequencies, whereas V4 tillers are relatively uncommon (Figure 5-17). Tiller interdependence averages out the growth and reproductive performance over an environment that is variable in both time and space. The vegetative reproduction characteristics of *Dupontia* and other graminoids are not an alternative to sexual reproduction but rather a strategy of expanding the number of loci at which flowering may eventually occur (Lawrence et al. 1978). Vegetative reproduction is important under situations where 1) a given tiller has a low probability of survival, e.g. due to grazing, 2) the probability of successful seed set in any given year is low, or 3) the probability of seedling establishment from the seed crop produced in a given year is low. All of these conditions characterize the coastal tundra at Barrow and may be important in selecting for extensive vegetative reproduction. The selected strategy, of allocating most resources to competition and to growth rather than to extensive short-term reproductive output, typifies tundra

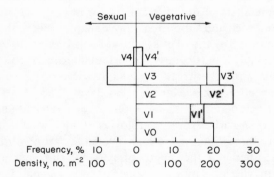

FIGURE 5-17. *Relative frequency and density of* Dupontia fisheri *tillers in various age classes and sexual conditions in moist meadow tundra in August 1973. (Lewis and Tieszen, unpubl.)*

species (Bliss 1971). Rough calculations based on carbon cost of inflorescence production, percentage seed set, percentage seedling survival, etc., suggest that the carbon cost of producing a new tiller in coastal tundra by sexual reproduction is 10,000 times greater than the cost of tiller production through vegetative reproduction. The fact that sexual reproduction receives substantial carbohydrate allocation in spite of the low frequency of seedling establishment points out the necessity of a long-term evolutionary framework within which to view growth and allocation processes. On successional and evolutionary time scales there must be substantial selection for sexual reproduction to maintain genetic variability and flexibility and to permit dispersal to new areas. The selective advantage of dispersal capability results from the heterogeneous nature of the microtopography that limits the expansion of clones, and the occasional creation of new unvegetated areas such as frost scars and drained lake basins that are not effectively colonized by clonal expansion. Population processes and evolutionary strategies deserve attention in future tundra studies.

EFFECT OF GRAZING ON ALLOCATION AND POPULATION STRUCTURE

Lemmings periodically graze wet meadow communities to such an extent that maximum aboveground biomass may be decreased from 100 g m^{-2} to as little as 5 g m^{-2} (Dennis 1968, Tieszen 1972b, Chapter 8). Simulations suggest that the long-term effect of lemming grazing is to reduce total foliage by an average of 33% (Lawrence et al. 1978). Grazing alters graminoid allocation patterns in the tundra at Barrow and affects plant survival and community structure. Certain gross morphological features of *Dupontia* and other graminoids appear to be adaptive under a grazing regime. The shoot meristem and virtually all the storage and perennial tissues are located below ground, protected from grazing. Tissues that are available to grazers are only weakly lignified and are potentially replaceable at a minimal biochemical cost. Grazing may be a critical factor leading to the dominance of the graminoid growth form at Barrow.

Clipping experiments on *Dupontia* indicate that the movement of carbohydrate from one tiller to another is important in allowing *Dupontia* to survive intensive grazing. *Dupontia* leaves regrow rapidly following grazing because of the abundance of belowground carbohydrate reserves (Mattheis et al. 1976). Light clipping to simulate grazing can even result in a slight increase in the available carbohydrate pool of the rhizome, provided the clipped tiller remains attached to the tiller system (Mattheis et al. 1976), perhaps due to decreased shading and increased photosynthesis. After six consecutive clippings in a single season, to simulate the

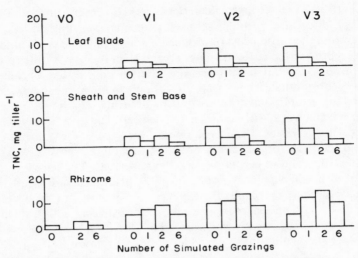

FIGURE 5-18. *Total nonstructural carbohydrate (TNC) content in various plant compartments and tiller age classes of* Dupontia fisheri *following clipping at various intensities. Plants were clipped at weekly intervals to simulate grazing and were sampled on 20 August in moist meadow tundra. (After Mattheis et al. 1976.)*

maximum grazing intensity that might be sustained in a lemming high, total nonstructural carbohydrate concentrations still remained high in rhizomes (Figure 5-18), and shoot weight was not affected. However, when a tiller no longer had access to the reserves of the entire tiller system, clipping decreased shoot weight substantially (Table 5-7), as has also been noted by Babb and Bliss (1974).

Results of clipping experiments suggest that even chronic grazing would have little effect upon survivorship of vegetative tillers, because the tiller meristem is normally not damaged. However, at times of high lemming densities and inadequate food supply, lemmings may grub in the moss layer and remove the shoot meristem, killing the shoot. The impact of grazing upon reproduction is most pronounced 1) through the grazing of flowering shoots, since the inflorescence is lost, and 2) through the general lowering of the reserve status of the entire tiller system so that the chances of successful seed set are diminished.

The number of new rhizomes produced is curtailed by grazing much less than is shoot production (Table 5-7). Grazing causes not only a decrease in reserves but also a shift in the allocation pattern from shoot production toward greater rhizome production and vegetative reproduction. Grazing causes a change in age class structure only because above-

TABLE 5-7 *Effect of Simulated Grazing upon Dry Weight of Shoot Regrowth and Number of Newly Initiated (V0) Rhizomes of* Dupontia fisheri *Growing in Moist Meadow Tundra*

Tiller age	Control	One clipping		Two clippings	
		Clipped only	Ringed and clipped	Clipped only	Ringed and clipped
Dry weight above ground (mg)					
First year tiller (V1)		7.7 ± 3.4	8.8 ± 2.4	2.5 ± 0.7	5.8 ± 1.8	0.3 ± 0.1
Established tiller (V2 or V3)		6.8 ± 2.8	11.4 ± 2.1	4.0 ± 3.0	0.0	2.0 ± 0.6
Number daughter tillers (no. V0s tiller⁻¹)					
First year tiller (V1)	0.8	1.1	0.7	0.6	0.4
Established tiller (V2 or V3)	0.2	0.7	0.2	0.0	0.3

Note: Treatments involved clipping all leaves of the tiller at the moss surface (clipping) and/or severing all rhizome connections between the treated tiller and the rest of the tiller system (ringing). Tillers were clipped or ringed and clipped on 25 July, leaves were reclipped on 4 August, and shoots and rhizomes were harvested on 16 August 1973 ($n = 10$).
Source: Mattheis et al. (1976).

average numbers of newly initiated (V0) tillers are recruited into the population in the year of a lemming high. Computer simulations suggest that the differential mortality and reduced competition due to grazing are not responsible for change in age structure (Lawrence et al. 1978). Hence, grazing by moderate lemming populations influences population structure more by increasing recruitment of new tillers than by increasing mortality.

The maximum stress that lemmings are likely to exert upon the nutrient reserves of the wet meadow vegetation is simulated and shown in Figure 5-19. Simulations suggest that grazing depletes nitrogen and phosphorus reserves more rapidly than carbohydrate reserves which, in turn, are depleted more rapidly than are calcium reserves. The strain on belowground nitrogen or phosphorus reserves may not differ significantly in grazed or ungrazed situations until after four or five defoliations, because the early part of the growing season is characterized by rapid upward nutrient translocation regardless of whether grazing occurs or not. Grazing would, however, prevent downward translocation of nutrients lost to herbivores and would likely affect growth primarily in subsequent years. In fact, detailed studies (Tieszen and Archer 1979) of various growth forms at Atkasook, Alaska, have not only shown that seasonal carbon balance is seriously affected (Chapter 3) but also that a single grazing event can reduce reserves in a manner which influences growth

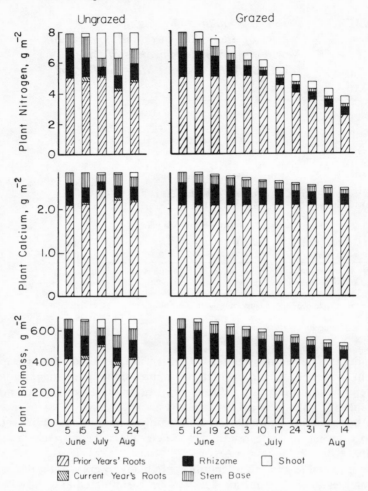

FIGURE 5-19. *Standing crops of plant nitrogen, calcium and biomass in moist meadow tundra with and without maximum lemming grazing, calculated assuming: 1) the total plant nutrient and biomass contents were altered through the season only by grazing (i.e. that no nutrient gain or loss occurred through uptake, senescence, or leaching, and that maintenance and growth respiration equaled photosynthesis); 2) translocation to aboveground parts after grazing occurred at the maximum rate observed during the 1970 growing season; 3) grazing occurred weekly and totally removed the aboveground compartment; 4) roots did not normally serve a storage function (nutrients and carbohydrates contained in roots were translocated upward only after all other reserves were exhausted); and 5) no new roots were produced when plants were intensively grazed. (After Chapin 1975.)*

and production the next year. Since this longer-term effect is most harm-ful to evergreen shrubs and then deciduous shrubs, and least harmful to graminoids, it is clear that vegetation units will change under different kinds of grazing regimes.

VARIABILITY IN GROWTH AND ALLOCATION PATTERNS

Substantial interspecific differences in the growth and allocation patterns of three dominant graminoids (*Dupontia fisheri, Eriophorum angustifolium* and *Carex aquatilis*) have resulted in niche differentiation. *Carex* is generally dominant in phosphorus-poor sites such as pond mar-gins and basins and rims of low-centered polygons, which receive low grazing pressure. In contrast, *Dupontia* predominates on phosphorus-rich sites such as polygon troughs. *Eriophorum* also tends to occur in more phosphorus-rich sites, particularly where vegetative cover has been broken by frost or human disturbance.

Differences in allocation pattern between the three principal gram-inoids partially explain distribution patterns (Table 5-8). Leaf produc-tion and elongation occur earlier in the growing season and are more syn-

TABLE 5-8   *Characteristics of the Growth and Allocation Patterns of* Dupontia fisheri, Carex aquatilis *and* Eriophorum angustifolium

	Dupontia fisheri	*Carex aquatilis*	*Eriophorum angustifolium*
Leaf production*	Asynchronous	Somewhat syn-chronous	Somewhat syn-chronous
Shoot longevity*	3 to 4 (5) yr	4 to 7 yr	5 to 7 (8) yr
Root longevity†	4 to 6 yr	5 to 8 (10) yr	1 yr
Root elongation ability†	1 yr	2 to 3 yr	1 yr
Seasonality of root elongation†	Mid–late season	Continuous	Continuous
Lateral root production†	90% 1st yr	2nd to 4th yr	None
Seasonality of lateral production†	Mid–late season	Continuous	—
Root origins†	Predominantly rhizome nodes	Stem base	Stem base

*Shaver (1976).
†Shaver and Billings (1975).

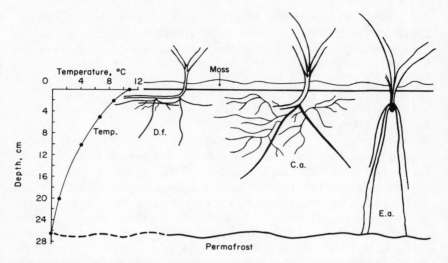

FIGURE 5-20. *Patterns of root distribution of* Dupontia fisheri *(D.f.),* Carex aquatilis *(C.a.) and* Eriophorum angustifolium *(E.a.) at peak season.*

chronous in *Carex* and *Eriophorum* than in *Dupontia* (Mattheis et al. 1976), suggesting that shoots of *Dupontia* might be able to regrow more rapidly following grazing than would shoots of the other two graminoids. However, in the ungrazed situation earlier canopy development by *Carex* and *Eriophorum* may give these two species a more favorable carbon balance that in turn allows them to invest in new structures, particularly roots and rhizomes, to a greater extent than can *Dupontia*.

The interspecific differences in growth and allocation patterns for the three species are more pronounced below ground than above ground (Shaver and Billings 1975), suggesting that at the Biome research area competition is more intense and niche differentiation more clearly delineated in soil than in air. Nutrient and oxygen concentrations, pH and temperature all vary substantially with depth. The three principal graminoid species have strikingly different rooting patterns and exploit different depths (Figure 5-20).

Roots of *Dupontia* are concentrated in the top 5 cm of the soil where phosphate and potassium are most abundant and where temperature and aerobic conditions are most favorable for absorption (Shaver and Billings 1975). *Eriophorum* has thin annual roots that grow vertically downward following the seasonal thaw (Bliss 1956, Shaver and Billings 1975). At the freeze/thaw interface, phosphorus may be highly available (Saebø 1969). The disadvantages of the deep-rooting habit are that soils are colder and less aerobic and that deep roots are locked in frozen soil the following season, which is perhaps why the entire root system of *Eriophorum* is replaced annually. Annual replacement avoids the cost of maintenance respiration during the second year when the roots may be less functional (Shaver and Billings 1975). *Carex* produces long-lived, thick primary roots that exploit intermediate soil horizons and thin secondary roots that are quite abundant in surface horizons. *Carex* invests proportionately more tissue in roots than do the other two species and is most successful in nutrient-poor situations.

Interspecific differences in growth and allocation, tiller interdependence, and age class distribution lead to distinct population structures in the three graminoid species. *Dupontia* from the nutrient-rich habitat shows considerable tiller interdependence, low tiller mortality, and a uniform age class structure (Shaver and Billings 1975, Allessio and Tieszen 1975a, Lawrence et al. 1978). Tiller interdependence may be important in allowing *Dupontia* to survive acute and chronic grazing.

In contrast, the longer-lived *Eriophorum* tillers lose rhizome connections and become physiologically independent within two or three years (Shaver 1976). Heavily grazed *Eriophorum* tillers cannot rely upon the reserves of an interconnected tiller system and tend to occur less frequently in heavily grazed polygon troughs. Lack of tiller interdependence may be important in explaining *Eriophorum's* apparent success in sexual reproduction, since its reserves may accumulate to support the inflorescence rather than being continuously siphoned away into the rest of the tiller system. Allocation to sexual reproduction and the windblown seed dispersal pattern in *Eriophorum* are in part responsible for its abundance in disturbed habitats. An annual rooting pattern is adaptive in disturbed sites, where roots are subject to breaking by frost heaving. Little is currently known about mortality of *Eriophorum* tillers, but the greater tiller independence in *Eriophorum* than in *Dupontia* may well lead to greater variability in recruitment and death in the former and hence more variation in age class structure.

Carex has a dual tillering pattern. Some tillers (clumping tillers) have very short rhizome internodes so that new shoots are produced adjacent to the parent tiller (Shaver and Billings 1975). Other (spreading) tillers have elongated rhizome internodes so that daughter tillers occupy space quite far from the parent tiller. The spreading pattern is most common in phosphorus-deficient sites like polygon basins. The low phosphorus-to-nitrogen ratio may stimulate rhizome elongation, minimizing competition between parent and daughter tillers. Such an effect has been proposed in temperate grasses (Evans et al. 1964, Langer 1966).

These consistent differences in allocation patterns among the various graminoids are consistent and appear to explain their distribution patterns. Differences in life forms are more pronounced and are discussed in Chapter 6.

SUMMARY

The component processes of growth and allocation in graminoids of the coastal tundra at Barrow have compensated for low temperature to such an extent that these processes occur at nearly the same rates in situ as those observed in temperate grasslands. Temperature compensation may be achieved at substantial carbon and protein cost and thus be accompanied by lowered reproductive output. Latitudinal temperature compensation has been demonstrated for shoot growth, photosynthesis, respiration and phosphorus uptake, but requires documentation for growth of belowground organs. Because the air warms faster than the soil, shoot growth and photosynthesis predominate early in the season, whereas root growth and uptake continue well after shoot senescence. Nutrients absorbed in one year have their most pronounced effect upon growth and reproduction in subsequent years.

The lower levels of annual plant production in tundra than in comparable temperate communities are more a consequence of shortness of the growing season than of the difference in ambient summer temperature. This hypothesis is supported by computer simulations but has not been tested by field experiments or long-term observations.

Allocation patterns are altered genetically and environmentally in a way that minimizes limitation to growth by any one environmental resource but maximizes long-term survival through vegetative and sexual reproduction. Growth is limited simultaneously by several factors. Experimental manipulations under field conditions indicate that phosphorus and nitrogen strongly limit plant growth. Simulations predict that light, carbon dioxide concentration, and water availability also limit growth to a lesser extent. Low temperature limits production in a complex fashion involving all of the above environmental variables. The high root-to-shoot ratio of the graminoids compensates for low nutrient availability. The environmental and genetic determinants of typical allocation patterns remain to be determined.

Plant growth at Barrow is generally more strongly limited by an inadequate supply of certain nutrients, especially nitrogen and phosphorus, than by inadequate carbohydrate. Available carbohydrate levels are high in the graminoids, particularly in habitats of low nitrogen and phosphorus availability. Carbohydrate levels are reduced by fertilization. We suggest that the low radiation environment of the Arctic limits plant growth more strongly by the indirect effects of low temperature upon nutrient availability than by a direct effect upon photosynthesis. Shoots also become photosynthetically self-sufficient quite early in the season and depend upon rhizome reserves for nutrients more than for carbohydrate. The decrease in rhizome weight that coincides with early season shoot growth is primarily a consequence of high rates of maintenance respiration and translocation to roots.

The evolutionary response of plants to the nutrient-limited environment is to limit production to the formation of a small amount of tissue that is well supplied with nutrients and highly effective metabolically. This would explain the apparent paradox of relatively high nitrogen and phosphorus concentrations in leaves of plants that respond dramatically to nitrogen and phosphorus fertilizers, in contrast to graminoid crop plants where nutrient deficiency is evident in foliar nutrient analysis.

Rapid upward translocation early in the season supports rapid shoot growth when radiation is most favorable for photosynthesis. Net downward translocation begins six weeks after growth commences, a full month before onset of obvious leaf senescence. The belowground carbohydrate and nutrient reserves appear to exceed levels required for growth in any given season and may allow the graminoids to successfully survive intensive lemming grazing and to regrow even after successive clippings.

6

The Vegetation: Pattern and Succession

P. J. Webber, P. C. Miller,
F. S. Chapin III, and B. H. McCown

INTRODUCTION

This chapter analyzes paths by which the environment acts upon tundra plants and interdependence between environmental factors and plant growth form characteristics (Figure 6-1). The analysis emphasizes the distinguishing characteristics and the environmental distributions of some of the principal growth forms recognized for tundra regions by Webber (1978) (Figure 6-2).

Although selection acts on whole individuals, growth form characteristics follow environmental gradients (Mooney et al. 1974) somewhat independently of each other. The objectives of this chapter are to identify the patterns of vegetation and plant growth forms in the coastal tundra at Barrow, the principal factors controlling these patterns, and the paths of influence between the major environmental controls and the plant growth forms which lead to the patterns of vegetation observed in the field. The major pathways of plant succession and the effect of natural and other perturbations are also examined.

To approach these objectives, the distribution of species, growth forms, and plant characteristics was determined along environmental gradients in the field, and the distribution of plant characteristics along environmental gradients was predicted from the physical and physiological information given in preceding chapters. The field distribution can be regarded as the realized niche, the predicted distribution as an indication of the fundamental niche (Hutchinson 1959).

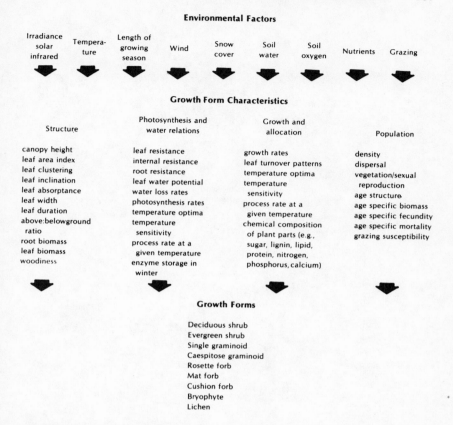

Environmental Factors

Irradiance solar infrared | Temperature | Length of growing season | Wind | Snow cover | Soil water | Soil oxygen | Nutrients | Grazing

Growth Form Characteristics

Structure	Photosynthesis and water relations	Growth and allocation	Population
canopy height	leaf resistance	growth rates	density
leaf area index	internal resistance	leaf turnover patterns	dispersal
leaf clustering	root resistance	temperature optima	vegetation/sexual
leaf inclination	leaf water potential	temperature	reproduction
leaf absorptance	water loss rates	sensitivity	age structure
leaf width	photosynthesis rates	process rate at a	age specific biomass
leaf duration	temperature optima	given temperature	age specific fecundity
above:belowground	temperature	chemical composition	age specific mortality
ratio	sensitivity	of plant parts (e.g.,	grazing susceptibility
root biomass	process rate at a	sugar, lignin, lipid,	
leaf biomass	given temperature	protein, nitrogen,	
woodiness	enzyme storage in	phosphorus, calcium)	
	winter		

Growth Forms

Deciduous shrub
Evergreen shrub
Single graminoid
Caespitose graminoid
Rosette forb
Mat forb
Cushion forb
Bryophyte
Lichen

FIGURE 6-1. *The principal environmental factors, plant growth form characteristics, and plant growth forms in the coastal tundra at Barrow.*

TOPOGRAPHIC VARIATION AND VEGETATION PATTERNS IN THE COASTAL TUNDRA

Topographic and Environmental Variations

Topographic variation in the coastal tundra at Barrow causes variation in the environmental factors which control the growth and distribution of different plant species and growth forms (Table 6-1). The controlling factors can be indicated by the techniques of factor analysis or ordination (Whittaker 1967). The phytosociological gradients formed by indirect ordinations are interpreted as complex environmental gradients which represent the probable major controlling factors. Using these techniques, 9 of a total of 17 measured environmental factors were sig-

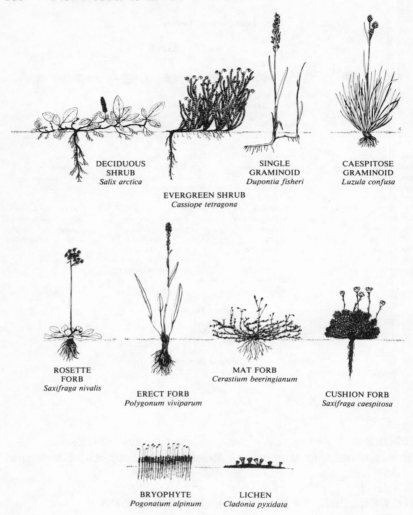

FIGURE 6-2. *Examples of the ten plant growth forms. (After Webber 1978.)*

nificantly correlated with the growth and distribution of different plant species and growth forms. The principal controlling factors were soil moisture, soil anaerobicity (indicated by soil odor of hydrogen sulfide), soluble phosphate in the soil and, to a lesser extent, snow cover.

Sampling sites were classified in terms of topography, hydrology and soil morphology. Samples were taken from six microtopographic units: ponds, meadows, polygon troughs, tops of high-centered polygons

TABLE 6-1. *Site Factors for Eight Vegetation Types Within the Biome Site at Barrow*

Site factor	Vegetation type							
	Luzula heath I (1)	*Salix* heath II (5)	*Carex–Poa* meadow III (11)	*Carex–Oncophorus* meadow IV (6)	*Dupontia* meadow V (6)	*Carex–Eriophorum* meadow VI (8)	*Arctophila* pond margin VII (2)	*Cochlearia* meadow VIII (4)
Snow depth (cm), 6 June 1973	0	4	21	29	43	36	28	86
Snow-free date	Before 1 June	13 June	23 June	23 June	30 June	20 June	13 June	12 July
Soil moisture (g cm⁻¹), 29 July 1973	0.31	0.45	0.97	0.92	0.96	0.80	0.90	0.38
Thaw depth (cm), 17 Aug 1973	37	54	36	32	32	32	37	76
Sand (g g⁻¹ mineral soil)	0.13	0.34	0.28	0.14	0.09	0.29	0.05	0.75
Surface organic matter (kgdw m⁻²)	4.4	3.0	13.0	23.6	17.1	27.3	2.0	0.6
Surface organic matter thickness (cm)	4	4	7	12	10	18	2	1
Bulk density (g cm⁻¹)	0.40	0.70	0.53	0.32	0.32	0.21	0.18	0.91
Soluble phosphate (g m⁻² 10 cm⁻¹ depth)*	0.62	1.51	0.98	0.32	1.91	0.09	0.74	0.55
Odor of hydrogen sulfide on 17 Aug 1973 (arbitrary scale: 0 = no odor)	0	0.4	0.3	2.2	1.7	17	2.0	0
Soil pH†	3.9	5.3	4.2	4.1	4.4	4.2	4.5	5.1

Note: Values are means from the plots within each type. The number of stands per type is given in parentheses.

*Water extract. Based on two samples per type except for I, in which only one sample was measured.

†Saturated water slurry.

Source: Webber (1978).

189

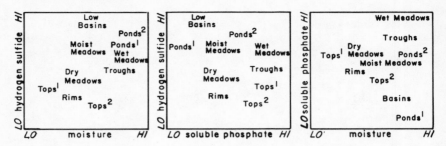

FIGURE 6-3. *The distribution of microtopographic units within the three principal axes of the ordination. The axes are soil moisture, soil odor of hydrogen sulfide, and soluble soil phosphate. Low basins are the centers of low-centered polygons, Tops¹ are the centers of high-centered polygons with little or no peat, Tops² are the centers of high-centered polygons with thick peat, Ponds¹ are those with no significant flow of water, and Ponds² are those with flowing water. (After Webber 1978.)*

and rims and basins of low-centered polygons. Two categories of ponds—those with and without flowing water—and three types of meadows—dry, moist and wet—were distinguished. Two categories of polygon tops—those with little or no peat at the surface and those with thick surface peat—were distinguished.

The different microtopographic units can be plotted within the axes of the indirect ordination (Figure 6-3). The sequence of units along the soil moisture gradient from low moisture to high is: tops of high-centered polygons with shallow soil, polygon rims, dry meadows, moist meadows, basins of low-centered polygons, tops of high-centered polygons with thick peat, polygon troughs, and wet meadows. The sequence along a gradient of soil hydrogen sulfide from low to high is: tops with thick peat, rims, tops with shallow soil, dry meadows, troughs, wet meadows, moist meadows and basins. The sequence along a gradient of soil soluble phosphate from low to high is: ponds with no flow, basins, dry meadows, moist meadows, rims, tops, troughs, and wet meadows. Basins of low-centered polygons and polygon troughs have the greatest snow accumulation and are the last microtopographic units to be free of snow, while polygon rims and tops of high-centered polygons have only a thin snow cover and are first to be snow-free. The duration of snow cover affects the length of the growing season, which varied from 30 to 42 days in 1973 (Table 6-1).

These observations coincide with the conclusions of Wiggins (1951) and Britton (1957) who emphasized the control by the microrelief of the substrate conditions, which in turn control the distribution of plants. In contrast to the results of most tundra ordinations (e.g. Webber 1971,

Webber et al. 1976) and other tundra studies (Gjaerevoll 1956, Bliss 1963, Scott and Billings 1964), snow cover does not emerge as a major controlling factor from these analyses. The variations in microrelief among most of the sampled locations are insufficient to produce a pronounced variation in snow cover. However, where ravines, creek banks, beach ridges and snow fences occur, snow cover becomes an important factor influencing vegetation distribution.

Vegetation Turnover Patterns

As discussed in Chapter 1 (Table 1-4), eight major vegetation types or noda were distinguished in the vegetation of the coastal tundra at Barrow. Most species occur in more than one vegetation type, but the types are distinguished by the presence of certain indicator species and the consistent importance of other species. Each vegetation type has a reasonably distinct standing crop composition at the period of peak aboveground biomass (Table 3-2). The *Cochlearia* meadow is a rudimentary vegetation restricted to recent alluvium and disturbed sites; it is therefore not included in the discussion.

Each vegetation type has a unique distribution within the three axes of the ordination (Figure 6-4). The vegetation types are numbered from *Luzula* heaths to *Arctophila* pond margins, following the primary controlling gradient of increasing soil moisture which is associated with increasing snow cover. Along a gradient of increasing hydrogen sulfide, the sequence of vegetation types is from *Luzula* heath, *Salix* heath, and *Carex–Poa* meadow, all found on well-drained sites, to *Carex* and *Dupontia* meadows, *Arctophila* pond margin, and *Carex–Oncophorus* meadow, all found on poorly drained sites with still or stagnant water. Along

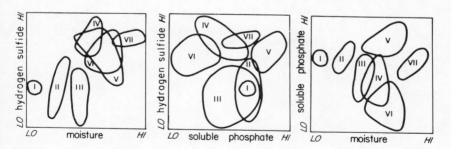

FIGURE 6-4. *The distribution of seven mature vegetation types within the ordination. I)* Luzula *heath, II)* Salix *heath, III)* Carex–Poa *meadow, IV)* Carex–Oncophorus *meadow, V)* Dupontia *meadow, VI)* Carex–Erio- phorum *meadow, VII)* Arctophila *pond margin. (From Webber 1978.)*

TABLE 6-2 *Above- and Belowground Turnover Rates for the Eight Vegetation Types Based on Data of Tables 3-1 and 3-2*

	Vegetation type							
Variables	Luzula heath I	Salix heath II	Carex-Poa meadow III	Carex-Oncophorus meadow IV	Dupontia meadow V	Carex-Eriophorum meadow VI	Arctophila pond margin VII	Cochlearia meadow VIII
Vascular plants								
Aboveground biomass								
Graminoids	0.99	0.97	0.91	0.99	0.97	0.98	0.96	0.99
Forbs	0.96	0.96	0.89	0.91	0.94	0.89	0.97	0.97
Woody dicotyledons	0.83	0.53	0.33	0.46	0.50	a	a	a
Vascular biomass	0.94	0.63	0.62	0.95	0.96	0.98	0.97	0.99
Standing dead	0.32	0.77	1.26	1.27	0.99	1.01	3.23	1.46
Litter and prostrate dead	0.44	0.20	0.32	0.67	0.68	0.94	1.80	0.56
Aboveground dead	0.18	0.16	0.26	0.44	0.40	0.49	0.16	0.40
All aboveground matter	0.15	0.13	0.18	0.30	0.28	0.33	0.53	0.30
Belowground biomass	0.10	0.10	0.14	0.14	0.17	0.13	0.20	0.33
Mosses								
Green	0.23	0.23	0.23	0.23	0.23	0.23	0.23	0.23

Note: Turnover rates are in units of g g^{-1} yr^{-1}. Turnover rates were calculated assuming steady state conditions and no respiration losses.
a—Absent.

the gradient of increasing soluble phosphate, the sequence of vegetation types runs from *Carex-Eriophorum* meadow, *Carex-Oncophorus* meadow and *Carex-Poa* meadow to the heaths, *Arctophila* pond margin and *Dupontia* meadow. The three vegetation types associated with the lowest phosphate concentrations occur on sites that receive no drainage water or influx of minerals, while the types associated with higher concentrations are found on mineral soils on sites receiving an influx of drainage water.

Turnover rates (grams incorporated annually per gram standing crop) in a particular vegetation type depend on the species or growth forms present (Table 6-2). Turnover rates for aboveground biomass are about 1.0 yr^{-1} for those vegetation types that are mainly composed of graminoids and forbs. In the *Salix* heath and *Carex-Poa* meadow, woody dicotyledons are common and biomass turnover rates are about 0.6 yr^{-1}. The woody dicotyledons in these vegetation types have low turnover rates; several individuals of *Salix pulchra* were at least 20 years old, as determined by counts of terminal bud scars on the branches.

Turnover rates of standing dead range from 0.3 yr^{-1} in the *Luzula* heath to 3.2 yr^{-1} in the *Arctophila* pond margin. The turnover rates for standing dead in the *Carex-Oncophorus*, *Dupontia* and *Carex-Eriophorum* meadows are 1.0 yr^{-1} to 1.3 yr^{-1}. The turnover rate of standing dead is affected by the rates at which standing dead is blown or washed away from the site or pressed prostrate by snow and rain.

Turnover rates of litter and prostrate dead are from about 0.2 yr^{-1} in the *Salix* heaths to 1.8 yr^{-1} in the *Arctophila* pond margin. Turnover rates are 0.6 to 0.9 yr^{-1} in the *Carex-Oncophorus*, *Dupontia* and *Carex-Eriophorum* meadows. These turnover rates are affected by the rates of removal of material from the site, by rates of decomposition and by rates of incorporation of the vascular material into belowground material, which depends partly on the rate of vertical growth by moss.

The turnover rates for all aboveground dead material are about 0.2 yr^{-1} in the heaths, 0.4 yr^{-1} in the *Dupontia* and *Carex-Eriophorum* meadows, and 1.2 yr^{-1} in the *Arctophila* pond margin. These turnover rates imply residence times of dead material of less than a year in the *Arctophila* pond margin, to 2 to 2.5 years in the meadows, to 6.3 years in the heaths. Residence times of aboveground material in all vegetation types are between 1.9 and 7.7 years, and are about 3.4 years in the *Dupontia* and *Carex-Eriophorum* meadows.

Belowground turnover rates are estimated from root longevity data when available (Chapter 5). Root longevities are about 5 years in *Dupontia* and 8 years in *Carex aquatilis*, giving turnover rates of 0.2 to 0.12 yr^{-1} for the *Dupontia* and *Carex-Eriophorum* meadow types. Lower turnover rates are expected for the belowground parts of the woody dicotyledons.

GROWTH FORMS AND ENVIRONMENTAL CONTROL

Definition of Growth Forms

The factors controlling the distribution of plant populations could not be analyzed at the scale of resolution of individual species, however desirable such analyses might be, because of the lack of complete data on all species. Thus the plant species were grouped into growth forms based on aboveground characteristics (Figure 6-2). Since the early work of Raunkiaer (1934), the importance of plant growth forms as strategic adaptations to the tundra environment has been emphasized (Bliss 1962a, Tikhomirov 1963, Chabot and Billings 1972). The evidence is that growth forms are selected in different habitats, and therefore are a meaningful basis on which to analyze different plant–environment interactions. The growth form categories are based primarily on the nature of the shoot habit, although some categories, such as bryophytes and lichens, are systematic or phylogenetic in character. Nevertheless, bryophytes and lichens seem to be valid growth forms in the tundra.

Woody shrubs in the coastal tundra at Barrow are all of low stature and many are prostrate. Shrubs are subdivided on the basis of being evergreen or deciduous. The genus *Salix* is the principal representative of the deciduous shrub while *Cassiope tetragona* and *Vaccinium vitis-idaea* represent the evergreen shrub. Herbaceous plants with elongated, narrow leaves are represented by the graminoids, i.e. grasses, sedges and rushes. The graminoids are subdivided into those with crowded, bunched shoots, here called caespitose graminoids, and those with well spaced individual shoots, here called single graminoids. *Luzula confusa* and *Eriophorum vaginatum* are examples of caespitose graminoids and *Dupontia fisheri* and *Carex aquatilis* represent the single graminoids.

Four growth forms are recognized for the broad-leaved herbs or forbs. Acaulescent, or essentially stemless, plants with a rosette of radicle leaves, such as *Saxifraga nivalis* and *Pedicularis lanata*, are called rosette forbs. Broad-leaved herbs with erect leaves or leaves supported into the canopy on long petioles or on an erect stem are called erect forbs and are represented by *Polygonum viviparum* and *Petasites frigidus*. Mat forbs such as *Cerastium jenisejense* and *Stellaria humifusa* have tightly matted, often long, prostrate stems with leaves along the length of the stems. Cushion forbs have short, crowded stems, often coming from a single tap root, which give the plant a hemispherical shape illustrated by *Saxifraga caespitosa* and *Silene acaulis*.

Distribution of Growth Forms

An analysis of the distribution of plant growth forms along the environmental gradients shows that some growth forms have high fidelity for a vegetation type, e.g. the evergreen shrub in the heaths, while other growth forms are distributed through several vegetation types, e.g. the single-stemmed graminoids and the mosses.

The above- and belowground standing crops and foliage area indices of the vascular plants form clear patterns along the complex environmental gradients (Figure 6-5). A comparison of the patterns of foliage area index and productivity shows a general correlation between these two variables similar to that described by Miller et al. (1976).

The principal factor controlling the distribution of bryophytes appears to be slight differences in microrelief which influence soil moisture regimes. Bryophyte biomass is low on sites with high hydrogen sulfide and highest in the presence of moderately low values for soil moisture and soluble phosphate. The standing crop of forbs and woody dicotyledons is highest in dry, well-aerated sites with moderate levels of phosphorus.

Aboveground biomass of graminoids increases along the moisture gradient from the *Salix* heath to the *Arctophila* pond margin. The *Luzula* heath has a higher graminoid biomass than the *Salix* heath because of the caespitose graminoids, such as *Luzula confusa*, which are abundant on dry sites. In all types except the two heaths, which are relatively dry, the aboveground standing dead is less than the aboveground live for both graminoids and forbs. The decay index for litter and prostrate dead vascular plant material, which is the ratio of net aboveground productivity to litter and prostrate dead, is lower on dry sites than on wet sites, and standing dead material is incorporated into prostrate dead and litter fractions more easily on the wet sites.

The distribution of belowground biomass in relation to environmental factors differs from that of aboveground material. Belowground biomass is greatest in the most anaerobic soils, and in soils with moderate moisture and high concentrations of soluble phosphate (Figure 6-5). The ratio of aboveground to belowground biomass presents yet another picture, with the lowest ratios (1:40) in moist, partly anaerobic soils with low soluble phosphate concentrations. The ratio increases along the moisture gradient and from anaerobic to aerobic soils. These patterns of belowground biomass support the conclusion (Chapin 1974a, Wielgolaski 1975c, Chapter 5) that vascular plants develop greater amounts of absorptive root tissue on anaerobic, phosphate-poor soils. But they are also partly an artifact of the changing growth form spectrum along these gradients, i.e. a shift from woody-stemmed species to rhizomatous spe-

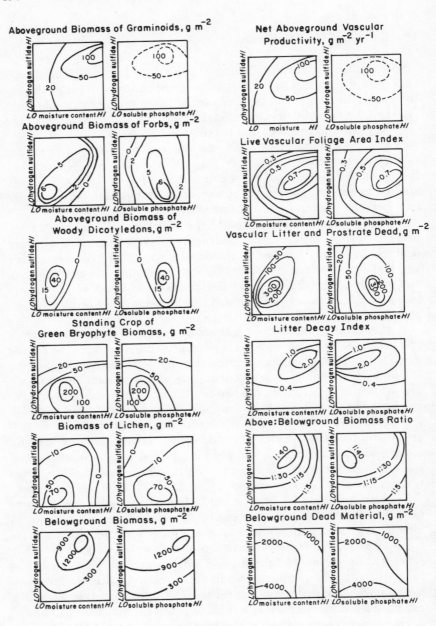

FIGURE 6-5. *Distribution within the principal axes of ordination of various above- and belowground standing crops, net aboveground productivity of vascular plants, foliage area index, above-to-belowground vascular biomass ratio, and vascular decay index. (After Webber 1978.)*

TABLE 6-3 *The Distribution of Major Growth Forms by Relative Cover for the Principal Vegetation Types of the Biome Sites at Barrow*

Site	Growth form/Example									
	Evergreen shrub *Vaccinium vitis-idaea*	Deciduous shrub *Salix lanata*	Caespitose graminoid *Luzula confusa*	Single graminoid *Carex aquatilis*	Cushion forb *Saxifraga caespitosa*	Mat forb *Cerastium beeringianum*	Rosette forb *Saxifraga nivalis*	Erect forb *Saxifraga cernua*	Bryophyte *Pogonatum alpinum*	Lichen *Cetraria islandica*
Luzula heath (I)	—	5.0	15.1	4.0	—	2.3	2.0	11.3	37.0	23.3
Salix heath (II)	3.3	16.5	4.4	8.1	0.8	2.3	3.0	11.1	31.7	18.8
Carex–Poa meadow (III)	1.5	3.2	2.1	16.7	—	1.4	1.3	4.9	45.3	23.6
Carex–Oncophorus meadow (IV)	1.3	1.4	2.8	26.5	—	3.4	2.5	8.8	46.2	7.1
Dupontia meadow (V)	—	0.4	0.4	28.4	—	6.4	1.5	12.1	45.4	5.4
Carex–Eriophorum meadow (VI)	—	—	0.6	40.2	—	0.5	3.2	3.8	47.4	4.3
Arctophila pond margin (VII)	—	—	—	35.5	—	1.0	—	32.3	31.2	—
Cochlearia meadow (VIII)	0.2	—	2.8	20.8	—	12.9	4.3	15.2	30.2	13.6

Source: Modified from Webber (1978).

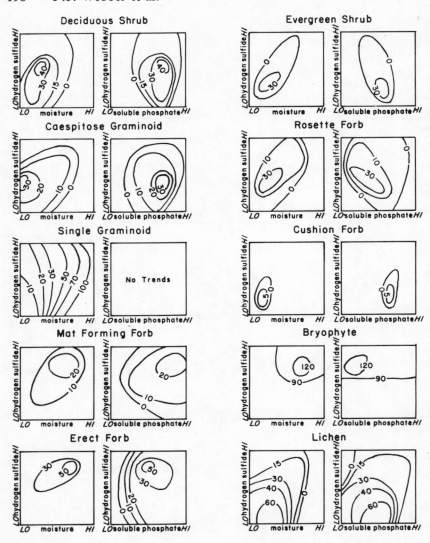

FIGURE 6-6. *The relative importance of growth forms within the principal axes of the ordination. The contour values are the sum of relative cover and relative frequency of the growth form. (After Webber 1978.)*

cies with increasing water-logging, and increasing moss growth which buries aboveground plant parts. The ratios and the magnitude of belowground biomass are similar to those reported by Dennis and Johnson (1970) and Dennis (1977).

The abundance of the graminoid-dominated vegetation types at the wet end of the moisture gradient is clearly apparent (Table 6-3). In wet meadows, single graminoids make up most of the vascular vegetation. Underlying the graminoid canopy is a discontinuous layer of moss. These two growth forms are the most important in primary production and nutrient cycling and have been studied the most intensively.

The importance of these growth forms, which is calculated from the relative cover plus relative frequency, varies in the different vegetation types and in the different microtopographic units, reflecting the different productivities of the growth forms along environmental gradients (Figure 6-6). Evergreen and deciduous shrubs, caespitose graminoids, cushion forbs, and lichens are more important on the drier microsites. The single graminoids, grasses, sedges and rushes, and the bryophytes are more important on the wetter sites. Caespitose graminoids occur with lower moisture, moderate soil anaerobicity, and moderate concentrations of soluble phosphorus (Figure 6-6). The importance of the single graminoids increases with moisture and is independent of soil aeration and phosphorus. Mat and erect forbs are most abundant in moist sites with moderate to high levels of phosphate and hydrogen sulfide, while rosette forbs prefer drier sites where phosphate and sulfide levels are moderate. Evergreen shrubs occur with low moisture, moderate concentrations of hydrogen sulfide and moderate phosphorus. Deciduous shrubs occur with slightly higher soil moisture, slightly higher hydrogen sulfide, and higher phosphorus. The importance of lichens is highest with moderately low moisture, low hydrogen sulfide, and moderate phosphorus. Bryophytes, by contrast, are most important with moderately high soil moisture, somewhat anaerobic soils, and low phosphorus.

Species Diversity Within Growth Forms

The number of species within a growth form, as well as overall cover and frequency, varies along the environmental gradients (Figure 6-7). The diversity of species within a given growth form does not always correspond with the importance of the form. The importance of single graminoids is highest in wet sites, and shows little relation to soil anaerobicity and phosphate. The species diversity is greatest with moderate moisture and phosphate and relatively high soil anaerobicity. Deciduous shrubs are more diverse with low soil hydrogen sulfide, but show high cover with higher soil hydrogen sulfide.

Production and diversity are related. Stands with lower diversity have high productivity; stands with moderate diversity have lower productivity. The highest diversity occurs on the drier sites, with growth forms of low productivity. The lowest diversity occurs at stream and pond edges, in monospecific graminoid stands with high production.

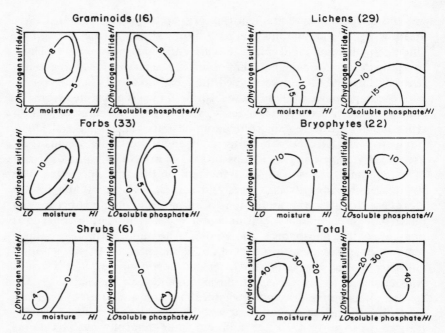

FIGURE 6-7. *The number of species per 10-m² plot of the most common growth forms and the total number of species within the principal axes of the ordination. The total number of species of each growth form is given in parentheses. (After Webber 1978.)*

FUNCTIONAL RELATIONSHIPS OF GROWTH FORMS AND ENVIRONMENTAL GRADIENTS

Functional Definition of Growth Forms

The growth forms defined on the basis of morphological habit differ in functional characteristics related to the environmental gradients. Functional characteristics include leaf longevity, timing of leaf growth, location of the perennating bud, location of stored organic and inorganic nutrients, leaf resistance to water loss, photosynthetic rates, carbon and nutrient costs of constructing new leaf material, and location of absorbing roots.

The graminoid forms are characterized by sequential leaf production and, for single graminoids, a rapid leaf turnover (Tieszen and Wieland 1975, Johnson and Tieszen 1976). The leaf longevity may be shorter than the growing season. This pattern results in a high annual growth respiration cost, and is generally associated with relatively high photosynthetic rates (Tieszen and Wieland 1975). Reserve materials are stored below ground (Allessio and Tieszen 1975a). The meristematic region that overwinters is either just below the moss or soil surface, or protected above ground by dead but persisting leaf sheaths. Forbs of the rosette, erect, mat or cushion types have high leaf growth rates and synchronous leaf production early in the season. The leaf duration is one growing season. The respiration rate during leaf growth is high, but net photosynthetic rates may be moderate (Tieszen 1973). Materials stored below ground in rhizomes and roots are mobilized early in the season to support the rapid growth (Mooney 1972). The perennating bud is located below ground or at the soil surface.

Deciduous shrubs have a high leaf growth rate and synchronous leaf production early in the growing season. Respiration rates are high during the leaf growth period, and photosynthesis rates are high; for example photosynthesis rates of *Salix* are higher than those of the graminoids (Chapter 4). The perennating buds are above ground and materials are stored in stems through the winter. The aboveground location of the perennating buds and stored materials makes the deciduous shrubs susceptible to grazing and to loss of plant parts due to abrasion by wind. The production of wood by the deciduous shrub involves a large biosynthetic cost, since the efficiency of lignin synthesis is comparatively low (Table 5-5). The deciduous shrub also has a relatively low root biomass (Chapter 3), which reduces the total maintenance cost.

Evergreen shrubs usually have synchronous leaf growth (Johnson and Tieszen 1976) with a low rate of leaf turnover, although some, e.g. *Dryas integrifolia*, have sequential but low rates of leaf production (Svoboda 1977). The respiration rates of evergreen woody shrubs are relatively low because of the low rates of growth. Photosynthesis rates based on leaf dry weight are also low, about half those of the graminoid form, but may be similar to the graminoid on a leaf area basis (Johnson and Tieszen 1976). Leaf resistance to water loss may be low in spite of their xerophytic appearance (Kedrowski 1976, Oberbauer 1978). Materials are stored in the stems and leaves through the winter, perhaps in the form of lipids. The perennating buds are located above ground. The evergreen form is found on exposed locations that are snow-free early in the season. It can photosynthesize early when the surface is warm, even though the soil and roots are frozen, since all the materials required for photosynthesis are stored in the leaf. It commonly survives desiccation and grows late in the season. The form also occurs in late-lying snowbeds.

The moss and lichen forms grow throughout the season whenever moisture and temperature conditions permit photosynthesis. Respiration and photosynthesis are low in relation to graminoids (Chapter 4). Materials are stored where they are formed; translocation is uncommon (Collins and Oechel 1974). The intake of minerals by moss depends largely upon inorganic nutrients being absorbed or deposited upon the moss surface or diffusing to the surface, since most mosses cannot absorb minerals through a root system from the soil profile.

Interrelations Between Environmental Factors and Plant Characteristics

The links between the major environmental factors and the patterns of plant characteristics can be diagrammed to clarify and assess the current state of understanding (Figure 6-8). Although the variation in environmental factors is continuous, a comparison of the interactions on exposed microtopographic units, such as tops of high-centered polygons, with those on more protected units, such as polygon troughs or sloping creek banks, provides some basis for assessing the direction of influence. Within the macroclimatic environment the patterns of vegetation are related to topographic gradients and associated environmental factors.

For example, the major environmental variables are all influenced by wind. Sites with relatively high wind have thin snow cover, low soil water and lower temperatures during the growing season (Table 6-1; Oberbauer and Miller 1979). High wind leads to increased removal of litter, which is indicated in the higher litter turnover rate of the unprotected *Luzula* heath relative to the *Salix* heath, and to reduced nutrients because of the wind-blown nutrient loss (Figure 6-4, Table 6-1). The low soil water also increases soil aeration, which can lead to increased acidity and phosphorus immobilization.

These environmental factors influence several plant processes. High wind and thin snow cover lead to increased loss of plant parts due to abrasion (Savile 1972), which favors low growth forms and species in which the buds are protected. The lower temperatures in the active season should lead to reduced growth (Warren Wilson 1966a, Larcher et al. 1973), although the relation between temperature and growth is poorly quantified for the Arctic (Miller et al. 1979). The reduced growth may also lead to low growth forms. The low growth forms lead to increased plant temperature, since ground surface temperatures are higher than air temperatures. The higher plant temperatures will cause higher vapor pressure differences from leaf to air, thus potentially increasing water loss and water stress unless compensated by high leaf resistance. High leaf resistances are associated with low photosynthesis rates, which lead to greater leaf longevity that provides time to recover the leaf construction costs (Johnson and Tieszen 1976, Miller and Stoner 1979). The need for greater leaf longevity is reinforced by the low nutrients (Beadle 1962, Monk 1966, Small 1972, Stoner et al. 1978b).

Thin snow cover results in earlier exposure of the surface in spring.

Leaf expansion cannot take place, since the ground may still be frozen and water unavailable, but photosynthesis is still possible (Larcher et al. 1973). In such a situation evergreen leaves containing photosynthetic enzymes stored through the winter are advantageous (Miller 1978). Thin snow cover also results in low soil water and the possibility of periodic summer drought, at least in the surface soil layers. The summer drought should select for leaves with structural thickenings and for plants with deep roots to exploit deeper, moister soil layers (Oberbauer 1978, Oberbauer and Miller 1979). Thus, on exposed sites the vegetation should comprise plants of low stature with long-lived leaves, low photosynthesis rates, high leaf resistance, buds protected by scales, hairs or persistent plant parts, rigid leaves and deep roots. These trends are exemplified in the vegetation turnover rate, growth form composition, and above- to belowground biomass ratios (Table 3-2, Table 6-2, Figure 6-5) of the heath vegetation types.

More protected sites have lower wind speeds, which lead to deeper snow cover, greater protection from winter abrasion, high soil water, higher temperatures in the active season, and increased litter deposition and nutrients. The decreased abrasion loss makes possible taller growth forms and the storage of nutrients above ground. The increased snow cover results in later exposure of the surface. Air and ground temperatures, when the surface is finally exposed, are higher than for the sites that are exposed earlier. Early in the season the ground is warmed by the influx of meltwater. Thus leaf expansion becomes possible as soon as photosynthesis is possible. Deciduous leaved plants, with nutrients stored in the aboveground stems, can occur. The vegetation of these sites includes many deciduous shrubs. With still greater snow cover the short snow-free season can favor evergreen forms which can regain the carbon cost of leaf construction through several seasons.

Increasing protection or impeded drainage leads to soils saturated with water, low soil aeration, and low soil temperatures because of the high heat capacity of the soil (Chapters 3 and 7). Low temperatures decrease mineralization and uptake ability, leading to reduced nutrient availability. The plant may compensate by increasing the number and biomass of absorbing roots. The lower soil oxygen can lead to greatly increased respiration demands to support the root biomass, unless aerenchyma are present. Thus, selection may be strong for plants with aerenchyma, which may have deep roots, or for plants with shallow roots, such as the evergreen shrub, or no roots, such as mosses. Saturated conditions are found in the *Dupontia* and *Carex–Eriophorum* meadows and in the *Arctophila* pond margins (Table 3-2, Table 6-2, Figure 6-5). Slightly better aeration allows plants without aerenchyma to occur and vegetation similar to *Salix* heath develops.

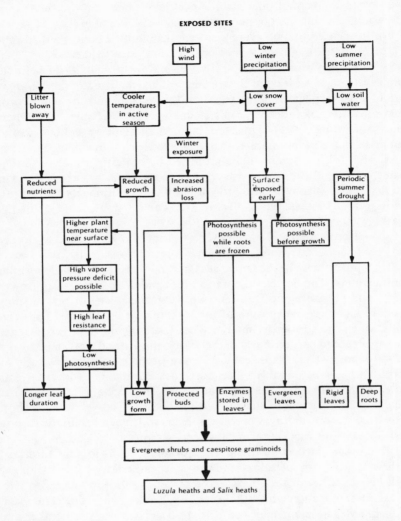

FIGURE 6-8. *Diagrammatic relationships between major environmental factors and plant characteristics. The diagram consists of two complexes: those for exposed sites which lead to plant characteristics to be found in evergreen shrubs and caespitose graminoids of* Luzula *and* Salix *heaths*

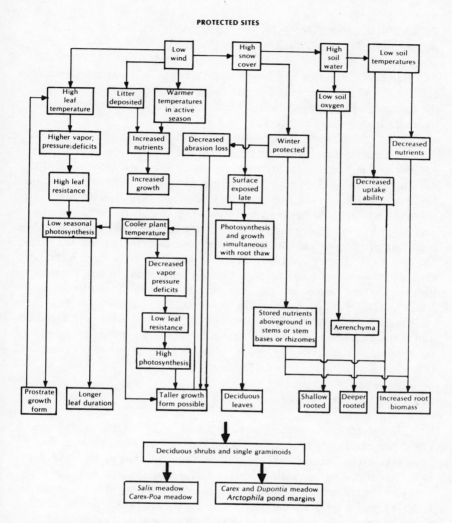

and those for protected sites which lead to the characteristics of the plants of Salix and Carex–Poa meadows, for example deciduous shrubs and graminoids, and the plants of Carex and Dupontia meadows and Arctophila pond margins, for example single graminoids.

PLANT SUCCESSION AND
RESPONSE TO PERTURBATIONS

The explanation of vegetation patterns can lie in the physiological constraints of the species and growth forms as already discussed and in the change in plant populations as the vegetation recovers from disturbance or invades new territory.

Plant colonization of new or disturbed surfaces and subsequent plant succession is an important topic in arctic tundra, especially with the prospect of increasing disturbance associated with the development of natural resources. Unfortunately the problem is complex and really no better understood at the present time than when Churchill and Hanson (1958) wrote their comprehensive review of tundra succession. Too often successional patterns are interpreted by inference without either an adequate set of observations through time or dated surfaces (Polunin 1935, Oosting 1956, Spetzman 1959, Johnson and Tieszen 1973). Although succession was not a main emphasis of the vegetation studies, a description of inferred succession patterns can be useful in interpreting such studies. The plant succession discussion is based largely on field inference and the literature. The rates of change in succession are variable and some changes may take a thousand years while others take only a few tens of years.

Thaw Lake Cycle

Short-term linear succession is apparent in the Biome research area, but the overriding patterns are cyclic and can be related either to the thaw lake cycle (Britton 1957) or to the colonization of alluvium (Figure 6-9). The resulting successional pattern is oversimplified and may only apply to the immediate Biome research area. Only the most commonly followed pathways are discussed; many others are possible. The successional changes are controlled primarily by changes in microrelief and thus drainage regimes.

Plant colonization on stable floodplain alluvium is rapid. In a few years a good cover develops, made up of species such as *Cochlearia officinalis, Stellaria laeta, Phippsia algida, Alopecurus alpinus, Poa arctica, Saxifraga cernua,* and *Bryum* spp. Other plants, including *Dupontia fisheri, Petasites frigidus* and lichens soon follow, and stands belonging to the *Cochlearia* meadow type develop. In areas that are not dominated by snow accumulation, stabilization of the sediments allows development of stands belonging to the *Carex–Poa* meadow type. Stabilized areas may become drier either by high-centered polygon formation, or by

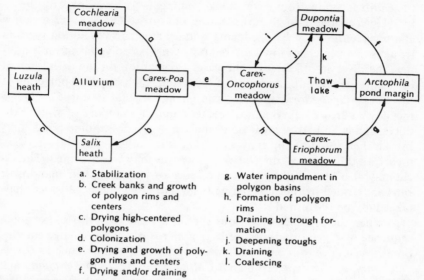

FIGURE 6-9. *Principal successional trends of vegetation types and principal allogenic geomorphic processes controlling them. (After Webber 1978.)*

increased drainage as local water courses deepen through thermokarst or frost heaving activity. Drier areas will support *Salix* and *Luzula* heaths. Although good field evidence exists for the transition to *Luzula* heath, such transitions are rare.

The colonization of drained lake sediments is also rapid. The basin of Footprint Lake has become covered with vegetation within 25 years (Dennis 1977). The present vegetation of the basin varies according to local drainage and substrate composition. It includes *Carex–Oncophorus, Dupontia* and *Carex* meadows, and *Arctophila* pond margins. The *Dupontia* meadow is the most abundant vegetation in the Footprint Lake basin at present. Once a surface has a complete cover of vegetation it seems slow to change to another vegetation type. As ice wedge polygons develop, with their attendant variety of microrelief and moisture regimes, the vegetation of the Footprint Lake basin should become similar to the highly polygonized Biome research area, but many decades must elapse before the same variety of vegetation types develops in the lake basin. The frequency with which thaw lakes drain and with which new alluvium is laid down is increased by man's activities.

The mechanisms responsible for changing vegetation types are predominantly geomorphic. The *Carex–Oncophorus* meadow can form when polygon troughs drain in a *Dupontia* meadow. The development of the *Carex* meadow from drained lake sediments forms a link with the alluvial succession. Trough formation in the *Carex–Oncophorus* meadow can reverse the trend by producing wetter areas and vegetation types in troughs and centers of low-centered polygons. As polygonization continues, the diversity of surfaces increases. Vegetation on the drier rims of low-centered polygons and tops of low-relief, high-centered polygons of the *Carex–Oncophorus* meadow can change to that of the *Carex–Poa* meadow. Further depression of centers and impounding of water produces ponds and *Arctophila* pond margin vegetation. Some ponds may breach their impounding rims and drain while others may fill with sediments. In this manner, the *Dupontia* meadow may be re-formed. The cycle may also be closed by the coalescence of ponds as their margins or rims are eroded by thermokarst activity, and large ponds and even thaw lakes may be re-formed.

When the presence of various species is plotted on this successional sequence of vegetation types, orderly patterns of species change emerge. Some species occur in only one type or successional stage, such as *Hierochloe alpina*, *Cassiope tetragona*, *Caltha palustris*, *Phippsia algida* and *Saxifraga rivularis*. Others occupy several types, such as *Poa arctica*, *Dupontia fisheri*, *Saxifraga foliolosa*, *Carex aquatilis* and *Eriophorum angustifolium*. Those species occurring in more than one type usually occur sequentially in the postulated successional sequences and this occurrence is not interrupted or haphazard. The single exception is *Arctophila fulva*, which dominates the pond margin vegetation, and also occurs in the *Dupontia* meadow and in the *Cochlearia* meadow.

Orderly patterns are also formed when the numbers of the species of different growth forms in each vegetation type and various productivity measures are plotted in the successional sequence (Figure 6-10). In the alluvial sequence from *Cochlearia* meadow to the *Luzula* heath on the tops of high-centered polygons, the total number of species increases from the *Cochlearia* meadow through the *Carex–Poa* meadow to the *Salix* heath but decreases abruptly from the *Salix* heath to the *Luzula* heath. In the thaw-lake cycle from the *Dupontia* meadow through the *Carex–Oncophorus* meadow, *Carex–Eriophorum* meadow and *Arctophila* pond margin, the total number of species first increases from the *Dupontia* meadow to the *Carex–Oncophorus* meadow and then decreases through the *Carex–Eriophorum* meadow to the *Arctophila* pond margin. The *Arctophila* pond margin has the lowest diversity in total number of species and in the number of species in each growth form. The highest proportion of graminoids is found in the *Carex–Eriophorum* meadow and the smallest in the *Salix* heath. The vegetation types found on dry sites have the highest proportion of dicotyledons. The *Cochlearia* meadow has several typical pioneer species which are dicotyledons, for example *Cochlearia officinalis*, *Saxifraga rivularis* and *Stellaria humifusa*.

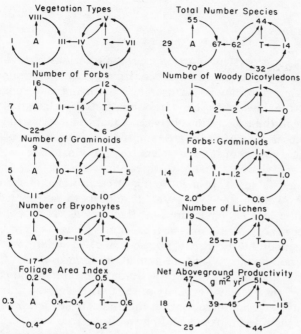

FIGURE 6-10. *The distribution of the species diversity (number of species per 10 m²) of the major growth forms, foliage area index, and annual net aboveground vascular productivity within the successional sequence diagram. The Roman numerals represent the positions of the vegetation types and the letters A and T represent the starting points of alluvium (A) and thaw lake (T) successions. Foliage Area Index refers only to vascular plants. See Figure 6-9 for vegetation types. (After Webber 1978.)*

Foliage area index is low in the *Cochlearia* meadow, increases in the alluvial sequence to the *Salix* heath and then decreases slightly in the *Luzula* heath. It is highest in the *Arctophila* pond margin and decreases in the thaw lake cycle to the *Carex–Oncophorus* meadow. Annual aboveground vascular productivity decreases steadily with succession. From the *Cochlearia* meadow through the *Carex–Poa* meadow and *Salix* heath to the *Luzula* heath, productivity decreases from 47 g m⁻² yr⁻¹ to 18 g m⁻² yr⁻¹. From the pond margin through the *Dupontia* meadow to the *Carex–Oncophorus* meadow productivity decreases from 115 g m⁻² yr⁻¹ to 45 g m⁻² yr⁻¹.

Natural Perturbations

The control over ecosystem function exerted by various factors can best be studied when the system is perturbed. Enlargement and drainage of lakes may be viewed as natural perturbations occurring in the coastal tundra as part of the thaw lake cycle. Ecosystem function changes drastically in response to these alterations between aquatic and terrestrial environment, and thousands of years are required for completion of the thaw-lake cycle and return of the ecosystem to its original state.

Tundra is often viewed as easily disturbed or changed (Bliss et al. 1970) but it is quite stable and resilient to major environmental changes (Bliss et al. 1970, Webber and Ives 1978). It appears to be adapted to large, natural, often sudden environmental fluctuations. For example, the pulse of water runoff during snowmelt is dramatic but does not have immediate effects upon most other factors such as an efflux of nitrogen or phosphorus, even though 40% of the annual phosphorus return from litter to the soluble pool occurs during this 10-day period (Chapin et al. 1978). Apparently, the exchange capacity of the mosses and the nutrient demands of plants and microorganisms at this time are sufficient to extract most of the dissolved nitrogen and phosphorus from runoff. During the growing season, microbial populations in the soil may build up and crash, releasing a large proportion of the annual nutrient flux in brief periods. However, the rapid nutrient uptake by plants and the high exchange capacity of peat are sufficient to remove nutrients as they are made available.

The recurrent peaks in lemming abundance at 3- to 4-year intervals constitute another natural perturbation of the coastal tundra at Barrow (Chapter 10). Heavy winter grazing removes dead leaves from the canopy, and computer simulations predict that the associated increase in light intensity will stimulate photosynthesis and increase net production the following summer (Miller et al. 1976). Moreover, litter decomposes more rapidly once it is felled and in contact with the wet ground surface, releasing nutrients and further stimulating production.

Heavy grazing during summer, removing 50% or more of leaf biomass, depletes plant carbon and nutrient reserves as new leaves are produced and reduces the length of time that new leaves can photosynthesize (Mattheis et al. 1976, Chapin 1975); computer simulations predict a reduced annual production. The tundra vegetation recovers from intense grazing perturbations within 3 to 4 years, as discussed in Chapter 10 and by Schultz (1964, 1969). Briefly, grazing increases nutrient availability through leaching of urine and feces and more rapid decomposition of felled leaves and litter. The stimulation of primary production by increased nutrient availability returns the vegetation to its original state.

Controlled Perturbations

Experimental alteration of selected ecosystem variables reveals their relative importance in the resilience or fragility of tundra and provides clues to the recovery time and thresholds beyond which the system does not quickly recover. Heavy fertilization increases primary production and plant nutrient concentrations initially, but subsequent increases in standing dead and litter tie up nutrients and reduce light penetration and photosynthesis, so that within 3 to 8 years little treatment effect upon primary production can be observed (Schultz 1964, 1969). Clipping and removal of all aboveground vegetation or addition of excess litter (to stimulate accumulation of standing dead) alter primary production and plant nutrient concentrations only slightly (Chapin 1978). Even multiple defoliations of single tillers have relatively small effect upon regrowth (Mattheis et al. 1976). All the above manipulations cause changes that are within the normal range of conditions in lemming cycles, and the tundra is highly resilient to these perturbations.

The anticipated effect on the tundra of the Trans-Alaska Pipeline System, which carries hot oil, led to an experiment in which a wet meadow substrate was heated in situ. Alteration of soil temperature markedly affects ecosystem function, but the nature of the response depends upon the similarity of the perturbation to those that occur naturally. A 10 °C soil temperature rise for one summer month at Barrow increased thaw depth, decomposition rate, nitrogen availability, plant nutrient absorption rates, and primary production (Chapin and Bloom 1976). Ten years later little treatment effect could be observed. However, when soils were heated for one full year, the increased thaw depth caused melting of ice in permafrost, subsidence of the ground surface and ponding of water. Rapid decomposition depleted soil oxygen and soils became anaerobic, killing all vegetation within one year. The site did not recolonize during the 10 years following the experiment. Thus, although temporary summer changes in soil temperature stimulate nutrient cycling and primary production, a chronic year-round soil temperature change in ice-rich soils leads to ponding of water, death of the vegetation and a long-term change in ecosystem function. Experimental heating of a relatively ice-free soil in interior Alaska throughout the year caused no subsidence and increased primary production 3- to 5-fold (McCown 1973), an effect comparable to that caused by temporary heating of the ice-rich soil at Barrow. Thus the detrimental effects of soil heating appear to be caused primarily by a perturbation in excess of any natural fluctuation which triggers a chain of circumstances associated with melting of ice, soil subsidence, and change in soil chemical and physical environment.

Vehicle Tracks

Human impact in the Arctic is a subject of current concern because of both increasing human activity associated with arctic resource development and the unexpectedly severe ecological impact of human activity over the past 25 years. The severity of vehicle impacts upon tundra depends upon the nature of both the disturbance and the community and can be predicted from an understanding of natural and controlled perturbations of tundra (Figure 6-11).

Vegetation changes triggered by tracked vehicle damage and by water impoundments resulting from road construction fit into the thaw lake successional scheme presented here (Figure 6-9). Total destruction of any vegetation type because of catastrophic thermokarst activity leads to either the alluvium or the thaw lake starting points. Most commonly, water impoundment results in deepening of troughs through partial ice-wedge melting. In some instances this has caused both drier inter-trough areas and wetter trough areas. For example, at one site following disturbance by tracked vehicles the vegetation type has changed from the *Dupontia* meadow to both the *Carex–Oncophorus* meadow and the *Arctophila* pond margin, and from the *Carex–Oncophorus* meadow to both the *Carex* meadow and the *Dupontia* meadow. Vegetation changes may occur within a very few years.

Multiple passes by ACV's or a single pass by a Rolligon (balloon-tire vehicle) produce similar effects in winter or early spring. However, if the traffic occurs during the summer months, live vascular plants and mosses are crushed; passage of a wheeled vehicle may also produce some depression of the tundra surface (Abele et al. 1978, Everett et al. 1978). Soil temperature and, in following years, depth of thaw, nutrient availability and primary production increase. Recovery time is estimated at 2 to 4 years and is comparable to that associated with intense winter grazing by lemmings (Bliss and Wein 1972, Hernandez 1973, Wein and Bliss 1974, Challinor and Gersper 1975, Gersper and Challinor 1975, Brown and Grave 1979). The effect is greater in shrub tundra due to greater breakage of rigid stems, and recovery time is longer. Vehicle passage with greater frequency and later in the season increases damage to live leaves, prolongs recovery, and makes the impact more nearly comparable to that of summer lemming grazing by removing productive tissue and decreasing primary production.

Use of tracked vehicles, or repeated passage by low pressure wheeled vehicles, frequently compacts the low-bulk-density organic mat and depresses the soil surface below the water table, particularly in poorly drained meadow soils (Gersper and Challinor 1975). Standing water decreases albedo and increases soil temperature and thawing of permafrost,

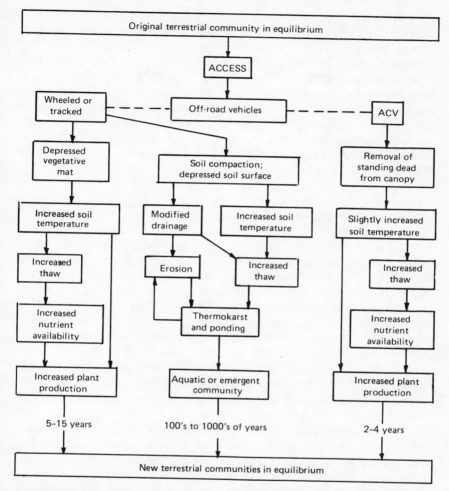

FIGURE 6-11. *Impact of air cushion vehicles (ACV) and wheeled and tracked vehicles upon the coastal tundra at Barrow. Recovery times are estimated from observations by Hok (1969), Hernandez (1973), Rickard and Brown (1974), Abele et al. (1978), and Lawson et al. (1978).*

causing increases in nutrient availability and primary production as well as further subsidence of the soil surface. Where the vehicle track crosses ice wedges or ice lenses, deep permanent ponds may form (Kryuchkov 1976, Peterson 1978). Sites with low ice content are less susceptible to this positive feedback and ponding (Webber and Ives 1978). On slopes, compaction by vehicles promotes drainage of water from surrounding areas, and thus speeds decomposition and permafrost thawing, increases nutrient availability, and changes community composition to that characteristic of wetter sites. Such communities are generally highly productive (Hernandez 1973, Wein and Bliss 1974). Drainage patterns also change naturally in tundra, with consequences similar to those described above, and are part of the thaw lake cycle (Britton 1957). Both natural and man-induced changes lead to irreversible permanent changes in the natural community, and recovery may require thousands of years until the landscape is modified by the thaw lake cycle. Vehicle impact upon various tundra communities can be predicted and mapped in order to manage vehicle use in areas of development (Everett et al. 1978, Webber and Ives 1978).

Vegetation and Organic Mat Removal

In general, tundra graminoids, if defoliated, regrow readily from belowground stems and rhizomes, especially in wet sites. Simulations suggest that wet meadow tundra can tolerate 50% foliage removal and still recover in 3 to 5 years. This situation is comparable to that which occurs naturally during lemming cycles (Bliss 1970, Babb and Bliss 1974). Vegetation in xeric sites generally recovers more slowly because of lower productivity, slower nutrient cycling, and greater exposure of dry-site species (e.g. evergreen shrubs) to disturbance (Hernandez 1973, Babb and Bliss 1974, Van Cleve 1977). The most serious consequences of removing aboveground vegetation are decreased albedo and increased heat penetration into the soil, which leads to thawing of permafrost, as described above, especially in wet sites.

The highly organic surface soil horizons of wet coastal tundra at Barrow serve an important function in nutrient retention. Removal of this organic mat from the tundra surface not only eliminates potentially resprouting vegetation but also removes a large proportion of the accumulated nutrient capital and most of the cation exchange capacity of the soil system. The 40 to 60% of the accumulated system nitrogen that is contained in the organic horizon of several tundra sites would require 5,000 to 10,000 years to replenish at current fixation rates (Chapin and Van Cleve 1978). In ice-rich permafrost, thermokarst continues over decades and relatively flat areas are recolonized by the native vegetation (Lawson et al. 1978). Perhaps the most serious consequence of organic mat removal has been serious erosion following thawing of permafrost on sloping terrain. An aquatic or emergent vegetation may eventually stabilize such erosion patterns (Hok 1969, Hernandez 1973, Haag and Bliss 1974), but the system probably will not return to its former state for thousands of years.

Although revegetation of naturally disturbed sites such as drained lake basins occurs by seedling establishment within 10 to 20 years in the Barrow area (Dennis 1968), seeding with grasses of temperate origin has often been attempted to speed the revegetation process in areas disturbed by man. These grasses have higher nutrient and soil temperature requirements than most native tundra graminoids (Chapter 5; McCown 1978) and become established only with heavy and repeated fertilization (Mitchell 1973, Younkin 1976, Van Cleve 1977). Such grasses are often effective in stopping erosion but generally slow down reinvasion by native species (Hernandez 1973, Younkin 1976, Johnson and Van Cleve 1976). The fertilization required to maintain cover of temperate-origin grasses may have secondary effects such as attraction of herbivores and eutrophication of adjacent aquatic systems.

Oil Spills

Oil is an environmental factor foreign to most tundra communities, so that recovery from oil spills cannot be readily predicted from our knowledge of the responsiveness of the natural vegetation. Alaskan crude oil and fuel oil are toxic to plant leaves, but if the oil does not penetrate the soil, the tundra system responds much as it would following 100% defoliation by lemmings (Figure 6-12). There is a temporary decrease in albedo and increased heating of the soil (Haag and Bliss 1974, Everett 1978), but regrowth of the vegetation allows the community to approach its original condition within a few years. Flooding of the community with water largely prevents oil penetration into the soil until toxic volatile fractions have evaporated and thereby minimizes the local impact of an oil spill.

Most of the live biomass of all trophic groups in the coastal tundra at Barrow is in the top 10 cm of the soil and is rapidly killed if oil penetrates into the soil before toxic volatile fractions evaporate (Jenkins et al. 1978). In wet soils, oil penetrates more slowly, much of the toxic fraction evaporates, and less vegetation dies than in dry sites (Walker et al. 1978). Species differ in their sensitivity to oil, and often the response is seen as decreased winter hardiness rather than as immediate mortality (Deneke et al. 1975, Linkins and Antibus 1978).

Other effects of oil upon system function are more subtle but equally important. Hydrocarbons may remain in the active layer for at least 30 years after an oil spill (Lawson et al. 1978). Addition of a large carbon-rich, nutrient-poor substrate to the soil increases the demands of microbes for nutrients from the available soil pools so that nutrients become less available to vascular plants. Moreover, oil kills at least certain mycorrhizal fungi, further decreasing the ability of plants to extract nutrients from the soil (Antibus and Linkins 1978). Thus, oil may effec-

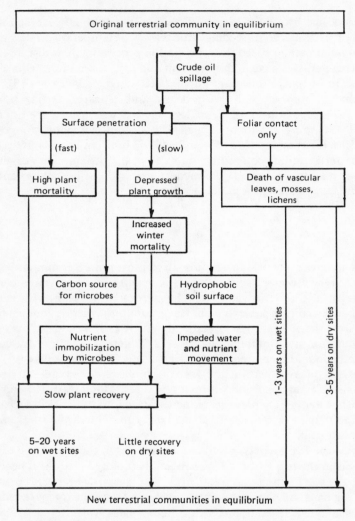

FIGURE 6-12. *Impact of crude oil upon the coastal tundra at Barrow. Recovery times are estimated from observations by Wein and Bliss (1973), Deneke et al. (1975), Hutchinson et al. (1976), and Walker et al. (1978).*

tively retard nutrient cycling and decrease nutrient availability in an ecosystem that is already nutrient-poor and highly dependent upon internal recycling of nutrients. Oil is hydrophobic and once within the soil greatly reduces water movement both into the soil and from the bulk soil to plant roots (Raisbeck and Mohtadi 1974, Everett 1978). Because nutrient movement within the soil is dependent upon water movement, the hydro-phobic nature of oil-contaminated soil may decrease nutrient as well as water availability to plants.

SUMMARY

Within the prevailing coastal tundra macroclimate, the topographic position of a site causes the variation in environmental factors which in turn control the growth and distribution over the tundra surface of different plant species and growth forms. The complexes of controlling environmental factors were identified by indirect ordination. They are, in order of importance in explaining the overall variation of the vegetation, the complexes of soil moisture, soil anaerobicity, soil phosphate, and snow cover. The distribution of vegetation types, plant growth forms, and various vegetation and growth form attributes such as standing crop of above- and belowground material, productivity, foliage area, turn-over rates, and diversity are described in terms of the controlling environmental complexes.

The principal growth forms recognized at Barrow are single graminoids, erect forbs, deciduous shrubs, and bryophytes. Others that may be locally abundant are caespitose graminoids; cushion, mat and rosette forbs; evergreen shrubs; and lichens.

Dry, exposed sites with little snow cover usually contain a preponderance of caespitose graminoids and lichens. They may also have evergreen and deciduous shrubs and cushion forbs. Mesic sites tend to have the most forbs but have an abundance of bryophytes and deciduous shrubs. Single graminoids are abundant over much of the tundra and are dominant in moist and wet sites along with bryophytes.

The distribution of plant growth forms within the tundra is related to structural and functional characteristics, such as leaf longevity, timing of leaf growth, location of perennating organs, location of stored nutrients, leaf resistance to water loss, photosynthetic rates, carbon and nutrient costs of making new leaf material, and the location of absorbing roots; to the availability or abundance of wind, water, light energy, heat, and inorganic nutrients; and to the influence of grazing animals.

A hypothetical scheme is presented for the major paths of plant succession in the Biome research area. The scheme is based on the thaw lake cycle, and the major vegetation types are seen as phases in the cycle. Plant colonization of stable surfaces may take only a few years, but the major vegetation types are generally long-lasting and change primarily in response to physical changes, such as microrelief and drainage, rather than in response to biological changes, as a result of competition.

Most human impacts upon tundra are within the range of natural perturbations, and their severity can be predicted from an understanding of the controls over ecosystem processes in natural tundra. Vehicle tracks that decrease canopy cover but do not destroy the vegetation or depress the soil surface create an impact comparable to intensive lemming grazing and the tundra may recover within a few years, or it may not. Disturbances that depress or destroy the vegetation mat initiate a series of changes in physical environment comparable to those occurring in the thaw lake cycle, and result in a corresponding recovery time, probably thousands of years.

7

The Soils and
Their Nutrients

P. L. Gersper, V. Alexander,
S. A. Barkley, R. J. Barsdate, and P. S. Flint

INTRODUCTION

Soils of the coastal tundra are formed under conditions of low temperature and high moisture. Mean annual precipitation is low, but relative humidity is high and drainage is impeded by permafrost; consequently, soil moisture content is high. Low temperatures and high moisture contents lead to the accumulation of organic matter. Because of the cold, impervious permafrost there are strong gradients of temperature and oxygen saturation within the thawed soil, but soil profile differentiation is retarded by the restriction of downward leaching and associated chemical transformations. Visibly distinct horizons are largely associated with organic matter, a product of organic input from primary production and physical redistribution via frost churning processes.

Overall, the soils of the coastal tundra at Barrow are similar to those of other tundra areas. In the data gathered by French (1974) on 27 soils from nine tundra sites studied during the International Tundra Biome effort, soil from a wet meadow of the Biome research area at Barrow falls near the middle of the range of values observed for most soil parameters, although this soil is somewhat wetter than those of most other circumpolar sites. In an analysis based on climate and soil factors (Rosswall and Heal 1975), five microtopographic units from the coastal tundra at Barrow (meadows, polygon troughs, rims and basins of low-centered polygons, and centers of high-centered polygons) were found to be similar to each other, but were also very similar to the meadow site on Devon Island and the moss turf and moss carpet on Signy Island, Antarctica. The soils near Barrow are different from those at Prudhoe Bay, 320 km to the east, which are calcareous and lower in organic matter (Douglas and Bilgin 1975, Everett and Parkinson 1977). The properties of the soils of the coastal tundra at Barrow are therefore the products of both the climatic factors common to arctic tundra regions and the specific geologic history of this area.

SOIL PHYSICAL PROPERTIES AND NUTRIENTS

Biological processes in the soils of the coastal tundra at Barrow occur in an organic-rich layer less than 50 cm thick that is thawed for less than four months of the year. This layer contains over 70% of the living biomass of the tundra ecosystem. In it, roots grow and take up nutrients and water, organic matter decomposes, invertebrates graze and prey upon one another, and lemmings burrow for summer protection from predators.

This shallow layer of thawed soil is the reservoir from which inorganic nutrients are initially supplied to the living organisms. Calcium, magnesium, potassium and sodium are all retained by the cation exchange complex, which is made up largely of humified soil organic matter. The organic matter itself contains the major pools of nitrogen and phosphorus. However, most of the available nitrogen is in the form of ammonium and is retained on the soil exchange complex, while most of the available phosphorus is bound to iron or aluminum ions. The pools of available nutrients are highly variable, both spatially, because of the different kinds of soils associated with the different microtopographic landforms, and temporally, in response to fluctuations in environmental conditions. The underlying permafrost affects the nutrient supply through its effects on temperature gradients in the thawed soil and by isolating large quantities of nutrients contained in the frozen soil.

Organic Matter

The predominant characteristic of the soils is their high proportion of organic matter. More than 95% of the total organic matter in the terrestrial tundra ecosystem is below the ground surface, and one-third is in the upper 10 cm of soil, where biological activity is concentrated. The large amounts of organic matter impose a particular structure on the soil, influence the flux of moisture, oxygen and heat, and modify the chemical properties, particularly in the cation exchange complex. The large proportion of organic matter in these soils has a strong effect on the nutrient supply, as is typical for arctic tundra soils (Babb and Whitfield 1977, Chapin and Van Cleve 1978).

Carbon and nitrogen, in an average ratio of 20:1, make up from 10 to 40% of the total soil weight (Figure 7-1). Total carbon contents in the upper 15 cm of soil typically range from about 12,000 to 16,000 g m^{-2} but may be less than 10,000 g m^{-2} in comparatively warm, nutrient-rich, wet Pergelic Cryaquepts of polygon troughs, where decomposition rates are high.

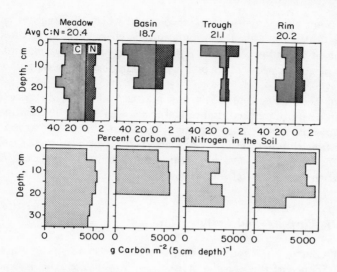

FIGURE 7-1. *The percentage of carbon and nitrogen in soils from different tundra microtopographic units, including meadows, basins of low-centered polygons, polygon troughs, and rims of low-centered polygons.*

In nearly all the soils, organic matter in the surface horizons is mostly fibric; the degree of decomposition increases with depth. Fibric organic matter includes slightly decomposed, reddish- to yellowish-brown fibrous materials whose generic characteristics can be recognized and which are usually interlaced by an abundance of living roots and rhizomes. Live belowground plant parts averaged 660 g m^{-2} in 1972, most of it in the upper 10 cm (Dennis et al. 1978). Fibric materials are commonly associated with wet meadow and polygon trough soils, but such materials rarely dominate the entire soil profile.

Sapric inclusions of black to dark reddish-brown, generically unidentifiable, fibrous to granular organic materials which disintegrate completely under the mildest mechanical manipulation are commonly found below the surface horizon. In the better drained, more highly oxidized soils such as are found on the tops of high-centered polygons and the rims of low-centered polygons, highly decomposed sapric organic matter may predominate throughout the entire active layer and continue down into the permafrost.

Hemic materials, those of intermediate decomposition, represent the most common form of organic matter in the soils. These generally range in color from dark grayish-brown to dark brown, and in nearly all cases identifiable plant components can be recognized which disintegrate only after considerable mechanical manipulation. Such materials commonly dominate the entire soil profile in basins of low-centered polygons and in some of the large, very low relief orthogonal polygons of mesic and wet meadows.

Differences in the amount of organic matter over lateral distances of only 1 m can be more marked than differences with depth. In an apparently uniform area of wet non-polygonal terrain, the organic carbon in two soil profiles sampled only a meter apart differed by a factor of 2. However, differences between microtopographic units are generally 1.5 to 2 times greater than variations within these units.

Bulk Density, Porosity, and Texture

The bulk density of a soil has a strong effect on heat conduction and temperature, depth of thaw, soil water content and movement, soil porosity and air content, and the penetration of roots. Bulk densities in the soils of the coastal tundra at Barrow range from about 0.05 to about 1.50 g cm^{-3}. Differences in bulk density (D_b) along a microtopographic gradient are strongly associated with the percentage of organic carbon (C_{org}) present:

$$C_{org}(\% \text{ by weight}) = 1.1 - 57.15 \log(D_b) \qquad r = 0.93, n > 200$$

The lowest bulk densities are found in surface horizons, which have high contents of fibric organic matter, live and dead roots and moss (Figure 7-2). Within the thawed layer, soils of wet and mesic meadows have bulk densities that range from moderately high to low, with a tendency toward increasing bulk density with increasing wetness. Rims of low-centered polygons and centers of high-centered polygons have soils that range in bulk density from low to intermediate, depending on the nature

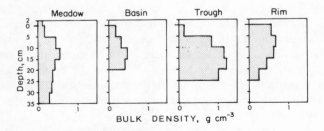

FIGURE 7-2. *Bulk density of soils from four different microtopographic units.*

of the soil formed before elevation of the rims and centers. Soils of the basins of low-centered polygons have low bulk densities. The general increase in bulk density between soils of basins and rims of these microtopographic units is partly due to the more highly decomposed organic matter in the rims and partly because the rims generally contain a higher content of fine-textured mineral matter. The relatively low content of organic matter in the Cryaquept soils found in most polygon troughs results in high bulk densities, although some soils in the troughs are highly organic, with correspondingly low bulk densities. The highest bulk densities of the coastal tundra at Barrow are generally encountered in the sandy soils along stream margins.

The bulk density of a tundra soil, as it reflects mineral content and water-holding capacity, is an important determinant of the depth of thaw (Gersper and Challinor 1975). Under similar moisture regimes, mineral soils generally thaw more deeply than organic soils because of their higher bulk density and consequent increased heat conduction. However, soils with low bulk density also tend to have high moisture content, which is also associated with deeper thawing. Although the variables are strongly covariant, multiple regression analysis suggests that bulk density alone accounts for 35% of the variation in thaw depth, while moisture content accounts for an additional 31%.

The soils are highly porous, with a range of porosity from 50 to 65% for mineral layers, increasing to more than 90% for organic layers (Figure 7-3). Thus, these soils are more porous than mineral soils of temperate regions, which range from 30 to 60% porosity (Hausenbuiller 1974).

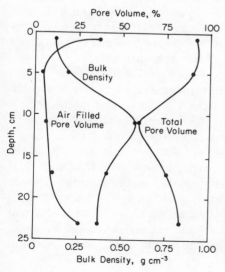

FIGURE 7-3. *Bulk density, percentage total pore volume, and percentage air-filled pore volume in soil of a moist meadow.*

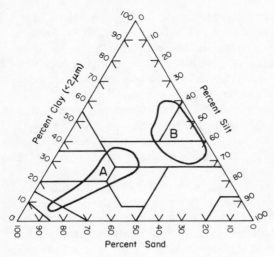

FIGURE 7-4. *Particle size distribution and texture of mineral horizons in soils from A) Aeric Pergelic Cryaquepts on sloping areas marginal to Footprint Creek (10 samples), and B) Histic Pergelic Cryaquepts and Pergelic Cryohemists in a moist meadow (86 samples). Textural diagram after Soil Survey Staff (1975).*

The very small particles and particle aggregates of sapric soils form a rather dense and relatively impermeable mass that is slow to transmit moisture or oxygen (Figure 7-3). Because of their highly aggregated condition, sapric soils have many small pores and retain large quantities of moisture, even in topographic positions that would normally be considered xeric. Further, the porosity of sapric soils may be high, especially in surface horizons, because of repeated ice segregation, which produces lenticular openings. However, vertical permeability is usually very low. In comparison, fibric materials are of low density and have a very large proportion of interconnected, free-draining macropores that permit rapid movement of air and water in all directions. Soils on low topographic positions have fibric surface horizons that remain filled with circulating water throughout much of the summer. Horizons containing hemic material have intermediate soil moisture properties.

Soils with high contents of clay- and silt-sized mineral materials generally tend to have very fine pores and consequently very low permeability to air and water. Mineral layers in soils of the coastal tundra at Barrow are generally of this type, although they are often admixed with porous organic matter and thus are more permeable. The dominant textures of the mineral horizons (Figure 7-4) are silty clay and silty clay loam, with some clays and a few soils of coarser texture. Mineral fractions of Histosols tend to be finer textured (silty clays) than the Inceptisols, which are silty clay loams, although Cryaquepts of polygon troughs and frost boils commonly have the finest textures. Sandy-textured and loam-textured soils are not common at the Biome research area, and appear to be restricted to alluvial positions and the stream banks along Footprint Creek.

TABLE 7-1 *Seasonal Averages of the Percentage of Moisture, Water Potential, and Redox Potential in the Upper 15 cm of Soil, and Soil Temperature During Summer 1972.*

Micro-topographic unit	Dominant vegetation type	Percent moisture (g water gdw⁻¹)	Water potential (bars)	Redox potential (mV)	Temperature, 10 cm (°C)
Slough	VII	292	ND	306	8.1
Meadow	IV	331	−0.009	405	6.3
Rim	II or III	118	−0.044	511	7.3
Basin	VI	208	−0.033	423	7.7
Trough	V	265	−0.008	430	8.0
Top	I or II	158	−0.041	487	6.5

Soil Moisture and Aeration

Because of their very high content of organic matter and related high porosity, soils of the Biome research area have a high capacity to hold water. Field moisture contents range to over 1000% dry weight. However, the extreme variability in bulk density and porosity makes expression of soil moisture content on the basis of volume, rather than weight, more useful. In terms of soil volume, *maximum* moisture content in the upper 15 cm of meadow soils averaged 47% during the summers of 1970 and 1971. The underlying mineral layers ranged between 55 and 60% by volume. In these soils the *minimum* moisture content in the upper 15 cm averaged 67% in 1970 and 65% by volume in 1971. During the summers of 1970–73 the soils in much of the nonpolygonal terrain and in the lower-lying areas of polygonized terrain remained almost completely water-saturated within approximately the 5-to 15-cm depth interval. On polygonized terrain, in the relatively warm and dry summer of 1972, only the centers of high-centered polygons had moisture contents of less than 65% by volume in the upper 10 cm of soil on 31 July.

In 1972, moisture tension was measured using tensiometers in soils along a moisture gradient in the polygonal terrain (Table 7-1). In the driest soils, on the top of a high-centered polygon and on a polygon rim, water potentials averaged over the 0- to 5-cm depth interval were never lower than −0.070 bar during the summer (Figure 7-5). Potentials at 0- to 5-, 5- to 10- and 10- to 15-cm depth intervals at a given location were similar, but with a tendency toward progressively higher potentials with depth. The low water potentials in the soil indicate that most of the water present is available for plant uptake. Variations with time were similar at all three depth intervals and within each microtopographic unit across the entire moisture gradient (Figure 7-5). Despite the general wetness,

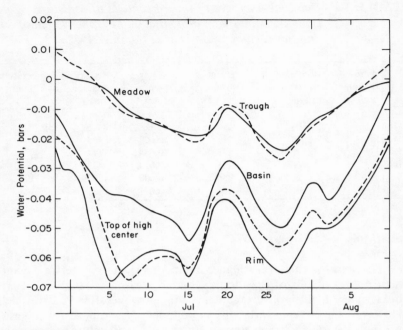

FIGURE 7-5. *Seasonal courses of soil water potential in the upper 5 cm of soils of different microtopographic units in 1972.*

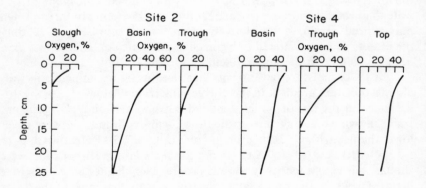

FIGURE 7-6. *Average oxygen saturation in soils of different microtopographic units in 1972. (Benoit, unpubl.)*

moisture regimes are sufficiently influenced by microtopography to result in differences in species composition and physiognomy of the above-ground plant community, and in the soil microflora and fauna.

Oxygen concentrations at 10 cm ranged from 40% saturation to 0%, with the highest values found in the tops of high-centered polygons and the lowest in the wet sloughs (Figure 7-6). As the soil thaws, the depth to fully anaerobic conditions follows the thaw front downward, and by mid-season oxygen saturation is zero at about 25 cm depth. Although the soil continues to thaw, the aerated layer in the wet meadow soil seldom exceeds 25 cm because oxygen flux is impeded by high bulk density and water saturation in the mineral horizons (Benoit, unpubl.).

Alternating organic and mineral layers in the soil can produce a very complicated pattern of air and water movement through the active layer (Figure 7-3). Histosols generally lack a continuous mineral layer and continue to drain freely as thaw progresses. These soils are unsaturated in the upper part, permitting air movement within the soil, except in wet summers. In contrast, the mineral layers of Inceptisols restrict drainage, and these soils often remain at or near saturation throughout the summer. Air movement is restricted, and reducing conditions prevail in and below the mineral layers.

Cation Exchange Capacity and Acidity

The cation exchange capacity (CEC) of the soils is dominated by the organic fraction. Thus there is a strong correlation between CEC and organic carbon content. For example, within the upper 30 cm of meadow soils this relationship was:

$$CEC[meq(100\ g)^{-1}] = 2.15\ C_{org}\ (\%) + 15.54 \qquad r = 0.97,\ n = 86.$$

This equation indicates that the mineral clay fraction, which makes up an average of 27% by weight within the upper 30 cm of these soils, contributes 15 milliequivalents (meq) per 100 grams of soil to the CEC, while the organic fraction, which averages approximately 20% carbon, contributes 40 meq $(100\ g)^{-1}$. These combine to give the average soil in the meadows a total CEC of 55 meq $(100\ g)^{-1}$, which is well above that of most mineral soils.

In general, poorly decomposed fibric organic matter contains relatively few phenolic hydroxyl and carboxyl groups, and thus contributes comparatively little CEC to soil horizons in which it occurs. On the other hand, well-humified sapric organic matter generally contains many such groups, and in many of the soils may be the main source of the CEC.

Cation exchange capacities ranged widely among soils of the differ-

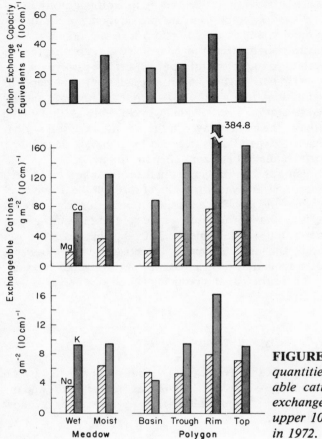

FIGURE 7-7. *Average quantities of exchangeable cations and cation exchange capacity in the upper 10 cm of the soils in 1972.*

ent microtopographic units. For example, average CEC within the upper 10 cm of soil in summer 1972 was approximately 50 meq $(100 \text{ g})^{-1}$ in wet meadows and 69 meq $(100 \text{ g})^{-1}$ in mesic meadows. In polygonized terrain the averages were 44, 70, 89 and 91 meq $(100 \text{ g})^{-1}$ in the troughs, rims, basins and tops of high-centered polygons, respectively.

Variations in CEC among the microtopographic units were different when measured on the basis of volume rather than weight of soil, because of variations in bulk density. For example, soils of polygon troughs had a CEC of approximately 27 meq $(100 \text{ cm})^{-3}$ in the upper 10 cm compared to 25 meq $(100 \text{ cm})^{-3}$ in the upper 10 cm of polygon basins (Figure 7-7), even though the CEC on a weight basis in the soil of the basins was more than double that of the troughs [89 versus 44 meq $(100 \text{ g})^{-1}$]. Thus, actual concentrations of nutrients in the soils of troughs were higher than those of basins (Figure 7-7) because of the much higher bulk density of the trough soils.

Soil pH values from the different microtopographic units generally range from 5.1 to 5.7; thus these soils are moderately to strongly acid by agricultural standards. They are, however, less acid than those of peat bogs, which have pH values between 3.0 and 4.0 (Moore and Bellamy 1974). The high concentrations of H^+ ions in the soil tend to favor their adsorption by the cation exchange complex, and decrease the adsorption of metallic cations.

Soil acidity varies both spatially and temporally, is generally constant with depth, and shows some association between the more basic values and high plant production. Polygon troughs and the rims of low-centered polygons have relatively high soil pH values of 5.6 to 5.7, while the basins of low-centered polygons and the centers of high-centered polygons with peaty soils are the most acid sites, with soil pH values of 5.1 to 5.3. In studies of vehicle track disturbance the soil pH in the depressions where vegetative growth was abundant was 5.8, while in the control area it was 5.5 (Challinor and Gersper 1975). A drop in the mean soil pH in the mesic meadow from 5.4 to 5.1 between 1970 and 1971 was associated with a 20% drop in primary production (Dennis et al. 1978).

Major Cations

Over the range of microtopographic units from wet meadows to tops of high-centered polygons, the quantity of exchangeable cations per square meter in the upper 10 cm of the soil ranges from 3.7 to 7.9 g Na, 4.4 to 16.2 g K, 19.6 to 76.9 g Mg and 71.3 to 384.5 g Ca. The rims of low-centered polygons have the largest pools of all cations; however, potassium is equally abundant in the centers of high-centered polygons. Wet meadows are lowest in all cations except potassium, which is lowest in the basins of low-centered polygons. Mesic meadows are generally richer than wet meadows, and troughs are richer than basins in exchangeable cations.

Patterns of cation concentration in soil solution (Figure 7-8) differ sharply from those of exchangeable pools. Soil solutions used for the analysis of metallic cations were obtained using porous ceramic cups in situ and a mild suction of -0.75 bar. High cation concentrations in the soil solution of polygon basins and the tops of high-centered polygons occur with low plant production while low concentrations in the troughs occur with high plant production (Webber 1978). The properties of the soil solution fluctuate during the summer and range widely between years in response to thaw, precipitation, evapotranspiration, surface and subsurface flow, nutrient uptake by roots, and microbial activity.

TABLE 7-2   *Mean (x̄) and Coefficient*
of Variation (C_v) for
Cations (meq m⁻²) in Soil
Solution Extracted from
the Upper 15 cm of Soil
in Moist Meadow, 1970
(n = 60) and 1971 (n = 90)

	1970		1971	
Cation	x̄	C_v (%)	x̄	C_v (%)
Calcium	48.2	17.0	59.4	13.6
Magnesium	40.9	12.2	58.4	16.7
Potassium	2.7	66.1	3.7	30.6
Sodium	62.8	11.1	79.7	6.3

The concentrations of soluble cations change markedly between years as well as throughout the season. Sampling in a mesic meadow site in 1970 and 1971 revealed changes in yearly averages up to 40% (Table 7-2). Averages of every nutrient were higher in 1971 than in 1970. The summer of 1971 was warmer and wetter than 1970. This may have produced an increase of mineral nutrients in solution due to increased mineralization of organic materials, or increased leaching of canopy and litter

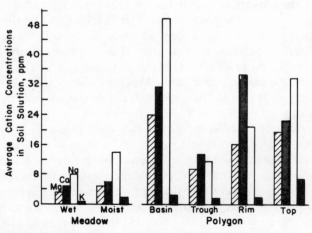

FIGURE 7-8. *Average concentrations of cations in solution extracted from the upper 10 cm of soils in 1972.*

as a result of more precipitation. Whenever soil solution was sampled immediately following precipitation, large increases in nutrient concentrations were observed, suggesting that leaching of aboveground plant materials may be a major factor in nutrient transport.

Of the major cations, only potassium occurs to a significant extent in a mineral form in soils. The clay mineral illite, which contains fixed potassium, is the dominant mineral in the clay fraction of the soils of the Barrow tundra (Douglas and Tedrow 1960). However, the bulk of the available potassium and almost all of the other metallic cations are bound on the exchange complex and are supplied from it to the soil solution.

Nitrogen and Phosphorus

The distribution of nitrogen and phosphorus is similar in that these elements are found mainly in the organic form in soil. The pools of nitrogen and phosphorus of the moist meadows were calculated for the upper 10 cm of the soil (Table 7-3), since this portion is relatively homogeneous and includes more than 75% of the live root biomass (Dennis et al. 1978) and microbial biomass (Chapter 8). A total of 432 g N m^{-2} was found in

TABLE 7-3 *Pools of Nitrogen and Phosphorus (g m^{-2} 10 cm^{-1}) in the Upper 10 cm of Soil in Moist Meadow*

	Nitrogen	Phosphorus
Living	**9**	**1.3**
Belowground plant parts	7	0.6
Microbial organisms		0.70
Bacteria (20 gdw)	2.3	0.64
Fungi (5.5 gdw)	0.1[1]	0.1[1]
Organic matter	**420**	**15.5**
Hydrolyzable N (6N HCl 15 hr)	336	
Readily hydrolyzable N (0.5N HCl 0.5 hr)	1.4	
Dissolved organic	0.2	0.0126
Inorganic matter	**3.0**	**7.8**
Resin-extractable P		0.0161
Dissolved inorganic	0.014	0.0006
NH$_4^+$	0.013	
NO$_3^-$	0.0006	
Total	**432**	**24.6**

[1]Nitrogen and phosphorus in fungi (Laursen 1975).

TABLE 7-4 *Exchangeable Ammonium Nitrogen of a Typical Pergelic Cryohemist in Moist Meadow, 1973*

Depth (cm)	Bulk density (g cm^{-3})	Exchangeable ammonium	
		(meq 100 g^{-1})	(g m^{-2} cm^{-1})
0–5	0.191	1.006	0.269
5–10	0.656	0.350	0.321
10–15	1.043	0.424	0.620
15–20	0.479	0.480	0.322
20–25	0.600	0.753	0.634

Source: Flint and Gersper (1974).

the upper 10-cm section, with more than 95% bound in organic matter (Flint and Gersper 1974). The organic nitrogen can be divided into hydrolyzable and nonhydrolyzable fractions. The hydrolyzable fraction makes up 80% of the nitrogen in the soil organic matter, while the non-hydrolyzable fraction, which probably represents the most resistant core of the humus, makes up approximately 19.5%. Most of the remaining 0.5% is in the form of readily hydrolyzable nitrogen. This latter fraction is seasonally variable, indicating that it may be an integral part of the labile nitrogen in the system.

The nitrogen content of the living soil microorganisms is uncertain since separation of the organisms from the soil material is difficult. Fungal biomass and nitrogen content of the fungi were both determined (Laursen 1975), but bacterial biomass may exceed fungal biomass by an order of magnitude (Chapter 8), and no measurements exist of the nitrogen concentrations in the natural bacterial population.

The inorganic nitrogen in the soil is almost entirely in the form of ammonium ions bound on the cation exchange complex, and in equilibrium with the ammonium and other cations in the soil solution. The vertical distribution of exchangeable nitrogen affects its availability to plants and soil organisms. Although the concentration of ammonium on a weight basis is highest in the surface 5 cm (Table 7-4), the amount in the 10-cm rooting zone is only a little more than 25% of the total exchangeable pool in the active layer (Flint and Gersper 1974). Thus, a large fraction of the nitrogen present in exchangeable form is not physically accessible to most of the plants or microorganisms.

Soil solutions for nitrogen and phosphorus determinations were obtained from sample cores using pressure up to 9.4 bars (Barèl and Barsdate 1978). The soil solution contains dissolved and colloidal organic nitrogen, ammonium, and nitrate, in approximately 10:1.0:0.1 ratios. Most of the organic nitrogen in solution is readily decomposed, but plant uptake is from the inorganic nitrogen in the soil solution, and diffusion processes act primarily within this pool. The average concentrations of ammonium and nitrate in the soil solution in 1973 were 145 and 6 ppb, respectively (Barèl and Barsdate, unpubl.).

The total amount of nitrogen in the soils of the drier microtopographic units is commonly greater than 500 g m^{-2} (10 cm)$^{-1}$, slightly more than in the moist meadow soils, but the amounts of exchangeable nitrogen are similar. The average nitrate concentration in the soil solution of the polygon rim was 5.9 ppm NO_3-N in 1973, almost three orders of magnitude higher than the nitrate concentration in the wet meadow. The ammonium concentration on the rim was 750 ppb, also higher than in the meadow. The ratios of ammonium to nitrate in the soil solution change from 10:1 in the moist meadow to 0.1:1 on the rims of low-centered polygons. Nitrate is also found in greater concentrations than ammonium in the centers of high-centered polygons with mineral soil, but ratios drop below 1 in the other, slightly moister high-centered polygons with peaty soil and in mesic meadows.

The total soil phosphorus in the upper 10 cm of the moist meadows is approximately 25 g m^{-2}, of which two-thirds is in organic form (Table 7-3). Dissolved organic phosphorus is not believed to be available to plant roots but it is apparently susceptible, like dissolved organic nitrogen, to rapid hydrolysis. The ratio of dissolved to total organic phosphorus is very low, 0.0008:1 (Barèl and Barsdate 1978), even when compared to that for organic nitrogen (0.002:1). The organic phosphorus contributed by soil microorganisms has not been determined, but calculations based on decomposer biomass and species composition indicate that the standing crop of decomposers ties up a far larger fraction of soil phosphorus than nitrogen, 3% vs 0.4%. Thus, fluctuations in microorganism populations may have a significant effect on the overall distribution of phosphorus.

The fraction of the inorganic phosphorus that is in equilibrium with the soil solution appears very small when measured by extraction onto an anion-exchange resin (Barèl and Barsdate 1978), and the concentration of inorganic phosphorus in the soil solution is correspondingly low, averaging 10 ppb in 1973. However, chemical fractionation of the inorganic phosphorus from the moist meadow soils indicated that a large fraction is extractable under reducing conditions (Chang and Jackson 1957). This fraction may contribute considerably more to the exchangeable and dissolved pools of phosphorus under anaerobic, reducing conditions such as exist in the soils of wet meadows and polygon troughs than is apparent in laboratory analyses performed under aerobic conditions (Khalid et al. 1977). Most of the available phosphorus is bound to iron or aluminum ions (Prentki 1976).

On the rims of low-centered polygons and the tops of high-centered polygons with mineral soil, total phosphorus in the surface horizon is somewhat more abundant than in the wet meadow soils, but a greater fraction of the total phosphorus is in an organic form, and inorganic phosphorus is less abundant. The inorganic phosphorus of the drier site is mainly NH_4-F soluble, and considered to be readily available to plants (Barèl and Barsdate 1978). Increased availability of phosphorus is also indicated by a higher average value of resin-extractable phosphorus (22.6 mg m^{-2}) in the drier soils. However, the amount of inorganic phosphorus in solution is lower than in the wet meadow. On the tops of high-centered polygons the phosphate in the soil solution drops from 8 to 4 ppb at the boundary between organic and mineral soil, 4 cm below the soil surface (Barèl and Barsdate 1978).

INPUTS AND OUTFLOWS
OF NITROGEN AND PHOSPHORUS

The major input of nitrogen to the soils of the coastal tundra at Barrow is through the fixation of atmospheric nitrogen by blue–green algae, either alone or in symbiotic relationships. The inorganic ions in precipitation are the major sources of phosphorus and also add to the pool of inorganic nitrogen. Inorganic forms of nitrogen move in the soil by diffusion, but phosphorus ions are relatively immobile. Losses of nitrogen and phosphorus, in both inorganic and dissolved or suspended organic forms, occur through surface and subsurface flow. Nitrogen can also be lost through reduction to gaseous forms, nitrogen oxides and nitrogen gas. Even though a large portion of the tundra surface is covered with lakes and small ponds, movement of nutrients between the terrestrial and aquatic subsystems seems to be restricted to the period of snowmelt, when there is a small net loss of nitrogen and phosphorus to the ponds (Prentki et al. 1980).

Nitrogen Fixation

Fixation supplies the bulk of the nitrogen input to the terrestrial system, although amounts entering by this pathway vary markedly between microtopographic units. Measured rates increase from 8 to 180 mg N m^{-2} yr^{-1} along a moisture gradient from dry polygon rims to wet meadows.

Blue–green algae are the most important agents of nitrogen fixation. These algae, primarily *Nostoc commune*, occur as free-living or moss-associated filaments, or symbiotically in lichens of several genera. Although *Peltigera aphthosa* is the most abundant nitrogen-fixing lichen,

Peltigera canina, Lobaria linita, Nephroma spp., *Solorina* spp., *Stereocaulon* spp. and other *Peltigera* spp. also occur in significant amounts. With ambient temperatures of about 15°C nitrogenase activity ranges from 4.5 μg N gdw^{-1} hr^{-1} in *Stereocaulon tomentosum* to 41.5 μg N gdw^{-1} hr^{-1} in *Nostoc commune*. Nitrogen fixation per unit of biomass in the *Peltigera* species is high (8.8 to 25.8 μg N gdw^{-1} hr^{-1} at 15°C), considering the large proportion of its biomass contributed by fungus and thus not directly involved in nitrogen fixation.

Heterotrophic bacteria also may contribute to nitrogen fixation (Chapter 8). *Azotobacter* was isolated from a mesic meadow, but the numbers were low, 10^2 to 10^3 cells (gdw soil)$^{-1}$, and nitrogen fixation within the soil was consistently less than 1 μg N m^{-2} hr^{-1}. If heterotrophic bacteria are indeed active fixers of nitrogen in the soils, their activity is very low compared with the free-living and symbiotic blue–green algae of lichens.

No significant nitrogen fixation was found to be associated with any higher plants (Alexander and Schell 1973). Alpine tundra soils in central Alaska, however, have a substantial input of nitrogen from vascular species, including *Dryas* spp., *Lupinus, Astragalus* and *Oxytropis* spp., which are abundant in the alpine sites and in the Prudhoe Bay region but absent or rare in the coastal tundra at Barrow.

Similar constellations of organisms have been found dominant in the nitrogen-fixation regimes of other tundra sites (Alexander 1974, 1975, Jordan et al. 1978). *Nostoc commune* is a cosmopolitan species that is important in nitrogen fixation in a variety of natural ecosystems (Fogg et al. 1973). In particular, the *Nostoc*-moss association, which has drawn much attention in circumpolar studies, also appears to be an important feature of the grassland ecosystem (Vlassak et al. 1973).

Biomass of Nitrogen-Fixing Organisms

Nitrogen fixation rates for any location on the tundra depend primarily on the distribution and biomass of the nitrogen-fixing organisms and secondarily on the various abiotic variables that influence nitrogenase activity within organisms. The distribution of nitrogen-fixing organisms is correlated with moisture regime and vegetation. *Nostoc commune* occurs in wet environments, and is especially abundant in wet, low-lying meadows, where it may occur as extensive mats floating over the moss layer. One low-lying area contained 19.5 g *Nostoc* m^{-2}, 10% of the standing crop (Williams et al. 1978). Additionally, *Nostoc* forms an epiphytic or intercellular association with various genera of mosses.

The nitrogen-fixing lichens, primarily *Peltigera aphthosa*, tend to occur at intermediate moisture levels such as the slopes between troughs and rims, although *P. aphthosa, P. canina* and *Lobaria linita* are common in wet meadows, as well as in depressions between clumps of *Eriophorum vaginatum* in better-drained meadows (Williams et al. 1978). In the microtopographic units that are more favorable for lichens, such as the rims of low-centered polygons, a total lichen biomass as high as 180 g m⁻² has been observed; however, only about 2 g m⁻² of this is capable of nitrogen fixation. Thus the biomass of nitrogen-fixing organisms increases from dry to wet areas, with the major fraction made up of free-living or moss-associated *Nostoc*, which is confined to wet areas, and the remainder composed of nitrogen-fixing lichens, which are relatively more abundant in the mesic areas.

Environmental Controls on Nitrogen Fixation

In laboratory studies the principal environmental factors modifying rates of nitrogenase activity in nitrogen-fixing organisms are temperature, moisture, light and oxygen tension. Response of *Nostoc* and *Peltigera* to climatic factors, and to some inorganic nutrients, is described by Alexander et al. (1978). Diurnal temperature fluctuations of 10 °C for the rim of a low-centered polygon and 15 °C for a polygon trough were recorded in July 1972. Thus rather high temperatures can be attained in the immediate vicinity of the maximum algal biomass. Fluctuations in both light and temperature appeared to exert a strong influence on field rates of nitrogen fixation (Alexander et al. 1974).

The most critical environmental factor in determining the rate of nitrogen fixation is moisture. The response of *Peltigera* to moisture (Figure 7-9) shows that saturation of nitrogenase activity does not occur until the moisture content exceeds 250% of dry weight (Alexander et al. 1978), a response similar to that shown by other nitrogen-fixing lichens (Kallio 1973). Although no similar data exist for *Nostoc*, it shows no activity at all when dry, but rapidly resumes activity when moistened above 100% dry weight. The nitrogen-fixing organisms appear to be well adapted to handle periodic desiccation, and are able to make effective use of moisture whenever it is available.

On a season-long basis, highest inputs from nitrogen fixation occur on wet, mossy areas. In drier areas, seasonal nitrogenase activity is limited by available moisture (Alexander et al. 1974), and overall rates are somewhat lower during summers with low rainfall. Extremely wet areas devoid of moss cover also have very low rates of nitrogen fixation. In dry summers, such as 1972, there was a decline in fixation in moderately moist areas as the season progressed and soil moisture declined. The total seasonal input from nitrogen fixation, integrated over an area comprising a variety of microtopographic units, was lower in 1972 (85 mg N m⁻²)

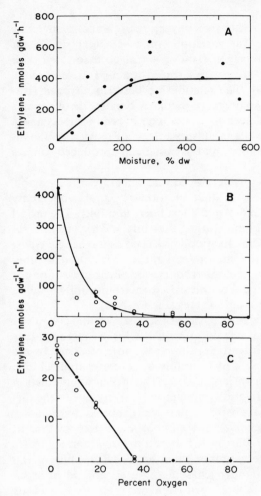

FIGURE 7-9. *Response of nitrogen fixation rates of* Peltigera aphthosa *to moisture (A) and oxygen concentration (B), and of* Nostoc commune *to oxygen concentration (C). (After Alexander et al. 1974 and Alexander 1978.)*

than in the wet summer of 1973 (119 mg N m^{-2}), the difference being due primarily to a higher rate of fixation in the relatively dry areas during the wetter year. These differences between years are considerably less than the differences between specific microtopographic units. For example, in the wetter summer seasonal input on the dry rim of a low-centered polygon was only 6.7 mg N m^{-2}, whereas in a nearby low, mossy area it was 150.4 mg N m^{-2}.

The response of *Nostoc commune* to oxygen tension is of special ecological interest, since the greatest nitrogenase activity of this organism occurs in wet, mossy areas, where these algae exist in extremely close association with mosses. In the water associated with the mosses, oxygen saturation may range from 5 to 24% over 24 hours (Alexander et al. 1974).

The strong inverse relationship between oxygen tension and nitrogenase activity (Figure 7-9) indicates the variation could be a very significant factor influencing rates of nitrogen fixation by algae associated with moss. Similar relationships have been described for a mire site in Sweden (Granhall and Selander 1973). The relationship between nitrogen fixation in lichens and oxygen is complex, particularly because there appears to be a strong interaction between light and oxygen requirements and a conflicting influence between the inhibitory effects of oxygen on the nitrogenase enzyme and the need for photosynthetically produced sources of energy.

A simple model, NFIXR, was developed that integrates the available laboratory measures and permits evaluation of their general applicability against field observations (Bunnell and Alexander, unpubl.). The model assumes that the influences of temperature, moisture and oxygen interact in a multiplicative fashion. Thus fixation is reduced as any single environmental control departs from the optimal range, even though other conditions may not be limiting. Seasonal courses of nitrogen fixation for specific genera can be predicted from measured environmental variables and compared with observed fixation rates (Figure 7-10).

Although actual magnitudes differ, the observed seasonal courses of nitrogen fixation in polygonal terrain at both the Biome research area and in a birch site at Kevo, Finland, are similar to those predicted by the model. Apparently, the measured relationships are broadly applicable to lichens and algae inhabiting a variety of sites. The inaccurate prediction of the magnitude of rates of fixation apparently is largely due to the difficulties in estimating biomass of the fixing organisms, particularly algae. Blue–green algae are relatively more important at Barrow than at Kevo, and the predictions for Barrow are therefore less accurate.

In light of the recent observation that non-heterocystous blue–green algae also contain the enzyme nitrogenase and are capable of nitrogen fixation under conditions of low oxygen (Kenyon et al. 1972, Stewart 1973), special interest centers on the ecology of these moss-associated algae. Present findings suggest that the majority of blue–green algal forms found in the moss layer may contribute to nitrogen fixation, and that estimates of nitrogen-fixing biomass based only on heterocystous algae may be greatly in error both in the wet, mossy layer and in soils.

There is no marked adaptation by the major nitrogen fixer, blue–green algae, to the arctic environment. The predominant nitrogen-fixing form, *Nostoc commune*, is found in the Antarctic and in all circumpolar tundra regions. Its temperature optimum is not greatly different from temperature optima for blue–green algae from temperate and tropical regions. Arctic lichens, however, appear to be rather well adapted. Nitrogenase activity of lichens recovers after freezing, with the rate of recovery depending on the length of time the lichens were kept frozen and the tem-

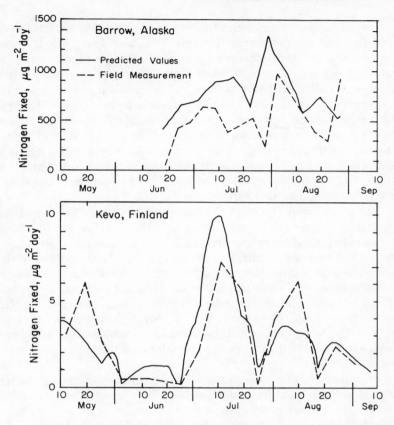

FIGURE 7-10. *Comparison of simulated and measured rates of nitrogen fixation at Barrow and at Kevo, Finland. (Bunnell and Alexander, unpubl.)*

perature at which recovery is taking place (Kallio and Alexander, un-publ., Kallio 1973). Rates of nitrogen fixation per unit of ground surface measured for arctic lichens are somewhat higher than those measured in other Biomes (Stewart 1969).

Inputs of Nitrogen and Phosphorus by Precipitation

Snowfall includes approximately 30% of the total nitrogen supplied by precipitation. Ammonium is the predominant form of nitrogen found in snowfall (Dugdale and Toetz 1961), although organic nitrogen has not been measured. The fraction of the inorganic nitrogen present as nitrate in snowfall declined from almost 30% to less than 10% between early September and late October of 1960 (Dugdale and Toetz 1961). Nitrite concentrations in fresh snow are extremely low, with an upper limit of about 1 μg N liter^{-1}. Comparisons of these values with nitrogen distribution in snow columns in May indicate that ammonium may be converted to nitrate in the snowpack. The concentration of inorganic nitrogen in both samples was similar, approximately 80 μg liter^{-1}, but the concentration of nitrate in the spring sample was higher by 15 μg N liter^{-1}. Concentrations of all three inorganic forms of nitrogen are higher in rain than in snow. The total concentration of nitrogen in summer precipitation is 340 μg liter^{-1}, of which ammonium contributes 75% and organic nitrogen less than 20% (Prentki et al. 1980).

The yearly input of nitrogen by precipitation was calculated by Barsdate and Alexander (1975) as 23.4 mg m^{-2}. However, revised values of total snowfall (Chapter 2) and the inclusion of organic nitrogen indicate that this value should be raised to 30.5 mg m^{-2} yr^{-1}. The majority of this input occurs during the summer. Although the amount of nitrogen in precipitation is very small in comparison with the total nitrogen pool, most of this nitrogen enters the system in inorganic forms and supplies an amount equal to 1% of the inorganic pool in the upper 10 cm of the soil. The nitrate content of precipitation seems particularly large from this viewpoint, more than seven times greater than the nitrate pool in the soil.

Precipitation is the major external source of phosphorus for the soil of the coastal tundra at Barrow (Table 7-5). As with nitrogen, phosphorus concentrations are lower in snow than in summer precipitation, 4.0 vs 7.9 μg liter^{-1} (Prentki et al. 1980); slightly more than half of the total input occurs during the summer. The inorganic phosphorus added by precipitation is equal to 6% of the labile phosphorus pool and is actually larger than the amount of dissolved inorganic phosphorus. The input of phosphorus in precipitation thus may be important in supplementing the small amounts of available phosphorus in the soil as well as in counteracting long-term losses to runoff.

Loss of Nitrogen and Phosphorus in Runoff

The major pathway for nitrogen outflow from the coastal tundra at Barrow is in surface runoff during the brief period of snowmelt (Table 7-5). The portion of winter precipitation that runs off during this time varies from as low as 51% at the Biome pond site to 95% at Esatkuat Creek (Miller et al. 1980). To produce a generalized nitrogen and phosphorus budget for the Barrow area, an intermediate runoff value of 83% was selected which corresponds to the spring runoff at the Biome pond

TABLE 7-5.   *Nitrogen, Phosphorus, and Water Budgets for the Coastal Tundra Land Surface*

	Inputs			Exports			
	Summer	Winter	Annual	Spring	Summer	Annual	Net
Nitrogen (mg m^{-2})							
Precipitation or runoff							
Ammonium	16.3	6.8	23.1	1.0	0.8	1.8	21.3
Nitrate	1.6	1.9	3.5	0.3	0.1	0.4	3.1
Nitrite	0.1	0.0	0.1	t	0.0	t	0.1
Organic*	3.8	ND	3.8	31.4	3.2	34.6	−30.8
Denitrification	—	—	—	ND	3.4	3.4	−3.4
Total without fixation	21.8	8.7	30.5	32.7	7.5	40.2	−9.7
N-fixation	69.5	ND	69.5	—	—	—	69.5
Total	91.3	8.7	100.0	32.7	7.5	40.2	59.8
Phosphorus (mg m^{-2})							
Precipitation or runoff							
Inorganic	0.46	0.16	0.62	0.21	0.01	0.22	0.40
Organic*	0.04	0.27	0.31	2.01	0.05	2.06	−1.75
Total	0.50	0.43	0.93	2.22	0.06	2.28	−1.35
Water (liters m^{-2})							
Precipitation or runoff	64	106	170	88	3	91	79
Dead storage and evapotranspiration	—	—	—	18	61	79	−79

t indicates trace.
ND indicates no data.
*Includes suspended particulates which are predominantly organic in origin.
Note: Concentrations of the various forms of nitrogen and phosphorus in precipitation and runoff were taken from Dugdale and Toetz (1961), Kalff (1965), Barsdate and Alexander (1975), Prentki (1976) and Prentki et al. (1980). Each input or export was calculated as the product of the appropriate nitrogen or phosphorus concentration and the water volume indicated in the table.

site in 1972. For the average winter precipitation of 106 mm (Chapter 2), this yields 88 mm of spring runoff, which is similar to the 85-mm June average discharge for Nunavak Creek for the period 1972-76 (U.S. Geological Survey 1971-76). During snowmelt 32.7 mg N m^{-2} is lost, more than the amount gained annually from precipitation. However, most of the nitrogen in the runoff is in organic form, and only a small fraction of the inorganic nitrogen present in the snowpack is lost. The retention of inorganic nitrogen from the snowpack is remarkable, since meltwater concentrations early in the snowmelt period range as high as 214 μg N liter^{-1}, almost twice as high as found in the snowpack (Barsdate and Alexander 1975). However, ammonium and nitrate concentrations decline rapidly, and were below those in the snowpack by 18 June in 1973 (Figure 7-11).

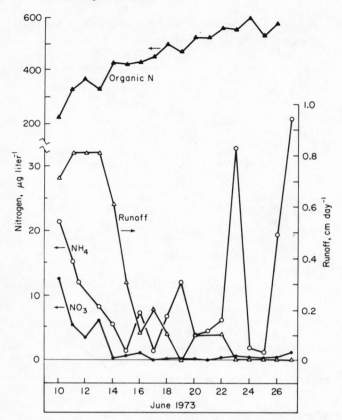

FIGURE 7-11. *Daily runoff and its concentration of NO₃-N, NH₄-N, and organic nitrogen during June 1973. (Data from Miller and Alexander, unpubl. and Barsdate and Alexander 1975.)*

The relatively low concentrations of nitrate at the start of snowmelt suggest that the high ammonium levels observed at this time are produced by leaching of animal excreta and plant material, rather than being the result of the concentration in the early meltwater of the ions already present in the snowpack. Leaching of biological material is also suggested by the high levels of organic nitrogen, since little or no organic matter is contributed by snowfall. During the summer, only an estimated 3 mm of the 64 mm of precipitation is lost in runoff. The loss to summer runoff is 7.5 mg N m⁻²—approximately 20% of the loss during snowmelt, or one-third of the input from precipitation during the summer.

The dynamics of phosphorus loss by runoff are somewhat different from those described above for nitrogen (Table 7-5). A phosphorus loss of 0.06 mg m^{-2} in summer runoff was calculated by the techniques used for nitrogen. Total phosphorus losses in runoff are 2.28 mg m^{-2} yr^{-1}, less than 0.01% of the total phosphorus in the upper 10 cm of soil. The phosphorus lost is mainly in the organic form, with particulate matter constituting almost 36% of the runoff loss (Prentki 1976). The high loss of phosphorus in particulate form is in contrast to nitrogen losses, where particulate organics make up less than 10% of the organic nitrogen fraction (Barsdate and Alexander 1975). The dissolved organic phosphorus lost in runoff constitutes approximately 10% of the pool of organic phosphorus in the soil solution. The major loss of phosphorus occurs during snowmelt, and the inorganic phosphorus lost during this period is greater than the input of inorganic phosphorus from snow.

The effects of precipitation and runoff on the nitrogen and phosphorus pools described above are integrated over a variety of microtopographic units. The effects of precipitation and, in particular, runoff differ among these units but quantitative assessment of this variation is difficult. In the absence of overland flow out of basins of low-centered polygons, these basins accumulate any nutrients that were present in the snowpack above them or on the inner sides of the polygon rims. Polygon troughs, on the other hand, are pathways for water flow, and may therefore be enriched in inorganic nitrogen and depleted of organic nitrogen and phosphorus by the meltwater. Drier areas retain a greater fraction of the water, and thus lose less of the inorganic nutrients associated with the rainfall or the dissolved or particulate organic matter that is assumed to be lost with the summer runoff.

Loss of Nitrogen in Gaseous Form

The soil nitrogen of the coastal tundra at Barrow is depleted by denitrification as well as by runoff losses. In anaerobic conditions such as are common in the soils, many bacteria can utilize nitrate rather than oxygen. This process can lead to denitrification, to the production of nitrogen oxide or nitrogen gas, to assimilation of nitrogen by the bacteria, or to the production of ammonia (Verstraete 1978). The population of facultative anaerobes in soils is large. Lindholm and Norrell (pers. comm.) measured the production of nitrite from nitrate in incubations at high nitrate levels. At 5 °C the microflora from a polygon trough showed average rates of nitrite production equivalent to the reduction of 430 μg N (g soil)$^{-1}$ day^{-1}. Samples from the tops of high-centered polygons showed a lower average rate, reducing 270 μg N (g soil)$^{-1}$ day^{-1}. The denitrifying bacteria isolated from the same soils were predominantly aerobic *Pseudomonas* spp. In a test of aerobically isolated bacteria from the upper 2 cm of a wet meadow soil, only 5 to 10% were capable of denitrification, although 68% were facultative anaerobes.

Direct measurements of denitrification in the field were made in midsummer. The rates of denitrification per gram of soil were six orders of magnitude lower than the rates of nitrate reduction measured *in vitro*. Although concentrations of nitrate were considerably lower in the field than in the laboratory incubations, 0.17 mg liter^{-1} vs 69 mg liter^{-1}, the extreme difference in rates suggests that most of the nitrate reduction that occurred in the laboratory tests did not result in denitrification. Focht (1978) discusses evidence that nitrate losses are significantly greater than denitrification when organic carbon is readily available and ammonium concentrations are low. The mean denitrification rate in the field results in a loss of 52 μg N m^{-2} day^{-1} from the surface of the wet meadow. The time course of denitrification in situ has not been established. However, the potential for nitrate reduction in soils from the wet meadow remained high for 65 days in 1972. If denitrification rates follow the same pattern, a net loss of 3.4 mg N m^{-2} yr^{-1} would occur, more than five times the amount of nitrate present in the upper 10 cm of the soil.

The rates of denitrification in other microtopographic units are generally lower than those in the wet meadow. No detectable denitrification occurred in field experiments on the top of a high-centered polygon. This is consistent with the low potential nitrate reduction rate in samples from similar microtopographic units. Nitrate concentrations in soils of tops of high-centered polygons are relatively high (2.5 ppm), indicating that the lack of denitrification activity here is not due to substrate limitation. In the mesic meadow, where nitrate concentrations were intermediate (0.33 ppm), denitrification rates in the field were 19 μg N$_2$ m^{-2} day^{-1}, only a third as high as those from the wetter area. Simultaneous addition of glucose and phosphate to these samples produced a more than four-fold increase, to 89 μg N$_2$ m^{-2} day^{-1}, over a 16-day incubation period. Munn (1973) also found a five-fold increase in apparent denitrification when a wet meadow was fertilized with urea.

Lack of denitrification in the soils from relatively dry polygon tops may be caused by the high aeration. Even though moisture contents remain high, the high pore volume and permeability of these soils may deter the development of anaerobic microenvironments. The strong response of denitrifying activity to glucose plus phosphate indicates that either energy or phosphorus is limiting under natural conditions in the mesic meadow. The stimulatory effect of easily decomposable organic matter on denitrification has been shown for temperate soils (Bremner and Shaw 1958). Lack of phosphorus can also inhibit the breakdown of organic matter (Chang 1940, Munevar and Wollum 1977), and this may occur in soils of the coastal tundra at Barrow. No analysis of the effect of pH on denitrification was made, but soil conditions are more acid than is optimal for denitrification in temperate soils (Bremner and Shaw 1958).

Overall, there is a net gain in the inorganic forms of both nitrogen and phosphorus because of the high level of conservation of incoming nutrients. Losses to denitrification do not eliminate the positive balance for inorganic nitrogen. When organic and inorganic forms are considered jointly, there is a net loss of both nitrogen and phosphorus from the combined activity of the abiotic processes of precipitation and leaching. However, the transformation of atmospheric nitrogen by nitrogen-fixing organisms into a form available to the rest of the system leads to a gain in total system nitrogen. Apparently, a net phosphorus loss has occurred, as has been documented in bog tundras of Glenamoy and Moor House (Heal et al. 1975, Moore et al. 1975).

TRANSFORMATION AND TRANSPORT OF NITROGEN AND PHOSPHORUS WITHIN THE SOIL

The preceding discussion presented the major pathways by which the total amounts of nitrogen and phosphorus in soils are increased or decreased. Changes in the locations and forms of these nutrients within the soil are also important in determining the supply available for biotic processes. The following section describes the major transformations of nitrogen and phosphorus that occur in the soils of the coastal tundra at Barrow and their transport within the soils.

Mineralization and Immobilization

Since plants take up nitrogen and phosphorus in inorganic forms and return these nutrients to the soil bound in organic matter, the process of remineralization must be a major source of inorganic nitrogen and phosphorus in any soil close to a steady state. Mineralization, the release of inorganic nutrients from dead organic material by microbial action, occurs whenever the concentrations of these nutrients in the organic material are greater than those necessary to support the production of new microbial biomass. As summarized by Frissel and Van Veen (1978), the net mineralization rate is controlled by the microbial decomposition rate, the concentrations of organic nitrogen and phosphorus in the material being decomposed and in the microbial biomass being produced, and the efficiency of the microbial population, i.e. the ratio of microbial biomass produced to organic matter decomposed. For any given ratio of mineralization to decomposition, the rate of release or uptake by the microflora will be affected by all the factors that control decomposition rate (Chapter 9).

The nutrient levels in the organic matter in soils, expressed by the ratios of carbon to nitrogen (C:N) and carbon to organic phosphorus

TABLE 7-6   *Ratios of Total Carbon to Organic Phosphorus in Soils of Different Microtopographic Units and Associated Vegetation Types and States of Organic Matter Decomposition*

Micro-topographic unit	Vegetation type	Decomposition state, top horizon	$C:P_o$ ratio				
			Depth in centimeters				Avg
			0–5	5–10	10–15	15–20	0–15
Meadow							
Wet	VI	Fibric	439	480	597	ND	517
Moist	IV	Fibric–hemic	448	531	681	1046	565
Basin	VI	Hemic–sapric	590	893	1072	1072	826
Trough	V	Fibric	505	346	352	322	385
Rim	III	Sapric	356	334	457	825	376
Top							
Low relief	I or II	Fibric	424	429	594	ND	472
High relief	I	Hemic	474	469	635	ND	507

ND indicates no data.

($C:P_o$), appear unfavorable for mineralization. The C:N ratio is close to 20:1 throughout the range of undisturbed soils in the tundra at Barrow. In general, C:N ratios below 20:1 produce net mineralization of nitrogen and ratios greater than 20:1 lead to the microbial transformation of inorganic nitrogen into organic forms, or immobilization (Frissel and Van Veen 1978). The ratios of carbon to phosphorus are calculated from organic rather than total phosphorus since a significant fraction of the total phosphorus is present in inorganic form rather than in the microbial substrate. The lowest $C:P_o$ ratios, which indicate the most favorable conditions for mineralization, are between 300 and 400:1 (Table 7-6). These values occur in the surface soils of all microtopographic units except rims and basins of low-centered polygons, and to depths of 10 to 15 cm in the polygon troughs. Ratios generally increase with depth, reaching values above 1000:1 in the 15- to 20-cm depth of rim soils and the 10- to 20-cm section of the basin soils. Cosgrove (1967) considered 0.2% (290:1) as the critical level of phosphorus in organic matter. Kaila (1949) found no net mineralization or immobilization of phosphorus from the decomposition of organic material with 0.3% P (194:1). It would appear that weak net immobilization of nitrogen and strong net immobilization of phosphorus should occur in the soils of the coastal tundra at Barrow.

However, mineralization must exceed immobilization in the soils since the net inputs are far too low to maintain the observed rates of plant production (Flint and Gersper 1974). Net mineralization could result from decreases in microbial efficiency as compared with values found in temperate soils. However, the tundra microflora appear relatively efficient when evaluated *in vitro*. Net mineralization might also be due to the microbial utilization of specific fractions of the organic matter containing above-average nutrient concentrations. The additional possibility is that tundra microorganisms produce biomass with concentrations of organic nitrogen and phosphorus below those found in temperate organisms. Some indication of this is given by the nitrogen levels of fungal hyphae, which were around 2% (Laursen 1975), considerably lower than the average levels of 5 to 6% reported from temperate regions (Cochrane 1958).

The efficiency of fungi (grams of fungal biomass produced per gram substrate degraded) is generally higher than that of bacteria (Alexander 1961), and the efficiency of bacteria decreases markedly under anaerobic conditions (Hattori 1973). Therefore, the anaerobic conditions that exist in the soils (Figure 7-6) may enhance mineralization by excluding fungi and decreasing bacterial efficiency. Low temperatures may also decrease microbial efficiency, since the microflora includes species which continue respiration, and therefore substrate degradation, at temperatures below the minimum for growth. Thus the environmental conditions of the soils lead to decomposer populations with average efficiencies lower than those of the same species in better drained and warmer soils.

Field and laboratory studies of nitrogen transformations support these conclusions. Maximum rates of immobilization are expected to occur during the early growing season, since overwintering, standing dead vegetation and fresh litter with C:N ratios from 30:1 to 60:1 (Flanagan and Veum 1974) have been incorporated into the soil surface, moisture from melting snow is plentiful, and temperatures are rising. Early season rates of nitrogen immobilization have been calculated from changes in the pools of available nitrogen and microbial biomass (Table 7-7). All these methods are indirect but agreement between them is reasonably good. The maximum rate observed was consistently around 0.025 g N m^{-2} cm^{-1} day^{-1} for the three organic horizons studied: moss, hemic and buried sapric.

Net rates of nitrogen mineralization in the field have been estimated by observing changes in size of nitrogen pools (Flint and Gersper 1974), in particular the buried sapric horizon of a wet meadow soil at 14 to 20 cm depth. Just after thaw there was a sudden increase in exchangeable ammonium in the horizon, which was interpreted as net mineralization. The computed rate, corrected for diffusion, is 0.077 g N m^{-2} cm^{-1} day^{-1}. Conditions were probably somewhat anoxic during the measurement period. Moreover, the horizon was cold, about 1 °C after thaw, indicating that nitrogen mineralization can occur at significant rates at very low temperatures. Phytotron experiments under anaerobic conditions showed a maximum mineralization rate of 0.075 g N m^{-2} cm^{-1} day^{-1} for a hemic horizon at 6°C, while the buried sapric horizon at 2°C gives an

TABLE 7-7   *Rates of Nitrogen Immobilization (g N m^{-2} cm^{-1} day^{-1})
in Soils During 1973, Estimated by Different Methods*

Horizon	Depth (cm)	Method			
		Change in pool size of NH_3-N*	Change in bacterial biomass†	Change in readily hydrolyzable N*	Change in fungal biomass**
Moss	0–2	0.0034 (15-29 June)	0.026 (10-29 June)	0.0019 (4-16 Aug)	0.006 (18-28 June)
Surface hemic	2–8	0.027 (15-19 June)	0.012 (29 June-27 July)	0.0093 (22-26 July)	
Subsurface sapric	14–20	ND	ND	0.026 (21-26 July)	ND

*From Flint (unpubl.).
†From Benoit (unpubl.).
**From Laursen and Miller (unpubl.).

estimated rate of 0.049 g m^{-2} cm^{-1} day^{-1}. The mineralization rates obtained in the phytotron experiments are close to those obtained in the field,
and both indicate that mineralization exceeds immobilization in the soil
during periods of rising temperature.

The mineralization of phosphorus was not studied in the field. However, simulations of decomposition and of nitrogen and phosphorus release in the soils (Barkley et al. 1978) indicate that anaerobic conditions
stimulate the net mineralization of phosphorus. Although anoxic conditions reduce the decomposition rate, the decrease in substrate breakdown
and gross phosphorus release is outweighed by the decrease in microbial
growth and phosphorus uptake per gram of organic matter decomposed.
Decreased microbial efficiency due to low temperatures will also increase
the release of phosphorus, as well as nitrogen, resulting from a given rate
of organic matter decomposition. However, Chapin et al. (1978) have
hypothesized that slow decomposition is the major limitation in the Barrow phosphorus cycle and that the mineralization rate is limited by the
microbial recovery rate following periodic population crashes.

The ratio of mineralization to decomposition may be enhanced by
selective degradation of high-nutrient substrates. The constancy of C:N
ratios exhibited by the soils over a wide range of decomposition states
and depths indicates that high-nitrogen material is not being selectively
degraded. However, for phosphorus, C:P_o ratios increase with depth,
and high C:P_o ratios are generally found in microtopographic units where
organic material shows the most advanced states of decomposition (Table

7-6). Decomposition may operate first on the material highest in phosphorus, leading to the release of mineralized phosphorus. If the phosphorus associated with the more resistant organic matter is insufficient to support microbial growth, decomposition of the accumulated organic matter might lead to lowering of phosphorus availability. Thus, the factors that have allowed the gradual accumulation of organic material, such as the occurrence of permafrost and the burial of the sapric organic layer beneath a relatively impermeable mineral horizon, may in fact be acting to increase the availability of phosphorus in the system. Further work would be necessary to evaluate this hypothesis.

Nitrification

Although nitrification neither produces nor removes available nitrogen from the soil, it affects nitrogen transport and utilization. The products of nitrification, nitrate and some small amounts of nitrite, are not involved in exchange processes with cation exchange sites. These anions are therefore much more mobile than ammonium in a system with high cation exchange capacity and move vertically and horizontally in the soil by diffusion and are lost by leaching or surface runoff. Nitrate, the major product of nitrification, is also available to denitrifying bacteria as an oxygen substitute, and may be reduced to dinitrogen gas or nitrous oxide and lost. In agricultural systems, nitrate is the form of nitrogen most readily taken up by plants, but in the tundra, as in natural grasslands (Porter 1975), ammonium may be equally preferred.

Nitrifying bacteria are scarce in the soils of the coastal tundra at Barrow. Munn (1973) attempted to measure the nitrification potential in soil samples taken from the moist meadows throughout the 1972 summer season. He detected no conversion of ammonium to nitrate in soil samples under aerobic conditions perfused with an ammonium sulfate solution at 23 °C and pH 5.6 to 6.3. No nitrifying bacteria were found among 200 aerobic isolates from the 0- to 2-cm horizon of the wet meadow soils, tested at 15 °C (Benoit, unpubl.). However, Viani (unpubl.), using the most probable number technique, was able to detect low numbers of nitrifying organisms in several soils from polygonal terrain. Norrell and Anderson (unpubl.) measured nitrification in the laboratory and reported average rates of 1.5 and 0.75 μg N (g soil)$^{-1}$ day^{-1} at 10 °C for dry and wet sites, respectively. These may represent the maximum potential ratesfor these soils, although alternate incubation conditions were not tested. Norrell and Anderson further indicated that temperature was a major limiting factor, nitrification being only occasionally detectable at temperatures below 5 °C. Efforts to isolate psychrophilic nitrifiers from the soils were unsuccessful, with no activity detected after 6 months of incubation at 2 °C.

While it is impossible to obtain absolute rates of nitrification from fluctuations in the amount of nitrate in the soil, it is possible to estimate rates that are equal to or usually less than the true rate. However, differences in concentration due to field variability or sample treatment may lead to overestimation. Since nitrification is the principal source of nitrate, an increase in the nitrate pool gives a minimum value for nitrification, disregarding small spatial transfers. The net rate observed is usually lower than the actual production of nitrate because some nitrate is denitrified or taken up by plants. Therefore, the most rapid rate of increase is used for the estimate. With this approach, data for the wet meadows from different investigators indicated nitrification rates in the surface 10-cm soil layer of 0.024 and 0.0045 mg N m^{-2} cm^{-1} day^{-1} in 1971 and 1973, respectively (Barèl and Barsdate, unpubl.). Rates in the deeper soil are consistently higher, 0.045 and 0.012 mg N m^{-2} cm^{-1} day^{-1} in 1971 and 1973. Denitrification in the 7- to 15-cm soil layer accounted for a total of 0.05 mg N m^{-2} day^{-1} at a similar site in 1972. The uptake of nitrate by the plants can also be added into the rates of change in the nitrate pool to produce another estimate of nitrification rate. In 1971, an experiment using ^{15}N indicated plant uptake rates in the wet meadow of 1.7 mg NO_3-N m^{-2} cm^{-1} day^{-1} (Munn, unpubl.). The apparent nitrification rates in the drier areas are much higher than those in the meadows. In 1973, the estimated rates of nitrification on the rims of low-centered polygons were 1.5 and 2.0 mg N m^{-2} cm^{-1} day^{-1} in the surface 10 cm and the buried organic layer (Barèl and Barsdate, unpubl.). The 1973 data indicate turnover times for the nitrate pools ranging from 5 to 25 days, with rates on the rims of low-centered polygons lower than those in the meadow soil.

Transport of Nitrogen and Phosphorus

Vertical transport of ammonium and nitrate ions in the soil solution should occur by diffusion if a concentration gradient exists with depth. The extremely wet conditions and low bulk densities in most soils of the coastal tundra at Barrow are favorable for diffusion, although it is slowed by low temperatures. The patterns of ammonium and nitrate concentrations with depth (Figure 7-12) suggest that the diffusive movement of ammonium during the summer of 1973 was into the silt loam mineral layer (8 to 16 cm), from both above and below. The diffusion gradient for nitrate, on the other hand, led to its movement into the surface organic layer (0 to 8 cm) from the mineral and buried peat material. In late September, concentrations of both ammonium and nitrate were highest in the mineral layer, leading to diffusion outward from this layer.

Preliminary results using ^{15}N document that ammonium is trans-

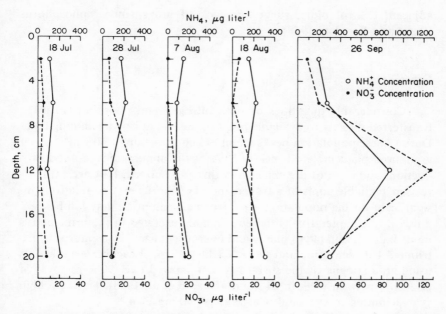

FIGURE 7-12. *Profiles of NH₄⁺ and NO₃⁻ concentrations in the soil solution from the moist meadow.*

ported from depths of 20 cm or more to the surface of a wet meadow soil during the growing season. In 1973 detectable transport began on about 20 July and continued into September. During this period the maximum net rate of flux from the well-decomposed organic layer into the mineral layer above it was about 0.049 g m^{-2} day^{-1}. At this rate at least 2 g N m^{-2} could be transferred from the subsoil to the rooting zone in a period of about 60 days. The mechanism of transport has not yet been verified. However, concentration profiles of exchangeable ammonium in the soil through the summer period indicate that a diffusion mechanism is operating along the soil exchange complex. This may be the primary mechanism of nitrogen transport, far exceeding the amounts that diffuse through the soil solution. Results also indicate that the amount of nitrogen transported by diffusion is strongly affected by soil temperature, thaw depth, and length of the thaw season.

No experimental studies have been conducted on phosphate diffusion in the soils of the coastal tundra at Barrow, but diffusion rates can be assumed to be generally low (Olsen et al. 1962) and added phosphorus fertilizer is strikingly immobile. Ten years after the last treatment, plots fertilized with phosphorus by Schultz (1964) still showed levels of labile and dissolved organic phosphorus that were 50 times as high as those of adjacent control plots, suggesting lack of movement of phosphorus (Barèl and Barsdate 1978).

Other Effects

Considerable quantities of both nitrogen and phosphorus can be transferred directly to available pools in the soil during a lemming high. During these population peaks lemmings consume up to 40 g m^{-2} yr^{-1} of graminoid plant material, nearly 50% of the annual aboveground production, and most of the minerals in this are excreted. However, this effect on available pools of nitrogen and phosphorus may be relatively insignificant during population lows, when consumption may fall below 1 g m^{-2} yr^{-1} (Chapter 10). Nitrogen is mainly excreted in the urine and is immediately available to plants and microorganisms. Phosphorus is distributed between urine and feces (Barkley 1976). Leaching experiments using an analogue of the surface runoff showed over 90% removal of phosphorus from feces in 24 hours (Chapin et al. 1978). During a high year, lemming feces would release about 90 mg P m^{-2}.

The freeze–thaw effect, described by Saebø (1968) for *Sphagnum* peat, is another way nutrients may be transferred from unavailable to available pools. After freezing and thawing, peat samples showed concentrations of dissolved and dilute acid-soluble phosphorus several times higher than did the control samples. The solution concentration returned to control values after remaining thawed for 48 hours, but values for acid-soluble phosphorus remained somewhat above controls for the same time period (Saebø 1968). Patterns of dissolved and resin-exchangeable inorganic phosphorus in the soils of the coastal tundra at Barrow indicate that the same effect is occurring (Barèl and Barsdate 1978). A similar effect was observed in solution concentrations of ammonium and nitrate (Barèl and Barsdate, unpubl.) and in soluble carbohydrates in soils of other areas (Gupta 1967). These similarities, and the lack of any effect on calcium levels, indicate that the freeze–thaw mechanism may involve a physical disruption of the organic matrix. The mechanics of the effect, and its magnitude, are still unclear.

The mineral fraction of the soil contains a significant fraction of the total phosphorus pool in non-exchangeable form (Chapin et al. 1978). Chemical transformation of the mineral matrix in which the phosphorus is bound would allow the transfer of some phosphorus to the exchangeable pool. Although weathering rates are low in arctic conditions (Douglas and Tedrow 1960), this source of inorganic phosphorus may not be negligible under the low-phosphorus regime of the wet meadow soils.

SUMMARY

Organic matter, generally in a partially decomposed (hemic) state, dominates the soil profiles of the coastal tundra at Barrow, and constitutes the major pool of fixed carbon in the ecosystem. The bulk density of the highly organic soil is low, but increases with advancing decomposition. The soils remain very moist throughout most summers, have high cation exchange capacities, and are moderately acid, with the lower pH levels correlated with lower primary productivity.

Almost all the nitrogen in the soil is present in organic form, and a large fraction of this is associated with poorly decomposed material. A small and variable amount of labile organic N is also present. In wet meadows inorganic nitrogen is mainly in the form of ammonium, and more than half is found below the primary rooting zone. In the wet areas, nitrate concentrations in the soil solution are very low, but in the driest units, nitrate concentrations exceed those of ammonium. Most of the soil phosphorus is also in organic forms, and the concentrations of inorganic phosphorus in the soil solution are extremely low.

Nitrogen fixation by blue–green algae is the major input mechanism for nitrogen. These algae may be free-living forms, but in many cases are associated with mosses or occur symbiotically in lichens. The predominant algal and lichen forms involved in nitrogen fixation are *Nostoc commune* and *Peltigera aphthosa*, respectively, although several other lichen species are also active. The biomass of nitrogen-fixing organisms is highest in wet, mossy areas, and is extremely low in dry areas. In mesic sites, moisture is usually the major factor controlling the input of nitrogen, but oxygen concentration and temperature are also important. The low oxygen concentrations that occur in wet, mossy areas may enhance the rates of nitrogen fixation. A simulation model indicates that a simple multiplicative interaction between these factors may be involved, and that the control mechanisms for nitrogen fixation may be similar at other tundra sites.

Inorganic nitrogen and phosphorus enter the system through precipitation. The amounts added are small in comparison to the total pools of these elements, but substantial with respect to available inorganic pools. The major losses of nitrogen and phosphorus occur in runoff during snowmelt and are mainly of organic forms. The combination of precipitation and runoff yields a net loss of nitrogen and phosphorus. Some nitrogen is also lost by denitrification, but the rate is low compared to the potential for nitrate reduction that exists in the wetter microtopographic units. Nitrogen fixation is sufficient to lead to a net accumulation of soil nitrogen.

The ratios of carbon to nitrogen and organic phosphorus are sufficiently high to suggest that weak nitrogen immobilization and strong phosphorus immobilization should be associated with decomposition. However, nitrogen mineralization has been shown to occur under cold, anaerobic conditions, perhaps because of low tissue nitrogen concentrations and low efficiency in the decomposer population. Phosphorus mineralization may respond to these same factors and be further facilitated by selective degradation of phosphorus-rich substrates.

Nitrifying bacteria are not common in the soil, and their activities are inhibited by low temperatures. Changes in the amount of nitrate present indicate low rates of nitrification in the wet meadows, and higher rates in drier microtopographic units.

Several internal pathways may aid in replenishing inorganic nutrients in the rooting zone. Studies with ^{15}N indicate a substantial flux of N from the subsoil to the surface. Freezing and rethawing of the soil liberate some available nitrogen and phosphorus. Weathering of minerals containing non-exchangeable phosphorus may also occur. In a high lemming year, lemming excreta contribute substantial amounts of available nitrogen and phosphorus.

8

The Microflora: Composition, Biomass, and Environmental Relations

F. L. Bunnell, O. K. Miller,
P. W. Flanagan, and R. E. Benoit

INTRODUCTION

Tundra microflora show the same low species diversity evident among the plants and herbivores. Two groups with broadly different dynamics dominate the microflora: rapidly changing bacterial populations that typically degrade smaller molecular compounds and more slowly changing fungal populations that are more capable of degrading larger molecules. The accumulation of organic matter in tundra systems reflects historical imbalances between production and decomposition. This chapter presents an overview of the composition, abundance and diversity of decomposer populations in the coastal tundra at Barrow as related to soil characteristics previously described (Chapter 7). Activities of the microflora are treated in Chapter 9.

The overview presented is unavoidably influenced by the isolation methods employed (Table 8-1). The usual cautions appropriate to interpretations of microfloral isolations apply. Isolation techniques select only a portion of the total viable flora. Microorganisms that grow readily on artificial media and appear to be dominant may not be dominant in their natural habitat. Similarly, fungi that fruit prolifically in the field may not contribute the greatest biomass of active vegetative cells. Therefore, the orientation of this discussion is broadly functional rather than strictly taxonomic, particularly when bacterial groups are being discussed. The bacteria are examined as they contribute to transformations of carbon, nitrogen and sulfur, whereas fungi are treated in more taxonomic detail.

TABLE 8-1 *Seasonal Averages of the Microflora Density and Biomass in Four Microtopographic Units in 1973 from the Barrow Research Area*

Density (units given below)

	Meadows	Basins	Troughs	Rims
Fungi				
standing dead[1]	2072	669	2004	2723
litter[1]	2127	1038	2649	2425
soil[1]	896	727	496	1445
Algae				
moss[2]	0.40	0.63	0.74	0.35
soil[2]	0.45	1.02	0.98	0.43
Yeasts, soil[1]	18.5×10^4	0.452×10^4	3.21×10^4	26.9×10^4
Bacteria, soil[10]				
plateable[4]	7.73×10^6	0.574×10^6	10.5×10^6	1.31×10^6
direct count[5]	8.29×10^9	4.59×10^9	9.76×10^9	5.52×10^9

Biomass (gdw m^{-2})

	Meadows	Basins	Troughs	Rims
Fungi				
standing dead[6]	0.18 (1.07)	0.07 (0.42)	0.24 (1.43)	0.18 (1.07)
litter[6]	0.47 (1.02)	0.12 (0.26)	0.51 (1.10)	0.75 (1.62)
soil[7]	0.86 (0.96)	0.75 (0.76)	0.38 (0.40)	1.87 (1.88)
Algae				
moss[8]	0.11 (0.69)	0.24 (1.5)	0.13 (0.81)	0.15 (0.94)
soil[8]	0.13 (0.58)	0.40 (1.78)	0.17 (0.76)	0.20 (0.89)
Yeasts, soil[9]	1.89×10^{-1} (1.02)	0.101×10^{-1} (0.05)	0.267×10^{-1} (0.14)	5.18×10^{-1} (2.78)
Bacteria, soil[10]				
plateable[4]	2.12×10^{-1} (2.46)	0.137×10^{-1} (0.16)	0.821×10^{-1} (0.95)	0.372×10^{-1} (0.43)
direct count[5]	1.12 (0.98)	1.00 (0.87)	0.94 (0.82)	1.52 (1.33)

Note: Soils measurements for the 1- to 2-cm depth. Organism volume V was estimated from the volume, density ϱ, and percentage dry weight %dw. Numbers in parentheses are relative biomass (seasonal average biomass divided by the average biomass from the four units).

[1] Meters of hyphae gdw^{-1} standing dead, litter, or soil microscopic measurement, unstained.

[2] Millimeters[3] gdw^{-1} moss or soil, microscopic counts and most probable number determinations, volume estimated from size classes.

[3] Colonies gdw^{-1} soil, plate counts on de Menna's medium.

[4] Number gdw^{-1} soil, at a 1- to 2-cm depth, spread plate counts on various media and most probable number determinations.

[5] Number gdw^{-1} soil, converted by regression from plate counts (direct $= 1.97 \times 10^4$ (plate)$^{0.2447}$, $r = 0.66$).

[6] $V = \pi r^2 \ell$, $r = 2.5$ μm, ℓ given above, $\varrho = 1.3$ g cm^{-1}, %$dw = 10$.

[7] $V = \pi r^2 \ell$, $r = 1.4$ μm, ℓ given above, $\varrho = 1.1$ g cm^{-1}, %$dw = 11.5$.

[8] V given above, $\varrho = 1$ g cm^{-1}, %$dw = 12.5$.

[9] $V = {}^4/_3 \pi r^2$, $r = 2.5$ μm, $\varrho = 1.1$ g cm^{-1}, %$dw = 11.5$

[10] $V = \pi r^2 \ell$, $r = 0.4$ μm, $\ell = 1.0$ μm, $\varrho = 1$ g cm^{-1}, %$dw = 12.5$.

TAXONOMIC STRUCTURE: ITS GENERAL CHARACTER AND HETEROGENEITY

Bacteria and Actinomycetes

Fewer species of bacteria are observed in tundra soils than in soils of the temperate zone, while actinomycetes are sharply reduced or entirely absent, presumably because of the acid, organic nature of the soils. Among tundra areas, greatest densities of actinomycetes relative to total bacterial populations have been reported from drier, less acid areas (Kriss 1947, Widden 1977). The dominant bacteria isolated from a wide variety of microtopographic units in the tundra at Barrow were gram negative short rods. In wet meadows *Pseudomonas, Achromobacter* and *Flavobacterium* were the most frequent genera. In drier areas, where polygonal terrain predominated, three species of *Achromobacter* along with *Cytophaga hutchinsonii* were most frequent. The dominance of these bacterial groups agrees with earlier reports by Soviet researchers working with northern soils (Mishustin and Mirzoeva 1972) and the review of Dunican and Rosswall (1974) of studies in arctic and antarctic tundra. The presence of *Cytophaga* at both wet and dry sites suggests that the potential for cellulose decomposition by bacteria is widespread in tundra.

Numbers of gram positive bacteria, including spore-forming bacteria that are largely gram positive, were generally less than 10^3 gdw^{-1} soil at the Biome research area. The low numbers are in agreement with findings from most other high latitude sites (Boyd et al. 1966, Fournelle 1967, Dunican and Rosswall 1974). Some genera, such as *Arthrobacter* and *Bacillus*, were isolated primarily from drier areas with polygonal terrain. In the wet meadow *Arthrobacter* had a frequency of occurrence of less than 5%, increasing in late season to 10% of the plateable flora. *Corynebacterium* (*C. equi, C. sepedonicum* and *C. pseudolipheucium*) isolated from polygonal terrain are reported from only one other tundra location (Truelove Lowland, Widden 1977).

The work of Nelson (1977) suggests some possible reasons for the relative frequency of *Pseudomonas, Arthrobacter* and *Bacillus*. She found *Pseudomonas* spp. to be very resistant to starvation stress, which is a possible adaptation to the low amounts of some soil nutrients. *Arthrobacter* spp. were tolerant of freezing and thawing effects when inoculated into sterile soil, while *Bacillus* spp., which are less commonly encountered, were more sensitive to both stresses under the conditions studied and less tolerant of low temperatures.

Anaerobic and Facultative Anaerobic Bacteria

While some earlier tundra studies (Levin 1899, Oméliansky 1911) failed to document the presence of anaerobes in tundra soils, recent reviews (Dunican and Rosswall 1974, Clarholm et al. 1975) reported anaerobes from Swedish and Norwegian tundra and a British peat bog. Evidence from the coastal tundra at Barrow indicates that anaerobic bacteria are present and may be important in decomposition.

The presence of anaerobic bacteria is indicated by low aerobic plate counts, but high direct microscopic counts and significant quantities of adenosine triphosphate (ATP) in regions of low concentrations of soil oxygen. The observations suggest a living microflora at depth, only a small portion of which can be attributed to fungi, which decrease markedly with depth. Significant amounts of methane were evolved only from artificially heated or extremely wet soils. Benoit (unpubl.) isolated both methane oxidizers and methane producers from wet meadow soils using enrichment cultures. Oxidizers would reduce the quantity of methane released from the system, making the detection of anaerobes such as *Methanomonas* more difficult. The most probable number (MPN) of soil anaerobes obtained in pre-reduced broth media in anaerobic jars was always tenfold greater than the most probable number from the same soil incubated under aerobic conditions. Many of these anaerobes are facultative; strict anaerobes constitute less than half of the anaerobic population. Although facultative anaerobic bacteria are estimated to constitute 50 to 70% of the aerobically plateable populations below 10 cm depth, they do not increase in numbers with depth as might be expected in wet soils (Clarholm et al. 1975). The reason appears to be lower temperatures with depth rather than lack of favorable substrates. Heated soils showed a marked loss in caloric content despite low oxygen concentrations.

Nitrogen, Sulfur, and Iron Bacteria

Free-living, aerobic, nitrogen-fixing bacteria (e.g. *Azotobacter* spp.) are generally absent in tundra soils (Dunican and Rosswall 1974), while anaerobic *Clostridium* spp. often occur (Mishustin and Mirzoeva 1972). Although *Azotobacter* has been identified from both arctic and antarctic soils, reported numbers are very low and fixation of nitrogen has not been demonstrated (Boyd and Boyd 1962, Boyd et al. 1966, Stutz 1977). Present studies confirm that all three species of *Azotobacter* described in Bergey's manual (Breed et al. 1957) occur in low numbers in the soils at Barrow, but nitrogen fixation by isolates could not be demonstrated. Some nitrogen-fixing activity has been observed in wet meadows in plots where nitrogen-fixing lichens or blue–green algae were absent or did not seem to be present in sufficient numbers to account for this fixation. Thus, heterotrophic, free-living, nitrogen-fixing bacteria may be active in some areas. In most other tundra locations nitrifying bacteria are similarly rare or absent; soils are generally too wet and acid. At Barrow, wet meadow soils are relatively rich in ammonia and low in nitrates. Nitrifying bacteria are present in these soils in extremely low numbers but the presence of some nitrate provides indirect evidence that nitrification is taking place. It is unlikely that rates of nitrification are low solely because of low temperatures (Alexander 1971) or the total lack of nitrifying bacteria propagules.

In contrast to nitrifiers, the presence of denitrifying bacteria in tundra is widely reported (Dunican and Rosswall 1974). Studies in the Biome research areas at Barrow and Eagle Summit suggest that denitrifying bacteria constitute 5% of the total aerobic population and are almost exclusively of the genus *Pseudomonas*. The two most prominent types, representing 65% of the isolates, were closely related to *Pseudomonas denitrificans*. Estimated rates of nitrogen transformation are presented in Chapter 7.

The role of sulfur may be especially important for two reasons. First, concentrations of inorganic sulfur in soils are very low, generally less than 1 ppm, within the range of possible sulfur deficiency for vascular plants and well below the values of 50 to 100 ppm reported for temperate regions (Starkey 1950, Walker 1957). Second, the wet, organic environment may favor accumulation of hydrogen sulfide as a terminal step in anaerobic mineralization of proteins. Hydrogen sulfide is toxic to many aerobic microorganisms and the precipitation of metallic sulfides could influence the mineral nutrition of vascular plants.

The low levels observed suggest that most of the sulfur in the system is resident in the protein of live cells. Boyd (1967) reported that chemoautotrophic, sulfur-oxidizing bacteria were absent in arctic and antarctic soils, while Cannon et al. (1970) documented their presence in low numbers in soils of blanket peat. Using enrichment cultures of pH 2 and 7, we found sulfur oxidizers to be rare or absent at Barrow. These observations are not surprising, for such organisms are found in low numbers even in soils of the temperate zone, except where enrichments of sulfur exist, as in mine tailings and pyrites (Starkey 1966). Photosynthetic sulfur bacteria have not been found in the soils at Barrow and are only reported from one subarctic site (Rosswall and Svensson 1974). Sulfate-reducing bacteria have been reported previously from both arctic (Russell et al. 1940, Dunican and Rosswall 1974) and antarctic soils (Barghoorn and Nichols 1961, Iizuka et al. 1969). They were isolated in low numbers in enrichment cultures from some of the wettest soils of the Biome research area and appear sufficiently rare that accumulation of hydrogen sulfide should not significantly modify the soil environment. However, where compaction by traffic impeded aeration and mixed plant and soil materials, sulfide evolution was evident and associated with rates of soil respiration four to six times greater than in adjacent, undisturbed areas. In such areas, the environment was likely made less favorable for vascular plant nutrition.

Iron bacteria are rarely found in tundra. In their review of International Tundra Biome research sites, Dunican and Rosswall (1974) reported iron bacteria only from Hardangervidda, a Norwegian subarctic site where they were abundant at only one sampling location. The high concentrations of iron in ponds and soils at Barrow certainly provide potential habitats for iron bacteria. Despite the availability of substrate, chemoautotrophs that can oxidize ferrous iron were not detected, although several heterotrophic species, which incorporate ferric iron into their cell envelopes, were isolated from surface soils.

In general, the available taxonomic information for tundra bacteria suggests that they have more limited diversity than bacterial flora from soils of temperate regions. However, there appear to be at least some bacterial species present that are capable of decomposing or mineralizing most of the major organic and inorganic substrates. Under laboratory conditions, at temperatures of 0 to 5 °C, many pure cultures of both tundra bacteria and fungi are capable of rapid metabolism. Experimental studies such as those with heated soils or sulfate enrichment demonstrate that in situ decomposition can increase dramatically under some field conditions (Benoit, pers. comm.). Together these observations suggest that existing rates of decomposition in tundra soils cannot be attributed to the absence of specific organisms.

Fungi and Yeasts

As with bacteria, the number of species of fungi in tundra is considerably less than in other Biomes, with the possible exception of the Desert Biome (Laursen 1975, Laursen and Miller 1977). Nevertheless the major classes of fungi are represented at Barrow. Proportions of Basidiomycetes in sterile hyphal counts with clamp connections generally range from 5 to 50%. Among the fungi in the vegetative, litter and soil layers, the sterile forms and/or Basidiomycetes not revealing clamp connections also show the greatest species diversity; the Fungi Imperfecti are next, followed by the Ascomycetes, including yeasts. In the relatively wet areas, including the ponds, there is a diverse and at times abundant flora of aquatic fungi.

Few endemics are present and the specific characteristics of the mycoflora lie in the relative importance of a given species or in the rarity of large groups such as families or orders commonly dominant in other Biomes. For example, the soils show a great preponderance of sterile forms combined with the absence or low incidence of common soil fungi such as *Aspergillus, Fusarium, Alternaria* and *Botrytis* in the Fungi Imperfecti, and *Rhizopus* in the Zygomycetes. On the other hand *Cladosporium herbarum*, a dominant phyllosphere fungus of the coastal tundra at Barrow, is common in other Biomes and is a circumpolar fungus as well (Flanagan and Scarborough 1974). The preponderance of sterile forms agrees well with data from Macquarie Island (Bunt 1965), Mackenzie Valley (Ivarsen 1965), British Moorlands (Latter et al. 1967), northern Sweden (Hayes and Rheinberg 1975) and Truelove Lowland (Widden 1977). The low incidence of species of *Penicillium, Fusarium* and *Aspergillus* relative to the mycoflorae of temperate regions also has been reported for the Canadian High Arctic (Widden et al. 1972) and northern Sweden (Hayes and Rheinberg 1975) in drier years. Data from the same sites in relatively wet years suggest that Hudson's (1968) assertion that *Penicillia* are rare and *Trichoderma* typically absent from tundra soil mycoflorae is not universally applicable.

Among the Zygomycetes, members of the Mucorales that are normally dominant in temperate soils (Pugh 1974) are poorly represented at Barrow and in other arctic areas (Widden et al. 1972). The species that do occur appear to have adapted to cold (see Chapter 9) and are often encountered in the early spring or under near-winter conditions. The cold tolerance of some Mucorales has also been observed and reported by Latter and Heal (1971) for the Antarctic.

The most important segment of the aquatic fungi are the algal parasites, and relatively few free-living species have been isolated from the soils and waters. Nearly 85% of the algae examined contained at least one fungal parasite, with *Lagenidium oedogonii* the most abundant parasitic form (Seymour, pers. comm.). Populations of Chytridiales and Saprolegniales are, however, common in polygon troughs, basins of low-centered polygons and slough areas. Members of the genera *Achlya, Apodachlya, Saprolegnia* and *Pythium* are the most commonly occurring water molds; *Nowakoskiella elegans* and *Rhizophylctis hyalina* are the most frequently encountered chytrid species. *Allomyces arbuscula* has been isolated at Barrow.

Yeasts, including Endomycetales and some sterile forms (Fungi Imperfecti), are relatively abundant (10^4 to 10^7 gdw^{-1} soil). Only three yeast isolates have been identified, each as *Cryptococcus laurentii* var. *magnus* (Shadomy, pers. comm.). Populations tend to be low in polygon troughs and basins of low-centered polygons but in wet meadows and rims of low-centered polygons, irregular, rapid increases and declines in populations have been observed. Similar observations of fluctuating yeast abundance have been made on Devon Island in the Canadian Arctic (Widden et al. 1972).

The Basidiomycetes and Ascomycetes, including the Discomycetes, which dominate the mycoflora, are distributed among 17 families including 30 genera and about 110 species (Kobayasi et al. 1967, 1969, Miller et al. 1973, Laursen 1975, Laursen et al. 1976). In the Deciduous and Coniferous Forest Biomes one would expect at least 50 families and not less than 250 genera. The number of species would be variable but the total would range from 400 to 1200 species or more, depending on the complexity of the plant community (Miller and Farr 1975).

Most species that are mycorrhizal associates of the coniferous or woody dicotyledonous plants are rarely encountered or are absent in tundra. Their absence is due in large part to the reduced higher plant flora. Similarly, the vast numbers of wood-rotting fungi (Aphyllophorales: Basidiomycetes) encountered in other Biomes are reduced to three species in the Barrow research area. One, *Thelephora terrestris*, is mycorrhizal and the other two, *Polyporus elegans* and *Thelephora anthocephala*, are decay organisms on the few woody substrates present, such as stems of *Salix* and *Cassiope*. Basidiomycete decomposers on leaf and litter substrates such as *Galerina subannulata* and *Naematoloma (Hypholoma) udum* are apparently dominant and found fruiting in large numbers. It is noteworthy that basidiolichens are represented by four species: *Omphalina ericetorum, O. hudsoniana, O. luteovitellinia* and *Multiclavula mucida*. For many years the only lichenized Basidiomycetes were thought to be the small groups in the tropics (Poelt 1973). While there are still only about 20 species known (Letrouit-Galinou 1973), they are clearly more cosmopolitan than initially thought.

The taxonomic information for fungi as well as bacteria documents a diversity much reduced from that of the microflorae of temperate regions. A portion of the reduction, in particular among the Phycomycetes, appears associated with lower temperatures while reduction in substrate diversity further limits mycorrhizal and wood-rotting fungi. Aquatic fungi, which exploit the common moist areas, show less reduction in diversity; 15 genera and 26 species are present.

The relative dominance of the Basidiomycetes in numbers of species and the relatively high contribution they make to the total fungal biomass at Barrow is in contrast to subarctic tundra sites (Pilát and Nannfeldt 1954, Rall 1965) and to temperate regions (Miller et al. 1975, Laursen 1975). The reason, in part, is their role as mycorrhizal symbionts of arctic plants (Miller and Laursen 1978). It is also possible that the more versatile, dikaryotic hyphal system of the Basidiomycetes has enabled many of these species to adapt physiologically to the rigorous environmental conditions of the Arctic. In contrast the monokaryotic hyphal system of many yeasts and imperfect fungi as well as ascomycetes may be less versatile and therefore less responsive to environmental stress.

Algae

Fifty-nine species of algae were found at Barrow. Blue–green algae and bacteria are included in this figure as they are in the following discussion of algae (Cameron et al. 1978). Green algae were represented by 35 species, diatoms by 12, blue–green algae by 7, euglenoids by 4, and yellow–green algae by 1. The dominance of green and blue–green species follows the pattern reported elsewhere in the tundra and in other Biomes (John 1942, Taylor 1956, Durrell 1959, Dorogostaiskaya and Novichkova–Ivanova 1967, Gollerbakh and Shtina 1969, Akiyama 1970, Clark and Paul 1970, Novichkova-Ivanova 1972). As with other flora and faunal groups, the aquatic green and blue–green algae are more poorly represented in the coastal tundra than they are farther south on the Arctic Slope (Prescott 1953, Maruyama 1967).

Prominent algal species include the green *Chlamydomonas* spp., *Chlorella vulgaris, Stichococcus bacillaris, Chlorococcum minutum* and *Ulothrix subtilissima.* A small *Navicula* sp. was the most frequently observed diatom, and *Schizothrix calcicola*, a small oscillatorioid blue–green form, was commonly cultured from many microtopographic units. This latter species is probably the most common of the blue–green algae in arctic tundra soils and appears cosmopolitan for it contributes a large biomass in temperate, desert and grassland soils as well (Cameron 1972). Another of the blue–green algae, *Nostoc commune*, was found frequently in a variety of microtopographic units. In the drier microtopographic units it sometimes formed microscopic plants, but it developed large, discrete mats in the moister units. This species is one that characteristically dominates other nitrogen-fixing species in virgin soils with moisture contents of 80 to 100% dry weight (Shtina 1972). Thus its frequent occurrence in polygon troughs and meadows is not unexpected. Because it is less mobile in mat form, *Nostoc* tends to become parasitized and lichenized in harsh environments, and in this climax form stabilizes as *Peltigera* and *Stereocaulon* spp., which are more resistant to desiccation.

Lemming fecal material is abundant in the upper soil, and several of the common algal genera (*Chlorella, Chlamydomonas, Scenedesmus, Schizothrix* and *Elakatothrix*) thrive in fecally contaminated habitats (Doyle 1964). The algal flora documents another striking feature of the tundra ecosystem—its high moisture levels. Several planktonic forms, including *Quadrigula lacustris* and *Scenedesmus quadricauda*, were cultured from wet meadows and polygon troughs.

The absence of certain groups within cultures is equally noteworthy. No desmids were encountered, although on the basis of observations in other organic soils or polar regions they should be expected. Prescott

(1961) stated that desmids constitute about 75% of the freshwater algal flora in the Arctic. Previous reviews of the arctic algal flora from fresh water and soil suggest that both *Prasiola* spp. and *Nostoc* spp. contribute importantly to the subaerial algal biomass or biomass in the surface soils (Ross 1956, Taylor 1956). *Nostoc commune* was commonly encountered in the field, although it was not common in culture. *Prasiola* spp. were not collected from any of the sampled microtopographic units. However, *Prasiola* spp. did form an observable cover over owl casts found in the Biome research area (E.A. Schofield, pers. comm.) and *Prasiola crispa* formed extensive green mats over caribou carcasses in the vicinity of Prudhoe Bay (Atlas et al. 1976).

Heterogeneity Within the Microflora

Given the extreme variability of the soils of the coastal tundra both laterally and with depth, dramatic changes in the taxonomic structure and biomass of the microflora can be expected over lateral distances of a meter and depths of a few centimeters. It is pertinent to document the magnitude of this heterogeneity, and to determine the degree to which the microflora constitutes groups that can be associated with specific microtopographic units. The variability in both taxonomic structure and amounts of biomass is important. Taxonomic heterogeneity is evaluated in the two broad groups for which the most taxonomic information is available, higher fungi (Basidiomycetes and Discomycetes) and algae.

Five microtopographic units are considered: wet meadows, polygon troughs, the rims of low-centered polygons, basins, and the tops of high-centered polygons. Beach ridges are treated together with the tops of high-centered polygons because of the similarity of the resident vascular plants and mosses present. Of the 33 fungal species collected, the highest numbers are present in the relatively well aerated soils of polygon rims and polygon tops (Figure 8-1). In contrast, fruiting higher fungi are strongly reduced and often absent in basins of low-centered polygons. Samples from basins revealed only three species (*Aleuria aphanodictyon,*

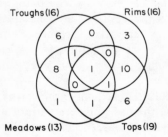

Troughs (16)   Rims (16)

6   0   3

1   0

8   1   10

0   1

1   1   6

Meadows (13)   Tops (19)

FIGURE 8-1. *The distribution of numbers of species of higher fungi in four microtopographic units. No fungal species were restricted to the basins of low-centered polygons. (Data of Laursen and Miller.)*

Laccaria striatula and *Galerina subannulata*), no one of which is restricted to this microtopographic unit.

Higher fungi inhabiting the wet meadow also show little specificity;
only 1 of 13 species recorded appears restricted to wet meadows, while 10
of the 19 species recorded from wet meadows and polygon troughs are
common to both microtopographic units. Rims of low-centered polygons
and tops of high-centered polygons show similar overlap, with 12 of the
23 species recorded being common to both (Figure 8-1). In all other comparisons there is a clear lack of common species; usually fewer than 10%
of the species recorded from a pair of microtopographic units are common to both. Much of the difference in commonality appears associated
with gradients in soil moisture and aeration and vascular plant assem-
blages. A relatively high percentage of the species on the extremes of the
moisture gradient are found in only one microtopographic unit, e.g. 31%
in troughs and 32% on tops. Similarly, a comparison between tops of
high-centered polygons and polygon troughs reveals only 1 of 35 species
in common. This species, *Galerina subannulata* (Sing.) Smith and Sing.,
is ubiquitous and found in all microtopographic units sampled.

Broad trophic distinctions exist between the meadow–trough complex and the rim–top complex (Figure 8-2). About 50% of the species in
each complex function as decomposers of dead plant material. Almost
all the mycorrhizal forms are restricted to the rim–top complex, where
the proportion of dicotyledonous plants in the vascular vegetation is
higher than in the wet meadows or polygon troughs. Conversely, the epiphytic fungi are restricted to the meadow–trough complex. Among the
basidiolichens, *Omphalina hudsoniana* is found only on rims and tops

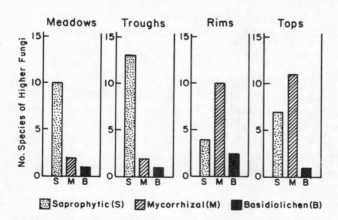

FIGURE 8-2. *The usual trophic status of higher fungi
within different microtopographic units. (Data of Miller
and Laursen.)*

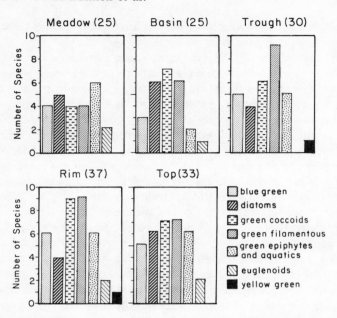

FIGURE 8-3. *The distribution of numbers of algal species in microtopographic units. (After Cameron and Knox, unpubl.)*

and *Omphalina luteovitellina* only on rims. In contrast *Omphalina ericetorum* has only been found in the relatively moist meadows and polygon troughs, where it often occurs on mats of *Sphagnum* mosses.

Algae, including blue–greens, are much more cosmopolitan than the higher fungi in their distribution over the microtopographic units of the tundra at Barrow (Figure 8-3). Diversity indices ($h = \sum\limits_{i=1}^{n} -p_i \log_2 p_i$) range from 4.30 in basins of low-centered polygons to 4.68 on tops of high-centered polygons (Cameron et al. 1978). Equitability measures ($h/\max h$, given n species) show a similarly small range, from 0.89 on rims of low-centered polygons to 0.94 in wet meadows, suggesting that species diversity is primarily a function of the number of species encountered rather than the distribution of relative abundance. Again the rims and tops show the highest number of species, 33 and 37 respectively of the 59 species recorded from culture. Basins and meadows yielded the fewest species, 25, but algae there do not show the same dramatic reduction as was apparent in the higher fungi. Ten algal species, six green algae and four blue–green forms, were found in all microtopographic units. Ten percent or fewer of the species recorded are restricted to any one unit and about 50% of the species recorded for any two units are common to

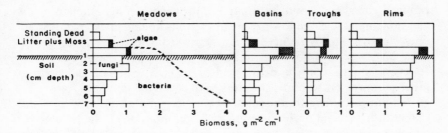

FIGURE 8-4. *Depth profiles of the average biomass of algae and fungi in 1973 and bacteria (direct count) in 1971. Direct counts for bacteria are only available for wet meadows. (Benoit, Cameron, Flanagan, Knox, Miller and Webber, unpubl., and Laursen 1975.)*

both. Green filamentous forms dominate in polygon troughs (25% of the species present); green coccoids are particularly dominant, in terms of number of species represented, in basins of low-centered polygons; and euglenoids are totally missing from troughs (Figure 8-3).

Even the relatively cosmopolitan algae differ in species composition among the microtopographic units considered. These differences are more marked among the soil fungi, which exhibit considerable taxonomic specificity (Figure 8-1) as well as broad trophic differences (Figure 8-2) among these units.

Differences in taxonomic structure are associated with differences in biomass. Among the algae the number of species represented and total biomass show positive correlations among microtopographic units (cf. Figure 8-3 and Figure 8-4). The most precise data available, however, are those for the soil fungi. When all samples of fungal biomass from 1 to 2 cm depth collected during the summer of 1973 are subjected to two-way analysis of variance, significant differences are found among microtopographic units for biomass levels of the soil-inhabiting mycelia. Recognition of different fungal habitats is justified on the basis of broad trophic differences and average biomass levels.

Functional Implications of Taxonomic Structure

Although the influences of an extreme environment are evident in the reduced diversity, the capacity to degrade all major organic and inorganic substrates is present (see also Chapter 9). The impact of low temperatures and the rigorous freeze–thaw cycle is evident in the relative sparsity of such taxa as *Bacillus* and common groups among the Mucorales. The influence of substrate is most evident in the marked reduction of mycorrhizal and wood-rotting fungi. Influences of high moisture, low aeration and associated low pH are ubiquitous among broad taxa: Actinomycetes are sharply reduced, gram negative bacteria dominate, planktonic algae are common, as are aquatic fungi, while yeasts and higher fungi are common only in better-aerated areas. The moist, acid environment supports a taxonomic structure with restricted potential for bacterial fixation of nitrogen, abundant denitrifiers and a similarly restricted potential for fungal decomposition of larger molecules. The presence of permafrost and impeded drainage maintains a zone of the soil with restricted potential for decomposition leading to accumulation of carbon. In the better-aerated microtopographic units where fungi are more abundant, levels of available nutrients in the soil are often higher and primary production greater.

MICROFLORA BIOMASS: ITS DISTRIBUTION IN THE ENVIRONMENT AND CHANGES THROUGH TIME

Although microbial biomass itself is of limited applicability in assessing kinetics of decomposition, and many assumptions must be used to calculate it, measures of biomass are useful in establishing broad relationships between the microflora and its environment (Table 8-1). Because of the marked differences in bulk density and organic matter within profiles of tundra soil, estimates of microbial biomass are computed on a volume basis as well as per gram of soil. Throughout the following discussion the term *density* refers to numbers of bacteria or meters of hyphae per gram substrate; the term *biomass* refers to weight of organisms per volume of substrate.

Spatial Distribution of Microbial Biomass

Differences Among Microtopographic Units

Within the soil the seasonal average of fungal biomass is highest on the rims of low-centered polygons, and lowest in polygon troughs (Table 8-1, Figure 8-4) (Laursen 1975). Algal biomass, in contrast, is highest in the basins of low-centered polygons and lowest in polygon troughs and wet meadows (Table 8-1). Unfortunately, direct counts of the bacterial component were not available when fungal data were collected. The direct counts obtained from wet meadow soils in 1971 suggest that the upper 7 cm of those soils contained about 16.5 g m^{-2} of microbial biomass of which, for a seasonal average, about 75% was bacterial. If the plate to direct count ratios observed in wet meadows hold in other soils as well, it appears that total microfloral biomass in the upper 7 cm of soil ranges from 12 to 20 g m^{-2}, with the greatest amounts of biomass in wet meadows and polygon troughs, less on rims of low-centered polygons, and least in basins of low-centered polygons. These values are considerably less than those observed for temperate grasslands. From the data of Clark and Paul (1970) the microfloral biomass in a grassland soil to a depth of 10 cm is 77 g m^{-2}, of which only 31% is bacterial.

Within the tundra environment the suitability of the various microtopographic units for different decomposer groups can be assessed by comparing the relative levels of average seasonal biomass of a particular group found in the different units (Table 8-1). Data for the aerobic soil-inhabiting organisms (fungi, yeasts and plateable bacteria) are presented to a depth of 2 cm only; during most of the summer season the activity of these organisms is concentrated in the surface layers of the soil. Eukaryotic decomposers (fungi and yeasts) are most abundant on rims of low-centered polygons (Table 8-1), which show somewhat greater concentrations of oxygen in soil solution. Furthermore, rims frequently support the *Carex–Poa* vegetation type in which primary production is dominated by mosses. Because mosses are richer in aromatic compounds than graminoids, and the decomposition of large molecular weight aromatics proceeds largely through fungal metabolism, the predominance of mosses may favor fungal dominance. Antagonism between yeasts and bacteria in tundra soils is suggested by these comparisons, and further corroborated by the seasonal courses of biomass for these groups.

In wetter microtopographic units the relative abundance of soil fungi decreases while that of bacteria increases, apparently in response to increasingly anaerobic conditions. Reasons for the particularly marked reduction of the decomposer flora in basins of low-centered polygons are unclear but it may be associated with low levels of available phosphorus. The relatively high algal biomass in the basins is composed largely of diatoms. Methodologies involved may have included a significant accumulation of dead diatomaceous cells, which also could be associated with low potential for decomposition rather than higher algal production.

Bacterial plate counts from the relatively productive polygon troughs and meadows (Table 8-2) are similar to those from mires and meadows of other arctic and subarctic locations (Parinkina 1974, Clarholm et al. 1975, Widden 1977), but are commonly one order of magnitude lower than those reported for temperate grasslands (Paul et al. 1973). Conversely, direct bacterial counts tend to be higher than in forest or grassland soils, but are broadly similar to counts from other tundra soils (Parinkina 1974). Measures of total bacterial biomass are thus similar to those at other tundra sites, and because of the relatively small size of tundra bacteria the biomass estimates made from direct counts are similar to those of more temperate regions as well. When plate counts are

TABLE 8-2   *Patterns of Bacterial Biomass with Depth and Time as Estimated by Plate and Direct Counts from Soils in Wet Meadows for 1971*

Date	Depth (cm)	Plate count	Direct count	Plate:Direct
		Bacterial biomass (gdw m^{-2} cm^{-1})		
26 June	0–2	4.0×10^{-1}	1.3	1:322
	2–7	0.91×10^{-1}	1.6	1.1750
	7–12	1.9×10^{-1}	3.3	1.1695
26 July	0–2	0.36×10^{-1}	0.91	1:2500
	2–7	0.45×10^{-1}	1.89	1:4200
	7–12	0.103×10^{-1}	2.85	1:27777
24 August	0–2	0.065×10^{-1}	0.65	1:10000
	2–7	0.245×10^{-1}	2.45	1:10000
	7–12	ND	ND	ND
		Bacterial numbers		
Seasonal avg.	0–2	22.6×10^{6}	1.22×10^{10}	1:539
	2–7	2.24×10^{6}	1.09×10^{10}	1:4866
	7–12	0.32×10^{6}	0.81×10^{10}	1:33750

corrected for bulk density, basins and rims of low-centered polygons still support the least bacterial biomass while polygon troughs and wet meadows support significantly more (Table 8-1).

The plate to direct count ratios observed for soil bacteria in the Biome research area commonly range from 1:1000 to 1:8000 in the upper 2 cm and become somewhat broader with depth (Table 8-2). These values are higher than many reported by Parinkina (1974) for tundra soils but do not exceed the range she reported. Parinkina also noted that comparison of data from amended soils of the tundra region and from soils of temperate and southern regions shows that the difference between direct and plate counts decreases both with cultivation and decreasing latitude. Two explanations for these trends may be offered. First, the trends may testify to greater availability of nutrients in cultivated or southern soils; second, they may document higher rates of decomposition and a smaller content of dead cells in those soils.

Seasonal averages of the plate counts for yeasts in the upper 1 to 2 cm of soil range from 4.5×10^{3} colonies (gdw soil)$^{-1}$ in basins to 2.7×10^{5} colonies (gdw soil)$^{-1}$ in rims of low-centered polygons (Table 8-1). The technique used for isolation of yeasts probably cultures a limited portion of the yeast population present, and these counts are likely conservative. The single taxon identified frequently occurs as an epiphyte and the relatively large biomass of yeast on polygon rims (5.2×10^{-3} g m^{-2}) probably exists on the abundant mosses. In other high latitude sites yeasts occur at about the same level of abundance, also commonly as epiphytes (Baker 1970a,b, Dowding and Widden 1974).

Seasonal averages of fungal density, expressed as mycelial length per gram of soil, in the upper 1 to 2 cm of soil range from 496 m (gdw soil)$^{-1}$ in polygon troughs to 1445 m (gdw soil)$^{-1}$ on the rims of low-centered polygons (Table 8-1). Although fungal abundance in the more favorable units is similar to that found in Irish blanket bog and in mesic to dry arctic meadows of Norway and Canada (Dowding and Widden 1974), it is much lower than in other Biomes. In woodland soils it is not uncommon to find 7000 m (gdw soil)$^{-1}$ or more in organic soil horizons (Parkinson 1971). In surface soils of the coastal tundra at Barrow, however, fungi are still an important component of the microflora biomass and their biomass in the top 1 to 2 cm ranges from 0.38 g m^{-2} in polygon troughs to 1.87 g m^{-2} on the better-aerated rims (Laursen 1975). In general, the relative proportions of fungi and bacteria in soils of polygon rims resemble those observed in temperate soils more closely than do proportions in other microtopographic units (Table 8-1). Conversely, the dominance of bacteria in the wet meadows and polygon troughs suggests that decomposition in wet tundra soils is governed by bacteria to a greater degree than in many soils examined in other Biomes.

Although mycelial densities per gram of substrate are generally two to three times higher in litter and standing dead than in soils, somewhat more fungal biomass is present in soil because of the greater density of substrate. Fungal densities per gram of substrate in litter and standing dead vegetation are similar in all microtopographic units examined with the exception of the basins of low-centered polygons (Table 8-1). On rims of low-centered polygons, as well as in wet meadows and polygon troughs, mycelial densities in both litter and standing dead vegetation range from about 2000 to 2700 m gdw^{-1} of substrate. In basins the average seasonal values for fungal density are 1038 m gdw^{-1} in litter and 669 m gdw^{-1} in standing dead vegetation. The relative inhospitality of basins for the decomposer flora is evident in the dead vegetation as well as the soil. Much of the difference in relative distribution of fungal biomass in litter and standing dead vegetation across microtopographic units (Table 8-1) is attributable to differences in amounts of substrate, not fungal densities.

Although algae are not members of the decomposer community they are considered here as a constituent of the total microflora. Volumes of blue–green, green and diatomaceous algae in the moss and surface soil do not show the same variability among microtopographic units as do the decomposer organisms (Table 8-1). Volumes in moss range from 0.35 mm^3 (gdw moss)$^{-1}$ on rims of low-centered polygons to 0.74 mm^3 (gdw moss)$^{-1}$ in polygon troughs. Volumes in the soil range from 0.43 mm^3 (gdw soil)$^{-1}$ on the rims of low-centered polygons to 1.02 mm^3 (gdw soil)$^{-1}$ in the basins. Differences in bulk density modify the ranking of algal biomass in soils. Although basins still contain the greatest amounts (0.40 g m^{-2} in the upper 1 to 2 cm of soil), wet meadow soils contain the least amount of algal cells, only 0.13 g m^{-2}, and amounts in trough soils are also low (Table 8-1).

Differences with Depth

The same broad relationships that influence the relative distribution of microflora groups across microtopographic units influence the distribution with depth. In marked contrast to temperate regions the presence of permafrost in tundra soils accentuates the rate of environmental change with depth (Chapters 2 and 7).

Except in the better-aerated microtopographic units such as rims, the eukaryotic organisms, yeasts and fungi, decline rapidly with depth (Figure 8-4), a phenomenon also common in other arctic sites (Hanssen and Goksøyr 1975, Widden 1977). In soils of wet meadows seasonal averages of yeast dilution counts in 1971 decline from 1.6×10^6 colonies (gdw soil)$^{-1}$ in the upper 2 cm to 9.7×10^4 colonies (gdw soil)$^{-1}$ in samples collected from 2 to 7 cm depth. Because of increasing bulk density with depth, total biomass declines less rapidly, from 0.011 g m^{-2} to 0.002 g m^{-2}.

Fungal density declines consistently with depth and the observed increase in fungal biomass below 6 cm in polygon troughs (Figure 8-4) is due to a sharp increase in bulk density from an organic to mineral horizon (Laursen 1975). The decrease in fungal densities parallels the increase in bulk density and the decrease in concentration of oxygen.

In wet meadows, bacteria constitute about 40 to 55% of the decomposer biomass in the upper 2 cm, and increase their contribution with increasing depth (Figure 8-4). Failure of bacteria to decrease with depth indicates their facultative anaerobic nature. The decline of plateable numbers with depth concomitant with an increase in direct counts changes the seasonal average ratio of plate to direct counts from 1:539 at 0 to 2 cm to 1:4866 at 2 to 7 cm and 1:33750 at 7 to 12 cm depth (Table 8-2). Direct microscopic measures invariably overestimate bacterial numbers, but ATP measurements indicate that most of the bacterial biomass at depths of 2 to 12 cm is viable. The wider plate to direct count ratio at depth may represent an increase in the strictly anaerobic bacterial flora. The shift from fungal to bacterial dominance with depth produces a shift in the enzymatic potential to utilize specific substrate constituents (Chapter 9) and compounds of larger molecular weight are degraded less readily.

Temporal Distribution and Productivity

Temporal patterns of decomposer biomass indicate the overall productivity of microflora populations and some effects of environmental factors. Comparison of these patterns among different microtopographic units provides a series of examples of the interactive effects of temperature and moisture.

Fungi in Standing Dead Vegetation and Litter

In wet meadows, fungi in both the litter and upper 1 cm of soil show a rapid early-season increase in density at the same time that fungi in standing dead are decreasing (Figure 8-5). The high amounts of moisture at runoff rapidly leach the standing dead substrate and enrich the litter and upper soil layers.

Seasonal patterns of fungal density in standing dead vary among microtopographic units largely as a function of moisture. The summer of

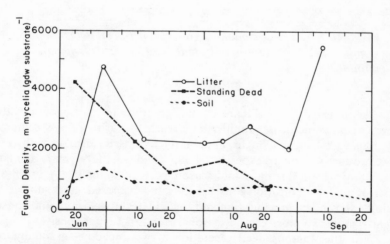

FIGURE 8-5. *The seasonal progression of fungal density in standing dead vegetation, plant litter and the 1- to 2-cm soil depth in wet meadows, 1973. (After Flanagan, unpubl., and Laursen 1975.)*

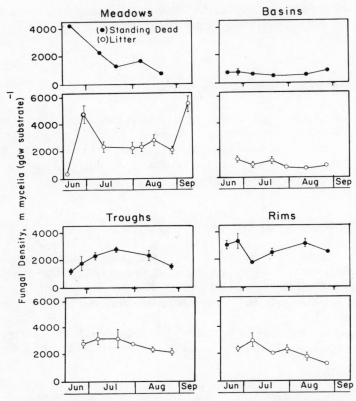

FIGURE 8-6. *The seasonal progression of fungal density in standing dead vegetation and plant litter, 1973. (Flanagan, unpubl.)*

1973 was unusually wet (Figure 2-2). High amounts of moisture in the more concave microtopographic units, such as basins of low-centered polygons and polygon troughs, apparently depressed fungal growth. The more productive troughs experience highest moisture levels early and late in the season, producing a mid-season peak in biomass (Figure 8-6). Rims of low-centered polygons are elevated, exposed, and subject to periodic wetting by precipitation and fog and drying by wind, and consequently show the most erratic seasonal trend in fungal density. Fungal density in the standing dead vegetation of wet meadows gradually declines through the season as drying progresses. Although the seasonal pattern was the same, during the moister summer of 1973 average fungal density within the standing dead vegetation of wet meadows was 12% higher than in 1972.

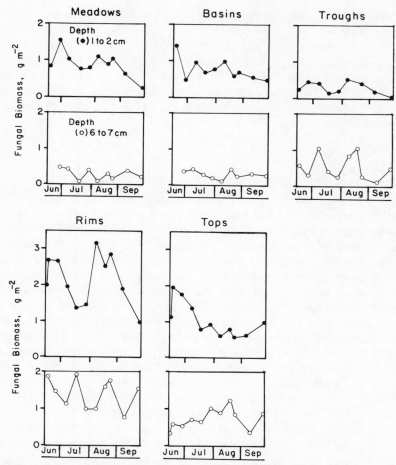

FIGURE 8-7. *The seasonal progression of fungal biomass at two soil depths, 1973. The values are the means of three to five replicate plots. (After Laursen 1975.)*

Seasonal courses of fungi in the litter layer show somewhat more consistency in pattern than is apparent in standing dead vegetation (Figure 8-6), but the variation among microtopographic units remains large. Generally, the pattern is more akin to that observed for fungi in the soil, with a peak in biomass shortly after snowmelt followed by a gradual decline (cf. Figure 8-7). The peak in fungal biomass is most evident in wet meadows and rims of low-centered polygons, which accumulate less moisture than do the concave microtopographic units. In the basins of low-centered polygons, fungal biomass in litter shows a gradual decline during the growing season, and never does attain the levels measured in other habitats.

In wet meadows, seasonal mean estimates of fungal densities in litter ($\bar{x} \pm$ SE) were 2442 $\pm$654 m mycelia (gdw litter)$^{-1}$ in 1972, and 2127 $\pm$664 m mycelia (gdw litter)$^{-1}$ in 1973. The microclimatic regime of the litter layer is typically moister than that for standing dead and the increased precipitation of 1973 apparently was insufficient to alter measures of average litter biomass.

Fungi in the Soil

The seasonal patterns of fungal biomass in the surface layer of soil (1 to 2 cm) show a peak immediately after snowmelt followed by a second peak in early August, which may be as pronounced as the first, moderate, or weak (Figure 8-7) (Laursen 1975). The magnitude of the first peak for troughs and basins may be underestimated because the soils were frozen at the time of the first sample and the highest levels may have been reached before the next measurement. More pronounced early peaks in fungal biomass were observed in the surface soil of polygon troughs in 1972 and 1974 (Laursen and Miller 1977). Except for the second, variably expressed increase, a general decline in biomass similar to that observed among litter fungi is evident over the season (Figures 8-6 and 8-7). The pattern of a moderate peak followed by a gradual decline that was observed in the wet meadow is also evident in data from Norwegian sites (Hanssen and Goksøyr 1975). The rapid early growth of fungal biomass in the surface layer of soil, as well as in the litter, may be a response to the release of nutrients during snowmelt. The second peak occurs just before the basidiomycetes fruit and is often more pronounced in the more productive microtopographic units (Figure 8-7). The same factors that restrict biomass of soil fungi in the polygon troughs and basins of low-centered polygons may also restrict the ability of these fungi to respond quickly to favorable conditions. Thus the seasonal courses of fungal biomass are not only lower, but less variable in troughs and basins than in the other microtopographic units.

Seasonal patterns at a depth of 6 to 7 cm do not mimic patterns at 1 to 2 cm depth (Figure 8-7). The only apparent consistency in the seasonal pattern among microtopographic units in the deeper soil is the peak in fungal biomass that occurs in all units around 22 August. The decline in fungal biomass in the surface soil that begins in late August is probably associated with freezing or near-freezing temperatures in that stratum. Fungal biomass in the deeper soil typically equals or exceeds the biomass in the surface soil by mid-September (Laursen and Miller 1977).

The taxonomic structure of both soil and litter fungi appears to shift during the season and provides further circumstantial evidence concerning the nature of the rapid early-season growth. In both litter and surface soil, some members of the Mucorales and common molds are more evident early in the season and become less evident as the season progresses. These species are cold-tolerant (Latter and Heal 1971, Flanagan and Veum 1974), fast-growing and can be termed "soft" decomposers since they are better able to exploit readily leachable compounds than cellulose or lignin (Chapter 9).

In deeper soil layers the fungal population includes "hard" decomposers, fungi with a relatively greater capacity to utilize cellulose and lignin than have the mucors and common molds. Many of these are basidiomycetes and ascomycetes, although zygomycetes are present at intermediate depths. The "hard" decomposers generally fluctuate less rapidly than the "soft" decomposers of the litter and surface soil layers, and tend to increase slowly in biomass over the season as soil temperatures increase and buried organic soils become drier (Laursen and Miller 1977).

A third broad component of the soil fungi are the mycorrhizal formers. Profiles of these fungi with depth approximate the profiles of roots of dicotyledonous plants, particularly *Salix, Cassiope* and *Vaccinium* species. On the rims of low-centered polygons, fungal biomass increases at depths of 2 to 4 cm and the average proportion of basidiomycete cells increases from well below 20% in the surface layers to 29% at 1 to 2 cm depth and 42% at 2 to 3 cm depth, declines to 37% at 3 to 4 cm, and subsequently drops sharply below 4 cm. The temporal pattern of mycorrhizal formers is marked by rather stable biomass levels which increase steadily from early season levels until fruiting, during July and early August (Miller and Laursen 1978).

In general, yeasts are most abundant in early, frozen samples. Numbers of yeasts decline as the soil thaws and bacterial biomass increases early in the season. The seasonal decrease in abundance is greater in soils with deeper thaw—about ten times greater from 26 June to 5 August in 1973. Yeast numbers thus appear negatively correlated with bacterial numbers, but the data are sparse. Differences in average population levels between years suggest that the differential response of yeast and bacteria is associated with amounts of moisture. In the moist summer of 1973, yeast counts in the upper 2 cm of wet meadow soil were less than 20% of the levels observed in 1971. At depths of 5 cm, counts in 1973 were at least 100-fold lower than in 1971, less than 10^2 (gdw soil)$^{-1}$.

Bacteria

In the surface soil, bacteria appear to follow the same seasonal pattern as fungi and may be responding similarly to changes in substrate.

Both groups have early- and late-season peaks. While the peak early in the summer may be associated with the release of organic material from both aboveground and belowground material, the second peak is more probably associated with the senescence and death of roots. Because the second peak appears to coincide with the first frost, this increase may also be associated with subsequent leaching of aboveground vegetation. Further evidence for the concept of substrate abundance influencing bacterial abundance is apparent in the differences with depth. Before the recovery of bacterial numbers in late August or early September, plate counts from meadow soils show a gradual decline from 10^7 to 10^6 in the upper 2 cm and a more marked decline from 10^6 to 10^4 at depths of 2 to 7 cm (Benoit, unpubl.). Direct counts from the surface soil are also depressed in mid-season, but show no mid-season decrease in numbers in the deeper soil. The lower soil layers depend more upon root growth and exudation for replenishment of potential substrate, and less upon leaching from aboveground organic matter. Root activity at mid-season is apparently sufficient to maintain the bacterial population in the deeper soil.

Although bacterial biomass and ratios of fungi to bacteria differ among microtopographic units (Table 8-1), seasonal courses of bacterial plate counts do not. Composition of the biomass does show some taxonomic shift and chromogenic bacteria appear relatively more abundant in late season. The consequences of such a shift to decomposition are unknown.

Estimates of Minimal Production

The estimates of production discussed below consist simply of the sum of the positive changes in measured biomass *sensu* Ivanov (1955) and are thus minimal and frequently confused by the variability of the microflora.

Although biomass varied considerably among sample points on a specific microtopographic unit, both fungal productivity and fungal density showed broad differences among these units (Figure 8-8). Fungal density was lower in the wetter summer of 1973. The difference in density between years was most consistent in the wetter microtopographic units, suggesting that the decrease was due to higher moisture levels. Although minimal fungal productivity is broadly correlated with average mycelial density, the nature of the relationship apparently shifts between years. Despite lower mean density, the total fungal growth in 1973 was generally higher than in 1972 for drier microtopographic units, in particular the rims of low-centered polygons, and for basins of low-centered polygons. Much of this growth occurred in late July to early August (Figure 8-7)

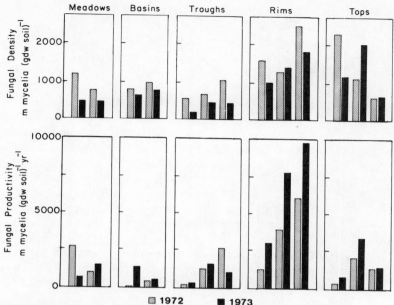

FIGURE 8-8. *The seasonal average density and estimates of minimal productivity (sum of positive changes in density) of soil fungi at the 1- to 2-cm depth in 1972 and 1973. The pairs of bars represent replicates from similar microtopographic units. (Laursen and Miller, unpubl.)*

TABLE 8-3 *Mean Biomass and Minimal Estimates of Productivity (Sum of Positive Changes in Biomass) of Soil Fungi in Different Microtopographic Units, 1973*

Depth (cm)	Meadows	Basins	Troughs	Rims	Tops
		Biomass			
		(g m^{-2})			
1–2	0.86	0.75	0.38	1.87	1.66
6–7	0.29	0.25	0.46	1.47	0.70
		Productivity			
		(g m^{-2} yr^{-1})			
1–2	1.32	1.47	1.36	5.59	3.95
6–7	0.96	0.80	2.84	5.33	2.05

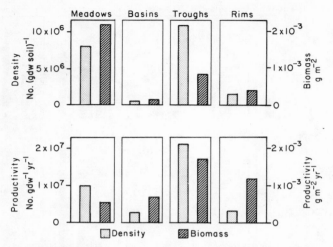

FIGURE 8-9. *The seasonal average density and bio-mass and estimates of minimal productivity (sum of positive changes in counts) of plateable bacteria in the 1- to 2-cm soil depth, 1973. (Benoit, unpubl.)*

and appears associated with fruiting of the basidiomycetes.

A comparison of estimates of minimal fungal productivity with mean biomass estimates (Table 8-3) indicates that minimal productivity ranges from about 2 to 3.6 times the average biomass in the surface soil, giving broad turnover rates of about 2 to 3.6 times per season, about 2 times the rates estimated by Hanssen and Goksøyr (1975) for Norwegian sites. Turnover rates in the deeper soil are generally about 20 to 70% greater. Although fungal biomass is low in the deeper soil layers, the existing biomass appears more productive than near the soil surface. This latter observation may be a result of grazing microbivores consuming more of the fungal growth near the surface (Chapter 11), a phenomenon that may confuse comparisons between years as well.

Estimated bacterial production is only broadly correlated with measured abundance among microtopographic units (Figure 8-9). Although basins of low-centered polygons show low counts of plateable bacteria in the upper soil, the population is relatively more productive than the more abundant populations in wet meadows. Widden (1977) reported a similar situation from Truelove Lowland: the more abundant bacteria of the sedge meadow were less productive than the sparser bacteria on the beach ridge. When dilution counts are converted to biomass, polygon troughs and rims of low-centered polygons are the most productive microtopographic units.

In the wet meadows, average seasonal abundance and productivity of plateable bacteria in the surface soil were higher in 1971 than in 1973. Because most of the increase in bacterial biomass occurs at the end of the season, these observations suggest that the bacteria in the surface of the soils were not encouraged by either the higher late season temperatures or increased precipitation during 1973. The low temperatures encountered in deeper soil apparently did not suppress bacterial growth severely. In 1971 direct counts gave an estimate of the minimal seasonal bacterial productivity in wet meadow surface soils of about 1.2 g m^{-2} (1 cm)$^{-1}$ yr^{-1} in the surface soil while the minimum productivity in the deeper soil was 3.7 g m^{-2} (1 cm)$^{-1}$ yr^{-1}. Again it is possible that microbivores, more active in surface soils, confuse these comparisons.

ENVIRONMENTAL CONTROLS ON MICROFLORAL BIOMASS

Empirical spatial and temporal patterns are presented above. In the following section, an attempt is made to account for the observed differences in microbial biomass among microtopographic units solely on the basis of measured variables: organic substrate, inorganic nutrients, temperature, moisture, and oxygen. The analysis is limited to field data for measured values from a number of different but natural environments. Soil fungi are the only group for which the data base is sufficiently large to address specific relationships.

Substrate

If no other factors are acting, the soil microflora should increase as the amount of organic substrate increases. The total amount of organic material available to microorganisms was seldom measured directly. However, the percentage organic carbon is strongly correlated with bulk density (Chapter 7). Soils of higher bulk density contain more inorganic matter and less organic substrate per gram of soil. Thus fungal density should decline with increasing bulk density. For samples of all but the lowest bulk densities, fungal density does decline with increasing bulk density (Figure 8-10). Regression of fungal biomass in the surface soil (g mycelia cm^{-3}) on amount of carbon per soil volume (g C cm^{-3}) suggests that the response is associated with available substrate:

fungal biomass $= 0.633 + 0.014$ (g C) $(F = 12.47, n = 406)$.

Thus, large differences in amounts of carbon on a volume basis are

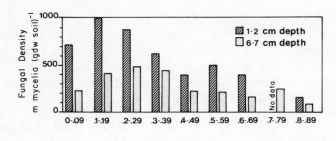

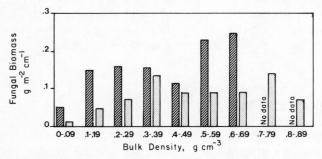

FIGURE 8-10. *The density and biomass of soil fungi arranged by soil bulk density and soil depth. (After Laursen 1975.)*

associated with differences in fungal biomass per volume of soil. Total carbon in the top 15 cm of polygon troughs (Figure 7-1) is about half that found in the wet meadows and the basins and rims of low-centered polygons; fungal biomass in soils of troughs is also lower than in basins, meadows or rims (Figure 8-4). However, fungal biomass per volume of soil shows no consistent relationship with bulk density alone (Figure 8-10). Apparently at the highest bulk densities some factor, such as poor aeration, reduces the "hospitality" of a volume of substrate regardless of the amount of organic substrate available.

Inorganic Nutrients

Observed relationships between soil fungi and amounts of phosphorus are equivocal but suggest that phosphorus is limiting to fungal growth in some microtopographic units. No clear relationship appeared in the surface soil between daily measurements of resin-extractable phosphorus expressed on a volume basis and fungal density (values of the correlation coefficient ranged from 0.10 in polygon troughs to 0.42 in basins of low-centered polygons). However, fungal density and biomass

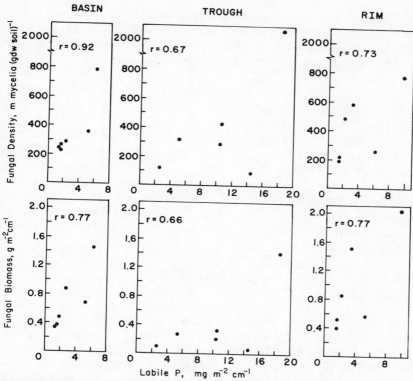

FIGURE 8-11. *The density and biomass of soil fungi in relation to available phosphorus 10 days earlier. An* r *value of 0.81 is statistically significant at the 0.05 level. (Barèl, Laursen and Miller, unpubl.)*

do appear to be related to amounts of resin-extractable phosphorus present ten days earlier (Figure 8-11). Correlation coefficients for phosphorus with density and biomass were 0.77 and 0.92 for the basins of low-centered polygons where concentrations of phosphorus are generally low. The correlations were poorest for polygon troughs, where concentrations of phosphorus are much higher than in basins. Low concentrations of phosphorus may reduce fungal biomass below the levels that can be supported by the amounts of organic substrate present. In the phosphorus-rich troughs fungal density and biomass appear limited by either the reduced amount of organic matter or other conditions associated with high bulk densities.

Regressions of resin-extractable phosphorus against levels of fungal biomass or density 5 or 10 days earlier reveal no significant relationships. Thus, low concentrations of phosphorus do not appear to be a function of low densities of fungi. It is impossible to evaluate the role bacterial biomass or activity may play in modifying levels of soil nutrients, a problem that is particularly disconcerting when considering nitrogen. No significant relationships were found between concentrations of ammonium and abundance of either blue–green algae or fungi.

Temperature, Moisture and Oxygen

Relationships between microbial activity and temperature, moisture and oxygen have been demonstrated in a variety of natural substrates from tundra, including soil (Bunnell et al. 1977a, Bunnell and Scoullar 1981). Relationships between microbial biomass and these abiotic variables are more equivocal. No relationship was found between fungal density or biomass in the soil and soil temperature. However, rates of fungal growth do show relationships with temperature. Relative growth rate (*rgr*) is defined as:

$$rgr = \frac{\ln(D_i / D_{i-1})}{\Delta t}$$

where ln is the natural logarithm, D_i and D_{i-1} represent fungal densities [m mycelia (gdw soil)$^{-1}$] at times t and $t-1$, and Δt represents the time in days between t and $t-1$. When values for relative growth rate are stratified by temperature regardless of microtopographic unit, statistically different distributions of growth rates are observed within different temperature classes based on the mean temperature during that 10-day interval (Figure 8-12). Using the Smirnov one-sided test the probability of temperatures 4 to 5 °C and 5 to 6 °C having the same distribution of growth rates is $\leqslant 0.1$. A similar value is obtained when temperature classes 5 to 6 °C and 6+ °C are compared. The probability that classes 4 to 5 °C and 6+ °C have the same distribution of growth rates is $\leqslant 0.0001$. At higher temperatures a greater proportion of the observed changes in

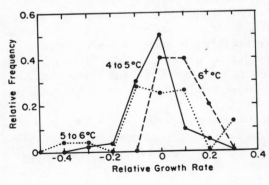

FIGURE 8-12. *The frequency of the relative growth rates of soil fungi at different temperatures. The temperatures used were the means of the 10-day interval. (Laursen, Miller and MacLean, unpubl.)*

biomass are positive and the mean growth rate is more rapid. Mean growth rates were also rapid when the 10-day mean temperatures were less than 4 °C. This temperature range includes the early part of the growing season when fungal densities increase rapidly (Figure 8-7). When organic and inorganic substrates are readily available, rates of fungal growth may be high despite low temperatures.

Within different microtopographic units, relative growth rates are normally distributed with a mean of near zero (−0.024) and a variance of 0.13. The distributions are most different between polygon troughs and rims of low-centered polygons, but cannot be distinguished statistically using the Smirnov test. Although temperature regimes differ between troughs and rims the difference is not sufficient to generate different patterns of fungal growth, and the relationship between temperature and fungal growth rates appears similar in all microtopographic units.

Under natural conditions temperature appears limiting to fungal growth in aboveground substrates only early and late in the season. In 1972 and 1973 growth appeared to respond rapidly to early-season increases in the temperature (Figure 8-13). Despite continued warming,

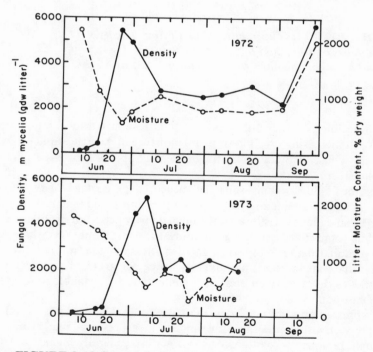

FIGURE 8-13. *Seasonal courses of fungal density and moisture content in* Eriophorum *litter from a wet meadow, 1972 and 1973. (Flanagan, unpubl.)*

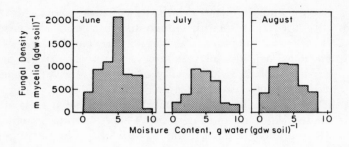

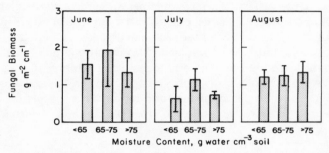

FIGURE 8-14. *The relationship of the density and biomass of soil fungi to soil expressed on a dry weight and on a volume basis for each summer month. (After Laursen 1975.)*

growth declined in early July, apparently in response to declining moisture. With increasing precipitation and moisture in August, rapid growth resumed. Thus, in plant litter, fungal density appears to be correlated with moisture.

In the highly organic soils the measured percentage of water by weight is largely a function of the amount of inorganic material present in the organic matrix. Estimates of fungal density per gram of soil show a clear but somewhat misleading relationship with amounts of water per gram of soil (Figure 8-14). As bulk densities and the amounts of inorganic material increase, amounts of water per gram of soil decrease and so does the relative amount of organic material available to support microbial biomass and growth.

Expressed on a volume basis, moisture content shows little variation seasonally or with depth. Over the range of measures available, estimates of fungal biomass per volume of substrate are generally highest for the moisture class of 0.65 to 0.75 g water cm^{-3} (Figure 8-14). Within this class the percentage moisture on a weight basis ranges from less than 120% to over 800% moisture. Thus, when moisture contents are expressed on a weight basis their potential influence on fungal biomass and bulk density may be confused by strong covariance between both factors. It is noteworthy that the form of the relationship between fungal biomass and moisture is similar to that between microbial respiration and moisture (Bunnell et al. 1977a). Relative growth rates of soil fungi show no relationship with soil moisture. These observations are consistent with the fact that soil moisture is only rarely limiting in the horizons where fungi are abundant.

Although there are few data on amounts of oxygen, those available (Figure 7-6), together with the documented relationships among fungal biomass, organic matter, soil moisture and bulk density, suggest that the low fungal biomasses of some microtopographic units are a function of excessive moisture and oxygen depletion or excessive carbon dioxide. Increases in bulk density resulting from additional fine mineral particles decrease total pore volume and the percentage of air-filled pores (Figure 7-3). With relatively high bulk densities, concentrations of oxygen decline rapidly with depth, carbon dioxide presumably increases, and amounts of fungal biomass are low despite the relatively large amounts of organic substrate. The decline in fungal biomass is due not simply to aeration, but also to available moisture (Bunnell et al. 1977a). In the more mineral layers, field moisture contents decline to 0.55 to 0.60 g cm^{-3}, below the optimal value for fungi (Figure 8-14). Total bacterial biomass is largely unaffected by the declining pore volume or oxygen saturation and appears to respond more directly to available substrate (Figure 8-4, Table 8-2).

Dominant Controls

The broad relations documented above plus the seasonal courses of biomass indicate which environmental factors exert the greatest control on microfloral biomass and productivity. Within the standing dead vegetation the relatively high quality of the substrate in June and, to a lesser extent, in September permit high levels of microfloral biomass and productivity despite relatively low temperatures. At these times, moisture is not limiting. As temperatures increase during the growing season, moisture becomes limiting, substrate quality declines, and microfloral biomass declines. The limitation by moisture is more pronounced for microtopographic units more exposed to wind and drying, such as rims of low-centered polygons and tops of high-centered polygons. The pattern is similar in litter with only slight modifications. The early-season period of positive influence by substrate quality lasts a few days longer in litter than in standing dead, and the mid-season period of control by low amounts of moisture is shorter, markedly so for concave microtopographic units. Temperature again exerts its greatest influence early and late in the season, but may be a controlling influence throughout the growing season in moist, concave microtopographic units.

Marked differences in bulk densities among soils of different microtopographic units modify the pattern of control for soil organisms. Again, enhanced substrate quality at snowmelt and late season leaching of aboveground vegetation encourage the microflora, especially in the surface horizons. Death of roots in the deeper soil provides a similar positive influence late in the season. At all but the highest bulk densities microfloral biomass is correlated with amounts of carbon present and amounts of resin-extractable phosphorus. These factors establish some upper value for potential biomass, while productivity is strongly governed by temperature. Temperatures do not differ sufficiently among microtopographic units to bring about the observed differences, which are largely a product of moisture and aeration. Throughout the top 10 cm of soil, moisture itself is seldom limiting to soil fungi, but insufficient oxygen or excessive carbon dioxide is. High bulk densities and low oxygen levels encourage bacteria over fungi, especially in deeper soil layers. The anaerobic flora is capable of rapid decomposition within heated soils, but under natural conditions the influences of impeded drainage and low amounts of oxygen appear more profound than those of temperature.

While relationships among mineral content, porosity, aeration and moisture appear to modify the apparent "hospitality" of the organic substrate available in some microtopographic units, the basins of low-centered polygons remain an enigma. Physical measures suggest that basins should be favorable to microbes, but populations in standing dead vegetation, litter and soil are consistently low. The high correlations between fungal abundance and resin-extractable phosphorus for basins, together with low amounts of phosphorus in basins, suggest a possible chemical limitation.

SUMMARY

All components of the microflora of the coastal tundra at Barrow are characterized by lower species diversity than is observed in other Biomes, with the possible exception of some deserts. As in other Biomes, algae (photosynthetic microorganisms) are best represented by green and blue-green forms, which in the Biome research area contribute 42 of the 59 species identified. Several algal species are characteristic of fecally contaminated environments, while others are planktonic, reflecting the high amounts of moisture. Bacteria present in the system similarly reflect the high amounts of moisture. Anaerobes, particularly facultative anaerobes, constitute 50 to 70% of the bacterial population and are important in decomposition. Sulfate-reducers are present, while sulfide-oxidizers are rare. The wet, acidic nature of the soils similarly discourages heterotrophic nitrogen-fixing and nitrifying bacteria, while denitrifiers are common, accentuating the importance of nitrogen fixation by algae. Although all major classes of fungi are present, their diversity also is low. Most fungi exhibit specificity for particular microtopographic units. Generally, endemics are few and sterile forms make up more than 50% of the isolates. In comparison to other Biomes, wood-rotting fungi are rare, reflecting the low availability of suitable substrate, while mycorrhizal fungi are common in some areas. Aquatic fungi are present primarily as algal parasites. The apparent dominance of basidiomycetes among the fungi is associated with their role as mycorrhizal formers and with their more versatile, dikaryotic hyphal system, which may facilitate adaptation to an extreme environment.

Average amounts of total microfloral biomass also differ significantly among microtopographic units. Total biomass ranges from 12 to 20 g m^{-2} in the upper 7 cm. Biomass is generally highest in wet meadows and polygon troughs, lower on rims of low-centered polygons, and lowest in basins of low-centered polygons. The inhospitality exhibited by basins is evident in fungal densities in standing dead vegetation and litter as well as in the soil. Generally the eukaryotic decomposers, fungi and yeasts, are much better represented in well aerated soils found on rims of low-centered polygons and tops of high-centered polygons, while bacteria become dominant in the wetter soils of polygon troughs and wet meadows. Plate counts of bacteria are commonly a factor of ten lower than values reported for soils of the temperate zone, while direct counts are higher. Because of the smaller size of the bacteria found in the coastal tundra at Barrow, total bacterial biomass is similar to that in temperate regions. Fungal biomass is frequently much lower than values reported for other Biomes and fungi-to-bacteria ratios approximate values for temperate regions only in the well aerated soils. In wet soils decomposition is governed by bacteria to a greater degree than in most soils from other Biomes.

The broad relationships with moisture and aeration that govern relative distribution across microtopographic units also influence patterns with depth. Densities of eukaryotic organisms decline rapidly with depth, producing a shift from fungal to bacterial dominance. This shift reduces the potential to degrade compounds of large molecular weight and total carbon declines much less rapidly with depth than does root production. Intra- and interseasonal differences in abundance also demonstrate the influence of moisture in the tundra system, with moister periods or moister microtopographic units generally showing depressed fungal biomass or productivity. Both bacteria and fungi exhibit a similar seasonal pattern of biomass with early- and late-season peaks. While the peak in early summer appears to be associated with release of organic material at thaw, the late peak may be associated with senescence and death of plant parts. This underlying pattern generated by availability of substrate is subsequently modified by the amounts of moisture present. Depending upon the microtopography and climate, fungi in the soil show minimal turnover rates for biomass of two to six times per season.

Although low temperatures may limit amounts of microbial biomass, temperature-related differences between years or among microtopographic units were not observed. Rates of activity (Chapter 9) and growth, however, are positively related to temperature. The organic substrate seldom governs the biomass of the microflora, but low concentrations of inorganic nutrients, particularly phosphorus, are limiting to growth rates in some microtopographic units. The major control on composition and biomass of the microflora appears to be moisture and associated aeration. These factors are indirectly controlled by temperature through the impeded drainage associated with permafrost, and are much modified by physical characteristics of the soils such as bulk density.

9

Microflora Activities and Decomposition

P. W. Flanagan and F. L. Bunnell

INTRODUCTION

Decomposition results in the disintegration and mineralization of organic residues. Most physical and chemical changes that occur in and around the decomposing substrate cannot be separated from the effects of microbial activity. However, degradation of plant and animal remains may be well advanced before significant ingress of microbes occurs (Dowding 1974, Flanagan and Veum 1974). Losses of weight and specific chemical constituents, which are often considered as measures of decomposition, may be initiated by plant–soil environment interactions that induce senescence and autolysis in moribund tissue. Important ecological phenomena that cause loss of weight from organic residues but occur somewhat independently of microbial activity include leaching, microfaunal activities, and chemical reactions that influence mineralization.

Soil invertebrates and protozoans are considered to influence decomposition rates indirectly by modifying the activities of the decomposer organisms or microbes. They modify the environment through comminution of organic matter, and the microbial populations by grazing upon them (Chapter 11). Plant components like soil algae and the roots of vascular plants alter the environment through the provision of particular substrates and physical structure, and by modification of pH and supply rates for oxygen and other chemical compounds.

Decomposition of organic matter is accompanied by synthesis of microbial tissues which themselves decompose, contributing to further microbial production. If the amount of substrate is limited, the potential for production of microbial biomass is dependent upon the efficiency of the microbial population in solubilizing, assimilating and incorporating organic remains, i.e. the efficiency of conversion of grams substrate to grams microbe, or the yield coefficient. The yield coefficient is influenced by climatic and substrate variables and is decreased significantly by the maintenance demands of preformed and forming tissues (Gray and Williams 1971). These aspects of microbial activities are best related to inputs from primary production.

Under aerobic conditions, microbes decomposing a substrate break down complex organic molecules to end-products that are primarily inorganic (carbon dioxide, water and minerals); under anaerobic conditions the end-products assume a variety of organic and inorganic forms. The breaking down is accompanied by a loss in weight and energy content of the substrate as well as disintegration of its physical structure. An observer of the decomposition phenomenon thus witnesses physical and chemical as well as biological changes. Measures of decomposition incorporate varying features of these changes, and no one measure quantifies decomposition perfectly. Belowground events are especially difficult to decipher because of the simultaneous respiration of heterotrophic and autotrophic organisms and the complex geometry of hundreds of substrates and microorganisms showing vastly different responses. Soils of the coastal tundra at Barrow are frozen for a large part of the year and this further complicates examination of biological processes within them.

Given the complex of physical, chemical and biological processes comprised in decomposition, diverse methods have been employed to relate the findings of individual, specialized techniques to general concepts. The concepts of decomposition used recognize that different microbes have different enzymatic potentials or capacities to utilize various chemical constituents of naturally occurring substrates. Not only do microbes have different capacities to exploit substrates, but their enzymatic potential, growth and respiration rates also respond differently to the temperature, moisture, oxygen and pH in their environment. Thus the capacity to decompose inherent in a particular microbial population is at any time modified by the environment.

Acknowledging this conceptual framework, our studies of decomposition have examined the physiological potentials of different microfloral constituents to utilize particular chemical compounds as substrates; the response of these potentials to environmental conditions; the biomass, biomass yield per gram of substrate, and maintenance demands of major microbial species; the response of rates of respiration and growth to changes in important environmental variables such as temperature, moisture, oxygen and dissolved nutrients; and the resultant loss rates of particular chemical constituents, carbon, calories and net weight. Measures of ability to utilize particular chemical compounds are *in vitro* assessments of an organism's ability to exploit selected natural substrates. Responses of respiration and growth to selected environmental variables and measures of biomass yields and maintenance demands are also evaluated, primarily by laboratory techniques, particularly Gilson respirometry. Laboratory measures are related to field observations by simulation models (Flanagan and Bunnell 1976, Bunnell et al. 1977a, b). Field measures of decomposition and decomposition-related phenomena are primarily measures of rates of loss of specific substrate components. Four field measures have been employed.

Weight losses from litter bags measure the rate at which litter becomes sufficiently disintegrated that it disappears from the litter bag. A portion of this loss is due to microbial activity but some weight is lost by leaching and physical comminution by invertebrates and by the freeze-thaw cycle. Ingress of microbial, plant, animal and mineral matter can confound estimates of weight loss.

Chemical analyses of substrate composition coupled with measured weight loss estimate the rate of disappearance of major chemical compounds such as cellulose or phosphorus. These measures are also an inaccurate estimate of microbial activity. Not only are other processes also acting (e.g. leaching) but the microbial populations and their chemical composition are inseparable from the substrates.

Measurements of rates of evolution of carbon dioxide represent the rate of mineralization of complex organic compounds to carbon dioxide, water and residual constituents such as minerals, and are perhaps the best measure of aerobic microbial activity. Depending on the substrate measured and the method used, various inaccuracies are introduced, either by the effects of methodology, as with the physical disturbance in Gilson respirometry, or by inclusion of carbon dioxide evolved from plant roots and soil invertebrates. Anaerobic decomposition processes are incompletely measured by carbon dioxide evolution and may present an important omission in some habitats.

Measurements of microbial biomass during decomposition of above- and belowground substrates permit one to relate the abundance of major decomposer agents to substrate availability and quality. These measures, coupled with laboratory data on microbial growth and yield from varying substrates and information indicating microbial maintenance demands, allow approximation of the microbial production in the field. Microbial biomass and production may then be compared with similar measures from leaves, roots, microfauna etc. Additionally, studies of microbial biomass permit compensation for underestimates of weight loss caused by growth of microbial tissue in litter bags. By knowing microbial mineral content per gram we can approximate values for mineral immobilization and cycling in microbial biomass and production, respectively.

In the subsequent discussion, both field and laboratory measures are employed to help define patterns of decomposition. Since decomposition is equated with the microbial mineralization of carbon, these measures are to varying degrees inaccurate. No one measure discretely encompasses decomposition as defined, but integrated with a knowledge of microbial biomass, dynamics, and physiology the measures contribute to a synthetic view of decomposition. Tools of integration include correlative analyses and computer simulation models. Although these tools are in some instances novel and sophisticated, the conceptual framework employed owes much to the seminal work of Douglas and Tedrow (1959) (see Bunnell and Tait 1974).

The approach in the following discussion moves through the conceptual framework as it is presented above, first examining the potential to exploit particular substrates that different microfloral constituents possess. Then we examine the manner in which this potential and other critical activities such as respiration are influenced by environmental variables such as temperature, moisture and oxygen. The discussion in the section on *Decomposer activities and decomposition* utilizes simulation models to combine the responses of microbial respiration to individual environmental variables and compares the predictions with integrative measures such as weight loss. Measures of microbial biomass, yield and efficiency are related to substrate availability and potentials for mineral cycling and immobilization.

POTENTIAL OF THE MICROFLORA
TO UTILIZE SUBSTRATES

The decomposition of organic remains proceeds mainly through the action of microorganisms that can use them as a source of energy and nutrients. Most soil microbial populations are heterotrophic and the organisms compete for available substrates. In the coastal tundra at Barrow, microbial saprophytes are more competitive and abundant than are parasites and the present discussion ignores the latter. Not all saprophytic microorganisms utilize and compete for the same substrates. Although an individual microorganism may be encouraged by the presence of a specific substrate that it can use, its potential to exploit that substrate is further modified by environmental conditions and "competitive saprophytic ability" (Garrett 1963). The composition of the microbial population inhabiting a particular substrate and thus the decomposition rate of the substrate are therefore dependent upon the environmental conditions and competitive ability of the microorganisms as well as the measured potential to utilize specific substrates. The data presented here are based almost entirely on *in vitro* measurements. The discussion is biased towards treatment of the mycoflora rather than of the total microbial population.

Major substrates for decomposer organisms at Barrow can be divided into two main categories on the basis of their chemical composition, pattern of dissolution and utilization by microorganisms. These categories are 1) low molecular weight, water- and/or 80%-ethanol-soluble fractions that are readily leachable, and 2) the more recalcitrant compounds, such as lignin, cellulose, hemicellulose, pectin and starch. The first, more soluble group contains approximately 25% of aboveground plant products, exits as leachate from moribund tissues and contains the bulk (> 80%) of plant leaf nitrogen, phosphorus and potassium. The second group represents the bulk of the available organic substrate and is relatively poor in nitrogen, phosphorus and potassium (Flanagan and Veum 1974, Van Cleve 1974). Substrates of the more soluble group are frequently utilized by organisms decomposing the more resistant group.

Microflora in all Biomes display a broad diversity of enzymatic potential to decompose the various organic substrates. Tundra microflora share this capacity, with the restriction that the cold-dominated environment has selected for taxa or strains that utilize these substrates under cooler conditions. The restricted number of taxa may or may not reduce the potential to complete a given phase of decomposition such as conversion of cellulose to carbon dioxide, but it does reduce the number of modes that such a reaction can follow in the ecosystem.

As in many temperate zone habitats, bacteria in tundra are often weak competitors with the fungi for those substrates that both groups have the enzymatic potential to metabolize. The competitive difference is especially obvious in such habitats as standing dead and litter, and in drier surface soils. Conversely, in wet habitats bacteria play a proportionately greater role in decomposition. In extremely wet or anaerobic habitats, such as sediments of tundra ponds or soils at depth, bacteria are the dominant group of decomposers. The potentials to utilize specific forms of nitrogen and phosphorus are addressed in Chapters 7 and 12; here we consider only carbon.

Bacteria

The sources of carbon most commonly exploited by soil bacteria are of intermediate molecular size (Table 9-1). Large molecules such as pectin and cellulose, which form major structural entities of plant cells, can be decomposed by relatively few of the plateable bacteria. *Cytophaga* appears important among the cellulose-decomposing bacteria since it frequently occurs on plate isolations. Enrichment studies of "most probable number" show *Cytophaga* populations varying from 10^5 (gdw soil)$^{-1}$ after thaw to 10^6 (gdw soil)$^{-1}$ at mid-season. No cultures of indigenous aerobic bacteria that could decompose humic substances were obtained.

The relative ability to utilize humic substances is one of the major enzymatic differences that separate bacteria from fungi (cf. Table 9-1 and Figure 9-1). Widden (1977) has documented similar differences between bacteria and fungi at Devon Island. Enzymes that cleave the aro-

TABLE 9-1 *Percentage of Bacterial Types at Barrow Capable of Utilizing Specific Carbon Sources*

Carbon source	Bacteria (%)
Succinic acid	92
Citric acid	84
Glucose	78
Maltose	66
Starch	42
Pectin	28
Lactic acid	25
Cellulose	5
Lactose	0
Lignin	0
Tannic acid	0

Note: Based on 200 randomly selected aerobic types isolated from the 0- to 2-cm soil depth in wet meadows and tested at 15 °C.
Source: Benoit (unpubl.).

matic ring of humic materials require the presence of oxygen. Thus, as humic materials move from the surface into the less aerobic subsurface layers of the soils, the probability of their decomposition is markedly reduced. The differential capacities of bacteria and fungi to survive low amounts of oxygen and to exploit humic material are instrumental in the accumulation of organic matter in the soil horizon.

The strictly anaerobic portion of the microflora remains the least known in terms of physiology and in situ activity. Rapid development and intense activity of anaerobes on the soil plots heated to 15 to 20 °C illustrates the potential of this group. Enrichment cultures of strictly anaerobic cellulose-decomposers and methane-producers were obtained from anaerobic soils on these plots. There is no evidence that anaerobic bacteria can degrade humic materials; therefore the activity of the anaerobes becomes limited when the pool of rapidly decomposable material originating from the death of belowground parts is exhausted. Continued decomposition requires the action of other microorganisms and a change of abiotic conditions.

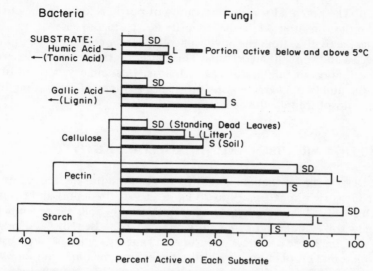

FIGURE 9-1. *Percentages of fungi and bacteria capable of exploiting specific organic substrates. Bacterial percentages are based on 200 randomly selected, aerobic types isolated from the 0- to 2-cm soil depth in wet meadows and tested at 15°C. Fungal percentages are based on percent frequency of major species and their ability to utilize specific substrates as sole carbon sources* in vitro. *(Benoit and Flanagan, unpubl.)*

Fungi

The major taxonomic groups of phyllosphere, litter and soil fungi have been discussed (Chapter 8). The ability of these groups to utilize pectin, starch, cellulose and lignin has been tested (Flanagan and Scarborough 1974). Comparison among the mycoflorae of the phyllosphere, litter and soil reveals different enzyme potentials for substrate degradation as integrated over the season (Figure 9-1). Generally, the mycoflorae of litter and soil are better able to degrade the more recalcitrant substrates than is the mycoflora of the phyllosphere. Fungi in standing dead leaves are infrequently cellulolytic (10%), while in litter and soil 27% and 35% respectively are cellulolytic. The pattern is repeated for polyphenol oxidizers, some of which (gallic acid oxidizers) are better represented in litter and soil than are cellulolytic forms. The potential to utilize humic acids also is represented better among litter and soil fungi than among fungi of the phyllosphere. Fungi decomposing pectin and starch make up the greatest portion of the mycoflora, whether from phyllosphere, litter or soil. The potential for decomposition of pectin is lower in the phyllosphere than in litter while the opposite is true in the case of potential amylase activities. Both the phyllosphere and litter contain more utilizers of pectin and starch than do soils. This pattern is the reverse of the trend in distribution of utilizers of lignocellulose. In summary, a trend of increasing ability to degrade larger molecules is apparent proceeding from the phyllosphere into the soil.

ABIOTIC VARIABLES AND MICROFLORA ACTIVITIES

Despite the low annual input of energy to tundra, the active layer of the soils is rich in carbon (9 to 20 kg m^{-2} to 20 cm depth) and contains much energy. The energy contents of wet meadow soils range from 13.8 kJ (gdw soil)$^{-1}$ in the 0- to 2-cm horizon to 9.6 kJ (gdw soil)$^{-1}$ at depths of 12 to 18 cm. These resources of carbon and energy could sustain substantial microbial production, provided other environmental conditions were satisfactory. Potentially limiting factors include low temperatures and reduced availability of moisture, oxygen and inorganic nutrients.

Here we treat two themes: 1) potentially adaptive responses to low temperatures, and 2) relationships between measured soil oxygen, associated moisture levels, and activities of microbial groups.

Responses to Temperature

Temperature influences microbial activity in at least three ways. Both growth rates and respiration rates of microorganisms are affected as well as the activities of specific enzymes used to degrade substrates. Cardinal influences of temperature on organisms and their enzymes determine the upper and lower temperature thresholds. The form of the response may differ between cardinal points. We have examined the influence of temperature on tundra microorganisms within the framework of two broad hypotheses:

1) Tundra microorganisms gain cold tolerance by extending their range of metabolism towards lower temperatures.
2) Tundra microorganisms enhance their effective metabolic range by showing linear rather than exponential responses to low temperature (Bunnell et al. 1977a).

The first hypothesis addresses the depression of the lower cardinal temperature; the second addresses the form of response to changing temperature. Both hypotheses relate to psychrophily. Definitions of psychrophily and mesophily vary (Ingraham 1958, Griffin 1972, Christophersen

1973). Psychrophilic organisms are here defined as having a growth optimum at or below 20 °C (Griffin 1972).

Temperature Influences on Microbial Growth and Respiration

Metabolic processes of decomposers are generally adapted to the cold-dominated environment. Respiration within soil and litter is measurable down to -6.5 °C and substantial increases in fungal biomass have been measured in soils when temperatures were between 0 ° and 2 °C. Data on growth and respiration of individual bacteria from the Biome research area and other cold-dominated systems (Boyd 1967, Christensen 1974, Mosser et al. 1976) have shown that strict psychrophiles are present, but their incidence is less than 5 to 10% of the total plateable flora.

Most fungi are cold-tolerant mesophiles able to respire heterotrophically to -6.5 °C but with optima for growth and respiration between 20 ° and 30 °C (Figure 9-2). Minimum and maximum temperatures at which

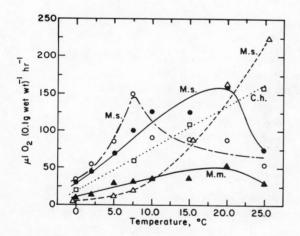

FIGURE 9-2. *Influence of temperature on respiration of tundra fungi growing on potato extract in Gilson respirometers (1 m extract: 0.1 g mycelium). M.s. = three different* Mycelia sterilia *from Barrow tundra soil; C.h. =* Cladosporium herbarum; *M.m. =* Mucor microsporus. *Each point is a mean of three samples; six readings per sample. Standard deviations ranged from 5 to 7.5% of mean. (After Flanagan and Scarborough 1974.)*

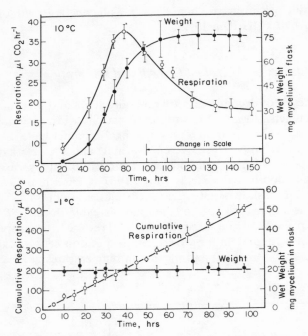

FIGURE 9-3. *Respiration and growth (wet weight) of a common tundra soil fungus,* Mycelium sterilium *B18, at 10° and –1 °C, growing on a mineral salt medium containing a known amount of glucose. Vertical bars represent the standard errors (*n = 6*). (After Flanagan and Bunnell 1976.)*

respiration was measurable using individual fungi were –6.5 °C and + 48 °C. Some psychrophilic fungi were present. Corresponding with the temperature gradient, there is a general increase in psychrophilic fungi from the phyllosphere (5.5%) to the litter (7.5%) and into the soil (15.6% of the mycoflora). Even among psychrophilic forms, however, growth of most organisms was not measurable below –3 °C. At 0 °C the psychrophiles cultured on potato extract broth did produce measurable growth; average growth rate of four psychrophiles at 0 °C was 3.6 mg g^{-1} day^{-1}. Fungi from other Alaskan sites, Eagle Summit and Prudhoe Bay, showed similar responses (Flanagan and Scarborough 1974), leading to the conclusion that both bacteria and fungi in tundra are capable of growth and respiration at subzero temperatures. These observations support hypothesis one.

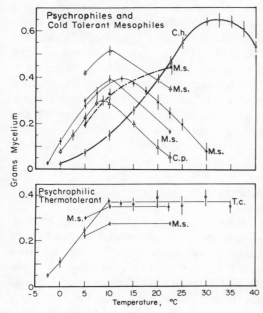

FIGURE 9-4. *Fungal growth responses to temperature among several different sterile forms (M.s.),* Chrysosporium pannorum *(C.p.),* Cladosporium herbarum *(C.h.), and* Trichosporiella cerebriformis *(T.c.) growing in liquid potato dextrose extract. Vertical bars represent the standard errors (n = 8). (Flanagan, unpubl.)*

Growth rates of fungi are not always closely coupled with rates of respiration (Figure 9-3), especially in the senescing phase of growth or at low temperatures (−3 °C) when growth has ceased but respiration is still measurable. The relationship between respiration and temperature can be either linear or exponential, depending on the isolate. Furthermore, certain fungi, e.g. CC8, may show an exponential relationship between respiration and temperature while the relationship of growth to temperature is linear, or the reverse may be the case as with *Cladosporium herbarum* (cf. Figures 9-2 and 9-4). Therefore no one specific organism or randomly collected group of organisms will emulate completely the response of respiration or growth to temperature found among field populations.

Summing individual rates of respiration (cf. growth) for the major fungal species shows an average Q_{10} (ratio of the rates at 10° and 0 °C) of 3.6. The measured Q_{10} for respiration of total litter over the same temperature range is between 3.8 and 4. Temperature fluctuations decrease and temperatures are generally lower with depth. According to the second hypothesis it is expected that with increasing depth microorganisms would show flatter and more linear responses to temperature for their various biological activities. A linear rather than exponential response to temperature can result in a higher rate of activity near the minimum temperatures (Bunnell et al. 1977a). In support of the second hypothesis it is noted that observed relations between respiration and temperature in soils do not depart statistically from linear, and computed Q_{10} values in the soil are frequently less than 2.0. Q_{10} values for respiration decrease from the surface litter downwards into the soil. Numbers of psychrophiles increase from the phyllosphere to the 10-cm depth in soil, and the majority of psychrophiles and several important cold-tolerant mesophiles have linear responses to increasing temperature (Figures 9-2 and 9-4). Because such organisms have not been recorded for temperate regions it would seem that the second hypothesis is further supported.

Temperature Influences on Substrate Utilization

About 80 to 90% of the tundra bacteria that are cellulolytic at 15 °C are unable to use cellulose as a sole source of carbon at 0 °C. But 82% of these same bacteria use glucose as a sole source of carbon at 0 °C. These observations are similar to those made in Canadian arctic lakes by Christensen (1974), who found 6% of the cellulolytic *Cytophaga* to be psychrophilic. The bacteria capable of decomposing hydrocarbons that were isolated from plots treated with oil at the Biome research area illustrate similar relations with temperature. Bacteria that could use mineral oil as a sole source of carbon at 15 °C could not metabolize the same substrate at 0 °C (Campbell et al. 1973). They could, however, use succinic acid or glutamic acid as sole sources of carbon at 0° and 15 °C.

The limited data suggest that a temperature near 0 °C eliminates specific metabolic pathways of bacteria while other metabolic activities, e.g. respiration, in the same organisms are only depressed. At low temperature bacteria can sustain themselves on substrates which at higher temperature they might ignore in favor of larger molecular compounds. Comparable data are not available for temperate forms of the organisms found at Barrow, but one interpretation of such a switch between substrates is that the tundra organisms are responding to the demands of a colder environment. Such a response broadly conforms to hypothesis one, and suggests that tundra bacteria extend their capabilities at lower temperature by exploiting compounds of lower molecular weight.

The influences of temperature on the potentials for substrate utilization by fungi are greatest for simple substrates (Figure 9-1). Utilization of cellulose and phenolic compounds does not cease below 5 °C and in most cases continues to sub-zero levels, although usually at lower rates. Potentials for fungal utilization of pectin and starch are substantially decreased when the temperature falls below 5 °C but do not cease. Decomposers of hemicelluloses have not been fully examined, but preliminary data suggest that the fungal potential for hydrolysis of hemicellulose resembles the pattern for utilization of pectin and starch.

The response of the fungi thus contrasts directly with that of bacteria which apparently use less recalcitrant substrates preferentially as temperature decreases. Widden (1977) made similar observations on Devon Island. The byproducts of fungal cellulolysis may serve as substrates for bacteria at temperatures below 5 °C and coevolution of interdependent cold acclimations may result in closer relationships between bacteria and fungi at lower temperatures.

Our second hypothesis relates to the form of response with changing temperature. Different enzymes produced by pure cultures of specific tundra fungi have very different responses to temperature (Figure 9-5). The low temperatures (< 10 °C) commonly encountered may encompass simultaneously the optimal range for utilization of one substrate and the unfavorable range for utilization of another. Flanagan and Scarborough (1974) have shown that some cellulolytic fungi decompose cellulose optimally below 10 °C, while in the same organism optimal amylase and pectinase activity occurs above 30 °C. The pectinase activities of four fungal isolates (Figure 9-5) have temperature optima between 18 ° and 30 °C, while those for cellulase activities are between 6 ° and 14 °C.

If such differences in enzyme activity through varying temperature ranges occur *in vivo*, then the optimum temperature range for cellulose decomposition in the field may be wider than for some other enzyme systems, e.g. pectinase and amylase. These observations help explain why pectinolytic and amylolytic fungi are less frequently isolated or active at low temperature than are cellulolytic forms (Figure 9-1).

Literature on fungi from temperate regions often examines temperature as a regulator of fungal respiration, but relationships between temperature and utilization of substrate have received less attention. Thus both hypotheses presented here are not fully testable with regard to utilization of substrate. However, tundra fungi at Barrow do appear to extend their effective metabolic activity over a wide temperature range, by incorporating different temperature optima for utilization of different substrates.

Temperature influences on microbial utilization of substrate, growth and respiration seem to fall into three broad groups (Figures 9-2, 9-3 and 9-4). All three groups have a range of activity that extends below 0 °C, while at the same time the population as a whole has the flexibility to take advantage of mesic and higher temperatures. One group, including several sterile soil fungi together with *Mucor microsporus*, shows very gradual responses of growth and respiration to temperature values in the range from –3 ° to + 20 °C. The second group shows a positive response to increasing temperature up to an optimal point, but thereafter shows no further response to increasing temperature in the range exam-

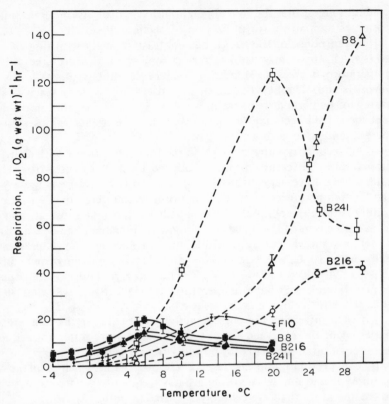

FIGURE 9-5. *Influence of temperature and substrates on fungal respiration for* Cylindrocarpon magnusianum *(B8),* Cladosporium *cf.* cladosporoides *(B216),* Phialophora hoffmannii *(B241) and* Chrysosporium pruinosum *(F10) in Gilson respirometers growing on media with cellulose (—) and pectin (---) as the sole sources of carbon. Substrate moisture content was 250% (dry weight) in all cases. Flasks contained 0.1 g fungus (wet weight). Measures began 48 hours after substrate inoculation. (After Flanagan and Scarborough 1974.)*

ined, e.g. *Trichosporiella cerebriformis* and several sterile forms like B1, CC17 and CSS4 (Figure 9-4). Fungi with responses to temperature like that of *T. cerebriformis* are new to the literature in microbial ecology and could be termed "psychrophilic thermotolerant." Roots of plants such as *Eriophorum angustifolium* show a similar response to temperature for uptake of phosphorus (Chapin 1974a). A third group of soil fungi displays psychrophilism, but demonstrates high exponential increases of respiration in its minimum–optimum temperature range, e.g. CC8 (Figure 9-2).

Together, the two hypotheses address extension of the lower temperature limits and the form of response with changing temperature. The microflora appears to have extended its capacity to degrade substrates, respire and grow at low temperatures. Respiration continues to $-7.5\,°C$, growth is positive at $0\,°C$, and oxidation of cellulose and phenols probably continues well below $+5\,°C$, possibly to $-7.5\,°C$, because psychrophilic and psychrophilic thermotolerant organisms show a propensity for utilizing these substrates at low temperature. Both interspecific differences and individual responses serve to increase the effective metabolic range of the microflora, by broadening the near-optimal metabolic range or form of response with changing temperature. Bacteria appear to increase their effective metabolic range by shifting to compounds of lower molecular weight (6-C compounds) at lower temperature, while fungi continue oxidation of cellulose and phenols. In terms of growth and respiration, evidence from tests of individual soil fungi and the calculation of the percentage of psychrophiles in soil as compared to above ground (7.5% in litter, 15.6% in soil) strongly suggests that soil organisms at Barrow are cold-adapted, while aboveground populations with wider ranges of near-optimal temperature occur. Adaptation to cold rather than acclimation is indicated. Progressing from aboveground to belowground environments, relations between temperature and respiration tend from exponential to linear, suggesting another form of adaptation to cold. Computed values of Q_{10} from soils of the Biome research area are typically lower (closer to linearity) than are values from temperate soils (Macfadyen 1970, de Boois 1974). Neither the first nor the second hypothesis can be rejected.

Responses to Moisture and Oxygen

As with temperature, moisture levels for microbial activity assume minimum and maximum thresholds and optima. These cardinal moisture levels differ between organisms and within a single organism for different processes. While there are some notable exceptions (Pitt and Christian 1968), most microbial activities in soil are limited by moisture potentials below -100 bars. The lower limit for bacteria generally is believed to be higher than that for fungi (Dommergues 1962, Griffin 1972). It is unlikely that soils of the Barrow research area were dry enough to restrict the activities of microorganisms, but in the standing dead canopy decomposition may be limited by lack of moisture. Within the soils, moisture effects are more likely to be indirect and associated with reduced flux of oxygen (Chapter 8).

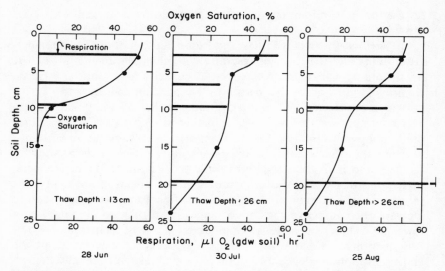

FIGURE 9-6. *Depth profiles of soil respiration and oxygen saturation on three days in wet meadows. Oxygen saturation measured by Polarographic analyses; respiration measured by Gilson respirometry. (Based on data from Benoit and Gersper, unpubl.)*

Oxygen concentrations are influenced by root metabolism and the associated rhizosphere effect as well as by soil moisture and respiration by decomposers. Because of the intense respiratory activity of the roots and the associated bacteria, the rhizosphere has a high demand for oxygen. Since tundra plants typically have high root-to-shoot ratios there is high demand for oxygen throughout the active layer.

Microaerobic or anaerobic conditions depress the overall activity and eliminate some functions of the soil microflora. Over short periods anaerobic conditions reduce the rate of decomposition because of the buildup of end-products which inhibit microbial activity. In the long term, anaerobic conditions may be the major reason organic matter can accumulate. All natural products except aromatic compounds can be decomposed under anaerobic and aerobic conditions. The aromatic compounds generally cannot be utilized as microbial substrates under anaerobic conditions. Furthermore, the decomposition of large molecular weight compounds is largely the province of the fungi. Therefore, lignicolous and phenolic polymer compounds will be decomposed primarily in the surface soil where oxygen values are higher and the fungal biomass is greatest (Chapter 8). When phenolic compounds reach the lower levels of the soil profile, either by leaching or transfer by microfauna, they enter a zone of changed abiotic conditions where oxygen levels and temperatures are lower. Here they can accumulate and thereby affect the long-term carbon balance of the system. Under anaerobic conditions these aromatic products may change their chemical structure, repolymerize and become highly recalcitrant organic matter.

However, decomposition occurs throughout the active layer (Figure 9-6) and the numbers of facultative and anaerobic bacteria appear sufficient to prevent rapid accumulation of carbon in the wetter microtopographic units. Roots that follow the thaw front down presumably can exploit nutrients mobilized by microbial activity.

Moisture and Microfloral Metabolism

Because of the interaction between moisture and temperature, a general optimal moisture level for microbial respiration in organic residues is indeterminable, but an optimal moisture range is determinable at optimal temperatures (Douglas and Tedrow 1959, Flanagan and Veum 1974). When moisture is less than 20% of the dry weight residues it is not possible to measure respiration at any temperature; thus moisture levels above 20% dry weight seem necessary to initiate microbial metabolism. The metabolic rates continue to increase throughout the moisture range 20 to 500% of dry weight. High moisture levels (> 500% dw) may depress microbial respiration. In a Gilson respirometer the depressant effect can be eliminated by increasing available oxygen (Flanagan and Veum 1974) and is likely associated with reduced rates of supply of oxygen. As temperatures increase, respiration in some substrates shows saturation of metabolic moisture demand at amounts of moisture less than 400% dw. Temperature–moisture interactions, as demonstrated by studies of microbial respiration from plant remains, may reflect differences in oxygen diffusivity in water or changes in microbial oxygen demand as temperature varies.

Oxygen and Microfloral Metabolism

Oxygen is critical in microbial metabolism because it serves as an electron acceptor in the breakdown of organic matter. In the soils at Barrow the potential alternate electron acceptors such as nitrate and sulfate are present in such low concentrations (< 1 ppm) that they can support little activity. Diffusion of oxygen into the soil is often below levels required for optimal microbial activity, and in very wet soils pore spaces become filled with moisture. The effect is decreased microbial activity among the aerobic component; the cause is not too much moisture, but apparently too little oxygen. It is equally plausible that carbon dioxide operating separately from or in concert with a deficiency of oxygen reduces microfloral metabolism (Burges 1958, Griffin 1972).

The highest oxygen levels measured within the upper 20 cm of soil were observed in the soils of the basins and rims of low-centered polygons and the tops of high-centered polygons (Figure 7-6). It is surprising to find that on the dates they were sampled the basins of low-centered polygons had high oxygen values throughout the soil profile. Soil thin sections from basins, unlike rims, indicate a structure that should impede drainage and aeration (Everett, pers. comm.). The data for both *in vitro* respirometry and measured evolution of carbon dioxide indicate that basins of low-centered polygons have low rates of decomposer activity (Figure 9-9). For example, in 1972 the mean seasonal rate of respiration, as measured by Gilson respirometry, for 0- to 2-cm basin soils was 10.06 μl O_2 (gdw soil)$^{-1}$ hr^{-1} whereas the values from similar depths in the trough and very wet meadow were 31.37 and 43.15 μl O_2 (gdw soil)$^{-1}$ hr^{-1} respectively. The consistently low decomposer activity and low primary productivity probably act to maintain relatively high levels of oxygen in the basin soils.

The shift of bacteria-to-fungi ratios along the oxygen gradient (Chapter 8) suggests that anaerobiosis does not eliminate decomposition of the soil organic matter but changes the quality of that decomposition. In the wet meadow, depressed oxygen concentrations in the deeper soils were associated with high levels of decomposer activity measured by Gilson respirometry (Figure 9-6). Thus the high values for respiration from subsurface samples represent activity of facultative bacteria after full induction of potential for oxidative phosphorylation in the Gilson respirometer. The rapid response to oxygen indicates the active enzymatic state of the cells. The zone of anaerobiosis at the front of the thaw zone appears to be a result of the rapid decomposition of readily available substrates.

Experiments with heated soil further demonstrate that anaerobic conditions *per se* do not prevent decomposer activity in tundra soils. Oxygen saturation in the soil solution in heated soils declined to 0% by the 3-cm depth. On these plots methane routinely composed 60% (with a range of 42 to 65% of the gas released), with the balance primarily of carbon dioxide. Methane production provides good evidence for anaerobic activity because methane producers represent one of the most strictly anaerobic groups, and can be killed easily by transitory exposure to oxygen. Despite anaerobic conditions, rates of decomposition were high in heated soils. Evolution of carbon dioxide over a 33-day period in late summer was 39% higher in heated soils, and after 12 months the energy content in the heated soil was less than in control soils by 21% in the upper 2 cm and by 16% at depths of 7 to 12 cm. The higher rates of microbial respiration in the heated soils are a result of the increased temperatures and approximate the rates expected, given the respiratory Q_{10} of 1.78 measured from unheated soils and a 4° to 6°C increase in mean daily soil temperature. The heat treatment documents the in situ potential for anaerobic decomposition present in tundra soils suggested by the high number of facultative bacteria relative to strictly aerobic species (Chapter 8).

DECOMPOSER ACTIVITIES AND DECOMPOSITION

Two general approaches are used in analyzing the response of decomposer organisms to temperature, moisture and other environmental phenomena. The first approach employs integrative measures of all microbial groups. The evolution of carbon dioxide, the rates of weight loss from selected substrates, and the patterns of nutrient concentration are each considered direct or indirect functions of the activities of all microbial groups. The second, more direct, approach examines the individual activities of specific microbial groups. The specific activities suggest the contribution particular groups make to the general integrative measures such as carbon dioxide evolution. We discussed some specific responses earlier in this chapter without relating them to patterns of weight loss or carbon dioxide evolution measured in the field. The present discussion illustrates how these activities are enacted in the changing environment to produce the observed patterns of weight loss or decomposition.

Decomposition of aboveground parts of graminoids begins at the time when necrotic patches appear on the leaves and stem bases. The necroses are most apparent from mid-August onwards. Before or concurrent with visual signs of senescence the leaves lose up to 12% of their weight as green healthy tissue (Figure 9-7). The initial loss, which occurs prior to substantial microbial ingress, and whether or not rain has fallen, is apparently caused by translocation to belowground parts. The freeze-thaw cycle and the physical throughput of water remove up to 18% of the dry weight of overwintering leaves by the spring. During and prior to the period of leaching substantial microbial activity may take place, contributing to overall weight loss, but microbial contributions to weight loss in this and the previous phase of aboveground plant weight losses are undetermined. During the period from mid-August to the end of spring runoff, up to 30% dry weight may be lost from leaves of graminoids (Figure 9-7, Table 9-5).

Three simulation models relate microbial activities quantitatively and unambiguously to the environmental phenomena that govern them. One model, GRESP (Bunnell et al. 1977a), relates the respiratory response of microbial populations to changing temperature and moisture. The second, DECOMP (Bunnell et al. 1977b), expresses the respiration rate as a

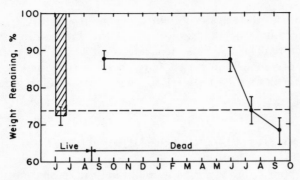

FIGURE 9-7. *Progression of leaf weight of* Carex aquatilis *and* Eriophorum angustifolium, *combined. Hatched bar shows the amount of material removed* in vitro *by warm water and 80% ethanol. Vertical bars indicate the standard errors. The dashed line indicates the weight loss before ingress of microorganisms is well under way. (Flanagan, unpubl.)*

function of substrate chemistry. The third, ABISKO II (Bunnell and Scoullar 1975), integrates the effects of changing meteorological conditions and substrate chemistry within an ecosystem framework. The models document relationships between weight loss and microbial activities, as they are influenced by abiotic variables and substrate chemistry and the relationship of the biomass of microbial populations to primary production and turnover of organic matter. Although the development of these models was based on tundra research, their predictive abilities have also been tested for conditions found in the taiga and moors (Bunnell et al. 1977a, Bunnell and Scoullar 1981).

Temperature, Moisture, and Microbial Respiration

The function GRESP represents a formal statement and complex hypothesis of the manner in which temperature, moisture and substrate features influence aerobic respiration of microbes. It treats aerobic respiration as a function of the supply rates of water, oxygen and organic nutrients. The critical features of the hypothesis are presented:

$$R(T,M) = [M/(a_1 + M)][a_2/(a_2 + M)] \ a_3 a_4^{(T-10)/10}$$

where $R(T,M) = \mu l \ CO_2$ respired (g substrate)$^{-1}$ hr^{-1} at temperature T and moisture M

T = temperature, °C
M = moisture, percent dry weight
$a_1,...,a_4$ = substrate specific parameters.

The rationale of the GRESP function has been presented elsewhere (Bunnell and Tait 1974, Bunnell et al. 1977a) and only a summary is repeated here. Microbial respiration is assumed to be related to the moisture potential of the substrate via two saturation processes. The first process is related to the metabolic water requirements of decomposer organisms and embodies a convention of soil mycologists, that is, the expression of water content on a relative basis, or as a percentage of the value when the soil is saturated (Griffin 1966). This process is expressed as $M/(a_1 + M)$, where M represents the percent water content on a dry weight basis and a_1 represents the percent water content at which the substrate is "half-saturated" with water or respiratory activity is at half its optimal level.

The second saturation process occurs at high moisture levels. It is assumed to represent the effect of water on gas exchange with the atmosphere either of oxygen, carbon dioxide or both. The simplest formulation is employed (Bunnell and Tait 1974). Since the degree to which gas exchange is inhibited can be expressed as $M/(a_2 + M)$, the degree to which it is not inhibited can be expressed as:

$$1 - [M/(a_2 + M)] \quad \text{or} \quad a_2/(a_2 + M).$$

Again M represents the moisture content, and a_2 represents the percent water content at which gas exchange is limited to half its optimal value.

The third and fourth factors, temperature and substrate characteristics, are treated as a substrate-specific Q_{10} relationship:

$$a_3 \times a_4^{(T-10)/10}$$

where a_3 is the substrate specific respiration rate that occurs at 10 °C when neither moisture nor oxygen are limiting and a_4 is the Q_{10} coefficient. Alternative formulations for both moisture and temperature influences on rates of nutrient supply are discussed by Bunnell et al. (1977a); the treatment of substrate characteristics is pursued later in this chapter. According to the GRESP function any one of the major determinants of rates of respiration (moisture, oxygen, temperature and substrate) can effectively reduce the rate of microbial respiration independently of the other factors. Thus, the rate determinants are combined multiplicatively.

Evaluation of the complex hypothesis represented by the GRESP function indicates that it predicts carbon dioxide evolution more accurately from aboveground substrates than from tundra soils. In the somewhat more aerobic soils of the taiga the model accounts for 78 to 84% of the variability in respiration rates (Bunnell et al. 1977a). The generality

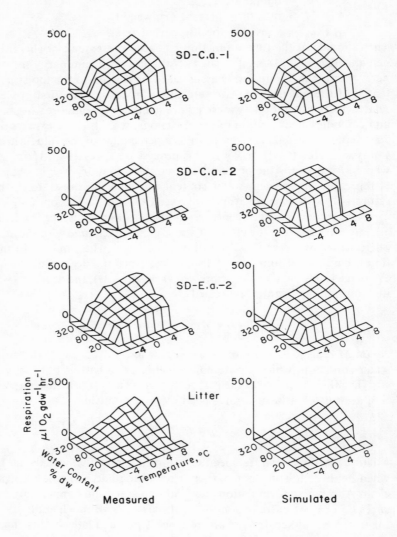

FIGURE 9-8. *Measured and simulated rates of microbial respiration in relation to moisture and temperature for: 1-yr-old standing dead of* Carex aquatilis *(SD-C.a.-1); 2-yr-old standing dead of* C. aquatilis *(SD-C.a.-2); 2-yr-old standing dead of* Eriophorum angustifolium *(SD-E.a.-2); and mixed graminoid litter. (After Bunnell et al. 1977a.)*

TABLE 9-2   *Parameter Values Giving the Best Fit of the* GRESP *Function to Data from Seven Substrates and Coefficients of Determination*

Substrate	No. of obs.	a_1 water (% dry wt)	a_2	a_3 (μl O_2 g^{-1} hr^{-1})	a_4 (Q_{10})	r^2	r_a^2*
Carex (1 yr old)	96	59	NE	204	3.33	0.79	0.86
Carex (2 yr old)	45	213	822	296	2.18	0.63	0.71
Eriophorum (newly dead)	54	416	416	777	8.79	0.65	0.96
Eriophorum (1 yr old)	79	74	NE	184	2.56	0.64	0.72
Eriophorum (2 yr old)	65	19	NE	107	2.79	0.72	0.77†
Dryas (2 yr old)	38	160	160	158	1.75	0.36	0.43
Total Barrow litter	346	116	2820	232	3.74	0.66	0.71

* r_a^2 is an estimate of the accountable variation explained by a nonlinear model.
† An optimum solution was not found.
NE—No estimate; number of measurements at moisture contents >500% moisture (% dry wt) are <10. Therefore $a_2/(a_2 + M)$ was set equal to 1.
Source: After Bunnell et al. 1977a.

and accuracy of the model in predicting measured microbial respiration from aboveground substrates, assessed visually (Figure 9-8) and statistically (Table 9-2), suggest that the hypothesis is applicable to a diversity of aboveground substrates.

Coefficients a_1 and a_2 assess the moisture range over which microbial respiration is little affected by changes in moisture levels. The range encompassed by these coefficients extends beyond the optimal moisture regime determined for individual species, particularly at the upper end. Excluding the poorly constrained values (NE in Table 9-2) the weighted mean of the mid-point between a_1 and a_2 for aboveground substrates is 461% moisture on a dry weight basis. For the microbial community *in toto*, respiration from dead vegetation is depressed far more as amounts of moisture approach the lower thresholds than near the upper thresholds. Within plant litter where aquatic fungi are more abundant, the upper limits to the moisture range may be greatly extended (Table 9-2; Flanagan and Veum 1974).

Some substrates, particularly in taiga soils, have computed half-saturation values that are equal for both a_1 and a_2 (e.g. newly dead *Eriophorum angustifolium*, Table 9-2). The resulting model with a_1 set equal to a_2 has only three parameters but accounts for 96% of the variation in respiration from that substrate (Bunnell et al. 1977a). However, Bunnell et al. (1977a) noted that equal values of a_1 and a_2 are likely an artifact of the model. Given the multiplicative form of the GRESP function, a narrow-peaked response of respiration versus moisture can be obtained only by having a_1 equal a_2.

Despite an uneven data base, trends in coefficients a_1 and a_2 are revealing. With increasing age and pitting within the substrate, the moisture range for effective respiration appears to broaden (see *E. angustifolium*, Table 9-2). Bunnell and Tait (1974) stated that the volume of water relative to the amount of organic matter was critical. Thus, they predicted that the moisture range over which respiration was unconstrained would broaden with age in aboveground substrates and narrow with increasing depth and bulk density below ground. The trend below ground has been documented most rigorously for aspen forest floor in the taiga, and does show a gradual decrease in the effective moisture range with depth (Bunnell et al. 1977a).

Coefficient a_3 represents the respiration rate at 10 °C when moisture and oxygen are not limiting. It is assumed to be a measure of substrate quality and as such should decline with the age of the substrate. Bunnell et al. (1977a) documented the expected pattern within the taiga forest floor; among substrates of the Biome research area it is evident among the *E. angustifolium* age classes (Table 9-2). The exponential response of respiration with temperature, defined by coefficient a_4, assumes Q_{10} values ranging from 2.2 to 8.8, with younger substrates showing a higher Q_{10} than older substrates (Table 9-2). There are two possible reasons. 1) Newly senescent substrates have not experienced a winter and may not be well colonized by psychrophilic organisms; thus they would show lower rates of respiration at lower temperatures and higher Q_{10} values. 2) Younger substrates contain greater proportions of constituents of low molecular weight which appear to have higher Q_{10} values associated with their utilization as discussed earlier in this chapter. Over the range 0° to 10 °C the weighted average of Q_{10} values for all aboveground substrates tested at the Biome research area is 3.65.

Observations suggest that while younger aboveground substrates have the chemical potential for higher respiration rates than do older substrates, respiration is more likely to be constrained by temperature and moisture. The high Q_{10} values from younger substrates imply a population poorly adapted to low temperatures. The narrower moisture range suggests that drying by wind frequently may reduce realized respiration. These environmental constraints act to ensure that nutrients present in newly dead standing vegetation are not released into the system until the spring thaw.

The same clear pattern of carbon dioxide evolution with temperature and moisture is not observed for decomposition processes below ground. The best fit of the GRESP function to Gilson respirometry measures of wet meadow soil accounts for only 10 to 20% of the variation. The computed Q_{10} is near 2.0 for a variety of soils and the optimal mois-

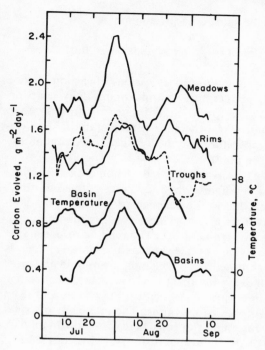

FIGURE 9-9. *Seasonal courses of the evolution of carbon dioxide from soils of four microtopographic units and soil temperature near the surface in the basin of a low-centered polygon. Carbon flux measured by KOH titrations in darkened lysimeters. Data are ten-day running means for 1973. (Benoit, unpubl.)*

ture level is about 75 to 80%. Few measures incorporating higher moisture levels were available and the estimate is likely low. Rates of soil respiration as measured by Gilson respirometry can be extrapolated only tenuously to estimate decomposition rates in the field. At best they represent a potential rate of decomposition that may not be realized.

Another estimate of field decomposition rate and the factors which control it can be made from in situ measurements of carbon dioxide evolution although these measures include respiration of roots as well as microflora. Field data were obtained by daily potassium hydroxide titration of gas collected from plastic cores sunk into the soil in 1973. Measures of carbon dioxide evolution from different microtopographic units all peak in early August (Figure 9-9). Although the peak appears correlated with temperature, early August is also the time of maximum aboveground biomass of vascular plants and intense activity by soil fauna. Logarithmic regression of the daily evolution of CO_2 m^{-2}, as measured by lysimeters in wet meadow soils, against mean daily soil temperature estimates a Q_{10} of 1.89:

$$R = 1465.6 \times 1.89^{Tmean/10} \qquad r^2 = 0.37, \ \alpha \leqslant 0.01$$

where R is ml CO_2 m^{-2} day^{-1} and $Tmean$ is the mean daily temperature.

Linear regression with the same data produces:

$$R = 1476 + 117.4 \times T\text{mean} \qquad r^2 = 0.39, \; \alpha = 0.01.$$

For all microtopographic units, linear regressions of carbon dioxide evolution versus mean daily temperature and maximum daily temperature consistently provided higher coefficients of determination, r^2, than regressions involving $2^{T/10}$ and $e^{T/10}$ (where T = temperature). The observed linear response to temperature may be a result of the summation of a number of exponential responses.

The contribution of plant roots to observed carbon dioxide production was analyzed by comparing undisturbed soil cores with cores effectively stripped of primary producers. Linear regressions of carbon dioxide evolution from stripped cores also provide better fits than do exponential models for the effect of temperature. The relative response (the predicted response at 10 °C divided by the predicted response at 0 °C) is higher for stripped cores than for cores on which the graminoid and moss canopy was left intact. Removing the plant cover increased the relative response from 2.08 to 3.1 in basins of low-centered polygons and from 1.59 to 1.89 on rims of low-centered polygons. The intercepts of equations for stripped cores of basin and rim soils were 155 and 634 ml CO_2 day^{-1}, about half the level of the intercepts of untreated cores (353 and 1121 ml CO_2 day^{-1}).

Direct comparisons between treated and untreated cores should be viewed with caution because microbial populations in treated cores are not experiencing the same environment as the controls. Further, there may have been increased root respiration associated with clipping. However, the results do suggest that the near-linear response of carbon dioxide evolution to temperature changes in soils is in part due to the influence of primary production. The lower relative response of soils on rims, which support higher primary production than do soils in basins, corroborates the suggestion, as do the high Q_{10} values observed for microbial respiration in standing dead and litter substrates (Table 9-2). In short, microbial activity below ground appears to respond more strongly to changes in temperature than do processes of primary production below ground.

Undoubtedly some of the differences in carbon dioxide evolution observed among microtopographic units (Figure 9-9) are associated with differing primary productivity. Rims of low-centered polygons and polygon troughs evolve approximately twice as much carbon dioxide as basins of low-centered polygons and support considerably greater primary production. Evolution of carbon dioxide from meadow soils is still greater, possibly reflecting the higher biomass of bacteria in these soils. We cannot distinguish between the influences of soil moisture and primary production on measured respiration, but acknowledge that the difference in soil respiration among microtopographic units is greater than that expected from differences in primary productivity alone.

In taiga soils coefficient a_3 and total respiration decrease with depth in the profile, while the measured Q_{10} increases (Bunnell et al. 1977a). Such findings suggest that the relative contribution from primary production in the taiga declines with depth and that the effect of temperature on microbial populations increases with depth. In both tundra and taiga, microorganisms in the litter layer continue respiration at lower temperatures than do organisms at depth in the soil. Surface layers are subject to wider ranges in both temperature and moisture than are deeper layers. Thus it is not surprising to find deeper communities apparently adapted to narrower ranges of temperature and moisture than surface communities. The tendency within tundra soils for more linear relationships with temperature may reflect an adaptation to low temperatures.

The sensitivity analyses of the model based on the function GRESP that were conducted by Bunnell et al. (1977a) have been extended using other substrates from tundra. In all cases the model is most sensitive to coefficient a_4, which determines the predicted Q_{10}. Relative sensitivities to other coefficients vary with the substrate. For those substrates where the overall fit of the model is close ($r^2 \geqslant 0.80$) we observe that the broad

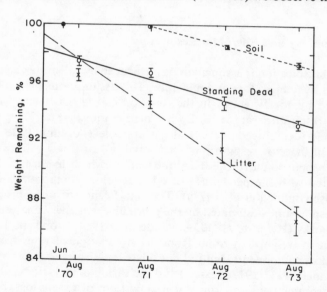

FIGURE 9-10. *Progression of weights of cellulose placed in surface soil, litter and standing dead material. Vertical bars give standard error. (After Bunnell et al. 1977b.)*

response of microbial respiration in substrates from tundra and taiga is most sensitive to temperature, then to substrate chemistry, and least sensitive to amounts of moisture, particularly high levels of moisture. Despite the variable response to moisture, elimination of moisture effects from the model reduces its predictive ability by a minimum of 23 to 31% (Bunnell et al. 1977a). Also, it is important to note that while respiration rates are relatively insensitive to moisture over the range of respirometry data collected, moisture levels in the field may become high enough to reduce respiration significantly. Temperature, moisture and oxygen are all important modifiers of the rate of respiration of tundra microorganisms.

The overall effect of the microbial population and micrometeorological factors can be seen in the relative decomposition rates of a uniform substrate, cellulose, placed in three different microhabitats (Figure 9-10). Over several years, the weight loss from the cellulose was greatest in the litter, intermediate in the standing dead, and lowest in the soil. As both soil and litter have more cellulolytic decomposers than standing dead (Figure 9-1), the results support the hypothesis that moisture may be limiting in the standing dead (Chapter 8). The considerable decrease in decomposition rate noted for the soil suggests that conditions in the soil are less favorable overall to decomposition than those above ground.

Substrate Chemistry and Microbial Respiration

Microbial respiration is assumed to be influenced by substrate chemistry as well as by temperature and moisture. This assumption is broadly accommodated by coefficient a_3 in the function GRESP. Coefficient a_3 represents the respiration rate at 10 °C when neither moisture nor oxygen are limiting, and is employed to establish the upper level or amplitude of the response surface for respiration. The "quality" of the substrate is thus directly proportional to the magnitude of a_3, which in turn is directly correlated with the percentage of ethanol-soluble compounds or percent glucose (Bunnell et al. 1977a). The significance of a_3 to broad patterns of respiration is estimated by the preceding sensitivity analyses.

Earlier works (Henin et al. 1959, Minderman 1968) proposed that observed rates of weight loss result from the summation of rates from specific chemical components, but did not relate these rates to microbial activities. Bunnell et al. (1977b) extended these earlier models of decomposition to encompass not only the observed patterns of weight loss, but the microbial activities producing these patterns. Ethanol-soluble compounds disappear five to six times as fast as other constituents of natural substrates (Figure 9-11). Combination of these two chemically defined groups produces the common departure from a simple exponential

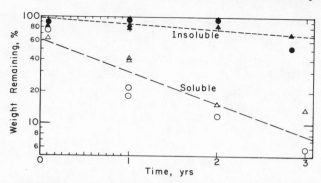

FIGURE 9-11. *Percentage of ethanol-soluble and ethanol-insoluble compounds remaining in decomposing* Carex aquatilis *(▲, △) and* Eriophorum angustifolium *(●, o). Percentages are based on weight per unit area. (After Bunnell et al. 1977b.)*

illustrated by many decomposing substrates (Burges 1958, Minderman 1968, Satchell 1974).

Here we address the manner in which the phenomenon of substrate "quality" represented in the function GRESP by the single coefficient a_3 can be related to substrate chemistry more directly. In accordance with earlier workers different constituents are assumed to have their own chemical-specific rates of decomposition. In addition the decomposition rate of each chemical constituent is assumed to be a function of the temperature and moisture-dependent respiration rate of the microflora, and thus changes seasonally or even daily. The observed decomposition rate of a substrate is assumed to be the sum of the temperature–moisture–chemical-specific rates of utilization times the amount of each chemical constituent present. Observed rates of decomposition thus change with the meteorologically induced changes in rates of microbial respiration and the changing capacity of the substrate to provide energy to the microbial population.

As developed by Minderman (1968), the decay rate of a substrate can be expressed as:

$$(dY/dt) = \sum_{i=1}^{n} (dy_i/dt)$$

$$(dY/dt) = \sum_{i=1}^{n} -k_i y_i$$

where Y = total weight of the decomposing substrate

y_i = weight of substrate component i; $\sum\limits_{i=1}^{n} y_i = Y$

k_i = decay rate of substrate component i.

The above equation states that each substrate component decomposes at a constant rate of decay specific for that substrate constituent and independent of the amount of other substrate components present. The relation of decomposition to temperature and moisture discussed earlier suggests that the above equation can be written

$$R(T,M) = \sum_{i=1}^{n} r_i(T,M)y_i$$

where $R(T,M)$ = respiration rate of the total substrate at temperature T and moisture M

$r_i(T,M)$ = respiration rate of substrate component i, a function of temperature and moisture

y_i = amount of substrate component i present, as before.

As expressed in the above equation, the model of decomposition not only accounts for the observed differences in response surfaces of respiration versus temperature and moisture for substrates of different chemical composition, but also accounts for the observed differences in rates of loss of different chemical components from a substrate in the field. To document the relative contributions of different chemical constituents to total respiration, the influences of temperature and moisture must be reduced or removed. Bunnell and Tait (1974) proposed several methods for separating the temperature and moisture effects from chemical-specific effects. Three methods have been evaluated by Bunnell et al. (1977b). Their evaluation suggests that dominating influences on the pattern of respiration for any specific constituent are levels of temperature and moisture. Only 1 to 4% of the variation in instantaneous respiration rates is due to chemical composition. These observations are not incompatible with the preceding sensitivity analyses, which suggest that the overall response surface of microbial respiration versus temperature and moisture is sensitive to substrate quality. The general amplitude of the response surface, and thus its overall shape, are sensitive to substrate quality (Bunnell et al. 1977a). Variations in temperature and moisture, however, account for more of the variation of the total surface (Figure 9-8) as it rises to the amplitude set by substrate quality. When summed over a year, even small differences associated with substrate chemistry will produce distinctly different annual rates of loss.

In their evaluation of the relationships expressed in the last equation, Bunnell et al. (1977b) initially treated five different substrate components: ethanol-soluble cellulose, lignin, pectin, starch and volatiles.

Several important points emerge from their analyses. The coefficients associated with the volatile and lignin components were occasionally negative, implying negative respiration. Analyses yielding negative coefficients for respiration usually had a disproportionately large number of *Dryas* substrates. The observations imply 1) that respiration rates of total substrates from any botanical taxon cannot be predicted consistently from independent consideration of the five substrate components mentioned above, and 2) that some substrate components may have an inhibitory effect on the respiration rate of other components.

In addition to generating inhibitory effects, specific substrate components also may provide energy for the degradation of more recalcitrant components. For example, the observed rates of weight loss from pure cellulose filter papers placed in the field are lower than rates of loss of cellulose from natural substrates.

As well as indicating the failure of the five selected chemical constituents to contribute independently to microbial respiration, the analyses of Bunnell et al. (1977b) indicate that the predictability of regression equations within temperature–moisture classes is little altered by ignoring amounts of pectin, starch and volatiles in the substrate being respired. When broader chemical groups (e.g. percent ethanol-soluble and percent ethanol-insoluble) are employed, and *Dryas* substrates are omitted, regression coefficients for the two substrate components are consistently different and significantly greater than 0 ($\alpha \leqslant 0.001$). Rates of respiration of ethanol-soluble components are about 5 to 10 times greater, depending on temperature, than the rates associated with other chemical constituents. It is noteworthy that ethanol-soluble compounds make a greater contribution to total respiration at higher temperatures.

The discussion of microfloral potential to utilize substrates noted that several fungal isolates show higher temperature optima for utilization of substances of lower molecular weight than they do for utilization of the more recalcitrant substances such as cellulose. The analyses associated with the last equation suggest that the phenomenon is general within the mycoflora of the coastal tundra at Barrow and applies to associated rates of respiration as well as to the physiological potential to degrade these substrates (Bunnell et al. 1977b). At lower temperatures tundra fungi not only maintain their competence to degrade more recalcitrant chemical constituents (Figure 9-1), but also have a greater proportion of their respiration associated with these constituents.

Microbial Respiration as a Measure of Weight Loss

Implicit in the preceding discussion is the assumption that the general form of the response surface for microbial respiration against temperature and moisture is characterized by the physical and chemical nature of the substrate. The model GRESP closely mimics this response surface for a variety of substrates (Figure 9-8, Table 9-2). Ignoring hysteresis effects and microbial succession, the assumption can further be made that given the initial characterization for a specific substrate one can predict the instantaneous respiration rate under any temperature and moisture condition during a year. Unfortunately, in situ measures of respiration from the soil are confused by plant and invertebrate activity, and there are no measurements of the pattern of weight loss during a specific annual cycle. However, annual measures of weight loss from a variety of substrates under markedly different meteorological conditions are available. These data were collected from different International Tundra Biome research sites.

Bunnell et al. (1977a) and Bunnell and Scoullar (1981) have compared measures of total weight loss from different litters with losses due to microbial respiration as simulated by the model. To project simulated weight losses due to microbial respiration they first estimated coefficients a_1 through a_4 (p. 310-311) from respirometry data collected at the specific site using the non-linear optimization techniques described by Bunnell et al. (1977a). The GRESP model was then used to project rates of microbial respiration during the year. Temperature and moisture data used in the projection were those collected from the appropriate site. Computations of weight loss assume that the substrate is 45% carbon and has a respiratory quotient of 1.0.

The annual weight losses computed from the simulated daily respiration rates are compared with the rates of weight loss as measured by litter bags (Table 9-3). Bunnell and Scoullar (1981) discuss the implications of computed coefficients a_1 through a_4 for each substrate and site. The hypothesis relating microbial respiration to measures of temperature and moisture accounts for 71 to 98% of the variation in rates of respiration measured from a variety of natural substrates and predicts annual loss rates under a wide range of environmental conditions that are 70 to 90% of the measured loss from litter bags. The values for loss of weight seem reasonable, given the additional losses due to leaching and physical reduction.

The equation on page 320 explicitly encompasses the additional influence of substrate chemistry. In nature, rates of weight loss from ethanol-soluble compounds and ethanol-insoluble compounds show a ratio of 5.75:1. When the effects of temperature and moisture are incorporated according to the central equation of GRESP, rates of respiration from the two chemical groups show ratios ranging from 5.1:1 to 8.7:1 (Bunnell et al. 1977b). Thus the rates of microbial respiration associated with the two chemical constituents show approximately the same ratio as rates of weight loss from these constituents in the field. If the simplifying

TABLE 9-3 *Annual Weight Losses of Various Litters Measured and Predicted from the Simulated Microbial Respiration*

Research area	Substrate	Weight loss (% of initial weight) Measured	Weight loss (% of initial weight) Simulated	Simulated as a percentage of measured
Abisko, Sweden	*Rubus chamaemorus* leaves	32[1]	23.3	73
Barrow, Alaska	*Dupontia fisheri* leaves	15[2]	13.4	89
	Carex aquatilis leaves	14.6[3]	13.4	
Moor House, United Kingdom	*Calluna vulgaris* shoots	15–20[4]		
	Calluna vulgaris stems	8[4]	7.1[5]	92
	Rubus chamaemorus leaves	36–38[4]	20.1	81

Note: Abiotic and respirometry data for the research areas were collected during development of the ABISKO model (Bunnell and Dowding 1974).
[1] Rosswall (1974).
[2] Benoit et al. (unpubl.).
[3] Benoit (unpubl.).
[4] Heal and French (1974).
[5] Shoots and stems combined in model.
Source: Bunnell et al. (1977b).

assumption is made that both chemical groupings contain the same percent carbon as the parent material, 45%, the respiration rates can be converted directly to weight loss. The rate of weight loss of ethanol-soluble compounds is:

$$\text{weight loss hr}^{-1} = 3.8 \text{ GRESP}(T,M)1.19WE$$

where GRESP = central equation of the model (p. 310) with coefficients appropriate to the specific substrate
1.19 = conversion factor from μl CO_2 to g substrate
WE = weight of ethanol-soluble compound in grams.

Following the same approach the rate of weight loss of ethanol-insoluble compounds is:

$$\text{weight loss hr}^{-1} = 0.76 \text{ GRESP}(T,M)1.19WNE$$

where WNE represents the weight of ethanol-insoluble compounds in grams. The annual rate of weight loss is given by:

$$1 - \prod_{i=1}^{365} (1 - k_i)$$

TABLE 9-4   *Measured and Simulated Chemical Composition After One Year and Rates of Weight Loss of* Eriophorum angustifolium *Standing Dead Material*

	Percentage	
	Measured*	Simulated†
Chemical composition of the substrate after one year:		
ethanol-soluble	7	10
ethanol-insoluble	93	90
Loss per year:		
ethanol-soluble	49	48
ethanol-insoluble	11	12
Total weight loss	27	31

*Measured values use changes in identified age classes.
†Simulated values used abiotic data from 1973.
Source: Bunnell et al. (1977b).

where k_i is the computed daily rate of weight loss due to respiration. The three equations above make up the model DECOMP. Using meteorological data from the Barrow site, Bunnell et al. (1977b) computed daily values of the function GRESP as determined by temperature and moisture and applied these to the chemical-specific coefficients. They obtained annual rates of weight loss of –0.66 and –0.13 for ethanol-soluble and ethanol-insoluble constituents respectively. Measured weight losses from the total litter in the field are –0.69 and –0.12 g g^{-1} yr^{-1}. The rates of weight loss computed from temperature–moisture–chemical-specific rates of respiration are thus in very close agreement with measured rates of weight loss. Because the loss rates are chemical-specific (Bunnell et al. 1977b), the model DECOMP can project not only total substrate weight loss but also chemical composition, which is also very similar to the observed value (Table 9-4).

The model DECOMP provides a framework that permits extrapolation of laboratory measures of microbial activity to predict total loss of substrate weight and changing composition of substrate. The concepts of decomposition embodied in the model appear supported by combined laboratory and field evidence. The reasonably close agreement between simulated and measured values for standing dead material (Table 9-4) suggests that at least during the initial period of decomposition many of the changes in substrate weight and chemical composition result from changing rates of microbial respiration which are chemical-specific and independently influenced by temperature and moisture (Bunnell et al. 1977b).

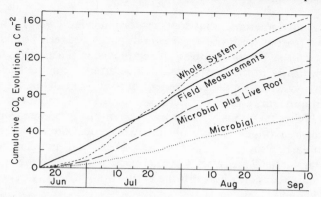

FIGURE 9-12. *Cumulative CO₂ release over a single growing season, simulated for soil microbes, microbes plus roots and the whole system, and measured by KOH titrations in darkened lysimeters. Root respiration includes that of microbes associated with the rhizosphere. Whole-system CO₂ evolution includes the flux from soil microbes, roots, aboveground decomposers and respiration of aboveground plant biomass. (After Bunnell and Scoullar 1975.)*

For the more advanced stages of decomposition, such as belowground substrates, the relationships of microbial activities to decomposition are not as well quantified. No data are available on the chemical composition of belowground substrates. Furthermore, measures of microbial activity are confused by the activities of invertebrates and vascular plants. To evaluate the hypothesis concerning decomposition below ground, a broader approach incorporating more ecosystem components but less chemical detail has been employed. The model ABISKO II (Bunnell and Scoullar 1975) incorporates the temperature and moisture influences expressed but also simulates contributions from dying roots and respiration of vascular plants.

Bunnell and Scoullar (1975) have evaluated the model ABISKO II for the Biome research area comparing in situ measures of carbon dioxide evolution with the cumulated totals of simulated respiration from relevant components of the system (Figure 9-12). The whole-system respiration of Figure 9-12 includes carbon dioxide evolution from soil microorganisms, roots, aboveground decomposers, and the growth plus maintenance respiration of aboveground live material.

Simulated microbial respiration follows a pattern very similar to that of the field measures of respiration, but shows a greater depression early in the season. The early season depression is most evident in the pattern of simulated microbial plus root respiration (Figure 9-12). There are at least two reasons for this early season disparity between simulated and measured values. The soil temperature employed in the model is that at 5 cm depth. Early in the season field temperatures near the surface permit respiration while simulated temperatures at 5 cm depth are too low to allow significant respiration. Because the lower threshold for root respiration is higher than that for microbes, the disparity between simulated and measured values is more obvious when roots are considered. The release of carbon dioxide trapped during freeze-up is not simulated but will appear in field measures (Benoit, pers. comm.; Coyne, pers. comm.), and this also contributes to the early spring disparity between field and simulated values.

Over the 85-day sample period the accumulated totals of measured respiration and simulated whole system respiration are 159 and 165 g C m^{-2} respectively. The difference between measured and simulated values over this period is thus 6 g C m^{-2} or 3.7% of the measured values. A disparity of less than 5% is well within the sample error associated with data for root biomass. Thus the simulated dynamics of respiration of microbe, root and other contributing compartments must be assumed realistic within the accuracy of available data. The proportion of simulated total soil respiration that originates with the roots on any given day varies between 33 and 70%, and lies at the lower end of the range of reported values of 50 to 93% (Billings et al. 1978). Errors in different processes might compensate to produce an invalid sense of accuracy. However, the generally realistic behavior of the model for other tundra areas, including Devon Island, Moor House and Abisko (Bunnell and Scoullar 1981), suggests that microbial respiration for specific substrates in the upper 10 cm of soil follows the relationship expressed by the function GRESP. The dynamics of microbial respiration at depth are much less clear and are confused by anaerobic conditions and poorly understood changes in substrate quality with advancing age.

In summary, the concepts of decomposition discussed above appear sufficiently comprehensive to allow laboratory measures to be related effectively to field measures through the vehicle of simulation models. The manner in which microbial respiration responds to temperature, moisture and broad chemical groups predicts not only weight loss but chemical composition of aboveground substrates. Upper limits on decay rates are established by chemical composition, but are modified by abiotic variables. Respiration is most sensitive to temperature and the microflora has responded by extending its capabilities to grow, respire and utilize substrates at low temperatures. Respiration declines with both increasing and decreasing moisture levels. At low moisture levels degradation and loss of chemicals from standing dead vegetation is temporarily suspended; at high moisture levels respiration becomes the province of bacteria which cannot degrade compounds of larger molecular weight. Decomposition of such compounds remains poorly understood, but it appears that accumulation of organic matter in tundra is more a product of high moisture levels than of low temperatures.

Microbes and Turnover of Organic Matter and Nutrients

The preceding models concentrate on rates of microbial activity and ignore microbial biomass. The accuracy of the predictions made by these models suggests that concentration on rates of processes is an insightful approach. That in no way obviates attempts to examine the consistency of the measures of microbial biomass with estimated turnover of organic matter. Growth, respiration, production efficiency, and maintenance demands of the microbial biomass in specific substrates can be related to weight loss from that substrate. Using the chemostat model of Marr et al. (1963) it is possible to examine compatibility between field and laboratory data and to evaluate the influence of microbial activities on turnover and accumulation of organic matter. Several workers (Babiuk and Paul 1970, Gray and Williams 1971, Flanagan and Bunnell 1976) have used this approach in attempting to balance budgets of energy or carbon in a variety of ecosystems. The biomass equation of Marr et al. (1963) is expressed as:

$$(dx/dt) + ax = Y(ds/dt)$$

where x = microbial biomass
s = substrate available for microbial growth
Y = yield coefficient, g microbial tissue (g substrate)$^{-1}$
a = specific maintenance rate—g microbial tissue required to maintain 1.0 g microbial tissue for a specific time, e.g. 1.0 hour.

When the rate of growth is zero, the above can be expressed:

$$ds/dt = ax/Y'.$$

The yield coefficient Y' is not identical to Y because at zero growth there is no actual yield. However, material for maintenance is believed to be utilized at very nearly the same level of efficiency as material assimilated for production of new tissue.

Gray and Williams (1971), following the approach of Babiuk and Paul (1970), utilized values for Y' and a of 0.3 g g^{-1} and 0.001 g g^{-1} hr^{-1} respectively. Their values for x and a were derived from field data collected at Meathop Wood in Great Britain. Utilizing these values they found that the annual maintenance demands of the microbial biomass in Meathop Wood were such that no organic matter would be available for microbial growth, or for growth or maintenance of any other soil organism. In commenting on the obvious unreality of the situation, Gray and Williams (1971) suggested a number of possible sources of error: 1) the yield coefficient used was too small, 2) the estimate of maintenance requirements was inflated, 3) microbial biomass was overestimated, and 4) primary productivity was underestimated.

In an analogous study, Flanagan and Bunnell (1976) attempted to minimize the potential errors inherent in the biomass equation by incorporating laboratory determinations of the specific maintenance rates and yield coefficients of major fungal species in the coastal tundra at Barrow. Values for a and Y' were calculated as 0.32×10^{-3} g g^{-1} hr^{-1} and 0.35 g g^{-1} respectively from data on growth and respiration. The value of Y' obtained by Flanagan and Bunnell (1976) is nearly identical to that calculated in studies of organisms from temperate regions, but the value of a is only one-third of that calculated by Marr et al. (1963) in chemostat studies and used by Babiuk and Paul (1970) and Gray and Williams (1971). Using these coefficients Flanagan and Bunnell (1976) estimated that the average standing crop of fungi in the standing dead grew, maintained and renewed itself at a cost of approximately 10 g substrate m^{-2} yr^{-1}. This estimate is compatible with the weight loss from standing dead leaves calculated by converting carbon dioxide respired annually by microbes in the tissue to organic matter (Flanagan and Veum 1974).

The following discussion is an attempt to 1) quantify the annual maintenance demands of an average standing crop of microorganisms in a unit area of *Carex–Oncophorus* meadow, 2) estimate the yearly potential for microbial production on the same area, and 3) examine whether microbial potentials for substrate utilization during growth and maintenance are compatible with estimates of the amount of organic matter produced and decomposed each year.

Microbial Maintenance and Production in the Coastal Tundra at Barrow

Direct counts of bacteria from the soils are sparse. Calculations of microbial utilization of substrate are constrained to estimates based primarily upon biomass, maintenance demands and yield coefficients of fungi.

Utilizing the biomass equation and replacing x by 18.1 g m^{-2} (the average standing crop of microbial biomass to 7 cm depth at the *Carex–Oncophorus* meadow), a by 0.32×10^{-3} g g^{-1}, and Y' by 0.35 g g^{-1}, calcu-

TABLE 9-5. *Standing Crops and Annual Weight Loss of Five Organic Matter Pools*

Organic residue	Standing crop (gdw m^{-2})[1]	Turnover rate (g g^{-1} yr^{-1})	Weight loss (gdw m^{-2} yr^{-1})
Moribund leaves	90	0.300[2]	27.0
Standing dead	50	0.075	4.0
Litter	75	0.100	8.0
Dead roots, 0–7 cm	100	0.025[3]	2.5
Soil organic matter, 0–7 cm	8000	0.020[3]	180.0
Total	8315		221.5

[1]Average values from data collected over 4 years at three sites.
[2]The losses are due primarily to the downward translocation of materials to roots in fall and to leaching in spring by meltwater.
[3]Estimated from decay rates of roots and cellulose paper in litter bags inserted in the soil, 1972–1977 (inclusive).

lated maintenance demands are 0.0166 g m^{-2} hr^{-1} or approximately 48 g m^{-2} for the period of microbial activity, which is about 100 days.

The annual primary productivity of the *Carex-Oncophorus* meadow both above and below ground, including phanerogams and cryptogams, is estimated to be approximately 200 g m^{-2}. If 48 g of organic matter m^{-2} yr^{-1} is necessary to maintain the average standing crop of microorganisms, 152 g m^{-2} yr^{-1} remains to be removed by microbial and invertebrate activity or organic matter will accumulate.

Litter-bag estimates of annual rates of decomposition for major substrates in the upper 7 cm of soil (Table 9-5) indicate that 222 g m^{-2} is decomposed annually. This is approximately one-half the rate for an ungrazed short-grass prairie (Van Dyne et al. 1978). Minimal annual maintenance requirements of microbes (48 g m^{-2}) and invertebrates (7 g m^{-2}, Chapter 11) could be met easily and would leave about 167 g m^{-2} annually for production of microbial and invertebrate tissue. Ignoring invertebrates, the potential number of microbial generations possible can be estimated using the equation of Gray and Williams (1971):

$$Y(s + Nx) = Nx$$

where s = total substrate available to microorganisms (total minus maintenance)

N = number of generations of average microbial biomass

Y and x are as in the two previous equations.

Allowance is made for recycling of microbial tissue towards its own production at a rate governed also by the yield coefficient Y, in the term $Y(Nx)$. Solving for N, the total number of average microbial standing crops possible per year, gives 5.0 and 4.3 generations based on measures of total decay and primary production respectively. Observed rates of turnover for fungi in *Carex–Oncophorus* meadows were markedly lower, 1.5 to 3.3 times, varying with depth (Table 8-3). In the troughs, however, observed turnover rates were similar to those calculated, 3.6 to 6.2 times, but fungal biomass was significantly lower. Only in the most productive areas do fungi exhibit values comparable to calculations based on laboratory measurements. In these areas the accumulation of organic matter is lowest (Chapter 7). The observation that litter bags in meadows estimate an annual rate of decomposition greater than annual input from primary production may result from overestimation of the decay rates of untested but apparently more recalcitrant material at depth. The observations do suggest that in the most favorable microhabitats decomposition can approximate primary production. Douglas and Tedrow (1959) observed similar variability in rates of decomposition of organic matter from tundra soils. Highest rates of decomposition were observed from the half-bog soil (*Dupontia* meadows and polygon troughs, Table 1-4). Those rates, 190 g m^{-2}, are comparable to the most rapid rates we have estimated and again suggest no accumulation of organic matter in sites most favorable for decomposition.

If all 222 g m^{-2} yr^{-1} of decomposable tissue undergoes dissolution to carbon dioxide, water and minerals through microbial processes, then, based on an average carbon content of 0.45 g g^{-1} organic matter, decomposers should release carbon dioxide to the atmosphere at an average rate of about 152 mg m^{-2} hr^{-1}. If annual primary production is matched by decomposition the estimate of average carbon dioxide evolution is 144 mg m^{-2} hr^{-1}.

Root and Microbial Respiration

The annual weight loss from belowground substrates plus surface litter is about 190 g m^{-2} yr^{-1} (Table 9-5). If all of this matter, or an equivalent amount minus the average standing crop of microbial biomass below ground (190–17.5 = 172.5 g m^{-2} yr^{-1}), is consumed annually by microbial metabolism, maintenance and growth, it is possible to calculate an average release of CO_2 m^{-2} hr^{-1} from Barrow soils that does not include the CO_2 emission of roots.

The average carbon concentration of the soil organic matter in the top 10 cm is about 45% so 172.5 g of organic matter could release 78 g C or 286 g CO_2. The amount of carbon dioxide released annually (100 days) by microbes would be equivalent to an average respiration rate of 119 mg CO_2 m^{-2} hr^{-1}.

The question concerning root contribution to total soil respiration is partially answered for Barrow tundra soils. Billings et al. (1977) estimated total soil respiration ranging from 75 to 125 mg CO_2 m^{-2} hr^{-1} in mid-June 1972. During the last week in July 1972, total soil respiration as measured by Billings et al. (1977) ranged from 150 to 300 mg CO_2 m^{-2} hr^{-1}. The values of Billings et al. are similar to calculations based solely on microbes, and are somewhat lower than actual field measurements made on root-free soils at Barrow (Benoit, unpubl.).

Flanagan and Veum (1974), using respiration data measured in situ in Barrow tundra soils, calculated the average release of CO_2 from these soils to be in the range 147 to 235 mg CO_2 m^{-2} hr^{-1}. The calculated rates do not include root respiration. They are about five times less than measurements made on temperate forest floors (Witkamp 1966) and about three times less than the average measurements made in tundra soils of the Taimyr peninsula, USSR (Aristoskaya and Parinkina 1972), which include root respiration. The comparison between the Soviet and U.S. data above suggests that microbes may contribute around 30% of total soil respiration. This speculation is in general agreement with rates of respiration simulated by ABISKO II (Figure 9-12) which indicate that root respiration may contribute from 33 to 70% of total soil respiration on any given day (Bunnell and Scoullar 1975). This range is somewhat lower than the 50 to 93% contribution by root respiration calculated by Billings et al. (1978).

In summary, the observed rates of microbial turnover in the most productive areas very nearly account for the total input of organic matter. Estimated rates of decomposition below ground are compatible with measures of soil respiration, and indicate that some microtopographic units may not be accumulating organic matter. Estimates of carbon dioxide evolution by decomposition above and below ground range from 2.8 to 5.6 g CO_2 m^{-2} day^{-1} (Flanagan and Veum 1974), in general agreement with estimates of carbon dioxide incorporation by atmospheric flux.

Microorganisms and Mineral Nutrient Cycling

The distribution of nitrogen and phosphorus in various ecosystem components can be calculated using data on nutrient content of live fungal tissues from Flanagan and Van Cleve (1977), and nitrogen and phosphorus content of soils and decaying matter from Chapter 12 and Flint and Gersper (1974). Flint and Gersper estimated that the wet meadow tundra required 6.4 g N m^{-2} yr^{-1} for plant and animal growth. According to the calculations above, gross release of nitrogen by decomposition is about 7.5 g m^{-2} yr^{-1}, while the combination of exchangeable and dissolved inorganic nitrogen amounts to 8.0 g m^{-2} (Figure 9-13).

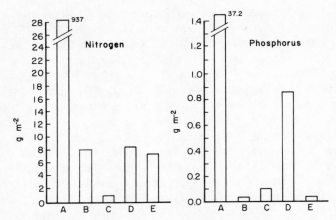

FIGURE 9-13. *Total and available pools and potential release rates of nitrogen and phosphorus in the soil calculated for the wet meadow. A) Total amount of nutrient to 20 cm. B) Amount available including dissolved and exchangeable (resin-extractable) phosphorus (Flint and Gersper 1974, Barèl and Barsdate 1978). C) Amount of nutrient in an average standing crop of microbial tissue to 7 cm. D) Potential annual release from tissue assuming 18.1 g m⁻² microbial biomass, 5.0 generations, and no internal microbial mineral recycling. E) Potential annual release calculated from the nutrient content of the material undergoing decay.*

Without including annual input to the system from rain and nitrogen fixation (Chapter 7) there appears to be more than adequate nitrogen for plant growth in the coastal tundra at Barrow. The amount of nitrogen immobilized by the average standing crop of microorganisms (0.8 g m⁻²) is almost insignificant in terms of available nitrogen plus that generated by decomposition.

The situation is quite different, however, in the case of phosphorus. The average amount of available phosphorus is small, as is the amount of phosphorus released annually in decay processes. The phosphorus immobilized in an average standing crop of microbial tissue is greater than the sum of labile pool plus the annual input via decay (Figure 9-13), suggesting a profound influence of microorganisms on availability of phosphorus in the system. Because tundra microorganisms, except for their resistant propagules, die off each year, they 1) release a relatively large quantity of phosphorus to the soil annually, and 2) are taking phosphorus from the system at levels that are greater than the normal size of the available pool. These observations indicate a pool of available phosphorus which turns over very rapidly and/or possible limitation to plant metabolism by microbial competition for and immobilization of soil phosphorus.

SUMMARY

Field and laboratory measures have been combined to provide an overall picture of decomposition. The ability of the tundra microflora to utilize substrates varies spatially, with aerobic decomposers showing a marked increase in capacity to degrade cellulose and phenols in the soil, as compared to the phyllosphere. This gradient in potential utilization is accompanied by an increase in anaerobes, and a marked decrease in both zymogenous forms and general microbial biomass. Fungi are better able to utilize cellulose and phenolic substrates than are bacteria. Unfortunately, the enzyme capabilities of the anaerobic microflora remain unknown, but no anaerobic decomposers of aromatic compounds are known from other areas.

Respiration rates of the microflora are governed in a predictable fashion by temperature, moisture, and substrate chemistry. Respiration rates are shown to be the dominant influence on weight loss from substrates. Substrate chemistry establishes a potential maximum rate which is modified by abiotic variables. Ethanol-soluble compounds generally are respired 5 to 7 times more rapidly than non-ethanol-soluble compounds, but some substrates (e.g. *Dryas* leaves) apparently contain substances inhibitory to microbial respiration.

Both bacteria and fungi show adaptations to cold. Microbial respiration continues to $-7.5\,°C$ and fungal growth is still positive at $0\,°C$, indicating greater levels of activity at low temperatures than are observed in vascular plants. Many microorganisms in colder strata of the environment show linear rather than exponential responses with increasing temperature, suggesting adaptation to cold through more rapid response to small increases in temperature. Cold-adapted microorganisms, especially fungi, increase in numbers from the phyllosphere into soils, while in the upper regions of the soil microbial populations display a wider range of temperature optima and mesophilic forms are more prominent. Among the fungi, psychrophiles, thermotolerant psychrophiles and cold-tolerant mesophiles retain the capacity to utilize structural plant carbohydrates at temperatures below $0\,°C$, while aerobic bacteria are largely restricted to non-structural plant components at $0\,°C$. As bacteria can use the products of fungal decomposition of large molecules, it is possible that co-evolution has permitted the development of different enzymatic responses to low temperatures.

Moisture levels above 20% dry weight are necessary to initiate microbial metabolism, while levels much above 400% dry weight attenuate microbial activity. Oxygen, carbon dioxide, and temperature relations interact with moisture levels to obscure definition of optimal moisture levels for decomposition. Shifting bacterial:fungal ratios along oxygen gradients indicate that oxygen availability and/or moisture alters the numbers and character of participants in decomposition. Large numbers of facultative anaerobic bacteria in litter and soil reflect a commonly occurring niche. Although present, obligate anaerobes are major contributors to decomposition only in heated soils.

Perhaps because of microbial adaptations to low temperatures, organic matter does not appear to be accumulating in some microtopographic units. Only the fungi are capable of degrading the larger compounds, particularly at low temperatures. The fungi, however, are restricted by high levels of moisture to the upper 7 to 10 cm of soil, and organic matter may accumulate at depth. The nutrient dynamics within the soil also suggest that phosphorus, but not nitrogen, immobilized within the standing crop of microbial tissue may be a factor limiting nutrient availability to vascular plants.

10

The Herbivore-Based Trophic System

G. O. Batzli, R. G. White, S. F. MacLean, Jr.,
F. A. Pitelka, and B. D. Collier

INTRODUCTION

The tundra is well known for its conspicuous and abundant animal populations. Indeed, tundra may be better characterized by caribou, wolves, lemmings, snowy owls, ptarmigan and hordes of flies than by any other feature, at least in popular literature. The next two chapters consider the composition and organization of animal communities, and their participation in the energy and nutrient dynamics of the coastal tundra ecosystem.

Ultimately, all heterotrophic activity, animal and microbial, depends upon the energy and nutrients fixed by green plants in net primary production. The amount of net primary production (Chapter 3) sets a limit upon the abundance and production of heterotrophic organisms. Two more or less distinct trophic systems based upon this net primary production may be recognized in virtually all ecosystems—a herbivore-based system that begins with the consumption of living autotroph tissue, and a detritus-based system that begins with the consumption of dead organic matter (Figure 10-1) (Batzli 1974, Heal and MacLean 1975). The distinction corresponds broadly to an aboveground and belowground division (perhaps reflecting a paucity of information on belowground herbivory). The two trophic systems may converge to some extent, particularly at the top carnivore level, and a single animal population may function in both trophic systems; this is a categorization of trophic functions rather than animals.

Several important conceptual differences distinguish the two trophic systems. The herbivore-based system begins with the consumption of living plant tissue, and thus impacts directly upon plant production, growth, and reproduction. Thus herbivores (or, indirectly, carnivores preying upon herbivores) modify the rate of input of chemical energy

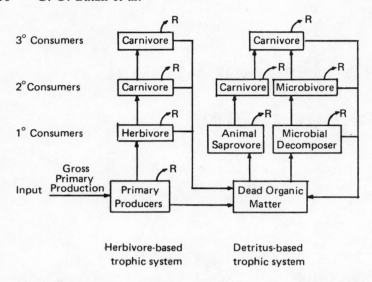

FIGURE 10-1. *A generalized trophic structure for terrestrial ecosystems, showing the distinction between herbivore-based and detritus-based trophic systems. Arrows represent the flow of energy and materials; R represents respiratory loss of energy. (After Heal and MacLean 1975.)*

(fixed carbon) into the ecosystem. The detritus-based system is based upon the consumption of dead organic matter. Saprovores and microorganisms influence the ecosystem through their control of the rate of decomposition and cycling of mineral nutrients. There is ample reason to believe that, in tundra, this is particularly important (Chapter 5). Other distinctions between the herbivore- and detritus-based trophic systems are discussed by Heal and MacLean (1975).

Herbivore-based food chains in arctic regions contain relatively few taxa. Whole groups of invertebrates that are common in grasslands at lower latitudes, e.g. insects and mollusks, have few representatives in the Arctic (MacLean 1975a). The most abundant herbivores are homeotherms, probably because they can maintain high rates of activity and growth at low temperatures.

Herbivorous birds, especially ptarmigan (*Lagopus* spp.) and geese (*Anser albifrons, Branta canadensis* and *Chen hyperborea*), use the North American tundra as a breeding ground during summer, but their occurrence and impact appear to be patchy. While avian herbivores generally migrate south in late summer, some ptarmigan do overwinter on inland tundra where they consume mostly willow buds and twigs (West and Meng 1966).

Some mammalian herbivores also occur sporadically on the tundra. Ground squirrels (*Spermophilus parryii*) may reach impressive densities along river banks and beach ridges, where substrate suitable for constructing their winter hibernacula can be found.Hares (*Lepus othus*, = *timidus*, and *L. arcticus*) rarely reach significant numbers on tundra, though summer herds of 100-150 occasionally appear (Batzli 1975a). The two remaining groups of mammalian herbivores, the microtine rodents (*Lemmus, Dicrostonyx* and *Microtus*) and the ungulates (*Rangifer* and *Ovibos*), frequently reach high densities over wide areas of tundra, and represent most of the biomass in the first link of the herbivore chain in tundras.

Differences in body size and mobility of the microtine rodents and ungulates lead to different tactics for dealing with the severe arctic climate (Batzli et al. 1981). The large ungulates have more insulation and can withstand lower temperatures (Scholander et al. 1950). When winter snow conditions or temperatures become intolerable, they can travel long distances to more favorable habitats. In contrast, the small microtines have poor insulation and must rely upon increased metabolism to maintain body temperature. Because they lack the ability to move long distances, they must select or create favorable microhabitats in order to survive severe winter conditions. Large body size gives ungulates the opportunity for a long life span and iterative reproduction. However, two other characteristics associated with large body size—a longer developmental period and an increased parental investment in each offspring (Pianka 1970)—reduce the ability of ungulates to respond rapidly to favorable conditions by reproducing, and populations remain relatively stable. Small microtines, by comparison, suffer greater mortality in severe environments, but their shorter developmental time and greater fecundity allow them to respond rapidly to favorable environmental conditions. The following exposition describes and compares the most important components of the herbivore-based trophic systems at Barrow, dominated by microtine rodents, and at Prudhoe Bay, dominated by ungulates.

HERBIVORY AT BARROW—LEMMINGS

Introduction

In the coastal tundra at Barrow the brown lemming (*Lemmus sibericus*, = *trimucronatus*) is the dominant herbivore. The density of trappable animals (post-weanlings) may reach 225 ha⁻¹. Collared lemmings (*Dicrostonyx torquatus*, = *groenlandicus*) are usually scarce, about 0.1 per hectare, though densities on elevated ground may be higher. They have reached substantial numbers only once in the last 20 years, 27 ha⁻¹ in 1971 (Figure 10-2). No other vertebrate herbivores regularly inhabit the Barrow peninsula, but a few caribou (*Rangifer tarandus*) and ptarmigan (*Lagopus lagopus*) visit occasionally. A discussion of herbivory can therefore center on a single species: the brown lemming.

Population Dynamics and Demography

Changes in the lemming population have been monitored for 20 summers, from 1955 to 1974. During that time densities have fluctuated between peaks of up to 225 trappable lemmings ha⁻¹ and lows of 0.02 ha⁻¹, with three to six years elapsing between peaks (Figure 10-2). Although reliable estimates of population size were not made before 1955, high densities were also observed in 1946, 1949 and 1953 (Pitelka 1957b). These fluctuations have traditionally been called cycles, largely because of their great amplitude (3 or more orders of magnitude), even though all aspects of successive cycles are not alike.

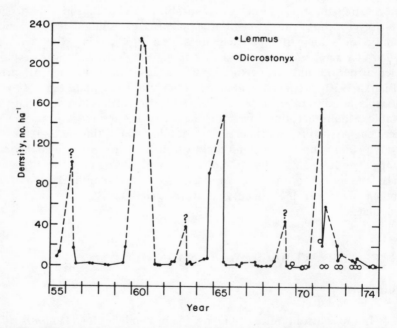

FIGURE 10-2. *Estimated lemming densities averaged for all habitats in the coastal tundra at Barrow for a 20-year period. The question marks indicate numbers based upon observations other than trapping.*

Mean densities for the entire tundra at Barrow are mainly useful for considering annual trends (Figure 10-2). The densities were calculated by calibrating results from extensive snap-trapping done at seven sites in five habitat types (Pitelka 1973). Local densities may depart markedly from overall densities, but the general trends from year to year were similar in all habitats.

A description of the sequence of events during a standard cycle can begin with the development of a high population. During the pre-high winter, lemmings reproduce in nests constructed out of dead grass and sedges and placed at the base of the snowpack. The population grows rapidly and reaches a peak in late spring. Breeding ceases during May, so few young are still in the nest during snowmelt, but juveniles continue to be recruited into the trappable population until early June. Before snowmelt there may be signs of stress. Many lemmings burrow to the surface and wander about, sometimes dying (Rausch 1950, Thompson 1955b). During snowmelt massive clipping of graminoids and disruption of moss and lichen carpets are revealed, and lemmings scurry everywhere. Large numbers of predators attack the exposed lemmings. Particularly prominent are pomarine jaegers (*Stercorarius pomarinus*), snowy owls (*Nyctea scandiaca*) and least weasels (*Mustela nivalis*). During the summer lemming survival declines, and the population crashes to a low level, where it remains for one to three years.

While this may be the general scenario, careful analysis of trapline data indicates that each cycle has peculiarities of its own (Pitelka 1973). In 1956, 1963 and 1969 populations increased under the snow, but declined before it was possible to measure maximum densities. In 1956, considered a peak year, an early snowmelt began in May, exposing the lemmings to avian predators. In 1963 and 1969 predation under the snow by weasels was unusually heavy (Pitelka 1973, MacLean et al. 1974), and normal peak densities of more than 100 ha^{-1} were never reached. The highest recorded density occurred during the 1960 peak, which lasted through the summer despite heavy predation and widespread destruction of habitat. In contrast, during 1965 the population declined to less than 1% of its initial density during the course of the summer. The decline following the population peak in 1971 was not as great, and, unlike all other post-high summers, in the summer of 1972 lemmings were present in moderate numbers. The population did not reach its usual low density of less than 0.5 ha^{-1} until 1974. During the pre-high summer of 1964 densities reached unusually high levels, but the population merely doubled during winter to produce the 1965 high. The pre-high summer of 1970 represents the other extreme: densities remained low, and the population increased by a factor of 250 during the ensuing winter. The combination of events since 1965, which has been especially peculiar compared with previous cycles, has been described in detail by Pitelka (1973).

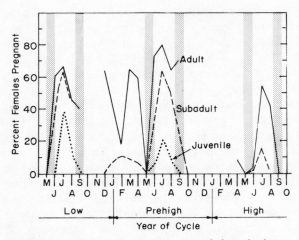

FIGURE 10-3. *The percentage of female lemmings pregnant in each age class during the course of a cycle. Sample sizes range from 10 to 746 and include all females collected by Pitelka (1973) during 1952-65. Data were collected for only one winter (1962-63). The shaded bars separate summer and winter and indicate times when mean air temperatures are near 0°C. (After Osborn 1975.)*

Demographic changes accompany these population fluctuations. Suppression of breeding, indicated by a low incidence of pregnancies, occurs in May just before snowmelt and in September during freeze-up (Figure 10-3). When lemmings do breed at these times, nests lie exposed on the surface because burrows are filled with ice or water or the snow cover is not well developed. Summer breeding appears to decline regularly in late August, although less so in pre-high years, but the resumption of breeding in early summer varies, depending upon temperature and the timing of snowmelt (Mullen 1968). During these breeding pauses the population structure shifts toward the older age classes, and density declines. Once the summer season begins, the population reproduces maximally—nearly every female is pregnant by mid-July—and the population structure shifts toward the younger age classes. If survival is high, the population increases rapidly. In general older females become pregnant more frequently than younger ones. The breeding intensity of adults varies little from summer to summer, but juveniles and subadults breed much less during the summer of a high population (Figure 10-3).

Little is known about the winter breeding season except that it lasts

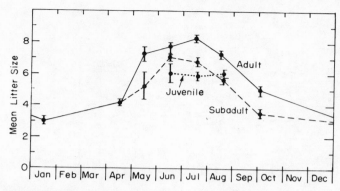

FIGURE 10-4. *Mean litter sizes for different age classes of lemmings throughout the year for the period 1952-65. Vertical bars represent ± 1 SE. (After Osborn 1975; based upon data of Pitelka 1974.)*

from November through April. Far fewer females are pregnant in midwinter than in summer. Breeding intensity varies more during winter than summer, probably depending upon the snowpack, thermal conditions and the availability of food, but there is little direct evidence for this. Lack of winter nests, lack of placental scars in adult females in spring and decreases in the population indicate that during some winters little, if any, reproduction occurs (MacLean et al. 1974).

Litter sizes differed among age classes of lemmings and among seasons (Figure 10-4). Older females have larger litters during summer; the mean litter size is eight for adults, seven for subadults and six for juveniles. During midwinter mean litter size declines to three. Although statistical analysis (ANOVA, $p < 0.05$) indicated significant, but minor, differences in average litter sizes from summer to summer, they did not appear to be related to the phase of the cycle (Osborn 1975).

Dramatic changes in survival rates from summer to summer do occur, from 70% per 28 days to 10% per 28 days for adults in July, but our knowledge of survival rates throughout a cycle is scanty. Changes in sex ratio indicate that survival of males tends to be lower than survival of females during the summer and higher during the winter, possibly as a result of differential predation. Osborn (1975) developed a computer simulation model that allows survival rates and density of sucklings, which are not trappable, to be estimated by a trial and error procedure, given information on age-specific reproductive rates and on population structure. Using the reproductive rates and litter sizes discussed above, together with field observations of age structure and population size during summer, he estimated density of sucklings and survival rates for each

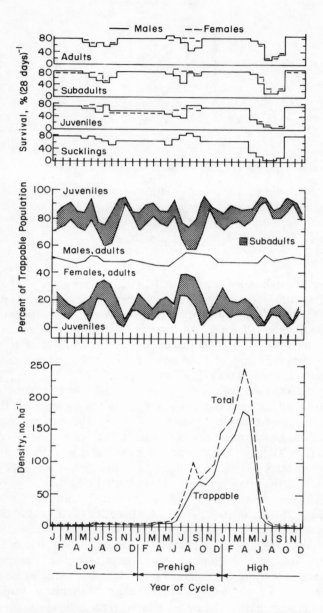

FIGURE 10-5. *The density and demography of brown lemmings through a standard three-year cycle calculated by a population model. (After Osborn 1975.)*

age, sex and reproductive class for a standard cycle based upon data from 1961–65 (Figure 10-5). In the model, survival rates for October through April were not varied with time and should be viewed as average values over the winter.

One of the most striking results of these simulations was the small increase in survival of lemmings required to build a peak population (Figure 10-5). Sucklings accounted for about half of the population during the pre-high summer and one-quarter of the peak population. During this time, reproductive rates were no better than the previous year, but suckling and female survival improved slightly. Even with high reproductive rates survival rates of sucklings and juveniles during the pre-high summer needed to be relatively high for the population to increase as observed in the field. During the population crash the survival rates of young animals remained very low so that at times the population became almost completely adult. Survival rates for sucklings are based only on litters whose mother also survives; when a nursing female dies her litter also dies. Thus, improvement of female survival has a double effect on population growth.

Habitat Use

Lemmings do not make equal use of various habitat types, so any analysis of herbivory must consider spatial patterns of habitat utilization. We use two scales in our analysis, mesotopographic units and microtopographic units (Figure 10-6).

Snap-trap lines run by Pitelka for 19 years in the Barrow area provided information on habitat utilization. These lines were divided into five habitat types, which can be arranged along a moisture gradient and

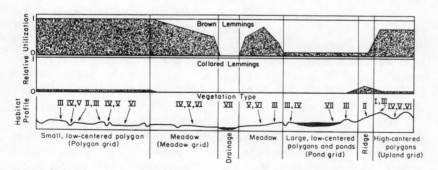

FIGURE 10-6. *The relative utilization by lemmings of habitat types on the Barrow research area. The numerals above the topographic profile indicate vegetation types (Table 1-4).*

correlated with the vegetation types given in Chapter 1 (Table 1-4):

1. Ridges: well-drained raised areas with *Salix* heath vegetation (I, II).
2. High-centered polygons: polygons with well-drained centers and with wet troughs and ponds between them (I, III, V, VI).
3. Low-centered polygons: polygons with mesic centers and with wet troughs between them (II, III, IV, V, VI).
4. Graminoid flats: wet meadow with mixed graminoid vegetation (V, VI).
5. *Carex* flats: wet meadow dominated by *Carex* (VI).

Although densities varied, the pattern of habitat use was fairly consistent from year to year. In early summer, well-drained areas dominated by high-centered polygons were the most heavily used, and twice as many lemmings were captured there as in any other habitat. By late summer the use of such areas decreased markedly, while use of areas dominated by low-centered polygons and of low-lying meadows increased. This pattern reflects the fact that low habitats are flooded in early summer but become drier as the summer progresses. The extremes of the moisture gradient, ridge and *Carex* meadow, received substantial use only when population densities were high. Collared lemmings, when present, usually were found in ridge or high-centered polygon habitats (Figure 10-6).

Density estimates and signs of activity on four 2.25-ha live-trapping grids in the immediate vicinity of the Biome research area gave a slightly different picture of habitat use. During winter nest densities were greater in high-centered polygons than other habitats, but population densities at snowmelt and winter clipping of vegetation were greater in low-centered polygons (Table 10-1). Clipping rates indicate the amount of winter foraging, while nests may reflect the intensity of reproduction. All indicators of activity support the notion that the polygon and pond habitats, which had relatively uniform vegetation heavily dominated by *Carex*, were used least by lemmings. Summer population densities and the rates of clipping indicate that the low-centered polygons and meadows were used most heavily, particularly in the summer of 1972 and the winter of 1973. At lower densities, in the summer of 1973 and the winter and summer of 1974, use of high-centered and low-centered polygons was more similar.

Use of the meadow depended upon moisture conditions. The summer of 1972 was relatively dry, so lemmings moved into the lower, wetter portions of the grid as standing water receded, and the overwintering population was similar to that on low-centered polygons (Table 10-1). The summer of 1973 had late rains, however, and much of the meadow was flooded at freeze-up. As a result, the overwintering population during 1974 was only a third of that on low-centered polygons.

TABLE 10-1   *Summary of Indicators of Brown Lemming Activity in Four Habitats at Barrow*

	1972	1973	1974
Winter nest density (no. ha⁻¹)			
High-centered polygons	—	24.9	18.5
Low-centered polygons	—	18.2	12.9
Meadow	—	17.2	4.2
Polygons and ponds	—	2.7	0.4
Summer population density (no. ha⁻¹)			
High-centered polygons	3.4–14.7	3.1–4.0	0.3–0.6
Low-centered polygons	12.9–46.1	3.1–4.9	0.3–0.6
Meadow	—	2.5–3.1	0.9–1.2
Polygons and ponds	1.6–7.7	0.3–1.5	0.0–0.6
Percentage of graminoid tillers clipped			
High-centered polygons	14.8	12.3	2.4
Low-centered polygons	—	25.1	6.7
Meadow	—	24.3	1.9
Polygons and ponds	—	5.4	0.3

Note: Densities are seasonal extremes. Habitat types are illustrated in Figure 10-6.

These observations support several generalizations. First, brown lemming activity, both summer and winter, tends to be concentrated in polygonal terrain, which has a mixture of relatively dry and wet habitat. Second, low, wet areas with vegetation heavily dominated by *Carex* and dry ridges with *Salix* heath are the areas least utilized by brown lemmings. Third, the use of low-lying meadows with mixed graminoids varies depending on seasonal and annual moisture conditions.

Lemming activity is neither randomly nor uniformly dispersed within the larger topographic units discussed above, and the use of local microtopographic units must also be considered. Habitats with well-developed high-centered and low-centered polygons have the greatest microtopographic relief and support the greatest winter nesting. Ninety-three percent of 139 nests examined in 1974 were located in polygon troughs. Winter clipping of vegetation is also concentrated in troughs, where the density of shoots is higher, but patches of clipping occur in all microtopographic units. In 1973 we found clipping percentages of 25 to 50% in troughs, where graminoid shoot densities were about 3000 m⁻², 15% on rims with 2000 shoots m⁻², and 5% in basins with 1000 to 1500 shoots m⁻².

Summer activity patterns have been more intensively studied than winter patterns. Using techniques of radio tracking, Banks et al. (1975) showed that individual lemmings may move over 1 km day⁻¹; however, most lemmings live in home ranges of highly variable size. Females tended

TABLE 10-2   *Home Ranges (Mean ± 1 SE in
Hectares) of Lemmings on
Low-centered Polygons*

	1972	1973
Males	1.33 ± 0.28 (12)	0.88 ± 0.28 (13)
Females	0.68 ± 0.37 (6)	0.41 ± 0.31 (11)

Note: Sample sizes are given in parentheses.
Source: Banks et al. (1975).

to have smaller home ranges than males (Table 10-2), but the variability
is such that differences were not statistically significant. Differences also
occurred from year to year, but again variability was high. Analysis of
the frequency of movements of 5 m or more indicated that males moved
more than females and that more movement occurred in 1972 than in
1973 (ANOVA, $p < 0.01$).

The greater movement of males probably results from the mating
system of lemmings, viz. promiscuous polygamy. Males can increase
their fitness by touring the habitat in search of females, whereas females
restrict their movements, usually moving between foraging sites and nesting burrows. A combination of increased energy requirements and vulnerability to predation when moving probably limits male movements.
The greater movement of lemmings in 1972 than in 1973 was correlated
with higher population density (Table 10-1), hence greater social interaction, and with a lower rate of predation in 1972.

Summer activity in polygonized terrain takes place primarily in the
troughs. Lemming burrows are concentrated on the sides of troughs
above the water line or on the sides of high-centered polygons. Summer
nests are usually located in these burrows or under elevated patches of
moss (*Sphagnum* spp.). Runways follow troughs, particularly the frost
cracks associated with them. Foraging activity is concentrated near the
burrows and along the sides of runways. About 95 to 100% of graminoid
shoots in the immediate vicinity of burrows are repeatedly clipped while
the burrow remains occupied. Away from the burrows, clipping is
patchy, and intensity decreases as distance from the runways increases.
Cheslak (pers. comm.) found only from 0 to 30% of shoots clipped at a
distance of 0.5 m from runways when lemming densities were moderate,
about 10 ha^{-1}. Maps of the locations of radio-tagged lemmings show patterns that match the patterns of polygon troughs (Banks, pers. comm.).
In nonpolygonized terrain the association with microtopographic
features is not so clear, and lemming activity appears to be located in
more randomly distributed patches, but, again, clipping is concentrated
near runways.

Although collared lemmings are not abundant on the coastal tundra at Barrow, they are more common than brown lemmings at many other tundra sites (Bee and Hall 1956, Krebs 1964, Fuller et al. 1975, Batzli and Jung 1980), and they present an interesting contrast. Collared lemmings generally prefer higher, drier habitats than brown lemmings, particularly areas where dicotyledonous plants are common. They excavate more elaborate burrow systems than brown lemmings and do not use runways, which are not required in habitats without dense graminoid growth.

Nutrition and Energetics

Diet

The food habits of lemmings, as of most herbivores, vary with season and habitat. In general, however, collared lemmings and brown lemmings specialize on different food types. Collared lemmings take primarily dicotyledons supplemented by graminoids, whereas brown lemmings take primarily graminoids supplemented by mosses. *Salix* appears to be the most important dietary item of collared lemmings in summer (40 to 50%) and may be even more important in winter. *Dicrostonyx* feces from winter nests contain large amounts of willow leaves. Dietary specialization reflects more than differences in habitat preference because dietary compositions remain distinct even at sites where both species occur (Batzli 1975a).

We have examined the food habits of brown lemmings in some detail. Significant seasonal changes in diet occur, from about 80% graminoids in mid-summer to 55% in mid-winter. Changes with habitat appear to be greater in summer than winter. During July graminoids may contribute only 70% of the diet in polygonal terrain but over 90% in low, wet meadows. During winter the variation of graminoid content between habitats is only ±5%. Dicotyledonous plants make up a fairly consistent 5 to 10% of the diet, and lichens contribute less than 1%; thus, most of the shifting to and from graminoids is matched by opposite trends for mosses.

Selection among graminoid species has been examined in the laboratory by Melchior (pers. comm.). Lemmings selected the sedges *Eriophorum russeolum* and *E. scheuchzeri* in greater amounts than other species when offered a choice of graminoid species in the form of sod blocks. Naturally occurring dicotyledonous species were ignored or consumed in very small amounts. Living green leaves and leaf sheaths were consumed; dead plant parts were rejected. Inflorescences were consumed by some lemmings and rejected by others. Thompson (1951) reported similar results; *Lemmus* preferred sedges and grasses and *Dicrostonyx* preferred

Salix and herbaceous dicotyledons. Only *Eriophorum* ranked highly as a preferred item for both lemmings.

Comparison of dietary composition in the field with the vegetational composition of the habitat shows that *Lemmus* selects *Dupontia fisheri.* The percentage in the diet is about twice the percentage in available forage during midsummer (Batzli 1981). Consumption of the most abundant and widely distributed graminoid, the sedge *Carex aquatilis,* is highly correlated with availability ($r = 0.91$, $p < 0.01$), and it is taken at a level of about half of its availability. Surprisingly, *Eriophorum (E. angustifolium, E. russeolum* and *E. scheuchzeri*, taken together) shows a lower preference rating despite its higher ranking in the laboratory trials.

In winter, graminoid shoots die back to about 1 cm above the ground, and tissue below this point freezes while green and nutritious. Food preferences are less apparent then, and lemmings consume the major graminoids approximately in proportion to their availability. Because polygon troughs, the favored winter habitat, contain much *Dupontia*, this species is also an important winter food of lemmings.

Energy Requirements

The total assimilated energy required by a lemming can be estimated by summing the energy demands for maintenance, growth and reproduction and the amount of energy lost in urine. Urinary loss of energy for lemmings on natural diets equals approximately 5% of respiratory energy (Batzli and Cole 1979). Maintenance energy requirement, or respiration, can be expressed as average daily metabolic rate, which is a function of body size, ambient temperature and activity. Collier et al. (1975) have developed a model of lemming energetics. The current version of that model (Peterson et al. 1976) is

$$\text{ADMR} = (1.28 W^{0.75} - 0.45 T + 6.40) 4.19$$

where ADMR is average daily metabolic rate in kJ day^{-1}, W is live body weight in grams and T is ambient temperature in °C. Measurements of the metabolic rate of free-living *Lemmus* using doubly labeled water, $D_2{}^{18}O$, indicated that extrapolations from laboratory results probably underestimate the metabolic rates of lemmings in the field by 40% (Peterson et al. 1976). Therefore, the following calculations based upon the curve of Collier et al. (1975) give conservative estimates of energy requirements.

The above equation was based upon animals with stable weights; additional energy is required for growing animals. The amount needed is determined by the growth rate of the individual and the efficiency with

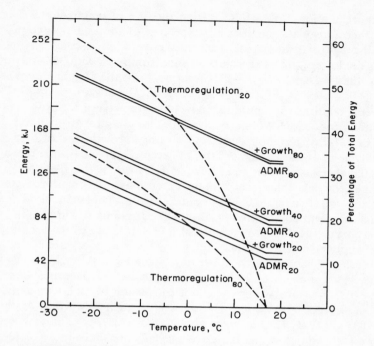

FIGURE 10-7. *The relationship of energetic requirements of non-reproducing lemmings (solid lines) and percentage of energy used for thermoregulation (dashed lines) to ambient temperatures. Subscripts give the body weight of lemmings in grams.*

which assimilated energy can be transformed into tissue. Growth rates of lemmings have been summarized by Batzli (1975a) and allow for the development of sexual dimorphism in size beginning as subadults, 30 to 60 days old. In order to calculate the total energy used for growth, 25% of the energy stored in new tissue must be added, given an efficiency of tissue growth of 0.80 (Blaxter 1967). Assuming that growth is independent of ambient temperature, growth adds a constant energy increment to the average daily metabolic rate.

Energy requirements for maintenance and growth as a function of ambient temperature differ markedly for juvenile and adult lemmings (Figure 10-7). The average daily metabolic rate increases significantly with declining ambient temperature; for the 20-g juvenile lemming it increases nearly 3-fold over the temperature range $+17°$ to $-25°C$, the annual range of temperature usually encountered by a lemming.

The average daily metabolic rate equation separates the energy cost of thermoregulation, 1.87 kJ °C⁻¹, from the cost of maintenance. The cost of thermoregulation expressed as percent of total energy requirements, average daily metabolic rate plus growth, is zero at +17 °C, which is the lower limit of thermoneutrality, compared with 36% of the total for the 80-g lemming at -25 °C and 60% for the 20-g lemming at -25 °C.

Energy required for reproduction includes that invested in growth of fetuses and production of milk for sucklings. Fetuses grow from 0 to 3.3 g over the 21-day gestation period, an average growth rate of 0.25 g day⁻¹. Given an average summer litter of seven (Figure 10-4), the reproductive female must support an average fetus growth of 1.75 g day⁻¹. Actually, the growth is concentrated in the latter phases of gestation. After a tissue growth efficiency of 0.80 is applied, the cost of pregnancy is about 75% greater than that for growth of the 20-g lemming (Figure 10-7).

The cost of suckling growth must also be supported by the breeding female. Applying a growth rate of 0.8 g day⁻¹ to a litter of seven gives a value of 5.6 g of suckling growth per day. Since 1 g suckling live weight has an energy content of 4.19 kJ, this is equal to 23.5 kJ. This must be divided by 0.3, the value for efficiency of conversion of milk to suckling tissue, and by 0.7, the value for efficiency of milk production by the mother (Brody 1945, Hashizume et al. 1965). The energy requirement is therefore 113 kJ day⁻¹, equal to the average daily metabolic rate of a 40-g lemming at 5 °C. Thus, lactation plays an immense role in the energetics of lemmings. Securing this additional energy requires more activity by reproducing females, which further increases energy demand. Lemmings usually are able to satisfy this demand during summer, but during winter, when the cost of thermoregulation is high and forage is sparse, litter size declines to three (Figure 10-4).

Reproduction would not be possible at all during winter without the construction of nests. The value of the nest to the lemming was explored by MacLean and Thomsen (pers. comm.) using a heat flow model. The model regards the lemming as a homeothermic body of temperature T_L and radius b, proportional to the cube root of body mass. The lemming must produce heat at a rate q that is equal to the heat flow from the warm lemming to the cold surroundings. The nest forms an insulating layer of inner radius b and outer radius a around the lemming.

The model shows that an equilibrium heat distribution is rapidly established in the inner layer of the nest around the lemming. At this time

$$q = 4\pi k(T_L - T_A)[ab/(a-b)]$$

where k is the thermal conductivity of the nest material in J s⁻¹ cm⁻¹ °C⁻¹ and T_A is the temperature of the snow around the nest. Heat flow is determined by the temperature gradient, the radius of the lemming and

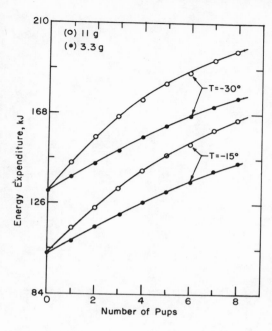

FIGURE 10-8. *The simulated daily energy expenditure by a reproducing female lemming with a winter nest in relation to litter size, weight of pups and ambient temperature T. (MacLean and Thomsen, pers. comm.)*

the radius of the nest. Under winter conditions heat flow from the nest is considerably less than the average daily metabolic requirement without a nest. For a 60-g lemming at an air temperature of –30 °C the average daily metabolic rate maintained over the entire day gives 199 kJ of energy used. The time that can be spent in a nest depends upon energy reserves, which can be estimated from the stomach capacity equation discussed below. Assuming 30-minute bouts of foraging with metabolism at the average daily rate, interspersed between bouts of nest use, total energy use by a 60-g lemming with a nest of 12-cm radius is 129 kJ day^{-1}.

A large nest is crucial for winter reproduction. It reduces the energy cost to the female and prevents rapid cooling and death of the sucklings prior to the development of homeothermy at 10 to 12 days of age. The physiological processes involved in reproduction are energy-demanding, especially lactation. However, much of the heat from respiration by the female goes into the nest, and thus contributes to homeothermy. Before the sucklings develop homeothermy the major costs of reproduction come from 1) the increased radius of the nest contents, the female plus young, which leads to greater heat flow from the nest; 2) the need to rewarm cooled sucklings following a period of absence; and 3) the growth of the sucklings. The estimated energy expenditure of a lemming supporting a maximum reproductive load, six 11-g heterothermic sucklings at an ambient temperature of –30 °C, is 186 kJ (Figure 10-8), or 144% of

TABLE 10-3 *Comparison of Population Dynamics and Energetics of Mammalian Herbivores at Two Coastal Tundra Sites*

	Barrow		Prudhoe Bay			
	Lemmus sibericus	*Dicrostonyx torquatus*	*Lemmus sibericus**	*Dicrostonyx torquatus**	*Spermophilus parryii**	*Rangifer tarandus*
Density (no. ha^{-1})	0.02–195	0.01–25	0.01–10	0.01–10	0.05	0.001–0.01
Animal residence (days ha^{-1} yr^{-1})	71–28,380	15–3,638	15–1,455	15–1,455	6.8	0.6–1.9
Biomass dry wt (kg ha^{-1})	0.0003–2.6	0.0002–0.3	0.0002–0.15	0.0002–0.15	0.05	0.04–0.52
Biomass residence (kg days ha^{-1} yr^{-1})	1.0–383	0.4–40	0.4–18	0.4–18	6.8	24–27
Ingestion (MJ ha^{-1} yr^{-1})	18–7000	2.9–669	5.7–531	2.9–271	3.0	24–78
Assimilation (MJ ha^{-1} yr^{-1})	5.9–2333	1.9–435	1.9–177	1.9–176	2.1	13–43
Respiration (MJ ha^{-1} yr^{-1})	5.4–2095	1.7–394	1.7–159	1.7–159	1.9	11–37
Production (MJ ha^{-1} yr^{-1})	0.27–105	0.036–8.3	0.085–8.0	0.036–3.3	0.095	0.24–0.78
Population efficiencies						
A/I	0.33	0.65				0.55
P/I	0.015	0.012				0.010
P/A	0.045	0.019				0.018
P/R	0.050	0.021				0.021
Turnover time (yr)	0.21	0.27				9.1

*Exact densities and year-to-year variations are unknown. Populations of ground squirrels are relatively stable (Carl 1971, Batzli and Sobaski 1980).

Note: Ranges of values for extreme years are shown. Densities and biomass values are instantaneous, others are cumulative totals of average monthly values.

the energy used by a nonreproductive female with a similar nest of 12-cm outer radius. The aditional energy cost of reproduction is rather low compared to earlier calculations because nonreproductive lemmings have a high rate of energy use at such low temperatures, even with a nest.

Total population energy demand for a high year (September of a pre-high year through August of a high year) has been calculated by summing energy requirements for the individuals of each category present each month. Monthly changes in density, population structure and reproductive intensity were estimated for a standard cycle in which trappable densities reached 150 ha^{-1} (Batzli 1975a). The low population was assumed to have a similar structure, but average densities for the whole year were 400 times less than for the high population (Table 10-3).

Grodziński and Wunder (1975) reported that production, the sum of all energy deposited in new tissue, averaged 2.3% of respiration for rodent populations in general, a value slightly higher than the 2% predicted by Turner (1970) for vertebrate homeotherms. When rising to a peak, production for a population of *Lemmus* at Barrow was 5% of respiration. This value is the highest known for a homeotherm and occurs despite the high energy requirements of thermoregulation. The high production results from nearly year-round reproduction and the high population turnover rate of *Lemmus*. Values calculated for *Dicrostonyx* are more similar to those for other small rodents.

Digestion and Ingestion

In order to calculate ingestion rates for the population, we must know the mean composition of the natural diet and the digestibility of natural forage as well as energetic demand. The information on the food habits of lemmings presented above has been averaged across habitats, and overall summer and winter digestibilities calculated (Figure 10-18). A mean digestive efficiency of 33% for energy is derived from these values and applied to assimilation to give an estimate of ingestion.

The digestive efficiency of *Lemmus* is strikingly low, much lower than that of *Dicrostonyx* and most other herbivorous mammals (Batzli and Cole 1979), and dramatically elevates the ingestion rate. The material within the plants may be separated into structural carbohydrate, composed of cellulose, hemicellulose and lignin, and nonstructural carbohydrate. Nonstructural carbohydrate is material contained in the cell cytoplasm and should be much more easily digested than structural carbohydrate. Total nonstructural carbohydrate (TNC) in graminoid shoots varied between 30 and 40% of the biomass for most of the growing season on moist meadows (Chapter 5, Figure 5-5). Lipid concentration found in shoots varied from 5 to 15%. Therefore, the observed 36% digestibility of graminoids can be accounted for by digestion of TNC and lipids.

Although digestibility of tundra graminoids by brown lemmings is low compared to the 45% to 55% digestibility of temperate grasses by other microtine rodents (Batzli and Cole 1979), tundra graminoids are higher in total nonstructural carbohydrate and lipids than are temperate graminoids (Chapter 5). Thus, the higher digestibilities achieved by temperate microtines must result from the breakdown of a significant portion of the structural tissue. For lemmings, however, the rate of energy and nutrient assimilation is maximized at the expense of efficiency. Food is passed rapidly through the gut and only the most easily digested fraction assimilated. Melchior (pers. comm.), in laboratory feeding trials using graminoids as food, showed that hunger reached maximal levels after two hours of food deprivation, and we found that guts were virtually empty after three hours. Following a change of diet, fecal pellets attributable to the new diet appeared in 35 minutes.

The rapid passage of food through the gut and the high daily energy demand require that a significant amount of each day be spent foraging. During summer adult lemmings spend about 60 to 70% of their time out of the burrow (Banks et al. 1975, Peterson et al. 1976). Melchior (pers. comm.) estimated the stomach capacity of adult male lemmings by feeding animals to satiation; food consumed was approximately 10% of body weight. This gives a stomach capacity of about 125 usable joules per gram of lemming:

$$\text{Stomach capacity} = 0.1\,W \times 0.20 \times 18,900 \times 0.33 = 125 \text{ J g}^{-1}$$

where W is the body weight of the lemming in grams, 0.20 is the proportion dry weight in forage, 18,900 represents the average number of joules per gram dry weight of forage and 0.33 is the proportion of joules assimilated. Given this stomach capacity, and assuming that the value derived for adult males holds for all age classes, we may calculate the number of times the gut must be filled each day to satisfy the energy requirements of average daily metabolic rate plus growth. Since both stomach capacity and body weight are proportional to the volume of the animal, we assume that stomach capacity increases linearly with weight, whereas average daily metabolic rate increases with $W^{0.75}$. Gut capacity increases more rapidly with size than does metabolism, and the number of gut fillings needed to satisfy average daily metabolic rate falls. Growth rate also decreases with size, further reducing the required number of fillings per day. Small lemmings (20 g) require 22 to 52 fillings per day while large lemmings (80 g) require only 14 to 22 as temperature varies from +15 to –25 °C. The large number of fillings does not represent the number of foraging bouts, however, as lemmings may spend an hour or more out of the burrow at a time, at least during summer, and probably refill the stomach before it is empty (Peterson et al. 1976).

Perhaps the most revealing expression of energy demand for the

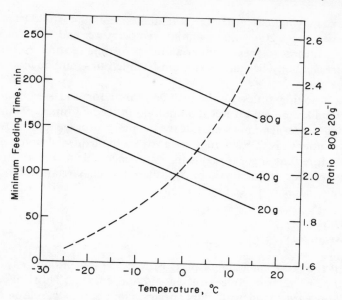

FIGURE 10-9. *The minimum feeding times required to meet the energetic demands of different-sized lemmings at several temperatures, assuming high availability of forage (no search time). Ratios of feeding times for large and small lemmings are shown by the dashed line.*

lemming is the time spent foraging. Each foraging bout requires the lemming to leave the warmth and protection of the nest or burrow and risk exposure to predators and/or lower temperatures. Melchior (pers. comm.) found that, with grasses and sedges provided *ad libitum*, mean food intake ($\pm$ 1 SE) was 0.14 $\pm$ 0.02 gdw min^{-1}. At this rate, a 40-g lemming could fill its stomach in slightly less than six minutes. Since no search was involved this rate is limited only by handling time, and provides an estimate of maximum ingestion rate. Minimum daily foraging time may now be calculated as a function of body weight and ambient temperature (Figure 10-9):

$$\text{Min. feeding time} = \text{Stomach capacity} \times \text{Max. ingestion rate}^{-1}$$
$$\text{(min day}^{-1}) \qquad \qquad \text{(gdw)} \qquad \qquad \text{(g min}^{-1})$$

$$\times \text{Required energy} \times \text{Stomach capacity}^{-1}$$
$$\text{(J day}^{-1}) \qquad \qquad \text{(J)}$$

Thus, small lemmings require more separate fillings, but less time to fill the gut and less feeding time even at low temperatures. Of course, rate of intake may increase with size, but an 80-g lemming would have to eat 66% faster than a 20-g lemming at low temperatures and 156% faster at high temperatures to spend similar amounts of time feeding. No relationship between body size and maximum feeding rate could be found in Melchior's data.

Actual foraging times would include search for and selection of food and would be much greater than minimum feeding times. Furthermore, during winter lemmings must leave the nest to forage under lower subnivean temperatures. While they are away from the nest, nest temperature falls. More time spent foraging increases energy demand, which increases the necessary foraging time. A positive feedback relationship exists and accentuates winter energy requirements.

Nutrient Relationships

One of the most intriguing aspects of lemming nutrition is its relationship to plant nutrient concentration and nutrient flux. Nutrient contents of plants vary widely with plant species, plant part, site, season and year (Chapter 5). Changes in forage quality have serious implications for lemming nutrition. For instance, the preference for *Dupontia fisheri* in midsummer may be related to the fact that it tends to grow in nutrient-rich areas. Indeed, the general propensity of lemmings to use vegetation more in troughs and wet meadows than in drier areas may be related to the higher nutrient status of graminoids in those areas.

Interest in the role of nutrients in lemming population dynamics led to examination of the nutrient dynamics of lemmings in relation to food habits and nutrient content of the forage. Of the energy ingested by the population as a whole, 1.5% is retained as production (Table 10-3):

$$P/I = A/I \times P/A = 0.33 \times 0.045.$$

The balance is lost as urine and feces, or through respiration. Since the energy and nutrients come from the same food, we may calculate the P/I value for nutrients as

$$P/I_{[N]} = 1.5(L/F_{[N]} \times 1.2^{-1}) = 1.3L/F_{[N]}$$

where $P/I_{[N]}$ is the percentage of a nutrient retained by the lemming population, 1.5 is the percentage of energy retained, $L/F_{[N]}$ is the ratio of nutrient concentration in lemmings to forage, and 1.2 is the ratio of energy concentration in lemmings to forage.

Calculated values for forage (Table 10-4) represent typical values and ignore wide variation for some nutrients, so only major trends

TABLE 10-4 *Relative Concentration of Energy (kJ gdw⁻¹) and Nutrients (mg gdw⁻¹) in Forage and Lemmings*

	Concentration in forage (F)*	Concentration in lemmings (L)†	Concentration factor (L/F)	P/I (%)
Energy	18.9	21.8	1.2	1.5
N	25	103	4.1	5.3
K	20	8	0.4	0.5
P	2	27	13.5	17.6
Mg	3	5	1.7	2.2
Ca	2	31	15.5	20.2
Na	1	5	5.0	6.5

*Data from Tieszen (unpubl.); Chapin et al. (1975).
†Data from Bunnell (unpubl.).
Note: Percentage of forage nutrients retained in lemming production given by ratio of production to ingestion (*P/I*) calculated from equation given on p. 356.

should be considered. Relatively large amounts of the calcium and phosphorus in forage are retained as lemming production, and these nutrients may be limiting for lemmings. If assimilation is low with high fecal loss, or if recycling within the body is inefficient with high urinary loss, the animal is in danger of entering negative nutrient balance, particularly during pregnancy and lactation when nutrient demands are high.

A simulation model of lemming nutrition was constructed to explore the nutrient balance in lemmings (Barkley et al. 1980). The model calculates the amount of nitrogen, phosphorus and calcium that a lemming could absorb from a given diet; the amount of nutrients required, given the lemming's body size, growth rate and reproductive condition; and the changes that occur in the lemming's nutrient pool. Normal nutrient pools were calculated from data of Bunnell (pers. comm.). Because little information was available on lemmings' ability to absorb nutrients or on their endogenous loss rates, which determine minimum nutrient requirements, this part of the model relied heavily upon nutritional information for the laboratory rat. In rats, and presumably in lemmings, absorption and losses are functions of ingestion, fecal output, metabolic rate and nutritional condition. Relatively high absorption rates and low loss rates were used, so the model was conservative and biased against the production of nutrient deficiencies.

The total amount of forage consumed was based upon lemmings' energetic requirements, food habits and forage digestibility. The standard model used a diet consisting of 80% graminoids and 20% mosses during midsummer and 60% graminoids and 40% mosses during midwinter. Continuous shifts in the diet mimicked the field situation. Nutrient concentrations in graminoids were those reported for the *Carex-Oncophorus* meadow for 1970 when nutrients were low and for 1973 when nutrients were high (Chapter 5; Chapin et al. 1975).

Early runs of the model, using a combination of starting ages, dates and nutrient concentrations, showed that only reproducing females would experience serious deficiencies—depletion of normal body pool by more than 25%. A series of runs were then conducted to compare the effects of different litter sizes, nutrient contents of forage, digestibility of forage and food habits of reproducing females. In years when there were low concentrations of nutrients in their forage, adult females (120 days old) could barely support litters of seven during midsummer, four during winter and two during late August. No offspring could be supported during late June of such years. In winter, reproduction was limited by nitrogen, calcium and phosphorus, but in early and late summer only calcium and phosphorus were limiting. During summers when there were high levels of nutrients in the vegetation, 30-day-old subadults could raise litters of eight. As expected, smaller litters and slower growth in older animals improved the nutrient status of the lemmings.

The simulation indicated that the condition of nutrient-deficient lemmings could be improved during summer by an increase in the intake of mosses or a reduction in digestive efficiency for energy and dry matter (Figure 10-10). In winter these tactics also improved calcium and phosphorus deficiencies, but they caused worse deficiencies in nitrogen. Reduced digestibility allowed the extraction of minerals from more total dry matter because the lemming had to eat more to meet energy requirements. These results help to explain some unusual aspects of lemming biology. The low digestibility of forage by lemmings, compared to temperate microtines, appears paradoxical since existence in an arctic environment increases energy requirements. However, the results of the model suggest that lemmings confront a nutritional situation where calcium and phosphorus availability are more critical than energy. Low digestive efficiency for energy requires greater food intake and thus increases nutrient availability. Adjusting the model so that energy digestibility was improved caused reproducing lemmings to become calcium- and phosphorus-deficient, even when nutrient levels in the forage were high. Calcium and phosphorus concentrations in arctic forage appear to be low compared to those in temperate forage (Table 10-5). Low digestive efficiency for energy by lemmings may have evolved to assure an adequate intake of inorganic nutrients. The lower limit of digestibility must be determined by the actual ability of lemmings to find enough food and pass it through the gut. The actual digestibilities are the result of several conflicting pressures.

The model also helps to explain the presence of relatively high

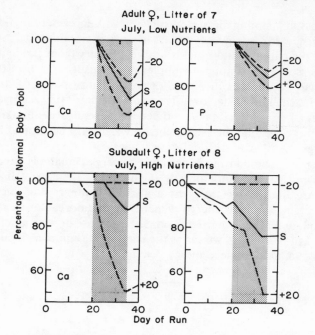

FIGURE 10-10. *Simulated nutrient pools in repro-ductive female lemmings with normal digestibility of energy in diet (S), 20% higher digestibility (+20) and 20% lower digestibility (-20). The assumptions of the model are given in the text. The shaded area represents lactation. (After Barkley 1976.)*

TABLE 10-5   *Concentrations (Mean ± 1 SE) of Nutrients in Shoots of Mature Graminoids from Four Temperate Grasslands and from Coastal Tundra at Barrow*

Habitat	No. of species	N	Ca	P	Reference
Great Basin	5	1.07 ± 0.22	0.53 ± 0.11	0.19 ± 0.07	Harner and Harper (1973)
Northern Great Plains	16	1.43 ± 0.34	0.28 ± 0.08	0.14 ± 0.05	Johnston and Bezeau (1962)
Tall Grass Prairie	4	1.13 ± 0.39	0.39 ± 0.26	0.19 ± 0.08	Gerloff et al. (1964)
Mown Grass-lands	6	1.47 ± 0.38	0.42 ± 0.06	0.29 ± 0.08	National Academy of Sciences (1969)
Coastal Tundra	7	1.86 ± 0.07	0.16 ± 0.01	0.13 ± 0.01	Chapin et al. (1975)

amounts of moss in lemming diets, up to 40% in winter, even though the digestive efficiency for energy of mosses is low. Lemmings fed only mosses reduce their intake and quickly starve. Results from the model suggest that mosses serve as nutrient supplements because they are 10 to 20% higher than graminoids in phosphorus concentration and 200 to 300% higher in calcium. The low digestive efficiency for energy of mosses requires a larger food intake, and hence assures a larger intake of nutrients. But mosses cannot be used exclusively as forage because of low digestible energy or other nutritional deficiencies.

Finally, reproduction during winter, when energy demand is already high, becomes more understandable with the hypothesis that growth and reproduction are limited by nutrient availability rather than energy availability. In fact, the high energy demand of thermoregulation may assure an adequate intake of nutrients, and conditions for reproduction may be nearly as favorable in winter as they are in late summer, if sufficient forage is available to meet energy demands.

PREDATION ON LEMMINGS

Introduction

Predators are conspicuous in the tundra at Barrow during the summer of a lemming high, and their populations have received considerable attention (Pitelka et al. 1955, Maher 1970, 1974, MacLean et al. 1974). A separation of avian and mammalian predators also distinguishes migratory predators from those remaining through the winter (Table 10-6). Their relative abundance throughout a standard lemming cycle is shown in Figure 10-11.

During the high winter, when the major increase to a high lemming population occurs, the only predators are the arctic fox and two species of weasels. Occasional snowy owls are seen in a pre-high winter, but they are so scarce as to be negligible. The immigration of snowy owls begins in late winter (April) of a high year and nesting commences in mid-May, well before snowmelt. At snowmelt they are joined by pomarine jaegers, glaucous gulls and, in some years, short-eared owls (Pitelka et al. 1955). The total intensity of predation rises dramatically and reaches its maximum at snowmelt, when lemmings are both most numerous and most exposed. A period of intense territorial activity follows, both within and between species. Nonbreeders are forced to marginal habitat, if they remain at all. The breeding population, with some attrition of unsuccessful birds, remains through the rest of the season. Migration of jaegers occurs in August, and snowy owls follow in September and early October. Following the departure of avian predators, foxes and weasels are again

TABLE 10-6 *Summary of Characteristics of Predator Populations in the Coastal Tundra at Barrow*

Predator	Mean adult body wt (g)	Characteristics of populations	Density (no. km^{-2})	Prey
Snowy owl (*Nyctea scandiaca*)	♀♀: 2120 ♂♂: 1730	Territorial when lemmings high; relatively stationary, non-breeding when lemmings moderate; absent when lemmings low.	0–2	Obligate lemming predator.
Short-eared owl (*Asio flammenus*)	♀♀: 400 ♂♂: 280	Irregular nester when lemmings high; absent in other years.	0–2	Obligate lemming predator.
Pomarine jaeger (*Stercorarius pomarinus*)	♀♀: 740 ♂♂: 650	Territorial when lemmings high; strong numeric response. Absent at low densities.	0–15	Obligate lemming predator.
Parasitic jaeger (*S. parasiticus*)	♀♀: 510 ♂♂: 420	Wanderer, singly or in small groups; occasional breeder, but may be excluded by territorial pomarines when lemmings high.	Great temporal and spatial variability (~60 bird-days yr^{-1})	Birds; facultative lemming predator.
Long-tailed jaeger (*S. longicaudus*)	♀♀: 315 ♂♂: 280	Wanderer, often in large groups, especially in July.	Great temporal and spatial variability (~50 bird-days yr^{-1})	Lemmings; bird eggs and young; adult craneflies in July.
Glaucous gull (*Larus hyperboreus*)	♀♀: 1230 ♂♂: 1510	Non-breeding flocks occur regularly, mainly at dump.	May be locally dense, usually just fly over.	Facultative lemming predator.
Arctic fox (*Alopex lagopus*)	~4000	Density appears unrelated to lemmings; common in winter when moves to coast, scarce in summer; affected by fur trappers.	0–2	Scavenger—both marine and terrestrial; bird eggs and young; lemmings.
Least weasel (*Mustela nivalis*)	40–70	Strong numerical response to lemming density; recolonizes each high; non-migratory.	0–25	Primarily lemming predator; may turn to bird eggs and young when lemmings crash.
Ermine (*M. erminea*)	100–110	Moderate numerical response to lemming density; non-migratory, but wanders.	0–2	Lemmings, birds and their eggs.

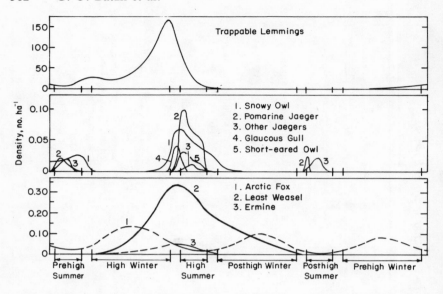

FIGURE 10-11. *The estimated densities of predators during the course of a standard lemming cycle for the coastal tundra at Barrow. Periods of snowmelt and freeze-up are indicated between summer and winter. (After Pitelka et al. 1955, and unpublished observations of authors.)*

the only predators. Presumably, these remain until the lemming population has declined to the point that it will no longer sustain predators. Foxes then switch to alternative food, especially dead waterfowl and sea mammals, but weasels may disappear from the Barrow peninsula altogether between lemming highs. Avian predators are usually scarce in the post-high summer.

Abundance of Predators—Numerical Response

The rate at which predators take lemmings is the product of the numerical response (number of predators per unit area) and the functional response (number of prey taken per predator) to prey density (Holling 1959). If lemming density is insufficient to support breeding when jaegers and owls arrive at Barrow, they quickly move on, and only nomadic individuals are seen throughout the summer. If the density of the lemmings is intermediate to high, both snowy owls and pomarine jaegers establish breeding territories, and in both species the density of the territories depends upon the abundance of lemmings. Maher (1970) concluded that pomarine jaegers did not establish territories if the density of trappable lemmings was below about 12 ha^{-1}. At higher lemming densities the density of breeding jaegers increased and approached an asymptote of about 7.3 nesting pairs km^{-2} at lemming densities above 100 ha^{-1}. The lemming density required for breeding is higher for snowy owls than it is for jaegers. Snowy owls have not bred on the Barrow peninsula in the absence of breeding jaegers, but jaegers have bred during periods of low to moderate lemming density when snowy owls did not. The density of owls during breeding is much lower than that of jaegers, and the owls' numerical response to the number of lemmings is less consistent. Pitelka et al. (1955) estimated the density of snowy owls on the Barrow peninsula to be 0.2 pair km^{-2} during the 1953 lemming high, and Pitelka (1973) estimated a density of about 1 pair km^{-2} during the 1960 high.

The difference in territory size in these two species may result from a difference in timing of nesting. Snowy owls arrive, establish territories, and begin their clutches well before snowmelt. The only exposed ground at this time is on ridges, bluffs and high-centered polygons, where the combination of wind and sublimation of snow produces small snow-free areas. Owls watch for lemmings while sitting on these vantage points. Thus, the extent of exposed ground in the spring may help to determine breeding density, along with amount of lemming movement over the snow.

Pomarine jaegers generally arrive later and establish territories around the time of snowmelt, when the tundra is rapidly becoming exposed and lemmings are maximally exposed. Jaegers search for lemmings while patrolling or hovering about 10 m above the ground. The strong numerical response in jaeger populations suggests that territory size is set by food supply. The territories are larger than necessary in June, but by July the demand for food is higher, since the young must be fed, while the lemming population has usually declined.

For the first few weeks of summer, there are often many more pomarine jaegers and snowy owls present than eventually establish territories and breed. At low to intermediate lemming densities, jaegers engage sporadically in territorial behavior. Unless mating and nesting ensue, the birds quickly abandon the territory and leave the area. In contrast, nonbreeding snowy owls may remain localized in an area for long periods of time. Even when lemming densities are high, some jaegers do not breed. Pitelka et al. (1955) estimated jaeger densities at 15 to 25 km^{-2} during early summer 1953; the breeding population later that summer was 6.9 pairs km^{-2}. Maher (1974) estimated the nonbreeding population as 25 to 50% of the breeding population in 1956 and less than 25% in 1960, two other peak years. Thus, in a pre-high season, the density of snowy owls may increase during the summer while jaeger density always declines after a spring peak (Figure 10-11).

The numerical response of other avian predators is less clear. Short-eared owls bred at a density of 1.0 pair km⁻² in the 1953 lemming high, were absent during the 1956 and 1960 highs and bred at low densities during the 1965 and 1971 highs. Parasitic and long-tailed jaegers occur primarily as nonbreeding nomads in late June and July, although a few parasitic jaegers may breed when lemming populations are high. These smaller jaegers are excluded by the aggressive behavior of the pomarine jaeger (Maher 1970, 1974).

Once breeding densities have been established, the density of avian predators during late summer depends upon breeding success. Jaegers lay no more than two eggs; clutches with one egg may occur when lemming densities are low to moderate (Maher 1970). The clutch size of snowy owls varies considerably. Nine nests in 1952–53 had a mean of 6.3 eggs per clutch and a range of 4 to 9 (Pitelka et al. 1955). Clutches as large as 14 have been observed in Lapland (Wasenius, cited by Watson 1957). Watson (1957) indicated that the clutch size of the snowy owl on Baffin Island was a function of lemming density, and this appears to be the case in the Barrow area as well.

The fledging success of both pomarine jaegers and snowy owls is highly variable and depends upon the continued availability of lemmings through the breeding season (Pitelka et al. 1955, Maher 1970). In each of the high years of 1956, 1960 and 1965 lemmings were sufficiently dense at snowmelt for jaegers to establish territories at their maximum density of about 7 pairs km⁻². In 1956 lemming density fell rapidly to less than 2 ha⁻¹ in August, and jaeger breeding success was 4%. In 1960 lemming density remained high all summer, with an estimated density of 215 animals ha⁻¹ in August, and jaeger breeding success was 55%. In 1965 lemming density fell from 150 ha⁻¹ in June to less than 1 ha⁻¹ in August, and almost no jaegers fledged (Maher 1970). Thus, a high lemming population in June does not guarantee that significant jaeger recruitment will occur. Indeed, Pitelka et al. (1955) found higher breeding success in the pre-high year of 1952 than in the high year of 1953. Given the tendency of the lemming population to increase during a pre-high summer and decline rapidly in the summer of a population high, breeding success of jaegers may often be better during years of moderate lemming density.

Snowy owls begin incubation with the first egg laid, resulting in an interval between hatchings of about 40 hours (Watson 1957). Hence, in a brood of eight chicks the youngest and oldest will differ in age by about 2 weeks. Since the parents tend to feed the more active and aggressive young first, the older chicks survive at the expense of the younger if lemmings become scarce. This mechanism allows a close adjustment of owl breeding success to changes in lemming density through the season. Pitelka et al. (1955) estimated fledging success of snowy owls to be less than 50% in 1952 and 1953. Even with prefledgling mortality of 75%, the mean clutch reported by Pitelka et al. (1955) of 6.3 eggs would produce

1.6 fledged young, well above the maximum of 1.1 fledged young per jaeger nest (2 eggs × 55% success rate) reported by Maher (1970) for 1960.

Mammalian predators are difficult to observe, and major population changes occur in winter, so less is known about their population fluctuations. The role of the arctic fox is modified by the proximity of the ocean and by human activities. Although foxes hunt lemmings, they also have access to an abundant supply of carrion, primarily carcasses of marine mammals and eiders that are crippled and lost by hunters. Foxes are trapped commercially by man during the winter. As a result, fox density shows little correlation with lemming density (Figure 10-11), although a strong numerical response is reported elsewhere (MacPherson 1969). An adult female fox regularly hunted and caught lemmings on the Biome research area throughout the summer of 1974, but foxes are usually more abundant in winter than in summer. The main denning areas are inland, possibly because of the low density of breeding waterfowl in the coastal tundra. In some areas foxes are known to take large numbers of waterfowl eggs (Underwood 1975).

Of all predators the least weasel appears most closely tied to the lemming. Least weasels may be absent from the coastal tundra at Barrow during years when the lemming population is low, but they appear during lemming peaks. Presumably, recolonization occurs from areas to the south where the lemming cycles are of lower amplitude and where local asynchrony of fluctuations of coexisting microtine species may allow maintenance of a more stable predator population (Pitelka 1957b). Nevertheless, the strong numerical response that occurs during most high winters results from reproduction. The reproductive cycle of *Mustela nivalis* differs from that of other small mustelids in that delayed implantation does not occur. This allows the least weasel to make a rapid reproductive response to increasing or high lemming populations. Juveniles collected at Barrow on 18 May and 6 June 1963 attest to the occurrence of winter breeding. Four pregnant females collected during summers with high lemming densities contained 15, 12, 12 and 3 ($\bar{x} = 10.5$) embryos, compared with an average of 4.8 for temperate zone females (B. Fitzgerald, pers. comm.). Thus, a dramatic reproductive response to lemming density appears to be present.

By immigration and reproduction least weasels can increase from nearly zero to maximum densities over the course of a pre-high summer and high winter (MacLean et al. 1974). Thompson (1955b) estimated the peak density at 25 km^{-2} during the 1953 lemming high, a value that Maher (1970) considered conservative. Maximum densities since 1969 have been far less than this. MacLean et al. (1974) reported 59 least weasels collected during summers following winters when lemming densities increased (1953, 1956, 1960, 1963, 1965, 1969), but only seven specimens in all other summers.

Ermine likewise show a numerical response to lemming density, although the response is less than that of the least weasel (MacLean et al. 1974). Ermine usually occur on the Barrow peninsula when lemming populations increase, but the density of ermine is probably less than 10% of the density of the least weasel.

Weasels differ from avian predators in their response to declining lemming populations. Low lemming density leads to reproductive failure and reduction of the population of adult jaegers and owls. By early fall, regardless of nesting success, all avian predators have departed. Weasels are less mobile; they remain through the summer into the post-high winter, and exert considerable predation pressure upon the declining lemming population. Eventually, by death or emigration, weasel density falls to undetectable numbers that characterize the low phase of the lemming cycle.

Nutrition and Energetics of Predators—Functional Response

Predators characteristic of the coastal tundra at Barrow are categorized as obligate or facultative lemming predators (Table 10-6). Obligate predators are those whose presence depends upon an adequate population of lemmings. Such predators show the largest numerical response and the absence of a strong functional response. Facultative predators are able to maintain a population at times of low lemming density by use of alternative food sources. Their numerical response to lemming density is small or even inverse, but they show a marked functional response. This section will consider two aspects of the functional response of predators: 1) changes in prey selection associated with changes in the density of primary and alternate prey, and 2) bioenergetic factors which determine rate of prey capture and consumption.

Clear differences in the food habits of jaegers are evident between years and between species (Maher 1974). Remains of lemmings were found in 98% of the pellets of pomarine jaegers taken in the high lemming years of 1956 and 1960, indicating the strong dependence of breeding pomarine jaegers upon lemmings. Lemmings were found in 100% of 75 pellets collected in 1959, when a few pairs of pomarine jaegers attempted breeding during a period of much lower lemming density. Even when lemming populations were low, lemmings were found in 41% of 56 stomachs of transient, nonbreeding pomarines collected in 1957 and 1958. This slight functional response was of little importance because the birds were rarely seen after mid-June

Parasitic jaegers preyed more on birds and their eggs than did the other jaegers, particularly when lemming densities were low (Maher 1974). However, during the 1956 lemming high, lemmings accounted for

75% of the food items in pellets of the parasitic jaeger. Data were available for the long-tailed jaeger only for the 1955-58 period when this species took fewer birds and many more insects than did the other jaegers. Long-tailed jaegers are most common in July, when adult craneflies (Tipulidae) are abundant on the tundra surface.

Comparable data on prey selection by snowy owls in relation to lemming density are lacking. Pitelka et al. (1955) noted that *Lemmus* makes up the bulk of the prey, but they also found owl pellets containing the remains of a variety of birds, ranging in size from the Lapland longspur to the old-squaw duck, as well as the remains of a least weasel. Examination of pellets over many years shows that the fraction of the diet consisting of lemmings is as large for snowy owls as for pomarine jaegers and may be even larger at low to moderate lemming densities.

Arctic foxes depend not only on lemmings but also on carrion during the winter and on birds and their eggs during summer. Using the lemming population dynamics model, a lemming mortality equivalent to 13.5 kg ha^{-1} was estimated during the winter (September–May) of a lemming high. These carcasses could constitute an important food source. Mullen and Pitelka (1972) investigated the disappearance of lemming carcasses by placing dead lemmings on the tundra in autumn. They found that virtually all carcasses disappeared by the following spring. In some cases other lemmings were implicated, but weasels were few, and winter observations indicated that foxes were primarily responsible for the removal of carcasses.

No data are available on the summer diet of foxes in the Barrow region, but in the Prudhoe Bay region Underwood (1975) found remains of *Lemmus* and *Dicrostonyx* in 86% of 50 fresh scats in an inland area and 75% of 24 scats in a coastal area, despite generally low densities of microtines during the 1971 summer. Birds were found in 50% of the scats from inland and 63% of the scats from the coast. Underwood (pers. comm.) reports finding as many as 30 lemming carcasses in a single fox den at other sites on the Arctic Slope. It is likely that the functional response of foxes to lemming density is much greater than their numerical response.

Data on the winter diet of both species of weasel derive from observations of remains and scats at lemming nests (MacLean et al. 1974), and thus may be biased in favor of lemmings. However, in the absence of alternative prey during winter, it seems safe to say that virtually the entire diet consists of lemmings. During summer weasels also take birds and their eggs, and a functional response to lemming density is probable.

Selective predation upon sex or age classes within the lemming population could influence the population dynamics of the lemmings. Since both jaegers and owls regurgitate pellets containing the bones of their prey, it is possible to estimate the frequency of capture of various classes of prey. Maher (1970) analyzed the remains of lemmings in pomarine jaeger pellets collected in the high lemming years of 1956 and 1960. The proportion of prey in the smallest size class, corresponding to nestlings, was greater in 1956, when lemming density declined rapidly during the summer, than in 1960, when lemmings remained abundant throughout the summer. Osborn (1975) compared the 1960 distribution of prey in jaeger pellets with estimates of relative abundance of different age classes and sexes from snap-trapping data. Little or no difference was evident. These observations do not rule out selectivity because snap trapping probably overestimated the frequency of males in the population. Greater movement by males than females exposes males to more traps, just as it exposes them to more predation. Although more male lemmings were found in jaeger pellets in 1960, Maher's 1956 sample contained a greater proportion of females (54%). Thus, there seems to be no consistent selection of males by jaegers.

Pitelka et al. (1955) determined the sex of 76 lemmings accumulated at a single snowy owl nest in June 1953; 25 were females and 51 were males. A similar preponderance of males was found by Thompson (1955c) in snowy owl pellets. The greater vulnerability of males to owl predation seems clear.

During the winter weasels prey heavily upon lemmings and live in the nests of their victims. MacLean et al. (1974) suggested that the large nests that are subject to the greatest predation are built by breeding females and that weasel predation may be concentrated upon reproductive females. This hypothesis may be tested by comparing the sex ratio of lemming populations after winters with heavy predation with the sex ratio after winters with little predation (Table 10-7). The sex ratio significantly favored males after the winters of 1959-60 and 1964-65; a sex ratio favoring males after the 1962-63 winter is marginally significant. During all three of these winters weasel predation was heavy (MacLean et al. 1974). Breeding also occurred during these winters, so the stress of breeding might have contributed to the skewed sex ratios.

The quantity of food removed per predator can be examined by calculating the number of prey needed to meet the energy requirement or by field observation of prey capture rate. The latter approach allows for the interaction of behavior and energy requirement in a natural setting, but such data are not easy to obtain.

Gessaman (1972) studied the metabolic rate of snowy owls by measuring both the oxygen consumption and the food intake of birds confined in outdoor pens. He concluded that the daily consumption of an average adult owl was 6.6 60-g lemmings during the coldest period of the winter ($T = -29\,°C$) and 4 lemmings in summer ($T > -5\,°C$). Pitelka et al. (1955) observed food consumption by a captive immature snowy owl kept in an outdoor cage during summer. During the late phase of growth,

TABLE 10-7   *Sex Ratios of Lemming Populations in Spring*

Year	Date	♂♂	♀♀	♂♂/♀♀	χ^2
1959	1–15 June	70	97	0.72	4.37**
1960	16 May–15 June	520	278	1.87	73.39†
1961	16 May–15 June	46	49	0.94	0.09
1962	1–15 June	248	226	1.10	1.02
1963	16 May–15 June	245	204	1.20	3.74*
1964	1–15 June	104	106	0.98	0.02
1965	16 May–15 June	308	215	1.43	16.54†

* $p < 0.10$.
** $p < 0.05$.
† $p < 0.001$.
Source: Data from Pitelka (unpubl.).

it consumed an average of 7.5 60-g lemmings day^{-1}. After its weight stabilized, food consumption fell to 5.4 lemmings day^{-1}, a value 35% greater than Gessaman found for summer.

Maher (1970) estimated the food requirement of pomarine jaegers by direct observation of adults, which were unfettered, and chicks, which were penned in the field. Chicks near the age of fledging consumed about 3.3 60-g lemmings day^{-1}, about one lemming less than adults.

Because of the very high insulating value of the winter pelage relative to the summer coat, the maintenance energy requirement of arctic foxes does not change appreciably through the year (Underwood 1971). Deposition of fat during summer, use of fat during winter and changing activity patterns modify the annual energy budget greatly. Total assimilated energy requirements for a single fox varied more than five-fold over the year. Requirements were greatest in August, about 4609 kJ day^{-1}, equivalent to 14.7 60-g lemmings, and least in April, about 838 kJ day^{-1} or 2.7 60-g lemmings. This remarkable difference may help to explain the greater density of foxes during winter than summer, even though food appears to be more available in summer.

The energy requirements of arctic weasel populations have not been measured. But extrapolating from Brown and Lasiewski's (1972) equations for *Mustela frenata*, MacLean et al. (1974) estimated that a 65-g least weasel living at an ambient temperature of –20 °C would have a resting metabolic rate of 409 kJ day^{-1}, which would require consumption of 1.3 60-g lemmings day^{-1}. However, weasels use lemming nests in winter, and maintaining a microclimate at 0 °C reduces the resting metabolic rate to 281 kJ day^{-1}, requiring only 0.9 60-g lemming day^{-1}.

Estimates of winter predation by weasels can be based upon remains

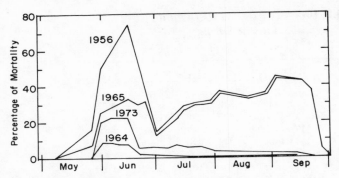

FIGURE 10-12. *The impact of avian predators on lemming populations in 4 years as indicated by the percentage of mortality accounted for by predators. Lemming densities are given in Figure 10-2. (After Osborn 1975.)*

found in winter nests. High predation rates—20% of nests on Banks Island (Maher 1967) and 35% of nests at Barrow (MacLean et al. 1974)—have been reported. The actual percentage of the population consumed was probably much higher since weasels usually consume more than one lemming per nest. But exact predation rates could not be calculated because the number of lemmings using each nest and the number of nests built by each lemming are unknown.

In order to assess the impact of avian predators on lemming populations, Osborn (1975) modeled the numerical and functional responses of snowy owls and pomarine jaegers. His model contains the information discussed above, plus growth curves of Watson (1957) for the snowy owl and Maher (1970) for the pomarine jaeger. He calculated the mortality rates for lemming populations when they were high enough to ensure breeding by the two avian predators, and expressed predation as the percentage of mortality (Figure 10-12).

In general, the model indicated that avian predation accounted for the greatest amount of mortality at snowmelt in early June when nonbreeding pomarine jaegers were still present. In 1956 and 1965, when the lemming population declined rapidly from peak levels, predation became an important source of mortality again in late summer when lemming populations were low. In 1964 and 1973, when lemming populations increased in late summer, percent predation declined. The simulation for the early summer of 1972 showed the maximum impact of predation: 88% of total mortality. In 1960, when lemming densities were at their highest recorded levels, absolute predation rates were also highest (79 g ha^{-1} day^{-1}), but avian predation accounted for only 39% of the mortality. Finally, Osborn found that in early June the amount of predation relative to standing crop of lemmings peaked at lemming densities of 25 ha^{-1} and dropped off rapidly at lower or higher densities.

Osborn did not simulate predation for summers when lemming populations were low, but there is some evidence suggesting that predation relative to standing crop is quite high. Pomarine jaegers do not defend territories when lemming populations in early June are less than 10 ha^{-1}. At these densities lemmings are distributed in small patches, upon which wandering predators prey. The percentage of lemmings taken may be greater than during years when lemmings are protected from other predators by pomarine jaegers.

During 1972 one of the live-trapping grids was located within an area that was defended by a nesting pair of pomarine jaegers and we observed minimum survival rates for adult lemmings of 40 to 70% per 28 days. On two other grids not defended by jaegers lemming survival rates were less than 20% per 28 days. During 1973 and 1974 no jaegers nested in the study area, and adult survival rates were less than 30% per 28 days on all grids. Wandering jaegers and owls were relatively common in all three years. Weasels were present in 1973, and in 1974 an arctic fox resided in the study area. Animals on trapping grids not defended by territorial jaegers appeared to be healthy, and all females were reproducing, so predation by other predators appeared to be the most likely cause of the high mortality.

FACTORS INFLUENCING LEMMING POPULATIONS

Abiotic Factors

One of the most dramatic features of tundra is the rapid transition between the mild summer and the severe winter. Because they neither migrate nor hibernate, lemmings must function throughout even the most extreme conditions. During the summer, temperatures near the ground are above freezing, but they are nearly always below the lower limit of thermoneutrality (17 °C) of lemmings (Figure 10-7). Hence, even summer temperatures cause metabolic rate and food demand to be elevated above the minimum value, but they pose little direct threat to survival.

Habitat flooding at the time of snowmelt and again, in some years, following July and August rains may be a greater danger to lemmings. Much of the low-lying habitat, including meadows, polygon troughs and basins of low-centered polygons, becomes inundated. Since water destroys the insulation value of lemming fur, and the high specific heat of water makes it an effective heat sink, lemmings must keep dry most of the time. Slight flooding (2 to 3 cm deep) can make a habitat unsuitable except for occasional foraging. At snowmelt the subnivean habitat collapses and the lemming population is concentrated into small areas of suitable habitat; when populations are dense, a period of intense social interaction may ensue. Lemmings may be forced into unfamiliar habitat where they may become more susceptible to predation. Thus, spring is a particularly traumatic period during which breeding subsides and mortality is high. In years of high rainfall much of the low-lying habitat continues to be flooded and unavailable to lemmings most of the summer. Polygon troughs and wet meadows, which are most susceptible to flooding, have the highest density of food plants and are preferred winter habitat. If these areas are flooded at freeze-up, they can remain unavailable to lemmings all winter long. The effect of late-season flooding may be greater than its spatial extent alone would suggest.

In August and early September lemmings encounter the only marked diurnal change in light intensity and temperature that they experience. The snowpack generally develops between mid-September and mid-October; delay poses two dangers for lemmings. First, if the vegetation becomes coated by freezing rains, the energy cost of foraging greatly increases. Second, in the absence of snow the ground surface is exposed to increasingly low nighttime temperatures. The reduction of breeding at this time attests to the severity of the period in the annual cycle of the lemming. Fuller (1967) has suggested that weather conditions in autumn can be a major factor influencing the population dynamics of lemmings.

The dense and shallow snow cover offers only modest protection from winter cold; very low temperatures are encountered at the ground/snow interface. In 1970-71 the temperature at the ground surface under 30 cm of snow at the *Carex–Oncophorus* meadow dropped below –20 °C in early December and to –25 °C in early March (Chapter 2). In March 1972 the mean temperature was –26 °C under 29 cm of snow (MacLean et al. 1974). Temperatures as low as –32 °C were recorded under 15 cm of snow.

Lemmings apparently take advantage of the higher temperatures that are found under deeper snow by concentrating their activity in polygon troughs. MacLean et al. (1974) found a significant correlation between nest density and amount of topographic relief ($r = 0.52, p < 0.01$), and presented evidence that winter reproduction was inhibited in years of shallow snow accumulation.

The structure of the snowpack may be just as important to lemmings as its depth. Once the snowpack accumulates, moisture is redistributed, and a strong structural profile develops (Chapter 2). The profile consists of two main layers: a fine-grained wind-packed layer of high density, and a large-grained layer of very low density (depth hoar). Where the snow is shallow the depth hoar layer may be thin or nonexistent. Although lemmings can move easily through depth hoar, dense snow may exclude them from a portion of the habitat. Freezing rains or partial thaws after the snowpack has developed can produce ice layers in the snowpack, and these also inhibit the formation of depth hoar.

The subnivean atmosphere has been suggested as another important feature of the winter environment of lemmings. The dense, wind-packed snow offers high resistance to gaseous diffusion. Kelley et al. (1968) and Coyne and Kelley (1974) demonstrated a buildup of subnivean carbon dioxide in fall, and again in spring. On two occasions, concentrations rose rapidly to 700 and 1500 ppm. While well above normal levels of 320 ppm, these values appear to be too low to influence the physiology of lemmings. Alveolar air in mammalian lungs is normally 5×10^4 ppm CO_2, and that level could easily be maintained by a slight change in respiratory rate (Johnson 1963).

Snow chimneys, tunnels dug by lemmings to the snow's surface, are frequent when lemming populations are high. Melchior (pers. comm.) found that they are used most during fall and spring, when release of gas under the snow is to be expected. Lemming tracks are often seen in fresh snow around the chimneys. Sometimes the tracks may be traced to the same or another chimney, indicating that the lemming returned to the subnivean environment. In other cases the tracks lead to a dead lemming or to signs of predation by foxes or owls. There are obviously risks associated with ventures above the snow. The advantages are unknown but may include escape from the toxicity of the subnivean atmosphere or dispersal to new habitat by an easier route when the depth hoar layer is poorly developed.

In summary, reproduction regularly subsides at snowmelt and during freeze-up before the snowpack develops, indicating that these are periods of stress for lemmings. Mortality rates, particularly from exposure to predators, are high at snowmelt. Circumstantial evidence suggests that a shallow snowpack and low winter temperatures inhibit winter reproduction, but we found no significant correlation between snow depth and spring population densities at Barrow over the past 25 years ($r = +0.18$; $p > 0.25$). If the depth hoar layer of the snowpack is poorly developed, winter populations decline, apparently because insufficient forage is accessible to them. Adequate snow depth and a well developed hoar layer are necessary but not sufficient to allow a population increase during winter. Unfavorable abiotic factors may contribute to the decline of high populations, but they do not appear to be necessary for the decline. Poor winter conditions can reduce populations to extremely low levels and prevent recovery of the population, thereby altering the timing of peaks. In summer, flooding may restrict the habitat available to lemmings, but reproduction and survival do not appear to be directly affected.

Predation

The general characteristics and feeding patterns of predator populations have been discussed above. In this section the impact of predation on the population dynamics of lemmings will be evaluated. Osborn's (1975) simulation indicated that in some years avian predators could account for 88% of the early summer mortality of lemmings. The major impact came at snowmelt when lemming densities were about 25 ha^{-1}, and percent predation dropped off rapidly at higher densities. Maher (1970) calculated the total impact of all predators on lemming populations during a high year. The calculations were based on the assumption that no young lemmings were weaned until mid-July and that mean litter size was six. Both assumptions are conservative (Batzli et al. 1974). He concluded that predation could not prevent population growth during the summer if lemming densities were greater than 65 ha^{-1} at snowmelt. Since lemming densities during high years are usually greater than 100 ha^{-1} at snowmelt, something in addition to predation must account for declines during the following summer. Predatory impact at high lemming densities is reduced by the protection afforded lemmings by territorial pomarine jaegers. During summers with lower population levels, when jaegers are not territorial, predation rates may be high enough to prevent population increases. Thus, predation contributes substantially to the rapid decline of lemming densities during some summers, and may even prevent population growth in others, but it is not sufficient to cause the decline of lemming densities from peaks.

During winter weasels are the most important lemming predators, and there is some evidence that winter predation rates may be sufficient to restrict the growth of lemming populations. During 1963 and 1969, lemming populations reproduced under the snow, but by snowmelt the populations had been reduced, and there was evidence of intense predation by weasels (Mullen 1968, MacLean et al. 1974). Maher (1967) reported a similar circumstance on Banks Island.

Pearson (1966) argued that the most significant effect of predators on cycling populations of microtines is the reduction of populations to extremely low levels, which delays their recovery. Maher (1970) and MacLean et al. (1974) supported this view as it applied to lemming populations. The increased mortality that adult lemmings experience during summers when populations are low lends further credence to such a role for predation. However, high populations of lemmings usually develop under the snow and not during summer, so the critical period is winter. If winter predation regulates lemming populations, intensity of predation should be negatively correlated with the change in lemming density. Our data for the winters of 1969 through 1974 do not show this trend. During four out of five winters populations did not increase even though predation was low. We conclude that high predation rates are not a necessary condition for the maintenance of low populations.

In summary, predation contributes to population declines and may be sufficient to prevent increases at low densities, but it is not sufficient to account for summer declines following a peak. Furthermore, relaxation of winter predation will not necessarily lead to population increases.

Nutrition

Weber (1950a) observed many dead lemmings and devastated vegetation following the spring 1949 population peak; he therefore proposed that exhaustion of food supplies and subsequent starvation caused the decline. However, Thompson (1955a) noted that after the peak in 1953 vegetation grew rapidly, even though total primary production was only half that expected with no grazing. Most of the dead lemmings that Thompson found appeared to be victims of predation. He suggested that lemming populations declined because of high predation rates and low reproductive rates, which resulted from low vegetative cover and poor forage availability. Pitelka (1957a, b) supported and expanded Thompson's views to include the possibility of changes in forage quality as a factor influencing lemming reproduction. Finally, Pitelka (1964) and Schultz (1964, 1969) proposed the nutrient-recovery hypothesis to account for the cyclic nature of lemming population dynamics. According to the hypothesis the nutrient concentration in vegetation declines following a lemming high and does not increase sufficiently to support good reproduction by lemmings for two or three years. The hypothesis is complex, involving several components of the ecosystem, and it will be considered in detail. Schultz's descriptions contain a few gaps concerning the mechanisms which drive the nutrient-recovery hypothesis, so we have embellished it slightly in the following treatment and tried to make explicit all the major causal links.

The fundamental interactions and mechanisms of the nutrient-recovery hypothesis are summarized in Figure 10-13. Intensive grazing takes place during the winter buildup of the lemming population and continues until the population crashes during the summer, apparently as a result of the combined effects of habitat destruction and predation. At snowmelt soluble nutrients released into the meltwater from urine, feces and clipped vegetation are rapidly taken up by growing plants. Thus, nutrient concentrations are high in the early summer forage. Later in the summer this growth becomes standing dead material, and locks up some nutrients that would otherwise be available the following summer.

In addition to releasing nutrients the lemmings' intensive grazing re-

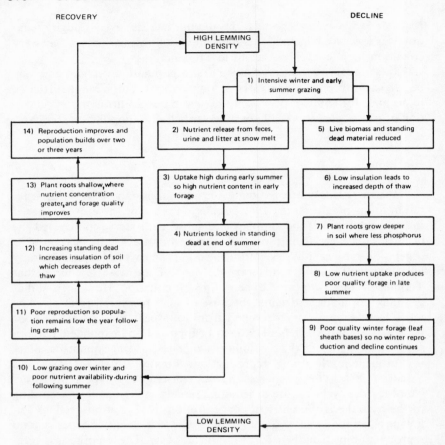

FIGURE 10-13. *Summary of steps in the nutrient-recovery hypothesis. (Adapted from Schultz 1964, 1969.)*

duces the amount of standing live and dead plant material during the summer of a lemming decline. This in turn reduces the albedo of the soil and its insulating cover, and the depth of thaw increases. As the depth of thaw increases, plant roots penetrate more deeply to where soil nutrient solutions (particularly phosphorus) are more dilute, and the available nutrients are distributed throughout a larger volume of soil. The low nutrient uptake of these roots leads to low nutrient concentrations in late summer growth, so that the leaf sheath bases produced then provide poor winter forage for lemmings. Because of the poor quality forage little lemming reproduction occurs during the winter, and the decline continues. There is little winter grazing, so the nutrient pulse in the spring is weak, and the nutrient quality of the vegetation stays low during that summer.

Lemming reproduction remains low during the summer and winter after a decline, and the standing dead material begins to accumulate. The increase in standing dead material and litter improves insulation over the soil and reduces the depth of thaw over the next two or three summers. As the depth of thaw decreases, plant roots are confined to soil with higher nutrient concentrations, and forage quality improves. Lemming reproduction then increases, and the population grows until a new peak is reached, usually 3 to 4 years after the last.

Our evaluation of the major premises of the nutrient-recovery hypothesis follows. Heavy grazing by lemmings can drastically reduce the standing crops of live and dead aboveground biomass (Dennis 1977) and increase feces and urine output (steps 1-3, Figure 10-13). The total consumption of graminoids by lemmings during a high year amounts to over 40 g m^{-2}, nearly 50% of the annual aboveground production and 20% of the total net production. Consumption is less than 1 g m^{-2} yr^{-1} when populations are low (Figure 10-14).

About 70% of the dry weight consumed is returned to the surface as feces and urine. Except for nitrogen, potassium and sulfur, minerals are primarily returned in feces (Wilkinson and Lowrey 1973). While the urinary minerals are readily available to plants, those in feces may not be. Most fecal phosphorus probably occurs as calcium diphosphate, a form that is soluble in a weakly acidic (pH 5) solution (Barrow 1975). The rate of nutrient loss from feces will depend upon where they are located. For instance, feces in ponded troughs or basins of low-centered polygons should lose their phosphorus more rapidly than feces on rims. Since most lemming feces are deposited in places where standing water occurs, at least during snowmelt, and since the tundra soil solution is acidic (pH 4.5 to 5.5), fecal phosphorus should be readily available to plants. Preliminary leaching experiments, using a solution that mimicked the soil solution, showed that over 80% of phosphorus was removed from feces in 24 hours (Chapin et al. 1978).

Standing dead plant material can amount to 40 g m^{-2} at snowmelt (Chapter 3), four to five times the dry weight of live material. Most of this represents the previous summer's production less those nutrients that have been removed by translocation and leaching. By felling standing dead over the winter, lemmings do add organic material to the tundra surface where it will decompose more rapidly, but its nutrient content is less than half of that from feces and urine deposited during the high winter. Disruption of mosses and lichens, which also takes place when the lemming population is at its peak, may also increase the rate of decomposition, but the amount is unknown.

The total influx of nutrients produced by lemming activity may be considerable. The average amount of soluble phosphorus in the top 5 cm of soil is 0.5 to 4 mg m^{-2}, whereas the amount deposited in lemming feces

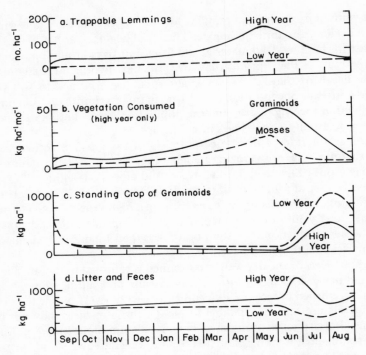

FIGURE 10-14. *Idealized comparison of lemming density, forage consumption, standing crop of forage and deposition of waste products during years with high and low populations. The calculations for lemmings are based on data presented earlier in the chapter. The density estimates include only animals usually caught in traps (> 20 days old), but consumption and waste are calculated for the entire population.*

during a year when the population is high, assuming 90% solubility, is about 90 mg m^{-2}. The phosphorus pool turns over very rapidly, and graminoids must absorb about 3 mg P gdw^{-1} of plant material produced, assuming an average of 0.3% total phosphorus. Since the peak aboveground standing crop averages 80 g m^{-2}, lemming feces would provide 35 to 40% of the required phosphorus. Most of the nutrient release from feces probably occurs during snowmelt in spring. That pulse spurs early nutrient uptake by plants and microbes since phosphorus uptake is proportional to phosphate concentration (Chapin and Bloom 1976). Hence, the first three premises of the nutrient-recovery hypothesis appear to be substantiated (Figure 10-13).

The idea that large quantities of nutrients may be tied up in organic matter during the summer following a lemming peak (step 4, Figure 10-13) is less tenable. Lemmings reduce the aboveground standing crop of vascular plants by about 50% at midsummer of a peak year (Figure 10-14) so nutrient storage in standing dead at the end of summer is also reduced. Furthermore, 75% of the phosphorus put into live biomass may be removed by translocation in late summer and by leaching the following spring (Chapin, pers. comm.). Although a few lemming carcasses may be found at snowmelt, large numbers of carcasses do not accumulate on the tundra, apparently because they are eaten by predators and scavengers (Mullen and Pitelka 1972). Nutrients from all tissues other than bones are probably returned rapidly to the soil. Phosphorus and calcium are concentrated in lemming bones, but only 10 to 20% of the total phosphorus and calcium in lemming forage is retained in bone. In a high year lemmings consume about half of the aboveground vascular plant production, so no more than 5 to 10% of the total phosphorus and calcium content of forage could be sequestered in lemming bones.

In some spots, where lemmings have grubbed for rhizomes, the standing crop of vascular plants may be reduced 90% (Schultz 1964, Dennis 1968). Thinning of the plant canopy does increase depth of thaw, although Schultz does not provide quantitative data. A simulation model suggests that complete removal of the canopy increases maximal depth of thaw by about 20% of normal, or about 5 cm, when the surface is saturated with water (Ng and Miller 1977). If the moss layer is drier, the effect on thaw is somewhat less. When lemmings are excluded from patches of tundra for long periods of time, standing dead plants continue to accumulate, and thaw depth is reduced as much as 25% (Batzli 1975b). Thus, the fifth and sixth premises are supported, although the effect on depth of thaw does not seem to be large.

Schultz (1964) presented evidence that total calcium and phosphorus decreased with depth in tundra soils; however, soluble soil nutrients do not necessarily follow the same pattern (Chapter 7), although soluble inorganic phosphorus usually does (Barèl and Barsdate 1978). The decline in nutrient absorption rates of temperate plants for 7 to 10 days after grazing, reported by Davidson and Milthorpe (1966), might also support the nutrient-recovery hypothesis. But the nutrient absorption rates of tundra graminoids increase following grazing under field conditions (Chapin 1980b). Moreover, the direct impact of grazing upon nutrient absorption rates would not last long.

Schultz's idea that roots would exploit greater soil depths does not seem likely when one considers that the plants could use the more concentrated nutrients in the upper soil horizons. In fact, all roots of *Dupontia fisheri* and the secondary absorbing roots of *Carex aquatilis*, the two most important forage plants for lemmings, are found in the upper soil horizon, regardless of thaw depth (Chapter 5). Furthermore, when soil temperatures and thaw depth increase as a result of human disturbance, nutrient availability and plant production increase (Bliss and Wein 1972, Challinor and Gersper 1975, Chapin and Van Cleve 1978), rather than decrease as the nutrient-recovery hypothesis predicts. For these reasons, the links between depth of thaw, nutrient availability in soil and nutrient concentrations in plants that are proposed by the hypothesis (steps 7–9, Figure 10-13) do not seem tenable. A more likely explanation for the decline in plant phosphorus concentration observed by Schultz (1964) in the years following peaks in the lemming population is that intensive grazing and grubbing for rhizomes sharply decrease plant phosphorus reserves. Simulations suggest that plant nutrient reserves may be severely depleted by grazing (Chapin 1978). The involvement of other ecosystem components need not be invoked.

Nutrient levels in forage may influence both litter size and the timing of reproduction of lemmings (steps 9-14, Figure 10-13). Phosphorus, calcium and nitrogen all have been implicated by a model of nutritional physiology of lemmings (see *Nutrition and Energetics*). Apparently lemmings have adapted to low nutrient availability through high forage intake rates, low digestive efficiency of energy and selection of mosses as a calcium supplement. Even if low nutrient quality of forage sometimes prevents lemming population growth, it probably is only one of several factors which can do so. Poor snow conditions and high weasel densities may also prevent population growth during winter. Hence, forage quality may influence the rate of lemming population growth, but other factors unrelated to nutrition may be equally important.

In 1973 the depth of thaw averaged about 10% less than in 1972. Low air temperatures caused peak standing crop of aboveground *Dupontia* to be 25% lower, but concentration of phosphorus was 200% greater (Chapter 5, Table 5-4). These changes are similar to those expected during the course of a lemming cycle according to the nutrient-recovery hypothesis. Yet in 1973 the lemming density was only 5 to 10 ha^{-1}, about half that of 1972, and the population declined during the winter of 1973-74. The nutrient-recovery hypothesis predicts that it should have increased.

Our general conclusion is that the nutrient-recovery hypothesis, as developed by Schultz, should be modified. Lemming activity does not appear to control the nutrient concentration of forage by changing depth of thaw, nor do trends in lemming populations necessarily follow trends in forage quality, at least as indicated by phosphorus concentration. Nevertheless, the hypothesis has been valuable because it pointed out the importance of considering vegetational quality as well as quantity for herbivore populations.

The quality of available forage is difficult to evaluate. About 40 spe-

The Herbivore-Based Trophic System   381

cific nutrients are known to be required by rodents (National Academy of Sciences 1972), but the exact requirements of lemmings are unknown. Some nutritional work has been done on lemmings and their forage, which forms the basis for our tentative conclusions regarding the role of forage quality in population dynamics.

Calculations of the energy requirements of lemmings during population buildup to a peak of 150 ha^{-1} showed that in a normal high year suitable forage would be completely utilized before snowmelt (Batzli 1975a). Some high population levels seem to reach 225 ha^{-1} or more before declining, so insufficient available energy appears to be contributing to population decline in late spring of some years. Death may occur directly by starvation since the average level of body fat in carcasses we collected before and during snowmelt was about 2%, the level at which starving lemmings die in the laboratory. The continued decline of populations through the summer can not be related to lack of available food, but there may be continuing effects of earlier undernutrition.

Reproducing females require considerably more energy than non-reproducing females. So insufficient forage relative to energy requirements may also explain why there are fewer pregnancies and smaller litters during the winter breeding season. The level of available graminoids then is one-tenth that of midsummer. Lemmings may not be able to maintain the necessary rate of forage intake on such a dispersed resource. Recent experiments show that rate of forage intake increases linearly with forage availability (Batzli et al., in press).

Although there is considerable variation from year to year and site to site, tundra graminoids are often low in calcium and phosphorus (Table 10-6). Batzli (unpubl. obs.) found that the temperate microtine *Microtus californicus* does not reproduce well when fed a diet with levels of calcium similar to the highest amounts found in tundra graminoids. Lemmings, however, perform well on such forage; and metabolic experiments have shown that nonreproductive subadults are in slight positive balance for all minerals except sodium. But when lemmings are reproducing and when the nutrients in forage are at their lowest levels, this may not be true. Laboratory animals fed natural forage ate more *ad libitum* than was required to meet their energy needs, and fat levels rose to 15 to 20% of body weight. In the field, where energy requirements are greater, fat averages only 3.5% of body weight. Apparently the ability to process large amounts of vegetation, which is related to low digestibility for energy, allows lemmings to do well on a diet that would not support temperate microtines. The simulation model of lemming nutrition (see *Nutrition and Energetics*) led to the same conclusion and indicated that reproductive success might be curtailed in years of poor forage quality.

Schultz (1969) conducted experiments in which the nutrient status of tundra vegetation was changed. By fertilizing heavily he increased the protein, calcium and phosphorus levels in graminoids well above those in nonfertilized areas. Fertilization apparently increased winter reproduction in 1968; there were about 75 winter nests ha^{-1} in the fertilized area and none in the control areas. The effect continued through 1971, although by then it was less dramatic. Melchior (pers. comm.) reported 14 nests ha^{-1} in the fertilized areas and 2 ha^{-1} on the control plots. These results suggest that, at least during some winters, reproductive performance of lemmings can be stimulated by improving vegetation quality.

In summary, lemming populations often increase up to a limit imposed by their food supply and begin to decline when there is not enough food to meet energy demands. However, in summer primary production exceeds the lemmings' requirements, and lack of food cannot explain the continued population decline. Several lines of evidence suggest that lemmings can survive on low quality forage because of nutritional adaptations, but the lack of nutrients may still reduce winter reproduction.

Intrinsic Factors

All the factors influencing lemming populations discussed so far are extrinsic, residing outside of the population itself. Several investigators have suggested that intrinsic factors such as behavior, physiology and genetics may be equally important and that social interactions and aggression increase with increasing population density. Christian and Davis (1965) proposed a hormonal imbalance to account for a population's decline. Chitty (1967) and Krebs et al. (1973) argued that some types of lemmings emigrate more or die sooner than others, thus changing the genetic composition of the remainder of the population. Changes in genotypic frequencies within the population are held to be responsible for changing reproductive and survival rates.

Some work has been done on physiological changes in lemmings at Barrow. Mullen (1965) looked at blood glucose and formed elements of blood during four summers. There was no evidence of physiological changes associated with population density. Krebs and Myers (1974) found no evidence that physiological stress played a role in the production of microtine cycles. Andrews et al. (1975) reported changes in adrenal activity and kidney disease associated with population density and climatic factors, but often these do not appear to be consistent or statistically significant. Thus the consequences of these endocrine adjustments for population dynamics of lemmings are unclear. Using a process of elimination Krebs (1964) concluded that genetic changes influenced lemming populations at Baker Lake, Canada, but gave no direct evidence. No studies of emigration or genetics have been done on lemmings at Barrow.

Summary

Even though little can be said about the role of intrinsic factors in lemming population dynamics, it seems clear that extrinsic factors can exert a strong and overriding influence. In order for lemming populations to reproduce and grow during winter, good quality forage must be available, the snowpack must be suitable and mammalian predators must

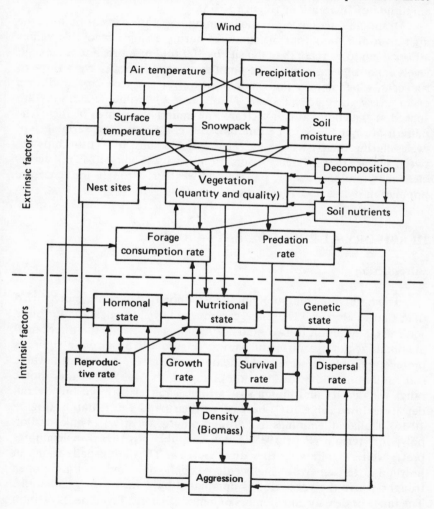

FIGURE 10-15. *Diagram of relationships among factors influencing lemming population density.*

be scarce. Only when all three of these conditions prevail can a high population be attained. A high population may begin to decline because of inadequate availability of forage, but only high mortality, resulting from predation or some other factor, and reduced recruitment can make the decline continue through the summer. Therefore, it does not seem that any single extrinsic or intrinsic factor can explain the population dynamics of lemmings. Rather, lemming populations respond to a number of factors that act and interact concurrently to determine the timing and amplitude of fluctuations (Figure 10-15).

Dramatic fluctuations in the lemming population occur because the high reproductive output of lemmings during a single favorable winter allows them to increase their density by 100-fold or more, and these high levels cannot be sustained. The population usually peaks every three to six years, which implies that winters meeting all the necessary conditions occur every three to six years. Why favorable winter conditions are spaced at that interval is not clear. The underlying causes of the cyclic pattern are not likely to be random. But considering the variability in cycles during the past 25 years (Figure 10-2), and the relationships between factors that influence population density (Figure 10-15), it seems clear that random factors, particularly weather, strongly influence the population dynamics of lemmings.

HERBIVORY AT PRUDHOE BAY—CARIBOU

Introduction

The herbivore community in the Prudhoe Bay region is more varied than that at Barrow. There are caribou, willow ptarmigan and ground squirrels in addition to two kinds of lemmings. Each of the three small mammals requires a different habitat (Figure 10-16). Ground squirrels prefer stream bluffs, stabilized sand dunes near rivers, and pingos, where soil conditions allow construction of deep burrows. Within their home range the density and biomass of ground squirrels is high, but overall density is low (Table 10-3) because of their patchy distribution (Figure 10-16). Collared lemmings live around pingos, on stream banks and on polygonal terrain (Feist 1975, Batzli, unpubl. obs.). Brown lemmings prefer wetter habitats, as they do at Barrow. They are usually found in polygonal terrain with high-centered polygons and well-developed troughs where the vegetation is dominated by a variety of graminoids. The range of density and biomass of lemmings in the Prudhoe Bay region is relatively low (0.01 to 10 animals ha^{-1} or 0.2 to 150 g dry wt ha^{-1}) compared with Barrow (Table 10-3). Much of the Prudhoe Bay vegetation is dominated by *Carex* and *Salix* spp., which grow on low, flat areas, often

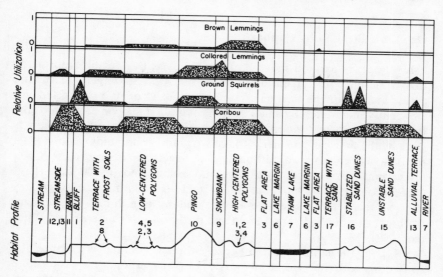

FIGURE 10-16. *Relative habitat utilization by herbivores near Prudhoe Bay. The numerals above the habitats refer to vegetation types identified by Webber and Walker (1975) for the Prudhoe Bay region.*

with large low-centered polygons, a habitat little used by lemmings at Barrow. Furthermore, the areas most favored by brown lemmings are also heavily utilized by caribou, whose trampling disturbs the habitat. Both factors may account for the modest lemming populations in the Prudhoe Bay region.

Caribou represent the largest biomass of herbivores in the Prudhoe Bay region (Table 10-3). Because of their mobility caribou utilize a wide variety of landforms and vegetation types, and a large study area must be considered. During 1972-73 a resident population of 200 to 500 animals inhabited the Prudhoe Bay region, a 2340-km² area of Coastal Plain bounded by the Kuparuk and Sagavanirktok Rivers in the west and east and by Prudhoe Bay on the north and the White Hills toward the south. These caribou constitute a portion of the Central Arctic caribou herd which has been identified in recent years by Cameron and Whitten (1979). During summer migratory herds of up to 3000 caribou may also pass through the region, and when they are under severe insect attack thousands may be concentrated in the coastal sand dunes associated with the river systems.

Habitat Utilization by Caribou

Migratory caribou move into the Prudhoe Bay region from herds that overwinter in Canada or south of the Brooks Range. The calving areas, located in the northern Foothills, consist of undulating terrain, frequently intersected by small streams. The first snowmelt north of the Brooks Range usually occurs in these areas (Hemming 1971). Snow is gone by the time caribou arrive for calving, and graminoids (*Eriophorum* spp.) have begun to grow, although green vegetation is very sparse. Calving commences as early as 25 May and usually ends by 20 June (Lent 1966, Skoog 1968, White et al. 1981), and the main influx of migratory caribou reaches the Prudhoe Bay region by late June. The resident caribou calve on the Coastal Plain and the Foothills (Cameron and Whitten 1979).

During the summer caribou graze either in small nursery groups of 2 to 10 cows with their calves and an occasional yearling, or in groups of 3 to 20 bulls and yearlings (White et al. 1975). Early grazing is concentrated on exposed ridges and pingos that are dominated by dicotyledons. As the snow melts, caribou begin to graze on polygonal terrain and drained lake beds whose vegetation is dominated by graminoids and dwarf willows. Some of the poorly drained centers of low-centered polygons and lake beds do not dry until late summer, and the graminoid-dominated vegetation of these areas is utilized then. For most of the summer, caribou prefer to graze on stream banks where the biomass and species diversity of the forage is high (White et al. 1975). The general summer movement pattern appears to be determined by the phenological progression of vegetation types and associated changes in their nutritional status.

As the season progresses caribou move back from the Coastal Plain to the Foothills, but daily movement patterns are less distinct due to the overriding effects of harassment by mosquitos (*Aedes* spp.) and warble flies (*Oedemagena tarandi*). During the warmest periods vegetation associated with standing water is avoided, presumably because it is prime mosquito habitat. Caribou gain some relief from mosquito harassment by grazing and walking into the prevailing wind. Or they move to the coastal sand dunes where it is cooler and windier than inland. Trail networks generally join the preferred grazing areas with those areas where they seek relief. Where several trails join at the shores of larger lakes the soil becomes deeply rutted and completely devoid of moss and vascular plants. Once the temperature drops and insect harassment abates, caribou graze slowly through the vegetation towards preferred habitat. Little use is made of the trail systems at this time (White et al. 1975).

In late October groups of caribou gather in herds of over a thousand, and the animals migrate south to the wintering grounds during October through December. Groups of the Central Arctic herd overwinter on the Coastal Plain and northern Foothills. Occasionally an early snowfall in the Brooks Range prevents the migration of most of the caribou, and large herds overwinter on the Arctic Slope (Lent 1966, Hemming 1971). Some of the surviving calves and yearlings of these herds may become adjusted to overwintering on the Arctic Slope and add to the nonmigratory component of the northern caribou populations.

Population Dynamics and Demography

The number of caribou grazing on the Coastal Plain varies according to migratory patterns, the number of resident caribou and the stage of their annual reproductive cycle. The number varies seasonally and annually in the Prudhoe Bay region. The estimates in Figure 10-17 are based on the total available area, not all of which is utilized by the caribou. Estimates based on the seasonal home range can be 5 to 15 times as high and give a good indication of habitat utilization during a season or year (Gaare and Skogland 1975). But the areas visited shift from year to

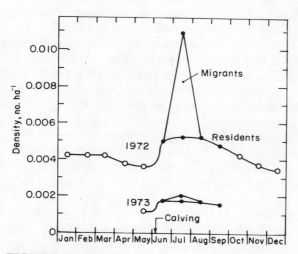

FIGURE 10-17. *The density of caribou in the Prudhoe Bay region during two years. The solid dots are based on observations of White et al. (1975); the open dots were calculated assuming reproductive performance equivalent to the Porcupine herd as reported by Calef and Lortie (1973).*

year and estimates based on total available area may give a better indication of the long-term population levels. The average resident caribou density in the Prudhoe Bay region was similar to recent estimates of the density of the Porcupine herd in 1972 (0.004 caribou ha⁻¹; Calef and Lortie 1973, Calef 1978), and the eastern Canadian Kaminuriak herd in 1973 (0.002 caribou ha⁻¹; Parker 1972). These densities seem small, but the biomass they represent in the region is greater than that of lemmings, particularly when large numbers of migratory caribou move into the area (Table 10-3).

In response to photoperiod, breeding activity commences with aggressive behavioral displays between adult males in mid- to late September. Peak rutting occurs in late October to early November (Kelsall 1968, Whitehead and McEwan 1973). Estrus in female caribou begins in late September, and estrus cycles recur at 10-day intervals (McEwan and Whitehead 1972). The date of peak calving varies from year to year, which suggests that secondary factors such as nutrition and climate may modify the timing of both rut and parturition. Gestation lasts about 210 days. The effects of winter nutrition on the gestation period are uncertain; however, nutrition can affect birth weights of calves and milk production in lactating females (Skjenneberg, pers. comm., White and Luick, unpubl. obs.). Normally one calf is born; twins are rare.

The age at which caribou first breed varies (Kelsall 1968). Female calves rarely breed, and frequently females are as old as 3½ years when they breed for the first time. Under good nutritional conditions up to 30% of females will conceive as yearlings, and caribou older than 4 years have peak pregnancy rates of 78 to 90% (Kelsall 1968). Female caribou breed until they are at least 16 years of age with little decline in fertility.

Mature female caribou generally breed annually. However, when severely undernourished some females do not come into estrus, and lactation continues through January (Reimers, pers. comm.). Under these circumstances breeding in alternate years would be expected. Disease, as well as nutrition, may affect fertility. For example, brucellosis probably caused lowered pregnancy rates in the Western Arctic herd in 1961 (Lent 1966).

In the Prudhoe Bay region, when calves were 4 to 6 weeks of age, 67% of non-yearling females had calves with them in 1972 and 31% had calves in 1973. Few caribou were observed in 1973, and the estimate may not be representative (White et al. 1975). The estimated number of females with calves in the Porcupine herd to the east of Prudhoe Bay was 50% for 1972 (Calef and Lortie 1973). Caribou calves have a high mortality rate, which can be attributed to inclement weather, predation and accidents. By the end of the first year the cohort has normally been reduced 40 to 50% (Kelsall 1968, Parker 1972). Lack of data on age-specific mortality precludes the construction of life tables, but survivorship curves have been compared. In reindeer herds with low early mortality, the mean expected life span may be as high as 4 years, but a value of 2.5 to 3.0 years has been reported for the Kaminuriak caribou herd west of Hudson Bay (Parker 1972, White et al. 1981).

Nutrition and Energetics

During the summer months caribou graze on both graminoids and dicotyledons while moving slowly at 0.5 to 1.2 km hr^{-1}. Bouts of grazing are interspersed with periods of rumination during which they lie down. There are four to six grazing periods daily with a high degree of synchrony within each group.

When not harassed by insects caribou spend 48 to 53% of the day grazing. Lactating females spend more time eating and less time searching and walking during a grazing period than do adult males, non-lactating females, and yearlings (White et al. 1975, Roby 1978). The activity cycle is highly modified on days of heavy insect harassment when as little as 30% of the day may be spent eating. On days of intense warble fly activity, trotting and running may take up 25% of the day. From late June through early August caribou suffer insect harassment for up to 25% of the entire period, and attacks may last for over an hour (White and Russell, unpubl. obs.). Thus, grazing periods are often interrupted, and trampling of the vegetation is increased.

Although the mouth parts of the caribou are large, grazing is selective. Rejected plant parts, particularly dead and coarse material, are expelled from the rear of the mouth and drop back to the tundra almost continuously while the caribou is eating. On summer range, rejection may be as high as 20% of all vascular plants clipped; foraging and trampling may waste considerably larger amounts of lichens (Gaare and Skogland 1975, White and Trudell 1980). When feeding on willow, caribou nip leaf parts, buds and some current year's stems, but they exclude older stems and twigs. Dead material of low nutritional value forms 15 to 20% of the diet in the Prudhoe Bay region (White et al. 1975), indicating some inefficiency in the selection and sorting processes.

Some selection of food results from selection of habitat type. Within the vegetation types there is further selection of plant species and parts. Early in the season an obvious preference is shown for the inflorescences of some dicotyledons, e.g. *Pedicularis sudetica* and *Saxifraga* spp. Because of their low availability, inflorescences do not make up a large component of the caribou diet, but selective grazing on flowers may be important because of its influence on plant populations.

Analysis of forage consumed by caribou in the Prudhoe Bay region showed that the dominant plant species in the diet were those that are

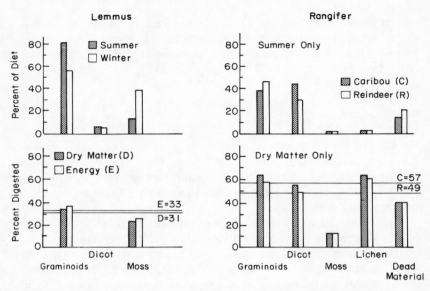

FIGURE 10-18. *The composition and digestibility of diet for lemmings and caribou. The horizontal lines represent mean digestibilities for the overall diet. (After White et al. 1975, Batzli and Cole 1979.)*

most available in the vegetation type. These include the graminoids *Eriophorum angustifolium, Carex aquatilis* and *Dupontia fisheri*, and several willows—*Salix pulchra, S. arctica, S. ovalifolia* and *S. lanata*. This generalized feeding was modified slightly by preferences for a few species of herbaceous dicotyledons and lichens (White et al. 1975). Dicotyledons made up a slightly higher percentage of the diet of caribou than did graminoids. Vascular plants contributed 92% of the diet (Figure 10-18). Mosses were eaten in such small amounts that intake may have been accidental.

Estimates of *in vitro* dry matter digestibility of hand-picked plant samples were used to calculate the mean digestibility of dietary components (Person 1975, White et al. 1975, Person et al. 1980, White and Trudell 1980). Rumen inoculum was obtained from caribou and rumen-fistulated reindeer while they were grazing on tundra. The ranges in digestibility of individual species were large for graminoids (52 to 79%) and shrubby dicotyledons (21 to 71%), but the mean ±1 SE digestibility of graminoids (54 ±3% to 64 ±3%, depending on species mixture) was not significantly different from shrubs (45 ±5%). Forb and lichen digestibility was similar to that of graminoids, but mosses had very low digestibility (Figure 10-18). Based on the relative occurrence of these dietary components mean summer estimates of digestibilities of all forage consumed were 57% for caribou and 49% for reindeer. The lower di-

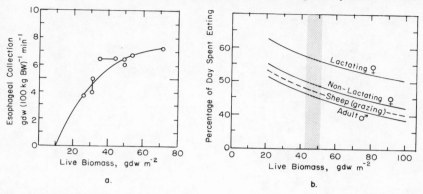

FIGURE 10-19. *Consumption of forage by esophageal-fistulated rein-deer (a) and the percentage of the day spent eating (b) in relation to the available green forage. The dashed line represents sheep grazing on range similar in available biomass to that of the Prudhoe Bay region. The solid lines represent the extrapolation of the relationship to caribou. The shaded column represents available biomass of vascular plants in the Prudhoe Bay region in July. (After White et al. 1975.)*

gestibilities estimated for reindeer may reflect the effects of confining them to specific vegetation types.

The potential digestibility of all material from the vegetation types in the Prudhoe Bay region varies considerably, but selection of green material would provide increased digestive efficiency. By following the phenological progression in vegetational development, caribou may be able to maintain maximum digestibilities of 57 to 63% throughout the summer (Person et al. 1975, White et al. 1975, White 1979).

Whether or not caribou can select individual plants for digestibility is not known, but Klein (1970) suggested that they select for protein and minerals, particularly phosphorus. *In vitro* digestibility is inversely related to nondigestible components such as lignin (White et al. 1975, Person et al. 1975). And selection for high digestibility should also provide higher intake of cell contents that contain most of the soluble protein and phosphorus. It seems likely that caribou select vegetational types and the plant species and parts within those types that are highest in general nutritional quality, but they avoid plant species and parts that contain toxic secondary compounds (White and Trudell 1980).

Selection of vegetational types may also maximize the quantity of food eaten. Non-lactating female reindeer grazing on *Carex–Eriophorum* meadows were used by White et al. (1975) to estimate food intake. The availability of green vascular plants was an important factor controlling the rate of consumption of food (Figure 10-19a).Studies with grazing

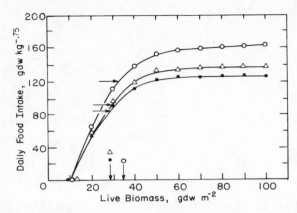

FIGURE 10-20. *Theoretical relationships between daily food intake and the availability of live biomass of vascular plants for lactating females (○), adult males (●), and non-lactating females (△). The relationships were calculated as the product of the relationships shown in Figure 10-19. The arrows indicate the daily food intake required to maintain body weight and, therefore, the amount of live biomass of available plants required before the caribou would gain weight. (After White et al. 1975.)*

sheep and reindeer have shown that the time spent grazing declines as available biomass increases (Allden and Whittaker 1970, Young and Corbett 1972, Trudell and White 1980). The curves for adult males and lactating females in Figure 10-19b were extrapolated from the data for non-lactating females. Presumably, curves for caribou would be similar.

The theoretical relationship between daily food intake and available plant biomass for reindeer can now be calculated (Figure 10-20, Trudell and White 1980). Food intake for lactating reindeer exceeds that for non-lactating reindeer because lactating females spend more time grazing. The theoretical relationships in Figure 10-20 are similar to actual observations of food intake in relation to plant biomass reported for domestic sheep grazing in Mediterranean grassland systems (Arnold 1964, Arnold and Dudzinski 1967).

Assuming that caribou and reindeer have similar grazing response functions, food intake of caribou in the Prudhoe Bay region during summer is directly related to seasonal changes in standing crop of green vascular plants, which peaks in midsummer (Chapter 3). In particular, food intake declines rapidly when the availability of green biomass becomes less than 40 to 50 g m^{-2}. Maximum food intake, when green biomass is greater than 50 g m^{-2}, would be expected only for the month of July and early August in *Carex–Eriophorum* meadows. By selecting vegetation

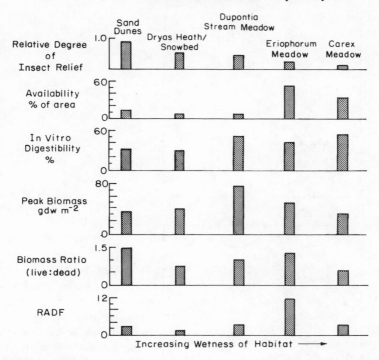

FIGURE 10-21. *Characteristics of the vegetation types in the Prudhoe Bay region. The relative degree of insect relief is an index scaled to the wetness of the habitat. RADF (relative availability of digestible forage) = availability × digestibility × biomass × biomass ratio. (After White et al. 1975.)*

types highest in green biomass caribou could maintain a period of maximum food intake from late June to mid-August.

Each vegetational type has different attributes with respect to caribou grazing in the Prudhoe Bay region (Figure 10-21). The product of four measured parameters—availability of habitat, digestibility of forage, peak green biomass and ratio of live-to-dead material—was used as a summary index of the relative availability of digestible forage for each habitat. The relative availability of digestible forage appeared to be positively correlated with the distribution of caribou on days without insect harassment, particularly in groups of ten or fewer individuals (Figure 10-22a). Caribou group size was generally between one and ten individuals following severe harassment as herds moved from relief areas to preferred grazing areas. On days with harassment, distributions changed noticeably, and there was no relationship to the relative availability of digestible forage (Figure 10-22b).

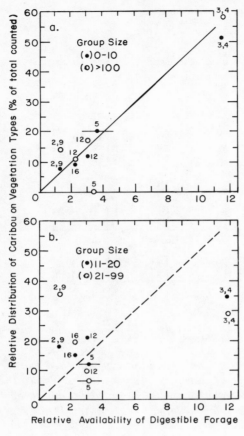

FIGURE 10-22. *The relationship of the distribution of caribou among habitats to the estimated relative availability of digestible forage for those habitats when under no insect attack (a) or mild to severe attack (b). The numbers refer to habitat types given in Figure 10-16. (After White et al. 1975.)*

To investigate the possible influence of food quality on factors regulating food intake a model of caribou rumen function (RUMENMET) was constructed (White et al. 1981). The model interfaced factors regulating food intake with factors responsible for digestion and outflow from the rumen. The rumination time required to reduce the particle size of unfermented material, so that it could leave the rumen, limited the amount of time available for grazing, particularly when forage digestibility was low. Thus, although the availability of green plant biomass regulates the actual eating rate, the digestibility of the food controls the amount of time the animal must ruminate and the amount of time left for grazing. Results from the model indicated that daily food intake may ultimately be regulated by the digestibility of the diet of caribou, a result well documented for domestic ruminants (Baumgardt 1970, Baile and Mayer 1970).

Seasonal changes in available plant biomass and digestibility of forage (White et al. 1975) were used to generate estimates of food and energy intake and rumen function parameters with RUMENMET. The number of grazing events, the time spent grazing, and the rate of ruminal volatile fatty acid production predicted by RUMENMET agreed with field observations in the Prudhoe Bay region (White et al. 1981) when the rumen capacity was expressed as:

$$\text{Rumen capacity} \cong 21\,W \times 18.9 \times 0.57 = 226 \text{ kJ kg}^{-1}$$

where $21\,W$ is the dry matter capacity of the rumen in relation to body weight (g kg^{-1}), 18.9 is the energy content of the forage (kJ g^{-1}) and 0.57 is the proportion of energy assimilated. This capacity is about half the daily energy requirement of an adult non-lactating caribou during summer.

At the end of summer, green biomass at Prudhoe Bay declines markedly to 10 g m^{-2} or less on all vegetational types except those on rims of low-centered polygons and pingos, where 20 g m^{-2} remains (Webber and Walker 1975, White et al. 1975). In most vegetation types a large amount of standing dead graminoid leaves is available. But this material is generally high in crude fiber and lignin, and expected digestibility would be only 30 to 40% (White et al. 1975). At this time caribou could continue to eat mostly green forage and maintain a relatively high digestibility, or they could consume larger amounts of dead material. RUMENMET was used to evaluate the effectiveness of these alternative tactics. If caribou continued to feed only on green material, then metabolizable energy intake would be about 30% of energy requirements. However, if both green and standing dead material were ingested, the model predicted that the daily metabolizable energy intake would be about 75% of energy requirements.

Even if caribou could consume almost all available food on exposed ridges and at the base of feeding craters, the Prudhoe Bay region appears to be poor winter range. In interior Alaska good winter range for caribou is characterized by shallow snow and high lichen biomass (>100 g m^{-2}; Hanson et al. 1975). Supplementation with frozen green graminoids is possible (Klein 1970, Hemming 1971), and maintenance requirements can probably be met. In the Prudhoe Bay region exposed ridges and pingos contain the highest lichen biomass. However. these areas constitute only 5% of the vegetated area (White et al. 1975), and the biomass of lichens is generally less than 10 g m^{-2} (Williams et al. 1975).

Population energetics can be calculated from estimates of energy expenditure by age and sex classes within the population combined with estimates of productivity by age class. A flow chart was used to calculate energy expenditures of adult male and female caribou (Table 10-8). Average daily metabolic rate was computed using the model ACTIVE (Bunnell et al., unpubl.), which was constructed to simulate the grazing

TABLE 10-8 *Flow Chart for Calculating Energy Requirements of Adult Grazing Caribou (kJ kg$^{-0.75}$ day^{-1})*

Standard Fasting Metabolism (FM)	$FM_s = 444$ $FM_w = 402$	McEwan (1970), caribou S = summer (1 June–31 Oct)
+		W = winter (1 Nov–31 May)
Energy required for maintaining body function		
↓		
Resting Metabolism (RM)	$RM = 536$ to 608	T. Hammel (unpubl.), reindeer
+		
Energy required for food inges- tion and digestion (energy cost of eating and specific dynamic effect)	$RM = 565$	White and Yousef (1978), White et al. (1975), reindeer
↓		
Maintenance Energy of Seden- tary Animal (MM$_R$)	$MM_R = 2FM_s = 888$ $= 2FM_w = 758$	Kleiber (1961), general
+		
Energy cost of locomotion and grazing activity		
↓		
Maintenance Energy of Grazing Animal (MM$_F$), equivalent to **Average Daily Metabolic Rate (ADMR)**	$MM_{F(S)} = 2.8$ FM_s $MM_{F(W)} = 2.2$ FM_w $ADMR = 884$ to 1244	See text
+		
Energy deposited in production (P) plus the energy cost of each process (tissue growth efficiency, E_G; efficiency of milk synthesis, E_M; efficiency of fattening, E_F)	$E_G = 0.80$ $E_M = 0.70$ $E_F = 0.81Q_M + 3.0$ $= 0.50$ to 0.70	Agricultural Research Council (1965), general Q_M = metabolizable energy of diet/gross energy of diet at maintenance
↓		
Metabolizable Energy Require- ments (MER)	$MER = ADMR + P_G/E_G$ $+ P_M/E_M + P_F/E_F$	
+		
Energy loss in urine and fer- mentation gases		
↓		
Assimilated Energy Requirement (AER)	$AER = MER/0.82$	Blaxter (1962), domestic ruminants
+		
Energy loss in feces (energy digestibility D$_F$)	$D_F = 0.57$ to 0.63	
↓		
Gross Energy Requirement (GER) or Ingestion	$GER = AER/D$ $= 1608$ to 1877	White et al. (1975), caribou

behavior and activity patterns of caribou. The model indicated that activity significantly affected the average daily metabolic rate and that the energy spent in grazing and evading insects needed to be determined. Grazing involves almost continuous movement, so it was necessary to estimate the energy cost of walking on tundra (White and Yousef 1978). ACTIVE calculated that, compared to days with no harassment, the average daily metabolic rate increased 1.06 times during mild harassment and 1.6 times during severe harassment, and averaged 2.8 times the standard rate during summer. Energy expended on locomotion increases from 17% of the average daily metabolic rate on insect-free days to approximately 60% during severe insect harassment.

Because of their heavy insulation, thermoregulation is not a problem for caribou in winter (White 1975), but the energy required for winter activities has not been determined. The assumption was made that energy expended in digging through snow was no higher than that expended during mild insect harassment. The average daily metabolic rate was then calculated to be 2.2 times the standard fasting rate. Thus, during the year the average daily metabolic rate in non-lactating caribou varied from 884 to 1244 kJ kg$^{-0.75}$.

Estimates of the production efficiency of each cohort of a caribou population were made from data of Krebs and Cowan (1962) and Kelsall (1968). In calves 3.0 and 4.6% of gross energy intake were used for production by males and females, respectively. Efficiencies declined to approximately 2% in animals between two and three years old and to zero in animals older than five years. Energy secreted in milk was taken as production of calves rather than a component of female production. The main reason for the low efficiency of production is the amount of energy required to support metabolism during winter, particularly from December to June when productivity is negative, and the animals lose weight.

The metabolic requirement for milk production during the first three weeks of lactation is very high—10.5 to 12.6 MJ day^{-1} or 40 to 50% of the average daily metabolic rate. This energy is required during May and June when primary production is negligible, and the predicted rates of energy intake would be low. Preliminary studies on reindeer grazing in shrub tundra in central Alaska indicate that the peak rate of milk secretion can vary from 0.8 to 2.2 liters day^{-1} (5.4 to 14.7 MJ day^{-1}), depending on food intake (White, unpubl. obs.). Thus, lactation can be less than optimal, and the growth rate and survival of calves may be related to the diet. Data for grazing reindeer show that the growth rate of calves depends on milk production for at least 50 days. After 50 days milk production declines rapidly (Holleman et al. 1974), and females begin to rebuild the nutrient pools in their bodies (Cameron and Luick 1972).

The general demographic pattern and data on production and gross intake were used to calculate population energetics for caribou (Table

10-3). At a density of 0.001 to 0.01 animal ha^{-1} annual production was 0.24 to 0.78 MJ ha^{-1} yr^{-1}. Energy retained, or productive energy, amounted to 1% of gross energy intake, 1.8% of assimilated energy, and 2.1% of respired energy.

Although calves make up only 15% of the population, they contribute 30% of the production. Seventy percent of the production is contributed by the 0- to 3-year-old caribou, which make up only 29% of the population. Thus, disturbances which affect the younger animals, e.g. adverse weather conditions, poor range quality or constant predation and harassment, have a marked effect on the population's productivity.

Population energetics in caribou can be compared with previous calculations for elephants (*Loxodonta africanus*—Petrides and Swank 1966) and white-tailed deer (*Odocoileus virginianus*—Davis and Golley 1963). Average caribou biomass (14 MJ ha^{-1}) was much lower than that of elephants (297 MJ ha^{-1}) or white-tailed deer (54 MJ ha^{-1}). Biomass and population turnover are reflected in absolute production of 0.78, 14 and 27 MJ ha^{-1} yr^{-1}, respectively, for the three species. However, efficiency of production with respect to energy intake, assimilation and respiration was similar for all species.

In addition to energy, caribou must receive sufficient nutrients from their forage to maintain a normal physiological state. Some insight into the relative importance of various nutrients for caribou can be gained by considering the degree to which nutrients in the diet must be retained. Similar calculations were made for lemmings.

TABLE 10-9   *Relative Concentration of Energy (kJ gdw^{-1}) and Nutrients (mg gdw^{-1}) in Vascular Plants and Caribou*

	Concentration in summer forage (F*)	Concentration in caribou (C)†	Concentration factor (C/F)	P/I** (%)
Energy	18.9	28.9	1.5	1.0
N	25	72	2.9	1.9
K	20	6	0.3	0.2
P	2	15	7.5	5.0
Mg	3	1	0.3	0.2
Ca	2	30	15.0	10.0
Na	1	5	5.0	3.3

* Data as in Table 10-4.
† Based on tissue values estimated for 100-kg domestic cattle (Agricultural Research Council 1965).
** Estimates based on equation analogous to that used for lemmings (p. 356).
Note: Retention of ingested nutrients in caribou represented by ratio of production to ingestion (P/I).

Nearly all production of caribou derives from summer range, so nutrient retention can be considered only in relation to summer forage. Retention of nutrients in the diet, the P/I ratio in Table 10-9, shows that nitrogen, phosphorus, calcium and sodium must be concentrated strongly, but not as strongly as for lemmings (Table 10-4). Nevertheless, nutrient availability could be as important for caribou as for lemmings.

No model has been constructed to explore the tactics open to caribou to maximize nutrient intake and to minimize nutrient loss by conservation and recycling processes as has been done for lemmings. However, if studies made on reindeer apply to caribou, then caribou may conserve nitrogen through urea recycling (Wales et al. 1975), and this mechanism may conserve use of energy, water and glucose as well (White 1975).

COMPARISON OF GRAZING SYSTEMS

Now that the main features of the herbivore-based food chains have been described, it should be clear that microtine rodents and ungulates represent very different approaches to herbivory. This section will compare the main features of these two grazing systems and point out their consequences for the coastal tundra ecosystem as a whole.

Population Characteristics

Perhaps the most conspicuous difference between microtines and ungulates is body size. Although that may seem to be a trivial observation, many life history characteristics of *Lemmus* and *Rangifer*, which determine characteristics of populations, appear to be a function of body size (Table 10-10).

The ratio of body size between lemmings and caribou remains nearly constant from birth through adulthood; caribou weigh about 1500 times as much as lemmings. Both species need to grow by a factor of 20 from birth to adulthood, but lemmings grow relatively faster. Thus, lemmings double their birth weight in four days and reach adult weights in 120 days whereas caribou take four times as long. The association of higher metabolic and growth rates with smaller body size is well known (Kleiber 1961). Generally, the efficiency of growth does not change. Small and large animals produce the same amount of new tissue for each unit of energy digested, but small animals produce the new tissue more rapidly.

Two other life history characteristics associated with small body size are a high reproductive rate and a short life span (Smith 1954). These relationships are dramatic in the lemming–caribou comparison.

Because lemmings have a large mean litter size (seven) and a rapid

TABLE 10-10 *Life History Characteristics of* Lemmus *and* Rangifer

	Lemmus	Rangifer	Ratio Lemmus/Rangifer
Body size			
Newborn (kg)	0.0033	5.0	0.0007
Weanling (kg)			
Individual	0.013	42	0.0003
Litter	0.091	42	0.0022
Adult (kg)	0.080	100	0.0008
Metabolic (kg$^{0.75}$)	0.15	32	0.0047
Growth			
Time to double birth wt (yr)	0.011	0.045	0.24
Total growth (kg)	0.077	95	0.0008
Adult/Newborn	24	20	1.2
Weanlings/Adult	1.1	0.42	2.6
Reproduction			
Litter size	7.0	1.0	7.0
Gestation (yr)	0.058	0.42	0.14
Lactation (yr)	0.041	0.44	0.094
Litters yr^{-1} (max.)	9.0	1.0	9.0
Age at first reproduction (yr)	0.15	2.0	0.075
Survival			
Maximum life span (yr)	1.5	20	0.075
Expected length of life (yr)	<0.1 to 0.3	2.9	0.069
Potential population growth*			
λ_{max} (yr)	1300	1.5	870

*Assume no deaths and that female lemming produces one litter per month (3.5 ♀♀ per litter), begins reproducing at two months and can produce nine months of the year. A female caribou produces one litter per year (0.5 ♀♀ litter⁻¹).

growth rate, the total weight of the litter at weaning is 1.1 times that of the mother. A weanling caribou weighs only 0.4 as much as its mother. The relative investment of a female lemming in each litter must therefore be much greater than that of a female caribou. The same would be true during a life span because the number of litters produced is similar. Surviving to maximum age and reproducing at a maximum rate, a lemming could produce 14 litters and a caribou 18. During a normal life span both species might be expected to produce one or two litters. A longer life appears to compensate somewhat for slower development and lower reproductive rates in caribou so that the total production of litters is similar. It is the number of individuals per litter, resulting in the large biomass of the litter relative to the mother, that produces a greater investment in offspring per female lemming. These results are consistent with those of Millar (1977), who concluded that litter size is the most important factor affecting the reproductive efforts of mammals in general.

Just as the ratio of body size remains similar for lemmings and caribou at any stage in their life cycle, two important measures of survival, the maximum and the mean expected lifetime, are about 14 times greater in caribou than in lemmings. Remarkably, the usual ages at first reproduction bear a similar relationship, which again suggests compensation between length of life and speed of development. Of course, the expected life span varies with any changes in the life table, so seasonal and annual differences will make its ratio between lemmings and caribou much more variable than that for maximum length of life.

The consequences of life history differences can be immense when considered at the population level. For instance, if we assume that survival is 100%, the potential population increase for lemmings during one year (λ_{max}) is a factor of 1300 while that for caribou is only 1.5 (Table 10-10). High reproductive potential allows lemmings to respond quickly to temporarily favorable conditions, but such high local densities are reached that they cannot be maintained. Thus, population densities fluctuate wildly. Caribou cannot respond quickly to short-term changes in the environmental conditions, and their population densities change slowly in response to long-term changes in environment.

Because of the great discrepancy in size of the major grazers, density figures (Table 10-3) do not give a good comparison of the two grazing regimes. The extreme changes in density of lemmings are modified somewhat if the time of residence is included (line 2), but the best comparative figure of the amount of grazers present is probably biomass residence (line 4), which compensates for both body size and time of residence. Even this measurement shows that the annual grazing population on the coastal tundra at Barrow is much more variable than that in the Prudhoe Bay region. The annual biomass residence at Barrow may vary between twenty times less and five times more than at Prudhoe Bay.

Energy flow through biomass is disproportionately large in lemmings compared with caribou because of the small body of the lemming. Maximum annual respiratory rates of lemming populations at Barrow are 50 times those of caribou in the Prudhoe Bay region, and relative production rates are even higher. Lemmings do not produce young any more efficiently than caribou, but in relation to their size they produce more. Among lemmings, *Lemmus* produces more than *Dicrostonyx* because litters are slightly larger and breeding seasons are longer (Batzli 1975a). The result of these relationships is that even in the Prudhoe Bay region, where caribou account for most of the biomass of grazers, the respiration and production of lemmings is often greater than that of caribou. Population efficiency and turnover time reflect the same relationships; lemming production efficiencies are greater than those of caribou, and turnover times are about 40 times shorter (Table 10-3).

Food Consumption and Foraging Patterns

The grazing regime imposed by these populations depends not only on their biomass but also on their rate of food consumption and on the composition of their diet. Rates of food consumption must allow at least sufficient assimilation to supply energy requirements. Because of their high energy requirements small mammals often put more grazing pressure on tundra vegetation, even in the Prudhoe Bay region, than do caribou. Although *Dicrostonyx* and *Rangifer* have similar assimilation efficiencies (~0.55 to 0.65) *Lemmus* has much lower efficiency (0.33), which further increases ingestion.

The gut capacity of *Lemmus* for digestible nutrients is 60% that of *Rangifer* in relation to body weight (Table 10-11), hence lemmings must fill their stomachs more often. However, for their size lemmings eat much faster, and the net result is that they need to spend only 20% as much time eating as caribou when forage is easily available. Interestingly, although the absolute turnover time of gut contents for lemmings is much less than for caribou, when corrected for metabolic weight (proportional to $W^{-0.25}$ according to Kleiber 1961), the relative turnover times are almost equal.

The distribution of grazing differs in its timing as well as in its intensity. Grazing by *Lemmus* becomes most intense during winter and at snowmelt when the vegetation lies dormant. Caribou migrate, and most of them leave the Prudhoe Bay region during winter, so the grazing pressure from caribou is highest during summer when plants are growing.

The species and parts of plants taken by the grazers also vary. *Lemmus* takes primarily graminoids with a supplement of mosses. During

TABLE 10-11 *Nutritional Characteristics of Mature* Lemmus *and* Rangifer, *Assuming Body Weights of 80 g and 100 kg, Respectively*

	Lemmus	Rangifer	Ratio Lemmus/Rangifer
Stomach or rumen capacity ($J \ g^{-1}$ body wt)	125	226	0.56
Fillings (no. day^{-1})	14	2.2	6.4
Turnover time (hr)	1.7	11	0.15
(hr kg$^{-0.25}$)	3.2	3.5	0.91
Maximum eating rate (g min^{-1})	0.14	6.0	0.023
(g kg$^{-0.75}$ min^{-1})	0.93	0.19	4.9
Foraging time (min day^{-1})	160	740	0.22

Note: Energetic calculations are for summer (15 °C).

summer caribou take equal amounts of the aboveground parts of dicotyledons and graminoids, about 15 to 20% of which may be dead material.
During winter caribou in the Prudhoe Bay region probably take mostly
dead plant material. *Dicrostonyx* specialize on dicotyledons, mostly *Salix*
spp., throughout the year, but graminoids form a supplement of about
10 to 20% of their diet (Batzli 1975a). Ground squirrels eat primarily
vegetative and reproductive parts of dicotyledons (Batzli and Sobaski
1980). The combined effects of these diets are that graminoids are most
heavily grazed on the coastal tundra at Barrow, while dicotyledons usually receive equal, if not more, grazing pressure than graminoids in the
Prudhoe Bay region.

Impact on Habitat

Five major characteristics of the grazing systems in the coastal tundras at Barrow and Prudhoe Bay can be compared (Table 10-12). Because small mammals at Barrow have been more intensively studied during the International Biological Program and because the literature on

TABLE 10-12   *Comparison of Mammalian Grazing Systems in the
Coastal Tundras at Barrow and Prudhoe Bay*

Characteristic	Barrow	Prudhoe Bay
1. Diversity of grazers	Two species One family One order	Four species Three families Two orders
2. Dominant grazer		
a. Biomass	Lemmings (*Lemmus*)	Caribou (*Rangifer*)
b. Consumption	Lemmings (*Lemmus*)	Lemmings (*Dicrostonyx* and *Lemmus*) and caribou
3. Grazing pressure		
a. Annual	Light to heavy (cyclic)	Light to moderate (stable)
b. Seasonal	Winter > summer	Winter ≅ summer
4. Forage taken	Graminoids and mosses	Graminoids and dicotyledons
5. Major impacts of grazers		
a. Microtopography	Burrows, runways and hummock formation.	Trampling, trails and burrows.
b. Vegetation	Favor graminoids and increase productivity.	Undocumented.
c. Soil	Speed nutrient cycling, increase depth of thaw and change dispersion patterns of nutrients.	Undocumented.

them is more extensive (see Batzli 1975a for review), ideas regarding their impact on tundra are more complete. The impacts can be considered in relation to three interacting components of the ecosystem, viz. microtopography, vegetation and soils. While some inferences can be drawn regarding the Prudhoe Bay region, they are largely speculative.

Lemmings at Barrow construct their burrows on elevated sites, e.g. centers of high-centered polygons or rims of low-centered polygons, which have favorable drainage. As a result, much of the drier tundra is riddled with burrows, and barren areas are formed at burrow entrances by deposition of soil. Runways connect the burrows, and hummocks often develop between runways owing to erosion of fine materials that are not stabilized by vegetation. In areas denuded by frost heaving, there seems to be progressively greater hummock development associated with increasing vegetation growth and lemming activity. Unfortunately, this sequence has not been documented by long-term observations in one area.

In the Prudhoe Bay region, where lemmings are less abundant, their impact is not as clear, although burrows and runways may be conspicuous in some areas. Ground squirrel diggings on river banks, sand dunes and pingos do create dramatic series of holes and mounds, but ground squirrels occupy only a small portion of the tundra. Caribou generally spread out as they graze, so compaction of soil caused by their trampling is not obvious except for systems of trails leading to sand dunes where they seek refuge from insect attack. Of course, the effects of grazers on microtopography presumably are reflected in the soil characteristics, such as soil temperature and depth of thaw.

Exclosure studies at Barrow, originally started in 1950, indicate that the elimination of lemming grazing causes several changes in vegetation (Batzli 1975b). At well-drained sites, carpets of mosses and lichens develop and graminoids become sparse. In low, wet sites graminoids continue to dominate, but standing dead material accumulates and productivity declines. Apparently, heavy lemming grazing disrupts mosses and lichens, which recover slowly. Graminoids, however, have their meristematic tissue under the moss layer and can replace shoots rapidly by drawing upon reserves in underground rhizomes. Chronic grazing by caribou during summer may have less effect on vegetation than the intensive grazing during winter and spring when lemming populations are high.

Grazers can affect vegetation indirectly as well as directly (Batzli 1975b). The bulbet saxifrage, *Saxifraga cernua*, appears to be concentrated around old lemming burrows and trails as does an acrocarpous moss, *Funaria polaris* (B. Murray, pers. comm.). *Saxifraga* is probably there because lemmings disperse their sticky bulbets, while *Funaria* may simply specialize on lemming feces as a substrate. Herds of caribou may have significant local effects owing to trampling and deposition of manure (Bee and Hall 1956, Steere, pers. comm.), but this impact has not been measured nor have long-term patterns been studied. The moss *Voitia hyperborea* is associated with musk ox and caribou dung (Steere 1974). Heavy mats of the grasses *Arctagrostis, Alopecurus* and *Calamagrostis* cover tops of sand dunes and pingos occupied by ground squirrels, apparently in response to disturbance and manuring. Caribou and ground squirrels also may influence the reproductive success of some dicotyledons, particularly *Pedicularis* and *Saxifraga*, since they seem to be especially fond of their flowering heads.

A particularly interesting interaction between lemmings, soil and vegetation may be occurring in areas with low-centered polygons. Microtopography produces large differences in soil moisture within a few meters. The deepest portions of polygon troughs may contain water all summer long, whereas the basins of low-centered polygons contain water only in early summer, and their rims are never submerged. Soil organic matter is greatest in the basins (bulk density < 0.5 g cm^{-3}) and least in the troughs (bulk density > 1 g cm^{-3}). Exchangeable phosphorus is greatest (240 μg g^{-1}) in the troughs and least (90 μg g^{-1}) in the basins (Barèl and Barsdate 1978). Differences in soil conditions produce different vegetational communities. Graminoid shoots are most robust and dense (~3000 m^{-2}) in troughs and least robust and dense in basins (1000 to 1500 m^{-2}). Phosphorus concentration in plant tissues and plant production are both highest in troughs. Decomposition and, therefore, nutrient cycling appear to be most rapid in troughs because that is where production of organic matter is greatest and accumulation is least. The highest activity rates of bacteria and the highest standing crops of soil invertebrates also occur in troughs, thus accounting for high rates of decomposition. Lemmings also concentrate their activities in troughs, apparently because the most palatable and nutritious food is concentrated there.

All these observations are consistent with one another, and they allow the microtopographic units to be ranked in order of decreasing biological activity: troughs, rims and basins. The one factor that seems most likely to account for the differences in biological activity is soil phosphorus. Higher levels of phosphorus allow greater production of more nutritious vegetation, which stimulates both decomposition and herbivory. Moisture conditions may also influence decomposition, and the troughs maintain greater soil moisture during the warmest part of the summer. But why should phosphorus be concentrated in the troughs?

One explanation might be that phosphorus is leached from the rims of low-centered polygons to the troughs. But if this were the only factor, phosphorus would accumulate on both sides of the rims, in the basins as well as the troughs. Then the basins and troughs would be expected to show similar levels of available phosphorus, which is not the case. A second possibility is called the nutrient-transport hypothesis: that lemmings transport nutrients from both basins and rims to troughs.

Polygons form in drained lake basins, which have relatively uniform topography and sediments and, therefore, an even distribution of soil nutrients before polygon formation begins. The nutrient-transport hypothesis provides an explanation for the development of the current patterns of biological activity as polygonal ground develops. The sequence of events can be hypothesized as follows.

Troughs develop over ice wedges, and the wedges continue to expand to produce the rims that surround the basins (Figure 1-10). Drainage is impeded in the central basins and the deepest parts of the troughs. Although the basins of low-centered polygons hold water during early summer, they are higher and relatively drier than the troughs by midsummer. Snow cover is deeper in the troughs during winter. Lemmings place their winter nests in troughs where deeper snow improves the microhabitat. Foraging lemmings move out from the troughs under the snow, but most feces and urine are deposited in the troughs near the nests. Nutrients accumulate in the troughs as a result of lemming activities. Nutrients are depleted in the basins where lemmings remove forage but deposit few wastes. Summer (June through September) burrows and nests are located on the relatively dry rims. The rims attain an intermediate nutrient status because they are the site of summer nests and near the winter nests. Accumulation of nutrients is associated with higher primary production and higher concentration of nutrients in the trough vegetation (Barèl and Barsdate 1978, Tieszen, pers. comm.). Improved forage reinforces the preference of lemmings for troughs. Nutrient depletion has the opposite effect in the basins. Increased activity of decomposers and soil invertebrates occurs in response to higher quality of litter and concentration of soil nutrients in troughs (see Chapter 11 for details). Accumulation of organic matter in the soil is slowed, and rates of nutrient cycling increase. Again, the opposite trends occur in the basins.

Although these events have been presented sequentially to emphasize causal relationships, all occur simultaneously. The result is a slow transition from relatively homogeneous distribution of soil properties and biological activity in drained lake basins to the marked spatial heterogeneity seen in polygonal terrain. According to the nutrient-transport hypothesis, spatial differences in biological activity are largely a result of different availability of nutrients. The pattern of nutrient availability is imposed by activities of lemmings.

Unfortunately, we do not have sufficient data to test the nutrient-transport hypothesis. The trends in soil properties and biological activity associated with polygonal terrain have been used to construct the hypothesis and cannot be used to test it. Ultimately, the causal links will need to be tested by field observations and experiments. In the absence of

TABLE 10-13   *Nutrients (kg ha⁻¹) Accumulated During a Standard Lemming Cycle (3 Years) as Calculated by a Simulation Model of Nutrient Transport by Lemmings*

	Habitats same			Habitats different		
	N	P	Ca	N	P	Ca
High plant nutrients						
Troughs	0.25	0.05	−0.07	−0.17	−0.33	−0.58
Rims	−1.03	−0.24	−0.28	−0.51	0.07	0.11
Basins	−0.32	−0.07	−0.08	−0.39	0.05	0.04
Carcasses	1.40	0.34	0.54	1.40	0.34	0.54
Low plant nutrients						
Troughs	−0.32	−0.08	−0.04	−0.31	−0.22	−0.61
Rims	−0.58	−0.13	−0.17	−0.43	−0.02	0.14
Basins	−0.16	−0.04	−0.05	−0.32	−0.02	0.04
Carcasses	1.40	0.34	0.54	1.40	0.34	0.54

Note: Four cases were run: with nutrient levels in forage high or low and with nutrient levels in forage the same or different in the three microhabitats at the beginning of the run.

such data, we have tried to determine the feasibility of the hypothesis by using computer models of lemming population dynamics and nutrition to calculate deposition of urinary and fecal nutrients in the various microtopographic units. The activity of lemmings in the various microtopographic units was distributed according to time spent in nests and percentage of shoots clipped in each unit. We assumed that excreta are formed and deposited continually. Thus, if lemmings spend 50% of their time in their nests, 50% of their excretions would be deposited in troughs, and the remaining amount would be distributed according to the amount of time spent foraging in each microenvironment. If the figures are adjusted for the relative area of each unit, the removal and deposition of nutrients can be put on an areal basis.

The results of these simulations indicate that net transportation of phosphorus from rims and basins to troughs only occurred when plant nutrient concentrations were high and the same in all habitats at the beginning of the run (Table 10-13). This would be the situation as polygonal development began in a recently drained lake basin.

In all cases the concentration of nutrients in lemming carcasses was sufficient to alter the results, depending on where those carcasses were deposited. Most carcasses found on tundra are in the troughs, near or in winter nests. This would increase nutrient deposition in troughs. Many, perhaps most, carcasses are taken by predators. Weasels deposit their scats near the winter nests of lemmings, but avian predators regurgitate pellets on higher ground, the rims of low-centered polygons and the centers of high-centered polygons. Deposition of pellets would therefore add nutrients to rims, and this would counteract the trend of greater nutrient removal from rims than from basins (Table 10-13).

The total movement of phosphorus to troughs, assuming half of the carcasses decayed in troughs, would be 0.2 kg ha^{-1} (20 mg m^{-2}) over a three-year period, five times the average amount of soluble phosphorus found there at present. While this simulation does not prove that consumers move nutrients to polygon troughs, it does show that the nutrient-transport hypothesis is feasible.

We do not know how effective predators are as nutrient-transport systems, but snowy owls spend long periods of time on favorite centers of high-centered polygons (owl mounds). Extremely high levels of phosphorus accumulate in the soils of these mounds, and grasses such as *Arctagrostis, Calamagrostis* and *Poa* dominate the vegetation there as nowhere else at Barrow. Jaegers deposit their pellets on lower mounds, such as the rims of low-centered polygons, as well. The deposition of these pellets affects the foraging patterns of shorebirds. MacLean (1974b) has shown that female shorebirds must consume lemming bones when laying eggs to obtain enough calcium for their eggshells. Shorebirds, which normally forage in lower areas, search on mounds for lemming bones. Thus, nutrient transport by consumers can affect other consumers as well as producers and decomposers.

More observations, calculations and experiments are required to determine the effectiveness of consumers as nutrient-transport systems in tundra. If confirmed, these systems will be an important example of the major impact consumers can have on ecosystem structure and dynamics, much greater than that predicted by simple measurement of their biomass.

Consideration of changes in tundra vegetation and soils after removal of lemming grazing provides additional insight into the effects of grazers òn coastal tundra. Batzli (1975b) sampled exclosures near Barrow that had been in place for 15 years (Schultz 1964) and 25 years (Thompson 1955c). Vegetation had changed little in low, wet sites that had standing water most of the summer. In mesic and dry sites, however, the net production of graminoid stems and leaves was almost twice as high in grazed areas as in the exclosures. Standing dead material and detritus were greater within the exclosures, suggesting that nutrient cycling had diminished in the absence of grazing. Reduced phosphorus in the soil solution under exclosed areas corroborates the hypothesis of decreased nutrient availability in the absence of grazing (Barèl, pers. comm.).

Batzli (1978) reviewed evidence for similar effects of herbivores in other ecosystems. Although the effects may not be as dramatic, herbivory in grasslands and forests may also increase the rate of nutrient cycling and change the distribution of nutrients.

SUMMARY

A single species, the brown lemming (*Lemmus sibericus*), dominates the herbivore community at Barrow. The number of trappable animals per hectare increases to a peak of 150 to 250 every three to six years and may drop to less than 1 in the years between.

A simulation model shows that a dramatic increase in the population can be produced by a slight improvement in the survival rate of adult females and their young. The population increases occur during those winters when the structure of the snowpack allows access to food, when forage quality is high, and when predatory mammals are scarce. The high reproductive potential of lemmings then allows the population to increase greatly before the snow melts.

Only catastrophic mortality can explain the radical declines. Current evidence suggests that the mortality, at least early in the summer, is caused by overgrazing accompanied by a rise in the number of predatory birds. However, the effects of increased social interactions on the dispersal and genetics of high populations have not been studied sufficiently.

Examination of the nutrient-recovery hypothesis as an explanation for cyclic fluctuations in lemming density leads to the conclusion that it requires modification. Although changes in the nutritional quality of the vegetation may affect lemming populations, lemming activity does not appear to produce the short-term effects required to alter nutrient concentrations in soil and plants as proposed.

The herbivore community in the Prudhoe Bay region is more diverse and more stable than that at Barrow. Caribou (*Rangifer tarandus*) provide the greatest herbivore biomass. The brown lemming and the collared lemming (*Dicrostonyx torquatus*) exist in about equal numbers, but their density is an order of magnitude less than at Barrow. Even so, lemmings may consume three to six times as much vegetation as caribou because their metabolic rates are higher and their forage is less digestible. Ground squirrels (*Spermophilus parryii*) are also important herbivores in more restricted habitats.

Comparison of ungulate and microtine grazers reveals two very different, but equally successful, suites of adaptation to herbivory on tundra. The short development times and large litters of the microtines give them a high population growth rate. In order to fuel its high metabolic rate a microtine must fill its gut often. But because it eats faster and has a faster turnover rate of gut contents than an ungulate, it requires less time for foraging. Caribou, on the other hand, being large and mobile, are less vulnerable to predators and can therefore spend more time foraging. During the summer they must make up for the undernutrition they suffer during winter. Their grazing patterns can be interpreted as an attempt to maximize their intake of high quality forage. But on some days harassment by mosquitoes and warble flies prevents them from obtaining adequate nutrients.

Owing to their periodic abundance lemmings can strongly affect vegetational composition and production on the coastal tundra at Barrow. There is little evidence of this in the Prudhoe Bay region, however, and the effects of grazing are not conspicuous there. Both lemmings and caribou influence soil characteristics by burrowing, trampling and manuring.

A proposed nutrient-transport hypothesis ascribes the uneven distribution of soil nutrients and biological activity in polygonized terrain to the redistribution of nutrients by animals.

11

The Detritus-Based
Trophic System

S. F. MacLean, Jr.

INTRODUCTION

The detritus-based trophic system is composed of animals that use energy only after it has passed from living components through the pool of dead organic matter. The system includes animals feeding directly upon dead organic matter (detritivores), upon microbial tissue (microbivores), or upon other animals (carnivores) (Figure 10-1). This chapter considers the abundance, energetics, and ecological function of animals in the detritus-based trophic system, and the contribution that they make to the decomposition of organic matter and cycling of mineral nutrients in the coastal tundra at Barrow.

Even in years with high lemming populations, assimilation of energy by herbivores amounts to only about 6% of net primary production (Chapter 10). Another 13% of net primary production is returned to the tundra as feces, while about 80% passes directly to the dead organic matter pool when unconsumed vegetation (including moss and vascular plant roots) senesces and dies. Thus, each year, 93 to 99% of the annual primary production enters the pool of dead organic matter and becomes available to microorganisms and invertebrate detritivores, which form the first link in the detritus-based trophic system.

The rate at which soil and litter organisms use this energy source is limited by the quality of the organic matter, the length and temperature of the period of biological activity, and other factors such as soil moisture and aeration. These influence both the population density and the rate of activity of individual organisms. The cumulative effect of these rate-limiting factors is seen in the large accumulation of organic matter in the soil which indicates that, by and large, the processes involved in the decomposition of organic matter have been more limited by arctic conditions than have the processes involved in the synthesis of organic matter by green plants. As a result, soil invertebrates live in an environment that is energy-rich, with up to 80% of the soil dry weight consisting of organic matter (> 1675 J cm^{-3}) in the top 5 cm, where most of the animals are found.

As in other functional units of the coastal tundra at Barrow, the diversity of animals in the detritus-based trophic system is low compared to that found in more temperate and tropical ecosystems; however, the diversity of soil invertebrates is not as limited as is that of herbivores. Some taxa that are important soil organisms in other ecosystems are missing altogether (earthworms, isopods, millipedes, ants, termites) or are poorly represented (beetles) in the fauna of the coastal tundra at Barrow. Other taxa, for example mites (Acari), springtails (Collembola), flies (Diptera), and enchytraeid worms (Enchytraeidae), show only a modest reduction in diversity compared with temperate ecosystems, and commonly are quite abundant in the coastal tundra ecosystem.

Invertebrate carnivores are few; the most conspicuous are the predatory cranefly larvae, *Pedicia hannai*, and beetles of the families Carabidae and Staphylinidae. Only two families of spiders, Linyphiidae and Lycosidae, are found, the latter with only a single species. During the summer months soil invertebrate communities support an abundant and diverse group of breeding birds, especially shorebirds or waders.

ABUNDANCE AND BIOMASS OF SOIL INVERTEBRATES

The array of microtopographic units that compose the coastal tundra was described in Chapter 1. Sample plots for the study of soil invertebrates were established in representative units of polygonal and meadow terrain (Table 11-1). The characteristics of the study areas and more detailed reports of the data are given by Douce (1976), Douce and Crossley (1977) and MacLean et al.(1977). This discussion draws heavily from these data, and emphasizes higher taxonomic categories. Community organization at the level of species is considered by Douce (1976), Douce and Crossley (1977), and MacLean et al. (1978). Energy budgets are calculated based upon abundance and biomass estimated in 1972, for which data were most complete.

Large differences among microtopographic units are apparent in mean abundance and biomass of the major faunal groups during the period of biological activity (Table 11-1). A two-way analysis of variance, using density as the dependent variable and plot and sample date as independent variables, was performed for free-living and plant-parasitic nematodes, Enchytraeidae, Collembola, and three major suborders of soil Acari (Prostigmata, Mesostigmata, and Oribatei). Location made

TABLE 11-1 *Abundance and Biomass of Soil Microfauna in Various Microtopographic–Vegetation Units of the Coastal Tundra at Barrow Arranged Along a Moisture Gradient (Wet–Dry)*

Unit	Nematoda[1]			Enchytraeidae			Acari[2]			Collembola		
	(no. m⁻²)	(μg ind⁻¹)	(mg m⁻²)	(no. m⁻²)	(μg ind⁻¹)	(mg m⁻²)	(no. m⁻²)	(μg ind⁻¹)	(mg m⁻²)	(no. m⁻²)	(μg ind⁻¹)	(mg m⁻²)
Carex–Oncophorus meadow[1]	199,400		20	52,000	50.4	2620	18,200	3.9	71	86,400		346
Carex–Oncophorus meadow[1]	226,500		23	44,200	51.0	2255	26,900	4.7	126	67,600		270
Dupontia meadow	304,500		30	84,400	32.2	2716	14,500	3.9	57	61,100		244
Polygon trough	276,700		28	93,600	44.1	4132	23,900	3.1	75	162,800		651
Dupontia meadow	307,700		31	50,100	32.4	1622	46,400	3.1	145	171,900		688
Polygon basin	46,200		5	25,200	73.3	1847	9,600	2.2	21	24,400		98
Polygon rim	448,400		45	12,900	50.5	651	72,700	2.0	147	83,700		335
Carex–Poa mesic meadow	723,800		72	40,700	54.1	2203	83,100	2.4	197	85,800		343
High-centered polygon	361,300		36	11,400	90.5	1032	69,500	3.2	224	72,400		290
Mean	321,600	(0.1)[4]	32	46,100	46.0	2119	40,500	2.9	118	90,700	(4)[4]	363

[1] Numbers as extracted and counted; biomass assuming 40% extraction efficiency.
[2] Numbers, and hence biomass, differ slightly from those reported by Douce and Crossley (1977), being based upon 28 rather than 14 cores per plot.
[3] Two different *Carex–Oncophorus* meadow plots located within the Biome intensive study area (site 2).
[4] Average values used to estimate biomass on all of the study locations.

the greatest contribution to total variation in five of the seven cases. The exceptions were mesostigmatid mites and Collembola, in which within-sample variation was greatest. Sampling date made a relatively small contribution to total variation, indicating that spatial variation is more important than temporal variation in determining the abundance of tundra soil invertebrates. A similar pattern is seen in the soil microflora (Chapter 8).

Mean annual density of nematodes, estimated by soil sieving followed by concentration through sugar solution centrifugation, varied between about 50,000 individuals m^{-2} in the basins of low-centered polygons and 724,000 m^{-2} in the mesic meadow. These values are very low, but have been confirmed by the use of three different extraction procedures. In a review of data on nematode density and biomass in a variety of terrestrial ecosystems, Sohlenius (1980) found that only in deserts were mean values below one million individuals m^{-2}, with coniferous forest, deciduous forest, and temperate grasslands averaging over three, six, and nine million individuals m^{-2}, respectively. Procter (1977) reported densities in the range of one to almost five million individuals m^{-2} in the tundra of Devon Island, N.W.T., Canada. Thus, the low densities found at Barrow are not characteristic of tundra. As at Barrow, the wet meadow at Devon Island supported the lowest density of nematodes.

Trophic function of nematodes was determined by examination of mouthparts. Although abundance varied by a factor of 15 among sample points, trophic structure of the population was remarkably constant. The free-living nematodes, which are largely bacterial and algal feeders, were most abundant overall. The plant-parasitic nematodes became relatively more abundant on the drier units, and were dominant on the mesic meadow. Predatory nematodes made up a small proportion of the population in all cases. The abundance of all three nematode groups was inversely correlated with soil moisture; the Spearmann rank correlation between total nematode abundance and moisture was -0.65 ($p < 0.05$).

Drier units contain more dicotyledonous plants, many of which are mycorrhizal (Miller and Laursen 1978). This is particularly so for Salix on the mesic meadow. The much greater abundance of plant-parasitic nematodes here may indicate that the root systems of dicotyledonous plants are more susceptible to the attack of nematodes than are roots of the graminoids that dominate wetter areas, or that the nematodes are feeding directly upon mycorrhizal fungi.

Biomass of nematodes was not directly determined. Based upon studies of nematodes at a variety of other locations (Sohlenius 1980), a mean biomass estimate of 0.1 μg dry weight per individual was used to approximate population biomass (Table 11-1). More elaborate functions relating density to biomass, for example based upon differences in trophic function, might be used, but hardly seem justified in light of the low abundance. These results indicate that nematodes are relatively unimportant in the coastal tundra at Barrow compared with other ecosystems.

The northern Coastal Plain near Barrow is totally lacking in earthworms (Annelida: Lumbricidae), but is rich in smaller worms of the family Enchytraeidae. These worms are largely aquatic, living in the soil interstitial water, and are less abundant in the drier areas. Mean densities ranged from 11,000 and 13,000 individuals m^{-2} on the well-drained polygon top and rim to 94,000 worms m^{-2} in the moist polygonal trough. The Spearmann rank correlation of enchytraeid abundance and soil moisture across the nine microtopographic units (Table 11-1) was positive and significant ($r = +0.75$; $p < 0.05$).

Biomass of Enchytraeidae was determined from the distribution of body lengths of each species, using the geometric equations of Abrahamson (1973). Biomass is dominated by a large species of the genus *Mesenchytraeus*, which had a mean individual biomass of 65 µg dry wt, and mean population biomass of 1500 mg m^{-2} in the polygon trough. The biomass of this one species exceeded the sum of nematode, mite, and collembolan biomass in this habitat, and the total enchytraeid biomass exceeded the sum of all other animal biomass in eight of the nine microtopographic units sampled. Mean enchytraeid biomass across all units was 2100 mg dry wt m^{-2}. Thus, Enchytraeidae achieve considerable abundance and biomass in the coastal tundra at Barrow and strongly dominate the soil fauna.

Mean density of Acari ranged from less than 10,000 individuals m^{-2} in the basins of low-centered polygons to 83,000 m^{-2} in the mesic meadow. The rank correlation with moisture ($r = -0.62$; $0.10 > p > 0.05$) indicated greatest density in drier areas. This trend occurred in all three of the major mite suborders: Prostigmata, Mesostigmata, and Oribatei. The Oribatei were particularly lacking from the basins of low-centered polygons.

In most ecosystems the Oribatei are the dominant group of Acari; however, the small prostigmatid mites are relatively abundant in tundra ecosystems (Behan 1978). Prostigmata comprised 16 of 37 species and 43% of all individuals in our samples (Table 11-2). The average individual weighed only 1 µg dry weight (Douce 1976); hence, the numerically dominant Prostigmata contributed relatively little to biomass. The most abundant oribatid species, *Liochthonius scalaris* Forsslund (= *L. sellnicki* S. thor) is also very small, with adults weighing only 0.5 µg; however, the mean weight of oribatid mites was 4.0 µg. Overall, the Oribatei composed 48% of the density but 66% of the biomass of mites. The predaceous Mesostigmata are the largest of the mites, averaging about 6.8 µg, and thus made a much larger contribution to biomass (18%) than to density (8%). Density and, especially, biomass of mites are generally low

TABLE 11-2 *Composition of the Mite (Acari) Fauna in the Coastal Tundra at Barrow*

Taxonomic group	Species (no.)	(%)	Density (ind m⁻²)	(%)	Weight (μg ind⁻¹)	Biomass (mg m⁻²)	(%)
Prostigmata	16	43	17,800	44	1.0	18	16
Mesostigmata	9	24	3,200	8	6.8	22	18
Oribatei	11	30	19,400	48	4.0	78	66
Astigmata	1	3					

compared with temperate forest and grassland ecosystems.

Density of Collembola varied between 24,400 individuals m⁻² in the basins of low-centered polygons and over 150,000 m⁻² in the polygon troughs and moist meadows, and was greater than that of mites in all nine microtopographic units sampled, although the difference was small in the three drier units. Collembolan density showed no relationship with soil moisture.

Biomass of Collembola was not determined directly. Population biomass was estimated using a standard value of 4 μg per individual, taken from Petersen's (1975) observations of adult *Folsomia quadrioculata* and from Fjellberg's (1975) observations of *F. diplophthalma* in arctic-alpine Norway. These two species made up 70% of the total collembolan density in our samples (MacLean et al. 1977). Using this value, estimated biomass of Collembola exceeded 0.5 gdw m⁻² in the most favorable areas.

The Diptera strongly dominated the numbers, biomass, and diversity of tundra macroarthropods (Table 11-3). Three cranefly species (Tipulidae) are particularly prominent: *Prionocera gracilistyla,* a large species with larvae in the wettest habitats; *Tipula carinifrons,* a large species of mesic and dry areas; and *Pedicia hannai,* a smaller species with carnivorous larvae that are most abundant in wet meadows and the polygon troughs. Larvae of other species of lower Diptera (Nematocera), including especially midges (Chironomidae) and fungus gnats (Mycetophilidae and Sciaridae), were recorded at densities of up to 685 individuals m⁻². This must be considered a minimum estimate due to uncertainties of sampling and extraction efficiency (Healey and Russell-Smith 1970). A large proportion of the smaller larvae may have been overlooked, which would lead to a serious underestimate of density, but not of biomass.

Rotifers, which are more commonly associated with freshwater habitats, occurred in all microtopographic units, with a mean annual density in the wettest meadows of 40,000 ind m⁻². Tardigrades occurred at densi-

TABLE 11-3 *Abundance and Biomass of Diptera Larvae in Various Microtopographic–Vegetation Units of the Coastal Tundra*

Habitat	Prionocera gracilistyla (no. m⁻²)	(mg)	(mg m⁻²)	Pedicia hannai (no. m⁻²)	(mg)	(mg m⁻²)	Tipula carinifrons (no. m⁻²)	(mg)	(mg m⁻²)	Other Nematocera (no. m⁻²)	(mg)	(mg m⁻²)	Muscidae (no. m⁻²)	(mg)	(mg m⁻²)	Total Diptera (mg m⁻²)
Carex–Oncophorus meadow[1]	29		824	328	0.50	164	2		32	249		125	10		10	1155
Carex–Oncophorus meadow[1]	4		113	234	0.27	63	2		32	288		144	18		18	270
Dupontia meadow	0		—	218	0.52	113	0		—	685		343	12		12	468
Polygon trough	0		—	250	1.53	382	12		193	127		64	2		2	641
Dupontia meadow	0		—	62	0.19	12	0		—	84		42	25		25	79
Polygon basin	0		—	31	2.35	73	6		97	125		63	0		—	233
Polygon rim	0		—	16	0.94	15	16		258	423		212	23		23	508
Carex–Poa mesic meadow	0		—	156	0.35	55	31		499	343		172	6		6	732
High-centered polygon	0		—	16	0.75	12	8		129	163		82	14		14	237
Mean	3.7	28.1	104	146	0.68	99	8.6	16.1	138	278	0.5	139	12	1.0	12	480

[1]Two different Carex–Oncophorus meadow plots located within the Biome intensive study area (site 2).

417

ties up to 15,000 ind m⁻² in the wet meadows; very few were found in the
drier areas. In both cases these must be regarded, cautiously, as minimum estimates since no special effort was made to census these animals.

Microtopographic units differ markedly in the abundance and composition of their invertebrate faunas, even using the gross taxonomic
units considered here. Total invertebrate biomass differed by a factor of
about three between the most productive polygon troughs and the least
productive basins and rims of low-centered polygons and tops of high-
centered polygons, although these units are separated by only a few
meters distance and about 20 cm of relief. We must be very cautious in
referring to a "mean" or "average" unit and its soil fauna in the very
heterogeneous coastal tundra at Barrow. Rather, the tundra is a repeat-
ing mosaic of polygon troughs, rims, tops and meadows that are quite
distinct habitats for soil invertebrates and microflora (Chapter 8).

Even within microtopographic units, populations of all major soil
arthropod groups were significantly clumped or aggregated in their patterns of dispersion. There was a significant tendency for coincidence in
the aggregations of total mites and Collembola (MacLean et al. 1977),
plant-parasitic and free-living nematodes, and prostigmatid and oribatid
mites, indicating that these groups respond similarly to microhabitat
suitability or richness.

A very consistent feature of the tundra soil fauna is the concentration of animals in the near-surface horizons of the litter and soil (Figure
11-1). In both Acari and Collembola over 90% of the individuals

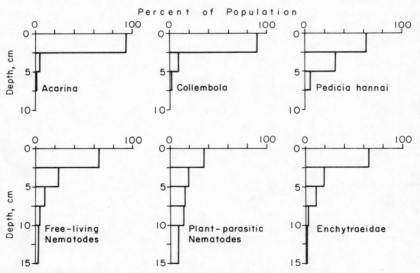

FIGURE 11-1. *The annual mean depth distribution of representative
groups of soil invertebrates.*

occurred in the top 2.5 cm, and over 98% in the top 5 cm of the soil. Sixty-six percent of the total Enchytraeidae occurred in the top 2.5 cm, and 86% in the top 5 cm. The Nematoda showed the greatest tendency to occur at depth. Approximately 85% of the free-living and predaceous and 55% of the plant-parasitic nematodes were found in the top 5 cm. The occurrence of plant-parasitic nematodes below 5 cm seems related to the presence of dicotyledonous plants. Plant-parasitic nematodes were the only animals to occur in significant numbers in the mineral soil beneath the peat. Their small size may allow them to exist within the small pores of mineral soil.

Depth distribution of Enchytraeidae showed a marked seasonal pattern (Figure 11-2); worms were concentrated near the surface at snowmelt, but moved to deeper layers by mid-season. After the first sample of the season, the three dominant enchytraeid species were segregated by depth. Individuals of the smallest species, *Cernosvitoviella atrata*, were found even below 15 cm in the tundra and, when sampling was concluded in late August, had shown no tendency to return to the surface. Over 50% of the populations of *Mesenchytraeus* sp. and *Henlea perpusilla* were found in the top 2.5 cm in all but the late July sampling.

Concentration of animals in the surface layer was greatest in the basins of low-centered polygons where well over 90% of the animal biomass, including 99% of the Collembola, 97% of the mites, and 89% of the Enchytraeidae, occurred in the top 2.5 cm. *C. atrata*, the deep-dwelling enchytraeid species, was entirely absent.

Although soil invertebrate densities are conventionally presented as number per unit area, the number per unit volume more accurately

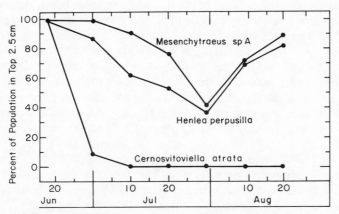

FIGURE 11-2. *The seasonal variation in depth distribution (percentage of the population in the top 2.5 cm) of the three dominant species of Enchytraeidae.*

expresses conditions encountered by an animal living in a three-dimensional environment. For example, an average cubic centimeter within the top 2.5 cm of the polygon trough contained 4.8 nematodes, 2.2 enchytraeid worms, 0.85 mite, and 5.8 Collembola. Although the densities of soil invertebrates in some other ecosystems may equal or exceed those of the coastal tundra at Barrow, it is unlikely that many have consistently greater concentrations of animals.

The abundance and vertical distribution of soil invertebrates can be compared with the vertical profiles of soil temperature and moisture, plant biomass and production, microbial biomass and production, and dead organic matter. The seasonal course of soil temperature in several microtopographic units was presented in Chapter 2. Temperatures significantly above air temperatures occur in the top few centimeters of the soil, but soil temperature declines rapidly with depth, and below 10 cm rises only slightly above 0°C even at mid-season. Low temperatures below 5 cm may contribute to the surface concentration of many soil invertebrate species. Conversely, winter season temperatures are lowest near the tundra surface. In temperate regions many soil invertebrates descend into deeper layers of the soil to avoid the frozen soil and cold. In tundra, this movement is prevented by permafrost. Soil animals could gain some protection by descending to lower depths, but to do so would result in a later onset of activity in the following spring. It appears that the advantage of the longer and warmer near-surface growing season outweighs the increased risk of mortality from winter cold, and soil animals remain near the surface during the winter. In fact, Enchytraeidae must move toward the surface late in the summer season (Figure 11-2).

Abundance of Nematoda, Enchytraeidae, and Acari all relate significantly to the moisture ranking of the microtopographic units, suggesting that moisture or some correlated factor is important in determining their distribution. The Enchytraeidae and Nematoda are basically aquatic organisms living in the soil interstitial water. The Enchytraeidae are relatively large, thus requiring larger water-filled pores and cavities in the soil. Increased soil moisture apparently increases the amount of habitat available to them, thus increasing population abundance. The Nematoda are much smaller, and can use the thin film of water that surrounds soil particles even in relatively dry soils. Since their abundance is negatively correlated with soil moisture some other factor must be involved.

At high soil moisture levels the soil pore volume is filled with water, and anaerobic conditions may develop. The commonly anaerobic conditions occur in the 5- to 15-cm depth interval (Chapter 7). Shortage of oxygen could well contribute to the observed depth distribution of Barrow soil invertebrates. The drier soils of high-centered polygons and rims of low-centered polygons probably have sufficient oxygen throughout the period of biological activity, and a larger proportion of soil invertebrate populations are found below 5 cm in these than in other microtopographic units. Soils of the meadows, troughs, and basins of low-centered polygons may become strongly anaerobic in early summer when saturated by snow meltwater, but less so, or even oxidizing, as the surface soil dries out in mid-season. The soil may again become anaerobic following late summer rains. Seasonal changes in depth distribution of Enchytraeidae follow the same pattern (Figure 11-2), suggesting that Enchytraeidae may use the resources occurring at depth only when the aeration of the deeper levels allows. Springett et al. (1970) showed that surface drying of peat soils in a British moorland resulted in downward movement of the enchytraeids *Cernosvitoviella briganta* and *Cognettia sphagnetorum*. In the present case, the fact that seasonal changes occur in even the wettest areas suggests that access to the deeper strata, determined by temperature and aeration, is responsible for population movements rather than exclusion from the surface layers by desiccation.

The basins of low-centered polygons are characterized by very low densities and high surface concentration of invertebrates. This could be a result of anaerobiosis developing when the basins are flooded in spring by meltwater confined within the surrounding rims. Over 90% of the invertebrate biomass in the polygon basin consisted of Enchytraeidae, which are known to be more tolerant of anaerobiosis than other invertebrates, as indicated by the very high densities achieved in sewage beds.

Little is known of the feeding habits of soil invertebrates, making it very difficult to discern the relationship of the animals to their food supply. Progress will probably require detailed examination on a spatial scale much smaller than is reported here, and careful experimental and manipulative study. We can, however, attempt to relate the abundance of soil fauna in major habitat units to estimates of microbial biomass and productivity.

From direct counts (Table 8-1), it appears that abundance of bacteria changes in the order rims >> meadows > basins > troughs. Free-living nematodes are largely bacterial feeders, and their abundance (Table 11-1) shows a similar pattern, rims >> meadows ≈ troughs >> basins, with the exception of the very low abundance in the basins.

Fungal biomass is greatest in dry habitats. The abundance of soil Acari corresponds; however, the Enchytraeidae, which are probably the major soil fungivores, are most abundant in wet habitats. Fungal biomass is higher in the basins than in the troughs, but low in both; however, fungal productivity, estimated as the sum of positive biomass increments between sampling occasions (Chapter 8), is highest in the troughs. This could account for the abundance of soil invertebrates found in troughs. Soil algae may also help support the abundance of invertebrates near the surface of the wet meadows and troughs. In all microtopographic units, abundance of soil invertebrates drops off much more rapidly

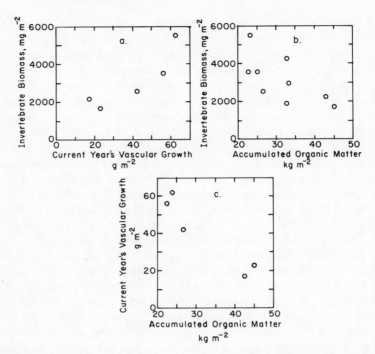

FIGURE 11-3. *The relationship of invertebrate biomass to current year's vascular plant growth (a) and total organic matter to 20 cm (b), and of vascular plant growth to total organic matter to 20 cm (c). (After MacLean 1974a.)*

with depth than does biomass of microorganisms.

Invertebrate abundance and biomass can also be compared to the amount and distribution of net primary production, which represents input of fresh substrate for heterotroph activity. Peak season aboveground vascular plant biomass was used as an index of annual input into the various microtopographic units. This measure is available for five of the study plots in which invertebrate populations were sampled. Total invertebrate biomass shows a strong positive correlation with this index of primary production on these five plots (Figure 11-3a).

In many ecosystems concentration of invertebrates near the soil surface maximizes their access to fresh substrate in the form of litter falling from a plant canopy to the ground surface. In tundra plants, however, the larger part of the annual primary production is invested in roots and rhizomes (Chapter 3). Billings et al. (1978) estimated the annual root turnover of the *Carex-Oncophorus* meadow as between 60 to 65 g m^{-2} yr^{-1} and 90 g m^{-2} yr^{-1}. Even the minimum estimate is in excess of annual aboveground production. In *Eriophorum angustifolium*, which makes the largest contribution to this total because of its annual root system, new roots occurred throughout the soil profile to a depth of 30 cm. New roots of *Carex* were concentrated between 10 and 20 cm depth, and roots of *Dupontia* were concentrated between 5 and 15 cm. Dennis (1977) found 62% of the belowground live plant biomass, including rhizomes, and 38% of the dead biomass in the top 5 cm of the soil.

The depth distribution of plant-parasitic nematodes resembles the distribution of live plant biomass below the ground. All other invertebrates show greater confinement to the surface layers than either biomass or production of belowground plant parts. Clearly, a significant part of the annual net primary production appears as growth below 10 cm in the soil and is very little used by soil invertebrates.

Since soil invertebrates constitute a detritus-based trophic system, a positive relationship might be expected between the quantity of soil organic matter at the base of the food chain and the abundance of organisms supported by this base, in much the same way that a rich plant biomass may support an abundance of herbivores. In fact the total biomass of soil fauna is inversely related to accumulated soil organic matter to a depth of 20 cm (Figure 11-3b) and the hypothesis that a large detritus base leads to an abundance of animals in the detritus-based trophic system must be rejected. Most of the organic matter lies below the layers of abundant fauna. The soil animals are concentrated in the near-surface organic-rich horizons, but they have access to only a small part of the total pool of organic matter. All of the habitats sampled are highly organic in the near-surface horizons, and no relationship between faunal density and organic matter between 0 and 2.5 cm or between 0 and 5 cm is evident.

Annual net primary production in the coastal tundra at Barrow also shows a strong inverse correlation with accumulated organic matter (Figure 11-3c). The most productive plots are characterized by little accumulation, hence rapid turnover of organic matter and recycling of nutrients. In the less productive habitats the annual production of organic matter and uptake of nutrients are small relative to the amounts tied up in accumulation.

Rate of organic matter turnover may be taken as an index of total microbial activity. The fact that it correlates poorly with microbial biomass (Chapter 8) indicates that much of the microbial biomass is inactive at any one time. Total invertebrate abundance, then, correlates positively with the input and turnover of dead organic matter and with microbial activity and productivity.

Much of the annual input of dead organic matter and microbial production lies below the depth of significant invertebrate density; thus, potential food goes uneaten. This does not necessarily indicate that food is unimportant in determining the distribution and abundance of tundra soil invertebrates. Rather, it appears that physical factors, among which temperature, moisture, and aeration are prominent, determine access to the habitat and the food that it contains.

Invertebrates reach their greatest abundance in the polygon troughs and meadows, where they are part of a syndrome that involves relatively little organic matter accumulation, rapid nutrient recycling, and high rates of primary production. Low invertebrate abundance is associated with more organic matter accumulation and low rates of primary production, suggesting a system that is constrained by a low rate of nutrient release and recycling.

This analysis does not show causation. A very large number of cause-and-effect relationships are doubtless included in these broad patterns. It would be of little value to debate whether an impoverished soil fauna is cause or effect of low decomposition rate; surely feedback relationships make both points, in part, true. The same can be said for soil nutrient concentration and decomposition rate. These data do suggest that the activity of soil invertebrates is interwoven with the pattern of production and decomposition that characterizes the coastal tundra ecosystem.

LIFE CYCLES OF TUNDRA SOIL INVERTEBRATES

The abundance, seasonal dynamics, and energy requirements of invertebrates derive, in large part, from the life cycle characteristics of the species involved. Life cycle characteristics have been studied in the cranefly species *Pedicia hannai* (MacLean 1973) and *Tipula carinifrons* (Clement 1975), and in the three dominant enchytraeid species, *Mesenchytraeus* sp., *Henlea perpusilla*, and *Cernosvitoviella atrata*. Life cycles of these groups differ in a fundamental way. The Diptera pass through four larval instars in the soil and then undergo a complete metamorphosis in a pupal stage to the adult form. The adults leave the soil to swarm over the tundra surface, where reproduction is quickly accomplished. In Enchytraeidae development is gradual, and reproduction may occur over a considerable part of the total life cycle. There is no marked change in habitat or life form associated with the onset of reproduction.

Tipulidae

The cranefly species require at least four years to complete larval development. The early instars are completed relatively quickly, while the final, fourth instar lasts about two years. As a result, the population at any time contains a high proportion of large, fourth-instar larvae. Average biomass is high, although the ratio of productivity to biomass is low. The slowing of development that leads to multi-annual life cycles with overlapping larval generations is an important contributor to the high density and biomass of Diptera larvae in the tundra.

In both cranefly species, respiration rate of larvae increases with temperature over the entire range observed: 0.5° to 20°C. Q_{10} values calculated over this range are virtually identical: 2.34 for *P. hannai* and 2.35 for *T. carinifrons*, comparing fourth instar larvae. In contrast, the growth responses to increasing temperature differ. The growth rate of *P. hannai* increases with increasing temperature over the range of temperatures observed in the field. Growth was fastest in mid-season, when temperatures are highest. Thus, in *P. hannai* assimilation of energy must increase by a factor greater than the increase in respiration rate as temperature increases; that is, the Q_{10} of assimilation is greater than 2.34. In contrast, Clement (1975) found a distinct growth optimum for *T. carinifrons* at 4° to 5°C. Growth rate was reduced at temperatures above or below this optimum. Assimilation of energy does not increase to compensate for the increase in respiration at temperatures above 5°C.

It follows from the differing growth responses to temperature that *Tipula carinifrons* is an obligate arctic species that is unable to complete development in warmer climates, while *Pedicia hannai* is a facultative arctic resident that might also occur in warmer climates. In fact, *P. hannai* is known from a number of locations in northern Alaska, including Anaktuvuk Pass in the Brooks Range, Umiat in the northern Foothills (Weber 1950b), Meade River, and the Prudhoe Bay region (MacLean 1975b), areas varying widely in summer-season length and climate. *T. carinifrons* occurs extensively in the Soviet far north (Chernov and Savchenko 1965), apparently always in arctic coastal localities. In Alaska it is known only from the coastal tundra at Barrow and Cape Thompson (Watson et al. 1966), and from coastal tundra in the Yukon–Kuskokwim River delta.

Following the long period of larval development, the adult life span is completed very quickly. Pupation begins in late June, and most adults emerge quite synchronously around mid-July (MacLean and Pitelka 1971). In both *P. hannai* and *T. carinifrons* females have very small, non-functional wings. In *P. hannai* the mouthparts, antennae, eyes, and legs of females are poorly developed. Males of both species are winged, but the wings are used only for feeble fluttering along the surface and they are incapable of sustained flight. The morphological reduction of females may lead to greater fertility (Byers 1969); the limited use of wings by males indicates that wings would probably be of small advantage to females anyway. Females of the third cranefly found in the coastal tundra at Barrow, *Prionocera gracilistyla*, do retain wings and are capable of flight on warm days. This species has the most restricted larval habitat, and thus may require more searching for oviposition sites.

Adults do not feed. Copulation may occur almost immediately after emergence, and egg-laying commences soon thereafter. Clement (1975) hypothesized the release of a sex pheromone by nearly emerged (or emerging) females to attract males. Given favorable conditions, males are quite active. The weight-specific respiration rate of adult male *T. carinifrons* is 3 to 4 times that of larvae at the same temperature, and the metabolic response to temperature (Q_{10}) is greater. All of this increases the likelihood of successful reproduction under the variable and unpredictable weather conditions of the arctic summer, a likelihood that is favored by emergence into a high-density population.

The advantage of synchronous emergence is further enhanced by predation. The abundant avian predators feed upon insect larvae early and late in the season, but switch almost entirely to adult Diptera, especially craneflies, when they are available. During the main period of emergence the density of adult flies far exceeds consumption by birds, and the impact of predation is relatively low. As discussed below, predation is more intense upon individuals emerging into low density populations, early and late in the emergence period. The result is selection for synchrony of emergence.

During the midsummer emergence period photoperiodic cues are weak, particularly for soil-dwelling pupae. It appears that the timing of emergence is controlled entirely by temperature as it affects rate of pupal development and ecdysis. For instance, MacLean (1975b) documented emergence at Prudhoe Bay in two seasons (1971–1972) differing by about one week in the time of snowmelt and the onset of activity, and found that emergence differed by a like amount in the two seasons.

Because of the length of the life cycle, differences between areas or years in the density of emerging adults may reflect differences in the larval population density or in the relative abundance of the cohorts composing the population. The large difference in emergence of adult *P. hannai* on the *Carex–Oncophorus* meadow in 1970 and 1971 (Table 11-4) can be attributed to differences in cohort size rather than total population; the population was actually much larger in June 1970 than in June 1971, as can be easily surmised, since the 1970 population also included the large cohort giving rise to adults in 1971.

The emergence of adult *P. hannai* increased from 1970 to 1971 on the *Carex–Oncophorus* meadow, declined on the *Dupontia* meadow, and remained essentially stable in the polygon trough (Table 11-4); thus, differences in emergence between years do not simply reflect weather patterns. In some years, however, cold weather before or, especially, during the emergence period can delay or even inhibit emergence, as was recorded in the very cold July of 1969 (MacLean and Pitelka 1971, MacLean 1973).

TABLE 11-4 *Emergence of Adult Craneflies (Diptera, Tipulidae) in Various Habitats of the Coastal Tundra in the Years 1970–1972*

	1970					1971					1972				
	Area sampled (m⁻²)	Tipula (no.)	Tipula (no. m⁻²)	Pedicia (no.)	Pedicia (no. m⁻²)	Area sampled (m⁻²)	Tipula (no.)	Tipula (no. m⁻²)	Pedicia (no.)	Pedicia (no. m⁻²)	Area sampled (m⁻²)	Tipula (no.)	Tipula (no. m⁻²)	Pedicia (no.)	Pedicia (no. m⁻²)
Site 2 *Carex–Oncophorus* meadow	7.6	4	0.5	67	8.8	10.0	39	3.9	271	27.1	2.3	4	1.8	18	7.9
Gradient site															
Dupontia meadow	2.0	3	1.5	63	31.5	4.5	11	2.4	47	10.4	3.0	0	0	28	9.3
Polygon trough	2.0	1	0.5	35	17.5	2.5	3	1.2	55	22.0	1.5	7	4.7	34	22.7
Carex–Poa mesic meadow	4.0	20	5.0	11	2.8	3.0	55	18.3	4	1.3					
Polygon basins						2.3	0	0	4	1.7	1.5	2	1.3	11	7.3
Low-centered polygon											1.5	4	2.7	0	0
High-centered polygon	4.0	4	1.0	0	0	3.0	12	4.0	3	1.0	1.5	2	1.3	0	0
Total	19.6	32	1.6	176	9.0	25.3	120	4.7	384	15.2	11.3	19	1.7	91	8.1

427

Taken over a number of years and cohorts, mean emergence of adults must reflect population size. *P. hannai* are clearly most abundant in wet meadows and polygon troughs (Table 11-4). *Tipula carinifrons* adults emerged at greatest density from mesic meadows. The overall density of emerging *T. carinifrons* (3.0 individuals m⁻²) was less than that of *P. hannai* (11.5 individuals m⁻²); however, because of the difference in size of adults, the biomass of emerging *T. carinifrons* (35.3 mg m⁻²) was greater than that of *P. hannai* (19.6 mg m⁻²).

Enchytraeidae

The life cycles of the three dominant enchytraeid species last from one to two years, and may include one or two distinct periods of recruitment each season (Figure 11-4). In both *Cernosvitoviella atrata* and *Mesenchytraeus* sp. early season recruits come from eggs that were deposited in cocoons the prior season, while the late season recruits hatch from eggs deposited in the same season. Thus, Enchytraeidae can overwinter successfully as eggs, immature worms, or mature worms.

Growth rates of these species are reflected in the ratio of production to average biomass, $P/\bar{B}$. *Mesenchytraeus* sp. grows to the largest size, over 300 μg dry weight over the two-year life cycle, and the $P/\bar{B}$ (annual production divided by average biomass, both in mg m⁻²) ratio is quite high, 3.22. *C. atrata* is much smaller with a maximum size of about 20 μg, but growth is accomplished in one year, and $P/\bar{B}$ is 2.89. The two-year growth period and modest size (maximum = 65 μg) of *Henlea perpusilla* gives rise to a $P/\bar{B}$ of 1.49. Although the average biomass of *C. atrata* (131 mg m⁻²) is half that of *H. perpusilla* (260 mg m⁻²), the estimated annual production of the two species is nearly equal. This emphasizes the danger of basing estimates of ecological importance upon density and biomass data alone. The relative growth rate of the three

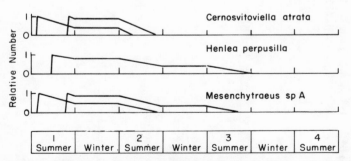

FIGURE 11-4. *A schematic view of the life cycles of the three dominant species of Enchytraeidae.*

enchytraeid species was well above those of the two cranefly species studied, and this is reflected in much higher $P/\bar{B}$ ratios in the Enchytraeidae (Table 11-6). Thus, the difference in energetic activity of Enchytraeidae and Diptera is even greater than the difference in biomass.

Evolution of Life Cycles

Life cycles lasting more than one year occur in many arctic invertebrates (Chernov 1978, MacLean 1975a). Given the short growing season and low temperatures of the Arctic, few species may be able to complete growth and development in a single season. Those species unable to overwinter and renew growth in the following season will be eliminated from the arctic fauna. An invertebrate species might be able to complete development in many, even most seasons; however, an obligate annual life cycle demands successful development and reproduction every season for maintenance of the population. Thus, a sequence of severe summers could eliminate annual species from the fauna. Many herbivorous insect species have obligate annual life cycles that are closely tied to the phenology of the plants upon which they feed. This may contribute to the shortage of foliage-dwelling insect herbivores in the coastal tundra at Barrow.

In the Arctic, life cycle length is determined by both temperature and length of the active season, that is, by growth rate and duration of the growth period. Thus, were the season lengthened with no change in mean temperature as, for instance, occurs in the subantarctic islands (Rosswall and Heal 1975), *Tipula carinifrons* and *Pedicia hannai* might achieve annual life cycles.

Relative growth rate of both Tipulidae and Enchytraeidae declines in larger individuals. This observation is not unique to arctic invertebrates. Consider a boreal and an arctic species characterized by the growth rate functions g_1 and g_2, respectively, with $g_2 < g_1$ due to lower temperatures in the arctic regions (Figure 11-5a). Such a growth rate function results in the pattern of growth shown in Figure 11-5b. Let W_m be the weight at maturity. The slower growth rate (g_2) of the arctic population requires a prolonging of the development period to reach W_m. This increases the period of exposure to mortality, and may lead to a smaller population, N_2 (Figure 11-5c), at maturity. Thus, many species that might be able to grow and complete the life cycle in the Arctic are unable to maintain a population due to the total mortality during the long development period. This may be one factor contributing to the reduced diversity of northern ecosystems. Reduction of development time and decreased generation mortality would help to explain the steep increase in species diversity found along climatic gradients away from the immedi-

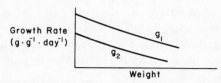

a. Growth rate functions relating growth rate to body weight for a subarctic (g₁) and an arctic (g₂) invertebrate.

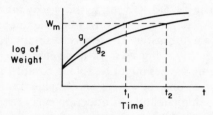

b. Growth curves resulting from growth rate functions g₁ and g₂. Different development periods (t₁ and t₂) are required to reach the size (Wₘ) necessary for pupation.

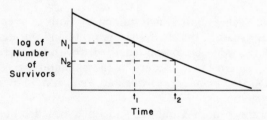

c. Survivorship curve showing the number of adults (N₁ and N₂) produced after development periods t₁ and t₂. Slower growth (g₂) leads to a longer development time (t₂) and fewer individuals (N₂) surviving to become reproducing adults.

FIGURE 11-5. *Effect of growth rate on survivorship.*

ate arctic coastal tundra (MacLean 1975b, MacLean and Hodkinson 1980).

In Diptera, larval development continues until some point (W_m) is reached. At this time, there is a complete change (pupation) from a growing larva to a reproducing adult. The onset of sexual maturity in Enchy-

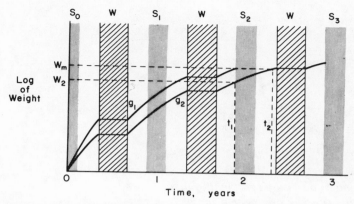

FIGURE 11-6. *Factors influencing the evolution of multi-annual life cycles of Diptera.* S = *summer,* W = *winter.*

traeidae is a much less radical change. The form of the animal remains much as before, and growth continues. In fact, most of the biomass is added after the onset of sexual maturity.

In Diptera, successful completion of the life cycle is influenced by constraints upon adult biology. The highly synchronous emergence of adult Diptera suggests that these constraints are rigorously imposed. Only flies emerging within a narrow time span successfully complete the life cycle. The short period each summer during which successful emergence may occur is indicated by the areas S_1, S_2, S_3 (Figure 11-6). In a particular climate larvae growing according to the growth function g_1 reach W_m and complete the life cycle in two years. In a somewhat more severe climate growth is slowed to that described by growth function g_2. In this case W_m is reached at t_2 which falls between S_2 and S_3, however emergence at time t_2 is disadvantageous. Some individuals in the population might retain the two-year life cycle and pupate in S_2, but at a smaller size (W_2) than in the less severe climate. Since fecundity in insects is related to body size, this carries with it a cost of reduced fecundity. Other individuals in the population may extend the life cycle and pupate in S_3 at a size equal to or even larger than W_m. In this case full fecundity is maintained, but at the cost of increased period of exposure to mortality. The strategy that maximizes expected reproduction (probability of survival × fecundity) should prevail in the population.

Body size and fecundity can change continuously with climatic severity and growth rate. Life cycle length, however, changes discontinuously, a year at a time. Thus it is likely that small changes in climatic severity will result in changes in body size and fecundity (Figure 11-7). This would explain the well-known decline in insect body size along elevational

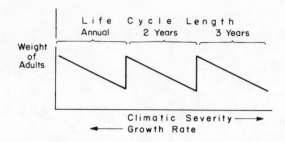

FIGURE 11-7. *The resulting changes in body size and life cycle length of Diptera along a continuous gradient of increasing climatic severity and decreasing growth rate.*

gradients (Mani 1962, 1968, Houston 1971). Similar changes, apparently, occur over latitudinal gradients (Hemmingsen and Jensen 1957).

Body size and fecundity should continue to fall until the disadvantage of reduced fecundity balances the disadvantage of increased mortality accompanying a lengthening of the life cycle. At this point the life cycle will change discontinuously. The unit lengthening of the life cycle should be associated with a discontinuous increase in adult size (Figure 11-7). Thus, we expect a saw-tooth pattern of size and life-cycle length in species that are widely distributed along gradients of environmental severity. Data are not available to test this prediction.

ENERGETICS OF SOIL INVERTEBRATES

Estimates of production, respiration, assimilation, and consumption of energy were made for each of the major invertebrate groups (Table 11-5). The source and reliability of the estimates varied with amount of information available. Information was most complete for the cranefly species *T. carinifrons* and *P. hannai*; production was estimated from changes in the size distribution of larval populations in the field, and respiration was estimated from laboratory measurements of respiration as a function of temperature and size of larvae, extrapolated to field temperature and size distribution (MacLean 1973, Clement 1975). A similar technique was used to estimate production of Enchytraeidae. Respiration of Nematoda, Enchytraeidae, Acari, and Collembola was estimated using equations or parameters derived from the literature. Calculation of energy budgets for these groups was then completed using bioenergetic ratios (e.g. production/respiration, assimilation/consumption; Table 11-6) derived from published values (summar-

TABLE 11-5   *Estimates of Energetic Function (J m⁻² yr⁻¹) of Major Invertebrate Groups in the Coastal Tundra Ecosystem*

	Production	Respiration	Assimilation	Consumption
Nematoda	970	1,940	2,910	7,265
Enchytraeidae	120,525	97,100	217,625	544,050
Acari				
Prostigmata	810	1,010	1,820	2,420
Mesostigmata	865	1,085	1,950	2,600
Oribatei	1,250	1,780	3,030	7,560
Collembola	13,770	13,770	27,540	68,850
Diptera				
P. hannai	3,810	4,310	8,120	10,150
T. carinifrons	5,020	3,850	8,870	22,180
P. gracilistyla	2,510	1,925	4,435	11,090
Other Nematocera	4,270	4,270	8,540	21,340
Muscidae	335	335	670	1,675

ized in Heal and MacLean 1975). Thus, estimates of consumption, assimilation, production, and respiration are not independent.

The results (Table 11-5) emphasize the importance of Enchytraeidae in this coastal tundra ecosystem. The energetic role of enchytraeids far exceeds the sum of all other invertebrates, and is exceeded by lemmings only in the year of a population high (Chapter 10). Even then, the enchytraeid value is achieved in an active period of about 100 days, while lemmings are active year-round. Enchytraeidae are similarly important in tundra-like moorland of the British Isles, where they accounted for 46 and 55% of the assimilation of energy by animals in two habitats on peat soils (Coulson and Whittaker 1978). On high arctic tundra on Devon Island, N.W.T., Canada, nematodes were the major invertebrate consumers on a dry cushion plant–lichen community, while Enchytraeidae were the dominant consumers in a sedge–moss meadow community (Ryan 1977).

The estimated annual production of the two abundant cranefly species, *Tipula carinifrons* and *Pedicia hannai*, was compared with the annual emergence of adult flies estimated earlier (Table 11-4), assuming an energy value of 22.6 J mg⁻¹ of tissue produced. The emergence values (35.3 and 19.6 mg m⁻² yr⁻¹ respectively) represent 15.9 and 11.6% of the estimated annual production of larvae. Since larvae lose approximately

TABLE 11-6 *Bioenergetic Parameters of Various Taxa of Soil Invertebrates*

	R $(\mu l\ O_2\ mg^{-1}\ hr^{-1})$	P/R[1]	P/B[2]	A/C[1]
Nematoda	1.6	0.50	1.34	0.4
Enchytraeidae	1.2	1.24	2.5	0.4
Acari				
Prostigmata	1.4	0.8	1.71	0.75
Mesostigmata	1.3	0.8	2.26	0.75
Oribatei	0.7	0.7	0.99	0.4
Collembola	1.0	1.0	1.43	0.4
Diptera				
P. hannai	1.1	0.88	0.70	0.8
T. carinifrons	0.7	1.30	1.61	0.4
P. gracilistyla	0.5	1.30	1.07	0.4
Other Nematocera	0.8	1.0	1.36	0.4
Muscidae	0.7	1.0	1.23	0.4

P—production; R—respiration; B—biomass; A—assimilation; C—consumption.

[1] joule joule^{-1} or cal cal^{-1}.

[2] mg mg^{-1}; production may be changed from milligrams to joules assuming 22 J mg^{-1}.

60% of their mass in pupation, the emergence actually represents approximately 88 and 49 mg of larval production. The remainder represents mortality of larvae prior to the emergence of adult flies: 134 mg m^{-2}, or 60% of annual production, for *Tipula carinifrons*, and 120 mg m^{-2}, or 71% of production, for *Pedicia hannai*.

In order to relate these calculations to ecosystem function, the energetic estimates must be partitioned according to the trophic role of the animals. Only the Nematode data were collected and reported according to trophic–functional categories. The literature abounds with observations of gut contents or feeding preferences of particular invertebrate species; however, generalizations are few and tenuous. Literature values and our field data were used to partition the activity of taxonomic categories according to the scheme shown in Table 11-7.

In view of the great importance of Enchytraeidae, it would be particularly valuable to know their feeding habitats. Unfortunately, direct observations are lacking. Enchytraeid guts commonly contain plant detritus in various stages of decomposition, microorganisms, and, where

TABLE 11-7   *Division of Energetic Activity According to Trophic Function (% of activity) Assigned to the Various Invertebrate Groups.*

| | | | Microbivore | | |
	Herbivore	Saprovore	Bacteria and algae	Fungi	Carnivore
Nematodes					
Free-living	0	20	60	20	0
Predaceous	0	0	0	0	100
Plant-parasitic	100	0	0	0	0
Enchytraeidae	0	20	20	60	0
Acarina					
Prostigmata	0	0	20	10	70
Mesostigmata	0	0	0	20	80
Oribatei	0	50	10	40	0
Collembola	5	50	15	25	5
Diptera					
P. hannai	0	0	0	0	100
T. carinifrons	25	50	10	15	0
P. gracilistyla	25	50	10	15	0
Other Nematocera	0	70	10	20	0
Muscidae	0	70	10	20	0
Coleoptera					
Carabidae	0	0	0	0	100
Staphylinidae	0	0	0	0	100
Chrysomelidae	100	0	0	0	0

available, mineral matter. O'Connor (1967) found fungi in greater proportion in the gut than in the available substrate for two of three enchytraeid species examined, while the third species showed no selectivity. Dash and Cragg (1972) found that boreal woodland Enchytraeidae were attracted to fungal baits placed on the soil surface. Nielsen (1962) examined the digestive enzymes of four species of Enchytraeidae, including one species of *Mesenchytraeus*, and concluded that they are unable to break down the complex structural polysaccharides of higher plants. Thus, it appears that Enchytraeidae are primarily microbivores, selectively ingesting fungi and also feeding upon bacteria and algae ingested with dead organic matter.

Most investigators emphasize the importance of fungal hyphae in the diet of Collembola (Peterson 1971); however, evidence from gut contents (Bodvarsson 1970), feeding preference and growth rate (Addison 1977), and digestive enzymes (Zinkler 1969) of Collembola of the genus *Folsomia* indicate that they feed directly upon dead organic matter. Since *Folsomia quadrioculata* and *F. diplophthalma*, together, constitute 70%

of the Collembola found in the coastal tundra at Barrow, the feeding activity of this group is biased toward saprophagy.

The litter and soil-dwelling prostigmatid and mesostigmatid mites are mainly predatory (Wallwork 1967); many Prostigmata feed upon the eggs and juvenile stages of Collembola. The Oribatei include species which feed upon microbial tissue, dead plant litter, and combinations of these (Luxton 1972, Behan and Hill 1978).

The Diptera include a variety of trophic types. Larvae of *Pedicia hannai* are predatory and have been observed preying upon Enchytraeidae in culture (MacLean 1973). Larvae of aquatic Tipulidae are commonly indiscriminate detritus feeders (e.g. Hall and Pritchard 1975). In British moorland blanket bog larvae of *Tipula subnodicornis* feed upon liverworts, and thus are herbivores (Coulson and Whittaker 1978). Smirnov (1958, 1961) examined gut contents of invertebrates in a *Sphagnum* bog and found large quantities of *Sphagnum* leaves only in *Tipula* larvae. In the coastal tundra at Barrow, *Prionocera gracilistyla* is restricted to mossy depressions and *Tipula carinifrons* is commonly found in dry moss hummocks. Although many of the invertebrates found living in moss do not actually consume living moss (Smirnov 1958, 1961), more than the estimated 25% of the energy consumed by these craneflies may come from living plants.

The majority of the remaining Diptera larvae are probably saprophagous (Raw 1967, Healey and Russell-Smith 1970), although microbial tissue is undoubtedly digested as it is consumed along with plant litter and humus.

ENERGY STRUCTURE OF THE DETRITUS-BASED TROPHIC SYSTEM

Estimates of trophic function can be applied to biomass and energetic estimates to infer the trophic structure of the invertebrate fauna of this coastal tundra ecosystem. The result (Table 11-8, Figure 11-8) is strongly determined by the division of trophic function assigned to Enchytraeidae, which makes the largest contribution to three of the five trophic categories: saprovores, bacterial and algal feeders, and fungivores.

Canopy-dwelling herbivores are virtually absent from the fauna, the only exception being sawfly (Tenthredinidae) larvae, which feed upon the prostrate willows that occur in drier habitats. Even with a fraction of the biomass and activity of the large and abundant cranefly larvae assigned to herbivory, invertebrate herbivores are of minor importance in this ecosystem. Consumption of 15.1 kJ m^{-2} yr^{-1} (Figure 11-8) amounts to less than 1 gdw m^{-2} yr^{-1}, a negligible part of annual net primary production.

TABLE 11-8 *Biomass of Invertebrates (mg m^{-2})in the Coastal Tundra at Barrow Partitioned According to Trophic Function*

| | Total | Herbivore | Saprovore | Microbivore | | Carnivore |
				Bacteria and algae	Fungi	
Nematodes						
Free-living	16	0	3	10	3	0
Predaceous	1	0	0	0	0	1
Plant-parasitic	15	15	0	0	0	0
Enchytraeidae	2119	0	424	424	1271	0
Acarina						
Prostigmata	25	0	0	5	3	18
Mesostigmata	21	0	0	0	4	17
Oribatei	72	0	36	7	20	0
Collembola	336	18	183	55	92	18
Diptera						
P. hannai	164	0	0	0	0	164
T. carinifrons	206	52	103	21	31	0
P. gracilistyla	104	26	52	10	16	0
Other Nematocera	139	0	97	14	28	0
Muscidae	12	0	8	1	2	0
Coleoptera						
Carabidae and Staphylinidae	14	0	0	0	0	14
Chrysomelidae	2	2	0	0	0	0
Total	3277	113	909	547	1481	227

The microbial feeders (bacteria and algae grazers, and fungivores) make up the majority of the biomass of the soil fauna. This contrasts with many forest ecosystems where large populations of saprovores such as earthworms, millipedes and isopods may dominate the litter and soil fauna. Consumption by saprovores amounts to approximately 9 gdw m^{-2}, about 4.5% of the total annual input to the detritus-based trophic system. In contrast, fungal-feeding invertebrates consume over 18 gdw m^{-2}, an amount in excess of the mean annual standing crop of fungi.

Animals are influenced by both availability and quality of their food. The food of microbivores is less abundant but of higher quality (higher in soluble carbohydrates and nutrients and more easily digested) than that of herbivores and saprovores. It may be that animals using a low-quality diet are at an extra disadvantage under the severe conditions of the Arctic. Schramm (1972) investigated the interaction of temperature and food quality as determinants of growth rate of herbivorous insects. Diets low in protein produced poor growth at all temperatures. Diets lacking in low molecular weight carbohydrates (starch and sugar)

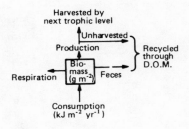

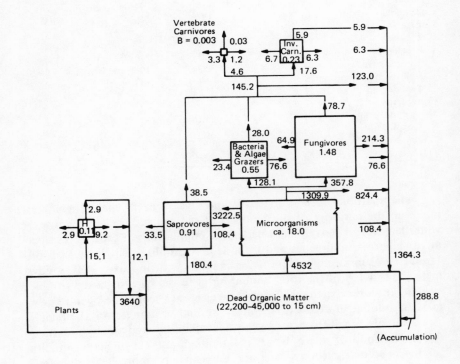

FIGURE 11-8. *The bioenergetic structure of the detritus-based trophic system in the coastal tundra at Barrow.*

produced poor or no growth only at low temperature (10 °C). Plant detritus, the food source of saprovores, contains little protein and consists largely of carbohydrate in the form of cellulose and other long-chain polysaccharides.

The quality of the diet may also provide an explanation for the relatively great abundance of prostigmatid compared with oribatid mites. Luxton's (1972) review of data for Oribatei indicates that approximately 25% are wholly (macrophytophages) and 50% are partially (panphytophages) dependent upon low-quality dead organic matter for food. In contrast, Prostigmata feed on microorganisms and on other animals and their eggs, a higher quality diet.

Larvae of the cranefly *Pedicia hannai* are the dominant soil carnivores in the coastal tundra at Barrow, followed by the predatory mites. Predatory beetles, Carabidae and Staphylinidae, were abundant only on the drier areas. Spiders were not accurately sampled and are not included in this analysis. The spider fauna is poorly developed, consisting almost entirely of small web-spinners of the family Linyphiidae that probably contribute minimally to energy flow. The total consumption by invertebrate carnivores of about 16.7 kJ m^{-2} yr^{-1} amounts to about 12% of the productivity and 27% of the average biomass of their prey, figures that indicate a modest level of predation.

The total consumption by invertebrates is about 700 kJ m^{-2} yr^{-1}. Consumption by carnivores represents energy consumed at least twice by animals. Subtracting this, the equivalent of about 35 g m^{-2} of input to the ecosystem passes through invertebrate animals each year, 34 g of this in the detritus-based trophic system. This is approximately 19% of the annual input, assuming an input of 190 g to the detritus-based system.

The fractions of consumption that appear as feces and as production remain within the detritus-based system. Feces and unharvested production are recycled through the dead organic matter pool (Heal and MacLean 1975). Through respiration, animals in the detritus-based trophic system are directly responsible for the loss of 128.5 kJ m^{-2} yr^{-1}, which is the equivalent of less than 7 g of input. Assuming that annual accumulation of organic matter is insignificant, 3.5% of the total annual input of 190 g m^{-2} is dissipated by respiration of invertebrates, and the remaining 96.5% by microbial respiration. Allowing for accumulation of up to 15 g organic matter m^{-2} yr^{-1} changes these figures only slightly, to 3.8% for animal respiration and 96.2% for microbial respiration. Invertebrate respiration varied between 65.3 kJ m^{-2} yr^{-1} in the low polygon rim and 242.3 kJ m^{-2} yr^{-1} in the adjacent trough, with the difference due primarily to Enchytraeidae; however, because of the relationship of invertebrate biomass to primary production (Figure 11-3a), it is unlikely that the proportionate contribution of invertebrates to total community respiration changed considerably between habitats.

TABLE 11-9 *Invertebrate Respiration and
Primary Production at a High Arctic
Tundra and North Temperate
Moorland Site*

	Invertebrate respiration (kJ m⁻² yr⁻¹)	Primary production (kJ m⁻² yr⁻¹)	IR/PP (%)
Devon Island, N.W.T., Canada			
Hummocky sedge–moss meadow	26.8	3,549	0.8
Cushion plant–lichen ridge	27.6	448	6.1
Moor House,U.K.			
Peat soils			
Blanket bog	352	12,351	2.8
Juncus squarrosus	829	14,962	5.5
Mineral soils			
Alluvial grassland	2263	9,790	23.1
Limestone grassland	1963	9,280	21.2

Source: Devon Island, Whitfield (1977); Moor House, Coulson
and Whittaker (1978).

Comparable data are available for high arctic tundra on Devon
Island, Canada, and for the tundra-like peat moorlands of the British
Isles (Table 11-9). Values for invertebrate respiration in two habitats at
Devon Island are about one-fifth the value reported here for the coastal
tundra. Primary production in the sedge–moss meadow at Devon Island
is about equivalent to that of the *Carex–Oncophorus* meadow of the Barrow area; thus, the estimated role of invertebrates in this habitat is much
smaller than we find in meadows of the coastal tundra of northern
Alaska. In the dry cushion plant–lichen community on Devon Island primary production is lower and invertebrates apparently play a greater direct role in community energetics.

Expressed as a proportion of primary production, invertebrate respiration in peat soils of the British moorland site is about the same as in
the arctic coastal tundra near Barrow. The higher invertebrate activity in
mineral soils results from the large populations of earthworms (Lumbricidae), which are scarce in peat soils. The difference between peat and
mineral soils is attributed to the low nutrient status of the vegetation and
resulting litter of peat soils (Coulson and Whittaker 1978), a situation
that may be shared with the coastal tundra ecosystem.

In Chapter 9 a theoretical estimate of annual production by microorganisms, based upon decomposition of the entire net primary production, was given as 75 g m^{-2} yr^{-1}. Using this estimate, the consumption by microbivores of 25 g m^{-2} yr^{-1} accounts for 33% of the annual production of microorganisms. If we hypothesize an annual accumulation of 10 g m^{-2} yr^{-1} and reduce the estimate of microbial production accordingly, estimated consumption by microbivores increases only slightly, to 35%. Alternatively, observed rates of decay indicated a maximum value of 90 g m^{-2} yr^{-1} for microbial production, which sets the level of consumption by microbivores at 28%.

Animal biomass and activity are strongly confined to the near-surface layers whereas microorganisms are more evenly distributed, at least through the organic layer. Overall, 71% of the invertebrate biomass occurs in the top 2.5 cm. Assuming 25% of the microbial biomass occurs there (Figure 8-4), the effect of invertebrate feeding activity is magnified nearly three-fold in the top 2.5 cm compared with estimates integrating over all depths. Thus, animals might consume an amount approximately equal to the annual microbial production in the top 2.5 cm. It is clear that, at least in the surface layers of the tundra, animal activity may exert a considerable influence upon microbial function, and hence upon the decomposition process. Below 5 cm depth the impact of animals is probably minimal.

THE ROLE OF SOIL INVERTEBRATES IN NUTRIENT CYCLES

Invertebrate production represents nutrients temporarily withdrawn from cycling and unavailable to plants, and biomass represents the amount of nutrients immobilized at any time. Since invertebrate biomass contains a number of important nutrients such as phosphorus and nitrogen in concentration much greater than either living plant tissue or detritus, these nutrients may be immobilized in amounts larger than dry matter or energy content might suggest. Can this amount be significant in ecosystem dynamics?

The density and surface concentration of soil invertebrates have previously been combined to express number of animals per unit volume of the soil. The maximum concentration, about 125 μg of biomass cm^{-3}, occurred in the top 2.5 cm of the polygon trough. The organic matter density (bulk density $\times$ percent organic matter) at the same place is 68 mg cm^{-3}. This value includes live plant parts, microorganisms, invertebrates, and dead organic matter. Thus, living invertebrates at their greatest average concentration represent less than 0.2% of the organic matter of the system. Even allowing for the approximately five-fold concentration of nitrogen and a three-fold concentration of phosphorus in animals relative to plant tissue (Coulson and Whittaker 1978), invertebrate biomass contains less than 1% of the nutrients of the system.

The high nutrient concentration of invertebrate biomass may be significant as a source of nutrients for microorganisms following death of the animal. Such a nutrient source might be sufficient to stimulate microbial decomposition of surrounding energy-rich but nutrient-poor organic matter. That is, local concentrations in an otherwise nutrient-poor environment may lead to a higher overall rate of decomposition.

For a brief period each summer the coastal tundra at Barrow is aswarm with adult insects, mainly Diptera, that have emerged from the soil to complete the life cycle. The emergence of the craneflies *P. hannai* and *T. carinifrons*, alone, represents 55 mg m^{-2} (Table 11-4); the total emergence of Diptera is, perhaps, twice this amount. Thus, each summer about 100 mg m^{-2}, including 1 mg of phosphorus and 10 mg of nitrogen, leaves the soil and becomes mobile over the tundra surface. This provides a considerable potential for nutrient transport.

It is likely that insect death and oviposition in most microtopographic units approximates emergence, resulting in no net movement. However, where insects develop in areas that are relatively uncommon and disperse in search of other similar areas, there is likely a net movement away from the preferred unit. This movement is increased when predators intercept dispersing individuals. Thus, it seems certain that there is a net movement of nutrients from pond sediments to surrounding tundra caused by the emergence of adult chironomids (midges), which are heavily preyed upon by terrestrial birds. This process would tend to reverse the movement of dissolved nutrients and detritus from the land surface into ponds with spring snowmelt each year. The net movement in any year is undoubtedly small, but accumulated over many years this mechanism may contribute to current patterns of nutrient distribution.

The action of soil saprovores in reducing the average particle size of litter, thereby increasing surface area available for attack by microorganisms, is frequently cited as an important factor in the decomposition process (van der Drift 1959, Crossley 1977, but see also Webb 1977). Given the estimated rate of consumption of detritus by saprovores, and even adding an additional amount for consumption of detritus by microbivores, it appears that less than 10% of the annual input of detritus is consumed by invertebrates each year. In contrast, where large earthworms dominate the fauna, as on the mineral soils at Moor House, consumption may approach the annual input of detritus (Satchell 1971).

In the coastal tundra at Barrow, the most important interaction of invertebrates in the decomposition process is their consumption of microorganisms and consequent effect upon the composition, biomass and activity of the microbial community. Direct evidence is scanty, but recent research suggests that the activity of soil invertebrates can significantly influence microbial decomposition, and that the magnitude of this effect is poorly represented by measures of direct energetic involvement (Chew 1974, Crossley 1977, Kitchell et al. 1979). Coleman et al. (1977) established soil microcosms containing bacteria as decomposers with and without amoebae and nematodes as grazers of the bacteria. Release of CO_2 and mineralization of N and P occurred more rapidly in the microcosms that included the grazers.

Parkinson et al. (1977) showed that selective grazing by Collembola influenced the growth and colonizing ability of competing fungal species, and that this effect was as marked at low experimental densities of Collembola as it was at higher densities. Addison and Parkinson (1978) found that addition of Collembola stimulated the release of carbon dioxide from tundra cores that had been sterilized, then inoculated with fresh litter and microorganisms. Addition of the saprovore species *Folsomia regularis* had a greater stimulatory effect than addition of the fungivore *Hypogastrura tullbergi* or of a mixture of the two Collembola species. In this regard, it may be significant that *Folsomia* species dominate the Collembola fauna of the coastal tundra ecosystem at Barrow.

Standen (1978) used litter bags to study the effect of soil fauna on decomposition of litter from a British peat moorland. Bags containing litter with either enchytraeid worms or tipulid larvae lost weight faster and showed a higher rate of oxygen uptake than did bags containing only the litter without animals. At Barrow, Douce (1976) compared the rate of weight loss of litter on control and chemically defaunated plots in polygon rim, basin, and trough habitats. Weight loss from litter was reduced on the defaunated plots. Similar results from a variety of other ecosystems were reviewed by Chew (1974) and Crossley (1977).

These data indicate that invertebrate activity stimulates the decomposition of organic matter. This is consistent with the correlation between invertebrate biomass and organic matter turnover rate. Because of the limited vertical distribution of invertebrates, any effect of their activity occurs only near the surface. The rate of microbial activity is also highest at the surface and drops off with depth because of the combined effects of lower temperature, poorer aeration, and reduced substrate quality. This produces an important interaction. A high rate of decomposition near the surface (to which invertebrates contribute) limits the proportion of the annual organic increment that reaches the lower depths, where its decomposition rate would be reduced. Anything that inhibits surface activity, such as reduced invertebrate populations, may allow material to reach the deeper layers, and thus will contribute to accumulation of organic matter and reduction of rates of nutrient cycling. The interaction of invertebrates and microorganisms in the near-surface layers may have an importance for overall ecosystem function that is beyond the proportion suggested by the amount of energy that is actually respired by animals.

ABUNDANCE, PRODUCTIVITY, AND
ENERGETICS OF AVIAN INSECTIVORES

Insectivorous birds are the top carnivores in the detritus-based trophic system. The avifauna of the coastal tundra at Barrow includes a large number of accidental or occasional breeding species; this probably results from the geography of northern Alaska (Pitelka 1974). Barrow lies at the apex of a triangle of land that concentrates birds that have made an error in navigation. The list of bird species recorded in the Barrow region includes 151 species, but only 22 of these are regarded as regular breeders (Table 11-10). This includes five species of waterfowl (loons and ducks), nine species of waders (plovers, sandpipers and phala-

TABLE 11-10   *Species of Birds Breeding Regularly in the Coastal Plain Tundra near Barrow*

Graviiformes
  Arctic loon — *Gavia arctica*
  Red-throated loon — *Gavia stellata*
Anseriformes
  Pintail — *Anas acuta*
  Oldsquaw — *Clangula hyemalis*
  Steller eider — *Polysticta stelleri*
Charadriiformes
  Golden plover — *Pluvialis dominica*
  Ruddy turnstone — *Arenaria interpres*
  Pectoral sandpiper — *Calidris melanotos*
  White-rumped sandpiper — *Calidris fuscicollis*
  Baird's sandpiper — *Calidris bairdii*
  Dunlin — *Calidris alpina*
  Semipalmated sandpiper — *Calidris pusilla*
  Western sandpiper — *Calidris mauri*
  Red phalarope — *Phalaropus fulicarius*
  Pomarine jaeger — *Stercorarius pomarinus*
  Parasitic jaeger — *Stercorarius parasiticus*
  Sabine gull — *Xema sabini*
  Arctic tern — *Sterna paradisaea*
Strigiformes
  Snowy owl — *Nyctea scandiaca*
Passeriformes
  Redpoll — *Carduelis flammea*
  Lapland longspur — *Calcarius lapponicus*
  Snow bunting — *Plectrophenax nivalis*

Source: After Pitelka (1974).

ropes), four gulls (including two jaegers and the arctic tern), the snowy owl, and three passerine species. Excluding the aquatic-feeding species, the terrestrial bird fauna consists of a group of carnivores (pomarine and parasitic jaegers, and snowy owl) that are conspicuous only in years when lemmings are abundant, and a large group of "insectivorous" birds.

The paucity of passerine species and abundance of waders contrasts sharply with temperate avifaunas. Of the three passerine species, the snow bunting is limited by lack of natural nesting cavities to areas around present or past human settlements, and the redpoll, a seed-eating finch, occurs sporadically in both time and space. Thus, the Lapland longspur is the only generally distributed passerine bird species of undisturbed tundra in the Barrow region.

The dominance of waders over passerines is limited to the northern Coastal Plain. Many more passerine species breed in the Foothills and the Brooks Range. This argues for the importance of ecological rather than biogeographic factors in limiting the diversity and composition of the breeding bird fauna of the arctic coastal tundra.

Studies on the birds of the Barrow area conducted for many years by F.A. Pitelka and his associates provide a firm foundation of information on natural history and breeding ecology. The present discussion will focus upon six species: the dunlin, pectoral sandpiper, Baird's sandpiper, semipalmated sandpiper, red phalarope and Lapland longspur. These six species are the major consumers of arthropods in the coastal tundra ecosystem. They form a guild of avian consumers linked to the detritus-based trophic system.

Phenology

The birds arrive on the tundra in early June, as the tundra is just beginning to emerge from the winter snow cover, and daily mean temperatures are still well below freezing. Establishment and defense of territories occurs as the snow melts; and courtship and nesting follow shortly. The median date of clutch completion falls on or before 15 June in both dunlin and Lapland longspurs (Table 11-11). On this date the tundra is normally about 50% snow covered (Chapter 2), and much of the exposed habitat is unavailable to feeding birds because of ponded meltwater. Breeding of other species follows shortly, with median dates of clutch completion falling within a two-week period. Except for the phalaropes, which are semi-aquatic, the early onset of egg-laying concentrates early season activities in areas of upland tundra.

Nesting synchrony within species is high. Custer and Pitelka (1977) found that the median date of egg-laying fell between 7 and 14 June, and followed the first by an average of only seven days in Lapland longspurs

TABLE 11-11 *Characteristics of Breeding Phenology, Density and Success for Avian Insectivores Breeding in the Barrow Region*

Species	Body weight (g wet wt)	Duration of residence (days)	Nesting density (nest ha⁻¹)	Median date of clutch completion	Incubation period (days)	Clutch size	Hatching success (%)	Fledging success (%)	Young fledged nest⁻¹	Young fledged ha⁻¹
Dunlin	♂ 55 ♀ 60	70 70	0.11 (0.07–0.14)[1]	12 June	22	3.95 (n = 55)	75 (n = 217)	(50)[2]	1.48	0.16
Baird's sandpiper	♂ 40 ♀ 45	50 30	0.18 (0.15–0.27)[1]	25 June	20.5	3.75 (n = 56)	49 (n = 210)	(50)[2]	0.92	0.17
Pectoral sandpiper	♂ 95 ♀ 65	25 55	0.09 (0.05–0.21)[1]	23 June	13.5	4.00 (n = 48)	63 (n = 192)	(50)[2]	1.30	0.12
Semipalmated sandpiper	♂ 25 ♀ 30	50 32	0.10 (0.06–0.14)[1]	20 June	20	(3.8)	(65)	44% of young hatched	1.1	0.11
Red phalarope	♂ 50 ♀ 55	50 20	0.12 (0.06–0.18)[1]	26 June	18–21	3.63 (n = 48)	56 (n = 174)	(50)[2]	1.02	0.12
Lapland longspur	♂ 28 ♀ 25	80 75	0.30 (0.12–0.88)[1]	15 June	12	5.06 (n = 251)	64 (n = 1244)	68% of young hatched (n = 792)	2.20	1.03

[1]Range of densities over years of measurement.
[2]Estimates used in the absence of data.

studied over seven seasons. Seastedt and MacLean (1979) found that no new male longspurs were successful in establishing a territory and obtaining a mate after 12 June, only eight days after the first arrival on the study area.

Incubation lasts from 12 days in Lapland longspurs to 22 days in dunlin (Table 11-11); thus, the peak of hatching occurs in late June in longspurs and in the first half of July in the wader species. The altricial longspur young remain in the nest for about eight days, during which they are fed and brooded by both adults. Young waders are very precocial. They usually abandon the nest within hours of hatching of the last egg, and they gather all of their own food; however, they are metabolically unable to maintain their own body temperature (Norton 1974) and require frequent brooding by adults (50 to 83% of the time during the first week for semipalmated sandpipers; Ashkenazie and Safriel 1979a). The young of both longspurs and waders appear on the tundra before the warmest weather of the season. A large proportion of the birds have left the tundra by the second week in August, when average temperatures are only slightly below the mid-July peak. Thus, avian activities are strongly skewed toward the early season and are not coincident with the warmest weather. Neither temperature nor length of the snow-free season can be considered major factors in the evolution of breeding phenology. It is more likely that the timing of breeding is determined by the emergence of adult Diptera.

Prior to the mass emergence of adult flies, adult birds feed heavily on dipteran larvae, which they capture by inserting the bill into the tundra. Young waders have growing, incompletely ossified bills. They are unable to probe into the tundra, and thus require surface-active prey for the first three to four weeks of life. The appearance of wader young closely follows the appearance of their prey. Longspur hatching precedes the emergence of adult Diptera, and larvae and pupae are the major prey fed to nestlings. The young leave the nest in early July, just as adult Diptera become abundant. Similarly, the abrupt decline in emergence of adult Diptera, which occurs sometime after mid-July, may limit the period in which newly hatched birds can forage successfully, and thus may be responsible for the synchrony of reproduction.

The phenological relationship of avian reproduction and insect emergence may help to explain an apparent paradox in incubation periods (Norton 1974). In dunlin both adults incubate, providing almost continuous attention to the eggs; incubation lasts about 22 days. In pectoral sandpipers, the eggs are slightly larger than those of dunlin; the female incubates alone and is present about 86% of the time, yet the incubation period is 19 to 20 days. Nest initiation is later in pectoral sandpipers than in dunlin, presumably because of the later snowmelt of the lowland meadows in which they feed. The shorter incubation period of pectoral sandpipers may have evolved to allow them to exploit the abundance of prey in lowland meadows while maintaining hatching at the optimal time of the season.

Use of Habitats and Food Habits

The bird species differ in their distribution over major habitat units (Figure 11-9) and their use of microhabitats within these (MacLean 1969, Custer 1974); however, there is considerable overlap in both habitat use and prey selection throughout the breeding season (Holmes and Pitelka 1968). Early in the season the birds make greatest use of upland habitats, with only pectoral sandpipers and red phalaropes making significant use of wet meadow and pond habitats. Longspurs feed mainly on seeds during the first ten days of June, and thus differ from the waders, but switch to larval Diptera once breeding commences (Custer and Pitelka 1978). All birds seem to feed preferentially along the edge of retreating snowfields, suggesting that insects just exposed are more easily located or captured than those that have achieved full activity in thawed tundra.

Territorial defense diminishes during incubation, and defense of the breeding territory ceases altogether when the young leave the nest in early July. The adults commonly lead the young from upland nesting habitats, which provide relatively little cover, to low-lying meadows, where vegetation provides greater cover from predators. It is unlikely that abundance of food is a serious factor influencing habitat choice at this time. Since emergence of adult insects is sensitive to weather, periods of food

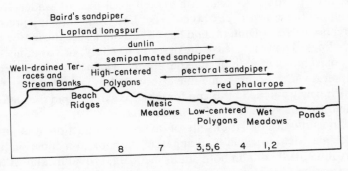

1. Carex–Oncophorus *meadow.*	5. *Basin of low-centered polygon.*
2. *Wet* Dupontia *meadow.*	6. *Rim of low-centered polygon.*
3. *Polygon trough.*	7. Carex–Poa *mesic meadow.*
4. *Moist* Dupontia *meadow.*	8. *High-centered polygon.*

FIGURE 11-9. *The distribution of preferred breeding habitat of birds along a mesotopographic gradient.*

scarcity may occur even during mid-July; however, such periods probably influence all habitats alike. Striking year-to-year differences in growth rates and survival of wader young appear to be closely related to weather conditions during this mid-summer period (Norton 1973, Myers and Pitelka 1979). Interspecific overlap in diet is greatest during this period of the season (Holmes and Pitelka 1968).

In August, after the period of adult insect abundance, dunlin and longspurs move back to upland tundra. Longspurs take large numbers of sawfly (Tenthredinidae) larvae and seeds, both items that are little used by the wader species. Dunlin feed on *Tipula* larvae and, if drying and exposure of pond margin sediments permit, on midge (Chironomidae) larvae. Holmes (1966) noted a segregation between adult and immature dunlin, the immatures making greater use of coastal, brackish lagoons.

In semipalmated and Baird's sandpipers the two adults share in incubation; however, females (occasionally males in *Calidris bairdii*) depart at or soon after the time of hatching, leaving only one adult to accompany the young. Adults, and then immatures, move to coastal lagoons as soon as the young become independent, and their southward migration begins soon thereafter.

In the polygamous pectoral sandpiper, females incubate alone; males form flocks in lowland marshes in late June and early July, and leave the tundra before the eggs hatch. Thus, male pectoral sandpipers that have migrated to arctic Alaska from southern South America remain on the tundra for a period of less than 30 days. The females remain with the young in July, but leave soon after the young become independent around the first of August. Flocks of immatures remain on the tundra throughout August, feeding mainly on pond-margin chironomid larvae.

In some years large numbers of immature pectoral sandpipers, clearly representing far more than local production of young, appear on the tundra in the Barrow area in August. Similarly, in some years large flocks of immature long-billed dowitchers (*Limnodromus scolopaceus*) may be found in August, although dowitchers breed only occasionally and sparsely in the immediate Barrow area. There is thus a premigratory coastward movement of shorebirds from inland breeding areas that contributes to the use of resources of the coastal tundra in August.

In the sex-reversed polyandrous red phalarope, females form flocks and depart soon after all nests are completed, and males incubate the eggs alone (Schamel and Tracy 1977). Coastal lagoons and even the coast of the open ocean are used as premigratory staging areas by red phalaropes, and large flocks may remain throughout August and even into September.

Although a variety of tundra arthropods appear in the diets of these birds, the majority of breeding activities are supported by larval and adult Diptera, especially of the three cranefly species, *Tipula carinifrons*,

Prionocera gracilistyla, and *Pedicia hannai* (Holmes and Pitelka 1968, Custer and Pitelka 1978). *T. carinifrons,* alone, makes up between 40 and 72% of the diet of adult longspurs between 10 June and 20 July (Custer and Pitelka 1978), and over 50% of the food fed to nestlings (Seastedt and MacLean 1979). Overall, about 40% of the longspur diet consists of *T. carinifrons.* Dunlin are almost entirely dependent upon *T. carinifrons* (Holmes 1966), and both Baird's and pectoral sandpipers feed largely upon larvae of this cranefly in June. Pectoral sandpipers feed more in lowland meadows, and consequently take more larvae of *Pedicia hannai* and *Prionocera gracilistyla* than do the other sandpiper species. Semipalmated sandpipers differ from the other sandpipers in specializing upon the smaller larvae of Chironomidae throughout the season. Overlap in diet between species is greatest in early June, when feeding sites are limited, and in mid- to late-July, when food is maximally available (Holmes and Pitelka 1968, Custer and Pitelka 1978).

Density and Reproductive Success

Both density and breeding success of these birds differ between years and between areas of the coastal tundra, with at least part of the variation due to differences in food supply. Average nesting density of the five wader species varied from 0.09 nest ha^{-1} in the pectoral sandpiper to 0.18 nest ha^{-1} in Baird's sandpiper (Table 11-11); however, these average values obscure both yearly and spatial variation. Baird's and semipalmated sandpipers occurred abundantly in census plots adjacent to coastal lagoons; dunlin and pectoral sandpipers were scarce or absent from these areas. Pectoral sandpipers are particularly variable in nesting density from year to year. Holmes (1966) found from 0 to 27 nests in a 40-ha study plot censused each season from 1960 to 1963. Average density varied between 0.02 and 0.20 nest ha^{-1} in the four years (1969–1972) included in this analysis. In contrast, nesting density of dunlin is more stable, varying from 0.07 to 0.14 nest ha^{-1} between 1968 and 1972 (Norton 1974). Pitelka et al. (1974) argued that some of the sandpipers, notably the pectoral sandpiper, have an "opportunistic" social system that allows maximum reproduction in favorable years and places; others, such as the dunlin, use a more "conservative" social system that provides for a modest level of reproduction in all years.

The waders are determinate layers. The vast majority of nests contain four eggs, with some tendency for clutches laid very late in the season (usually replacement clutches) to be smaller. Hatching success varied considerably between species, from 49% in Baird's sandpiper to 75% in dunlin (Table 11-11). Most egg loss was caused by predation from jaegers and least weasels. Baird's sandpipers, which suffer the greatest losses, nest in the most exposed sites. Given this strong selection pressure, the continued use of exposed nesting sites by Baird's sandpipers at Barrow seems paradoxical. The solution to the paradox may lie in the lack of tenacity in this species, indicated by the paucity of return sightings of the many breeding birds and juveniles banded in the Barrow area.

Soon after hatching, adults may lead the chicks a distance of up to 2 to 3 km from the nest site (Ashkenazie and Safriel 1979a); thus, broods are difficult to follow, and data on survival of young are rarely collected. Safriel (1975), however, was able to follow the fate of 39 broods of semipalmated sandpipers, and found a mean of 1.74 young fledged per brood, for a success rate of 44%. As with eggs, most losses of juveniles were attributed to predation.

The average density of a population of longspurs studied over a seven-year period (1967–1973) was 0.47 nest ha^{-1} (Custer and Pitelka 1977), a value well above the wader species. Density was highest (0.82 and 0.88 nest ha^{-1}) in 1967 and 1968, but dropped steadily to a low of 0.12 nest ha^{-1} in 1972. The population showed some recovery in 1973 and 1975 (Seastedt and MacLean 1979). In longspurs, year-to-year variation in productivity of nesting habitat cannot be detected at the time of territory establishment because most of the ground is still covered by snow; hence, territory size and nesting density are related to average or "expected" productivity of the habitat (Seastedt and MacLean 1979). Nesting success should be more responsive than nesting density to year-to-year variation in habitat productivity. The decline in nesting density of longspurs recorded between 1968 and 1972, then, should reflect changes in the size of the potential breeding population, as influenced, in part, by breeding success in preceding years (Figure 11-10). Since the study area used by Custer and Pitelka was placed in optimal longspur habitat, a slightly more conservative estimate of 0.30 nest ha^{-1} is used for the area as a whole (Table 11-11).

Lapland longspurs are indeterminate layers, and clutches of four, five, and six eggs are common. The modal clutch size, five eggs, occurred in 45% of the nests examined. Mean clutch size was 5.06 eggs, and varied between only 4.76 and 5.50 between years (Custer and Pitelka 1977). Over this period as a whole, 64% of the eggs hatched and 68% of the chicks survived to fledging, about eight days after hatching. Thus, the average female produced about 2.2 fledged young.

The occurrence of starved nestlings in longspur nests after some of the young have fledged indicates that food supply can influence reproductive success; however, only 3.7% of all nestlings observed over the seven-year period died of starvation. Loss to starvation was greatest (7.1%) in the very cold summer of 1969.

By far the major source of reproductive failure was predation; 22.3% of all eggs were taken by predators prior to hatching, and 22.7%

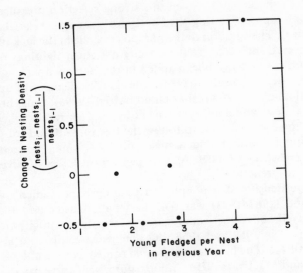

FIGURE 11-10. *Relationship of nesting density and breeding success during previous year. (Data from Custer and Pitelka 1977.)*

of chicks were lost before fledging. Predation accounted for 73% and 72% of losses of eggs and nestlings, respectively, and for most of the variance in reproductive success (Figure 11-10). The decline in nesting density from 1968 to 1972 was attributed to a sequence of years with heavy predation. As with the waders, the major predators upon eggs and nestlings are pomarine and parasitic jaegers and least weasels. Since the densities of these predators are primarily determined by density of lemmings (Chapter 10), the reproductive success of insectivorous birds may be determined primarily by events in the herbivore-based trophic system.

Energetics and Impact Upon Prey Populations

Norton (1974, West and Norton 1975) used gas exchange techniques to study the bioenergetics of sandpipers breeding at Barrow. An alternative time–energy budget approach was used by Custer (1974) on Lapland longspurs and by Ashkenazie and Safriel (1979b) on semipalmated sandpipers. Energy budgets calculated for semipalmated sandpipers using these alternative approaches yielded virtually identical estimates.

Norton found that the temperatures ordinarily encountered by the birds during the summer season are below thermoneutrality, so that energy must be expended for thermoregulation throughout the season, and particularly in early June. Various energy-demanding processes and activities—territorial defense and display, egg formation, incubation, care and brooding of chicks, molt (in dunlin and longspurs), and pre-migratory fat deposition—are distributed through the season. This led Norton (1974) to suggest that the daily energy requirement for maintenance plus productive activities remains near the maximum metabolic rate throughout the period of residence on the tundra.

Differences among species in the energy requirement for reproduction stem primarily from differences in body size and in duration of residence on the tundra (Table 11-12). Energy required per nesting attempt (Figure 11-11) is greatest in pectoral sandpipers and dunlin, and least in semipalmated sandpipers; however, when differences in nesting density are included to estimate total energy removed from the tundra (Table

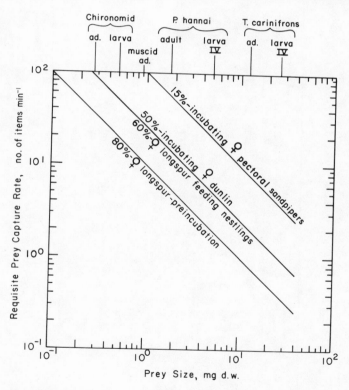

FIGURE 11-11. *The requisite rate of prey capture (items per minute of foraging) to satisfy daily energy requirements for birds with different energy requirements and different proportions of the day available for foraging.*

TABLE 11-12 *Energetic Characteristics of Avian Insectivores of the Barrow Region*

Species		Adult[1] net energy requirement (kJ day⁻¹)	Adult residence (bird-days ha⁻¹)	Adult net energy requirement (kJ ha⁻¹)	Gross adult energy requirement (kJ ha⁻¹)	Gross energy of chick growth (kJ chick⁻¹)	Gross energy of chicks (kJ ha⁻¹)	Gross energy of post-fledging young (kJ ha⁻¹)	Total gross energy [kJ (nesting attempt)⁻¹]	Total gross energy (kJ ha⁻¹)
Dunlin	♂	280	7.7	2160	2879	4750	1160	1256	76,625	8450
	♀	306	7.7	2352	3135					(5440–10,500)
Baird's sandpiper	♂	218	9.0	1959	2611	3440	854	209	30,467	5482
	♀	251	5.4	1356	1808					(4478–8316)
Pectoral sandpiper	♂	460	2.3	1038	1381	6863	1168	2720†	84,956	7638
	♀	360	5.0	1783	2377					(3910–17,500)
Semipalmated sandpiper	♂	163	5.0	816	1088	2063	368	146	23,896	2390
	♀	184	3.2	590	787					(1360–3323)
Red phalarope	♂	(260)	6.0	1557	2076	(4604)	841	251	33,900	4068
	♀	(280)	2.4	674	900					(2034–6102)
Lapland longspur	♂	159	24	3817	5089	1448	1180	4428	51,060	15,350
	♀	155	22.5	3486	4645					(6140–45,025)

* Data from Norton (1973), Custer (1974) and West and Norton (1975).
† 1046 local and 1674 wanderers.

454

11-12), the average value for longspurs is almost twice that of the next species, the dunlin, and accounts for 35% of the energy removed from the tundra by the complex of avian insectivores.

The total food requirement for these birds (4.35 kJ m^{-2} yr^{-1}) amounts to only 3% of the productivity of invertebrates in the detritus-based food chain, which suggests a modest intensity of predation; however, a large proportion of invertebrate productivity is accounted for by taxa, particularly Enchytraeidae, that are not eaten by the birds. It appears that about 40% of the total consumption by avian insectivores is supported by the cranefly species *Tipula carinifrons*, and about 60% by the three cranefly species. Thus, about 35% of the annual production of *T. carinifrons*, and 23% of total cranefly production, is taken by avian predators.

The annual emergence of adult craneflies amounts to about 35 mg m^{-2} in *T. carinifrons* and 20 mg m^{-2} in *P. hannai*, and is largely confined to a three-week period. MacLean and Pitelka (1971) recorded the median 67% of the total captures within a period of 5.3 to 11.6 days for *T. carinifrons*, and within 3.8 to 6.3 days for *P. hannai*. Thus, during this peak period emergence of each species is on the order of 3 mg m^{-2} day^{-1}.

During this period 66% of the diet of adult dunlin and 79% of the diet of juvenile dunlin consists of adult tipulids (Holmes 1966). In order to satisfy the gross energy requirement of two adults plus three juvenile dunlin (3.95 eggs clutch $^{-1}$ × 75% hatching success) at these proportions, 52 g of adult craneflies would be required each day, the equivalent of the total emergence of adult *Tipula carinifrons* and *Pedicia hannai* from 9600 m^2. At 0.11 dunlin nest ha^{-1}, even at the peak of emergence dunlin alone consume about 11% of the daily emergence of craneflies. Each longspur family (two adults plus an average of 3.25 chicks hatched per nest) requires about 55 grams of prey each day. In early July, adult craneflies compose about 70% of the diet (Custer and Pitelka 1978). This removes another 11.6 g ha^{-1} day^{-1} or 19% of the peak emergence. The addition of other avian insectivore species may raise the daily intake above 40% of the peak emergence of adult craneflies. It is easy to appreciate the impact that these predators must have, particularly upon adult insects that emerge into less than peak populations, when loss to predation must approach 100%.

Earlier, I estimated the mortality of cranefly larvae prior to pupation at 134 mg m^{-2} for *T. carinifrons* and 120 mg m^{-2} for *P. hannai*. Over the season, 76% of the diet of adult dunlin consists of larvae of *T. carinifrons*. This results in a consumption of 202 g of *T. carinifrons* larvae ha^{-1}, or 15% of estimated larval mortality. Addition of other avian species might double this value. Predation by birds is heavily concentrated on fourth instar larvae; mortality at earlier stages of development must be due to other causes.

Varying amounts of time are available to the birds for foraging, depending upon the time demands of other activities, notably incubation. Female pectoral sandpipers incubate their eggs 85% of the time (Norton 1972), leaving no more than 15% of the day for foraging. They must obtain food at a rate of about 100 mg dry wt min^{-1} during foraging bouts. This might be satisfied by taking about 100 chironomid larvae, 20 *P. hannai* larvae, or 4 larvae of *T. carinifrons* per minute (Figure 11-10). The advantage of feeding on the large cranefly larvae is clear. Female dunlin have a similar energy demand, but by sharing incubation with the males they have much more time available for foraging, and their requisite rate of prey capture is about one-fourth that of the female pectoral sandpiper during incubation.

Shortly after arrival female longspurs forage about 80% of the day (Custer 1974), and must find food at a rate of about 10 mg dry wt min^{-1}. During this period longspurs feed on seeds, Collembola, and small chironomid larvae, items too small to be used by other species with higher energy requirements, or by longspurs later in the season when time available for foraging is reduced.

Thus, as is so often the case in studying animal populations, the impact of avian predators stated in relation to the total energy budget of the ecosystem appears small (Figure 11-8); however, because of the concentration of predation upon Diptera and particularly upon the craneflies, avian predation may have a large influence as a force in the evolution of life cycles and in the reproduction and population dynamics of Diptera populations.

SUMMARY

The coastal tundra ecosystem supports abundant populations of Enchytraeidae, Collembola, and Diptera, modest populations of Acari, and small populations of Nematoda. Soil invertebrates are concentrated near the surface of the tundra, where the number of individuals per cubic centimeter can be quite high. Large differences in abundance are found among the various microtopographic units that compose the coastal tundra. These differences are related to soil moisture, aeration, and annual input of detritus. Both invertebrate abundance and biomass and plant production are inversely correlated with accumulated soil organic matter.

Tundra soil invertebrates have long life cycles, often extending over several seasons. Craneflies require four years to complete larval development and their ratio of annual production to average biomass is consequently small.

The energetics of the detritus-based trophic system in the coastal ecosystem is dominated by Enchytraeidae. The fauna is lacking in large, abundant saprovores, and microbivory is the most important trophic function of soil invertebrates. Invertebrate respiration accounts for about 130 kJ m^{-2} yr^{-1}, which is 3.5% of the annual input of detritus. Consumption of microorganisms is greater than average biomass and accounts for 33 to 37% of estimated microbial production. Near the tundra surface the entire annual production of microorganisms may be consumed by invertebrate microbivores. Evidence suggests that grazing upon detritus and microorganisms by soil invertebrates stimulates the decomposition of organic matter and accelerates the turnover of energy and cycling of mineral nutrients in the ecosystem.

Soil invertebrate populations, especially Diptera, support an abundant and diverse community of breeding birds; four sandpiper species, the red phalarope, and the Lapland longspur are the most important of these. Bird breeding is timed so that the young can feed on the adult Diptera that emerge in early and mid-July. In June and August dipteran larvae, especially those of craneflies, are the most important prey. Energy requirements are determined by body size and duration of residence on the tundra. When breeding density is also considered, longspurs are the most important consumers of tundra arthropods. Birds may consume 35% of the annual production of the cranefly *Tipula carinifrons*, and 50% of the peak emergence of adult craneflies. This level of predation must influence the evolution of life cycles and contemporary population dynamics of tundra Diptera.

12

Carbon and Nutrient Budgets and Their Control in Coastal Tundra

F. S. Chapin III, P. C. Miller,
W. D. Billings, and P. I. Coyne

INTRODUCTION

Arctic tundra ecosystems are characterized by low productivity, slow energy flow, slow nutrient cycling, and, in many cases, peat accumulation, despite a diversity of parent material and variable species composition (Billings and Mooney 1968, Bliss et al. 1973, Rosswall and Heal 1975, Dowding et al. 1981). These common features derive in some fashion from the low annual solar irradiance and consequent low temperatures that prevail at high latitudes. Earlier chapters have shown that most organisms inhabiting the wet meadow tundra have adaptations that minimize the effect of low temperature upon vital processes. How then do low irradiance and associated low temperature help to generate the unique characteristics of coastal tundra, and to what extent are other factors responsible? In this chapter we summarize, from information presented in earlier chapters, pool sizes and average annual fluxes of carbon and selected inorganic nutrients. Through comparisons with other ecosystems we attempt to identify those aspects of energy flow and nutrient cycling that are peculiar to the Arctic and consider the nature of causal links with climate.

STANDING CROPS

Two sets of standing crop data are presented for Barrow. Pool sizes and fluxes at the intensive study site in a *Carex–Oncophorus* meadow were measured in considerable detail in 1970 and 1971(Figures 12-1, 12-2 and 12-3). Biomass was also measured in 1972 in all major microtopographic units and then weighted by relative abundance to give average pool sizes (Chapter 3, Table 12-2). The *Carex–Oncophorus* meadow values are based upon more thorough study and may thus be more accurate, whereas the data for the mosaic of wet meadow vegetation types are more representative of the coastal tundra of northern Alaska. Unless otherwise specified (e.g. Table 12-2) data refer to the *Carex–Oncophorus* meadow.

Although relatively little carbon is fixed by tundra vegetation in any one year, up to 20 kg m^{-2} of carbon has accumulated in the top 20 cm of tundra (Table 12-1). This is similar to the carbon content of other wet tundras (17 to 32 kg m^{-2}), tropical rain forests (17 to 34 kg m^{-2}) and a red alder shrub stand (20 kg m^{-2}). It is greater than the carbon accumulation in grassland (3 kg m^{-2}), chaparral (6 kg m^{-2}), and a Douglas fir forest (12 kg m^{-2}) (Table 12-1). Many tundra communities, including those near Barrow, have buried organic horizons preserved in the permafrost. Temperate communities with their deeper soil profiles often contain considerable carbon which has been leached from upper horizons and thus also have more total carbon than is shown in Table 12-1. Because tundra constitutes a significant fraction (5%) of the total terrestrial landscape (Whittaker 1975) and because wet and moist tundra (including coastal and tussock tundra) make up a substantial proportion of all tundra communities, a major alteration of the carbon balance of tundra could significantly modify the global carbon balance.

Tundra differs from most other ecosystems in that the bulk of its carbon is contained in soil, rather than in live biomass (Table 12-1; Schlesinger 1977). At Barrow over 96% of the organic carbon is bound in dead organic matter or peat, and only 1.7% or less is in living organisms. The remainder is dead plant parts. In contrast, 50 to 75% of the organic carbon in forests and 10% of the carbon in grasslands is in living organisms (Table 12-1). This implicates decomposer organisms as a major bottleneck for carbon and energy flow at Barrow and other wet tundra sites. Like the tundra, mid-latitude grasslands contain a substantial proportion of carbon in dead organic matter. But in grasslands, roots penetrate 1 to 2 m so that carbon from dead roots and associated microorganisms is distributed throughout the soil (Weaver 1958, Clark 1977). In contrast, tundra soils typically exhibit a distinct surface horizon 10 to 20 cm thick, in which the percentage of organic matter is 90 to 96%. Such high concentrations of organic matter are associated with low pH and consequently with reduced nutrient availability, as discussed in Chapters 7 and 8.

Most of the carbon in living organisms is in plants, and most of this is below ground in roots and rhizomes (Figure 12-1, Table 12-2). The average aboveground vascular standing crop for the coastal tundra at Barrow is 24 g C m^{-2} (Table 12-2), half that of the intensive study site (Figure 12-1). The greater vascular aboveground standing crop in the

TABLE 12-1 *Total Quantity of Carbon, Nitrogen, and Phosphorus to a Depth of 20 cm Present in Various Ecosystems and the Percentage of Each Element Contained in Vegetation*

Ecosystem	Latitude	Site	Total quantity in system (g m^{-2})*			Percent in vegetation			Reference
			C	N	P	C	N	P	
Wet meadow	75°	Devon Island, Canada	17,435	1170	81.1	4.7	2.0	2.3	Babb and Whitfield (1977); Muc (1977)
Polar desert	75°	Devon Island, Canada	4,936	158	15.4	1.2	1.4	1.0	Babb and Whitfield (1977); Svoboda (1977)
Wet meadow tundra	71°	Barrow, Alaska	19,768	960	63.2	1.6	0.9	1.3	This volume
Spot tundra	71°	Agapa, U.S.S.R.	—	378	33.5	—	4.3	4.5	Dowding et al. (1981)
Mire	68°	Abisko, Sweden	9,446	225	10.9	4.2	4.0	—	Rosswall et al. (1975)
Tussock tundra	65°	Eagle Creek, Alaska	18,767	964	48.7	0.6	0.4	0.3	Chapin and Van Cleve (1978)
Wet meadow	60°	Hardangervidda, Norway	—	1014	—	—	2.1	—	Østbye (1975)
Grassland	60 °S	Signy Island	—	829	269	—	0.8	2.2	Dowding et al. (1981)
Calluna bog	55°	Moor House, U.K.	—	466	—	—	2.7	—	Dowding et al. (1981)
Grassland	54 °S	Macquarie Island	24,640	1869	—	4.8	15.6	—	Jenkin (1975)
Tussock grassland	54 °S	South Georgia	—	1260	—	—	2.3	—	Lewis Smith and Walton (1975)
Peat bog	54°	Glenamoy, Ireland	—	330	30	—	2.8	1.3	Moore et al. (1975)
Subalpine heath	47°	Washington							
a) residual soil			13,379	979	—	2.2	0.5	—	Grier (1973)
b) organic soil			32,096	1276	—	2.7	0.9	—	

TABLE 12-1 *(cont'd)*.

Ecosystem	Latitude	Site	Total quantity in system (g m⁻²)*			Percent in vegetation			Reference
			C	N	P	C	N	P	
Grassland									
Cottonwood	43°	South Dakota	—	275	—	—	4.0	—	Bokhari and Singh (1975)
Pawnee	40°	Colorado	3,204	273	—	9.8	3.2	—	Clark (1977)
Osage	36°	Oklahoma	—	261	—	—	2.1	—	
Temperate pasture	—	—	—	—	139	—	—	4.2	Wilkinson and Lowrey (1973)
Grassland	23°	Ratlam, India	—	336	—	—	1.4	—	Billore and Mall (1976)
Red alder (20 yr)	65°	Fairbanks, Alaska	4,276	154	146	76.1	36.0	3.3	Van Cleve et al. (1971)
									Van Cleve and Viereck (1972)
Chaparral	32°	San Diego, California	5,750	—	—	30.4	—	—	Mooney (1977)
Red alder (35 yr)	46°	Cascades, Washington	19,527	701	—	49.3	9.9	—	Cole et al. (1977)
Temperate deciduous forest (50 yr)	44°	Hubbard Brook, New Hampshire	—	179	—	—	29.7	—	Likens et al. (1977)
Temperate deciduous forest (48 yr)		Germany	11,735	—	—	—	—	—	Olson (1963)
Douglas fir forest (35 yr)	46°	Cascades, Washington	12,276	160	166	73.7	20.4	4.0	Cole et al. (1977)
Oak forest	35°	Oklahoma	12,884	250	37.7	75.0	42.3	25.2	Johnson and Risser (1974)
Tropical rain forest	18°	El Verde, Puerto Rico	16,966	—	—	64.1	—	16.7	Odum (1970)

*Multiply by 10 to obtain kg ha⁻¹.

461

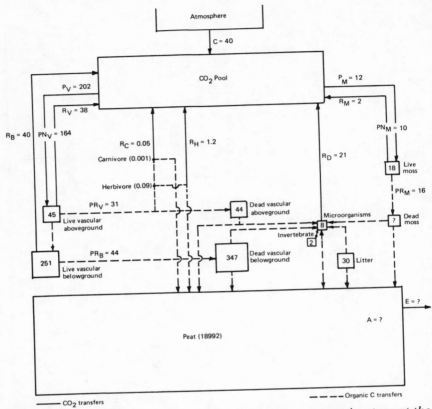

FIGURE 12-1. *Carbon budget of the wet meadow vegetation type at the intensive study site to a depth of 20 cm. The number in each box is the pool size of carbon for that compartment expressed in g C m⁻² to a depth of 20 cm. We assume that carbon constitutes 44% of organic material, the average measured at another Alaskan tundra site (Chapin et al. 1979). The area of each box is proportional to its compartment size. Values next to arrows indicate the annual carbon fluxes between respective compartments (g C m⁻² yr⁻¹). P_V and P_M = net daytime photosynthesis of vascular plants and moss, respectively; PN_V and PN_M = net annual carbon exchange between atmosphere and aboveground vascular plants and mosses, respectively; R_B, R_D, R_H, R_C = respiration of vascular belowground, decomposers, herbivores and carnivores, respectively; PR_B, PR_V, PR_M = net annual production of vascular belowground, vascular aboveground and mosses, respectively; C = net carbon flux from atmosphere to community; A = net annual accumulation; E = export in runoff. Animal compartment sizes assume peak lemming abundance to indicate maximal animal role. All other data were collected in 1970 and 1971, years of low lemming abundance. All values shown were obtained independently by direct field measurements, extrapolated to an annual basis, and corrected for light and temperature. Values for vascular plant and litter carbon are calculated from Tieszen (1972b) and Dennis (1977), moss carbon from Oechel and Sveinbjörnsson (1978), and soil carbon from Flint and Gersper (1974). References for transfer values are given in Table 12-4.*

TABLE 12-2 *Standing Crops of Carbon in the Coastal Tundra at Barrow*

	g C m^{-2}	Chapter
Carnivores	0.001	12
Herbivores	0.12 (max)	10
Standing dead	16	3
Litter	40	3
Moss	51	3
Algae	0.15	8
Lichens	0.12	3
Aboveground vascular	24	3
Belowground vascular	374	3
Nematodes	0.01	11
Enchytraeids	0.95	11
Acarina	0.051	11
Collembola	0.16	11
Fungi	2.0	8
Bacteria	6.0	8
Total live plant	461	3
Soil organic matter	18992	12 (Fig. 12-1)
TOTAL	19518	

Note: The moist meadow is a mosaic of vegetation types. Standing crops of each vegetation type are weighted by relative area (Chapter 3). Localized variations in these values are discussed in the text.

intensive study site (Figure 12-1). The greater vascular aboveground standing crop in the intensive site in 1971 (Figure 12-1) than in a variety of other *Carex–Oncophorus* meadows in 1972 (Table 3-2) suggests substantial yearly and/or microtopographic differences in production. Estimates of belowground standing crop range from 207 to 574 g C m^{-2}, depending upon the microtopographic unit (Chapters 3 and 6). The above-to belowground ratio of live vascular plants is about 1:10 (Dennis and Johnson 1970, Dennis 1977), similar to that found in a shortgrass prairie (Clark 1977). The carbon in moss at Barrow (51 g C m^{-2}) is twice that in vascular aboveground parts. Algae and lichens are less important components of biomass (Table 12-2). Standing dead and litter constitute a larger standing crop (56 g C m^{-2}) than the live vascular material above ground and retard nutrient cycling by altering the radiation regime within the canopy (Chapter 3) and by directly immobilizing nutrients (Chapters 8 and 9).

Bacteria constitute the largest standing crop of decomposer organisms (6.0 g C m^{-2}), three times that of fungi, although the balance between fungal and bacterial biomass varies strikingly with habitat and soil depth (Chapter 8). Soil invertebrates account for 1.8 g C m^{-2} (Chapter

11). The standing crop of lemmings, the only major herbivore, ranges from 0.00002 to 0.12 g C m⁻², depending upon the stage in the lemming cycle. Carnivorous birds attain a maximum standing crop of only 1.4×10^{-6} g C m⁻². The small size of the herbivore-based relative to the saprovore-based trophic system emphasizes the importance of below-ground interactions in the Barrow region.

The amounts of nitrogen and phosphorus in the coastal tundra at Barrow are comparable to those in other ecosystems (Table 12-1). In fact, tundra communities generally have more accumulated nitrogen (960 g N m⁻² at Barrow) than do temperate systems, including grasslands (270 g N m⁻²), alder shrub (700 g N m⁻²), Douglas fir forest (250 g N m⁻²), and oak forest (250 g N m⁻²). The parent materials of tundra soils at Barrow are not unusually phosphorus-deficient, because they are derived largely from marine sediments (Chapter 1). Limitation of primary production by nitrogen and phosphorus (Chapter 5) is thus not a result of small quantities in the system but rather of their slow rate of cycling. It should be noted that in tundra permafrost limits the quantity of nutrients available for exploitation whereas deeper soil horizons often play an important role in long-term replenishment in temperate and tropical ecosystems. As with carbon, the proportion of nutrients in the living components of the tundra system is quite small, approximately 1% in the case of nitrogen and phosphorus. This is typical of wet tundra (e.g. Babb and Whitfield 1977, Dowding et al. 1981) and differs from forests, where the biota constitute a significant reservoir of nutrients (Table 12-1).

Tundra thus appears to represent an end-point on the latitudinal spectrum by having the smallest proportion of the system's nutrient capital tied up in live biomass. Ovington (1968), Marks and Bormann (1972), and Whittaker et al. (1979) have pointed out the importance of vegetation as a nutrient reservoir that retains nutrients within the system by absorption from soil and internal recycling. In the tundra it is primarily the dead soil organic matter that serves this function by structurally binding a large proportion of the nutrients, by providing exchange sites for cations that otherwise would move through the soil during runoff, and by physically preventing thermokarst (thawing and subsidence) and erosion of the underlying mineral soils.

The distribution of nitrogen and phosphorus among biomass compartments follows a pattern similar to that of carbon. However, living soil organisms, microbes plus invertebrates, contain 8% of the nitrogen and 18% of the phosphorus, but only 2.5% of the carbon in living material. The live belowground vegetation contains almost 80% of the carbon but only 68% of the nitrogen and less than 60% of the phosphorus in living material. Thus, soil organisms are more concentrated sources of nutrients than are plants or plant-derived detritus, and form the major avenue of nutrient and energy flow through the saprovore-based trophic

TABLE 12-3 *Distribution of Carbon and Nutrient Pools in Vascular Plants on 4 August, Time of Maximum Aboveground Biomass in the Intensive Study Site*

| Plant part | Nutrient (g m^{-2}) | | | | | |
	C	N	P	K	Ca	Fe
Shoot	44.7	1.79	0.12	0.90	0.17	0.01
Stem base	37.4	1.18	0.10	0.08	0.29	0.41
Rhizome	38.7	0.90	0.10	0.06	0.24	0.82
Root	174.5	4.71	0.40	0.11	1.92	6.12
Total	295.3	8.58	0.71	1.15	2.65	7.36
Percent belowground	85	79	84	22	92	100

system (Chapter 11). The bulk of the nutrient pools of each trophic level occur below ground. Except for potassium, 80% or more of all vascular plant nutrient pools also are localized below ground (Table 12-3). Animal nutrient pools are concentrated below ground and are associated with turnover of organic matter. Even during lemming population highs, 3 to 10 times more nutrients are present in soil invertebrates than in lemmings (Figure 12-2).

AVERAGE ANNUAL FLUXES

Carbon Budget

During the growing season, the long period of daylight compensates for low sun angle and consequent low light intensities, so that during July the total daily input of photosynthetically active radiation is similar in arctic and in temperate ecosystems (Billings and Mooney 1968). The vegetation is seldom light-saturated and captures more than 1% of the available energy in July (Chapter 4), an efficiency comparable to or higher than that of most other natural communities (Ricklefs 1973). Aboveground plant parts maintain a positive carbon balance 24 hours a day during most of the growing season (Chapter 4), and 81% of the photosynthate is converted to aboveground biomass or translocated below ground. This aboveground net production efficiency is higher than that of most temperate communities (Ricklefs 1973). Because of the minor amount of dark respiration and the high photosynthetic and net production efficiencies, relative production rates (g g^{-1} day^{-1}) for the coastal tundra at Barrow are similar to rates observed at much higher temperatures in the shortgrass prairie (Chapter 5). However, at Barrow the growing season is short, and 90% of the aboveground vascular biomass senesces each fall. Consequently, the tundra exhibits a small standing crop of photosynthetic tissue. The net quantity of carbon fixed by photosynthesis at Barrow (174 g m^{-2} season^{-1}; Figure 12-1) is about half the quantity fixed by a shortgrass prairie. This corresponds to a Barrow growing season which is half as long as that in the prairie (Coleman et al. 1976). It thus appears that the annual carbon input into the coastal tundra ecosystem at Barrow is limited not so much by light and temperature effects upon photosynthesis as by the shortness of the growing season, which in turn limits the standing crop of photosynthetic tissue (Miller et al. 1976). Carbon flux through the tundra at Barrow is slow. Less than 1% of the ecosystem carbon pool turns over annually. This contrasts sharply with tropical systems, where 40% of the organic carbon in a rain forest is fixed and respired each year (calculated from Odum 1970). Radiocarbon dating of surface and buried organic matter from soils in the Barrow region yields ages of as much as 10,000 years (Brown 1965). These suggest that there are large pools of soil organic matter with very slow turnover rates and other pools that turn over much more rapidly than the ecosystem average, as demonstrated in temperate and tropical soils (Jenkinson and Rayner 1977, Jenkinson and Ayanaba 1977).

The partitioning of photosynthetic carbon and its subsequent loss in respiration emphasize the belowground nature of the system. Of the 214 g m^{-2} of total carbon fixed annually (total net daytime photosynthesis), only 19% is lost as aboveground dark respiration, in part because of the long periods of daylight during summer (Figure 12-1). Another 22% is converted to aboveground biomass, and the remaining 59% is translocated below ground. Of the carbon translocated below ground, approximately half is converted to new tissue and half is lost in respiration. This contrasts with the shortgrass prairie (Coleman et al. 1976), where 34% of the total carbon fixed is respired above ground, 9% is converted to aboveground production, and of the 57% translocated below ground, 85% is converted to new biomass. Apparently tundra plants produce shoots efficiently because of the long period of daylight, but much of the belowground carbon is used in maintenance respiration for the large standing crop of roots and rhizomes. The large proportion of litter released below ground, where decomposition rates are low, may be one factor leading to organic accumulation in tundra. However, in grasslands, where a substantial proportion of the litter is also shed below ground, soil conditions are more favorable for decomposition, and there is less accumulation of soil organic matter.

The relative importance of plants and soil organisms as sources of soil CO_2 is unclear. The proportion of soil respiration accounted for by plant roots and rhizomes has been variously estimated as 68% (Billings et al. 1977 using gas exchange), 30 to 70% (Bunnell and Scoullar 1975 using computer simulations), and 37% (Chapter 9 from litter bag weight loss). Belowground plant respiration may constitute a proportionately larger CO_2 source in tundra than in ecosystems of warmer climates (Coyne and Kelley 1975, 1978, Billings et al. 1977). For example, roots contribute 17 to 30% of soil respiration in a tallgrass prairie (Herman 1977, Redmann and Abouguendia 1978) and 35% in a temperate forest (Edwards and Sollins 1973). Root respiration is estimated to be 70% of total soil respiration in a tundra-like heath ecosystem (Chapman 1979). In tundra the period of active decomposition is only slightly longer than the period of primary production, whereas in many temperate ecosystems decomposition continues throughout the year, and primary production exhibits a more restricted season. Thus, the short duration of the arctic summer may affect decomposition even more than primary production when compared with temperate ecosystems.

The saprovore-based food web is clearly the predominant pathway of energy flow in the coastal tundra ecosystem at Barrow (Figure 12-1; Chapter 11), as it is at Devon Island (Whitfield 1977) and in grassland systems (Woodmansee et al. 1978). Even during a lemming high at Barrow, herbivores consume only 20% of the net primary production.

In the Barrow region, 60 to 80% of the annual ecosystem respiration occurs when plants are photosynthetically active (Coyne and Kelley 1975). Because photosynthesis occurs 24 hours a day, much of the respiratory CO_2 is fixed immediately by photosynthesis so that the net CO_2 flux between atmosphere and canopy is small. The CO_2 concentration within the canopy is seldom reduced more than 5% below free atmospheric values (Coyne and Kelley 1975). In mid-latitude forest and grassland ecosystems a larger proportion of the respiratory CO_2 is released at night and during the non-photosynthetic season, so that the bulk atmosphere plays a greater role as net CO_2 source and sink than in arctic tundra (Coyne and Kelley 1975). During the winter, particularly in April and May, there is a net CO_2 flux from the ground to the atmosphere (Kelley et al. 1968, Coyne and Kelley 1974).

Plant forms differ considerably in the role they play in energy flow in the coastal tundra at Barrow. Although mosses constitute 40 to 70% of the maximum standing crop of aboveground plant biomass, they are responsible for only 6% of the carbon fixed by wet meadow vegetation. Clearly mosses do not play a major role in carbon flux in the Barrow system in the short term.

Estimates of the total carbon flux for the Barrow intensive site suggest that during the period of study this ecosystem was not in steady state but fixed three times as much carbon annually as it lost in respiration of nonphotosynthetic organs and organisms (Figure 12-1):

TABLE 12-4 *Barrow Carbon Budget Calculated by Three Methods*

	Method		
Compartment	Aerodynamic*	Turf chamber†	KOH absorption**
Total C fixed	$GCU' = 210$	$PN_V + PN_M + R_T' = 202$	$PN_V + PN_M + R_V + R_M = 214$
Ecosystem respiration	$R_E = 170$	$R_B + R_T' + R_D' = 82$	$R_B' + R_V + R_M + R_D' = 155$
Net ecosystem C gain	$C = 40$	$C = 120$	$C = 59$
Subcompartments of ecosystem respiration		$R_B = 40$	$R_B' = 93$
		$R_T' = 29$	$R_V + R_M = 38 + 2 = 40$
		$R_D' = 13$	$R_D = 22$

Note: All values are direct measurements unless indicated as calculated by prime notation. Fluxes given as g C m^{-2} yr^{-1}.

GCU = gross community CO_2 uptake
R_T = total dark respiration above ground
R_E = total carbon efflux from ecosystem in dark
R_D = decomposer plus saprovore respiration

PN_V and PN_M = net photosynthesis, vascular and nonvascular, respectively
R_V and R_M = dark respiration, aboveground vascular and moss, respectively
R_B = belowground vascular respiration
C = net carbon flux from atmosphere

*Coyne and Kelley (1975).
† PN_V (Tieszen 1978b); PN_M (Oechel and Sveinbjörnsson 1978); R_B, $(R_B + R_D)$, and C (Billings et al. 1978).
**PN_V and PN_M (as above); R_V (Tieszen 1978b); R_M (Oechel and Sveinbjörnsson 1978), calculated by extrapolating photosynthesis/light curves to 0 light intensity; R_D (field) (Benoit pers. comm.); R_B' (Miller 1979) calculated from theoretical respiration costs of growth and maintenance.

$$(PN_V + PN_M) - (R_B + R_D + R_H + R_C) = 173 - 53 = 120 \text{ g C m}^{-2}.$$

Terms are defined in Figure 12-1.

With a carbon budget constructed for only one year, it is unwise to extrapolate and assume that this large imbalance is responsible for the observed organic accumulation at Barrow. Such an imbalance would generate the observed organic accumulation in 160 years, whereas radiocarbon dating indicates that accumulation has occurred for thousands of years (Chapter 1). August was 5 °C cooler in 1971 than the long-term average and may have reduced respiration below the norm and partially accounted for the net carbon gain measured in that year. June and July, when most of the growth and photosynthesis occur, were close to the long-term temperature average. Furthermore, for the years 1972–1977 litter bag data suggest that, on the average, decomposition exceeded production at the same site (Chapter 9). Because of the many possibilities for error, we used various independent methods and combinations of methods to calculate the carbon budget of wet meadow tundra. These methods differ in the calculated magnitude of carbon imbalance in 1971, but all agree that there was a net gain of 40 to 120 g C m^{-2} in that year (Table 12-4). Therefore, although methodology may be responsible for part of the observed discrepancy between total ecosystem carbon fixation and ecosystem respiration, this carbon imbalance was probably real. The carbon budget in Figure 12-1 is based on actual field measurements, where possible, rather than calculated values. Although the latter show greater self-consistency, they require steady state assumptions. The extent of agreement between field methods indicates that the carbon balance of coastal tundra and other terrestrial ecosystems may deviate substantially from steady state in any given year. Similarly, Woodmansee et al. (1978) suggest that steady state conditions are an unrealistic assumption in ecosystem nutrient budgets.

Inorganic Nutrients

Nutrient Input

The presence of permafrost within tens of centimeters of the ground surface limits the amount of thawed soil that is available for weathering. The remainder of the frozen nutrient capital could be tapped only in the event of disturbance or climatic fluctuations that result in deeper thaw. Judging from clay mineralogy, the rate of chemical weathering of minerals in thawed soil is negligible, due primarily to low temperature (Hill and Tedrow 1961). Hence, the coastal tundra at Barrow apparently depends largely upon the atmosphere for nutrient input. This contrasts strongly with most temperate systems where weathering represents the primary source of nutrient supply (Cole et al. 1967, Ovington 1968, Likens and Bormann 1972).

The arctic climate and the general global atmospheric circulation patterns severely limit atmospheric nutrient input. Arctic tundra regions receive little precipitation. The presence of sea ice minimizes the amount of sea spray that could carry nutrients inland from the Beaufort Sea. Snow cover, wet surfaces and distance from agricultural and urban centers render dry nutrient fallout negligible. The annual atmospheric inputs of nitrogen and phosphorus (Figure 12-2) are an order of magnitude less than those characteristic of temperate systems (Ovington 1968). The resupply of phosphorus and cations to the ecosystem must occur not

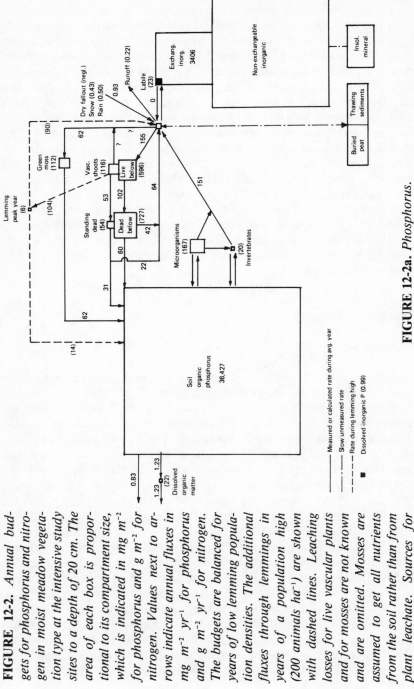

FIGURE 12-2. *Annual budgets for phosphorus and nitrogen in moist meadow vegetation type at the intensive study sites to a depth of 20 cm. The area of each box is proportional to its compartment size, which is indicated in mg m⁻² for phosphorus and g m⁻² for nitrogen. Values next to arrows indicate annual fluxes in mg m⁻² yr⁻¹ for phosphorus and g m⁻² yr⁻¹ for nitrogen. The budgets are balanced for years of low lemming population densities. The additional fluxes through lemmings in years of a population high (200 animals ha⁻¹) are shown with dashed lines. Leaching losses for live vascular plants and for mosses are not known and are omitted. Mosses are assumed to get all nutrients from the soil rather than from plant leachate. Sources for*

FIGURE 12-2a. *Phosphorus.*

470

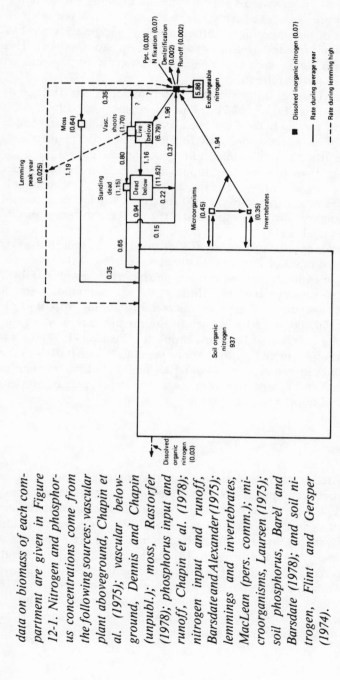

data on biomass of each compartment are given in Figure 12-1. Nitrogen and phosphorus concentrations come from the following sources: vascular plant aboveground, Chapin et al. (1975); vascular belowground, Dennis and Chapin (unpubl.); moss, Rastorfer (1978); phosphorus input and runoff, Chapin et al. (1978); nitrogen input and runoff, Barsdate and Alexander (1975); lemmings and invertebrates, MacLean (pers. comm.); microorganisms, Laursen (1975); soil phosphorus, Barèl and Barsdate (1978); and soil nitrogen, Flint and Gersper (1974).

FIGURE 12-2b. *Nitrogen.*

471

through regular annual fluxes but through the sea spray from rare summer or autumn storms and through geologic and successional processes such as the cyclic occurrence of frost action and draining and colonization of phosphorus-rich lake basins. In the absence of such renewing inputs, the rates of decomposition, nutrient cycling, and primary production decline, and the standing crops of all trophic groups diminish. This situation is most clearly seen in the basins of low-centered polygons on the coastal tundra (Chapter 3).

Nitrogen accrues at Barrow primarily through nitrogen fixation, as in most ecosystems (Figure 12-2b). Blue–green algae associated with mosses account for the bulk of nitrogen fixation (Alexander and Schell 1973). Even in the Arctic, nitrogen fixation is strongly temperature-dependent, so that the total annual nitrogen input to coastal tundra is 10-fold smaller than precipitation inputs alone in temperate latitudes (Barsdate and Alexander 1975). In fact, the total annual nitrogen input is only 5% of that which annually cycles through the vegetation in coastal tundra as compared with an estimated 21% in the shortgrass prairie (Woodmansee et al. 1978).

The annual input of carbon is 1.0% of the total amount in the system. The annual input of nitrogen is only about 0.01% of the total ecosystem nitrogen content, and the input of phosphorus is about 0.0014% of the total phosphorus content. Thus, at the current input rates, it would take 10,000 years to regenerate the present standing crop of nitrogen and over 70,000 years to regenerate the present standing crop of phosphorus. By contrast, at Hubbard Brook (Likens et al. 1977) the annual inputs of nitrogen and phosphorus are about 1% and 0.01% of the total standing crop respectively, about 100- and 7-fold higher than in coastal tundra. This comparison emphasizes the importance of nutrient conservation within the tundra system.

Nutrient Loss

In the Arctic, where climate dictates that nutrient input must be small, the system can remain in steady state only if it has characteristics that lead to low rates of nutrient loss. Some of these characteristics are associated with climate and landform, others with development of the system during succession. Low precipitation and flat terrain reduce the amount of runoff, so that nutrient loss from the coastal tundra is small. Ninety-five percent of summer precipitation normally evaporates (Brown et al. 1970). Only during the ten days of snowmelt is runoff from the Barrow tundra appreciable, and at this time the organic mat readily absorbs available nutrients such as ammonium and phosphate (Chapin et al. 1978). Permafrost prevents downward leaching of nutrients.

Nitrogen is lost from the system primarily in spring runoff, but these losses are less than the annual gain through precipitation and N fixation. The large accumulation of nitrogen in tundra systems (Table 12-1) suggests that nitrification and/or denitrification are restricted more severely than nitrogen fixation under tundra conditions. Denitrification rates are very low, even though facultative denitrifying organisms are abundant in the tundra at Barrow (Chapter 7). Low phosphorus availability is one factor limiting denitrification rates (Barsdate and Alexander 1975), and phosphorus thereby plays a role in the accumulation of organic nitrogen. Assuming that organic carbon accumulates in parallel with organic nitrogen, the continued accumulation of organic matter will further reduce phosphorus availability (Chapter 7) and hence denitrification rate. This positive feedback loop may continue to operate in the absence of large external inputs, as discussed above.

Transfer Within the Ecosystem

Because of the low nutrient input to the coastal tundra the functioning of this ecosystem depends greatly upon internal recycling of the existing nutrient capital, more so than do temperate systems. Yet the low temperature regime of tundra restricts these rates of nutrient cycling, both directly through temperature effects upon biological processes and weathering and indirectly through the occurrence of permafrost, which restricts drainage and results in poorly oxygenated soil.

Fungi are important in the breakdown of nutrient-containing compounds in litter and in better drained soils (Chapter 9). However, in waterlogged, low-oxygen soils, fungal metabolism is depressed and bacteria dominate (Chapter 8). In contrast to fungi, bacteria at Barrow lack the capacity to break down complex substrates at low temperature (Chapter 9). Thus, any nitrogen and phosphorus contained in complex organic molecules might tend to accumulate in the anaerobic zone because of the absence of fungi and the inability of bacteria to attack such substrates at low temperature and low oxygen. Such nutrients would be largely removed from active cycling within the ecosystem. Low temperature also has direct and indirect effects upon microbial growth (Chapter 9), such that microbial biomass is an order of magnitude less than that characteristic of temperate grasslands (Chapter 8). As soil organic matter accumulates, the soil becomes more acid, restricting the kinds of bacteria and further constraining decomposition. In short, the arctic climate restricts decomposition, but many of the temperature effects are indirect and complex as consequences of permafrost, low oxygen and acidity.

The cycling of some nutrients is more directly dependent upon decomposition than the cycling of others. Eighty-two percent of the potas-

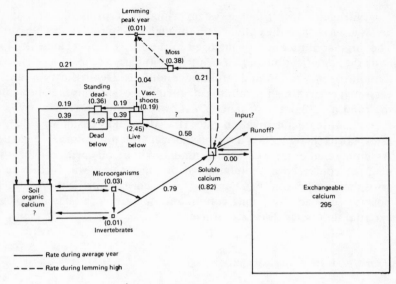

a. Calcium.

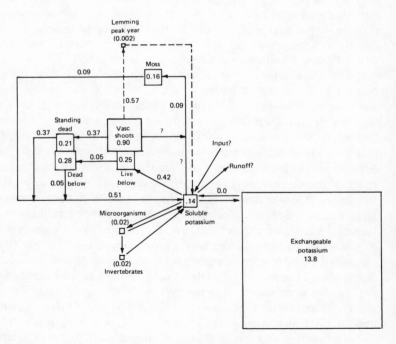

b. Potassium.

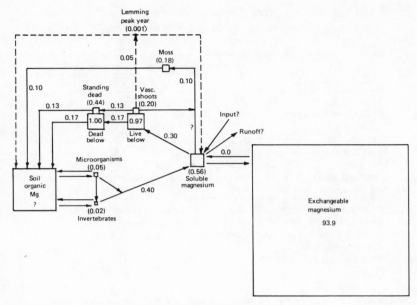

c. Magnesium.

FIGURE 12-3. *Annual budgets for calcium, potassium and magnesium in the Barrow wet meadow tundra intensive study sites to a depth of 20 cm. The area of each box is proportional to its compartment size, which is indicated in g m^{-2}. Values next to arrows indicate annual fluxes in g m^{-2} yr^{-1}. Assumptions for budgets and sources of data are presented in Figures 12-1 and 12-2. Soil nutrient pools are calculated from Gersper (unpubl.).*

sium content of litter is leached during snowmelt, so that decomposition plays only a minor role in the cycling of this element (Figure 12-3). In contrast, almost no calcium is leached from litter, so calcium must recycle exclusively through the decomposition process. However, this element is relatively abundant in the marine sediments from which soils of the Coastal Plain are derived. The soil contains a large exchangeable pool (Figure 12-3), suggesting that calcium does not strongly limit primary productivity. Calcium addition does not stimulate production in cottongrass tundra at Atkasook, 100 km south–southwest of Barrow (McKendrick et al. 1980). Sixty percent of the phosphorus and 80% of the nitrogen contained in litter must be recycled through the decomposition process (Figure 12-2), and both may occur in compounds that are not readily broken down. Both of these nutrients have been found to limit primary productivity in the coastal tundra at Barrow and at other

TABLE 12-5 *Nutrient Turnover Rate in Various Compartments of the Moist Meadow Vegetation Type*

Compartment	Net turnover rate (% of pool yr⁻¹)*				
	N	P	K	Ca	Mg
Dissolved soil inorganic	6,089	21,919	371	96	54
Soil organic	0.21	0.41	†	**	**
Live vascular	23	22	36	22	17
Dead vascular	15	21	85	11	18
Live moss	55	55	55	55	55
Lemmings (peak year)	4,760	1,733	28,600	571	4,545
Soil organisms	243	82	**	2,015	249

*Assumes a one-way transfer of material. The actual turnover rate will be much greater in pools where there are multiple paths of nutrient flow through the compartment, as in soil organisms.
†Pool nonexistent.
**Not measured.

tundra sites (Chapter 5). Hence, the role of decomposition and nutrient mineralization is extremely important in the cycling of these elements and in the functioning of the system in general.

Nutrient turnover rates of soil organic matter are 5 orders of magnitude lower than those of the soluble soil pools (Table 12-5). The turnover times (= total/input) for carbon, nitrogen and phosphorus averaged for the top 20 cm of soil organic matter are 220 years for carbon, 480 years for nitrogen and 240 years for phosphorus. This compares with an average world carbon turnover time of 40 years (Schlesinger 1977). Such turnover estimates mask complexities associated with different soil organic fractions, each with distinct turnover times (Jenkinson and Rayner 1977). The slow turnover of organic nutrient pools in the soil seems responsible for the slow overall cycling of nutrients in the coastal tundra at Barrow. Slow nutrient cycling characterizes high latitude ecosystems generally (Jordan and Kline 1972, Babb and Whitfield 1977, Dowding et al. 1981). Soluble inorganic phosphorus and nitrogen pools are extremely small and turn over rapidly (Table 12-5), contributing to microorganisms and vascular plants while receiving input from a variety of sources. The soluble nitrogen must be replenished at least 60 times in the course of the growing season to supply the quantity absorbed by plants. Soluble phosphorus must be replenished 220 times a season, an average of three times a day. The soluble pools for mineral cations turn over less rapidly (Table 12-5).

Although the dissolved nutrient pools are small, they are presumably in equilibrium with larger exchangeable pools. The input into the dissolved inorganic nutrient pools from vegetation, microflora, animal wastes, etc., is strongly seasonal. The exchangeable inorganic nutrient pools may perform an important buffering function by diminishing the size of soluble pools when concentrations are high and replenishing them as concentrations decrease. Although the net annual flux into and out of the exchangeable pool is small, the flux at any moment may be large. The labile phosphorus pool, which replenishes phosphorus removed by plants, is smaller in coastal tundra and may provide less seasonal buffering of soil solution concentration than in most soils (Brewster et al. 1975, Barèl and Barsdate 1978).

The absorption of phosphorus (and presumably of other nutrients) by vascular plants is much more strongly limited by the soluble nutrient concentration in the soil than by temperature (Chapin and Bloom 1976). Because the soluble nutrient pools are small relative to the annual plant requirement, particularly for nitrogen and phosphorus, uptake by the vegetation must depend upon simultaneous nutrient release by decomposition or chemical exchange processes. Nutrient release by decomposition and nutrient absorption by the vegetation are thus apparently closely coupled.

Nutrient release and nutrient uptake do not occur at constant rates through the season. Microbial populations are characterized by several population increases and crashes each growing season, due to a variety of factors such as changing soil moisture and grazing by invertebrates. One microbial population crash releases enough phosphorus to supply 90% of the annual vascular plant requirement. Such population crashes reduce the biomass of microbes that might otherwise effectively compete with vascular plants for nutrients. Thus, conditions that cause crashes in microbial populations may be essential for nutrient uptake by vascular plants. Further evidence for this hypothesis is presented elsewhere (Chapin et al. 1978).

Vascular plants of the coastal tundra are relatively conservative with nutrients and replenish only about 20% of their nutrient capital each year (Table 12-5). This estimate ignores losses from leaching, which may be considerable for elements such as potassium. Much of the plant nutrient capital invested in leaves is retranslocated to rhizomes during the latter half of the growing season (Chapter 5).

Mosses play an important role in nutrient cycling as well, although this role has not been documented for the coastal tundra at Barrow. Mosses appear to derive their nutrients from plant leachates as well as from the soil and snowmelt water and may effectively filter these nutrients before they become available to vascular plants or microorganisms (Tamm 1964). The nutrient concentration of brown moss tissue is very similar to that of green tissue (Rastorfer 1978), and moss decomposition rates are low. Therefore, mosses represent an important avenue by which nutrients become bound in peat (Moore and Bellamy 1974). However, slow decomposition of mosses is probably due more to low nutrient content and tundra environmental conditions than to any inherent resistance of mosses to decay (Heal et al. 1978, Coulson and Butterfield 1978). Therefore, the idea that mosses are a major path of nutrients to soil organic matter deserves further critical examination.

The importance of animals in the coastal tundra at Barrow is much greater than is indicated by their biomass, owing to their ability to recycle nutrients, as shown by high turnover rates (Table 12-5). Lemmings recycle 80 to 90% of the ingested plant phosphorus directly back to the soluble inorganic pool, whereas most phosphorus contained in standing dead material must recycle through the soil organic pool at a much lower rate. Thus herbivores can short-circuit the decomposition process, just as cattle do in the shortgrass prairie (Dean et al. 1975). The annual phosphorus turnover in vascular plants more than doubles in years of peak lemming abundance. The annual absorption of phosphorus by vascular plants that would be necessary to balance this loss to herbivores exceeds the calculated annual uptake rate by 25%. In contrast, most of the calcium recycled through lemming feces is contained in undigested cell walls and must still cycle largely through the decomposition process before becoming available again to plants. Soil invertebrates also apparently increase the rate of nutrient release from organic matter, perhaps by grazing upon microbes (Chapter 11).

A given group of organisms may play very different roles in cycling of different elements. The roles of mosses and vascular plants in cycling of nitrogen and of carbon are quite different (Figures 12-1 and 12-2). In the case of carbon, mosses and vascular plants function in parallel, both fixing carbon photosynthetically and then passing it on to herbivore- or saprovore-based trophic systems. In the case of nitrogen, mosses act in series with vascular plants. Mosses probably receive a large proportion of their nitrogen as leachate from vascular plant leaves and are thus an intermediate step in the movement of nutrients from vascular plants to the soil. Moreover, because blue–green algae associated with mosses are responsible for the bulk of the nitrogen fixation at Barrow, mosses represent a major point of entry of nitrogen into the ecosystem. Mosses undoubtedly retain some elements more effectively than others, e.g. divalent cations more than monovalent cations.

LONG-TERM CHANGES IN COASTAL TUNDRA

Lakes and ponds, which constitute 30% or more of the surface area of arctic coastal tundra, are continually forming, enlarging and draining in a cyclic process which encompasses thousands of years (Chapter 1).

Virtually the entire coastal landscape has at some time been part of this thaw lake cycle. Nutrient cycles and nutrient budgets of terrestrial systems and their yearly variations must be viewed in this cyclic successional context. Furthermore, the extensive interdigitation of aquatic and terrestrial systems has important implications for the function of coastal tundra as a landscape unit. Our concept of the exchanges between terrestrial and aquatic nutrient pools and changes in nutrient availability during the thaw lake cycle is shown in Figure 12-4.

The annual carbon and nitrogen budgets of wet meadow tundra suggest a gradual accumulation of these elements through time, and this view is supported by the accumulation of peat. Some of this accumulation may have occurred in the past. In contrast, tundra ponds exhibit negative carbon balances and virtually no peat accumulation in the sediments (Stanley and Daley 1976). The more effective recycling of organic carbon in ponds than in wet meadow may result from higher temperatures, better aeration, more intensive aquatic grazing, a more elaborate food web, or some combination of these factors (Barsdate et al. 1974, Hobbie 1980). Considerable organic matter of terrestrial origin decomposes in tundra ponds, including dissolved and particulate organic matter that flows into the ponds during snowmelt and some of the accumulated soil organic matter at the pond margin. Small tundra ponds may enlarge, although others may be invaded by emergent macrophytes. Similarly, large tundra thaw lakes enlarge by erosion and eventually drain.

Nitrogen accumulates slowly in both terrestrial and aquatic systems. On land, nitrogen accumulates primarily in peat. When organic nitrogen enters the aquatic system, either through runoff or erosion, much of the carbon portion of the organic matter is respired, but the nitrogen cycles through the aquatic system and is eventually deposited in the sediments as ammonium.

In contrast to carbon and nitrogen, phosphorus may exhibit a net loss from wet meadow tundra but accumulates in sediments of small ponds as iron hydroxy-phosphate compounds (Prentki 1976). The phosphorus in the sediments of the lakes and ponds is insoluble and is not recycled within the aquatic system to any significant extent.

Lakes and ponds eventually drain, either through the process of enlargement or when captured by a headward eroding stream (Britton 1957; Chapter 6). When lake sediments are exposed, they are characterized by low organic accumulation and presumably by relatively high phosphorus and nitrogen availability. In spite of low rates of seed production in coastal tundra, complete cover of drained lake basins can be attained within 20 to 25 years by seedling establishment and subsequent vegetative spread (Dennis 1968, Peterson 1978, Webber 1978). Such early successional communities are relatively productive, presumably because of high nutrient availability in the lake sediments.

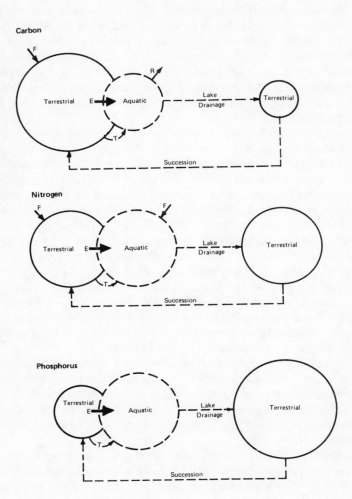

FIGURE 12-4. *Comparison of nutrient pools in terrestrial and aquatic systems on tundra during the course of thaw lake cycles. The relative sizes of the circles on the left indicate differences between terrestrial and aquatic habitats in pool sizes of organic carbon or available N or P. Solid arrows represent annual net transfers by fixation (F), respiration (R), erosion (E) and transport by runoff at thaw (T). Dashed arrows indicate conversion of habitat from aquatic to terrestrial or vice versa.*

The movement of carbon and nutrients from terrestrial to aquatic systems plays a relatively minor role in the annual budgets of these systems. Nonetheless, awareness of the slow alternation of the terrestrial and aquatic landforms across any point in the landscape is essential to an understanding of the overall functioning of coastal tundra, because this alternation prevents long-term nutrient accumulation in soil organic matter. The impact of industrial activities on the whole biosphere and on the tundra itself, either directly or indirectly, is likely to speed up these cycles and processes. From the present work, we have gained considerable knowledge about the coastal tundra ecosystem. Needed now are quantitative data on rates of ecosystem change through time. Upon these, we can construct models of what this tundra ecosystem may be like in the future. The initiation of such long-term ecological research is required so that utilization of this coastal ecosystem can proceed in the most rational and scientific manner possible.

SUMMARY AND CONCLUSIONS

This study of energy flow and nutrient cycling examined the causal relationships linking low solar irradiance with the unique features of the wet coastal tundra at Barrow (Figure 12-5). Although the low light intensity limits photosynthetic rate directly, low annual solar irradiance exerts its influence most strongly by limiting the length of the season for most

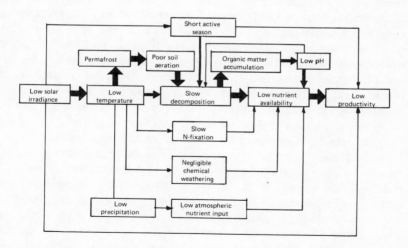

FIGURE 12-5. *Causal relationships between low solar irradiance and low primary productivity of arctic coastal tundra. Thickness of arrows indicates magnitude of effect.*

biological activity and by causing a low ambient temperature during that season. Because they have evolved numerous characteristics that enhance activity at low temperature and lengthen the season of activity, tundra organisms are generally relatively insensitive to the direct effects of low temperature, while still strongly influenced by the indirect temperature effects upon other environmental factors, such as length of growing season, permafrost formation and soil aeration.

Low temperature and precipitation and a short growing season limit nutrient input to the tundra ecosystem from precipitation, weathering and nitrogen fixation. Therefore, the system depends almost entirely upon recycling of organically bound nutrients. Decomposition, the main bottleneck in nutrient recycling, is ultimately limited by low temperature. The nature of this limitation is largely indirect: the presence of permafrost, resulting from negative mean annual temperature, restricts drainage and soil aeration and thereby decomposition. In lower soil horizons aerobic decomposition is severely restricted, so nutrients accumulate in organic matter and pH declines. Soil microorganisms, and therefore decomposition, are more severely restricted in their activity by tundra conditions than are other trophic groups, not because they are any less well adapted, but because they must bear the full brunt of interaction between low temperature and anaerobiosis. Moreover, tundra decomposers have a season of activity only slightly longer than that of primary producers, whereas in temperate regions the season of decomposition may greatly exceed that of most primary producers. Nutrients slowly accumulate in soil organic matter, where they are unavailable to plants until decomposed. As a result, primary productivity, and therefore energy flow, are strongly limited.

Animals may increase nutrient release to plants by stimulating or by short-circuiting the slow decomposition process. Soil invertebrates consume microorganisms, and lemmings consume vegetation. Both release much of the nutrient content from their food into the soil in soluble form, thus bypassing the decomposition process. Lemmings also fell standing litter and live plant biomass, thereby improving the quality of the substrate and the temperature regime for decomposition.

The gradual accumulation of nutrients in soil organic matter through succession reduces rates of primary production and nutrient cycling. The continued functioning of the tundra ecosystem may depend upon perturbations in the steady-state nutrient cycles. Perturbations that assist long-term cycling of nutrients include grazing, thaw lake cycles, and frost action. Thus the present functioning of the tundra system must be viewed in the context of processes that operate on time scales of hundreds and thousands of years.

References

Abele, G., D.A. Walker, J. Brown, M.C. Brewer and D.M. Atwood (1978) Effects of low ground pressure vehicle traffic on tundra at Lonely, Alaska. U.S. Army Cold Regions Research and Engineering Laboratory Special Report 78-16, 63 pp.

Abrahamsen, G. (1973) Studies on body volume, body-surface area, density and live weight of Enchytraeidae (Oligochaeta). *Pedobiologia,* **13:** 6-15.

Addison, J.A. (1977) Population dynamics and biology of Collembola on Truelove Lowland. In *Truelove Lowland, Devon Island, Canada: A High Arctic Ecosystem* (L.C. Bliss, Ed.). Edmonton: The University of Alberta Press, pp. 363-382.

Addison, J.A. and D. Parkinson (1978) Influence of Collembolan feeding activities on soil metabolism at a high arctic site. *Oikos,* **30:** 529-538.

Agricultural Research Council (1965) The nutrient requirements of farm livestock. In *No. 2 Ruminants. Technical Reviews and Summaries. Section 2* (Technical Committee on the Nutrient Requirements of Farm Livestock, Agricultural Research Council, Ed.). London: Her Majesty's Stationery Office, pp. 71-85.

Ahmadjian, V. (1970) Adaptations of Antarctic terrestrial plants. In *Antarctic Ecology* (M.W. Holdgate, Ed.). London: Academic Press, pp. 801-811.

Akiyama, M. (1970) Some soil algae from the arctic Alaska, Canada and Greenland. *Shimane University of Natural Science, Memoir of the Faculty of Education,* **4:** 53-75.

Alexander, M (1961) *Introduction to Soil Microbiology.* New York: John Wiley, 472 pp.

Alexander, M. (1971) *Microbial Ecology.* New York: John Wiley, 511 pp.

Alexander, V. (1974) A synthesis of the IBP Tundra Biome circumpolar study of nitrogen fixation. In *Soil Organisms and Decomposition in Tundra: Proceedings of the Microbiology, Decomposition and Invertebrate Working Groups Meeting, Fairbanks, Alaska, August 1973* (A.J. Holding, O.W. Heal, S.F. MacLean, Jr., and P.W. Flanagan, Eds.). Stockholm: International Biological Programme Tundra Biome Steering Committee, pp. 109-121.

Alexander, V. (1975) Nitrogen fixation by blue–green algae in polar and subpolar regions. In *Nitrogen Fixation by Free-living Microorganisms* (W.D.P. Stewart, Ed.). Cambridge: Cambridge University Press, pp. 175-188.

Alexander, V. and D.M. Schell (1973) Seasonal and spatial variation in nitrogen fixation in the Barrow, Alaska, tundra. *Arctic and Alpine Research,* **5:** 77-88.

Alexander, V., M. Billington and D.M. Schell (1974) The influence of abiotic factors on nitrogen fixation rates in the Barrow, Alaska, arctic tundra. *Reports from the Kevo Subarctic Research Station,* **11:** 3-11.

Alexander, V. and R.J. Barsdate (1975) Studies of nitrogen cycle processes in arctic tundra systems. In *Proceedings of the Circumpolar Conference on Northern Ecology, Ottawa 1975.* Ottawa: National Research Council of Canada, pp. III-53 to III-64.

Alexander, V., M. Billington and D.M. Schell (1978) Nitrogen fixation in arctic and alpine tundra. In *Vegetation and Production Ecology of an Alaskan Arctic Tundra* (L.L. Tieszen, Ed.). New York: Springer-Verlag, pp. 539-558.

Allden, W.G. and I.A. McD. Whittaker (1970) The determinants of herbage intake by grazing sheep: The interrelationship of factors influencing herbage intake and availability. *Australian Journal of Agricultural Research,* **21:** 755-766.

Allessio, M.L. and L.L. Tieszen (1975a) Patterns of carbon allocation in arctic tundra grass, *Dupontia fisheri* (Gramineae), at Barrow, Alaska. *American Journal of Botany,* **62:** 797-807.

Allessio, M.L. and L.L. Tieszen (1975b) Leaf age effect on translocation and distribution of ^{14}C photoassimilate in *Dupontia* at Barrow, Alaska. *Arctic and Alpine Research,* **7:** 3-12.

Allessio, M.L. and L.L. Tieszen (1978) Translocation and allocation of ^{14}C-photoassimilate by *Dupontia fisheri.* In *Vegetation and Production Ecology of an Alaskan Arctic Tundra* (L.L. Tieszen, Ed.). New York: Springer-Verlag, pp. 393-413.

Anderson, E.A. and N.H. Crawford (1964) The synthesis of continuous snowmelt runoff hydrographs on a digital computer. Stanford University Department of Civil Engineering, Technical Report No. 36.

Anderson, J.E. and S.J. McNaughton (1973) Effects of low soil temperature on transpiration, photosynthesis, leaf relative water content, and growth among elevationally diverse plant populations. *Ecology,* **54:** 1220-1233.

Anderson, L.E. and P.F. Bourdeau (1955) Water relations of two species of terrestrial mosses. *Ecology,* **36:** 206-212.

Anderson, M.C. (1966) Stand structure and light penetration. II. A theoretical analysis. *Journal of Applied Ecology,* **3:** 41-54.

Andrews, R.V., K. Ryan, R. Strohbehn and M. Ryan-Klein (1975) Physiological and demographic profiles of brown lemmings during their cycle of abundance. *Physiological Zoology,* **48:** 64-83.

Antibus, R.K. and A.E. Linkins (1978) Ectomycorrhizal fungi of *Salix rotundifolia* Trautv. I. Impact of surface applied Prudhoe Bay crude oil on mycorrhizal structure and composition. *Arctic,* **31**: 366-380.

Aristoskaya, T.V. and O.M. Parinkina (1972) Preliminary results of the IBP studies of soil microbiology in tundra. In *Proceedings, IV International Meeting on the Biological Productivity of Tundra, Leningrad* (F.E. Wielgolaski and Th. Rosswall, Eds.). Stockholm: International Biological Programme Tundra Biome Steering Committee, pp. 80-92.

Arnborg, L., H.J. Walker and J. Peippo (1966) Water discharge in the Colville River, 1962. *Geografiska Annaler,* **48A**: 195-210.

Arnold, G.W. (1964) Factors within plant associations affecting the behavior and performance of grazing animals. In *Grazing in Terrestrial and Marine Environments: A Symposium of the British Ecological Society, Bangor, 11-14 April 1962* (D.J. Crisp, Ed.). Oxford: Blackwell Scientific Publications, pp. 133-154.

Arnold, G.W. and M.L. Dudzinski (1967) Studies on the diet of the grazing animal. III. The effect of pasture species and pasture structure on the herbage intake of sheep. *Australian Journal of Agricultural Research,* **18**: 657-666.

Ashkenazie, S. and U.N. Safriel (1979a) Breeding cycle and behavior of the semipalmated sandpiper at Barrow, Alaska. *The Auk,* **96**:56-67.

Ashkenazie, S. and U.N. Safriel (1979b) Time–energy budget of the semipalmated sandpiper *Calidris pusilla* at Barrow, Alaska. *Ecology,* **60**: 783-799.

Atlas, R.M., E.A. Schofield, F.A. Morelli and R.E. Cameron (1976) Effects of petroleum pollutants on arctic microbial populations. *Environmental Pollution,* **10**: 35-43.

Auclair, A.N.D., A. Bouchard and J. Pajazkowski (1976) Productivity relations in a *Carex*-dominated ecosystem. *Oecologia,* **26**: 9-31.

Babb, T.A. and L.C. Bliss (1974) Effects of physical disturbance on arctic vegetation in the Queen Elizabeth Islands. *Journal of Applied Ecology,* **11**: 549-562.

Babb, T.A. and D.W.A. Whitfield (1977) Mineral nutrient cycling and limitation of plant growth in the Truelove Lowland ecosystem. In *Truelove Lowland, Devon Island, Canada: A High Arctic Ecosystem* (L.C. Bliss, Ed.). Edmonton: The University of Alberta Press, pp. 589-606.

Babiuk, L.A. and E.A. Paul (1970) The use of fluorescein isothiocyanate in the determination of the bacterial biomass of grassland soil. *Canadian Journal of Microbiology,* **16**: 57-62.

Baile, C.A. and J. Mayer (1970) Hypothalamic centres: feedbacks and receptor sites in the short term control of feed intake. In *Physiology of Digestion and Metabolism in the Ruminant* (A.T. Phillipson,

486   References

Ed.). Newcastle Upon Tyne: Oriel Press, pp. 254-263.

Baker, J.H. (1970a) Quantitative study of yeasts and bacteria in a Signy Island peat. *British Antarctic Survey Bulletin,* **23**: 51-55.

Baker, J.H. (1970b) Yeast, moulds, and bacteria from an acid peat on Signy Island. In *Antarctic Ecology* (M.W. Holdgate, Ed.). New York: Academic Press, pp. 717-722.

Banks, E.M., R.J. Brooks and J. Schnell (1975) Radiotracking study of home range and activity of the brown lemming (*Lemmus trimucronatus*). *Journal of Mammalogy,* **56**: 888-901.

Barèl, D. and R.J. Barsdate (1978) Phosphorus dynamics of wet coastal tundra soils near Barrow, Alaska. In *Environmental Chemistry and Cycling Processes: Proceedings of Symposium, Augusta, Georgia, April 28-May 1, 1976* (D.C. Adriano and I.L. Brisbin, Jr., Eds.). U.S. Department of Energy, CONF-760429, pp. 516-537.

Barghoorn, E.S. and R.L. Nichols (1961) Sulfate-reducing bacteria in pyritic sediments in Antarctica. *Science,* **134**: 190.

Barkley, S.A. (1976) The influence of mineral nutrients on the lemmings of Point Barrow, Alaska. M.S. thesis, San Diego State University, 110 pp.

Barkley, S.A., D. Barèl, W.A. Stoner and P.C. Miller (1978) Controls on decomposition and mineral release in wet meadow tundra—A simulation approach. In *Environmental Chemistry and Cycling Processes: Proceedings of Symposium, Augusta, Georgia, April 28-May 1, 1976* (D.C. Adriano and I.L. Brisbin, Jr., Eds.). U.S. Department of Energy, CONF-760429, pp. 754-778.

Barkley, S.A., G.O. Batzli and B.D. Collier (1980) Nutritional ecology of microtine rodents: a simulation model of mineral nutrition for brown lemmings. *Oikos,* **34**: 103-144.

Barrow, N.J. (1975) Chemical form of phosphorus in sheep faeces. *Australian Journal of Soil Research,* **13**: 63-67.

Barry, R.G. (1967) Seasonal location of the Arctic Front in North America. *Geographical Bulletin,* **9**: 79-95.

Barry, R.G. and J.D. Ives (1974) Introduction. In *Arctic and Alpine Environments* (J.D. Ives and R.G. Barry, Eds.). London: Methuen, pp. 1-13.

Barry, R.G., R.E. Moritz and J.C. Rogers (1976) Studies of climate and fast ice interaction during the decay season along the Beaufort Sea coast. In *Science in Alaska, 1976: Proceedings Twenty-seventh Alaska Science Conference, Fairbanks, Alaska, August 4 to August 7, 1976,* Vol. II, *Resource Development—Processes and Problems.* Fairbanks, Alaska: Alaska Division, AAAS, pp. 213-228.

Barsdate, R.J., R.T. Prentki and T. Fenchel (1974) The phosphorus cycle of model ecosystems: Significance for decomposer food chains and effect of bacterial grazers. *Oikos,* **25**: 239-251.

Barsdate, R.J. and V. Alexander (1975) The nitrogen balance of arctic tundra: pathways, rates and environmental implications. *Journal of Environmental Quality,* **4**: 111-117.

Batzli, G.O. (1974) Production, assimilation, and accumulation of organic matter in ecosystems. *Journal of Theoretical Biology,* **45**: 205-217.

Batzli, G.O. (1975a) The role of small animals in arctic ecosystems. In *Small Mammals: Their Productivity and Population Dynamics* (F.B. Golley, K. Petrusewicz and L. Ryszkowski, Eds.). Cambridge: Cambridge University Press, pp. 243-268.

Batzli, G.O. (1975b) The influence of grazers on tundra vegetation and soils. In *Proceedings of Circumpolar Conference on Northern Ecology, Ottawa, 1975.* Ottawa: National Research Council of Canada, Scientific Committee on Problems of the Environment, pp. I-215 to I-225.

Batzli, G.O. (1978) The role of herbivores in mineral cycling. In *Environmental Chemistry and Cycling Processes: Proceedings of Symposium, Augusta, Georgia, April 28-May 1, 1976* (D.C. Adriano and I.L. Brisbin, Jr., Eds.). U.S. Department of Energy, CONF-760429, pp. 95-112.

Batzli, G.O. (1981) Populations and energetics of small mammals in the tundra ecosystem. In *Tundra Ecosystems: A Comparative Analysis* (L.C. Bliss, O.W. Heal and J.J. Moore, Eds.). Cambridge: Cambridge University Press, pp. 377-396 (in press).

Batzli, G.O., N.S. Stenseth and B.M. Fitzgerald (1974) Growth and survival of suckling brown lemmings *Lemmus trimucronatus. Journal of Mammalogy,* **55**: 828-831.

Batzli, G.O. and F.R. Cole (1979) Nutritional ecology of microtine rodents: Digestibility of forage. *Journal of Mammalogy*, **60**: 740-750.

Batzli, G.O. and H.G. Jung (1980) Nutritional ecology of microtine rodents: Resource utilization near Atkasook, Alaska. *Arctic and Alpine Research,* **12**: 483-499.

Batzli, G.O. and S.T. Sobaski (1980) Distribution, abundance, and foraging patterns of ground squirrels near Atkasook, Alaska. *Arctic and Alpine Research,* **12**: 501-510.

Batzli, G.O., R.G. White and F.L. Bunnell (1981) Herbivory: a strategy of tundra consumers. In *Tundra Ecosystems: A Comparative Analysis* (L.C. Bliss, O.W. Heal and J.J. Moore, Eds.). Cambridge: Cambridge University Press, pp. 359-375 (in press).

Batzli, G.O., H.G. Jung and G. Gunterspergen (In press) Nutritional ecology of microtine rodents: Linear functional response curves for brown lemmings. *Oikos.*

Baumgardt, B.R. (1970) Control of feed intake in the regulation of energy balance. In *Physiology of Digestion and Metabolism in the Ruminant* (A.T. Phillipson, Ed.). Newcastle Upon Tyne: Oriel Press, pp. 235-253.

Beadle, N.C.W. (1962) Soil phosphate and the delimitation of plant communities in eastern Australia II. *Ecology,* **43**: 281-288.

Bee, J.W. and E.R. Hall (1956) *Mammals of Northern Alaska on the Arctic Slope.* University of Kansas Miscellaneous Publication of the Museum of Natural History 8, 309 pp.

Behan, V.M. (1978) Diversity, distribution, and feeding habits of North American Arctic soil Acari. Ph.D. dissertation, MacDonald College, McGill University, 428 pp.

Behan, V.M. and S.B. Hill (1978) Feeding habits and spore dispersal of Oribatid mites in the North American Arctic. *Revue d'Ecologie et de Biologie du Sol,* **15**: 497-516.

Benson, C.S. (1969) The seasonal snow cover of arctic Alaska. Arctic Institute of North America Research Paper 51, 47 pp.

Benson, C., B. Holmgren, R. Timmer, G. Weller and S. Parrish (1975) Observations on the seasonal snow cover and radiation climate at Prudhoe Bay, Alaska, during 1972. In *Ecological Investigations of the Tundra Biome in the Prudhoe Bay Region, Alaska* (J. Brown, Ed.). Biological Papers of the University of Alaska, Special Report 2, pp. 13-50.

Bergman, R.D., R.L. Howard, K.F. Abraham and M.W. Weller (1977) Water birds and their wetland resources in relation to oil development at Storkersen Point, Alaska. U.S. Department of Interior, Fish and Wildlife Service Resource Publication 129, 38 pp.

Bernard, J.M. (1974) Seasonal changes in standing crop and primary production in sedge wetland and an adjacent dry oil-field in central Minnesota. *Ecology,* **55**: 350-359.

Beschel, R.E. (1970) The diversity of tundra vegetation. In *Proceedings of the Conference on Productivity and Conservation in Northern Circumpolar Lands, Edmonton, Alberta, 15 to 17 October 1969* (W.A. Fuller and P.G. Kevan, Eds.). IUCN Publication N.S. 16. Morges, Switzerland: International Union for Conservation of Nature and Natural Resources, pp. 85-92.

Biederbeck, V.O. and C.A. Campbell (1971) Influence of simulated fall and spring conditions on the soil system. I. Effects on soil microflora. *Soil Science Society of America, Proceedings,* **35**: 474-479.

Bieleski, R.L. (1973) Phosphate pools, phosphate transport and phosphate availability. *Annual Review of Plant Physiology,* **24**: 225-252.

Bilello, M.A. (1966) Survey of arctic and subarctic temperature inversions. U.S. Army Cold Regions Research and Engineering Laboratory Technical Report 161, 35 pp.

Billings, W.D. (1973) Arctic and alpine vegetations: Similarities, differences and susceptibility to disturbances. *BioScience,* **23:** 697-704.

Billings, W.D. (1974a) Arctic and alpine vegetation: Plant adaptations to cold summer climates. In *Arctic and Alpine Environments* (J.D. Ives and R.G. Barry, Eds.). London: Methuen, pp. 403-444.

Billings, W.D. (1974b) Adaptations and origins of alpine plants. *Arctic and Alpine Research,* **6:** 129-142.

Billings, W.D. and R.J. Morris (1951) Reflection of visible and infrared radiation from leaves of different ecological groups. *American Journal of Botany,* **38:** 327-331.

Billings, W.D. and H.A. Mooney (1968) The ecology of arctic and alpine plants. *Biological Reviews of the Cambridge Philosophical Society,* **43:** 481-529.

Billings, W.D., P.J. Godfrey, B.F. Chabot and D.P. Bourque (1971) Metabolic acclimation to temperature in arctic and alpine ecotypes of *Oxyria digyna. Arctic and Alpine Research,* **3:** 277-289.

Billings, W.D., G.R. Shaver and A.W. Trent (1973) Temperature effects of growth and respiration of roots and rhizomes in tundra graminoids. In *Primary Production and Production Processes: Proceedings of the Conference, Dublin, Ireland, April 1973* (L.C. Bliss and F.E. Wielgolaski, Eds.). Stockholm: International Biological Programme Tundra Biome Steering Committee, pp. 57-63.

Billings, W.D., K.M. Peterson, G.R. Shaver and A.W. Trent (1977) Root growth, respiration, and carbon dioxide evolution in an arctic tundra soil. *Arctic and Alpine Research,* **9:** 129-137.

Billings, W.D., K.M. Peterson and G.R. Shaver (1978) Growth, turnover, and respiration rates of roots and tillers in tundra graminoids. In *Vegetation and Production Ecology of an Alaskan Arctic Tundra* (L.L. Tieszen, Ed.). New York: Springer-Verlag, pp. 415-434.

Billore, S.K. and L.P. Mall (1976) Nutrient composition and inventory in a tropical grassland. *Plant and Soil,* **45:** 509-520.

Black, R.F. (1954) Precipitation at Barrow, Alaska, greater than recorded. *Transactions, American Geophysical Union,* **35:** 203-206.

Black, R.F. (1964) Gubik formation of Quaternary age in northern Alaska. U.S. Geological Survey Professional Paper 302-C, pp. 59-91.

Blair, W.F. (1977) *Big Biology: The US/IBP.* Stroudsburg, Pa.: Dowden, Hutchinson and Ross, 261 pp.

Blaxter, K.L. (1962) *The Energy Metabolism of Ruminants.* Springfield, Ill.: C.C. Thomas, 332 pp.

Blaxter, K.L. (1967) The efficiency of energy transformation in ruminants. In *Energy Metabolism of Farm Animals* (K.L. Blaxter et al., Eds.). European Association of Animal Production Publication No. 12, pp. 21-28.

Bliss, L.C. (1956) A comparison of plant development in microenvironments of arctic and alpine tundras. *Ecological Monographs,* **26**: 303-337.

Bliss, L.C. (1962a) Adaptations of arctic and alpine plants to environmental conditions. *Arctic,* **15**: 117-144.

Bliss, L.C. (1962b) Caloric and lipid content in alpine tundra plants. *Ecology,* **43**: 753-757.

Bliss, L.C. (1963) Alpine plant communities of the Presidential Range, New Hampshire. *Ecology,* **44**: 678-697.

Bliss, L.C. (1966) Plant productivity in alpine microenvironments on Mt. Washington, New Hampshire. *Ecological Monographs,* **36**: 125-155.

Bliss, L.C. (1970) Oil and the ecology of the Arctic. *Transactions of the Royal Society of Canada,* 4th Series, **VII**: 1-12.

Bliss, L.C. (1971) Arctic and alpine plant life cycles. *Annual Review of Ecology and Systematics,* **2**: 405-438.

Bliss, L.C. (Ed.) (1977) *Truelove Lowland, Devon Island, Canada: A High Arctic Ecosystem.* Edmonton: The University of Alberta Press, 714 pp.

Bliss, L.C., W.O. Pruitt, Jr., R.A. Hemstock, F.K. Hare, J.D. Ives and G.A. McKay (1970) The tundra environment: a symposium of Section III of the Royal Society of Canada, Winnipeg. *Transactions of the Royal Society of Canada,* 4th Series, **VII**: 50 pp.

Bliss, L.C. and R.W. Wein (1972) Plant community responses to disturbances in the western Canadian Arctic. *Canadian Journal of Botany,* **50**: 1097-1109.

Bliss, L.C., G.M. Courtin, D.L. Pattie, R.R. Riewe, D.W.A. Whitfield and P. Widden (1973) Arctic tundra ecosystems. *Annual Review of Ecology and Systematics,* **4**: 359-399.

Bliss, L.C., O.W. Heal and J.J. Moore (Eds.) (1981) *Tundra Ecosystems: A Comparative Analysis.* Cambridge: Cambridge University Press, 813 pp. (in press).

Bodvarsson, H. (1970) Alimentary studies of seven common soil-inhabiting Collembola of Southern Sweden. *Entomologica Scandinavica,* **1**: 74-80.

Bokhari, U.G. and J.S. Singh (1975) Standing state and cycle of nitrogen in soil–vegetation components of prairie ecosystems. *Annals of Botany,* N.S., **39**: 273-285.

Bormann, F.H. and G.E. Likens (1979) *Pattern and Process in a Forested Ecosystem.* New York: Springer-Verlag, 253 pp.

Bowen, E.J. (1931) Water conduction in *Polytrichum commune. Annals of Botany,* **45**: 175-200.

Bowen, E.J. (1933) The mechanism of water conduction in the Musci considered in relation to habitat. *Annals of Botany,* **47**: 401-422, 635-661, 889-912.

Bowen, G.D. and A.D. Rovira (1967) Phosphate uptake along attached and excised wheat roots measured by an automatic scanning method. *Australian Journal of Biological Science,* **20**: 369-378.

Boyd, W.L. (1967) Ecology and physiology of soil microorganisms in polar regions. In *Proceedings of the Symposium on Pacific–Antarctic Sciences.* National Science Museum, Tokyo, JARE Scientific Report, Special Issue 1, pp. 265-275.

Boyd, W.L. and J.W. Boyd (1962) Presence of *Azotobacter* species in polar regions. *Journal of Bacteriology,* **83**: 429-430.

Boyd, W.L., T.J. Staley and J.W. Boyd (1966) Ecology of soil microorganisms in Antarctica. In *Antarctic Soils and Soil Forming Processes* (J.C.F. Tedrow, Ed.). Washington, D.C.: American Geophysical Union, pp. 125-159.

Breed, R.S., E.G.D. Murray and N.R. Smith (1957) *Bergey's Manual of Determinative Bacteriology.* 7th edition. London: Tindall and Cox, 1094 pp.

Bremner, J.M. and K. Shaw (1958) Denitrification in soil. II. Factors affecting denitrification. *Journal of Agricultural Science,* **51**: 40-52.

Brewer, M.C. (1958) Some results of geothermal investigations of permafrost in northern Alaska. *Transactions, American Geophysical Union,* **39**: 19-26.

Brewster, J.L., K.S.S. Bhat and P.H. Nye (1975) The possibility of predicting solute uptake and plant growth response from independently measured soil and plant characteristics. III. The growth and uptake of onions in a sod fertilized to different initial levels of phosphate and a comparison of the results with model predictions. *Plant and Soil,* **42**: 197-226.

Breymeyer, A.I. and G.M. Van Dyne (Eds.) (1980) *Grasslands, Systems Analysis and Man.* Cambridge: Cambridge University Press, 950 pp.

Britton, M.E. (1957) Vegetation of the arctic tundra. In *Arctic Biology: Eighteenth Annual Biology Colloquium* (H.P. Hansen, Ed.). Corvallis: Oregon State University Press, pp. 26-61.

Britton, M.E. (Ed.) (1973) *Alaskan Arctic Tundra: Proceedings of the 25th Anniversary Celebration of the Naval Arctic Research Laboratory.* Arctic Institute of North America Technical Paper 25, 224 pp.

Brody, S. (1945) *Bioenergetics and Growth.* New York: Reinhold, 1023 pp.

Brouwer, R. (1962) Nutritive influences on the distribution of dry matter in the plant. *Netherlands Journal of Agricultural Science,* **10**: 399-408.

Brouwer, R. (1965) Root growth of grasses and cereals. In *The Growth of Cereals and Grasses: Proceedings of the Twelfth Easter School of Agricultural Science, University of Nottingham* (F.L. Milthorpe and J.D. Ivins, Eds.). London: Butterworth, pp. 153-166.

Brown, J. (1965) Radiocarbon dating, Barrow, Alaska. *Arctic,* **18:** 36-48.

Brown, J. (1969) Soil properties developed on the complex tundra relief of northern Alaska. *Biuletyn Peryglacjalny,* **18:** 153-167.

Brown, J. (1970) Tundra Biome applies a new look to ecological problems in Alaska. *Northern Engineer,* **2:** 9.

Brown, J. (Ed.) (1975) *Ecological Investigations of the Tundra Biome in the Prudhoe Bay Region, Alaska.* Biological Papers of the University of Alaska, Special Report 2, 215 pp.

Brown, J., S.L. Dingman and R.I. Lewellen (1968) Hydrology of a small drainage basin on the Coastal Plain of northern Alaska. U.S. Army Cold Regions Research and Engineering Laboratory Research Report 240, 18 pp.

Brown, J., W. Rickard and D. Vietor (1969) The effect of disturbance on permafrost terrain. U.S. Army Cold Regions Research and Engineering Laboratory Special Report 138, 13 pp.

Brown, J., H. Coulombe and F.A. Pitelka (1970) Structure and function of the tundra ecosystem at Barrow, Alaska. In *Proceedings of the Conference on Productivity and Conservation in Northern Circumpolar Lands, Edmonton, Alberta, 15 to 17 October 1969* (W.A. Fuller and P.G. Kevan, Eds.). IUCN Publication N.S. 16. Morges, Switzerland: International Union for Conservation of Nature and Natural Resources, pp. 41-71.

Brown, J., R.K. Haugen and S. Parrish (1975) Selected climatic and soil thermal characteristics of the Prudhoe Bay region. In *Ecological Investigations of the Tundra Biome in the Prudhoe Bay Region, Alaska* (J. Brown, Ed.). Biological Papers of the University of Alaska, Special Report 2, pp. 3-11.

Brown, J. and N.A. Grave (1979) Physical and thermal disturbance and protection of permafrost. In *Proceedings of the Third International Conference on Permafrost, July 10–13, 1978, Edmonton, Alberta, Canada.* Vol. 2. Ottawa: National Research Council of Canada, pp. 51-91.

Brown, J.H. and R.C. Lasiewski (1972) Metabolism of weasels: The cost of being long and thin. *Ecology,* **53:** 939-943.

Bryson, R.A. (1966) Air masses, streamlines and boreal forest. *Geographical Bulletin,* **8:** 228-269.

Bryson, R.A. and P.M. Kuhn (1961) Stress–differential induced divergence with application to littoral precipitation. *Erdkunde,* **15:** 287-294.

Bunnell, F.L. (1973) Theological ecology or models and the real world. *Forestry Chronicle,* **49:** 161-171.

Bunnell, F.L. and P. Dowding (1974) ABISKO—A generalized decomposition model for comparisons between tundra sites. In *Soil Organisms and Decomposition in Tundra: Proceedings of the Microbiol-*

ogy, Decomposition and Invertebrate Working Groups Meeting, Fairbanks, Alaska, August 1973 (A.J. Holding, O.W. Heal, S.F. MacLean, Jr., and P.W. Flanagan, Eds.). Stockholm: International Biological Programme Tundra Biome Steering Committee, pp. 227-247.

Bunnell, F.L. and D.E.N. Tait (1974) Mathematical simulation models of decomposition processes. In *Soil Organisms and Decomposition in Tundra: Proceedings of the Microbiology, Decomposition and Invertebrate Working Groups Meeting, Fairbanks, Alaska, August 1973* (A.J. Holding, O.W. Heal, S.F. MacLean, Jr. and P.W. Flanagan, Eds.). Stockholm: International Biological Programme Tundra Biome Steering Committee, pp. 207-225.

Bunnell, F.L., S.F. MacLean, Jr. and J. Brown (1975) Barrow, Alaska, U.S.A. In *Structure and Function of Tundra Ecosystems: Papers Presented at the IBP Tundra Biome V International Meeting on Biological Productivity of Tundra, Abisko, Sweden, April 1974* (T. Rosswall and O.W. Heal, Eds.). Ecological Bulletins 20. Stockholm: Swedish Natural Science Research Council, pp. 73-124.

Bunnell, F.L. and K.A. Scoullar (1975) ABISKO II—A computer simulation model of carbon flux in tundra ecosystems. In *Structure and Function of Tundra Ecosystems: Papers Presented at the IBP Tundra Biome V International Meeting on Biological Productivity of Tundra, Abisko, Sweden, April 1974* (T. Rosswall and O.W. Heal, Eds.). Ecological Bulletins 20. Stockholm: Swedish Natural Science Research Council, pp. 425-448.

Bunnell, F.L., D.E.N. Tait, P.W. Flanagan and K. Van Cleve (1977a) Microbial respiration and substrate weight loss. I. A general model of the influence of abiotic variables. *Soil Biology and Biochemistry, 9*: 33-40.

Bunnell, F.L., D.E.N. Tait and P.W. Flanagan (1977b) Microbial respiration and substrate weight loss. II. A model of the influence of chemical composition. *Soil Biology and Biochemistry, 9*: 41-47.

Bunnell, F.L. and K.A. Scoullar (1981) Between-site comparisons of carbon flux in tundra using simulation models. In *Tundra Ecosystems: A Comparative Analysis* (L.C. Bliss, O.W. Heal and J.J. Moore, Eds.). Cambridge: Cambridge University Press, pp. 685-715 (in press).

Bunt, J.S. (1965) Observations on the fungi of Macquarie Island. *ANARE Scientific Reports,* Series B (II) *Botany, 78*: 22 pp.

Burges, A. (1958) *Micro-organisms in the Soil.* London: Hutchinson, 188 pp.

Byers, G.W. (1969) Evolution of wing reduction in crane flies (Diptera: Tipulidae). *Evolution, 23*: 346-354.

Caldwell, M.M. (1970a) The effect of wind on stomatal aperture, photosynthesis, and transpiration of *Rhododendron ferrugineum* L. and *Pinus Cembra* L. *Centralblatt für das Gesamte Forstwesen,* **87**: 193-201.

Caldwell, M.M. (1970b) Plant gas exchange at high wind speeds. *Plant Physiology,* **46**: 535-537.

Caldwell, M.M., L.L. Tieszen and M. Fareed (1974) The canopy structure of tundra plant communities at Barrow, Alaska, and Niwot Ridge, Colorado. *Arctic and Alpine Research,* **6**: 151-159.

Caldwell, M.M., D.A. Johnson and M. Fareed (1978) Constraints on tundra productivity: Photosynthetic capacity in relation to solar radiation utilization and water stress in arctic and alpine tundras. In *Vegetation and Production Ecology of an Alaskan Arctic Tundra* (L.L. Tieszen, Ed.). New York: Springer-Verlag, pp. 323-342.

Calef, G.W. (1978) Population status of caribou in the Northwest Territories. In *Parameters of Caribou Population Ecology in Alaska. Proceedings of a Symposium and Workshop* (D.R. Klein and R.G. White, Eds.). Biological Papers of the University of Alaska, Special Report No. 3, pp. 9-16.

Calef, G.W. and G.M. Lortie (1973) Observations of the Porcupine caribou herd, 1972. Section I, Appendix I, Wildlife. Interim Report No. 3. Winnipeg: Environment Protection Board, Canada, 127 pp.

Callaghan, T.V. (1976) Growth and population dynamics of *Carex bigelowii* in an alpine environment. *Oikos,* **27**: 402-413.

Cameron, R.D. and J.R. Luick (1972) Seasonal changes in total body water, extracellular fluid, and blood volume in grazing reindeer. *Canadian Journal of Zoology,* **50**: 107-116.

Cameron, R.D. and K.R. Whitten (1979) Seasonal movements and sexual segregation of caribou determined by aerial survey. *Journal of Wildlife Management,* **43**: 626-633.

Cameron, R.E. (1972) Ecology of blue–green algae in Antarctic soils. In *First International Symposium on Taxonomy and Ecology of Blue–Green Algae, Madras, 1970* (T.V. Desikachary, Ed.). Madras: Bangalore Press, pp. 353-384.

Cameron, R.E., A.D. Knox and F.A. Morelli (1978) The role of algae in tundra soils. In *Vegetation and Production Ecology of an Alaskan Arctic Tundra* (L.L. Tieszen, Ed.). New York: Springer-Verlag, pp. 207-227.

Campbell, W.B., R.W. Harris and R.E. Benoit (1973) Response of Alaskan tundra microflora to crude oil spill. In *Proceedings of the Symposium on the Impact of Oil Resource Development on Northern Plant Communities: Presented at the 23rd AAAS Alaska Science Conference, Fairbanks, Alaska, 17 August 1972* (B.H. McCown and D.R. Simpson, Coords.). University of Alaska, Institute of Arctic Biology, Occasional Publications on Northern Life 1, pp. 53-62.

Cannon, F.C., L.K. Dunican and P.V. Jennings (1970) The significance of sulphur bacteria in blanket peat. In *Sulphur in Agriculture*. Dublin: An Foras Taluntias, pp. 134-157.

Cantlon, J.E. (1961) Plant cover in relation to macro-, meso- and micro-relief. Final report to Arctic Institute of North America on Contracts ONR-208 and ONR-212, 128 pp.

Carey, R.W. and J.A. Berry (1978) Effects of low temperature on respiration and uptake of rubidium ions by excised barley and corn roots. *Plant Physiology*, **61**: 858-860.

Carl, E.A. (1971) Population control in arctic ground squirrels. *Ecology*, **52**: 395-413.

Carlson, R.F., W. Norton and J. McDougall (1974) Modeling snowmelt runoff in an arctic coastal plain. University of Alaska Institute of Water Resources Report IWR-43, 72 pp.

Carson, C.E. (1968) Radiocarbon dating of lacustrine strands in arctic Alaska. *Arctic*, **21**: 12-26.

Carson, C.E. and K. Hussey (1962) The oriented lakes of arctic Alaska. *Journal of Geology*, **70**: 417-439.

Chabot, B.F. and W.D. Billings (1972) Origins and ecology of the Sierran alpine flora and vegetation. *Ecological Monographs*, **42**: 163-199.

Chabot, B.F., J.F. Chabot and W.D. Billings (1972) Ribulose–1,5 diphosphate carboxylase activity in arctic and alpine populations of *Oxyria digyna*. *Photosynthetica*, **6**: 364-369.

Challinor, J.L. and P.L. Gersper (1975) Vehicle perturbation effects upon a tundra soil–plant system. II. Effects on the chemical regime. *Soil Science Society of America, Proceedings*, **39**: 689-695.

Chang, S.C. (1940) Assimilation of phosphorus by a mixed soil population and by pure cultures of soil fungi. *Soil Science*, **49**: 197-210.

Chang, S.C. and M.L. Jackson (1957) Fractionation of soil phosphorus. *Soil Science*, **84**: 133-144.

Chapin, F.S., III (1974a) Morphological and physiological mechanism of temperature compensation in phosphate absorption along a latitudinal gradient. *Ecology*, **55**: 1180-1198.

Chapin, F.S., III (1974b) Phosphate absorption capacity and acclimation potential in plants along a latitudinal gradient. *Science*, **183**: 521-523.

Chapin, F.S., III (1975) Nutrient/carbon costs associated with tundra adaptations to a cold nutrient-poor environment. *Proceedings of the Circumpolar Conference on Northern Ecology, Ottawa 1975*. Ottawa: National Research Council of Canada, Scientific Committee on Problems of the Environment, pp. I-183 to I-194.

Chapin, F.S., III (1977) Temperature compensation in phosphate absorption occurring over diverse time scales. *Arctic and Alpine Re-*

search, **9**: 139-148.

Chapin, F.S., III (1978) Phosphate uptake and utilization by Barrow tundra vegetation. In *Vegetation and Production Ecology of an Alaskan Arctic Tundra* (L.L. Tieszen, Ed.). New York: Springer-Verlag, pp. 483-507.

Chapin, F.S., III (1980a) The mineral nutrition of wild plants. *Annual Review of Ecology and Systematics,* **11**: 233-260.

Chapin, F.S., III (1980b) Nutrient allocation and responses to defoliation in tundra plants. *Arctic and Alpine Research,* **12**: 553-563.

Chapin, F.S., III, K. Van Cleve and L.L. Tieszen (1975) Seasonal nutrient dynamics of tundra vegetation at Barrow, Alaska. *Arctic and Alpine Research,* **7**: 209-226.

Chapin, F.S. and A.J. Bloom (1976) Phosphate absorption: Adaptation of tundra graminoids to a low temperature, low phosphorus environment. *Oikos,* **26**: 111-121.

Chapin, F.S., III, R.J. Barsdate and D. Barèl (1978) Phosphorus cycling in Alaskan coastal tundra: a hypothesis for the regulation of nutrient cycling. *Oikos,* **31**: 189-199.

Chapin, F.S., III, and K. Van Cleve (1978) Nitrogen and phosphorus distribution in an Alaskan tussock tundra ecosystem: natural patterns and implications for development. In *Environmental Chemistry and Cycling Processes: Proceedings of Symposium, Augusta, Georgia, April 28-1 May, 1976* (D.C. Adriano and I.L. Brisbin, Jr., Eds.). U.S. Department of Energy, CONF-760429, pp. 738-753.

Chapin, F.S., III, K. Van Cleve and M.C. Chapin (1979) Soil temperature and nutrient cycling in the tussock growth form of *Eriophorum vaginatum. Journal of Ecology,* **67**: 169-189.

Chapin, F.S., III, D.A. Johnson and J.D. McKendrick (1980) Seasonal movement of nutrients in plants of differing growth form in an Alaskan tundra ecosystem: Implications for herbivory. *Journal of Ecology,* **68**: 189-209.

Chapman, S.B. (1979) Some interrelationships between soil and root respiration in lowland *Calluna* heathland in southern England. *Journal of Ecology,* **67**: 1-20.

Chernov, Yu.I. (1978) Adaptive features of the life cycles of tundra zone insects. *Journal of General Biology,* **39**(3): 394-402 (in Russian).

Chernov, Yu.I. and E.N. Savchenko (1965) Ecology and premarginal development phases of the arctic *Tipula (Pterolachisus) carinifrons* Holm. (Diptera: Tipulidae). *Zoologicheskii Zhurnal,* **44**: 777-779.

Chew, R.M. (1974) Consumers as regulators of ecosystems: an alternative to energetics. *Ohio Journal of Science,* **74**: 359-370.

Chitty, D. (1967) The natural selection of self-regulatory behaviour in animal populations. *Proceedings of Ecological Society of Australia,*

2: 51-78.

Christensen, P.J. (1974) A microbiological study of some lake waters and sediments from the Mackenzie Valley with special reference to Cytophagas. *Arctic,* **27**: 309-311.

Christian, J.J. and D.E. Davis (1965) Endocrines, behavior and population. *Science,* **146**: 1550-1560.

Christophersen, J. (1973) I. Basic aspects of temperature action on microorganisms. In *Temperature and Life* (H. Precht, J. Christophersen, H. Hensel and W. Larcher, Eds.). New York: Springer-Verlag, pp. 3-59.

Churchill, E.D. and H.C. Hanson (1958) The concept of climax in arctic and alpine vegetation. *Botanical Review,* **24**: 127-191.

Clarholm, M., V. Lid-Torsvik and J.H. Baker (1975) Bacterial populations of some Fennoscandian tundra soils. In *Fennoscandian Tundra Ecosystems.* Part I. *Plants and Microorganisms* (F.E. Wielgolaski, Ed.). New York: Springer-Verlag, pp. 251-260.

Clark, F.E. (1967) Bacteria in soil. In *Soil Biology* (A. Burges and F. Raw, Eds.). London: Academic Press, pp. 14-49.

Clark, F.E. (1977) Internal cycling of nitrogen in shortgrass prairie. *Ecology,* **58**: 1322-1333.

Clark, F.E. and E.A. Paul (1970) The microflora of grassland. *Advances in Agronomy,* **22**: 375-435.

Clebsch, E.E.C. and R.E. Shanks (1968) Summer climatic gradients and vegetation near Barrow, Alaska. *Arctic,* **21**: 161-171.

Cleland, R. (1971) Cell wall extension. *Annual Review of Plant Physiology,* **22**: 197-222.

Clement, L.E. (1975) The ecology of *Tipula carinifrons* Holm. (Diptera: Tipulidae) in the arctic coastal tundra of northern Alaska. M.S. thesis, University of Alaska, Fairbanks, 96 pp.

Cochrane, V.W. (1958) *Physiology of Fungi.* New York: John Wiley, 524 pp.

Cole, C.V., D.L. Grunes, L.K. Porter and S.R. Olsen (1963) The effect of nitrogen on short-term phosphorus absorption and translocation in corn (*Zea mays*). *Soil Science Society of America, Proceedings,* **27**: 671-674.

Cole, D.W., S.P. Gessel and S.F. Dice (1967) Distribution and cycling of nitrogen, phosphorus, potassium and calcium in a second-growth Douglas fir ecosystem. In *Symposium on Primary Productivity and Mineral Cycling in Natural Ecosystems* (H.E. Young, Ed.). Orono, Maine: University of Maine Press, pp. 197-232.

Cole, D.W., J. Turner and C. Bledsoe (1977) Requirement and uptake of mineral nutrients in coniferous ecosystems. In *The Belowground Ecosystem: A Synthesis of Plant-Associated Processes* (J.K. Marshall, Ed.). Colorado State University, Range Science Department

Science Series 26, pp. 171-176.

Coleman, D.C., R. Andrews, J.E. Ellis and J.S. Singh (1976) Energy flow and partitioning in selected man-managed and natural ecosystems. *Agro-Ecosystems,* **3**: 45-54.

Coleman, D.C., C.V. Cole, R.V. Anderson, M. Blaha, M.K. Campion, M. Clarholm, E.T. Elliot, H.W. Hunt, B. Schaefer and J. Sinclair (1977) An analysis of rhizosphere–saprophage interactions in terrestrial ecosystems. In *Soil Organisms as Components of Ecosystems: International Soil Zoology Colloquium, Uppsala, Sweden, June 21–25, 1976* (U. Lohm and T. Persson, Eds.). Ecological Bulletins 25. Stockholm: Swedish Natural Science Research Council, pp. 299-309.

Colinvaux, P.A. (1964) Origin of ice ages: pollen evidence from arctic Alaska. *Science,* **145**: 707-708; **147**: 633.

Collier, B.D., N.C. Stenseth, S. Barkley and R. Osborn (1975) A simulation model of energy acquisition and utilization by the brown lemming (*Lemmus trimucronatus*) at Barrow, Alaska. *Oikos,* **26**: 276-294.

Collins, N.J. and W.C. Oechel (1974) The pattern of growth and translocation of photosynthate in a tundra moss, *Polytrichum alpinum. Canadian Journal of Botany,* **52**: 355-363.

Conover, J.H. (1960) Macro- and micro-climatology of the Arctic Slope of Alaska. U.S. Army, Headquarters Quartermaster Research and Engineering Command, Natick, Massachusetts, Technical Report EP-139, 65 pp.

Cosgrove, D.J. (1967) Metabolism of organic phosphates in soil. In *Soil Biochemistry,* Vol. I (A.D. McLaren and G.H. Peterson, Eds.). New York: Marcel Dekker, pp. 216-228.

Coulson, J.C. and J. Butterfield (1978) An investigation of the biotic factors determining the rates of plant decomposition on blanket bog. *Journal of Ecology,* **66**: 631-650.

Coulson, J.C. and J.B. Whittaker (1978) Ecology of moorland animals. In *Production Ecology of British Moors and Montane Grasslands* (O.W. Heal and D.F. Perkins, Eds.). Berlin: Springer-Verlag, pp. 52-93.

Courtin, G.M. (1968) Evapotranspiration and energy budgets of two alpine microenvironments, Mt. Washington, N.H. Ph.D. dissertation, University of Illinois (Urbana), 177 pp.

Courtin, G.M. and J.M. Mayo (1975) Arctic and alpine plant water relations. In *Physiological Adaptations to the Environment* (F.J. Vernberg, Ed.). New York: Intext Educational Publishers, pp. 201-224.

Courtin, G.M. and C.L. Labine (1977) Microclimatological studies on Truelove Lowland. In *Truelove Lowland, Devon Island, Canada: A High Arctic Ecosystem* (L.C. Bliss, Ed.). Edmonton: The University of Alberta Press, pp. 73-106.

Coyne, P.I. and J.J. Kelley (1974) Variations in carbon dioxide across an arctic snowpack during spring. *Journal of Geophysical Research,* **79**: 799-802.

Coyne, P.I. and J.J. Kelley (1975) CO_2 exchange over the Alaskan arctic tundra: Meteorological assessment by an aerodynamic method. *Journal of Applied Ecology,* **12**: 587-611.

Coyne, P.I. and J.J. Kelley (1978) Meteorological assessment of CO_2 exchange over an Alaskan arctic tundra. In *Vegetation and Production Ecology of an Alaskan Arctic Tundra* (L.L. Tieszen, Ed.). New York: Springer-Verlag, pp. 299-321.

Crafts, A.S. and C.E. Crisp (1971) *Phloem Transport in Plants.* San Francisco: W.H. Freeman, 481 pp.

Crossley, D.A., Jr. (1977) The roles of terrestrial saprophagous arthropods in forest soils: current status of concepts. In *The Role of Arthropods in Forest Ecosystems* (W.J. Mattson, Ed.). New York: Springer-Verlag, pp. 49-56.

Custer, T.W. (1974) Population ecology and bioenergetics of the Lapland longspur (*Calcarius lapponicus*) near Barrow, Alaska. Ph.D. dissertation, University of California (Berkeley), 189 pp.

Custer, T.W. and F.A. Pitelka (1977) Demographic features of a Lapland longspur population near Barrow, Alaska. *The Auk,* **94**: 505-525.

Custer, T.W. and F.A. Pitelka (1978) Seasonal trends in summer diet of the Lapland longspur near Barrow, Alaska, U.S.A. *Condor,* **80**: 295-301.

Czapek, F. (1899) Zur Chemie der Zellmembranen bei den Laubund Lebermoosen. *Flora,* **86**: 361-381.

Dadykin, V.P. (1954) Peculiarities of plant behavior in cold soils. Akademii Nauk SSSR, *Voprosy Botaniki,* **2**: 455-472 (in Russian), 473-489 (in French).

Dahlman, R.C. and C.L. Kucera (1965) Root productivity and turnover in native prairie. *Ecology,* **46**: 84-89.

Dash, M.C. and J.B. Cragg (1972) Selection of microfungi by Enchytraeidae (Oligochaeta) and other members of the soil fauna. *Pedobiologia,* **12**: 282-286.

Davidson, J.L. and F.L. Milthorpe (1966) The effect of defoliation on the carbon balance in *Dactylis glomerata. Annals of Botany* N.S., **30**: 185-198.

Davidson, R.L. (1969) Effect of root/leaf temperature differentials on root/shoot ratios in some pasture grasses and clover. *Annals of Botany* N.S., **33**: 561-569.

Davis, D.E. and F.B. Golley (1963) *Principles in Mammalogy.* New York: Reinhold, 335 pp.

Dean, R., J.E. Ellis, R.W. Rice and R.E. Bement (1975) Nutrient removal by cattle from a short grass prairie. *Journal of Applied Ecology,* **12**: 25-29.

de Boois, H.M. (1974) Measurement of seasonal variations in the oxygen uptake of various litter layers of an oak forest. *Plant and Soil,* **40**: 545-555.

de la Roche, I.A., C.J. Andrews, M.K. Pomeroy and M. Kates (1972) Lipid changes in winter wheat seedlings (*Triticum aestivum*) at temperatures inducing cold hardiness. *Canadian Journal of Botany,* **50**: 2401-2409.

Deneke, F.J., B.H. McCown, P.I. Coyne, W. Rickard and J. Brown (1975) Biological aspects of terrestrial oil spills: USA CRREL oil research in Alaska, 1970–1974. U.S. Army Cold Regions Research and Engineering Laboratory Research Report 346, 66 pp.

Dennis, J.G. (1968) Growth of tundra vegetation in relation to arctic microenvironments at Barrow, Alaska. Ph.D. dissertation, Duke University, 289 pp.

Dennis, J.G. (1977) Distribution patterns of belowground standing crop in arctic tundra at Barrow, Alaska. *Arctic and Alpine Research,* **9**: 113-127.

Dennis, J.G. and P.L. Johnson (1970) Shoot and rhizome root standing crops of tundra vegetation at Barrow, Alaska. *Arctic and Alpine Research,* **2**: 253-266.

Dennis, J.G., L.L. Tieszen and M.A. Vetter (1978) Seasonal dynamics of aboveground and belowground production of vascular plants at Barrow, Alaska. In *Vegetation and Production Ecology of an Alaskan Arctic Tundra* (L.L. Tieszen, Ed.). New York: Springer-Verlag, pp. 113-140.

deWit, C.T. (1965) *Photosynthesis of Leaf Canopies.* Institute of Biological and Chemical Research on Field Crops and Herbage, Wageningen, Agricultural Research Reports 663, 57 pp.

deWit, C.T., R. Brouwer and F.W.T. Penning deVries (1970) The simulation of photosynthetic systems. In *Prediction and Measurement of Photosynthetic Productivity: Proceedings of the IBP/PP Technical Meeting, Trebon, 14-21 September 1969.* Wageningen: Center for Agricultural Publishing and Documentation, pp. 47-70.

Dingman, S.L. (1973) The water balance in arctic and subarctic regions: Annotated bibliography and preliminary assessment. U.S. Army Cold Regions Research and Engineering Laboratory Special Report 187, 133 pp.

Dommergues, Y. (1962) Contribution à l'étude de la dynamique microbienne des sols en zone semi-aride et en zone tropicale sèche. *Annales Agronomiques,* **13**: 265-324, 391-468.

Dorogostaiskaya, E.V. and L.M. Novichkova-Ivanova (1967) On the changes in the algal flora of tundra soils resulting from their cultivation. *Botanicheskii Zhurnal,* **52**: 461-468 (in Russian).

Douce, G.K. (1976) Biomass of soil mites (Acari) in arctic coastal tundra. *Oikos,* **27**: 324-330.

Douce, G.K. and D.A. Crossley (1977) Acarina abundance and community structures in an arctic coastal tundra. *Pedobiologia,* **17**: 32-42.

Douglas, L.A. and J.C.F. Tedrow (1959) Organic matter decomposition rates in arctic soils. *Soil Science,* **88**: 305-312.

Douglas, L.A. and J.C.F. Tedrow (1960) Tundra soils of arctic Alaska. *Transactions of the 7th International Congress of Soil Science, Madison, Wisconsin,* **4**: 291-304.

Douglas, L.A. and A. Bilgin (1975) Nutrient regimes of soils, landscapes, lakes and streams, Prudhoe Bay, Alaska. In *Ecological Investigations of the Tundra Biome in the Prudhoe Bay Region, Alaska* (J. Brown, Ed.). Biological Papers of the University of Alaska, Special Report 2, pp. 60-70.

Dowding, P. (1974) Nutrient losses from litter on IBP tundra sites. In *Soil Organisms and Decomposition in Tundra: Proceedings of the Microbiology, Decomposition and Invertebrate Working Groups Meeting, Fairbanks, Alaska, August 1973* (A.J. Holding, O.W. Heal, S.F. MacLean, Jr. and P.W. Flanagan, Eds.). Stockholm: International Biological Programme Tundra Biome Steering Committee, pp. 363-373.

Dowding, P. and P. Widden (1974) Some relationships between fungi and their environment in tundra regions. In *Soil Organisms and Decomposition in Tundra: Proceedings of the Microbiology, Decomposition and Invertebrate Working Groups Meeting, Fairbanks, Alaska, August 1973* (A.J. Holding, O.W. Heal, S.F. MacLean, Jr. and P.W. Flanagan, Eds.). Stockholm: International Biological Programme Tundra Biome Steering Committee, pp. 123-149.

Dowding, P., F.S. Chapin III, F.E. Wielgolaski and P. Kilfeather (1981) Nutrients in tundra ecosystems. In *Tundra Ecosystems: A Comparative Analysis* (L.C. Bliss, O.W. Heal and J.J. Moore, Eds.). Cambridge: Cambridge University Press, pp. 647-683 (in press).

Doyle, W.T. (1964) *Nonvascular Plants: Form and Function.* Belmont, California: Wadsworth, 147 pp.

Drew, J.V. and J.C.F. Tedrow (1962) Arctic soil classification and patterned ground. *Arctic,* **15**: 109-116.

Dugdale, R.C. and D.W. Toetz (1961) Sources of nitrogen for arctic Alaskan lakes. In *Final Report on Investigations of the Nitrogen Cycle in Alaskan Lakes.* Arctic Institute of North America, Subcontract ONR-253, University of Pittsburgh, Department of Biological Sciences, pp. 1-21.

502   References

Dunbar, M.J. (1968) *Ecological Development in Polar Regions: A Study in Evolution.* Englewood Cliffs, N.J.: Prentice-Hall, 119 pp.

Duncan, W.G., R.S. Loomis, W.A. Williams and R. Hanau (1967) A model for simulating photosynthesis in plant communities. *Hilgardia,* **38**: 181-205.

Dunican, L.K. and T. Rosswall (1974) Taxonomy and physiology of tundra bacteria in relation to site characteristics. In *Soil Organisms and Decomposition in Tundra: Proceedings of the Microbiology, Decomposition and Invertebrate Working Groups Meeting, Fairbanks, Alaska, August 1973* (A.J. Holding, O.W. Heal, S.F. MacLean, Jr. and P.W. Flanagan, Eds.). Stockholm: International Biological Programme Tundra Biome Steering Committee, pp. 79-92.

Durrell, L.W. (1959) Algae in Colorado soils. *American Midland Naturalist,* **61**: 322-328.

Edwards, N.T. and P. Sollins (1973) Continuous measurement of carbon dioxide evolution from partitioned forest floor components. *Ecology,* **54**(2): 406-412.

Ehleringer, J.R. and P.C. Miller (1975) Water relations of selected plant species in the alpine tundra, Colorado. *Ecology,* **56**: 370-380.

Elton, C.S. (1966) *The Pattern of Animal Communities.* London: Methuen, 432 pp.

Evans, L.T., I.F. Wardlaw and C.N. Williams (1964) Environmental control of growth. In *Grass and Grasslands* (C. Barnard, Ed.). London: Macmillan, pp. 102-125.

Everett, K.R. (1978) Some effects of oil on the physical and chemical characteristics of wet tundra soils. *Arctic,* **31**: 260-276.

Everett, K.R. and R.J. Parkinson (1977) Soil and landform associations, Prudhoe area, Alaska. *Arctic and Alpine Research,* **9**: 1-19.

Everett, K.R., P.J. Webber, D.A. Walker, R.J. Parkinson and J. Brown (1978) A geoecological mapping scheme for Alaskan coastal tundra. In *Proceedings of the Third International Conference on Permafrost, July 10-13, 1978, Edmonton, Alberta, Canada.* Vol. 1. Ottawa: National Research Council of Canada, pp. 359-365.

Feist, D.D. (1975) Population studies of lemmings on the arctic coastal tundra near Barrow, Alaska. In *Ecological Investigations of the Tundra Biome in the Prudhoe Bay Region, Alaska* (J. Brown, Ed.). Biological Papers of the University of Alaska, Special Report 2, pp. 135-143.

Fjellberg, A. (1975) Organization and dynamics of Collembola populations on Hardangervidda. In *Fennoscandian Tundra Ecosystems. Part 2. Animals and Systems Analysis* (F.E. Wielgolaski, Ed.). New York: Springer-Verlag, pp. 73-79.

Flanagan, P.W. (1978) Microbial ecology and decomposition in arctic tundra and subarctic taiga ecosystems. In *Microbial Ecology* (M.W. Loutit and J.A.R. Miles, Eds.). New York: Springer-Verlag, pp. 161-168.

Flanagan, P.W. and A.M. Scarborough (1974) Physiological groups of decomposer fungi on tundra plant remains. In *Soil Organisms and Decomposition in Tundra: Proceedings of the Microbiology, Decomposition and Invertebrate Working Groups Meeting, Fairbanks, Alaska, August 1973* (A.J. Holding, O.W. Heal, S.F. MacLean, Jr. and P.W. Flanagan, Eds.). Stockholm: International Biological Programme Tundra Biome Steering Committee, pp. 159-181.

Flanagan, P.W. and A.K. Veum (1974) Relationships between respiration, weight loss, temperature and moisture in organic residues on tundra. In *Soil Organisms and Decomposition in Tundra: Proceedings of the Microbiology, Decomposition and Invertebrate Working Groups Meeting, Fairbanks, Alaska, August 1973* (A.J. Holding, O.W. Heal, S.F. MacLean, Jr. and P.W. Flanagan, Eds.). Stockholm: International Biological Programme Tundra Biome Steering Committee, pp. 249-277.

Flanagan, P.W. and F.L. Bunnell (1976) Decomposition models based on climatic variables, substrate variables, microbial respiration, and production. In *The Role of Terrestrial and Aquatic Organisms in Decomposition Processes: The 17th Symposium of the British Ecological Society, 15-18 April 1975* (J.M. Anderson and A. Macfadyen, Eds.). London: Blackwell Scientific Publications, pp. 437-457.

Flanagan, P.W. and K. Van Cleve (1977) Microbial biomass, respiration and nutrient cycling in a black spruce taiga ecosystem. In *Soil Organisms as Components of Ecosystems: International Soil Zoology Colloquium, Uppsala, Sweden, June 21-25, 1976* (U. Lohm and T. Persson, Eds.). Ecological Bulletins 25. Stockholm: Swedish Natural Science Research Council, pp. 261-273.

Flint, P.S. and P.L. Gersper (1974) Nitrogen nutrient levels in arctic tundra soils. In *Soil Organisms and Decomposition in Tundra: Proceedings of the Microbiology, Decomposition and Invertebrate Working Groups Meeting, Fairbanks, Alaska, August 1973* (A.J. Holding, O.W. Heal, S.F. MacLean, Jr. and P.W. Flanagan, Eds.). Stockholm: International Biological Programme Tundra Biome Steering Committee, pp. 375-387.

Focht, D.D. (1978) Methods for analyses of denitrification in soils. In *Nitrogen in the Environment. Vol. II. Soil–Plant–Nitrogen Relationships* (D.R. Nielsen and J.G. MacDonald, Eds.). New York: Academic Press, pp. 433-490.

Fogg, G.E., W.D.P. Stewart, P. Fay and A.E. Walsby (1973) *The Blue-Green Algae.* London: Academic Press, 459 pp.

Fonda, R.W. and L.C. Bliss (1966) Annual carbohydrate cycle of alpine plants on Mt. Washington, New Hampshire. *Bulletin of the Torrey Botanical Club,* **93**: 268-277.

Ford, J.A. (1959) *Eskimo Prehistory in the Vicinity of Point Barrow, Alaska.* Anthropological Papers of the American Museum of Natural History 47, Pt. 1, 272 pp.

Formozov, A.N. (1961) On the significance of the structure of the snow cover in the ecology and geography of mammals and birds. In *Role of Snow Cover in Natural Processes: Presentation volume to G.D. Rikhter on his 60th birthday.* Moscow: Akademii Nauk SSSR, pp. 166-209.

Fournelle, H.J. (1967) Soil and water bacteria in the Alaskan subarctic tundra. *Arctic,* **20**: 104-113.

French, D.D. (1974) Classification of IBP Tundra Biome sites based on climate and soil properties. In *Soil Organisms and Decomposition in Tundra: Proceedings of the Microbiology, Decomposition and Invertebrate Working Groups Meeting, Fairbanks, Alaska, August 1973* (A.J. Holding, O.W. Heal, S.F. MacLean, Jr. and P.W. Flanagan, Eds.). Stockholm: International Biological Programme Tundra Biome Steering Committee, pp. 3-25.

French, H.M. (1976) *The Periglacial Environment.* New York: Longman, 309 pp.

Frissel, M.J. and J.A. Van Veen (1978) Critique of: Computer simulation modeling for nitrogen in irrigated croplands. In *Nitrogen in the Environment.* Vol. I. *Nitrogen Behavior in Field Studies* (D.R. Nielsen and J.G. MacDonald, Eds.). New York: Academic Press, pp. 145-162.

Fuller, W.A. (1967) Ecologie hivernale des lemmings et fluctuations de leurs populations. *Terre et Vie,* **2**: 97-115.

Fuller, W.A., A.M. Martell, R.F.C. Smith and S.W. Speller (1975) High arctic lemmings, *Dicrostonyx groenlandicus.* II. Demography. *Canadian Journal of Zoology,* **53**: 867-879.

Gaare, E. and T. Skogland (1975) Wild reindeer food habits and range use at Hardangervidda. In *Fennoscandian Tundra Ecosystems.* Part 2. *Animals and Systems Analysis* (F.E. Wielgolaski, Ed.). New York: Springer-Verlag, pp. 195-205.

Garrett, S.D. (1963) *Soil Fungi and Soil Fertility.* Oxford: Pergamon Press, 165 pp.

Gates, D.M. (1962) *Energy Exchange in the Biosphere.* New York: Harper and Row, 151 pp.

Gates, D.M. (1965) Energy, plants and ecology. *Ecology,* **46**: 1-13.

Gerloff, G.C., D.D. Moore and J.T. Curtis (1964) Mineral content of native plants of Wisconsin. Wisconsin Experimental Research Station Report 14, 27 pp.

Gersper, P.L. and J.L. Challinor (1975) Vehicle perturbation effects upon a tundra soil–plant system. I. Effect of morphological and physical environmental properties of the soils. *Soil Science Society of America, Proceedings,* **39**: 737-744.

Gessaman, J.A. (1972) Bioenergetics of the snowy owl (*Nyctea scandiaca*). *Arctic and Alpine Research,* **4**: 223-238.

Gimingham, C. and R. Smith (1971) Growth form and water relations of mosses in the maritime Antarctic. *British Antarctic Survey Bulletin,* **25**: 1-21.

Gjaerevoll, O. (1956) *The Plant Communities of the Scandinavian Alpine Snow-beds.* Det Kongelige Norske Videnskabers Selskabs Skrifter, 1956(1), 405 pp.

Gollerbakh, M.M. and E.A. Shtina (1969) *Soil Algae.* Leningrad: Publishing House Nauka, Leningrad Branch, 228 pp. (in Russian).

Goodman, G.T. and D.F. Perkins (1959) Mineral uptake and retention in cotton-grass (*Eriophorum vaginatum* L.). *Nature,* **184**: 467-468.

Goodwin, C.W. (1976) Process interaction and soil temperature near Point Barrow, Alaska. Ph.D. dissertation, University of Michigan, 258 pp.

Grace, J. and J.R. Thompson (1973) The after-effect of wind on the photosynthesis and transpiration of *Festuca arundinacea. Physiologia Plantarum,* **28**: 541-547.

Granhall, U. and H. Selander (1973) Nitrogen fixation in a subarctic mire. *Oikos,* **24**: 8-15.

Gray, T.R.G. and S.T. Williams (1971) Microbial productivity in soil. In *Microbial Productivity: 21st Symposium of the Society of General Microbiology* (D.E. Hughes and A.H. Rose, Eds.). Cambridge: Cambridge University Press, pp. 255-286.

Grier, C.C. (1973) Organic matter and nitrogen distribution in some mountain heath communities of the Source Lake Basin, Washington. *Arctic and Alpine Research,* **5**: 261-267.

Griffin, D.M. (1966) Soil water terminology in mycology and plant pathology. *British Mycological Society, Transactions,* **49**: 367-368.

Griffin, D.M. (1972) *Ecology of Soil Fungi.* Syracuse: Syracuse University Press, 193 pp.

Grime, J.P. (1977) Evidence for the existence of three primary strategies in plants and its relevance to ecological and evolutionary theory. *American Naturalist,* **111**: 1169-1194.

Grodziński, W. and B.A. Wunder (1975) Ecological energetics of small mammals. In *Small Mammals: Their Productivity and Population Dynamics* (F.B. Golley, K. Petrusewicz and L. Ryszkowski, Eds.). Cambridge: Cambridge University Press, pp. 173-204.

Gunn, W.W. (1973) Bibliography of the Naval Arctic Research Laboratory. Arctic Institute of North America Technical Paper 24, 176 pp.

Gupta, U.C. (1967) Carbohydrates. In *Soil Biochemistry*. Vol. 1. (A.D. McLaren and G.H. Peterson, Eds.). New York: Marcel Dekker, pp. 91-118.

Guymon, G.L. (1976) Summer moisture–temperature for arctic tundra. *ASCE: Journal of the Irrigation and Drainage Division*, **102**(IR 4): 403-411.

Haag, R.W. (1974) Nutrient limitations to plant production in two tundra communities. *Canadian Journal of Botany*, **52**: 103-116.

Haag, R.W. and L.C. Bliss (1974) Energy budget changes following surface disturbance to upland tundra. *Journal of Applied Ecology*, **11**: 355-374.

Hadley, E.B. and L.C. Bliss (1964) Energy relationships of alpine plants on Mt. Washington, New Hampshire. *Ecological Monographs*, **34**: 331-357.

Hall, H.A. and G. Pritchard (1975) The food of larvae of *Tipula sacra* Alexander in a series of abandoned beaver ponds (Diptera: Tipulidae). *Journal of Animal Ecology*, **44**: 55-66.

Hanson, W.C., F.W. Whicker and J.F. Lipscomb (1975) Lichen forage ingestion rates of free-roaming caribou estimated with fallout cesium-137. *Proceedings of the First International Caribou and Reindeer Symposium, 9-11 August 1972, University of Alaska, Fairbanks, Alaska* (J.R. Luick, P.C. Lent, D.R. Klein and R.G. White, Eds.). Biological Papers of the University of Alaska, Special Report 1, pp. 71-79.

Hanssen, J.F. and J. Goksøyr (1975) Biomass and production of soil and litter fungi at Scandinavian tundra sites. In *Fennoscandian Tundra Ecosystems*. Part 1. *Plants and Microorganisms* (F.E. Wielgolaski, Ed.). Berlin: Springer-Verlag, pp. 239-243.

Hare, F.K. and J. Ritchie (1972) The boreal bioclimates. *Geographical Review*, **62**: 333-365.

Harner, R.F. and K.T. Harper (1973) Mineral composition of grassland species of the Eastern Great Basin in relation to stand productivity. *Canadian Journal of Botany*, **51**: 2037-2046.

Harper, J.L. (1968) The regulation of numbers and mass in plant populations. In *Population Biology and Evolution: Proceedings of the International Symposium, June 7-9, 1967, Syracuse, New York* (R.C. Lewontin, Ed.). Syracuse, N.Y.: Syracuse University Press, pp. 138-158.

Harris, W.F., R.S. Kinerson and N.T. Edwards (1977) Comparison of belowground biomass of natural deciduous forests and loblolly pine plantations. In *The Belowground Ecosystem: A Synthesis of Plant-Associated Processes* (J.K. Marshall, Ed.). Colorado State University, Range Science Department Series 26, pp. 29-37.

Hashizume, T., H. Morimoto, T. Mosubuchi, M. Abe and T. Hamada (1965) Some aspects of energy utilization by cows during gestation and lactation. In *Energy Metabolism (of Farm Animals)* (K.L. Blaxter, Ed.). New York: Academic Press, pp. 111-120.

Hatch, M.D., C.B. Osmond and R.O. Slatyer (Eds.) (1971)*Photosynthesis and Photorespiration: Proceedings of a Conference Held at Australian National University, Canberra, Australia, 23 November to 5 December 1970*. New York: Wiley-Interscience, 565 pp.

Hattori, I. (1973) *Microbial Life in the Soil: An Introduction*. New York: Marcel Dekker, 427 pp.

Haugen, R.K. and J. Brown (1980) Coastal–inland distributions of summer air temperature and precipitation in northern Alaska. *Arctic and Alpine Research*, **12**: 403-412.

Hausenbuiller, R.L. (1972) *Soil Science Principles and Practices*. Dubuque, Iowa: Wm.C. Brown, 504 pp.

Hayes, A.J. and P. Rheinberg (1975) Microfungal populations of the Abisko area, northern Sweden. In *Fennoscandian Tundra Ecosystems. Part 1. Plants and Microorganisms* (F.E. Wielgolaski, Ed.). New York: Springer-Verlag, pp. 244-250.

Heal, O.W. and D.D. French (1974) Decomposition of organic matter in tundra. In *Soil Organisms and Decomposition in Tundra: Proceedings of the Microbiology, Decomposition and Invertebrate Working Groups Meeting, Fairbanks, Alaska, August 1973* (A.J. Holding, O.W. Heal, S.F. MacLean, Jr. and P.W. Flanagan, Eds.). Stockholm: International Biological Programme Tundra Biome Steering Committee, pp. 279-309.

Heal, O.W., H.E. Jones and J.B. Whittaker (1975) Moor House, U.K. In *Structure and Function of Tundra Ecosystems: Papers Presented at the IBP Tundra Biome V International Meeting on Biological Productivity of Tundra, Abisko, Sweden, April 1974* (T. Rosswall and O.W. Heal, Eds.). Ecological Bulletins 20. Stockholm: Swedish Natural Science Research Council, pp. 295-320.

Heal, O.W. and S.F. MacLean, Jr. (1975) Comparative productivity in ecosystems—secondary productivity. In *Unifying Concepts in Ecology: Report of the Plenary Sessions of the First International Congress of Ecology, The Hague, The Netherlands, September 2-14, 1974* (W.H. van Dobben and P.H. Lowe-McConnell, Eds.). The Hague: Dr. W. Junk, pp. 89-108.

Heal, O.W., P.M. Latter and G. Howson (1978) A study of the rates of decomposition of organic matter. In *Production Ecology of British Moors and Montane Grasslands* (O.W Heal and D.F. Perkins, Eds.). Berlin: Springer-Verlag, pp. 136-159.

Heal, O.W. and D.F. Perkins (Eds.) (1978) *Production Ecology of Brit-*

ish Moors and Montane Grasslands. Berlin: Springer-Verlag, 426 pp.

Heal, O.W., P.W. Flanagan, D.D. French and S.F. MacLean, Jr. (1981) Decomposition and accumulation of organic matter in tundra. In *Tundra Ecosystems: A Comparative Analysis* (L.C. Bliss, O.W. Heal and J.J. Moore, Eds.). Cambridge: Cambridge University Press, pp. 587-633 (in press).

Healey, I.N. and A. Russell-Smith (1970) The extraction of fly larvae from woodland soils. *Soil Biology and Biochemistry*, 2: 119-129.

Healey, I.N. and A. Russell-Smith (1971) Abundance and feeding preferences of fly larvae in two woodland soils. IV Colloquium Pedobiologiae, Dijon 1970. *Annales de Zoologie-Ecologie Animale, Inst. Nat. Recherche Agr.*, hors serie, 177-191.

Hemming, J.E. (1971) The distribution and movement patterns of caribou in Alaska. Alaska Department of Fish and Game, Game Technical Bulletin 1, 60 pp.

Hemmingsen, A. and B. Jensen (1957) The occurrence of *Tipula (Vestiplex) arctica* Curtis in Greenland and its decreasing body length with increasing latitude. *Meddelelser om Grønland*, 159(1), 20 pp.

Henin, S., G. Monnier and L. Turc (1959) *C. R. Seanc. Soc. Biol.*, 248: 138. (Original not seen; cited in Satchell 1974.)

Herman, R.P. (1977) Root contribution to 'total soil respiration' in a tallgrass prairie. *American Midland Naturalist*, 98: 227-232.

Hernandez, H. (1973) Natural plant recolonization of surficial disturbances, Tuktoyaktuk Peninsula Region, Northwest Territories. *Canadian Journal of Botany*, 51: 2177-2196.

Hicklenton, P.R. and W.C. Oechel (1976) Physiological aspects of the ecology of *Dicranum fuscescens* in the subarctic. I. Acclimation and acclimation potential of CO_2 exchange in relation to habitat, light, and temperature. *Canadian Journal of Botany*, 54: 1104-1119.

Hill, D.E. and J.C.F. Tedrow (1961) Weathering and soil formation in the arctic environment. *American Journal of Science*, 259: 84-101.

Hoagland, D.R. and T.C. Broyer (1936) General nature of the process of salt accumulation by roots with description of experimental methods. *Plant Physiology*, 11: 471-507.

Hobbie, J.E. (Ed.) (1980) *Limnology of Tundra Ponds, Barrow, Alaska*. Stroudsburg, Pa.: Dowden, Hutchinson and Ross, 514 pp.

Hocking, B. and C.D. Sharplin (1965) Flower basking by arctic insects. *Nature*, 206: 215.

Hok, J.R. (1969) A reconnaissance of tractor trails and related phenomena on the North Slope of Alaska. U.S. Department of Interior, Bureau of Land Management Publication, 66 pp.

Holleman, D.F., R.G. White and J. Luick (1974) New isotope methods for measuring milk intake and yield. *Journal of Dairy Science*, 58:

1814-1821.

Holling, C.S. (1959) The components of predation as revealed by a study of small-mammal predation of the European pine sawfly. *The Canadian Entomologist*, **91**: 293-320.

Holmes, R.T. (1966) Feeding ecology of the red-backed sandpiper (*Calidris alpina*) in arctic Alaska. *Ecology*, **47**: 32-45.

Holmes, R.T. and F.A. Pitelka (1968) Food overlap among coexisting sandpipers on northern Alaskan tundra. *Systematic Zoology*, **17**: 305-318.

Holmgren, B., C. Benson and G. Weller (1975) A study of the breakup on the Arctic Slope of Alaska by ground, aircraft and satellite observations. In *Climate of the Arctic: Twenty-fourth Alaska Science Conference Proceedings, Fairbanks, Alaska, August 1973* (G. Weller and S.A. Bowling, Eds.). Fairbanks: Geophysical Institute, University of Alaska, pp.358-366.

Holzworth, G.C. (1974) Summaries of the lower few kilometers of rawinsonde and radiosonde observations in the United States. Preprint, Climatology Conference and Workshop of the American Meteorological Society, 8-11 October 1974, Asheville, North Carolina. (Data available from National Climatic Center, Asheville, N.C., Job No. 13105, "Inversion Study.")

Horne, A.J. (1972) The ecology of nitrogen fixation on Signy Island, South Orkney Islands. *British Antarctic Survey Bulletin*, **27**: 1-18.

Hosokawa, T., N. Odani and H. Tagawa (1964) Causality of the distribution of corticolous species in forests with special reference to the physio-ecological approach. *The Bryologist*, **67**: 396-411.

Houston, W.W.K. (1971) Carabidae (Col.) from two areas of the North Pennines. *Entomologists' Monthly Magazine*, **107**: 1-4.

Hsiao, T. (1973) Plant responses to water stress. *Annual Review of Plant Physiology*, **24**: 519-570.

Hudson, H. (1968) The ecology of fungi on plant remains above the soil. *The New Phytologist*, **67**: 837-874.

Huffaker, R.C. and L.W. Peterson (1974) Protein turnover in plants and possible means of its regulation. *Annual Review of Plant Physiology*, **25**: 363-392.

Hultén, E. (1968) *Flora of Alaska and Neighboring Territories: A Manual of the Vascular Plants*. Stanford, Calif.: Stanford University Press, 1008 pp.

Hutchinson, G.E. (1959) Homage to Santa Rosalia or why there are so many kinds of animals. *American Naturalist*, **93**: 145-159.

Hutchinson, T.C., J.A. Hellebust and M. Telford (1976) Oil spill effects on vegetation and soil microfauna at Norman Wells and Tuktoyaktuk, N.W.T. Department of Indian Affairs and Northern Development, Ottawa, *Arctic Land Use Research*, 74-75-83, 143 pp.

Hyder, D.N. (1972) Defoliation in relation to vegetative growth. In *The Biology and Utilization of Grasses* (V.B. Youngner and C.M. McKell, Eds.). New York: Academic Press, pp. 304-317.

Iizuka, H., H. Okazaki and N. Seto (1969) A new sulphate-reducing bacterium isolated from Antarctica. *Journal of General and Applied Microbiology,* **15**: 11-18.

Ingraham, J.L. (1958) Growth of psychrophilic bacteria. *Journal of Bacteriology,* **76**: 75-80.

Ivanov, M.W. (1955) Method of determination of bacterial production in the reservoirs. *Mikrobiologiia,* **24**: 79-89 (in Russian).

Ivarson, K.C. (1965) The microbiology of some permafrost soils in the Mackenzie Valley, N.W.T. *Arctic,* **18**: 256-260.

Jarvis, P.G. and M.S. Jarvis (1963) The water relations of tree seedlings. IV. Some aspects of the tissue water relations and drought resistance. *Physiologia Plantarum,* **16**: 501-516.

Jenkin, J.F. (1975) Macquarie Island subantarctic. In *Structure and Function of Tundra Ecosystems: Papers Presented at the IBP Tundra Biome V International Meeting on Biological Productivity of Tundra, Abisko, Sweden, April 1974* (T. Rosswall and O.W. Heal, Eds.). Ecological Bulletins 20. Stockholm: Swedish Natural Science Research Council, pp. 375-397.

Jenkins, T.F., L.A. Johnson, C.M. Collins and T.T. McFadden (1978) The physical, chemical and biological effects of crude oil spills on black spruce forests, interior Alaska. *Arctic,* **31**: 305-323.

Jenkinson, D.S. and A. Ayanaba (1977) Decomposition of carbon-14 labeled plant material under tropical conditions. *Soil Science Society of America, Proceedings,* **41**: 912-915.

Jenkinson, D.S. and J.H. Rayner (1977) The turnover of soil organic matter in some of the Rothamsted classical experiments. *Soil Science,* **123**: 298-305.

Johansson, L.-G. (1974) The distribution and fate of ^{14}C photoassimilated by plants on a subarctic mire at Stordalen. In *International Biological Programme Progress Report 1973* (J.G.K. Flower-Ellis, Ed.). Swedish Tundra Biome Project, Technical Report 16, pp. 165-172.

John, R.P. (1942) An ecological and taxonomic study of the algae of British soils. I. The distribution of the surface-growing algae. *Annals of Botany,* N.S., **6**: 323-349.

Johnson, A.W. and J.G. Packer (1965) Polyploidy and environment in arctic Alaska. *Science,* **148**: 237-239.

Johnson, A.W., L.A. Viereck, R.E. Johnson and H. Melchior (1966) Vegetation and flora. In *Environment of the Cape Thompson Region, Alaska* (N.J. Wilimovsky and J.N. Wolfe, Eds.). Oak Ridge, Tenn.: U.S. Atomic Energy Commission, pp. 277-354.

Johnson, D.A. and M.M. Caldwell (1974) Field measurements of photosynthesis and leaf growth rate on three alpine plant species. *Arctic and Alpine Research*, **6**: 245-251.

Johnson, D.A. and L.L. Tieszen (1976) Aboveground biomass allocation, leaf growth, and photosynthesis patterns in tundra plant forms in arctic Alaska. *Oecologia* (Berl.), **24**: 159-173.

Johnson, F.L. and P.G. Risser (1974) Biomass, annual net primary production and dynamics of six mineral elements in a post oak–blackjack oak forest. *Ecology*, **55**: 1246-1258.

Johnson, L. and K. Van Cleve (1976) Revegetation in arctic and subarctic North America—A literature review. U.S. Army Cold Regions Research and Engineering Laboratory CRREL Report 76-15, 32 pp.

Johnson, P.C. (1963) Nervous and chemical control of respiration. In *Physiology* (E.E. Selkurt, Ed.). 2nd edition. Boston: Little, Brown, pp. 471-487.

Johnson, P.L. and F.B. Kistner (1967) Breakup of ice, Meade River, Alaska. U.S. Army Cold Regions Research and Engineering Laboratory Special Report 118, 12 pp.

Johnson, P.L. and L.L. Tieszen (1973) Vegetative research in arctic Alaska. In *Alaska Arctic Tundra: Proceedings of the 25th Anniversary Celebration of the Naval Arctic Research Laboratory* (M.E. Britton, Ed.). Arctic Institute of North America Technical Paper 25, pp. 169-198.

Johnston, A. and L.M. Bezeau (1962) Chemical composition of range forage plants of the *Festuca scabrella* association. *Canadian Journal of Plant Science*, **42**: 105-115.

Jordan, W.R. and J.T. Ritchie (1971) Influence of soil water stress on evaporation, root absorption, and internal water status of cotton. *Plant Physiology*, **48**: 783-788.

Jordon, C.F. and J.R. Kline (1972) Mineral cycling: Some basic concepts and their application in a tropical rain forest. *Annual Review of Ecology and Systematics*, **3**: 33-50.

Jordon, D.C., P.S. McNichol and M.R. Marshall (1978) Biological nitrogen fixation: The terrestrial environment of a high arctic ecosystem (Truelove Lowland, Devon Island, N.W.T.). *Canadian Journal of Microbiology*, **24**: 643-649.

Kaila, A. (1949) Biological absorption of phosphorus. *Soil Science*, **68**: 279-289.

Kalff, J. (1965) Primary production rates and the effects of some environmental factors on algal photosynthesis in small arctic tundra ponds. Ph.D. dissertation, Indiana University, 122 pp.

Kallio, P., S. Suhonen and H. Kallio (1972) The ecology of nitrogen fixation in *Nephroma arcticum* and *Solorina crocea*. *Reports from the Kevo Subarctic Research Station*, **9**: 7-14.

Kallio, P. and S. Heinonen (1973) Ecology of *Rhacomitrium lanugino-*

sum (Hedw.) Brid. *Reports from the Kevo Subarctic Research Station,* **10**: 43-54.

Kallio, P. and L. Kärenlampi (1975) Photosynthesis in mosses and lichens. In *Photosynthesis and Productivity in Different Environments: IBP Synthesis Meeting on the Functioning of Photosynthetic Systems in Different Environments, Aberystwyth, 1973* (J.P. Cooper, Ed.). Cambridge: Cambridge University Press, pp. 393-423.

Kallio, S. (1973) The ecology of nitrogen fixation in *Stereocaulon paschale. Reports from the Kevo Subarctic Research Station,* **10**: 34-42.

Kane, D.L. and R.F. Carlson (1973) Hydrology of the central arctic river basins of Alaska. University of Alaska, Institute of Water Resources Report IWR-41, 57 pp.

Kedrowski, R.A. (1976) Plant water relations in the arctic tundra near Meade River, Alaska. M.S. thesis, San Diego State University, 83 pp.

Kedrowski, R.A. and F.S. Chapin, III (1978) Lipid properties of *Carex aquatilis* from hot springs and permafrost-dominated sites in Alaska: Implications for nutrient requirements. *Physiologia Plantarum,* **44**: 231-237.

Kelley, J.J., Jr., D.T. Bailey and B.J. Lieske (1964) Radiative energy exchange over arctic land and sea: Data 1962. University of Washington, Department of Atmospheric Science, Scientific Report, 205 pp.

Kelley, J.J., Jr., D.F. Weaver and B.P. Smith (1968) The variation of carbon dioxide under the snow in the Arctic. *Ecology,* **49**: 358-361.

Kelley, J.J., Jr. and D.F. Weaver (1969) Physical processes at the surface of the arctic tundra. *Arctic,* **22**: 425-437.

Kelsall, J.P. (1968) *The Migrating Barren-ground Caribou of Canada.* Canada Wildlife Service Monograph 3. Ottawa: Queen's Printer, 340 pp.

Kenyon, C.N., R. Rippka and R.Y. Stanier (1972) Fatty acid composition and physiological properties of some filamentous blue–green algae. *Archiv für Mikrobiologie,* **83**: 216-236.

Kessel, B. and T.J. Cade (1958) *Birds of the Colville River, Northern Alaska.* Biological Papers of the University of Alaska 2, 83 pp.

Ketellapper, H.J. (1963) Stomatal physiology. *Annual Review of Plant Physiology,* **14**: 249-270.

Khalid, R.A., W.H. Patrick, Jr. and R.D. Delaune (1977) Phosphorus sorption characteristics of flooded soils. *Soil Science Society of America, Proceedings,* **41**: 305-310.

Kilday, G.D. (1974) Mean monthly and annual precipitation, Alaska. NOAA Technical Memorandum NWS AR-10, 13 maps.

Kitchell, J.F., R.V. O'Neill, D. Webb, G.W. Gallepp, S.M. Bartell, J.F. Koonce and B.S. Ausmus (1979) Consumer regulation of nutrient cycling. *BioScience,* **29**: 28-34.

Kleiber, M. (1961) *The Fire of Life: An Introduction to Animal Energetics.* New York: John Wiley, 454 pp.

Klein, D.R. (1970) Tundra ranges north of the boreal forest. *Journal of Range Management,* **23**: 8-14.

Klein, D.R. and R.G. White (Eds.) (1978) *Parameters of Caribou Population Ecology in Alaska; Proceedings of a Symposium and Workshop.* Biological Papers of the University of Alaska, Special Report 3, 49 pp.

Kleinendorst, A. and R. Brouwer (1970) The effect of temperature of the root medium and of the growing points of the shoot on growth, water content, and sugar content of maize leaves. *Netherlands Journal of Science,* **18**: 140-148.

Klikoff, L.G. (1966) Temperature dependence of the oxidative rates of mitochondria in *Danthonia intermedia, Penstemon davidsonii* and *Sitanion hystrix. Nature,* **212**: 529-530.

Kobayasi, Y., H. Hiratsuku, R.P. Korf, K. Tubaki, K. Aoshima, M. Soneda and J. Sugiyama (1967) Mycological studies of the Alaskan Arctic. *Annual Report of the Institute of Fermentation, Osaka,* **3**: 1-138.

Kobayasi, Y., H. Hiratsuku, Y. Otani, K. Tubaki, S. Udagawa and M. Soneda (1969) The second report on the mycological flora of the Alaskan Arctic. *Bulletin of the Natural Science Museum, Tokyo,* **12**: 311-316.

Koller, D. and J. Kigel (1972) The growth of leaves and tillers in *Oryzopsis miliacea.* In *The Biology and Utilization of Grasses* (V.B. Youngner and C.M. McKell, Eds.). New York: Academic Press, pp. 115-134.

Komárková, V. and P.J. Webber (1978) An alpine vegetation map of Niwot Ridge, Colorado. *Arctic and Alpine Research,* **10**: 1-29.

Köppen, W. (1936) Das geographische System der Klimate. In *Handbuch der Klimatologie* (W. Köppen and R. Seiger, Eds.). Vol. I.C. Berlin: Borntraeger, 44 pp.

Koranda, J.J., B. Clegg and M. Stuart (1978) Radio-tracer measurement of transpiration in tundra vegetation, Barrow, Alaska. In *Vegetation and Production Ecology of an Alaskan Arctic Tundra* (L.L. Tieszen, Ed.). New York: Springer-Verlag, pp. 359-369.

Kramer, P.J. (1969) *Plant and Soil Water Relationships: A Modern Synthesis.* New York: McGraw Hill, 482 pp.

Krebs, C.J. (1964) The lemming cycle at Baker Lake, Northwest Territories, during 1959-62. Arctic Institute of North America Technical Paper 15, 104 pp.

Krebs, C.J. and I.McT. Cowan (1962) Growth studies of reindeer fawns. *Canadian Journal of Zoology,* **40**: 863-869.

Krebs, C.J., M.S. Gaines, B.L. Keller, J.H. Myers and R.H. Tamarin

514   References

(1973) Population cycles in small rodents. *Science,* **179**: 35-41.

Krebs, C.J. and J.H. Myers (1974) Population cycles in small mammals. *Advances in Ecological Research,* **8**: 268-399.

Kressin, G. (1935) Beiträge zur vergleichenden Protoplasmatik der Mosszelle. Dissertation, Greifswald.

Kriss, A.E. (1947) Microorganisms of the tundra and desert soils of the Arctic. *Mikrobiologiia,* **16**: 437-448.

Krogg, J. (1955) Notes on temperature measurements indicative of special organization in arctic and subarctic plants for utilization of radiated heat from the sun. *Physiologia Plantarum,* **8**: 836-839.

Kryuchkov, V.V. (1976) *Sensitive Subarctic.* Moscow: Nauka, 137 pp. (Translation published as U.S. Army Cold Regions Research and Engineering Laboratory Draft Translation 556, 130 pp., 1976.)

Kuiper, P.J.C. (1964) Water uptake of higher plants as affected by root temperature. *Mededelingen Landbouwhogeschool Wageningen,* **63**: 1-11.

Kuramoto, R.T. and L.C. Bliss (1970) Ecology of subalpine meadows in the Olympic Mountains, Washington. *Ecological Monographs,* **40**: 317-347.

Lachenbruch, A.H. (1962) Mechanics of thermal contraction cracks and ice-wedge polygons in permafrost. Geological Society of America Special Paper 70, 69 pp.

Lachenbruch, A.H. and B.V. Marshall (1969) Heat flow in the Arctic. *Arctic,* **22**: 300-311.

Lachenbruch, A.H. and B.V. Marshall (1977) Sub-sea temperatures and a simple tentative model for offshore permafrost at Prudhoe Bay, Alaska. U.S. Geological Survey Open-file Report 77-395, 34 pp.

Langer, R.H.M. (1966) Mineral nutrition of grasses and cereals. In *The Growth of Cereals and Grasses* (F.L. Milthorpe and J.D. Ivins, Eds.). London: Butterworths, pp. 213-226.

Larcher, W., L. Schmidt, G. Grabherr and A. Cernusca (1973) Plant biomass and production of alpine shrub heaths at Mt. Patscherkofel, Austria. In *Primary Production and Production Processes: Proceedings of the Conference, Dublin, Ireland, April 1973* (L.C. Bliss and F.E. Wielgolaski, Eds.). Stockholm: International Biological Programme Tundra Biome Steering Committee, pp. 65-73.

Latter, P.M., J.B. Cragg and O.W. Heal (1967) Comparative studies on the microbiology of four moorland soils in the northern Pennines. *Journal of Ecology,* **55**: 445-464.

Latter, P.M. and O.W. Heal (1971) A preliminary study of the growth of fungi and bacteria from temperate and Antarctic soils in relation to temperature. *Soil Biology and Biochemistry,* **3**: 365-379.

Laursen, G. (1975) Higher fungi in soils of coastal arctic tundra plant communities. Ph.D. dissertation, Virginia Polytechnic Institute and

State University, 370 pp.

Laursen, G.A., O.K. Miller, Jr. and H.E. Bigelow (1976) A new Clitocybe from the Alaskan Arctic. *Canadian Journal of Botany,* **54**: 976-980.

Laursen, G.A. and O.K. Miller, Jr. (1977) The distribution of fungal hyphae in arctic soil on the International Biological Programme Tundra Biome site, Barrow, Alaska. *Arctic and Alpine Research,* **9**: 149-156.

Lawrence, B.A., M.C. Lewis and P.C. Miller (1978) A simulation model of population processes of arctic tundra graminoids. In *Vegetation and Production Ecology of an Alaskan Arctic Tundra* (L.L. Tieszen, Ed.). New York: Springer-Verlag, pp. 599-619.

Lawson, D.E., J. Brown, K.R. Everett, A.W. Johnson, V. Komárková, B.M. Murray, D.F. Murray and P.J. Webber (1978) Tundra disturbances and recovery following the 1949 exploratory drilling, Fish Creek, northern Alaska. U.S. Army Cold Regions Research and Engineering Laboratory CRREL Report 78-28, 81 pp.

LeDrew, E.F. and G. Weller (1978) A comparison of the radiation and energy balance during the growing season for an arctic and alpine tundra. *Arctic and Alpine Research,* **10**: 665-678.

Lemon, E.R. (1963) Energy and water balance of plant communities. In *Environmental Control of Plant Growth: Proceedings of a Symposium held at Canberra, Australia, August 1962* (L.T. Evans, Ed.). New York: Academic Press, pp. 55-78.

Lent, P.C. (1966) The caribou of northwestern Alaska. In *Environment of the Cape Thompson Region, Alaska* (N.J. Wilimovsky and J.N. Wolfe, Eds.). Oak Ridge, Tenn.: U.S. Atomic Energy Commission, pp.481-517.

Leonard, E.R. (1962) Interrelations of vegetative and reproductive growth, with special reference to indeterminate plants. *Botanical Review,* **28**: 353-410.

Letrouit-Galinou, M.-A. (1973) Sexual reproduction. In *The Lichens* (V. Ahmadjian and M.E. Hale, Eds.). New York: Academic Press, pp. 59-90.

Levin, E.I. (1899) Les microbes dans les régions arctiques. *Annales de l'Institute Pasteur,* **13**: 558-567.

Lewellen, R.I. (1972) *Studies on the Fluvial Environment, Arctic Coastal Plain Province, Northern Alaska.* Published by the author, P.O. Box 1068, Littleton, Colorado 80120, 282 pp.

Lewellen, R.I. (1977) Subsea permafrost research techniques. *Geosciences and Man,* **XVIII**: 29-34.

Lewis, J.K., J.L. Dodd, H.L. Hutcheson and C.L. Hanson (1971) Abiotic and herbage dynamic studies on the cottonwood site, 1970. Grasslands Technical Report 111, Fort Collins, Colorado.

Lewis Smith, R.I. and D.W.H. Walton (1975) South Georgia, subantarctic. In *Structure and Function of Tundra Ecosystems: Papers
Presented at the IBP Tundra Biome V International Meeting on Biological Productivity of Tundra, Abisko, Sweden, April 1974* (T.
Rosswall and O.W. Heal, Eds.). Ecological Bulletins 20. Stockholm: Swedish Natural Science Research Council, pp. 399-423.

Lieske, B.J. and L.A. Stroschein (1968) Radiative regime over arctic tundra. University of Washington Department of Atmospheric Sciences, Scientific Report on Contract ONR-477(24), 31 pp.

Likens, G.E. and F.H. Bormann (1972) Nutrient cycling in ecosystems.
In *Ecosystem Structure and Function: Proceedings of the Annual
Biology Colloquium, 31* (J.H. Wiens, Ed.). Corvallis: Oregon State
University Press, pp. 25-67.

Likens, G.E., F.H. Bormann, R.S. Pierce, J.S. Eaton and N.M.
Johnson (1977) *Biogeochemistry of a Forested Ecosystem.* New
York: Springer-Verlag, 146 pp.

Linell, K.A. (1973) Long-term effects of vegetative cover on permafrost stability in an area of discontinuous permafrost. In *Permafrost: North American Contribution to the Second International
Conference.* Washington, D.C.: National Academy of Sciences, pp.
688-693.

Linkins, A.E. and R.K. Antibus (1978) Ectomycorrhizal fungi of *Salix
rotundifolia* Trautv. II. Impact of surface applied Prudhoe Bay
crude oil on mycorrhizal root respiration and cold acclimation. *Arctic,* **31**: 381-391.

Lord, N.W., J.P. Pandolfo and M.A. Atwater (1972) Simulation of
meteorological variations over arctic coastal tundra under various
physical interface conditions. *Arctic and Alpine Research,* **4**: 189-
209.

Luxton, M. (1972) Studies on the oribatid mites of a Danish beech wood
soil. I. Nutritional biology. *Pedobiologia,* **12**: 434-463.

McCown, B.H. (1973) The influence of soil temperature on plant growth
and survival in Alaska. *Proceedings of the Symposium on the Impact of Oil Resource Development on Northern Plant Communities:
Presented at the 23rd AAAS Alaska Science Conference, Fairbanks,
Alaska, 17 August 1972* (B.H. McCown and D.R. Simpson, Coordinators). University of Alaska, Institute of Arctic Biology, Occasional Publications on Northern Life 1, pp. 12-33.

McCown, B.H. (1975) Physiological responses of root systems to stress
conditions. In *Physiological Adaptations to the Environment* (F.J.
Vernberg, Ed.). New York: Intext Educational Publishers, 225-237.

McCown, B.H. (1978) The interaction of organic nutrients, soil nitrogen, and soil temperature on plant growth and survival in the arctic
environment. In *Vegetation and Production Ecology of an Alaskan*

Arctic Tundra (L.L. Tieszen, Ed.). New York: Springer-Verlag, pp. 435-456.

McCown, D.D. and F.J. Deneke (1973) Plant germination and seedling growth as affected by the presence of crude petroleum. *Proceedings of the Symposium on the Impact of Oil Resource Development on Northern Plant Communities: Presented at the 23rd AAAS Alaska Science Conference, Fairbanks, Alaska, 17 August 1972* (B.H. Mc-Cown and D.R. Simpson, Coordinators). University of Alaska, Institute of Arctic Biology, Occasional Publications on Northern Life 1, pp. 44-51.

McCree, K.J. (1974) Equations for the rate of dark respiration of white clover and grain sorghum as functions of dry weight, photosynthetic rate, and temperature. *Crop Science,* **14**: 509-514.

McEwan, E.H. (1970) Energy metabolism of barren-ground caribou (*Rangifer tarandus*). *Canadian Journal of Zoology,* **48**: 391-392.

McEwan, E.H. and P.E. Whitehead (1970) Seasonal changes in the energy and nitrogen intake in reindeer and caribou. *Canadian Journal of Zoology,* **48**: 905-913.

McEwan, E.H. and P.E. Whitehead (1972) Reproduction in female reindeer and caribou. *Canadian Journal of Zoology,* **50**: 43-46.

McKendrick, J.D., C.E. Owensby and R.M. Hyde (1975) Big bluestem and Indiangrass vegetative reproduction and annual reserve carbohydrate and nitrogen cycles. *Agro-Ecosystems,* **2**: 75-93.

McKendrick, J.D., V.J. Ott and G.A. Mitchell (1978) Effects of nitrogen and phosphorus fertilization on the carbohydrate and nutrient levels in *Dupontia fisheri* and *Arctagrostis latifolia.* In *Vegetation and Production Ecology of an Alaskan Arctic Tundra* (L.L. Tieszen, Ed.). New York: Springer-Verlag, pp. 509-537.

McKendrick, J.D., G.O. Batzli, K.R. Everett and J.C. Swanson (1980) Some effects of mammalian herbivores and fertilization on tundra soils and vegetation. *Arctic and Alpine Research,* **12**: 565-578.

McNaughton, S.J., R.S. Campbell, R.A. Freyer, J.E. Mylroie and K.D. Rodland (1974) Photosynthetic properties and root chilling responses of altitudinal ecotypes of *Typha latifolia* L. *Ecology,* **55**: 168-172.

Macfadyen, A. (1970) Soil metabolism in relation to ecosystem energy flow and to primary and secondary production. In *Methods of Study in Soil Ecology* (J. Phillipson, Ed.). Paris: UNESCO, pp. 167-172.

MacLean, S.F., Jr. (1969) Ecological determinants of species diversity of arctic sandpipers near Barrow, Alaska. Ph.D. dissertation, University of California (Berkeley), 188 pp.

MacLean, S.F., Jr. (1973) Life cycle and growth energetics of the arctic cranefly *Pedicia hannai antenatta. Oikos,* **24**: 436-443.

MacLean, S.F., Jr. (1974a) Primary production, decomposition, and the activity of soil invertebrates in tundra ecosystems: A hypothesis. In *Soil Organisms and Decomposition in Tundra: Proceedings of the Microbiology, Decomposition and Invertebrate Working Groups Meeting, Fairbanks, Alaska, August 1973* (A.J. Holding, O.W. Heal, S.F. MacLean, Jr. and P.W. Flanagan, Eds.). Stockholm: International Biological Programme Tundra Biome Steering Committee, pp. 197-206.

MacLean, S.F., Jr. (1974b) Lemming bones as a source of calcium for arctic sandpipers (*Calidris* spp.). *Ibis,* **116**: 522-557.

MacLean, S.F., Jr. (1975a) Ecological adaptations of tundra invertebrates. In *Physiological Adaptation to the Environment* (F.J. Vernberg, Ed.). New York: Intext Educational Publishers, pp. 269-300.

MacLean, S.F., Jr. (1975b) Ecology of tundra invertebrates at Prudhoe Bay, Alaska. In *Ecological Investigations of the Tundra Biome in the Prudhoe Bay Region, Alaska* (J. Brown, Ed.). Biological Papers of the University of Alaska, Special Report 2, pp. 114-123.

MacLean, S.F., Jr. and F.A. Pitelka (1971) Seasonal patterns of abundance of tundra arthropods near Barrow. *Arctic,* **24**: 19-40.

MacLean, S.F., Jr., B.M. Fitzgerald and F.A. Pitelka (1974) Population cycles in arctic lemmings: Winter reproduction and predation by weasels. *Arctic and Alpine Research,* **6**: 1-12.

MacLean, S.F., Jr., G.K. Douce, E.A. Morgan and M.A. Skeel (1977) Community organization in the soil invertebrates of Alaskan arctic tundra. In *Soil Organisms as Components of Ecosystems: International Soil Zoology Colloquium, Uppsala, Sweden, June 21-25, 1976* (U. Lohm and T. Persson, Eds.). Ecological Bulletins 25. Stockholm: Swedish Natural Science Research Council, pp. 90-101.

MacLean, S.F., Jr., V. Behan and A. Fjellberg (1978) Soil Acari and Collembola from Chaun Bay, northern Chukotka. *Arctic and Alpine Research,* **10**: 559-568.

MacLean, S.F., Jr. and I.D. Hodkinson (1980) The distribution of psyllids (Homoptera: Psylloidea) in arctic and subarctic Alaska. *Arctic and Alpine Research,* **12**: 369-376.

MacPherson, A.H. (1969) Reproduction of Canadian arctic fox populations. Canadian Wildlife Service Report 8, 52 pp.

Mägdefrau, K. (1937) Der Wasserhaushalt der Moose. *Annales Bryologici,* **10**: 141-150.

Maher, W.J. (1967) Predation by weasels on winter population of lemmings, Banks Island, Northwest Territories. *Canadian Field Naturalist,* **81**: 248-250.

Maher, W.J. (1970) The pomarine jaeger as a brown lemming predator in northern Alaska. *Wilson Bulletin,* **82**: 130-157.

Maher, W.J. (1974) Ecology of pomarine, parasitic and long-tailed jaegers in northern Alaska. *Pacific Coast Avifauna,* **37**: 148 pp.

Mani, M.S. (1962) *Introduction to High Altitude Entomology.* London: Methuen, 302 pp.

Mani, M.S. (1968) *Ecology and Biogeography of High Altitude Insects.* The Hague: Dr. W. Junk, 527 pp.

Marks, P.L. and F.H. Bormann (1972) Revegetation following forest cutting: mechanisms for return to steady-state nutrient cycling. *Science,* **176**: 914-915.

Marr, A.G., E.H. Nelson and D.J. Clark (1963) The maintenance requirement of *Escherichia coli. Annals of the New York Academy of Sciences,* **102**: 536-548.

Marshall, C. and G.R. Sagar (1968) The distribution of assimilates in *Lolium multiflorum* Lam. following differential defoliation. *Annals of Botany,* N.S., **32**: 715-719.

Maruyama, K. (1967) Blue–green algae in the Alaskan Arctic. In *Phycological Report of the Japanese Microbiological Expedition to the Alaskan Arctic* (Y. Kabayashi, Compiler). *Bulletin of the National Science Museum, Tokyo,* **10**: 221-239.

Mather, J.R. and C.W. Thornthwaite (1958) *Microclimate Investigations at Point Barrow, Alaska, 1957-1958.* Drexel Institute of Technology, Publications in Climatology, **XI**(2), 239 pp.

Mattheis, P.J., L.L. Tieszen and M.C. Lewis (1976) Responses of *Dupontia fisheri* to lemming grazing in an Alaskan arctic tundra. *Annals of Botany,* N.S., **40**: 179-197.

May, D.C.E. (1973) Model for predicting composition and production of alpine tundra vegetation from Niwot Ridge, Colorado. M.A. thesis, University of Colorado (Boulder), 99 pp.

Maykut, G.A. and P.E. Church (1973) Radiation climate of Barrow, Alaska, 1962-66. *Journal of Applied Meteorology,* **12**: 620-628.

Mayo, J.M., D.G. Despain and E.M. van Zinderen Bakker, Jr. (1973) CO_2 assimilation by *Dryas integrifolia* on Devon Island, Northwest Territories. *Canadian Journal of Botany,* **5**: 581-588.

Mayo, J.M., A.P. Hartgerink, D.G. Despain, R.G. Thompson, E.M. van Zinderen Bakker, Jr. and S.D. Nelson (1977) Gas exchange studies of *Carex* and *Dryas*, Truelove Lowland. In *Truelove Lowland, Devon Island, Canada: A High Arctic Ecosystem* (L.C. Bliss, Ed.). Edmonton: The University of Alberta Press, pp. 265-280.

Millar, J.S. (1977) Adaptive features of mammalian reproduction. *Evolution,* **31**: 370-386.

Miller, J.F. (1963) Probable maximum precipitation and rainfall frequency data for Alaska for areas to 400 square miles, durations to 24 hours, and return periods from 1 to 100 years. U.S. Weather Bureau Technical Paper No. 47, 69 pp.

Miller, J.H., J.E. Giddens and A.A. Foster (1957) A survey of the fungi of forest and cultivated soils of Georgia. *Mycologia,* **49**: 779-808.

Miller, M.C., R.T. Prentki and R.J. Barsdate (1980) Physics. In *Limnology of Tundra Ponds, Barrow, Alaska* (J.E. Hobbie, Ed.). Stroudsburg, Pa.: Dowden, Hutchinson and Ross, pp. 51-75.

Miller, O.K., Jr., G.A. Laursen and B.M. Murray (1973) Arctic and alpine agarics from Alaska and Canada. *Canadian Journal of Botany,* **51**: 43-49.

Miller, O.K., Jr. and D.E. Farr (1975) Index of the common fungi of North America (synonymy and common names). *Bibliotheca Mycologia,* **44**: p. 206.

Miller, O.K., Jr. and G.A. Laursen (1978) Ecto- and endomycorrhizae of arctic plants at Barrow, Alaska. In *Vegetation and Production Ecology of an Alaskan Arctic Tundra* (L.L. Tieszen, Ed.). New York: Springer-Verlag, pp. 229-237.

Miller, P.C. (1978) Problems of synthesis in mineral cycling studies: The tundra as an example. In *Environmental Chemistry and Cycling Processes: Proceedings of Symposium, Augusta, Georgia, April 28–May 1, 1976* (D.C. Adriano and I.L. Brisbin, Jr., Eds.). U.S. Department of Energy, CONF-760429, pp. 59-71.

Miller, P.C. (1979) Quantitative plant ecology. In *Analysis of Ecosystems* (D. Horn, G.R. Stairs and R.D. Mitchell, Eds.). Columbus: Ohio State University Press, pp. 179-232.

Miller, P.C. and L.L. Tieszen (1972) A preliminary model of processes affecting primary production in the arctic tundra. *Arctic and Alpine Research,* **4**: 1-18.

Miller, P.C., B.D. Collier and F.L. Bunnell (1975) Development of ecosystem modeling in the Tundra Biome. In *Systems Analysis in Ecology,* **3**: 95-115.

Miller, P.C., W.A. Stoner and L.L. Tieszen (1976) A model of stand photosynthesis for the wet meadow tundra, Barrow, Alaska. *Ecology,* **57**: 411-430.

Miller, P.C., W.C. Oechel, W.A. Stoner and B. Sveinbjörnsson (1978a) Simulation of CO_2 uptake and water relations of four arctic bryophytes at Point Barrow, Alaska. *Photosynthetica,* **12**: 7-20.

Miller, P.C., W.A. Stoner and J.R. Ehleringer (1978b) Some aspects of water relations of arctic and alpine plants. In *Vegetation and Production Ecology of an Alaskan Arctic Tundra* (L.L. Tieszen, Ed.). New York: Springer-Verlag, pp. 343-357.

Miller, P.C., W.A. Stoner, L.L. Tieszen, M. Allessio, B. McCown, F.S. Chapin and G. Shaver (1978c) A model of carbohydrate, nitrogen, phosphorus allocation and growth in tundra production. In *Vegetation and Production Ecology of an Alaskan Arctic Tundra* (L.L. Tieszen, Ed.). New York: Springer-Verlag, pp. 577-598.

Miller, P.C., W.D. Billings and W.C. Oechel (1979) A modeling approach to low temperatures. In *Comparative Mechanics of Cold Adaptation in the Arctic* (L.S. Underwood, L.L. Tieszen, A.B. Callahan and G.E. Folk, Eds.). New York: Academic Press, pp. 181-214.

Miller, P.C. and W.A. Stoner (1979) Canopy structure and environmental interactions. In *Topics in Plant Population Biology* (O. Solbrig, S. Jain, G.B. Johnson and P.H. Raven, Eds.). New York: Columbia University Press, pp. 428-458.

Milthorpe, F.L. and J. Moorby (1974) *An Introduction to Crop Physiology.* Cambridge: Cambridge University Press, 202 pp.

Minderman, G. (1968) Addition, decomposition and accumulation of organic matter in forests. *Journal of Ecology, 56*: 355-362.

Mishustin, E.W. and V.A. Mirzoeva (1972) Soil microflora in the northern USSR. In *Microflora of the Soils of the Northern and Central USSR.* Jerusalem: Israel Programme for Scientific Translations.

Mitchell, W.W. (1973) Adaptations of species and varieties of grasses for potential use in Alaska. In *Proceedings of the Symposium on the Impact of Oil Resource Development on Northern Plant Communities: Presented at the 23rd AAAS Alaska Science Conference, Fairbanks, Alaska, 17 August 1972* (B.H. McCown and D.R. Simpson, Coordinators). University of Alaska, Institute of Arctic Biology, Occasional Publications on Northern Life 1, pp. 2-6.

Monk, C.D. (1966) An ecological significance of evergreenness. *Ecology, 47*: 504-505.

Monteith, J.L. (1965) Light distribution and photosynthesis in field crops. *Annals of Botany*, N.S., *29*: 17-37.

Monteith, J.L. (1974) *Principles of Environmental Physics.* London: Edward Arnold, 241 pp.

Mooney, H.A. (1972) The carbon balance of plants. *Annual Review of Ecology and Systematics, 3*: 315-346.

Mooney, H.A. (1977) *Convergent Evolution in Chile and California, Mediterranean Climate Ecosystems.* Stroudsburg, Pa.: Dowden, Hutchinson and Ross, 224 pp.

Mooney, H.A. and W.D. Billings (1960) The annual carbohydrate cycle of alpine plants as related to growth. *American Journal of Botany, 47*: 594-598.

Mooney, H.A. and W.D. Billings (1961) Comparative physiological ecology of arctic and alpine populations of *Oxyria digyna. Ecological Monographs, 31*: 1-29.

Mooney, H.A. and A.W. Johnson (1965) Comparative physiological ecology of an arctic and an alpine population of *Thalictrum alpinum. Journal of Ecology, 46*: 721-727.

Mooney, H.A., S.L. Gulmon, D.J. Parsons and A.T. Harrison (1974)

Morphological changes within the chaparral vegetation type as related to elevational gradients. *Madroño*, **22**: 281-316.

Moore, J.J., P. Dowding and B. Healy (1975) Glenamoy, Ireland. In *Structure and Function of Tundra Ecosystems: Papers Presented at the IBP Tundra Biome V International Meeting on Biological Productivity of Tundra, Abisko, Sweden, April 1974* (T. Rosswall and O.W. Heal, Eds.). Ecological Bulletins 20. Stockholm: Swedish Natural Science Research Council, pp. 321-343.

Moore, P.D. and D.J. Bellamy (1974) *Peatlands.* New York: Springer-Verlag, 221 pp.

Moritz, R.E. (1977) On a possible sea-breeze circulation near Barrow, Alaska. *Arctic and Alpine Research,* **9**: 427-431.

Morton, A.J. (1977) Mineral nutrient pathways in a Molinietum in autumn and winter. *Journal of Ecology,* **65**: 993-999.

Moser, T.J., T.H. Nash, III and J.W. Thomson (1979) Lichens of Anaktuvuk Pass, Alaska, with emphasis on the impact of caribou grazing. *Bryologist,* **82**: 393-408.

Mosser, J.L., G.M. Herdrich and T.D. Brock (1976) Temperature optima for bacteria and yeasts from cold-mountain habitats. *Canadian Journal of Microbiology,* **22**: 324-325.

Muc, M. (1977) Ecology and primary production of sedge–moss meadow communities, Truelove Lowland. In *Truelove Lowland, Devon Island, Canada: A High Arctic Ecosystem* (L.C. Bliss, Ed.). Edmonton: The University of Alberta Press, pp. 157-184.

Mullen, D.A. (1965) Physiologic correlations with population density and other environmental factors in the brown lemming, *Lemmus trimucronatus.* Ph.D. dissertation, University of California (Berkeley), 171 pp.

Mullen, D.A. (1968) Reproduction in brown lemmings (*Lemmus trimucronatus*) and its relevance to their cycle of abundance. *University of California Publications in Zoology,* **85**: 1-24.

Mullen, D.A. and F.A. Pitelka (1972) Efficiency of winter scavengers in the Arctic. *Arctic,* **25**: 225-231.

Muller, K. (1909) Untersuchung uber die Wasseraufnahme durch Moose und verschiedene andere Pflanzen und Pflanzenteile. *Jahrbuch für Wissenschaftliche Botanik,* **46**: 587-598.

Munervar, F. and A.G. Wollum II (1977) Effects of the addition of phosphorus and inorganic nitrogen on carbon and nitrogen mineralization in Andepts from Colorado. *Soil Science Society of America, Journal,* **41**: 540-545.

Munn, N.R. (1973) An examination of the inorganic nitrogen status of a soil of the Alaskan coastal tundra plain. M.Sc. thesis, Utah State University, 52 pp.

Murray, B.M. and D.F. Murray (1978) Checklists of vascular plants, bryophytes, and lichens for the Alaskan U.S. IBP Tundra Biome study areas; Barrow, Prudhoe Bay, Eagle Summit. In *Vegetation and Production Ecology of an Alaskan Arctic Tundra* (L.L. Tieszen, Ed.). New York: Springer-Verlag, pp. 647-677.

Murray, D.F. (1978) Ecology, floristics, and phytogeography of northern Alaska. In *Vegetation and Production Ecology of an Alaskan Arctic Tundra* (L.L. Tieszen, Ed.). New York: Springer-Verlag, pp. 19-36.

Myers, J.P. and F.A. Pitelka (1979) Variations in summer temperature patterns near Barrow, Alaska: analysis and ecological interpretation. *Arctic and Alpine Research,* **11**: 131-144.

Nakano, Y. and J. Brown (1972) Mathematical modeling and validation of the thermal regimes in tundra soils, Barrow, Alaska. *Arctic and Alpine Research,* **4**: 19-38.

National Academy of Sciences (1969) *United States–Canadian Tables of Feed Composition.* 2nd revision. Washington, D.C.: U.S. National Academy of Sciences, Publication 1684, 92 pp.

National Academy of Sciences (1972) *Nutrient Requirements of Domestic Animals.* 2nd revised edition. Washington, D.C.: U.S. National Academy of Sciences, No. 10, 117 pp.

National Academy of Sciences (1974) *U.S. Participation in the International Biological Program. Report No. 6 of the U.S. National Committee for the International Biological Program.* Washington, D.C.: U.S. National Academy of Sciences, 166 pp.

Nelson, L. (1977) Growth and survival characteristics of three arctic soil bacteria on Truelove Lowland. In *Truelove Lowland, Devon Island, Canada: A High Arctic Ecosystem* (L.C. Bliss, Ed.). Edmonton: The University of Alberta Press, pp. 547-565.

Ng, E. and P.C. Miller (1975) A model of the effect of tundra vegetation on soil temperatures. In *Climate of the Arctic: Twenty-fourth Alaska Science Conference Proceedings, Fairbanks, Alaska, August 1973* (G. Weller and S.A. Bowling, Eds.). Fairbanks: Geophysical Institute, University of Alaska, pp. 222-226.

Ng, E. and P.C. Miller (1977) Validation of a model of the effects of tundra vegetation on soil temperatures. *Arctic and Alpine Research,* **9**: 89-104.

Ng, E. and P.C. Miller (1980) Soil moisture relations in the southern California chaparral. *Ecology,* **61**: 98-107.

Nielsen, K.F. and E.C. Humphries (1966) Effects of root temperature on plant growth. *Soils and Fertilizers,* **29**: 1-7.

Nielson, C.O. (1962) Carbohydrases in soil and litter invertebrates. *Oikos,* **13**: 200-215.

Norton, D.W. (1972) Incubation schedules of four species of Calidridine sandpipers at Barrow, Alaska. *Condor,* **74**: 164-176.

Norton, D.W. (1974) Ecological energetics of Calidridine sandpiper breeding in northern Alaska. Ph.D. dissertation, University of Alaska, 163 pp.

Norton, D.W., I.W. Ailes and J.A. Curatolo (1975) Ecological relationships of the inland tundra avifauna near Prudhoe Bay, Alaska. In *Ecological Investigations of the Tundra Biome in the Prudhoe Bay Region, Alaska* (J. Brown, Ed.). Biological Papers of the University of Alaska, Special Report 2, pp. 124-133.

Novichkova-Ivanova, L.N. (1972) Soil and aerial algae of polar deserts and arctic tundra. In *Proceedings, IV International Meeting on the Biological Productivity of Tundra, Leningrad, USSR* (F.E. Wielgolaski and T. Rosswall, Eds.). Stockholm: International Biological Programme Tundra Biome Steering Committee, pp. 261-265.

Oberbauer, S. (1978) The influence of plant water relations on species distribution in alpine and tussock tundra. M.S. thesis, San Diego State Univeristy, 172 pp.

Oberbauer, S. and P.C. Miller (1979) Plant water relations in montane and tussock tundra vegetation types in Alaska. *Arctic and Alpine Research,* **11**: 69-81.

O'Connor, F.B. (1967) The Enchytraeidae. In *Soil Biology* (A. Burges and F. Raw, Eds.). London: Academic Press, pp. 213-257.

Odum, H.T. (1970) Rain forest structure and mineral-cycling homeostasis. In *A Tropical Rain Forest: A Study of Irradiation and Ecology at El Verde, Puerto Rico* (H.T. Odum, Ed.). Oak Ridge, Tenn.: U.S. Atomic Energy Commission, pp. H-3 to H-52.

Oechel, W.C. (1976) Seasonal patterns of temperature response of CO_2 flux and acclimation in arctic mosses growing in situ. *Photosynthetica,* **10**: 447-456.

Oechel, W.C. and N.J. Collins (1973) Seasonal patterns of CO_2 exchange in bryophytes at Barrow, Alaska. In *Primary Production and Production Processes: Proceedings of the Conference, Dublin, Ireland, April 1973* (L.C. Bliss and F.E. Wielgolaski, Eds.). Stockholm: International Biological Programme Tundra Biome Steering Committee, pp. 197-203.

Oechel, W.C., P. Hicklenton, B. Sveinbjörnsson, P.C. Miller and W.A. Stoner (1975) Temperature acclimation of photosynthesis in *D. fuscescens* growing *in situ* in the arctic and subarctic. In *Proceedings of the Circumpolar Conference on Northern Ecology, Ottawa, 1975.* Ottawa: National Research Council of Canada, pp. I-131 to I-144.

Oechel, W.C. and N.J. Collins (1976) Comparative CO_2 exchange patterns in mosses from two tundra habitats at Barrow, Alaska. *Canadian Journal of Botany,* **54**: 1355-1369.

Oechel, W.C. and B. Sveinbjörnsson (1978) Primary production processes in arctic bryophytes at Barrow, Alaska. In *Vegetation and*

Production Ecology of an Alaskan Arctic Tundra (L.L. Tieszen, Ed.). New York: Springer-Verlag, pp. 269-298.

Ohmura, A. (1972) Heat and water balance on arctic tundra. In *International Geography 1972: Papers Submitted to the 22nd International Geographical Congress, Canada* (W.P. Adams and F.M. Helleiner, Eds.). Toronto: University of Toronto Press, pp. 175-176.

Ohmura, A. and F. Müller (1976) Heat balance measurement on arctic tundra, Axel Heiberg Island, Canadian Arctic Archipelago. *Proceedings, 23rd International Geographical Congress, Moscow 1976*, pp. 80-84.

Olsen, S.R., W.D. Kemper and R.D. Jackson (1962) Phosphate diffusion to plant roots. *Soil Science Society of America, Proceedings,* **26**: 222-227.

Olson, J.S. (1963) Energy storage and the balance of producers and decomposers in ecological systems. *Ecology,* **44**: 322-331.

Olson, J.S. (1970) Carbon cycles and temperate woodlands. In *Analysis of Temperate Forest Ecosystems* (D.E. Reichle, Ed.). New York: Springer-Verlag, pp. 226-241.

Oméliansky, V.L. (1911) Etude bactériologique du Mammouth de Sanga Jorach et du sol adjacent. *Archives des Sciences Biologiques publiées par l'Institute Impérial de Médecine Expérimentale à St. Petersbourg,* **16**: 355-367.

Oosting, H.J. (1956) *The Study of Plant Communities: An Introduction to Plant Ecology.* 2nd edition. San Francisco: W.H. Freeman, 440 pp.

Orians, G.H. and O.T. Solbrig (1977) A cost-income model of leaves and roots with special reference to arid and semiarid areas. *American Naturalist,* **111**: 677-690.

Osborn, R.G. (1975) Models of lemming demography and avian predation near Barrow, Alaska. M.S. thesis, San Diego State University, 106 pp.

Østbye, E. (Ed.) (1975) Hardangervidda, Norway. In *Structure and Function of Tundra Ecosystems: Papers Presented at the IBP Tundra Biome V International Meeting on Biological Productivity of Tundra, Abisko, Sweden, April 1974* (T. Rosswall and O.W. Heal, Eds.). Ecological Bulletins 20. Stockholm: Swedish Natural Science Research Council, pp. 225-264.

Outcalt, S.I. (1974) Gradient mapping of patterned ground characteristics from a photomosaic of the IBP Tundra Biome site near Barrow, Alaska. *Mathematical Geology,* **6**: 235-244.

Outcalt, S.I., C. Goodwin, G. Weller and J. Brown (1975) A digital computer simulation of the annual snow and soil thermal regimes at Barrow, Alaska. *Water Resources Research,* **11**: 709-715.

Ovington, J.D. (1968) Some factors affecting nutrient distribution within ecosystems. In *Functioning of Terrestrial Ecosystems at Primary Production Level: Proceedings of the Copenhagen Symposium* (F.E. Eckardt, Ed.). Natural Resources Research 5. Paris: UNESCO, pp. 95-105.

Parinkina, O.M. (1974) Bacterial production in tundra soils. In *Soil Organisms and Decomposition in Tundra: Proceedings of the Microbiology, Decomposition and Invertebrate Working Groups Meeting, Fairbanks, Alaska, August 1973* (A.J. Holding, O.W. Heal, S.F. MacLean, Jr. and P.W. Flanagan, Eds.). Stockholm: International Biological Programme Tundra Biome Steering Committee, pp. 65-77.

Parker, G.R. (1972) Biology of the Kaminuriak population of barren-ground caribou. Part I. Total numbers, mortality, recruitment, and seasonal distribution. Canadian Wildlife Service Report Series 20, 95 pp.

Parkhurst, D.F. and O.L. Loucks (1972) Optimal leaf size in relation to environment. *Journal of Ecology,* **60**: 505-537.

Parkinson, D. (1971) Studies on fungi in Canadian aspen forest soils. In *Productivity of Forest Ecosystems: Proceedings of the Brussels Symposium* (P. Duvigneaud, Ed.). Paris: UNESCO, pp. 425-430.

Parkinson, D., S. Visser and J.B. Whittaker (1977) Effects of Collembolan grazing on fungal colonization of leaf litter. In *Soil Organisms as Components of Ecosystems: International Soil Zoology Colloquium, Uppsala, Sweden, June 21–25, 1976* (U. Lohn and T. Persson, Eds.). Ecological Bulletins 25. Stockholm: Swedish Natural Science Research Council, pp. 75-79.

Patterson, P.M. (1943) Some ecological observations on bryophytes. *The Bryologist,* **46**: 1-13.

Patterson, R.P., D.L. Grunes and D.J. Lathwell (1972) Influence of root-zone temperature and P supply on total and inorganic P, free sugars, aconitase and soluble amino N in corn. *Crop Science,* **12**: 227-230.

Paul, E.A., V.O. Biederbeck, W.E. Lowe and J.R. Willard (1973) Soil microorganisms. I: Population dynamics of bacteria and actinomycetes. Canadian Committee for the International Biological Program Technical Report No. 37, Matador Project.

Payne, T.C. et al. (1951) Geology of the Arctic Slope of Alaska. Oil and Gas Investigation Map OM 126. U.S. Geological Survey, Washington, D.C.

Payton, I.J. and D.J. Brasch (1978) Growth and nonstructural carbohydrate reserves in *Chionochloa rigida* and *C. macra*, and their short-term response to fire. *New Zealand Journal of Botany,* **16**: 435-460.

Pearson, O.P. (1966) The prey of carnivores during one cycle of mouse abundance. *Journal of Animal Ecology,* **35**: 217-233.

Penning de Vries, F.W.T. (1972a) A model for simulating transpiration of leaves with special attention to stomatal functioning. *Journal of Applied Ecology,* **9**: 57-77.

Penning de Vries, F.W.T. (1972b) Respiration and growth. In *Crop Processes in Controlled Environments* (A.R. Rees, K.E. Cockshull, D.W. Hand and R.G. Hurd, Eds.). London: Academic Press, pp. 327-347.

Penning de Vries, F.W.T. (1973) Substrate utilization and respiration in relation to growth and maintenance in higher plants. Ph.D. dissertation, Agricultural University, Wageningen, 357 pp.

Penning de Vries, F.W.T. (1974) Substrate utilization and respiration in relation to growth and maintenance in higher plants. *Netherlands Journal of Agricultural Sciences,* **22**: 40-44.

Penning de Vries, F.W.T. (1975) The cost of maintenance processes in plant cells. *Annals of Botany,* N.S., **39**: 77-92.

Penning de Vries, F.W.T., A.H.M. Brunsting and H.H. van Laar (1974) Products, requirements and efficiency of biosynthesis: a quantitative approach. *Journal of Theoretical Biology,* **45**: 339-377.

Person, S.J. (1975) Digestibility of indigenous plants utilized by *Rangifer tarandus.* Ph.D. dissertation, University of Alaska, 97 pp.

Person, S.J., R.G. White and J.R. Luick (1975) *In vitro* digestibility of forages utilized by *Rangifer tarandus.* In *Proceedings of the First International Caribou and Reindeer Symposium, 9–11 August 1972, University of Alaska* (J.R. Luick, P.C. Lent, D.R. Klein and R.G. White, Eds.). Biological Papers of the University of Alaska, Special Report 1, pp. 251-256.

Person, S.J., R.E. Pegau, R.G. White and J.R. Luick (1980) *In vitro* and nylon bag digestibilities of reindeer and caribou forages. *Journal of Wildlife Management,* **44**: 613-622.

Petersen, H. (1971) The nutritional biology of Collembola and its ecological significance. A review of recent literature with a few original observations (in Danish, English summary). *Entomologiske Meddelelser,* **39**: 97-118.

Petersen, H. (1975) Estimation of dry weight, fresh weight, and calorific content of various Collembolan species. *Pedobiologia,* **15**: 222-243.

Peterson, K.M. (1978) Vegetational successions and other ecosystemic changes in two arctic tundras. Ph.D. dissertation, Duke University, 305 pp.

Peterson, K.M. and D.W.. Billings (1975) Carbon dioxide flux from tundra soils and vegetation as related to temperature at Barrow, Alaska. *American Midland Naturalist,* **94**: 88-98.

Peterson, R.M, Jr. and G.O. Batzli (1975) Activity patterns in natural populations of the brown lemming *(Lemmus trimucronatus).* *Jour-*

nal of Mammalogy, **56**: 718-720.

Peterson, R.M, Jr., G.O. Batzli and E.M. Banks (1976) Activity and energetics of the brown lemming in its natural habitat. *Arctic and Alpine Research,* **8**: 131-138.

Peterson, W.L. and J.M. Mayo (1975) Moisture stress and its effect on photosynthesis in *Dicranum polysetum. Canadian Journal of Botany,* **53**: 2897-2900.

Petrides, G.A. and W.G. Swank (1966) Estimating the productivity and energy relations of an African elephant population. In *Proceedings of the Ninth International Grasslands Congress, São Paulo, Brazil,* pp. 832-842.

Pianka, E.R. (1970) On r- and K- selection. *American Naturalist,* **140**: 594-597.

Pilát, A. and J.A. Nannfeldt (1954) Notulae ad cognitionem Hymenomycetum Lapponiae Tornensis (Sueciae). *Friesia,* **1**: 6-38.

Pitelka, F.A. (1957a) Some aspects of population structure in the short-term cycle of the brown lemming in northern Alaska. *Cold Spring Harbor Symposium on Quantitative Biology,* **22**: 237-251.

Pitelka, F.A. (1957b) Some characteristics of microtine cycles in the Arctic. In *Arctic Biology: Eighteenth Annual Biology Colloquium* (H.P. Hansen, Ed.). Corvallis: Oregon State University Press, pp. 73-88.

Pitelka, F.A. (1964) The nutrient-recovery hypothesis for arctic microtine cycles. I. Introduction. In *Grazing in Terrestrial and Marine Environments: A Symposium of the British Ecological Society, Bangor, 11-14 April 1962* (D.J. Crisp, Ed.). Oxford: Blackwell Scientific Publications, pp. 55-56.

Pitelka, F.A. (1973) Cycling pattern in lemming populations near Barrow, Alaska. In *Alaskan Arctic Tundra: Proceedings of the 25th Anniversary Celebration of the Naval Arctic Research Laboratory* (M.E. Britton, Ed.). Arctic Institute of North America Technical Paper 25, pp. 199-215.

Pitelka, F.A. (1974) An avifaunal review for the Barrow region and North Slope of arctic Alaska. *Arctic and Alpine Research,* **6**: 161-184.

Pitelka, F.A., P.Q. Tomich and G.W. Treichel (1955) Ecological relations of jaegers and owls as lemming predators near Barrow, Alaska. *Ecological Monographs,* **25**: 85-117.

Pitelka, F.A., R.T. Holmes and S.F. MacLean, Jr. (1974) Ecology and evolution of social organization in arctic sandpipers. *American Zoologist,* **14**: 185-204.

Pitt, J.I. and J.H.B. Christian (1968) Water relations of xerophilic fungi isolated from prunes. *Applied Microbiology,* **16**: 1853-1858.

Poelt, J. (1973) Appendix A: Classification. In *The Lichens* (V. Ahmadjian and M.E. Hale, Eds.). New York: Academic Press, pp. 599-632.

Polunin, N. (1935) The vegetation of Akpatok Island, Part II. *Journal of Ecology,* **23**: 161-209.

Porter, L. (1975) Nitrogen transformation in ecosystems. In *Soil Biochemistry.* Vol. 4 (E.A. Paul and A.D. McLaren, Eds.). New York: Marcel Dekker, pp. 1-30.

Prentki, R.T. (1976) Phosphorus cycling in tundra ponds. Ph.D. dissertation, University of Alaska, 275 pp.

Prentki, R.T., M.C. Miller, R.J. Barsdate, V. Alexander, J. Kelley and P. Coyne (1980) Chemistry. In *Limnology of Tundra Ponds, Barrow, Alaska* (J.E. Hobbie, Ed.). Stroudsburg, Pa.: Dowden, Hutchinson and Ross, pp. 76-178.

Prescott, G.W. (1953) Preliminary notes on the ecology of freshwater algae of the Arctic Slope, Alaska, with descriptions of some species. *American Midland Naturalist,* **50**: 463-470.

Prescott, G.W. (1961) Ecology of freshwater algae in the Arctic. In *Recent Advances in Botany: From Lectures and Symposia Presented to the IX International Botanical Congress, Montreal, 1959.* Vol. 1. Toronto: University of Toronto Press, pp. 201-207.

Procter, D.L.C. (1977) Nematode densities and production on Truelove Lowland. In *Truelove Lowland, Devon Island, Canada: A High Arctic Ecosystem* (L.C. Bliss, Ed.). Edmonton: The University of Alberta Press, pp. 347-361.

Pruitt, W.O. (1960) Animals in the snow. *Scientific American,* **202**(1): 61-68.

Pugh, G.J.F. (1974) Terrestrial fungi. In *Biology of Plant Litter Decomposition* (C.H. Dickinson and G.J.F. Pugh, Eds.). London: Academic Press, pp. 303-336.

Putnins, P. (1966) The sequences of baric weather patterns over Alaska. In *Studies on the Meteorology of Alaska.* First Interim Report of the Environmental Data Service, Environmental Science Services Administration, Washington, D.C., 81 pp.

Raisbeck, J.M. and M.F. Mohtadi (1974) The environmental impacts of oil spills on land in the arctic regions. *Water, Air and Soil Pollution,* **3**: 195-208.

Rall, G. (1965) Soil fungi from the alpine zone of the Medicine Bow Mountains, Wyoming. *Mycologia,* **57**: 872-881.

Rastorfer, J.R. (1972) Comparative physiology of four West Antarctic mosses. In *Antarctic Terrestrial Biology* (G.A. Llano, Ed.). Washington, D.C.: American Geophysical Union, pp. 143-161.

Rastorfer, J.R. (1978) Composition and bryomass of the moss layers of two wet-tundra meadow communities near Barrow, Alaska. In *Vegetation and Production Ecology of an Alaskan Arctic Tundra* (L.L. Tieszen, Ed.). New York: Springer-Verlag, pp. 169-183.

Raunkiaer, C. (1934) *The Life Forms of Plants and Statistical Plant Geography.* Oxford: Clarendon Press, 632 pp.

Rausch, R. (1950) Observations of a cyclic decline of lemmings *(Lemmus)* on the arctic coast of Alaska during spring 1949. *Arctic,* 3: 166-177.

Raw, F. (1967) Arthropoda (except Acari and Collembola). In *Soil Biology* (A. Burges and F. Raw, Eds.). London: Academic Press, pp. 323-362.

Rayner, J.M. (Ed.) (1960a) Temperature and wind frequency tables for North America and Greenland. Vol. 1. January–June. McGill University, Arctic Meteorology Research Group, Publication in Meteorology 24, 275 pp.

Rayner, J.M. (Ed.) (1960b) Temperature and wind frequency tables for North America and Greenland. Vol. 2. July–December. McGill University, Arctic Meteorology Research Group, Publication in Meteorology 25, 275 p.

Redmann, R.E. and Z.M. Abouguendia (1978) Partitioning of respiration from soil, litter and plants in a mixed-grassland ecosystem. *Oecologia* (Berl.), 36: 69-79.

Reed, J.C. and A.G. Ronhovde (1971) Arctic laboratory: A history of the Naval Arctic Research Laboratory at Point Barrow, Alaska. Arctic Institute of North America Technical Report, 748 pp.

Rickard, W.E., Jr. and J. Brown (1974) Effects of vehicles on arctic tundra. *Environmental Conservation,* 1: 55-62.

Ricklefs, R.E. (1973) *Ecology.* Newton, Mass.: Chiron Press, 861 pp.

Roby, D.D. (1978) Behavioral patterns of barren-ground caribou of the Central Arctic herd adjacent to the Trans-Alaska oil pipeline. M.S. Thesis, University of Alaska, 200 pp.

Rochow, T.F. (1967) The ecology of *Thlaspi alpestre* in the central Rocky Mountains along altitudinal gradients. Ph.D. dissertation, Duke University, 265 pp.

Rodin, L.E., N.I. Bazilevich and N.N. Rozov (1975) Productivity of the world's main ecosystems. In *Productivity of World Ecosystems: Proceedings of Symposium, August 31–September 1, 1972, Seattle, Washington.* Washington, D.C.: National Academy of Sciences, pp. 13-26.

Rogers, J.C. (1978) Meteorological factors affecting interannual variability of summertime ice extent in the Beaufort Sea. *Monthly Weather Review,* 106: 890-897.

Ross, R. (1956) The cryptogamic flora of the Arctic. III. Algae: Planktonic. *Botanical Review,* 20: 400-416.

Rosswall, T. (1974) Decomposition of plant litter in Stordalen—A summary. In *Progress Report 1973* (J.G.K. Flower-Ellis, Ed.). International Biological Programme, Swedish Tundra Biome Project Technical Report 16, pp. 207-212.

Rosswall, T. and B.H. Svensson (1974) Chemolithotrophic and photo-synthetic bacteria at Stordalen. In *Progress Report 1973* (J.G.K. Flower-Ellis, Ed.). International Biological Programme, Swedish Tundra Biome Project Technical Report 16, pp. 73-79.

Rosswall, T., J.G.K. Flower-Ellis, L.G. Johansson, S. Jonsson, B.E. Rydén and M. Sonesson (1975) Stordalen (Abisko), Sweden. In *Structure and Function of Tundra Ecosystems: Papers Presented at the IBP Tundra Biome V International Meeting on Biological Productivity of Tundra, Abisko, Sweden, April 1974* (T. Rosswall and O.W. Heal, Eds.). Ecological Bulletins 20. Stockholm: Swedish Natural Science Research Council, pp. 265-294.

Rosswall, T. and O.W. Heal (Eds.) (1975) *Structure and Function of Tundra Ecosystems: Papers Presented at the IBP Tundra Biome V International Meeting on Biological Productivity of Tundra, Abisko, Sweden, April 1974.* Ecological Bulletins 20. Stockholm: Swedish Natural Science Research Council, 450 pp.

Rouse, W.R., P.F. Mills and R.B. Stewart (1977) Evaporation in high latitudes. *Water Resources Research,* **13:** 909-914.

Russell, R.S. (1940) Physiological and ecological studies on an arctic vegetation. III. Observations on carbon assimilation, carbohydrate storage and stomatal movement in relation to the growth of plants on Jan Mayen Island. *Journal of Ecology,* **28:** 289-309.

Russell, R.S., D.W. Cutler, S.E. Jacobs, A. King and A.G. Pollard (1940) Physiological and ecological studies on an arctic vegetation. II. The development of vegetation in relation to nitrogen supply and soil micro-organisms on Jan Mayen Island. *Journal of Ecology,* **28:** 269-288.

Ryan, J.K. (1977) Synthesis of energy flows and population dynamics of Truelove Lowland invertebrates. In *Truelove Lowland, Devon Island, Canada: A High Arctic Ecosystem* (L.C. Bliss, Ed.). Edmonton: The University of Alberta Press, pp. 325-346.

Rydén, B.E. (1977) Hydrology of Truelove Lowland. In *Truelove Lowland, Devon Island, Canada: A High Arctic Ecosystem* (L.C. Bliss, Ed.). Edmonton: The University of Alberta Press, pp. 107-136.

Saebø, S. (1968) The autecology of *Rubus chamaemorus* L. I. Phosphorus economy of *Rubus chamaemorus* in an ombrotrophic mire. *Scientific Reports from the Agricultural College of Norway,* **47**(1): 1-67.

Saebø, S. (1969) On the mechanism behind the effect of freezing and thawing on dissolved phosphorus in *Sphagnum fuscum* peat. *Scientific Reports from the Agricultural College of Norway,* **48**(14): 1-10.

Safriel, U.N. (1975) On the significance of clutch size in nidifugous birds. *Ecology,* **56:** 703-708.

Satchell, J.E. (1971) Feasibility study of an energy budget for Meathop Wood. In *Productivity of Forest Ecosystems: Proceedings of the Brussels Symposium* (P.E. Duvigneaud, Ed.). Paris: UNESCO, pp. 619-630.

Satchell, J.E. (1974) Introduction: Litter-interface of animate/inanimate matter. In *Biology of Plant Litter Decomposition* (C.H. Dickinson and G.J.F. Pugh, Eds.). New York: Academic Press, pp. xiii-xliv.

Savile, D.B.O. (1972) Arctic adaptations in plants. Research Branch, Canada Department of Agriculture Monograph 6, 81 pp.

Schamel, D. and D. Tracy (1977) Polyandry, replacement clutches, and site tenacity in the red phalarope (*Phalaropus fulicarius*) at Barrow, Alaska. *Bird-Banding,* **48**: 314-324.

Schlesinger, W.H. (1977) Carbon balance in terrestrial detritus. *Annual Review of Ecology and Systematics,* **8**: 51-81.

Scholander, P.F., V. Walters, R. Hock and L. Irving (1950) Body insulation of some arctic and tropical mammals and birds. *Biological Bulletin,* **99**: 225-236.

Schramm, U. (1972) Temperature–food interactions in herbivorous insects. *Oecologia* (Berl.), **9**: 399-402.

Schultz, A.M. (1964) The nutrient recovery hypothesis for arctic microtine cycles. II. Ecosystem variables in relation to arctic microtine cycles. In *Grazing in Terrestrial and Marine Environments: A Symposium of the British Ecological Society, Bangor, 11–14 April 1962* (D.J. Crisp, Ed.). Oxford: Blackwell Scientific Publications, pp. 57-68.

Schultz, A.M. (1969) A study of an ecosystem: The arctic tundra. In *The Ecosystem Concept in Natural Resource Management* (G.M. Van Dyne, Ed.). New York: Academic Press, pp. 77-93.

Schwerdtfeger, W. (1975) Mountain barrier effect on the flow of stable air north of the Brooks Range. In *Climate of the Arctic: Twenty-fourth Alaska Science Conference Proceedings, Fairbanks, Alaska, 15–17 August 1973*. Fairbanks: Geophysical Institute, University of Alaska, pp. 204-208.

Scott, D. (1970) Relative growth rates under controlled temperatures of some New Zealand indigenous and introduced grasses. *New Zealand Journal of Botany,* **8**: 76-81.

Scott, D. and W.D. Billings (1964) Effects of environmental factors on standing crop and productivity of an alpine tundra. *Ecological Monographs,* **34**: 243-270.

Sculthorpe, C.D. (1967) *The Biology of Aquatic Vascular Plants.* New York: St. Martin's Press, 610 pp.

Searby, H.W. and M. Hunter (1971) Climate of the North Slope, Alaska. NOAA Technical Memorandum AR-4, 54 pp.

Seastedt, T.R. and S.F. MacLean, Jr. (1979) Territory size and composition in relation to resource abundance in Lapland longspurs breeding in arctic Alaska. *Auk,* **96**: 131-142.

Sellmann, P.V., K.L. Carey, C. Keeler and A.D. Hartwell (1972) Terrain and coastal conditions on the Arctic Alaska Coastal Plain: Arctic environmental data package supplement 1. U.S. Army Cold Regions Research and Engineering Laboratory Special Report 165, 72 pp.

Sellmann, P.V. and J. Brown (1973) Stratigraphy and diagenesis of perennially frozen sediment in the Barrow, Alaska, region. In *Permafrost: North American Contribution to the Second International Conference.* Washington, D.C.: National Academy of Sciences, pp. 171-181.

Sellmann, P.V., J. Brown, R.I. Lewellen, H.L. McKim and C.J. Merry (1975) The classification and geomorphic implications of thaw lakes on the Arctic Coastal Plain, Alaska. U.S. Army Cold Regions Research and Engineering Laboratory Research Report 344, 20 pp.

Šesták, Z., J. Čatský and P.G. Jarvis (Eds.) (1971) *Plant Photosynthetic Production. Manual of Methods.* The Hague: Dr. W. Junk, 818 pp.

Sextone, A., K. Everett, T. Jenkins and R.M. Atlas (1978) Fate of crude and refined oils in North Slope soils. *Arctic,* **31**: 339-347.

Shaver, G.R. (1976) Ecology of roots and rhizomes in graminoid plants of the Alaskan coastal tundra. Ph.D. dissertation, Duke University, 213 pp.

Shaver, G.R. and W.D. Billings (1975) Root production and root turnover in a wet tundra ecosystem, Barrow, Alaska. *Ecology,* **56**(2): 401-409.

Shaver, G.R. and W.D. Billings (1976) Carbohydrate accumulations in tundra graminoid plants as a function of season and tissue age. *Flora,* **165**: 247-267.

Shaver, G.R. and W.D. Billings (1977) Effects of day length and temperature on root elongation in tundra graminoids. *Oecologia* (Berl.), **28**: 57-65.

Shtina, E.A. (1972) Some peculiarities of the distribution of nitrogen-fixing blue–green algae in soils. In *First International Symposium on Taxonomy and Ecology of Blue–Green Algae, Madras, 1970* (T.V. Desikachary, Ed.). Madras: Bangalore Press, pp. 294-295.

Skoog, R.D. (1968) Ecology of the caribou (*Rangifer tarandus granti*) in Alaska. Ph.D. dissertation, University of California (Berkeley), 699 pp.

Slaughter, C.W., M. Mellor, P.V. Sellmann, J. Brown and L. Brown (1975) Accumulating snow to augment the fresh water supply at Barrow, Alaska. U.S. Army Cold Regions Research and Engineering Laboratory Special Report 217, 21 pp.

Small, E. (1972) Photosynthetic rates in relation to nitrogen cycling as an adaptation to nutrient deficiency in peat bog plants. *Canadian Journal of Botany,* **50**: 2227-2233.

Smirnov, N.N. (1958) Some data about the food consumption of plant production of bogs and fens by animals. *Verhandlung Internationale Vereinigung für Theoretische und Angewandte Limnologie,* **13**: 363-368.

Smirnov, N.N. (1961) Food cycles in sphagnous bogs. *Hydrobiologia,* **17**: 175-182.

Smith, F.E. (1954) Quantitative aspects of population growth. In *Dynamics of Growth Processes* (E.J. Boell, Ed.). Princeton, N.J.: Princeton University Press, pp. 277-294.

Sohlenius, B. (1980) Abundance, biomass, and contribution to energy flow by soil nematodes in terrestrial ecosystems. *Oikos,* **34**: 186-194.

Soil Survey Staff (1975) *Soil Taxonomy: A Basic System of Soil Classification for Making and Interpreting Soil Surveys.* Soil Conservation Service, U.S. Department of Agriculture Handbook 436, 754 pp.

Sonesson, M. (Ed.) (1980) *Ecology of a Subarctic Mire.* Ecological Bulletins 30. Stockholm: Swedish Natural Science Research Council, 313 pp.

Sørenson, T. (1941) Temperature relations of phenology of the northeast Greenland flowering plants. *Meddelelser om Grønland,* **125**(9): 1-305.

Sørenson, T. (1948) A method of establishing groups of equal amplitude in plant sociology based on similarity of species content and its application to analyses of the vegetation of the Danish commons. *Biologiske Skrifter,* **5**: 1-34.

Spetzman, L.A. (1959) Vegetation of the Arctic Slope of Alaska. U.S. Geological Survey Professional Paper 302B, pp. 19-58.

Springett, J.A., J.E. Brittain and B.P. Springett (1970) Vertical movement of Enchytraeidae (Oligochaeta) in moorland soils. *Oikos,* **21**: 16-21.

Stålfelt, M.G. (1937) Der Gasaustausch der Moose. *Planta,* **27**: 30-60.

Standen, V. (1978) The influence of soil fauna on decomposition by micro-organisms in blanket bog litter. *Journal of Animal Ecology,* **47**: 25-38.

Stanley, D.W. and R.J. Daley (1976) Environmental control of primary productivity on an Alaskan tundra pond. *Ecology,* **51**: 1025-1033.

Starkey, R.L. (1950) Relations of microorganisms to transformations of sulfur in soils. *Soil Science,* **70**: 55-65.

Starkey, R.L. (1966) Oxidation and reduction of sulfur compounds in soils. *Soil Science,* **101**: 297-306.

Steere, W.C. (1974) The status and geographical distribution of *Voitia hyperborea* in North America (Musci: Splachnaceae). *Bulletin of the*

Torrey Botanical Club, **101**: 55-63.

Steere, W.C. (1976) Ecology, phytogeography, and floristics of arctic Alaskan bryophytes. *Journal of the Hattori Botanical Laboratory,* **41**: 47-72.

Steere, W.C. (1978a) Floristics, phytogeography, and ecology of arctic Alaskan bryophytes. In *Vegetation and Production Ecology of an Alaskan Arctic Tundra* (L.L. Tieszen, Ed.). New York: Springer-Verlag, pp. 141-167.

Steere, W.C. (1978b) *The Mosses of Arctic Alaska.* Bryophytorum Bibliotheca 14. Vaduz: J. Cramer, 508 pp.

Steere, W.C. and H. Inoue (1978) The Hepaticae of arctic Alaska. *Journal of the Hattori Botanical Laboratory,* **44**: 251-345.

Stewart, R.G. and W.R. Rouse (1976) Simple models for calculating evaporation from dry and wet tundra surfaces. *Arctic and Alpine Research,* **8**: 263-274.

Stewart, W.D.P. (1968) Nitrogen input into aquatic ecosystems. In *Algae, Man and the Environment: Proceedings of an International Symposium held at Syracuse University, June 18-30, 1967* (D.F. Jackson, Ed.). Syracuse, N.Y.: Syracuse University Press, pp. 53-72.

Stewart, W.D.P. (1969) Biological and ecological aspects of nitrogen fixation by free-living micro-organisms. *Proceedings of the Royal Society* B, **172**: 367-388.

Stewart, W.D.P. (1973) Nitrogen fixation by photosynthetic micro-organisms. *Annual Review of Microbiology,* **27**: 283-316.

Stoner, W.A. and P.C. Miller (1975) Water relations of plant species in the wet coastal tundra at Barrow, Alaska. *Arctic and Alpine Research,* **7**: 109-124.

Stoner, W.A., P.C. Miller and P.M. Miller (1978a) A test of a model of irradiance within vegetation canopies at northern latitudes. *Arctic and Alpine Research,* **10**: 761-767.

Stoner, W.A., P.C. Miller and W.C. Oechel (1978b) Simulation of the effect of the tundra vascular plant canopy on the productivity of four moss species. In *Vegetation and Production Ecology of an Alaskan Arctic Tundra* (L.L. Tieszen, Ed.). New York: Springer-Verlag, pp. 371-387.

Stoner, W.A., P.C. Miller, S.P. Richards and S.A. Barkley (1978c) Internal nutrient recycling as related to plant life form: A simulation approach. In *Environmental Chemistry and Cycling Processes: Proceedings of Symposium, Augusta, Georgia, April 28–May 1, 1976* (D.C. Adriano and I.L. Brisbin, Jr., Eds.). U.S. Department of Energy, CONF-760429, pp. 165-181.

Stoner, W.A., P.C. Miller and L.L. Tieszen (1978d) A model of plant growth and phosphorus allocation for *Dupontia fisheri* in coastal, wet tundra. In *Vegetation and Production Ecology of an Alaskan Arctic Tundra* (L.L. Tieszen, Ed.). New York: Springer-Verlag, pp. 559-576.

Streten, N.A. (1974) A satellite view of weather systems over the northern American Arctic. *Weather,* **29**: 369-380.

Stutz, R.C. (1973) Nitrogen fixation in a high arctic ecosystem. Ph.D. dissertation, University of Alberta, 62 pp.

Stutz, R.C. (1977) Biological nitrogen fixation in high arctic soils, Truelove Lowland. In *Truelove Lowland, Devon Island, Canada: A High Arctic Ecosystem* (L.C. Bliss, Ed.). Edmonton: The University of Alberta Press, pp. 301-314.

Sutton, C.D. (1969) Effect of low soil temperature on phosphate nutrition of plants: a review. *Journal of Science, Food, and Agriculture,* **20**: 1-3.

Sveinbjörnsson, B. (1979) Controls of CO_2 exchange in arctic *Polytrichum* mosses. Ph.D. dissertation, McGill University, Montreal, 190 pp.

Svoboda, J. (1977) Ecology and primary production of raised beach communities, Truelove Lowland. In *Truelove Lowland, Devon Island, Canada: A High Arctic Ecosystem* (L.C. Bliss, Ed.). Edmonton: The University of Alberta Press, pp. 185-216.

Swanson, C.A. and D.R. Geiger (1967) Time course of low temperature inhibition of sucrose translocation in sugar beets. *Plant Physiology,* **42**: 751-756.

Tamm, C.O. (1964) Growth of *Hylocomium splendens* in relation to tree canopy. *The Bryologist,* **67**: 423-426.

Taylor, W.R. (1956) The cryptogamic flora of the Arctic. II. Algae: Non-planktonic. *Botanical Review, 20*: 363-399.

Tedrow, J.C.F. (1977) *Soils of the Polar Landscapes.* New Brunswick, N.J.: Rutgers University Press, 638 pp.

Tedrow, J.C.F. and J.E. Cantlon (1958) Concepts of soil formation and classification of arctic regions. *Arctic,* **11**: 166-179.

Thompson, D.Q. (1951) Summer food preferences of the brown and collared lemmings. In *Science in Alaska 1951: Proceedings Second Alaska Science Conference, Fairbanks,* p. 347.

Thompson, D.Q. (1955a) The role of food and cover in population fluctuations of brown lemming at Point Barrow, Alaska. In *Transactions of the 20th North American Wildlife Conference,* pp. 166-176.

Thompson, D.Q. (1955b) The 1953 lemming emigration at Point Barrow, Alaska. *Arctic,* **8**: 37-45.

Thompson, D.Q. (1955c) The ecology and population dynamics of the brown lemming (*Lemmus trimucronatus*) at Point Barrow, Alaska. Ph.D. dissertation, University of Missouri, 138 pp.

Thomson, J.W. (1979) *Lichens of the Alaskan Arctic Slope.* Toronto:

University of Toronto Press, 314 pp.

Thomson, L.W. and S. Zalik (1973) Lipids in rye seedlings in relation to vernalization. *Plant Physiology,* **52**: 268-273.

Tieszen, L.L. (1972a) Photosynthesis in relation to primary production. In *Proceedings IV International Meeting on the Biological Productivity of Tundra, Leningrad, USSR* (F.E. Wielgolaski and T. Rosswall, Eds.). Stockholm: International Biological Programme Tundra Biome Steering Committee, pp. 52-62.

Tieszen, L.L. (1972b) The seasonal course of aboveground production and chlorophyll distribution in a wet arctic tundra at Barrow, Alaska. *Arctic and Alpine Research,* **4**: 307-324.

Tieszen, L.L. (1973) Photosynthesis and respiration in arctic tundra grasses: field light intensity and temperature responses. *Arctic and Alpine Research,* **5**: 239-251.

Tieszen, L.L. (1974) Photosynthetic competence of the subnivean vegetation of an arctic tundra. *Arctic and Alpine Research,* **6**: 253-256.

Tieszen, L.L. (1975) CO_2 exchange in the Alaskan arctic tundra: Seasonal changes in the rate of photosynthesis of four species. *Photosynthetica,* **9**: 376-390.

Tieszen, L.L. (Ed.) (1978a) *Vegetation and Production Ecology of an Alaskan Arctic Tundra.* New York: Springer-Verlag, 686 pp.

Tieszen, L.L. (1978b) Photosynthesis in the principal Barrow, Alaska, species: A summary of field and laboratory responses. In *Vegetation and Production Ecology of an Alaskan Arctic Tundra* (L.L. Tieszen, Ed.). New York: Springer-Verlag, pp. 241-268.

Tieszen, L.L. (1978c) Summary. In *Vegetation and Production Ecology of an Alaskan Arctic Tundra* (L.L. Tieszen, Ed.). New York: Springer-Verlag, pp. 621-645.

Tieszen, L.L. and D.C. Sigurdson (1973) Effect of temperature on carboxylase activity and stability on some Calvin cycle grasses from the Arctic. *Arctic and Alpine Research,* **5**: 59-66.

Tieszen, L.L. and D.A. Johnson (1975) Seasonal pattern of photosynthesis in individual grass leaves and other plant parts in arctic Alaska with a portable $^{14}CO_2$ system. *Botanical Gazette,* **136**: 99-105.

Tieszen, L.L. and N.K. Wieland (1975) Physiological ecology of arctic and alpine photosynthesis and respiration. In *Physiological Adaptation to the Environment* (F.J. Vernberg, Ed.). New York: Intext Educational Publishers, pp. 157-200.

Tieszen, L.L. and S. Archer (1979) Physiological responses of plants in tundra grazing systems. In *Special Management Needs of Alpine Ecosystems* (D.A. Johnson, Ed.). Symposium of the Society for Range Management, February 14, 1977, Casper, Wyoming. Range Science Series No. 5, Denver, Colorado, pp. 22-42.

Tieszen, L.L., M.C. Lewis, P.C. Miller, J. Mayo, F.S. Chapin, III and W. Oechel (1981) An analysis of processes of primary production in tundra forms. In *Tundra Ecosystems: A Comparative Analysis* (L.C. Bliss, O.W. Heal and J.J. Moore, Eds.). Cambridge: Cambridge University Press, pp. 285-356 (in press).

Tikhomirov, B.A. (1963) *Contribution to the Biology of Arctic Plants.* Doklady Akademii Nauk SSSR, 154 pp.

Trabant, D. and C. Benson (1972) Field experiments on the development of depth hoar. In *Studies in Mineralogy and Precambrian Geology.* Geological Society of America Memoir 135, pp. 309-322.

Treharne, K.J. (1972) Biochemical limitations to photosynthetic rates. In *Crop Processes in Controlled Environments* (A.R. Rees, K.E. Cockshull, D.W. Hand and R.G. Hurd, Eds.). London: Academic Press, pp. 280-303.

Trudell, J. and R.G. White (1980) The effect of forage structure and availability on food intake, biting rate, bite size and daily eating time of reindeer. *Journal of Applied Ecology* (in press).

Tukey, H.B., Jr. (1970) The leaching of substances from plants. *Annual Review of Plant Physiology,* 21: 305-324.

Turner, F.B. (1970) The ecological efficiency of consumer populations. *Ecology,* 51: 741-742.

Ulrich, A. and P.L. Gersper (1978) Plant nutrient limitations of tundra plant growth. In *Vegetation and Production Ecology of an Alaskan Arctic Tundra* (L.L. Tieszen, Ed.). New York: Springer-Verlag, pp. 457-481.

Underwood, L.S. (1971) The bioenergetics of the arctic fox (*Alopex lagopus* L.). Ph.D. dissertation, Pennsylvania State University, 92 pp.

Underwood, L.S. (1975) Notes on the arctic fox (*Alopex lagopus*) in the Prudhoe Bay area of Alaska. In *Ecological Investigations of the Tundra Biome in the Prudhoe Bay Region, Alaska* (J. Brown, Ed.). Biological Papers of the University of Alaska, Special Report 2, pp. 144-149.

University of Alaska, Arctic Environmental Information and Data Center (1975) *Alaska Regional Profiles: Arctic Region* (L.L. Selkregg, Ed.). Office of the Governor, 218 pp.

U.S. Department of Commerce. Local climatological data. Annual summary with comparative data (Barrow and Barter Island, Alaska). National Oceanic and Atmospheric Administration, Asheville, North Carolina.

U.S. Geological Survey (1971-1976) Water resources data for Alaska. U.S. Geological Survey, Water Resources Division, Anchorage, Alaska.

Vaizey, J.R. (1887) On the absorption of water and its relation to the constitution of the cell wall in mosses. *Annals of Botany,* 1: 147-152.

Van Cleve, K. (1974) Organic matter quality in relation to decomposition. In *Soil Organisms and Decomposition in Tundra: Proceedings of the Microbiology, Decomposition and Invertebrate Working Groups Meeting, Fairbanks, Alaska, August 1973* (A.J. Holding, O.W. Heal, S.F. MacLean, Jr. and P.W. Flanagan, Eds.). Stockholm: International Biological Programme Tundra Biome Steering Committee, pp. 311-324.

Van Cleve, K. (1977) Recovery of disturbed tundra and taiga surfaces in Alaska. In *Recovery and Restoration of Damaged Ecosystems* (J. Cairns, Jr., K.L. Dickson and E.E. Herricks, Eds.). *Proceedings of the International Symposium on the Recovery of Damaged Ecosystems held at Virginia Polytechnic Institute and State University, Blacksburg, Virginia, March 23–25, 1975.* Charlottesville: University Press of Virginia, pp. 422-455.

Van Cleve, K., L.A. Viereck and R.L. Schlenter (1971) Accumulation of nitrogen in alder (*Alnus*) ecosystems near Fairbanks, Alaska. *Arctic and Alpine Research,* **3**: 101-114.

Van Cleve, K. and L.A. Viereck (1972) Distribution of selected chemical elements in even-aged alder (*Alnus*) ecosystems near Fairbanks, Alaska. *Arctic and Alpine Research,* **4**: 239-255.

van der Drift, J. (1959) The role of the soil fauna in the decomposition of forest litter. In *Proceedings of 15th International Congress of Zoology* (H.R. Hewer and N.D. Riley, Eds.). London: Burlington House, pp. 357-360.

Van Dyne, G., F.M. Smith, R.L. Czaplewski and R.G. Woodmansee (1978) Analyses and syntheses of grassland ecosystem dynamics. In *Glimpses of Ecology* (J.S. Singh and B. Gopal, Eds.). Jaipur, India: International Scientific Publications, pp. 1-79.

Verstraete, W. (1978) Critique of "Methods for analysis of denitrification in soils." In *Nitrogen in the Environment.* Vol. 2. *Soil–Plant–Nitrogen Relationships* (D.R. Nielsen and J.G. MacDonald, Eds.). New York: Academic Press, pp. 491-501.

Viereck, L.A. and E.L. Little, Jr. (1975) Atlas of United States trees. Vol. 2. Alaska trees and common shrubs. U.S. Department of Agriculture, Forest Service, Miscellaneous Publication No. 1293, 19 pp. and 81 maps.

Vlassak, K., E.A. Paul and R.E. Harris (1973) Assessment of biological nitrogen fixation in grassland and associated sites. *Plant and Soil,* **38**: 637-649.

Wales, R.A., L.P. Milligan and E.H. McEwan (1975) Urea recycling in caribou, cattle and sheep. In *Proceedings of the First International Reindeer and Caribou Symposium, 9–11 August 1972, University of*

Alaska, Fairbanks, Alaska (J.R. Luick, P.C. Lent, D.R. Klein and R.G. White, Eds.). Biological Papers of the University of Alaska, Special Report 1, pp. 297-307.

Walker, D.A. (1977) Analysis of effectiveness of a television scanning densitometer for indicating geobotanical features in an ice wedge polygon at Barrow, Alaska. M.A. thesis, University of Colorado, 132 pp.

Walker, D.A., P.J. Webber, K.R. Everett and J. Brown (1978) Effects of crude and diesel oil spills on plant communities at Prudhoe Bay, Alaska, and the derivation of oil spill sensitivity maps. *Arctic,* **31**: 242-259.

Walker, D.A. and P.J. Webber (1979) Relationships of soil acidity and air temperature to the wind and the effect on vegetation at Prudhoe Bay, Alaska. *Arctic,* **32**: 224-236.

Walker, H.J. (1973) Morphology of the North Slope. In *Alaskan Arctic Tundra: Proceedings of the 25th Anniversary Celebration of the Naval Arctic Research Laboratory* (M.E. Britton, Ed.). Arctic Institute of North America Technical Paper 25, pp. 49-92.

Walker, T.W. (1957) The sulphur cycle in grassland soils. *Journal of British Grassland Society,* **12**: 10-18.

Wallace, L.L. and A.T. Harrison (1978) Carbohydrate mobilization and movement in alpine plants. *American Journal of Botany,* **65**: 1035-1040.

Wallwork, J.A. (1967) Acari. In *Soil Biology* (A. Burges and F. Raw, Eds.). London: Academic Press, pp. 363-395.

Walsh, J.E. (1977) Measurement of the temperature, wind and moisture distribution across the northern coast of Alaska. *Arctic and Alpine Research,* **9**: 175-182.

Warren Wilson, J. (1957) Arctic plant growth. *Advancement of Science,* **13**: 383-388.

Warren Wilson, J. (1966a) An analysis of plant growth and its control in arctic environments. *Annals of Botany,* N.S., **30**: 383-402.

Warren Wilson, J. (1966b) Effect of temperature on net assimilation rate. *Annals of Botany,* N.S., **30**: 753-761.

Watson, A. (1957) The behavior, breeding and food-ecology of the snowy owl *Nyctea scandiaca. Ibis,* **99**: 419-462.

Watson, C.E. (1959) Climates of the states, Alaska. Climatography of the United States No. 60-49. U.S. Department of Commerce, 24 pp.

Watson, D.G., W.C. Hanson, J.J. Davis and C.E. Cushing (1966) Limnology of tundra ponds and Ogotoruk Creek. In *Environment of the Cape Thompson Region, Alaska* (N.J. Wilimovsky and J.N. Wolfe, Eds.). Oak Ridge, Tenn.: U.S. Atomic Energy Commission, pp. 415-435.

Weaver, D.F. (1969) Radiation regime over arctic tundra, 1965. University of Washington, Department of Atmospheric Sciences, Scientific Report, 260 pp.

Weaver, D.F. (1970) Radiation regime over arctic tundra and lakes, 1966. University of Washington, Department of Atmospheric Sciences, Scientific Report, 112 pp.

Weaver, J.E. (1954) *North American Prairie.* Lincoln, Neb.: Johnsen, 348 pp.

Weaver, J.E. (1958) Summary and interpretation of underground development in natural grassland communities. *Ecological Monographs,* **28**: 55-78.

Weber, N.A. (1950a) The role of lemmings at Point Barrow, Alaska. *Science,* **111**: 552-553.

Weber, N.A. (1950b) A survey of the insects and related arthropods of arctic Alaska. Part I. *Transactions of the American Entomological Society,* **76**: 147-206.

Webb, D.P. (1977) Regulation of deciduous forest litter decomposition by soil arthropod feces. In *The Role of Arthropods in Forest Ecosystems* (W.J. Mattson, Ed.). New York: Springer-Verlag, pp. 57-69.

Webber, P.J. (1971) Gradient analysis of the vegetation around the Lewis Valley, north-central Baffin Island, Northwest Territories, Canada. Ph.D. dissertation, Queen's University at Kingston, 366 pp.

Webber, P.J. (1978) Spatial and temporal variation of the vegetation and its productivity, Barrow, Alaska. In *Vegetation and Production Ecology of an Alaskan Arctic Tundra* (L.L. Tieszen, Ed.). New York: Springer-Verlag, pp. 37-112.

Webber, P.J. and D.A. Walker (1975) Vegetation and landscape analysis at Prudhoe Bay, Alaska: A vegetation map of the Tundra Biome study area. In *Ecological Investigations of the Tundra Biome in the Prudhoe Bay Region, Alaska* (J. Brown, Ed.). Biological Papers of the University of Alaska, Special Report 2, pp. 80-91.

Webber, P.J., J.C. Emerick, D.C.E. May and V. Komárková (1976) The impact of increased snowfall on alpine vegetation. In *Ecological Impacts of Snowpack Augmentation in the San Juan Mountains, Colorado* (H.W. Steinhoff and J.D. Ives, Eds.). Final Report to the Bureau of Reclamation, Colorado State University FNR-7052-1. Fort Collins: College of Forestry and Natural Resources, Colorado State University, pp. 201-264.

Webber, P.J. and D.E. May (1977) The distribution and magnitude of belowground plant structures in the alpine tundra of Niwot Ridge, Colorado. *Arctic and Alpine Research,* **9**: 157-174.

Webber, P.J. and J.D. Ives (1978) Damage and recovery of tundra vegetation. *Environmental Conservation,* **5**: 171-182.

Wein, R.W. and L.C. Bliss (1973) Experimental crude oil spills on arctic plant communities. *Journal of Applied Ecology,* **10**: 671-682.

Wein, R.W. and L.C. Bliss (1974) Primary production in arctic cottongrass tussock tundra communities. *Arctic and Alpine Research,* **6**: 261-274.

Weiser, C.J. (1970) Cold resistance and injury in woody plants. *Science,* **169**: 1269-1278.

Weller, G., S. Cubley, S. Parker, D. Trabant and C. Benson (1972) The tundra microclimate during snow-melt at Barrow, Alaska. *Arctic,* **25**: 291-300.

Weller, G. and B. Hoimgren (1974a) The microclimates of the arctic tundra. *Journal of Applied Meteorology,* **13**: 854-862.

Weller, G. and B. Holmgren (1974b) Summer global radiation and albedo—Data for three stations in the Arctic Basin: Ice Island T-3, Barrow, Prudhoe Bay, 1971-1973. University of Alaska, Geophysical Institute Technical Report 2, 31 pp.

Wendler, G., N. Ishikawa and N. Streten (1974) The climate of the McCall Glacier, Brooks Range, Alaska, in relation to its geographical setting. *Arctic and Alpine Research,* **6**: 307-318.

West, G.C. and M.S. Meng (1966) Nutrition of willow ptarmigan in northern Alaska. *Auk,* **83**: 603-615.

West, G.C. and D.W. Norton (1975) Metabolic adaptations of tundra birds. In *Physiological Adaptation to the Environment* (F.J. Vernberg, Ed.). New York: Intext Educational Publishers, pp. 301-329.

White, L.M. (1973) Carbohydrate reserves in grasses: a review. *Journal of Range Management,* **26**: 13-18.

White, R.G. (1975) Some aspects of nutritional adaptations of arctic herbivores. In *Physiological Adaptation to the Environment* (F.J. Vernberg, Ed.). New York: Intext Educational Publishers, pp. 239-268.

White, R.G. (1979) Nutrient acquisition and utilization in arctic herbivores. In *Comparative Mechanisms of Cold Adaptation* (L.S. Underwood, L.L. Tieszen, A.B. Callahan and G.E. Folk, Eds.). New York: Academic Press, pp. 13-50.

White, R.G., B.R. Thomson, T. Skogland, S.J. Person, D.E. Russell, D.F. Holleman and J.R. Luick (1975) Ecology of caribou at Prudhoe Bay, Alaska. In *Ecological Investigations of the Tundra Biome in the Prudhoe Bay Region, Alaska* (J. Brown, Ed.). Biological Papers of the University of Alaska, Special Report 2, pp. 150-201.

White, R.G. and M.K. Yousef (1978) Energy expenditures in reindeer walking on roads and on tundra. *Canadian Journal of Zoology,* **56**: 215-223.

White, R.G. and J. Trudell (1980) Habitat preference and forage consumption by reindeer and caribou near Atkasook, Alaska. *Arctic and Alpine Research,* **12**: 511-529.

White, R.G., F.L. Bunnell, E. Gaare, T. Skogland and B. Hubert (1981) Ungulates on arctic ranges. In *Tundra Ecosystems: A Comparative Analysis* (L.C. Bliss, Jr., O.W. Heal and J.J. Moore, Eds.). Cambridge: Cambridge University Press, pp. 397-483 (in press).

Whitehead, P.E. and E.H. McEwan (1973) Seasonal variation in the plasma testosterone concentration of reindeer and caribou. *Canadian Journal of Zoology,* **51**: 651-658.

Whitfield, D.W.A. (1977) Energy budgets and ecological efficiencies on Truelove Lowland. In *Truelove Lowland, Devon Island, Canada: A High Arctic Ecosystem* (L.C. Bliss, Ed.). Edmonton: The University of Alberta Press, pp. 607-620.

Whittaker, R.H. (1967) Gradient analysis of vegetation. *Biological Reviews of the Cambridge Philosophical Society,* **42**: 207-264.

Whittaker, R.H. (1975) *Communities and Ecosystems.* 2nd edition. New York: Macmillan, 385 pp.

Whittaker, R.H., G.E. Likens, F.H. Bormann, J.S. Eaton and T.G. Siccama (1979) The Hubbard Brook ecosystem study: forest nutrient cycling and element behavior. *Ecology,* **60**: 203-220.

Widden, P. (1977) Microbiology and decomposition on Truelove Lowland. In *Truelove Lowland, Devon Island, Canada: A High Arctic Ecosystem* (L.C. Bliss, Ed.). Edmonton: The University of Alberta Press, pp. 505-530.

Widden, P., T. Newell and D. Parkinson (1972) Decomposition and microbial populations of Truelove Lowland, Devon Island. *Devon Island I.B.P. Project, High Arctic Ecosystem, Project Report 1970 and 1971* (L.C. Bliss, Ed.). Edmonton: Department of Botany, University of Alberta, pp. 341-358.

Wielgolaski, F.E. (Ed.) (1975a) *Fennoscandian Tundra Ecosystems.* Part 1. *Plants and Microorganisms.* Berlin: Springer-Verlag, 366 pp.

Wielgolaski, F.E. (Ed.) (1975b) *Fennoscandian Tundra Ecosystems.* Part 2. *Animals and Systems Analysis.* Berlin: Springer-Verlag, 337 pp.

Wielgolaski, F.E. (1975c) Productivity of tundra ecosystems. In *Productivity of World Ecosystems: Proceedings of a Symposium, August 31–September 1, 1972, Seattle, Washington.* Washington, D.C.: National Academy of Sciences, pp. 1-12.

Wielgolaski, F.E., S. Kjelvik and P. Kallio (1975) Mineral content of tundra and forest tundra plants in Fennoscandia. In *Fennoscandian Tundra Ecosystems.* Part 1. *Plants and Microorganisms* (F.E. Wielgolaski, Ed.). Berlin: Springer-Verlag, pp. 316-332.

Wiggins, I.L. (1951) The distribution of vascular plants on polygonal ground near Point Barrow, Alaska. *Contributions from the Dudley Herbarium,* **4**: 41-56.

Wilkinson, S.R. and R.W. Lowrey (1973) Cycling of mineral nutrients in pasture ecosystems. In *Chemistry and Biochemistry of Herbage,* Vol. II (G.W. Butler and R.W. Bailey, Eds.). New York: Academic Press, pp. 247-315.

Williams, J.R. (1970) Ground water in the permafrost regions of Alaska. *U.S. Geological Survey Professional Paper* 696, 83 pp.

Williams, M.E., E.D. Rudolph and E.A. Schofield (1975) Selected data on lichens, mosses and vascular plants on the Prudhoe Bay tundra. In *Ecological Investigations of the Tundra Biome in the Prudhoe Bay Region, Alaska* (J. Brown, Ed.). Biological Papers of the University of Alaska, Special Report 2, pp. 213-215.

Williams, M.E., E.D. Rudolph, E.A. Schofield and D.C. Prasher (1978) The role of lichens in the structure, productivity and mineral cycling of the wet coastal Alaskan tundra. In *Vegetation and Production Ecology of an Alaskan Arctic Tundra* (L.L. Tieszen, Ed.). New York: Springer-Verlag, pp. 185-206.

Williams, R.F. (1955) Redistribution of mineral elements during development. *Annual Review of Plant Physiology,* 6: 25-42.

Witkamp, M. (1966) Rates of carbon dioxide evolution from the forest floor. *Ecology,* 47: 492-493.

Woo, M.-K. (1976) Evaporation and water level in the active layer. *Arctic and Alpine Research,* 8: 213-217.

Woodmansee, R.G., J.L. Dodd, R.A. Bowman, F.E. Clark and C.E. Dickinson (1978) Nitrogen budget of a shortgrass prairie ecosystem. *Oecologia* (Berl.), 34: 363-376.

Young, B.A. and J.L. Corbett (1972) Maintenance energy requirement of grazing sheep in relation to herbage availability. *Australian Journal of Agricultural Research,* 23: 57-76.

Younkin, W.E. (1976) Revegetation studies in the northern Mackenzie Valley region. *Arctic Gas Biological Report Series,* 38. Various pagination.

Zinkler, D. (1969) Vergleichende Untersuchungen zum Wirkungsspekdrum der Carbohydrasen von Collembolen (Aplerygola). *Verhandlingen der Deutsche Zoologischen Gesellschaft,* Zoologischer Anzeiger 32, Supplementband, pp. 640-644.

APPENDIX 1

U.S. IBP Tundra Biome Projects, Personnel, Site Locations 1970–1974

Project title	Personnel and affiliation	Arctic Barrow	Arctic Prudhoe	Alpine Eagle Summit	Alpine Niwot Ridge	Other
	Producers					
Primary production, photosynthesis and nutrient dynamics in tundra vegetation	Dr. Larry L. Tieszen, Augustana College (Sioux Falls)	70-73	70		73	
	Dr. Mary L. Allessio Leck, Rider College	72				
	Dr. John G. Dennis, National Park Service	70-71	71			
	Dr. Brent McCown, Univ. of Wisconsin	71-72				73L
	John Ahrendt	70				
	David Albright	72				
	Michael W. Battrum	71	71			
	Rick Bohnsack	71				
	Dr. Terry V. Callaghan, British Antarctic Survey	72				
	Dr. Nigel Collins, The University, Birmingham, England	72				
	Elizabeth Collins	72				
	Carol Dennis	71				
	Margaret Dillon	74				
	Gary Fischer	71	71			
	David Greiner	70				
	Dale Harrison	70				
	Donald L. Hazlett	71	71			
	Dr. Douglas A. Johnson (M.S., Ph.D.), USDA, SEA, Utah	70-71	71	72-73		
	Claire Lewellen	71				
	Dr. Martin C. Lewis, York Univ., Ontario	73				
	Richard Mandsager	72-73				
	Philip Mattheis	73				
	Corrine Mikhelson	71				
	Gregory E. Mowers	71	71			
	Richard Nelson	71-72	71			
	Bruce Oksol	72				
	Ken Olson	70	70			
	Robert Pritchard					72L
	Donna C. Sigurdson	71				
	Jerel Tieszen	71				
	Sharon Tieszen	70-71				
	Robert Vaughn	70				
	Mary Vetter	74				
	Nancy Wieland	73				
Carbon dioxide dynamics on arctic coastal tundra	Dr. Patrick I. Coyne, USDA, SEA, Okla.	71-72				
	Dr. John J. Kelley, Univ. of Alaska	70-72				
	Barry Corell	72				
	Mary Ann Coyne	71-72				

Principal investigators listed first, remaining personnel alphabetically with senior personnel's current affiliation. ( ) degrees awarded as part of Biome research (* cooperative with other programs).
L = Laboratory or office; dates primarily refer to period of field activity and not subsequent lab and office analyses.

Project title	Personnel and affiliation	Barrow	Prudhoe	Eagle Summit	Niwot Ridge	Other
		Location and years				
		Arctic		Alpine		
		Barrow	Prudhoe	Eagle Summit	Niwot Ridge	Other

Producers (cont'd)

Project title	Personnel and affiliation	Barrow	Prudhoe	Eagle Summit	Niwot Ridge	Other
Root and rhizome growth and respiration in arctic tundra soils	Dr. W. Dwight Billings, Duke Univ.	71-74				
	Dr. Kim Peterson (Ph.D.)	73-74				
	Dr. Gaius R. Shaver (Ph.D.), Marine Biology Laboratory, Woods Hole	72-74				
	Alex W. Trent (M.A.)	71				
Water relations of selected arctic tundra plants	Dr. Philip C. Miller, San Diego State Univ.	72-73		71	71-72	
	James Ehleringer (M.S.)				72	
	Patsy Miller	73				
	Russ Moore				72	
	Wayne Stoner (M.S.)	72				
	Nancy Wieland				72	
Tundra lichen productivity and the role of lichens in nutrient cycling and tundra structure	Dr. Emanuel D. Rudolph, Ohio State Univ.	72-73	72-73			
	Douglas C. Prasher	73				
	Dr. Edmund A. Schofield, Sierra Club (formerly)	72	72			
	Michael S. Williams (M.S.)	72-73	72-73			
Physiological ecology of arctic bryophytes	Dr. James R. Rastorfer, Chicago State Univ.	72-73	72			
	James Haeberlin	73				
	Allen Skorepa	73				
	Dr. David K. Smith (Ph.D.*), Univ. of Tennessee	72	72			
	Dr. Harold J. Webster, Fordham Univ.	72	72			
Patterns of carbon dioxide exchange in principal arctic bryophyte species	Dr. Walter C. Oechel, McGill Univ.	72-74				
	Patrick W.C. Leung	73				
	Janet Mailey	74				
	Therese Ruszczynski	74				
	Dr. Bjartmar Sveinbjornsson (Ph.D.*), University of Alaska (Anchorage)	73-74				
	Halldora Sveinbjornsson	74				
Measurement of transpirational water flux by tritium method	Dr. John J. Koranda, Lawrence Radiation Laboratory	73				
	Bruce Clegg	73				
	John Martin	73				
	Marshall Stuart	73				
Annual nitrogen and reserve carbohydrate cycle in two arctic grass species as affected by nitrogen and phosphorus fertilization	Dr. Jay D. McKendrick, Univ. of Alaska	73-74				
	Gary Michaelson	74				
	George A. Mitchell	73-74				
	Valerie Ott	73				
	Peter C. Scorup	74				
Phosphate uptake and internal cycling in tundra plants	Dr. F. Stuart Chapin III (Ph.D.*), Univ. of Alaska	72-73				
	Arnold Bloom	73				
Critical plant analysis values for growth of tundra plants	Dr. Albert Ulrich, Univ. of California (Berkeley)	72				
	Clifford Carlson					72-74L
	Kwok Fong					72-74L
	Carlos Llano					72-74L
	M.S. Mustafa					72-74L
	Jeffrey Tennyson	73				

		Location and years				
		Arctic		Alpine		
Project title	Personnel and affiliation	Barrow	Prudhoe	Eagle Summit	Niwot Ridge	Other

Producers (cont'd)

Project title	Personnel and affiliation	Barrow	Prudhoe	Eagle Summit	Niwot Ridge	Other
Canopy structure, gas exchange and water relations in alpine–arctic species	Dr. Martyn M. Caldwell, Utah State Univ.	70			72-73	
	James Ehleringer (M.S.)				72	
	Marcee Fareed (M.S.)				71	
	Diane Hanson				71	
	Roger Hanson				71	
	Dr. Douglas A. Johnson				72-73	
	Thomas Shoemaker				71	
	James R. Vickland				73	
Response of arctic, boreal, and alpine biotypes in reciprocal transplants	Dr. William W. Mitchell, Univ. of Alaska		71-74	71-73		71-74L
	Dr. Frank J. Wooding, Univ. of Alaska			71-74		71-73L
	Dr. Jay D. McKendrick, Univ. of Alaska		72-73	72-73		71-74L
	William Folkstead			71		
	Charles Knight					72L
	Paul Michaelson		72-73			
	Keith Poppert					72L
	David Scharon			71		
Growth rates, phenology and production of certain alpine and arctic plants in Colorado transplant gardens	Dr. Erik K. Bonde, Univ. of Colorado				71-73	
	Dr. Maxine Foreman, Community College of Denver				71-72	
	James K. Mitchell					
Gradient analysis and primary production in transects from arctic and alpine tundra to taiga	Dr. James H. Anderson, Univ. of Alaska			71-73		70
	Frank Bogardus	70				70
	Bruce K. Bright					70
	Bruce P. Burba			71		
	Patrick D. Cahill			71		
	Dr. Aureal T. Cross,			71		
	Christopher Cross			71		
	David Densmore			72		
	Roseann Densmore			72		
	Kent P. Gormley					70
	Rebecca A. Ludlum			71		
	J. Page Spencer			71		
	Stephen E. Tilmann			71		
Ordination, productivity and mapping of tundra vegetation	Dr. Patrick J. Webber, Univ. of Colorado	71-74	71-74	71	71-74	
	Dr. John Andrews, Univ. of Colorado	74	74			
	John Batty	72-74	72-74			
	John Davidson	74			73	
	Dr. Diane Ebert (May) (M.S., Ph.D.), Husson College	72			71-74	
	Dr. John C. Emerick (Ph.D.), Colorado School of Mines				71-74	
	Dr. JoAnn W. Flock (Ph.D.*), Univ. of Colorado					
	Dr. Vera Komárková (Ph.D.*), Univ. of Colorado				71-74	
	Gregory E. Mowers	72				
	Rachel Sherer	73				
	Marie Slack				73	
	Anne Stilson	73			72	
	Kim Sutherland	72-73				

Project title	Personnel and affiliation	Arctic Barrow	Arctic Prudhoe	Alpine Eagle Summit	Alpine Niwot Ridge	Other
Producers (cont'd)						
	Sue Vetter (Clark)	72			73	
	Donald A. Walker (M.A.)	73-74	73-74			
	J. Wied				72	
	Robyn Willey				73	
Taxonomy, biogeography and documentation of tundra flora	Dr. David F. Murray, Univ. of Alaska	71-72	71			71-74
	Dr. Palle Gravensen, Univ. of Alberta	71		71		
	Dr. Albert W. Johnson, San Diego State Univ.	72				72
	Alan Batten					72-74
	Janet Leon					72
	Barbara Murray		71			71-73
	Dr. William Steere, New York Botanical Garden	71-72	71-72			
Vegetation survey of the Prudhoe Bay region	Dr. Bonita J. Neiland, Univ. of Alaska		71			
	Jerome Hok	71	71			
A cytological and floristic survey of the vascular plants in the vicinity of Barrow	Dr. John G. Packer, Univ. of Alberta	72				
	Marc Galeski	72				
	Gordon D. McPherson	72				
Ecological effects of oil spills and seepages in cold-dominated environments	Dr. Jerry Brown, CRREL	70-73				70
	Dr. Brent McCown, Univ. of Wisconsin	71-73				71-73
	Dr. Patrick I. Coyne	70				73L
	Dr. Frederick Deneke, USFS, Minn.	71-72				71-73
	Richard Haugen	70				70
	Dr. Patrick J. Hunt, USDA/SEA, S.C.	71				71
	Fleetwood Koutz	71				71-72
	Dr. R.P. Murrmann, USDA/SEA, Calif.	70	70			
	Warren E. Rickard, Jr.	71-72				70-73
	Donald Vietor	70				
Natural landmarks of the Alaskan arctic lowlands	Dr. John J. Koranda	74				74
	Charles D. Evans, Univ. of Alaska	74				74
	Dr. George C. West, Univ. of Alaska					74
Consumers						
Population studies of the brown lemming	Dr. Frank A. Pitelka, Univ. of Calif. (Berkeley)	70-74				
	Dr. Guy N. Cameron, Univ. of Houston	70				70-71L
	William E. Glanz	71				
	Lawrence S. Goldstein	72				
Population determination and nutrient flux through lemmings in the tundra ecosystem	Dr. George O. Batzli Univ. of Illinois (Urbana)	72-74				
	David Best	73-74				
	David Cappetta	74				
	Ronald Cherry	73				
	Fred R. Cole (M.S.)	72				
	Joan Fitzgerald	73				
	Mark Ginder	73				
	Glenn Gunterspergen	74				
	Nancy Hikes	74				
	Roy M. Peterson (M.S.)	72-73				
	Gary Ullinsky	73				

Project title	Personnel and affiliation	Location and years				
		Arctic		Alpine		
				Eagle	Niwot	
		Barrow	Prudhoe	Summit	Ridge	Other
Consumers (cont'd)						
Determination of lemming home range by radio-tracking	Dr. Edwin M. Banks, Univ. of Illinois (Urbana)	72-73				
	Ronald J. Brooks	72				
	Michael Kirton	73				
	Tom Kron	73				
	Michael Melampy	72				
	Jay Schnell	72-73				
	Virginia Schnell	73				
The interaction of brown lemmings, vegetation and habitat characteristics during the winter	Dr. Stephen F. MacLean, Jr., Univ. of Alaska	72-73				
	Herbert R. Melchior, Univ. of Alaska	72-73				
Lemming herbivory in arctic tundra	Herbert R. Melchior, Univ. of Alaska	70-72	70			
	Dr. Boyd D. Collier, San Diego State Univ.	72				
	Edward F. Cheslak (M.S.)	71-72				
	Jon Keely	71				
	Walter Koenig	73				
	Stephen Temple	70				
Small mammal populations and energetics in arctic and subarctic ecosystems	Dr. Dale D. Feist, Univ. of Alaska	71	71-72	71-72		71-72
	Dr. George C. West					
	Dr. John W. Coady (Ph.D.*), Alaska Department of Fish and Game			70		70
	Wayne Couture		71-72	71-72		71-72
	Lawrence Frank					70
	Ray Kendel					70
	Tom Lahey		71-72	71-72		71-72
	Randy Pitney				70	70
	Dr. Paul H. Whitney (Ph.D.*), Lombard North Group, Ltd., Calgary		70	70		70
The role of weasels as lemming predators on arctic coastal tundra	Dr. Stephen F. MacLean, Jr.	72-73				
	Dr. B. Michael Fitzgerald, DSIR, New Zealand	72-73				
	Andrew Grossman	73				
Ecology and bioenergetics of small mammalian carnivores on the Arctic Coastal Plain	Dr. Larry S. Underwood, Univ. of Alaska	71	71-72			71
	Dr. Robert E. Henshaw, N.Y. State Dept. of Environmental Conservation	71				
Food intake, energy expenditure and ecology of caribou in arctic tundra	Dr. Robert G. White Univ. of Alaska		72-73			71
	Dr. Jack R. Luick, Univ. of Alaska		72-73			71
	Dianne Caley					71L
	Dr. Raymond D. Cameron, Alaska Dept. of Fish and Game		72			71
	Robert A. Dieterich, DVM, Univ. of Alaska		72			
	Paul Frelier		72			
	A.M. Gau		72			72-73
	Dr. Dan F. Holleman, Univ. of Alaska		72-73			
	Dr. Steven J. Person (Ph.D.*), Univ. of Alaska		72			71
	Donald E. Russell (M.S.)		73			
	Dr. Terje Skogland, Norwegian State Wildlife Research Institute					

| Project title | Personnel and affiliation | Arctic | | Alpine | | |
		Barrow	Prudhoe	Eagle Summit	Niwot Ridge	Other
	Consumers (cont'd)					
	Dr. Brian R. Thomson, Univ. of Edinburgh		72			
	Dr. M.K. Yousef, Univ. of Nevada		73			73
Social organization and habitat utilization in the Lapland longspur at Barrow, Alaska	Dr. Frank A. Pitelka,	71-74				
	Dr. Thomas W. Custer (Ph.D.), U.S. Fish and Wildlife Service	71-73				
	Michael W. Monroe	73				
	James V. Remsen	72				
	Alan P. Romspert	71				
Avian populations and bio- energetics in arctic and subarctic ecosystems	Dr. George C. West	70	70	70		70-73
	Dr. David W. Norton (Ph.D), Univ. of Alaska	70-72	71-72			71
	Dr. Uriel N. Safriel, Hebrew Univ., Jerusalem	71-73				
	Zvi Abramski	72				
	Irwin W. Ailes	71	71			71
	David Anderson	72				
	Shoshana Ashkenazie (M.S.)	73				
	James Curatolo		72			
	Dr. Barbara B. DeWolfe, Univ. of Calif. (Santa Barbara)					70-71
	Scott Kronberg	72				
	Stephen McDonald	70	71	71		71
	Jeffrey O. Myll	71-72				
	Arnold Newman	73		71		
	Douglas Schamel	73				
Ecology and current status of cliff-nesting raptors in arctic tundra	Dr. Tom J. Cade, Cornell Univ.					71
	Dr. John R. Haugh, U.S. Geological Survey					71
	Dr. Clayton M. White, Brigham Young Univ.					71
	Kim Sikoryak					71
	Paul R. Spitzer					71
	Dr. Walter R. Spofford					71
	Dr. L.G. Swartz					71
	Stanley A. Temple					71
	James D. Weaver					71
Population ecology and habitat selection of whist- ling swans on the Alaskan Arctic Coastal Plain	Dr. William J.L. Sladen, Jr., Johns Hopkins Univ.	71	71			71
	John Moore	71	71			71
	Robert Munro	71	71			
	Frank Pines	71	71			71
	Peter Whitehouse	71				71
Population and habitat utilization of white-tailed ptarmigan in the Colorado alpine	Dr. Clait E. Braun, Color- ado Division of Wildlife				71-73	
	Dr. Terry A. May (Ph.D.), Univ. of Maine				71-73	
	Juliet Gee				71	
	Jeff Norton				72	
	Gary Slagel				72	
	Marie A. Vendeville				71	
Population ecology and energetics of tundra soil arthropods and their role in decomposition processes	Dr. Stephen F. MacLean, Jr.	70-73	70-72			
	Lawrence E. Clement (M.S.)	72-73				
	James Bumgartner	70				
	Mark Deyrup		71			
	Craig Hollingsworth		72			
	Margaret Miller (Skeel)	72				

Project title	Personnel and affiliation	Arctic		Alpine		
		Barrow	Prudhoe	Eagle Summit	Niwot Ridge	Other
Consumers (cont'd)						
	Thomas McGrath	73				
	Edward A. Morgan	71-72	71			
	Ray Price			72		
	Donald W. Smith	70				
	J. Ward Testa	73				
	Louis Verner	71	71			
	April D. Volk					71
Abundance, age structure and respiration rates of ground-dwelling spiders in arctic coastal tundra	Dr. Boyd D. Collier, San Diego State Univ.	72	72			
Energy budgets and elemental turnover of tundra invertebrates near Barrow, Alaska	Dr. D.A. Crossley, Jr., Univ. of Georgia	72				
	Dr. G. Keith Douce (M.S., Ph.D.), Univ. of Georgia	72&74				
Abundance and trophic function of tundra nematodes	Dr. Grover C. Smart, Jr., Univ. of Florida	71				
	Thomas H. Atkinson	72				
Composition and abundance of the lepidopteran fauna of arctic and alpine Alaskan tundra	Dr. Kenelm W. Philip, Univ. of Alaska	71				71
Abundance of soil arthropods and their effects on soil microorganisms in alpine tundra	Dr. John S. Edwards, Univ. of Washington	71	71	71-72		71
	Paul Banko			72		
	David A. Dailey			71		
Populations and production of major arthropods	Dr. Ronald Schmoller Univ. of Tennessee	71		71	71-72	
	Richard Ambrose				71	
	Martha Commins				72	
	Dayle Donaldson				71	
	Barry Lumpkin				71	
	Mary McGrade				71	
	Irene Rosenberg				71	
	Virginia Tolbert				71	
	Wayne Tolbert				72	
Decomposer, Soils, and Nutrient Flux						
Metabolic activities of bacteria and yeast in wet meadow tundra soil	Dr. Robert E. Benoit, Virginia Polytechnic Institute	70-73	70			
	Robert Breedlove	70				
	Walton B. Campbell (M.S.)	70-72				
	Gregory Dickenson	73				
	Richard W. Harris (M.S.)	71-72				
	Tryree Kessler	74				
	Robert E. Moffit	72				
	Leland S. Warren	71				
	Ton Rau	73				
Basidiomycetes biomass and function in the arctic and alpine tundras	Dr. Orson K. Miller, Virginia Polytechnic Institute	71-74				
	Dr. Gary A. Laursen (Ph.D.) Office of Naval Research	71-74		71		71
The role of algae and protozoan associates in tundra soils	Dr. Roy E. Cameron, Argonne National Laboratory	71-73				
	Anne Dalton (Knox)	73				72L
	Frank A. Morelli	73				

		Location and years				
		Arctic		Alpine		
				Eagle	Niwot	
Project title	Personnel and affiliation	Barrow	Prudhoe	Summit	Ridge	Other

Decomposer, Soils, and Nutrient Flux (cont'd)

Project title	Personnel and affiliation	Barrow	Prudhoe	Eagle Summit	Niwot Ridge	Other
Decomposition processes in arctic and alpine tundra	Dr. Patrick W. Flanagan Univ. of Alaska	70-73	70	70-73		70
	Alan Crawford	71-72	71	71-72		71L
	Diane Duvall					71L
	John Ho					70
	Arla Scarborough	71-73		70		70-73
Soil–plant interactions and associated multivariate analyses	Dr. Paul L. Gersper, Univ. of Calif. (Berkeley)	70-72		71	71	
	Dr. Rodney J. Arkley, Univ. of Calif. (Berkeley)	70-72		71		
	Douglas Anderson	73				
	William Bauman					72L
	Josephine L.Challinor	70			71	
	Dr. Harvey F. Donner, Univ. of Calif. (Berkeley)	72				
	Philip S. Flint	71-73				
	Karen Fuller	70				
	Dr. Rudi Glaser, Univ. of Calif. (Berkeley)					73-74
	Brian Hicks	72				
	Dr. L. Jacobsen, Univ. of Calif. (Berkeley)	72				
	Dr. Hans Jenny, Univ. of Calif. (Berkeley)	70				
	Merril Misam	72				
	Norton R. Munn (M.S.)	71				
	Dr. Arnold M. Schultz, Univ. of Calif. (Berkeley)	70				
	Alex P. Simons (M.S.)	70			71	
	Dean Williams	71				
	John N. Zorich	71				
Nitrogen fixation in arctic and alpine terrestrial and aquatic ecosystems	Dr. Vera Alexander, Univ. of Alaska	70-73		71		70
	Dr. Donald M. Schell, Univ. of Alaska	70-73		71		70
	Margaret Billington	70-74				
	Sinikka Kallio	73				73
	Linda Peyton	70-73				
	G.B. Threlkeld	70		71		70
Rates of nitrification and denitrification in tundra soils	Dr. Stephen A. Norrell, Univ. of Alaska	72-73		71-73		71-73L
	Carol M. Anderson	72-73		72-73		72-73L
	Mary Johnston (M.S.)	73				73L
	George Lindholm (M.S.)	71		71-72		71-72L
Nitrogen cycling in tundra and taiga soils as influenced by temperature and moisture (and laboratory plant nutrient analysis)	Dr. Keith Van Cleve, Univ. of Alaska	72	70-71			70-74L
	Nancy Anthony					70L
	Carol Brass					70L
	Carol Campbell					71
	Rudolph Candler					70-71L
	Robert Hardy			71		
	Joan Holland					71-72L
	Joyce Meador					71L
	Mark Metcalf			72		
	Lorraine Noonan					70-72L
	Tom Pearce			71		71
	Harold Piene (M.S.)					72
	Benjamin Sands					70L
	Robert Schlentner			71		71-72L
	Bonita Snarski					70L
	Patricia Troth					72L
Phosphorus characterization in tundra soil	Dr. Robert J. Barsdate Univ. of Alaska	73				

Project title	Personnel and affiliation	Arctic Barrow	Prudhoe	Alpine Eagle Summit	Niwot Ridge	Other

Location and years

Project title	Personnel and affiliation	Barrow	Prudhoe	Eagle Summit	Niwot Ridge	Other
Decomposer, Soils and Nutrient Flux (cont'd)						
	Dr. Dirk Barèl, Arheim, Netherlands	73				
Tundra soil land–water nutrient interactions	Dr. Lowell A. Douglas, Rutgers Univ.	71	71-72			
	Dr. Aytekin Bilgin (Ph.D.) (Deceased)	71-72	71-72			
Peat structure and soil mapping of arctic soils	Dr. K. R. Everett, Ohio State Univ.	72-74	72-74			
	Robert Parkinson (M.S.)		74			
Abiotic Interface						
The micro- and regional climate of the Alaskan arctic tundra	Dr. Gunter Weller, Univ. of Alaska	70-72	71			70-71
	Dr. Carl S. Benson, Univ. of Alaska	70-74	72-74			
	Stewart Cubley	71				72
	Gary Hess					70
	Dr. Bjorn Holmgren, Meteorological Institute. Sweden	73-74	73-74			
	Gilbert Mimken	70				70
	Stanley Parker	71-72	72			
	Scott Parrish (Deceased)	73	72-73			
	Richard Schwartz	71	71			
	Robert Timmer		72			
	Dennis Trabant (M.S.)	70-71				
	Dr. Gerd Wendler, Univ. of Alaska	70				
Prediction and validation of temperature and thaw in arctic tundra soils	Dr. Jerry Brown	70-71				
	Dr. Yoshisuke Nakano, CRREL	71				
	Robert Arnold	71				
	Gregor Fellers					70-71L
	Richard McGaw	70				
	William Powell	70				
	Vaughn Rockney	70-71				
	David Schaeffer	70				
	Leander Stroschein					70L
	Donald Vietor	70				
Soil and plant canopy temperature regimes in alpine tundra	Dr. Erwin R. Berglund, Oregon State Univ.			71		
Soil moisture balance in the alpine tundra	Dr. Dwane J. Sykes, Eyring Research Institute, Provo, Utah			71		
	Thomas R. Ford				71	
	William A. Quirk				71	
Ground temperature regimes and energy budgets in the Colorado alpine	Dr. John D. Ives, Univ. of Colorado				71-72	
	Dr. Roger G. Barry, Univ. of Colorado	73		73	72-73	
	Carol Batty				71	
	John Clark				72	
	Jed Fuhrman				73	
	Bonnie Gray				72	
	Edway Hinckley				73	
	Barbara Jarvis				71	
	Patricia Jenson				72	
	Kathleen Laughlin				73	
	Dr. Ellsworth LeDrew (M.S.), Univ. of Waterloo				72-73	

		Location and years				
		Arctic		Alpine		
Project title	Personnel and affiliation	Barrow	Prudhoe	Eagle Summit	Niwot Ridge	Other
Abiotic Interface (cont'd)						
	Evan F. Meltzer				72	
	David Rowe				71	
Terrestrial Modeling and Synthesis						
The analysis of the structure and function of the wet tundra ecosystem at Point Barrow, Alaska	Dr. Harry N. Coulombe, USFWS, Colorado	70				70
	Dr. Jerry Brown, CRREL	70				70
	Dr. Philip C. Miller	70				70
A tundra model	Dr. K.W. Bridges, Univ. of Hawaii	71				71
Simulation modeling of the Barrow tundra ecosystem	Dr. Mitchell E. Timin, San Diego State Univ.	71-72				71-73
	Paul Nobbs	72				
	Jean Rannells					72
	Jon S. Zich	72				
Modeling tundra primary production processes	Dr. Philip C. Miller	70-73				70-74
	Dr. Edward G. Brittain, Australian National Univ.	72-73				73
	John Hom	73				73
	Bruce Lawrence (M.S.)	73				73
	Edward Ng (M.S.*)	73				73
	Wayne Stoner (M.S.)	71-73				73
Modeling vertebrate consumers in the arctic tundra	Dr. Boyd D. Collier	73				72-74
	Sylvia A. Barkley (M.S.)	73	73-74			
	Ronald Osburn (M.S.)	72-73	73-74			
	Nils Stenseth	72				72
Decomposition–nutrient flux and caribou model development	Dr. Fred L. Bunnell (Ph.D.*), Univ. of British Columbia	70&73				72-74
	Dr. Pille Bunnell, Univ. British Columbia	73				73-74
	Penny Lewis	73				73-74
	Donald E. Russell (M.S.)	73				73-74
	David Tait	73				72-74
Simulation of meteorological variation over arctic coastal tundra under perturbed physical interface conditions	Dr. Joseph Pandolfo, Center for the Environment and Man		70			
	Dr. Norman W. Lord, Center for the Environment and Man					70-72
	Dr. Marshall Atwater, Center for the Environment and Man					70-72
Geomorphic and near-surface thermal regime model of tundra terrain	Dr. Samuel I. Outcalt, Univ. of Michigan	72-73				72-74
	Dr. Cecil W. Goodwin (M.S., Ph.D.), Pennsylvania State Univ.	72-73				72-74
	Roger Lachenbruch	73				
Snow-melt and hydrologic modeling of coastal tundra	Dr. S. Lawrence Dingman, Univ. of New Hampshire	72				72-74
	Dr. Robert I. Lewellen, Littleton, Colorado					
Central Program						
Administrative, technical and logistic support	Dr. Jerry Brown	70-74	71-74	71	73	70-80
	Dr. George C. West			71-72		70-74
	James Baldridge					70

Project title	Personnel and affiliation	Arctic Barrow	Prudhoe	Alpine Eagle Summit	Niwot Ridge	Other
Central Program (cont'd)						
	Dr. Patrick I. Coyne	71				70
	Christopher C. Cross			71		
	Dann Farquhar					72
	Bobby Fox					72-73
	David Grantz	72-73				
	Johanne Harper					73-74
	Dr. John E. Hobbie	73				
	Jule Loftus					72
	Dr. Stephen F. MacLean, Jr.	73				
	Jean Herb Moore					71
	Scott Parrish		72-74			73-74
	John Polhemus					72
	James Prill	72				
	Donval Simpson			71		71
	Dr. Larry L. Tieszen	71-73		71		
	C. Ray Vest			71		
	Dr. Patrick J. Webber				71-74	
	David Witt					72-74
Data processing and storage, computer research design and modeling†	Barry Campbell	73				73
	Brucilla Campbell	73				73
	Dr. Frederick C. Dean, Univ. of Alaska	71				71-73
	James Dryden					71-72
	Stephen Geller	72				71-72
	Dr. Samuel J. Harbo, Jr., Univ. of Alaska	71				71-72
	Dr. Jere Murray, Homer, Alaska	71-72				71-72
	Evelyn M. Porter	71				71-73
	Robert A. Porter	71				71-73
	Frances Randall					71-74
	David VanAmburg					73
	Dr. Keith Van Cleve	73				71-74
Publications (CRREL)	Stephen L. Bowen, CRREL					70-80
	Mary Aho, University of Alaska, Anchorage					74
	Cheryl Clark					74
	Norma Coutermanche					73
	Harold Larsen					70-80
	Laurie McNicholas, Univ. of Alaska					74
	Donna Murphy					70-80
	Matthew Pacillo					70-74
	Cheryl Richardson					70-73
	Hazel Sanborn					70-74
	Sandra Smith					70
	Audrey Vaughan					74
Aquatic Program (see Hobbie 1980)						
Primary productivity and phytoplankton dynamics in arctic ponds and lakes	Dr. Vera Alexander, Univ. of Alaska	70-74				
	Cathleen M. Chmielowski	71				
	Robert Clasby	71	71			
	Christopher Coulon	71-73				
	Elizabeth Coulon	73				
	Dr. Staffan Holmgren, Uppsala University	71				
Bacteria and benthic algae activity and productivity in arctic ponds	Dr. John E. Hobbie, Marine Biological Laboratory, Woods Hole	71-73				
	Mary E. Bennett	71				
	Michael Crezee	71				

Project title	Personnel and affiliation	Arctic Barrow	Prudhoe	Alpine Eagle Summit	Niwot Ridge	Other
Aquatic (cont'd)						
	Dr. Ralph Daley, Inland Waters, W. Vancouver, B.C.	73				
	Dr. Tom Fenchel, Univ. of Aarhus, Denmark	73				
	Polly Penhale	71-72				
	Park Rublee (M.S.)	73				
	Dr. Donald W. Stanley (Ph.D.), University of East Carolina	71-73	71			
	Tor S. Traaen	72				
Primary production of vascular aquatic plants in arctic ponds	Dr. C. Peter McRoy, Univ. of Alaska	71-72				
	Thomas Leue	72				
Daily rhythms, productivity, and seasonal cycles of zooplankton in arctic coastal ponds and lakes	Dr. Raymond G. Stross, State Univ. of New York	71-73				
	Dr. Sally W. Chisholm (Ph.D.), Univ. of Calif. (Berkeley)	72				
	Thomas Casady	73				
	Dr. Stanley Dodson Univ. of Wisconsin	73				
	James C. Edwards	72				
	Stephen Goldstone	73				
	Gary V. Gulezian	72				
	Dr. Donald Kangas, Northeast Missouri State Univ.		73			
	William A. Shapse	71	71			
	Peter L. Starkweather	71	71			
Seasonal cycles and energetics of benthic communities in coastal tundra ponds and lakes	Dr. Raymond D. Dillon, Univ. of South Dakota	71	71			
	Dennis G. Buechler (M.S.)	71	71			
	John T. Hobbs	71-72				
Dynamics of freshwater microbenthic communities in arctic ponds and lakes	Dr. Donald A. Bierle, St. Paul Bible College	71-72	71			
	Sharon Bierle	72				
	Ted Boal					72L
	Donald G. Hardy	71-72				
	Karen L. Hart	71				
Benthic carbon dynamics and the ecological role of *Lepidurus arcticus* in coastal tundra ponds	Dr. Michael C. Miller, Univ. of Cincinnati	71-73				
	T.W. Federle (M.S.)					
	Kathleen Kallendorf	73				
	Robert J. Kallendorf (M.S.)					
	Constance Menefee	73				
	James P. Reed (M.S.)	71-72	71			
	Linda R. Reed	72				
	D.J. Stromme (M.S.)					
Nutrient metabolism and water chemistry in ponds and lakes of the Arctic Coastal Plain	Dr. Robert J. Barsdate, Univ. of Alaska	70-73	71			
	Alex Fu	70				
	Norman A. King	71				
	Mary Nebert					70-73L
	Cathy Prentki	71				
	Dr. Richard Prentki (Ph.D.), Univ. of Wisconsin	70-73				
	Thomas Tribble	70				

		Location and years				
		Arctic		Alpine		
Project title	Personnel and affiliation	Barrow	Prudhoe	Eagle Summit	Niwot Ridge	Other
	Aquatic (cont'd)					
Energetics of the fish population in Ikroavik Lake	Dr. James N. Cameron, Univ. of Texas (Port Aransas)	71-72	71			
	Jon Kostoris	72				
	Polly A. Penhale (M.S.)	71-72				
Modeling the aquatic pond system at Barrow, Alaska	Dr. Jawahar Tiwari, Univ. of California (L.A.)	73				73-74
	Paul Nobbs	73				73-74

APPENDIX 2
Location of Principal Biome Plots

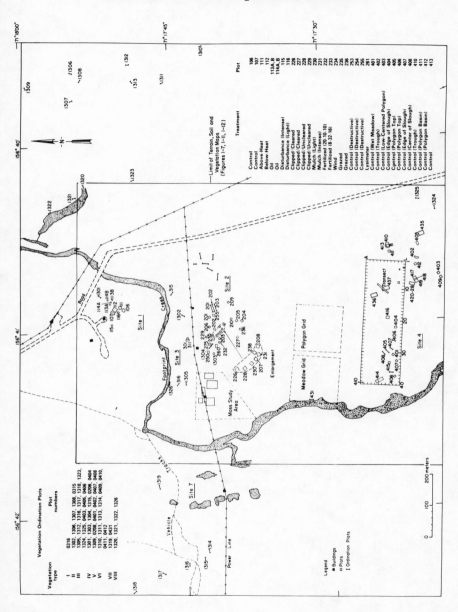

Subject Index